P9-ECS-667
Las Vegas, NV.

The Oxford Dictionary of

Political Quotations

edited by **Antony Jay**

Oxford New York

OXFORD UNIVERSITY PRESS

1996

Oxford University Press, Walton Street, Oxford OX2 6DP
Oxford New York
Athens Auckland Bangkok Bogota Bombay
Buenos Aires Calcutta Cape Town Dar es Salaam
Delhi Florence Hong Kong Istanbul Karachi
Kuala Lumpur Madras Madrid Melbourne
Mexico City Nairobi Paris Singapore
Taipei Tokyo Toronto
and associated companies in
Berlin Ibadan

Oxford is a trade mark of Oxford University Press

First published 1996

British Library Cataloguing in Publication Data
Data available

Library of Congress Cataloging in Publication Data
The Oxford dictionary of political quotations
edited by Antony Jay.
p. cm.
1. Political science—Quotations, maxims, etc. 2. Politicians—Quotations, maxims, etc.
I. Jay, Antony, 1930–
320—dc20 96-11425 PN6084.P6094 1996

ISBN 0-19-863158-8

Designed by Jane Stevenson
Typeset in Monotype Photina and Meta by Barbers Ltd.

Printed in Great Britain
on acid-free paper by
The Bath Press
Bath

Project Team

Managing Editor	Elizabeth M. Knowles
Index Editors	Susan Ratcliffe Christina Malkowska Zaba
Library Research	Ralph Bates Marie G. Diaz
Reading Programme	Helen McCurdy Verity Mason Penelope Newsome
Data Capture	Sandra Vaughan
Proof-reading	Fabia Claris Penny Trumble

We are grateful to George Chowdharay-Best for contributions to our file of incoming quotations, and to Gerald Blick, Jon Ross Simon, and Jeanne Croft for additional research.

Introduction

'The hard pressed writer in turning over these pages may find and note many excellent phrases, whether to give a pleasing touch of erudition or to save the trouble of thinking for himself.' Bernard Darwin's words in his introduction to the first *Oxford Dictionary of Quotations* are as true today as they were fifty-five years ago. But there are more honourable reasons for using quotations, especially in the world of politics. In mobilizing support for a project or a policy it is especially agreeable to be able to call upon the distinguished dead; their distinction adds intellectual weight and moral force to the argument, and their death makes it impossible for them to appear on television later and say that they meant something completely different.

Even more important, perhaps, than the support of the eminent is the wisdom of the ages. New ideas in politics are always suspect, but recourse to quotation can show that your ideas, far from being new and tender shoots, are rooted deep in the history of political society. Those who argue for punishment as deterrent rather than rehabilitation may find themselves out of the fashion, but a quick look at Aeschylus will enable them to demonstrate the two and a half thousand year pedigree of their belief. Those who oppose closer ties with Europe can quote Bagehot, 'Are they [the English people] not above all nations divided from the rest of the world?... Are they not out of the current of common European causes and affairs?' from the nineteenth century, and Gibbon, 'The division of Europe into a number of independent states is productive of the most beneficial consequences to the liberty of mankind,' from the eighteenth, to show that there is nothing new in their belief that there is strength and logic in their resistance, while Europhiles can adduce the dictum of the nineteenth century Prime Minister Lord Salisbury: 'We are part of the community of Europe and we must do our duty as such.' Just occasionally, too, quotations can be used not just for intellectual support, but for dramatic effect, as if they carried some magical power. Two Prime Ministers in living memory have felt the force of it. The first was Chamberlain in 1940, when Leo Amery quoted Cromwell's historic words to the Rump Parliament 'You have sat too long for any good you have been doing. Depart, I say, and let us have done with you. In the name of God, go!' Chamberlain went. The second was Macmillan in 1963, when a fellow Conservative, Nigel Birch, quoted just as lethally from Browning's *The Lost Leader*:

> Life's night begins; let him never come back to us!
> There would be doubt, hesitation and pain,
> Forced praise on our part—the glimmer of twilight,
> Never glad confident morning again!

Perhaps Macmillan was doomed anyway, but Birch's quotation made certain of his fall as surely as Brutus' dagger.

This Dictionary, it is hoped, will be of service to those who want to support their arguments and opinions with evidence of their distinguished pedigree and ancient lineage, as well as those looking for no more than a pleasing touch of erudition or the avoidance of thought. It is not, however, simply an anthology of political wit and wisdom. It is, first, foremost, and above all, a work of reference. The primary qualification for an entry is not its antiquity or its profundity but its familiarity. There is a bank of political quotations which are part of the currency of political speeches and writings throughout the English-speaking world. All of them should be in these pages, and if they are not (and I am sure time and alert readers will expose some glaring omissions) then the editor is to blame.

Beyond the central core of universally recognized political quotations there is a much wider circle of entries which, while they are quoted from time to time, are not immediately recognizable to all of those to whom they are addressed. These are subject to editorial judgment, and here the editor might try to defend an omission rather than apologize for it. But in both cases the key question has been 'Should this be in a work of reference?' The two principal users for whom the book is intended are those who have encountered or partly recall a quotation and want to verify or source it, and those who are looking for a quotation on a particular subject or from a given writer.

Many works of reference, however, have an appeal to browsers and grazers as well as hunters, and a dictionary of political quotations must be very close to the top of the list; it offers the delight of discovery as well as confirmation and verification. While this one is not designed as an anthology, it is bound to give the reader most of the pleasure of an anthology, and so in many cases I have tried to supply more contextual information than might be necessary in a work of pure reference. Some quotations (for instance Wellington's 'If you believe that you'll believe anything') make little sense to any but the expert reader, unless accompanied by some indication of the context. Others, while intelligible (like Margaret Thatcher's 'Now it must be business as usual'), can become much more interesting with some knowledge of the circumstances in which they were uttered. For the same reason the Dictionary is organized not by theme but by the name of the speaker or writer. I have never myself been entirely at ease with thematic organization—I always have a niggling suspicion that any thematic entry could legitimately have been included under a different heading, and often under several—whereas entries grouped under the name of the source cannot suffer under this disability, and arrangement by source is just as helpful as arrangement by theme for reference purposes. In a collection of political quotations, this form is particularly advantageous, especially for the random dipper: reading through the citations from one individual—Lloyd George, de Tocqueville, Halifax—gives a quick but vivid sense not only of what he said but also of his quality and individuality. So although this is indeed a work of reference, it is hoped that many people will also use it as an illuminating, if wildly unsystematic, compendium of opinions, ideas, and personalities that have marked our progress towards the political society we live in today.

So what makes a quotation into a political quotation? Often, of course, the answer is obvious. General truths about politics are immediate candidates: Aeschylus's 'Everyone's quick to blame the alien', Bacon's 'All rising to great place is by a winding stair', and Burke's 'To tax and to please, no more than to love and be wise, is not given to men.' Then there are quotations specific to an event or an individual which have passed into the language: Disraeli's 'I have climbed to the top of the greasy pole' or Mary Tudor's 'When I am dead and opened, you shall find "Calais" lying in my heart', even though it is more often misquoted than quoted. Some quotations would not merit inclusion but for the source; if you or I had said 'No woman in my time will be Prime Minister' we would hardly expect to find ourselves in the Dictionary. The fact that Margaret Thatcher said it makes all the difference.

There is however a disputed territory between what is obviously a political quotation and what is obviously not. There is nothing remotely political about the words 'I can't tell a lie, Pa; you know I can't tell a lie. I did cut it with my hatchet,' but because it illuminates Washington's character, and because its frequent quotation testifies to his reputation, there can be no question of leaving it out. But what about the sayings of great men when they are writing fiction and the words come from the mouths of their characters, as in Macaulay's poems or Disraeli's novels? Surely it can not be cheating to include them if exclusion would mean omitting 'A Jacobite's Epitaph'? And the 'Two nations' speech in *Sybil* is currently at the heart of the Conservative Party's internal strife.

Another obscure territorial boundary is that which divides, or fails to divide, political quotations from those which, while having large areas that overlap politics, might more properly be classified under headings such as law, warfare, royalty, or economics. If these subjects had their own Oxford quotation dictionaries, there might have been some debate about where to place Adam Smith's observation that 'people of the same trade seldom meet together, even for merriment and diversion, but the conversation ends in a conspiracy against the public, or in some contrivance to raise prices.' Since there is however (as yet) no Oxford Dictionary of Economics Quotations, there was no argument. There is however an excellent *Oxford Book of Political Anecdotes* and, while some anecdotes are the source of quotation, anecdotes as such are not included. Obviously there were temptations. After losing office in 1964 Iain McLeod was a conspicuous absentee from the opposition front bench, which Wilson knew was a cause of much critical comment among Conservative back-benchers. One day however he did appear, to put a challenging question to the Prime Minister. Wilson rose, paused, and then said 'Do you come here often?' It produced one of the biggest laughs ever heard from a party against one of its own front-benchers. But somehow 'Do you come here often?' did not sound like a political quotation; it belongs only in that anecdote and had to be excluded.

Of course not all political quotations are either by politicians or about politics. Lewis Carroll was certainly not a politician and *Alice Through the Looking Glass* is equally certainly not a political work, but 'Jam tomorrow' and 'When I use a word it means just what I choose it to mean' are regularly quoted in political debate—as witness the quotation from Tony Benn, 'Some of that jam we thought was for tomorrow we have already eaten.' The Dictionary would be failing its readers if it left them out. Politicians may no longer quote poetry as freely as they used to, but students of the politics of the recent past will find many quotations from and references to poets, and even today they may encounter Kipling's 'Paying the Dane-geld', Chesterton's 'The Secret People', and copious allusions to the Vicar of Bray. And there is of course one poet who stands out above all the others for frequency of quotation: it is not just the power and range of Shakespeare's writing that makes him so quotable in a political context, it is the fact that so many of his plays are so intensely political in their themes, characters, and conflicts. If readers feel that he is over-represented here, I can only say that I have been acutely aware of the apparently excessive space he has been given, and that the original section was considerably longer. Much weeding has been done, and the surviving entries represent the editor's judgement of those that could not be omitted without loss.

Shakespeare is not the only writer (though he is the only poet) to occupy what might seem to be a disproportionate amount of space. Four great national leaders—Churchill, Disraeli, Jefferson, and Lincoln—have been endlessly quoted by their contemporaries and successors. Certainly they had the gift of language, but it also seems as if the fame they achieved during their lifetime may have led to their words being more diligently recorded and more frequently repeated than those of their less famous contemporaries. There are however two people who figure prominently in these pages without having achieved the same world wide fame. Burke, though he was indeed a statesman, was not in their class, and Bagehot was never even a member of parliament. Both, however, consistently found a way of expressing ideas and arguments that everyone could remember and no one could improve on. Some of their ideas were original, but even those that were not have proved to be endlessly quotable. They exemplify Pope's definition:

> True wit is Nature to advantage dressed,
> What oft was thought, but ne'er so well expressed.

The editor feels no need to apologize for the amount of space they command.

There is one particular danger which confronts all quotation dictionaries: the danger of including only those quotations which have already appeared in other dictionaries. It is of course inevitable that many of the quotations will be found in other collections, but it is equally important that lexicographers should not be endlessly recycling the same material. If quotations are to refresh and invigorate political communication, they should be drawn from a living stream and not a stagnant pond. So while the starting point for this Dictionary was the existing corpus of political quotations held on the files of the Oxford University Press, it was only the starting point. The principal means of bringing in new material was a team of researchers who combed the daily papers and the periodicals, and listened to radio and television programmes, to record every significant quotation they came across and submit it for consideration. Another important source has been correspondence. A living dictionary of quotations will necessarily include quotations from the living, and many of them have been kind enough not only to verify and source entries attributed to them, but also to supply other of their writings and sayings that they have found being quoted. The living have also interceded for the dead: for example, the first draft selection, like all the quotation dictionaries I have encountered, was disturbingly short of quotations from one of Britain's most distinguished Prime Ministers, Robert Peel. It was hard to believe that he had left so few quotable remarks behind him, and a letter to the leading authority on Peel, Professor Norman Gash, produced evidence that it was not Peel but the record that was at fault. Peel's entry is now of a respectable length. Equally, one of the most politically astute civil servants of the nineteenth century would have remained unrepresented if Lord Dacre had not directed me to Henry Taylor's *The Statesman*.

This leads to the final aspect of the question 'What is a political quotation?', namely does it have to have been quoted, or is it sufficient for it to be quotable? Once you accept quotability as the criterion, you are on a slippery slope, at the bottom of which lie the broad acres of anthologies and commonplace books. The compilers of the first edition of the *Oxford Dictionary of Quotations* were in no doubt: 'During the whole work of selection a great effort was made to restrict the entries to actual current quotations and not to include phrases which the various editors or contributors believed to be quotable or wanted to be quoted.' Of course they were right. And yet even they said only that a great effort was made, not that it was successful in every case. I must confess to not having been quite so purist. Certainly this is essentially a dictionary of what has been quoted, but here and there I have taken one or two small steps down the slippery slope and included lines that I believed modern readers would like to quote. After all, how can one know that they have not been quoted somewhere at some time? I took the liberty of including Polonius's advice to Ophelia about marriage to the heir to the throne:

> His greatness weighed, his will is not his own
> For he himself is subject to his birth.
> He may not, as unvalued persons do,
> Carve for himself, for on his choice depends
> The sanity and health of the whole state;
> And therefore must his choice be circumscribed
> Unto the voice and yielding of that body
> Whereof he is the head.

I had no record of its being politically quoted anywhere, but in view of the continuing current debate about the divorce and remarriage of the Prince of Wales it seemed to me that many people might like to be reminded of it. It was only after it had been passed for the press that I discovered that Stanley Baldwin had quoted that same speech in the House of Commons, in relation to the abdication of King Edward VIII. So the reader will find here a small number—and an exceedingly small percentage—of entries that I cannot swear have been previously quoted, though equally I cannot swear that they have not. They are also another way of stopping the pool of political quotation from stagnating. And another aspect of this question is, when does a political quotation stop being a political quotation? It would have been easy to decide that Bismarck's observation that the Balkan conflict was 'not worth the healthy bones of a single Pomeranian grenadier' had passed into history's out-tray; but it surfaced again in 1995 in a House of Commons debate on the role of the UN forces in Bosnia.

If I may have taken slight liberties with the quotable as opposed to the quoted, this has not been the case with verification and sourcing. My colleagues at the Press have been rigorous and scrupulous about the tracing of quotations, and many promising runners fell at this last fence. They include familiar lines like *Pas d'ennemi à gauche* and 'Whoever is in office, the Conservatives are always in power', but among the omissions are a few whose absence I particularly regret. I am sure Bacon said 'Councils to which Time hath not been called, Time will not ratify' (and I am absolutely certain I did not make it up), and I am fairly sure he said 'Great events may have small occasions, but seldom small causes', but no amount of research has been able to track either of them down. I also wish we could have found who it was who said of Gladstone that when making a speech he not only followed every bay and headland along the coastline of his argument, but also insisted on tracking every river to its source. And I believe it was the American scholar Donald Schon who said that government bureaux are memorials to dead problems, but alas I cannot prove it. Another source of regret is the quotations that appeared just too late for inclusion, in particular Shimon Peres's observation 'Television has made dictatorship impossible, but democracy unbearable.' But we were not too late for President Izetbegović's words after signing the Dayton Accord: 'And to my people I say, this may not be a just peace, but it is more just than a continuation of war.'

Perhaps the most problematic of all the quotations are the very recent ones. Ultimately, time is the judge of whether an observation can be accepted as a quotation, and whether 'Tough on crime and tough on the causes of crime' is a full member of the club or merely a short-term visitor, only time will tell. On the other hand, to set an arbitrary limit of ten or twenty years from the first citation as a qualifying period would mean excluding many quotations to which readers would want to refer. I suspect that in any future edition it will be the most topical recent entries that are the least likely to survive.

And what about speech-writers? This is surely a recent problem. It may be that politicians in the past had help from time to time, but it is hard to picture Lincoln or Disraeli or Lloyd George or Churchill asking the boys in the back room to come up with some ideas for the next speech. Today a team of speech writers is part of the standard entourage of an international leader, and on occasions we learn, at least informally, that some famous phrase or other was coined by a hand unconnected to the tongue that uttered it. Should we seek out the names of the writers and give them due recognition? It would be an impossible task, and moreover the reader would look for the phrase under the name of the politician who delivered it. This is also true of quotations that were in circulation some time before a politician gave them national or international currency. Where we can trace the original we attribute it, but it has to be accepted that some of the quotations attributed to politicians were probably not their own coinage. Nevertheless they will always be associated with the words, just as Clark Gable, and not Margaret Mitchell or Sidney Howard, will always be associated with the line 'Frankly, my dear, I don't give a damn' (which would probably be the politician's comment on this question).

The other difficulty presented by the most recent quotations is the possibility that in their original form they reached a national or international audience without ever appearing on a printed page. Radio and television archives are not always accessible, and slow to plough through even when you know exactly what you are looking for; but when you have only an imprecise recollection or reference it can be effectively impossible to locate what would be fairly easy to find in a newspaper or press cuttings library. Of course all the memorable quotations eventually find their way into print, but not always in their original form. The chief whip's famous phrase in Michael Dobbs's *House of Cards*, 'You might very well think that. I couldn't possibly comment', is taken from the television script; it does not appear in the book. Equally, transcripts from radio and television can miss important emphases and nuances: when Neil Kinnock spoke to the Labour Party Conference about Liverpool Council, his stress on 'Labour' in the phrase, 'the grotesque chaos of a Labour council—a *Labour* council—hiring taxis to scuttle round the city handing out redundancy notices to its own workers' did not come through in the press reports as it did in the television news bulletins. And the televising of parliamentary debates has exposed the difference between the semi-incoherence of some members' speeches and the comparative lucidity and logic of the phrasing that appears subsequently in the august pages of Hansard.

Finally I must acknowledge with gratitude the large number of people whose help has been invaluable. Christopher Booker, Simon Heffer, Norman Rees, and Peter Hennessy all read the whole of the first draft and made numerous comments and suggestions of which many were immediately incorporated. All of them are extremely busy professionals and I was astonished as well as delighted at the amount of time and care they were willing to give to the task. Indeed one of the happiest aspects of an unusually happy assignment has been the willingness of almost everyone I contacted to give up time and take trouble to make the Dictionary as full and accurate as possible. Of those who helped out on specific topics or authors I would like to offer especial thanks to the following: Lord Bauer, Tony Benn, John Biffen, John Blundell, Dr Eamonn Butler, the Bishop of Coventry, Lord Dacre, Lord Deedes, Oliver Everett, Milton Friedman, Norman Gash, Martin Gilbert, Henry Hardy, Lord Healey, Sir Bernard Ingham, Simon Jenkins, Bernard Levin, Kenneth Morgan, Nigel Nicolson, Matthew Parris, Enoch Powell, Stanley Wells, and Chris Wrigley. Above all, I want to thank the editorial team of the Quotations Dictionaries department of the Oxford University Press. Not only have they done the bulk of the work; their knowledge, expertise, and scholarly rigour have contributed immeasurably to the quality of the book.

Any credit for the final result must be shared with all of the above; the blame remains exclusively the editor's.

ANTONY JAY

Somerset, January 1996

How to Use the Dictionary

The sequence of entries is by alphabetical order of author, usually by surname but with occasional exceptions such as imperial or royal titles, or authors known by a pseudonym ('**Saki**'), or a nickname (**Caligula**). In general authors' names are given in the form by which they are best known, so that we have **Harold Macmillan** (not Lord Stockton), **Lord Melbourne** (not William Lamb), **H. G. Wells** (not Herbert George Wells), and **Harold Wilson** (not James Harold Wilson). Collections such as **Anonymous** and the **Bible** are included in the alphabetical sequence.

Author names are followed by dates of birth and death (where known) and brief descriptions; where appropriate, cross-references are then given to quotations about that author elsewhere in the text (*on Acheson:* see **Pearson** 200:7). Within each author entry, quotations are arranged according to date, with material from novels, plays, letters, diaries, and speeches forming a single chronological sequence. (The **Anonymous** section is an exception to this rule: quotations under this heading are arranged alphabetically according to the first word of the quotation.) Foreign-language text is given where it is felt that the quotation is more familiar in the language of origin (*'L'État c'est moi'*).

Where the information is available (the composition date of a letter or diary, the publication date of a book), a quotation can be accorded a precise date. Some quotations are dated according to the circumstances with which the remark or comment is associated (Stanton's comment following the assassination of Abraham Lincoln, 'Now he belongs to the ages', dates the quotation as 1865). When the date is uncertain or unknown, and the quotation cannot be related to a particular event, the author's date of death has been used to date the quotation. A few entries (such as that for Winston Churchill) have a number of such attributed items; they are arranged alphabetically ('a' and 'the' being ignored).

Contextual information regarded as essential to a full appreciation of the quotation precedes the relevant text in an italicized note; information seen as providing helpful information follows in an italicized note. Bibliographical information as to the source from which the quotation is taken appears in a marginal note; titles and dates of publication are supplied, but full finding references are not given. Every attempt has been made to trace quotations to citable sources, but where necessary 'attributed' is used to indicate that while attribution to a particular author is popularly made, a specific reference has not been traced. It is felt more helpful to include widely known material with an account of its status, than to omit the item because it is not susceptible of final verification.

Cross-references are made both to individual quotations (cf. **Disraeli** 121:1) and to whole entries. References to specific quotations consist of the author's name followed by the page number and the number of the quotation on the page (**Burke** 63:1). Authors who have their own entries are typographically distinguished by the use of bold (epitaph for John **Adams,** of Lord **Halifax**) in context or source notes, or in the author descriptions (son of Joseph **Kennedy**).

The Index

Both the keywords and the entries following each keyword, including those in foreign languages, are in strict alphabetical order. Singular and plural nouns (with their possessive forms) are grouped separately.

The references show the author's name, usually in abbreviated form (SHAK/Shakespeare), followed by the page number and the number of the quotation on that page: 183:8 therefore means quotation 8 on page 183.

Diane Abbott 1953–

British Labour politician

1 Being an MP is the sort of job all working-class parents want for their children—clean, indoors and no heavy lifting. — in *Independent* 18 January 1994

Bella Abzug 1920–

American politician

2 Richard Nixon impeached himself. He gave us Gerald Ford as his revenge. — in *Rolling Stone*; Linda Botts *Loose Talk* (1980)

Accius 170–*c.*86 BC

Latin poet and dramatist

3 Let them hate, so long as they fear. — *Atreus*

Dean Acheson 1893–1971

American statesman
on Acheson: see **Pearson** 287:5

4 I will undoubtedly have to seek what is happily known as gainful employment, which I am glad to say does not describe holding public office. — in *Time* 22 December 1952

5 Great Britain has lost an empire and has not yet found a role. — speech at the Military Academy, West Point, 5 December 1962

6 The first requirement of a statesman is that he be dull. — in *Observer* 21 June 1970

7 A memorandum is written not to inform the reader but to protect the writer. — in *Wall Street Journal* 8 September 1977

of President **Eisenhower**:
8 I doubt very much if a man whose main literary interests were in works by Mr Zane Grey, admirable as they may be, is particularly equipped to be the chief executive of this country, particularly where Indian Affairs are concerned. — attributed

Lord Acton 1834–1902

British historian

9 Power tends to corrupt and absolute power corrupts absolutely. — letter to Bishop Mandell Creighton, 3 April 1887
often quoted as 'All power corrupts . . .'

10 Great men are almost always bad men, even when they exercise influence and not authority. — letter to Bishop Mandell Creighton, 3 April 1887

Abigail Adams 1744–1818

wife of John **Adams**, 2nd President of the USA, and mother of John Quincy **Adams**

1 In the new code of laws which I suppose it will be necessary for you to make I desire you would remember the ladies, and be more generous and favourable to them than your ancestors. Do not put such unlimited power into the hands of the husbands. Remember all men would be tyrants if they could.
letter to John Adams, 31 March 1776

2 These are times in which a genius would wish to live. It is not in the still calm of life, or the repose of a pacific station, that great characters are formed... Great necessities call out great virtues.
letter to John Quincy Adams, 19 January 1780

3 Patriotism in the female sex is the most disinterested of all virtues. Excluded from honours and from offices, we cannot attach ourselves to the State or Government from having held a place of eminence... Yet all history and every age exhibit instances of patriotic virtue in the female sex; which considering our situation equals the most heroic of yours.
letter to John Adams, 17 June 1782

Franklin P. Adams 1881–1960

American journalist and humorist

4 When the political columnists say 'Every thinking man' they mean themselves, and when candidates appeal to 'Every intelligent voter' they mean everybody who is going to vote for them.
Nods and Becks (1944)

5 The trouble with this country is that there are too many politicians who believe, with a conviction based on experience, that you can fool all of the people all of the time.
Nods and Becks (1944)

6 Elections are won by men and women chiefly because most people vote against somebody rather than for somebody.
Nods and Becks (1944)

Henry Brooks Adams 1838–1918

American man of letters

7 Politics, as a practice, whatever its professions, has always been the systematic organization of hatreds.
The Education of Henry Adams (1907)

8 A friend in power is a friend lost.
The Education of Henry Adams (1907)

9 [Charles] Sumner's mind had reached the calm of water which receives and reflects images without absorbing them; it contained nothing but itself.
of the American politician and orator Charles **Sumner**
The Education of Henry Adams (1907)

10 The progress of evolution from President Washington to President Grant was alone evidence to upset Darwin.
The Education of Henry Adams (1907)

1 Practical politics consists in ignoring facts. — *The Education of Henry Adams* (1907)

John Adams 1735–1826

1st Vice-President of the United States and 2nd President; father of John Quincy **Adams** and husband of Abigail **Adams**

2 I always consider the settlement of America with reverence and wonder, as the opening of a grand scene and design in providence, for the illumination of the ignorant and the emancipation of the slavish part of mankind all over the earth. — notes for *A Dissertation on the Canon and Feudal Law* (1765)

3 The jaws of power are always opened to devour, and her arm is always stretched out, if possible, to destroy the freedom of thinking, speaking, and writing. — *A Dissertation on the Canon and the Feudal Law* (1765)

4 Liberty cannot be preserved without a general knowledge among the people, who have a right…and a desire to know; but besides this, they have a right, an indisputable, unalienable, indefeasible, divine right to that most dreaded and envied kind of knowledge, I mean of the characters and conduct of their rulers. — *A Dissertation on the Canon and Feudal Law* (1765)

5 There is danger from all men. The only maxim of a free government ought to be to trust no man living with power to endanger the public liberty. — Notes for an Oration at Braintree (Spring 1772)

of the Boston Tea Party:

6 There is a dignity, a majesty, a sublimity, in this last effort of the patriots that I greatly admire. The people should never rise without doing something to be remembered—something notable and striking. — diary 17 December 1773

7 A government of laws, and not of men. — in *Boston Gazette* (1774)

later incorporated in the Massachusetts Constitution (1780)

8 I agree with you that in politics the middle way is none at all. — letter to Horatio Gates, 23 March 1776

9 Yesterday, the greatest question was decided which ever was debated in America, and a greater perhaps never was nor will be decided among men. A resolution was passed without one dissenting colony, 'that these United Colonies are, and of right ought to be, free and independent States.' — letter to Abigail Adams, 3 July 1776

10 The happiness of society is the end of government. — *Thoughts on Government* (1776)

11 Fear is the foundation of most governments. — *Thoughts on Government* (1776)

12 The judicial power ought to be distinct from both the legislative and executive, and independent upon both, that so it may be a check upon both, as both should be checks upon that. — *Thoughts on Government* (1776)

13 I must study politics and war that my sons may have liberty to study mathematics and philosophy. — letter to Abigail Adams, 12 May 1780

of the vice-presidency:

1 My country has in its wisdom contrived for me the most insignificant office that ever the invention of man contrived or his imagination conceived. — letter to Abigail Adams, 19 December 1793

2 Democracy never lasts long. It soon wastes, exhausts, and murders itself. There never was a democracy that did not commit suicide. — letter to John Taylor, 15 April 1814

3 The fundamental article of my political creed is that despotism, or unlimited sovereignty, or absolute power, is the same in a majority of a popular assembly, an aristocratic council, an oligarchical junto, and a single emperor. — letter to Thomas Jefferson, 13 November 1815

4 Thomas—Jefferson—still surv—
Jefferson *died on the same day* — last words, 4 July 1826

John Quincy Adams 1767–1848

6th President of the USA and son of the 2nd President, John **Adams**, and Abigail **Adams**

5 Think of your forefathers! Think of your posterity! — *Oration at Plymouth* 22 December 1802

6 *Fiat justitia, pereat coelum* [Let justice be done, though heaven perish]. My toast would be, may our country be always successful, but whether successful or otherwise, always right. — letter to John Adams, 1 August 1816; cf. **Decatur** 111:4, **Mansfield** 249:6, **Watson** 380:3

7 America, with the same voice which spoke herself into existence as a nation, proclaimed to mankind the inextinguishable rights of human nature, and the only lawful foundations of government. — address, 4 July 1821

8 America ... well knows that by once enlisting under other banners than her own, were they even the banners of foreign independence, she would involve herself beyond the power of extraction, in all the wars of interest and intrigue, of individual avarice, envy, and ambition, which assume the colours and usurp the standard of freedom. The fundamental maxims of her policy would insensibly change from liberty to force ... She might become dictatress of the world. She would be no longer the ruler of her own spirit. — address, 4 July 1821

9 Individual liberty is individual power, and as the power of a community is a mass compounded of individual powers, the nation which enjoys the most freedom must necessarily be in proportion to its numbers the most powerful nation. — letter to James Lloyd, 1 October 1822

10 His letter is a dissertation to prove that the whole science of diplomacy consists in giving dinners.
of a letter sent by **Canning** *to Christopher Hughes, US minister to Sweden* — diary 1825; Charles Francis Adams *Memoirs of John Quincy Adams*

11 This house will bear witness to his piety; this town [Braintree, Massachusetts], his birthplace, to his — epitaph for John **Adams**, 1829

munificence; history to his patriotism; posterity to the depth and compass of his mind.

on collapsing in the Senate, 21 February 1848 (he died two days later):

1 This, this is the end of earth. I am content. — William H. Seward *Eulogy of John Quincy Adams to Legislature of New York* 1848

Samuel Adams 1722–1803

American revolutionary leader

2 Let us contemplate our forefathers, and posterity, and resolve to maintain the rights bequeathed to us by the former, for the sake of the latter. — speech, 1771

on hearing gunfire at Lexington, 19 April 1775:

3 What a glorious morning is this. — J. K. Hosmer *Samuel Adams* (1886)
traditionally quoted as 'What a glorious morning for America'

4 A nation of shopkeepers are very seldom so disinterested. — *Oration in Philadelphia* 1 August 1776 (the authenticity of this publication is doubtful); cf. **Napoleon** 270:1, **Smith** 341:6

5 Driven from every other corner of the earth, freedom of thought and the right of private judgement in matters of conscience direct their course to this happy country as their last asylum. — speech in Philadelphia, 1 August 1776

6 We cannot make events. Our business is wisely to improve them... Mankind are governed more by their feelings than by reason. Events which excite those feelings will produce wonderful effects. — J. N. Rakove *The Beginnings of National Politics* (1979)

Frank Ezra Adcock 1886–1968

British classicist and historian of Greece and Rome

7 Rome under Sulla was like a bus, with half the passengers trying to drive, and the rest trying to collect the fare. — lecture at Cambridge in the 1940s

Joseph Addison 1672–1719

English poet, playwright, and essayist; co-founder of *The Spectator*

8 What pity is it
That we can die but once to serve our country! — *Cato* (1713)

9 From hence, let fierce contending nations know
What dire effects from civil discord flow. — *Cato* (1713)

Konrad Adenauer 1876–1967

German statesman, first Chancellor of the Federal Republic of Germany, 1949–63

1 A thick skin is a gift from God. — in *New York Times* 30 December 1959

Aeschylus *c.*525–456 BC

Greek tragedian

2 Do not taint pure laws with mere expediency
Guard well and reverence that form of government
Which will eschew alike licence and slavery.
And from your policy do not wholly banish fear
For what man living, freed from fear, will still be just? — *The Eumenides*

3 Everyone's quick to blame the alien. — *The Suppliant Maidens*

Herbert Agar 1897–1980

American poet and writer

4 The truth which makes men free is for the most part the truth which men prefer not to hear. — *Time for Greatness* (1942)

Spiro T. Agnew 1918–

American Republican politician, Vice-President 1968-73; he resigned the vice-presidency on 10 October 1973 amid charges of financial wrong-doing while Governor of Maryland

5 I didn't say I wouldn't go into ghetto areas. I've been in many of them and to some extent I would say this: If you've seen one city slum you've seen them all. — in *Detroit Free Press* 19 October 1968

6 A spirit of national masochism prevails, encouraged by an effete corps of impudent snobs who characterize themselves as intellectuals. — speech in New Orleans, 19 October 1969

7 In the United States today, we have more than our share of the nattering nabobs of negativism. — speech in San Diego, 11 September 1970

Alcuin *c.*735–804

English scholar and theologian

8 And those people should not be listened to who keep saying the voice of the people is the voice of God [*Vox populi, vox Dei*], since the riotousness of the crowd is always very close to madness. — letter 164 in *Works* (1863)

Richard Aldington 1892–1962

English poet, novelist, and biographer

9 Patriotism is a lively sense of collective responsibility. Nationalism is a silly cock crowing on its own dunghill. — *The Colonel's Daughter* (1931)

Cecil Frances Alexander 1818–95

Irish poet

1 The rich man in his castle,
The poor man at his gate,
God made them, high or lowly,
And ordered their estate.

'All Things Bright and Beautiful' (1848)

Henry Southworth Allen

American writer

2 America is like a bar-room drunk. One minute it brags about its money and muscle, and then for the next hour it bleats into its beer about failure and hopelessness… Right now, we're in a bleating phase.

Going Too Far Enough (1994)

William Allen 1803–1879

American Democratic politician; US Senator

3 Fifty-four forty, or fight!
slogan of expansionist Democrats in the presidential campaign of 1844, in which the Oregon boundary definition was an issue (in 1846 the new Democratic president, James K. Polk, compromised on the 49th parallel with Great Britain)

speech in the US Senate, 1844

Woody Allen 1935–

American film director, writer, and actor

4 I believe there is something out there watching over us. Unfortunately, it's the government.

Peter McWilliams *Ain't Nobody's Business If You Do* (1993); attributed

Joseph Alsop b. 1910

American journalist

5 Gratitude, like love, is never a dependable international emotion.

in *Observer* 30 November 1952

Leo Amery 1873–1955

British Conservative politician

of H. H. **Asquith**:

6 For twenty years he has held a season-ticket on the line of least resistance and has gone wherever the train of events has carried him, lucidly justifying his position at whatever point he has happened to find himself.

in *Quarterly Review* July 1914

7 Speak for England.

said to Arthur Greenwood in House of Commons, 2 September 1939, in *My Political Life* (1955) vol. 3; cf. **Boothby** 52:4

1 I will quote certain other words. I do it with great reluctance, because I am speaking of those who are old friends and colleagues of mine, but they are words which, I think, are applicable to the present situation. This is what Cromwell said to the Long Parliament when he thought it was no longer fit to conduct the affairs of the nation: 'You have sat too long here for any good you have been doing. Depart, I say, and let us have done with you. In the name of God, go.'

in the House of Commons, 7 May 1940; cf. **Cromwell** 105:8

Fisher Ames 1758–1808

American politician

2 A monarchy is a merchantman which sails well, but will sometimes strike on a rock, and go to the bottom; whilst a republic is a raft which would never sink, but then your feet are always in the water.

attributed to Ames, speaking in the House of Representatives, 1795; quoted by R. W. Emerson in *Essays* (2nd series, 1844), but not traced in Ames's speeches

Anacharsis

Scythian prince of the sixth century BC

3 Written laws are like spider's webs; they will catch, it is true, the weak and poor, but would be torn in pieces by the rich and powerful.

Plutarch *Parallel Lives* 'Solon'

Anonymous

4 All human beings are born free and equal in dignity and rights.

Universal Declaration of Human Rights (1948) article 1

5 All the 'isms are wasms.

said to have been the comment of a Foreign Office spokesman on the signing of the Molotov–Ribbentrop Pact in August 1939

Peter Hennessy *Whitehall* (1990)

6 All the way with LBJ.

US Democratic Party campaign slogan supporting Lyndon Baines **Johnson**

in *Washington Post* 4 June 1960

7 *Arbeit macht frei.*
Work makes free.

on the gates of Dachau concentration camp, and subsequently on those of Auschwitz

inscription, 1933

8 Bad money drives out good.

proverbial expression of a principle attributed to Sir Thomas Gresham (*c.*1519–79), founder of the Royal Exchange

9 Ban the bomb.

US anti-nuclear slogan, 1953 onwards

adopted by the Campaign for Nuclear Disarmament

10 A bayonet is a weapon with a worker at each end.

British pacifist slogan (1940)

11 The best defence against the atom bomb is not to be there when it goes off.

contributor to *British Army Journal*, in *Observer* 20 February 1949

1 Better red than dead.

slogan of nuclear disarmament campaigners, late 1950s

2 A bigger bang for a buck.

Charles E. **Wilson**'s defence policy, in *Newsweek* 22 March 1954

3 Black is beautiful.

slogan of American civil rights campaigners, mid-1960s

4 Browne was like a hawk, he swooped down upon us;
Grey was like a rat, he undermined us.

Maori comment on Thomas Gore Browne and George Grey, successively Governors of New Zealand in the mid nineteenth century

in *Dictionary of National Biography*

5 Burn, baby, burn.

Black extremist slogan in use during the Los Angeles riots, August 1965

6 But this is terrible—*they've* elected a Labour Government, and *the country* will never stand for that!

unidentified lady diner in the Savoy Hotel, 26 July 1945

Michael Sissons and Philip French (eds.) *The Age of Austerity 1945–51* (1964)

7 Careless talk costs lives.

Second World War security poster

8 A Company for carrying on an undertaking of Great Advantage, but no one to know what it is.

Company Prospectus at the time of the South Sea Bubble (1711)

9 Confound their politics,
Frustrate their knavish tricks.

'God save the King', attributed to various authors, including Henry Carey

10 Crisis? What Crisis?

summarizing James **Callaghan***'s remark of 10 January 1979: 'I don't think other people in the world would share the view* [that] *there is mounting chaos'*

Sun headline, 11 January 1979

11 *Ein Reich, ein Volk, ein Führer.*
One realm, one people, one leader.

Nazi Party slogan

early 1930s

12 Every country has its own constitution; ours is absolutism moderated by assassination.

of Russia

Ernst Friedrich Herbert, Count Münster, quoting 'an intelligent Russian', in *Political Sketches of the State of Europe, 1814–1867* (1868)

13 Everyone has the right to freedom of movement and residence within the borders of each state. Everyone has the right to leave any country, including his own, and to return to his country. Everyone has the right to seek and to enjoy in other countries asylum from persecution.

Universal Declaration of Human Rights (1948)

14 Expletive deleted.

Submission of Recorded Presidential Conversations to the Committee on the Judiciary of the House of Representatives by President Richard M. Nixon 30 April 1974

1 Exterminate...the treacherous English, walk over General French's contemptible little army.
often attributed to Kaiser Wilhelm II, but most probably fabricated by the British; source of the nickname 'the Old Contemptibles'
Annexe to British Expeditionary Force Routine Orders of 24 September 1914; Arthur Ponsonby *Falsehood in Wartime* (1928)

2 For the sake of brevity we have followed the common practice of using the phrase 'Communists' throughout to include Fascists.
Radcliffe Report 'Security Procedures in the Public Service' April 1962

3 Frederick the Great lost the battle of Jena.
attributing the Prussians' defeat at Jena by **Napoleon** *in 1806 to their rigid adherence to the strategy of* **Frederick** *(who had died in 1786)*
Walter Bagehot *The English Constitution* (1867)

4 Happy is that city which in time of peace thinks of war.
inscription found in the armoury of Venice
Robert Burton *The Anatomy of Melancholy* (1621–51)

5 Hark the herald angels sing
Mrs Simpson's pinched our king.
contemporary children's rhyme on the abdication of **Edward VIII**
Clement Attlee letter 26 December 1938; Kenneth Harris *Attlee* (1982)

6 Have you heard? The Prime Minister has resigned and Northcliffe has sent for the King.
a joke (c.1919) suggesting that Lord **Northcliffe**, *the press baron and* **Lloyd George**'s *implacable enemy, would succeed him as Prime Minister*
Hamilton Fyfe *Northcliffe, an Intimate Biography* (1930)

7 He talked shop like a tenth muse.
of **Gladstone**'s *Budget speech*
G. W. E. Russell *Collections and Recollections* (1898)

8 He who writes the minutes rules the roost.
Civil Service maxim

9 *Ils ne passeront pas.*
They shall not pass.
slogan used by French army defence at Verdun in 1916
variously attributed to Marshal Pétain and to General Robert Nivelle; cf. **Ibarruri** 186:6

10 I'm backing Britain.
slogan coined by workers at the Colt factory, Surbiton, Surrey, and subsequently used in a national campaign
in *The Times* 1 January 1968

11 I met wid Napper Tandy, and he took me by the hand,
And he said, 'How's poor ould Ireland, and how does she stand?'
She's the most disthressful country that iver yet was seen,
For they're hangin' men an' women for the wearin' o' the Green.
'The Wearin' o' the Green' (*c.*1795 ballad)

12 In good King Charles's golden days,
When loyalty no harm meant;
A furious High-Churchman I was,
And so I gained preferment.
Unto my flock I daily preached,
Kings are by God appointed,
And damned are those who dare resist,
Or touch the Lord's Anointed.
And this is law, I will maintain,
Unto my dying day, Sir,
That whatsoever King shall reign,
I will be the Vicar of Bray, sir!
'The Vicar of Bray' in *British Musical Miscellany* (1734) vol. 1

1 I never vote. It only encourages them.

elderly American lady quoted by comedian Jack Parr; William Safire *The New Language of Politics* (1968)

2 The iron lady.

name given to Margaret **Thatcher**, *then Leader of the Opposition, by the Soviet Defence Ministry newspaper* Red Star, *which accused her of trying to revive the cold war*

in *Sunday Times* 25 January 1976

3 It became necessary to destroy the town to save it.

comment by unidentified US Army major on Ben Tre, Vietnam

in Associated Press Report, *New York Times* 8 February 1968

4 It'll play in Peoria.

catch-phrase of the **Nixon** *administration (early 1970s) meaning 'it will be acceptable to middle America'*

originating in a standard music hall joke of the 1930s

5 It's that man again...! At the head of a cavalcade of seven black motor cars Hitler swept out of his Berlin Chancellery last night on a mystery journey.

headline in *Daily Express* 2 May 1939; the acronym ITMA became the title of a BBC radio show, from September 1939

6 The King over the Water.

Jacobite toast to the deposed and exiled James II and his heirs

current in the 18th century

7 King's Moll Reno'd in Wolsey's Home Town.

US newspaper headline on Wallis Simpson's divorce proceedings in Ipswich

Frances Donaldson *Edward VIII* (1974)

8 Labour isn't working.

caption to Conservative Party poster, 1978–9, showing a long queue outside an unemployment office

Philip Kleinman *The Saatchi and Saatchi Story* (1987)

9 Lacking any capacity for political passion, he has made it as nearly an unpolitical office as any man could.

of Walter **Monckton** *as Minister of Labour*

in *New Statesman* 8 January 1954

10 The land for the people.

Communist slogan, *c.*1917

11 LBJ, LBJ, how many kids have you killed today?

anti-Vietnam War marching slogan during the presidency of Lyndon **Johnson**

Jacquin Sanders *The Draft and the Vietnam War* (1966)

12 Let's run it up the flagpole and see if anyone salutes it.

Reginald Rose *Twelve Angry Men* (1955); recorded as an established advertising expression in the 1960s

13 *Liberté! Égalité! Fraternité!*
Freedom! Equality! Brotherhood!

motto of the French Revolution (though of earlier origin)

the Club des Cordeliers passed a motion, 30 June 1793, 'that owners should be urged to paint on the front of their houses, in large letters, the words: Unity, indivisibility of the Republic, Liberty, Equality, Fraternity or death'; in *Journal de Paris* no. 182 (from 1795 the words 'or death' were dropped)

14 Liberty is always unfinished business.

title of 36th Annual Report of the American Civil Liberties Union, 1 July 1955–30 June 1956

1 [Like] watching a stream of blood coming from beneath a closed door.
a contemporary expression of the feelings evoked by news of the executions after the Easter Rising
Robert Kee *Ourselves Alone* (1916)

2 Lloyd George knew my father,
My father knew Lloyd George.
two-line comic song, sung to the tune of 'Onward, Christian Soldiers' and possibly by Tommy Rhys Roberts (1910–75)

3 Lost is our old simplicity of times,
The world abounds with laws, and teems with crimes.
On the Proceedings Against America (1775)

4 CHILD: Mamma, are Tories born wicked, or do they grow wicked afterwards?
MOTHER: They are born wicked, and grow worse.
G. W. E. Russell *Collections and Recollections* (1898)

5 Men said openly that Christ and His saints slept.
of twelfth-century England during the civil war between Stephen and Matilda
Anglo-Saxon Chronicle for 1137

6 Ministers say one of two things in Cabinet. Some say, 'Look, Daddy, no hands.' Others say, 'Look, Daddy, me too.'
unidentified senior official to Sarah Hogg on her arrival to take over the Prime Minister's policy unit
in *Sunday Times* 9 April 1995

7 The ministry of all the talents.
name given ironically to William Grenville's coalition of 1806, and also applied to later coalitions
G. W. Cooke *The History of Party* (1837) vol. 3

8 The nearest thing to death in life
Is David Patrick Maxwell Fyfe,
Though underneath that gloomy shell
He does himself extremely well.
of David Maxwell Fyfe, later Lord **Kilmuir**, *and said to have been current on the Northern circuit in the late 1930s*
E. Grierson *Confessions of a Country Magistrate* (1972)

9 Never stand when you could sit, and never miss a chance to relieve yourself.
advice given by a private secretary or equerry to **George V** or **George VI**

10 No man's life, liberty or property are safe while the legislature is in session.
view of an unidentified New York State Surrogate Court Judge
in 1866; unattributed

the defenders of the besieged city of Derry to the Jacobite army of James II, April 1689:

11 No surrender!
adopted as a slogan of Protestant Ulster
Jonathan Bardon *A History of Ulster* (1992)

12 Now that the Cabinet's gone to its dinner,
The Secretary stays and gets thinner and thinner,
Racking his brains to record and report
What he thinks they think they ought to have thought.
anonymous verse, undated; S. S. Wilson *The Cabinet Office* (1975)

13 One Cartwright brought a Slave from Russia, and would scourge him, for which he was questioned: and it was resolved, That England was too pure an Air for Slaves to breathe in.
'In the 11th of Elizabeth' (17 November 1568–16 November 1569); John Rushworth *Historical Collections* (1680–1722)

1 Order reigns in Warsaw.
after the brutal suppression of an uprising

the newspaper *Moniteur* reported, 16 September 1831, 'Order and calm are completely restored in the capital'; on the same day Count Sebastiani, minister of foreign affairs, declared: 'Peace reigns in Warsaw'

2 Please to remember the Fifth of November,
Gunpowder Treason and Plot.
We know no reason why gunpowder treason
Should ever be forgot.

traditional rhyme on the Gunpowder Plot (1605)

3 *Plus royaliste que le roi.*
More of a royalist than the king.
noted as a current catch-phrase which was not in fact new; 'it was coined under Louis XVI: it chained up the hands of the loyal, leaving free only the arm of the hangman'

François René, Vicomte de Chateaubriand *De la monarchie selon la charte* (1816)

4 Power to the people.

slogan of the Black Panther movement, from *c.*1968 onwards

5 *Sic transit gloria mundi.*
Thus passes the glory of the world.
said during the coronation of a new Pope, while flax is burned to represent the transitoriness of earthly glory

used at the coronation of Alexander V in Pisa, 7 July 1409, but earlier in origin

6 The silly, flat, dishwatery utterances of the man who has to be pointed out to intelligent observers as the President of the United States.

review of **Lincoln**'s Gettysburg Address, in *Chicago Times* 20 November 1863; cf. **Everett** 134:4

7 *Tempora mutantur, et nos mutamur in illis.*
Times change, and we change with them.

William Harrison *Description of Britain* (1577); attributed to the Emperor Lothar I (795–855) in the form '*omnia mutantur, nos et mutamur in illis* [all things change, and we change with them]'

8 There is one thing stronger than all the armies in the world; and that is an idea whose time has come.

in *Nation* 15 April 1943; cf. **Hugo** 184:5

9 There's no such thing as a free lunch.
colloquial axiom in US economics from the 1960s, much associated with Milton **Friedman**

first found in printed form in Robert Heinlein *The Moon is a Harsh Mistress* (1966)

an unnamed Labour MP commenting on the unusually pale eyes of Hugh **Dalton**:

10 They have a habit of looking at you intently and conveying unfathomable depths of insincerity.
sometimes quoted as 'eyes blazing with insincerity'

Patricia Strauss *Bevin and Co. The Leaders of British Labour* (1941)

annotation to a ministerial brief, said to have been read out inadvertently in the House of Lords:

11 This is a rotten argument, but it should be good enough for their lordships on a hot summer afternoon.

Lord Home *The Way the Wind Blows* (1976)

12 Though I yield to no one in my admiration for Mr Coolidge, I do wish he did not look as if he had been weaned on a pickle.
of President Calvin **Coolidge**

anonymous remark, in Alice Roosevelt Longworth *Crowded Hours* (1933)

1 Three acres and a cow.
regarded as the requirement for self-sufficiency; associated with the radical politician Jesse Collings (1831–1920) and his land reform campaign begun in 1885
Jesse Collings in the House of Commons, 26 January 1886, although used earlier by Joseph **Chamberlain** in a speech at Evesham (in *The Times* 17 November 1885), by which time it was already proverbial

2 'Tis bad enough in man or woman
To steal a goose from off a common;
But surely he's without excuse
Who steals the common from the goose.
'On Inclosures'; in *The Oxford Book of Light Verse* (1938)

3 To secure for the workers by hand or by brain the full fruits of their industry and the most equitable distribution thereof that may be possible upon the basis of the common ownership of the means of production, distribution, and exchange.
Clause Four of the Labour Party's Constitution, adopted 1918/26; cf. **Blair** 49:2

4 Ulster says no.
slogan coined in response to the Anglo-Irish Agreement of 15 November 1985
in *Irish Times* 25 November 1985

5 Under capitalism man exploits man. And under Communism it is just the reverse.
joke told to J. K. **Galbraith** *at a dinner given for him during his lecture tour of Poland by the Polish Economic Society, May 1958*
J. K. Galbraith *A Life in Our Times* (1981)

6 War will cease when men refuse to fight.
pacifist slogan (often quoted 'Wars will cease ...')
from *c.*1936

7 We hold these truths to be self-evident, that all men are created equal, that they are endowed by their Creator with certain unalienable rights, that among these are life, liberty and the pursuit of happiness.
The American Declaration of Independence, 4 July 1776

8 We shall not be moved.
title of labour and civil rights song (1931) adapted from an earlier gospel hymn

9 We shall overcome.
revived in 1946 as a protest song by Black tobacco workers, and in 1963 during the Black Civil Rights Campaign
title of song, originating from before the American Civil War, adapted as a Baptist hymn ('I'll Overcome Some Day', 1901) by C. Albert Tindley

10 We want eight, and we won't wait.
on the construction of Dreadnoughts
George Wyndham's speech in *The Times* 29 March 1909

11 A well-regulated militia, being necessary to the security of a free State, the right of the people to keep and bear arms, shall not be infringed.
Constitution of the United States (Second Amendment, 1791)

12 What did the President know and when did he know it?
question current at the time of Watergate, associated particularly with Howard Baker, Vice-Chairman of the Senate Watergate Committee

13 When war enters a country
It produces lies like sand.
epigraph to Arthur Ponsonby *Falsehood in Wartime* (1928)

1 Whose finger do you want on the trigger?
headline alluding to the atom bomb, apropos the failure of both the Labour and Conservative parties to purge their leaders of proven failures
in *Daily Mirror* 21 September 1951

2 Why is there only one Monopolies Commission?
British graffito; incorporated in the Official Monster Raving Loony Party Manifesto, 1987

3 A willing foe and sea room.
Naval toast in the time of Nelson
W. N. T. Beckett *A Few Naval Customs, Expressions, Traditions, and Superstitions* (1931) 'Customs'

4 Winston is back.
Board of Admiralty signal to the Fleet on Winston **Churchill***'s reappointment as First Sea Lord, 3 September 1939*
Martin Gilbert *Winston S. Churchill* (1976) vol. 5

Susan Brownell Anthony 1820–1906

American feminist and political activist

5 The men and women of the North are slaveholders, those of the South slaveowners. The guilt rests on the North equally with the South.
Speech on No Union with Slaveholders 1857

6 Join the union, girls, and together say *Equal Pay for Equal Work.*
in *The Revolution* 8 October 1869

7 Here, in the first paragraph of the Declaration [of Independence], is the assertion of the natural right of all to the ballot; for how can 'the consent of the governed' be given, if the right to vote be denied?
speech in 1873 before her trial for voting
Is It a Crime for a Citizen of the United States to Vote?

John Arbuthnot 1667–1735

Scottish physician and pamphleteer

8 He [the writer] warns the heads of parties against believing their own lies.
The Art of Political Lying (1712)

9 All political parties die at last of swallowing their own lies.
Richard Garnett *Life of Emerson* (1988)

Hannah Arendt 1906–75

American political philosopher

10 The most radical revolutionary will become a conservative on the day after the revolution.
in *New Yorker* 12 September 1970

11 Under conditions of tyranny it is far easier to act than to think.
W. H. Auden *A Certain World* (1970)

Marquis d'Argenson 1694–1757

French politician and political essayist

1 *Laisser-faire.*
No interference.
term applied to the doctrine of minimum state intervention in economic affairs
Mémoires et Journal Inédit du Marquis d'Argenson; cf. **Quesnay** 299:2

Aristotle 384–322 BC

Greek philosopher

2 Therefore, the good of man must be the objective of the science of politics.
Nicomachean Ethics

3 We make war that we may live in peace.
Nicomachean Ethics

4 Politicians also have no leisure, because they are always aiming at something beyond political life itself, power and glory, or happiness.
Nicomachean Ethics

5 Man is by nature a political animal.
Politics

6 He who is unable to live in society, or who has no need because he is sufficient for himself, must be either a beast or a god.
Politics

7 For that some should rule, and others be ruled, is a thing not only necessary but expedient, for from the hour of their birth some are marked for subjection, others for rule.
Politics

8 Poverty is the parent of revolution and crime.
Politics

9 Where some people are very wealthy and others have nothing, the result will be either extreme democracy or absolute oligarchy, or despotism will come from either of those excesses.
Politics

10 The most perfect political community is one in which the middle class is in control, and outnumbers both of the other classes.
Politics

11 No tyrant need fear till men begin to feel confident in each other.
Politics

Robert Armstrong 1927–

British civil servant, Head of the Civil Service, 1981–7

12 It contains a misleading impression, not a lie. It was being economical with the truth.
referring to a letter during the 'Spycatcher' trial, Supreme Court, New South Wales, November 1986
in *Daily Telegraph* 19 November 1986; cf. **Burke** 68:2

William Armstrong 1915–80

British civil servant, Head of the Civil Service 1968–74
on Armstrong: see **Rothschild** 313:7

1 The business of the Civil Service is the orderly management of decline.
in 1973: Peter Hennessy *Whitehall* (1990)

Matthew Arnold 1822–88

English poet and essayist; son of Thomas **Arnold**

2 Our society distributes itself into Barbarians, Philistines, and Populace; and America is just ourselves, with the Barbarians quite left out, and the Populace nearly.
Culture and Anarchy (1869) preface

3 The men of culture are the true apostles of equality.
Culture and Anarchy (1869)

4 When I want to distinguish clearly the aristocratic class from the Philistines proper, or middle class, [I] name the former, in my own mind *the Barbarians.*
Culture and Anarchy (1869)

5 That vast portion...of the working-class which, raw and half-developed, has long lain half-hidden amidst its poverty and squalor, and is now issuing from its hiding-place to assert an Englishman's heaven-born privilege of doing as he likes, and is beginning to perplex us by marching where it likes, meeting where it likes, bawling what it likes, breaking what it likes—to this vast residuum we may with great propriety give the name of Populace.
Culture and Anarchy (1869)

Thomas Arnold 1795–1842

English historian; Headmaster of Rugby School from 1828; father of Matthew **Arnold**

6 As for rioting, the old Roman way of dealing with that is always the right one; flog the rank and file, and fling the ringleaders from the Tarpeian rock.
from an unpublished letter written before 1828

Raymond Aron 1905–

French sociologist and political journalist

7 Political thought, in France, is retrospective or utopian.
L'opium des intellectuels (1955)

Henry Fountain Ashurst

American politician

8 I am not in Washington as a statesman. I am there as a very well paid messenger boy doing your errands. My chief occupation is going around with a forked stick picking up little fragments of patronage for my constituents.
Thomas C. Donnelly *Rocky Mountain Politics* (1940); attributed

Herbert Henry Asquith 1852–1928

British Liberal statesman; Prime Minister, 1908–16
on Asquith: see **Churchill** 88:2, **Hennessy** 175:2

1 We had better wait and see.
phrase used repeatedly in speeches in 1910, referring to the rumour that the House of Lords was to be flooded with new Liberal peers to ensure the passage of the Finance Bill
Roy Jenkins *Asquith* (1964)

2 Happily there seems to be no reason why we should be anything more than spectators [of the approaching war].
Letters to Venetia Stanley (1982) 24 July 1914

3 We shall never sheath the sword which we have not lightly drawn until Belgium recovers in full measure all and more than all that she has sacrificed, until France is adequately secured against the menace of aggression, until the rights of the smaller nationalities of Europe are placed upon an unassailable foundation, and until the military domination of Prussia is wholly and finally destroyed.
speech at the Guildhall, London, 9 November 1914

4 There is no more striking illustration of the immobility of British institutions than the House of Commons.
Fifty Years of Parliament (1926) vol. 2

5 The office of the Prime Minister is what its holder chooses and is able to make of it.
Fifty Years of Parliament (1926) vol. 2

6 [The War Office kept three sets of figures:] one to mislead the public, another to mislead the Cabinet, and the third to mislead itself.
Alistair Horne *Price of Glory* (1962)

7 It is fitting that we should have buried the Unknown Prime Minister [Bonar Law] by the side of the Unknown Soldier.
Robert Blake *The Unknown Prime Minister* (1955)

8 He is a Chimborazo or Everest among the sandhills of the Baldwin Cabinet.
of Winston **Churchill**
Roy Jenkins *Asquith* (1964)

Margot Asquith 1864–1945

political hostess; wife of Herbert **Asquith**

on hearing that **Campbell-Bannerman**, *in planning the Liberal administration of 1905, intended to make R. B.* **Haldane** *Home Secretary instead of Lord Chancellor:*

9 I was reminded of George Eliot's remark, 'When a man wants a peach it is no good offering him the largest vegetable marrow.'
Roy Jenkins *Asquith* (1964)

10 Kitchener is a great poster.
More Memories (1933)

11 No amount of education will make women first-rate politicians. Can you see a woman becoming a Prime Minister? I cannot imagine a greater calamity for these islands than to be put under the guidance of a woman in 10 Downing Street.
Off the Record (1943)

1 Lord Birkenhead is very clever but sometimes his brains go to his head.

in *Listener* 11 June 1953 'Margot Oxford' by Lady Violet Bonham Carter

2 He can't see a belt without hitting below it.
of **Lloyd George**

in *Listener* 11 June 1953 'Margot Oxford' by Lady Violet Bonham Carter

Nancy Astor 1879–1964

American-born British Conservative politician

3 NANCY ASTOR: If I were your wife I would put poison in your coffee.
WINSTON CHURCHILL: And if I were your husband I would drink it.

Consuelo Vanderbilt *Glitter and Gold* (1952)

Brooks Atkinson 1894–1984

American journalist and critic

4 After each war there is a little less democracy to save.

Once Around the Sun (1951) 7 January

5 In every age 'the good old days' were a myth. No one ever thought they were good at the time. For every age had consisted of crises that seemed intolerable to the people who lived through them.

Once Around the Sun (1951) 8 February

6 There is a good deal of solemn cant about the common interests of capital and labour. As matters stand, their only common interest is that of cutting each other's throat.

Once Around the Sun (1951) 7 September

Clement Attlee 1883–1967

British Labour statesman; Prime Minister, 1945–51
on Attlee: see **Churchill** 93:13, 94:17, **Hennessy** 175:2, **Nicolson** 272:5, **Orwell** 278:8

7 Why does Mosley always speak to us as though he were a feudal landlord abusing tenants who are in arrears with their rent?
at a meeting of the Parliamentary Labour Party, 20 November 1930, a few months before Oswald Mosley was expelled from the Party

Hugh Dalton *Political Diary* (1986) 20 November 1930

8 A period of silence on your part would be welcome.
in reply to a letter from the Chairman of the Labour Party, Harold **Laski**, *asking (for the second time and at length) that Attlee should not form a new government until the Parliamentary Labour Party had had the chance to elect a new leader*

letter to Harold Laski, 20 August 1945; Francis Williams *A Prime Minister Remembers* (1961)

9 If the King asks you to form a Government you say 'Yes' or 'No', not 'I'll let you know later!'

Kenneth Harris *Attlee* (1982)

10 A monologue is not a decision.
to Winston **Churchill**, *who had complained that a matter had been raised several times in Cabinet*

Francis Williams *A Prime Minister Remembers* (1961)

1 The voice we heard was that of Mr Churchill but the mind was that of Lord Beaverbrook.
speech on radio, 5 June 1945; Francis Williams *A Prime Minister Remembers* (1961)

at a Cabinet Meeting, when Aneurin **Bevan** *as Minister of Housing complained that he could not get enough people for his building programme:*

2 BEVAN: Where are all the people I need for my programme?
ATTLEE: Looking for houses, Nye!
Michael Foot *Aneurin Bevan* (1973) vol. 2

3 Always was a loud-mouthed fellow.
of Hugh **Dalton**, *who had resigned as Chancellor of the Exchequer after a Budget leak*
Kenneth Harris *Attlee* (1982)

4 I should be a sad subject for any publicity expert. I have none of the qualities which create publicity.
Harold Nicolson *Diary* 14 January 1949

5 I think the British have the distinction above all other nations of being able to put new wine into old bottles without bursting them.
in the House of Commons, 24 October 1950

response to a memorandum from the Ministry of Works saying, 'We have read the Cabinet's proposals':

6 The Cabinet does not propose, it decides.
Tony Benn diary 20 May 1974

7 I believe that conscience is a still small voice and not a loudspeaker.
attributed, 1955

8 [Russian Communism is] the illegitimate child of Karl Marx and Catherine the Great.
speech at Aarhus University, 11 April 1956, in *The Times* 12 April 1956

9 Few thought he was even a starter
There were many who thought themselves smarter
But he ended PM
CH and OM
An earl and a knight of the garter.
describing himself in a letter to Tom Attlee, 8 April 1956
Kenneth Harris *Attlee* (1982)

10 Generally speaking the Press lives on disaster.
attributed, 1956

11 Democracy means government by discussion, but it is only effective if you can stop people talking.
speech at Oxford, 14 June 1957

12 Often the 'experts' make the worst possible Ministers in their own fields. In this country we prefer rule by amateurs.
speech at Oxford, 14 June 1957

13 It's a good maxim that if you have a good dog you don't bark yourself. I had a very good dog in Mr Ernest Bevin.
attributed, 1960

definition of the art of politics:

14 Judgement which is needed to make important decisions on imperfect knowledge in a limited time.
attributed

15 Queer bird, Halifax. Very humorous, all hunting and Holy Communion.
of Lord **Halifax**
in an interview; Peter Hennessy *Never Again* (1992)

W. H. Auden 1907–73

English poet

1 Private faces in public places
Are wiser and nicer
Than public faces in private places.

Orators (1932) dedication

2 There is no such thing as the State
And no one exists alone;
Hunger allows no choice
To the citizen or the police;
We must love one another or die.

'September 1, 1939' (1940)

3 Our researchers into Public Opinion are content
That he held the proper opinions for the time of year;
When there was peace, he was for peace; when there was war, he went.

'The Unknown Citizen' (1940)

4 This marble monument was erected by the state.
Was he free? Was he happy? The question is absurd:
Had anything been wrong, we should certainly have heard.

'The Unknown Citizen' (1940)

5 He knew human folly like the back of his hand,
And was greatly interested in armies and fleets;
When he laughed, respectable senators burst with laughter,
And when he cried the little children died in the streets.

'Epitaph on a Tyrant' (1940)

6 To save your world you asked this man to die:
Would this man, could he see you now, ask why?

'Epitaph for the Unknown Soldier' (1955)

Augustus 63 BC–AD 14

first Roman emperor

on Augustus: see **Cicero** 95:13

7 Quintilius Varus, give me back my legions.
after the annihilation by the German leader Arminius of three Roman legions under Quintilius Varus

Suetonius *Lives of the Caesars*

8 He could boast that he inherited it brick and left it marble.
of the city of Rome

Suetonius *Lives of the Caesars*

Marcus Aurelius AD 121–80

Roman emperor from AD 161

9 Man, you have been a citizen in this world city, what does it matter whether for five years or fifty?

Meditations

Jane Austen 1775–1817

English novelist

10 From politics, it was an easy step to silence.

Northanger Abbey (1818)

Francis Bacon 1561–1626

English lawyer, courtier, philosopher, and essayist

1 For also knowledge itself is power. — *Meditationes Sacrae* (1597) 'Of Heresies'

2 It is well to observe the force and virtue and consequence of discoveries, and these are to be seen nowhere more conspicuously than in those three which were unknown to the ancients, and of which the origins, though recent, are obscure and inglorious; namely, printing, gunpowder, and the magnet [Mariner's Needle]. For these three have changed the whole face and state of things throughout the world. — *Novum Organum* (1620)

3 To worship the people is to be worshipped. — *De Dignitate et Augmentis Scientiarum* (1623)

4 In civil business; what first? boldness; what second and third? boldness: and yet boldness is a child of ignorance and baseness. — *Essays* (1625) 'Of Boldness'

5 [Some] there be that can pack the cards and yet cannot play well; so there are some that are good in canvasses and factions, that are otherwise weak men. — *Essays* (1625) 'Of Cunning'

6 Nothing doth more hurt in a state than that cunning men pass for wise. — *Essays* (1625) 'Of Cunning'

7 There is surely no greater wisdom than well to time the beginnings and endings of things. — *Essays* (1625) 'Of Delays'

8 The difficulties in princes' business are many and great, but the greatest difficulty is often in their own mind. — *Essays* (1625) 'Of Empire'

9 Men in great place are thrice servants: servants of the sovereign or state, servants of fame, and servants of business. — *Essays* (1625) 'Of Great Place'

10 It is a strange desire to seek power and to lose liberty. — *Essays* (1625) 'Of Great Place'

11 The rising unto place is laborious, and by pains men come to greater pains; and it is sometimes base, and by indignities men come to dignities. The standing is slippery, and the regress is either a downfall, or at least an eclipse. — *Essays* (1625) 'Of Great Place'

12 Severity breedeth fear, but roughness breedeth hate. Even reproofs from authority ought to be grave, and not taunting. — *Essays* (1625) 'Of Great Place'

13 All rising to great place is by a winding stair. — *Essays* (1625) 'Of Great Place'

14 New nobility is but the act of power, but ancient nobility is the act of time. — *Essays* (1625) 'Of Nobility'

15 Fame is like a river, that beareth up things light and swollen, and drowns things weighty and solid. — *Essays* (1625) 'Of Praise'

16 So when any of the four pillars of government are mainly shakened or weakened (which are religion, justice, counsel, and treasure) men had need to pray for fair weather. — *Essays* (1625) 'Of Seditions and Troubles'

1 The surest way to prevent seditions (if the times do bear it) is to take away the matter of them.
Essays (1625) 'Of Seditions and Troubles'

2 Suspicions amongst thoughts are like bats amongst birds, they ever fly by twilight.
Essays (1625) 'Of Suspicion'

3 Neither is money the sinews of war (as it is trivially said).
Essays (1625) 'Of the True Greatness of Kingdoms'

4 Neither will it be, that a people overlaid with taxes should ever become valiant and martial.
Essays (1625) 'Of the True Greatness of Kingdoms'

5 What is truth? said jesting Pilate; and would not stay for an answer.
Essays (1625) 'Of Truth'

6 All colours will agree in the dark.
Essays (1625) 'Of Unity in Religion'

7 In the youth of a state arms do flourish; in the middle age of a state, learning; and then both of them together for a time; in the declining age of a state, mechanical arts and merchandise.
Essays (1625) 'Of Vicissitude of Things'

8 He is the fountain of honour.
An Essay of a King (1642); attribution doubtful; cf. **Bagehot** 24:12

9 There be three things which make a nation great and prosperous: a fertile soil, busy workshops, easy conveyance for men and goods from place to place.
attributed; S. Platt (ed.) *Respectfully Quoted* (1989)

10 For my name and memory, I leave it to men's charitable speeches, and to foreign nations, and the next ages.
his last will, 19 December 1625

Joan Baez 1941–

American singer and songwriter

11 The only thing that's been a worse flop than the organization of non-violence has been the organization of violence.
Daybreak (1970) 'What Would You Do If?'

Walter Bagehot 1826–77

English economist and essayist

12 Dullness in matters of government is a good sign, and not a bad one—in particular, dullness in Parliamentary government is a test of its excellence, an indication of its success.
in *Saturday Review* 16 February 1856

13 The English people never expect any one to be original.
in *Saturday Review* 19 April 1856

14 A constitutional statesman is in general a man of common opinion and uncommon abilities.
in *National Review* July 1856

15 The most influential of constitutional statesmen is the one who most felicitously expresses the creed of the moment, who administers it, who embodies it in laws and institutions, who gives it the highest life it is capable of, who induces the average man to think: 'I could not have done it any better if I had had time myself.'
in *National Review* July 1856

1 Public opinion is a permeating influence, and it exacts obedience to itself; it requires us to think other men's thoughts, to speak other men's words, to follow other men's habits.
in *National Review* July 1856

2 The path of great principles is marked through history by trouble, anxiety, and conflict.
in *Saturday Review* 16 February 1856

3 It has been the bane of many countries which have tried to obtain freedom, but failed in the attempt, that they have regarded popular government rather as a means of intellectual excitement than as an implement of political work.
in *Saturday Review* 16 February 1856

4 No real English gentleman, in his secret soul, was ever sorry for the death of a political economist.
Estimates of some Englishmen and Scotchmen (1858)

5 He believes, with all his heart and soul and strength, that there *is* such a thing as truth; he has the soul of a martyr with the intellect of an advocate.
of **Gladstone**
in *National Review* July 1860

6 There is no method by which men can be both free and equal.
in *The Economist* 5 September 1863

7 The American nation has very much the sort of faults which 'only children' are said to have. It has no correct measure of its own strength. Having never entered into close competition with any other nation, it indulges in that infinite braggadocio which a public school so soon rubs out of a conceited boy.
in *The Economist* 14 November 1863

8 Persecute a sect and it holds together, legalize it and it splits and resplits, till its unity is either null or a non-oppressive bond.
in *The Economist* 27 April 1867

9 The mystic reverence, the religious allegiance, which are essential to a true monarchy, are imaginative sentiments that no legislature can manufacture in any people.
The English Constitution (1867)

10 In such constitutions [as England's] there are two parts...first, those which excite and preserve the reverence of the population—the *dignified* parts...and next, the *efficient* parts—those by which it, in fact, works and rules.
The English Constitution (1867)

11 No orator ever made an impression by appealing to men as to their plainest physical wants, except when he could allege that those wants were caused by some one's tyranny.
The English Constitution (1867)

12 The Crown is, according to the saying, the 'fountain of honour'; but the Treasury is the spring of business.
The English Constitution (1867); cf. **Bacon** 23:8

13 A cabinet is a combining committee—a *hyphen* which joins, a *buckle* which fastens, the legislative part of the state to the executive part of the state.
The English Constitution (1867)

14 It has been said that England invented the phrase, 'Her Majesty's Opposition'; that it was the first government which made a criticism of administration as much a part
The English Constitution (1867); cf. **Hobhouse** 180:10

of the polity as administration itself. This critical opposition is the consequence of cabinet government.

1 *The Times* has made many ministries.

The English Constitution (1867) 'The Cabinet'

2 The great qualities, the imperious will, the rapid energy, the eager nature fit for a great crisis are not required—are impediments—in common times.

The English Constitution (1867) 'The Cabinet'

3 By the structure of the world we often want, at the sudden occurrence of a grave tempest, to change the helmsman—to replace the pilot of the calm by the pilot of the storm.

The English Constitution (1867) 'The Cabinet'

of Queen **Victoria** *and the future* **Edward VII**

4 It is nice to trace how the actions of a retired widow and an unemployed youth become of such importance.

The English Constitution (1867) 'The Monarchy'

5 The best reason why Monarchy is a strong government is, that it is an intelligible government. The mass of mankind understand it, and they hardly anywhere in the world understand any other.

The English Constitution (1867) 'The Monarchy'

6 It is often said that men are ruled by their imaginations; but it would be truer to say they are governed by the weakness of their imaginations.

The English Constitution (1867) 'The Monarchy'

7 The characteristic of the English Monarchy is that it retains the feelings by which the heroic kings governed their rude age, and has added the feelings by which the constitutions of later Greece ruled in more refined ages.

The English Constitution (1867) 'The Monarchy'

8 Women—one half the human race at least—care fifty times more for a marriage than a ministry.

The English Constitution (1867) 'The Monarchy'

9 Royalty is a government in which the attention of the nation is concentrated on one person doing interesting actions. A Republic is a government in which that attention is divided between many, who are all doing uninteresting actions. Accordingly, so long as the human heart is strong and the human reason weak, Royalty will be strong because it appeals to diffused feeling, and Republics weak because they appeal to the understanding.

The English Constitution (1867) 'The Monarchy'

10 Throughout the greater part of his life George III was a kind of 'consecrated obstruction'.

The English Constitution (1867) 'The Monarchy'

11 There are arguments for not having a Court, and there are arguments for having a splendid Court; but there are no arguments for having a mean Court.

The English Constitution (1867) 'The Monarchy'

12 The Queen…must sign her own death-warrant if the two Houses unanimously send it up to her.

The English Constitution (1867) 'The Monarchy'

13 Above all things our royalty is to be reverenced, and if you begin to poke about it you cannot reverence it…Its mystery is its life. We must not let in daylight upon magic.

The English Constitution (1867) 'The Monarchy'

1 The Sovereign has, under a constitutional monarchy such as ours, three rights—the right to be consulted, the right to encourage, the right to warn.

The English Constitution (1867) 'The Monarchy'

2 The only fit material for a constitutional king is a prince who begins early to reign—who in his youth is superior to pleasure—who in his youth is willing to labour—who has by nature a genius for discretion. Such kings are among God's greatest gifts, but they are also among His rarest.

The English Constitution (1867) 'The Monarchy'

3 The order of nobility is of great use, too, not only in what it creates, but in what it prevents. It prevents the rule of wealth—the religion of gold. This is the obvious and natural idol of the Anglo-Saxon.

The English Constitution (1867) 'The House of Lords'

4 A severe though not unfriendly critic of our institutions said that 'the cure for admiring the House of Lords was to go and look at it.'

The English Constitution (1867) 'The House of Lords'

5 Nations touch at their summits.

The English Constitution (1867) 'The House of Lords'

a 'cynical politician''s view of the parliamentary county members:

6 The finest brute votes in Europe.

The English Constitution (1867) 'The House of Commons'

7 The House of Commons lives in a state of perpetual potential choice: at any moment it can choose a ruler and dismiss a ruler. And therefore party is inherent in it, is bone of its bone, and breath of its breath.

The English Constitution (1867) 'The House of Commons'

8 An Opposition, on coming into power, is often like a speculative merchant whose bills become due. Ministers have to make good their promises, and they find a difficulty in so doing.

The English Constitution (1867) 'The House of Commons'

9 It is an inevitable defect, that bureaucrats will care more for routine than for results.

The English Constitution (1867) 'On Changes of Ministry'

10 A bureaucracy is sure to think that its duty is to augment official power, official business, or official members, rather than to leave free the energies of mankind; it overdoes the quantity of government, as well as impairs its quality.

The English Constitution (1867) 'On Changes of Ministry'

11 But would it not have been a miracle if the English people, directing their own policy, and being what they are, had directed a good policy? Are they not above all nations divided from the rest of the world, insular both in situation and in mind, both for good and for evil? Are they not out of the current of common European causes and affairs? Are they not a race contemptuous of others? Are they not a race with no special education or culture as to the modern world, and too often despising such culture? Who could expect such a people to comprehend the new and strange events of foreign places?

The English Constitution (1867) 'On Changes of Ministry'

1 It has been said, not truly, but with a possible approximation to truth, that in 1802 every hereditary monarch was insane.
The English Constitution (1867) 'Its Supposed Checks and Balances'

2 As soon as we see that England is a disguised republic we must see too that the classes for whom the disguise is necessary must be tenderly dealt with.
The English Constitution (1867) 'Its History'

3 The natural impulse of the English people is to resist authority.
The English Constitution (1867) 'Its History'

4 In plain English, what I fear is that both our political parties will bid for the support of the working man; that both of them will promise to do as he likes, if he will only tell them what it is; that, as he now holds the casting vote in our affairs, both parties will beg and pray him to give that vote to them. I can conceive of nothing more corrupting or worse for a set of poor ignorant people than that two combinations of well-taught and rich men should constantly offer to defer to their decision, and compete for the office of executing it.
The English Constitution: introduction to the second edition

5 A political country is like an American forest: you only have to cut down the old trees, and immediately new trees come up to replace them; the seeds were waiting in the ground, and they began to grow as soon as the withdrawal of the old ones brought in light and air.
The English Constitution: introduction to the second edition (1872)

6 If we know that a nation is capable of enduring continuous discussion, we know that it is capable of practising with equanimity continuous tolerance.
Physics and Politics (1872)

7 In happy states, the Conservative party must rule upon the whole a much longer time than their adversaries. In well-framed politics, innovation—great innovation that is—can only be occasional. If you are always altering your house, it is a sign either that you have a bad house, or that you have an excessively restless disposition—there is something wrong somewhere.
'The Chances for a Long Conservative Régime in England' (1874)

8 A great Premier must add the vivacity of an idle man to the assiduity of a very laborious one.
in *The Economist* 2 January 1875

9 The being without an opinion is so painful to human nature that most people will leap to a hasty opinion rather than undergo it.
in *The Economist* 4 December 1875

10 Good government depends at least as much on an impartial respect for the rights of all as it does on energy in enforcing respect for the authority which protects those rights.
in *The Economist* 27 May 1876

11 In every country the extreme party is most irritated against the party which comes nearest to itself, but does not go so far.
in *The Economist* 22 April 1876

12 The characteristic danger of great nations, like the Romans or the English, which have a long history of continuous creation, is that they may at last fail from not comprehending the great institutions which they have created.
in *Fortnightly Review* 1 November 1876

1 There never was a worse blunder than the supposition that the more states there are to suffer by a sanguinary quarrel, the sooner will the motives prevail for bringing it to a conclusion.

in *The Economist* 17 March 1877

2 Capital must be propelled by self-interest; it cannot be enticed by benevolence.

Economic Studies (1880)

Jacques Bainville 1879–1936

French historian

of the Treaty of Versailles:

3 Written by Bible readers *for* Bible readers.

'Les Consequences Politiques de la Paix' (1920)

Michael Bakunin 1814–76

Russian revolutionary and anarchist

4 The urge for destruction is also a creative urge!

in *Jahrbuch für Wissenschaft und Kunst* (1842)

5 We wish, in a word, equality—equality in fact as corollary, or rather, as primordial condition of liberty. From each according to his faculties, to each according to his needs; that is what we wish sincerely and energetically.

declaration signed by forty-seven anarchists on trial after the failure of their uprising at Lyons in 1870

J. Morrison Davidson *The Old Order and the New* (1890)

James Baldwin 1924–87

American novelist and essayist

6 It comes as a great shock around the age of 5, 6 or 7 to discover that the flag to which you have pledged allegiance, along with everybody else, has not pledged allegiance to you. It comes as a great shock to see Gary Cooper killing off the Indians and, although you are rooting for Gary Cooper, that the Indians are you.

speaking for the proposition that 'The American Dream is at the expense of the American Negro' at the Cambridge Union, England, 17 February 1965

in *New York Times Magazine* 7 March 1965

7 Freedom is not something that anybody can be given; freedom is something people take and people are as free as they want to be.

Nobody Knows My Name (1961) 'Notes for a Hypothetical Novel'

8 At the root of the American Negro problem is the necessity of the American white man to find a way of living with the Negro in order to be able to live with himself.

in *Harper's Magazine* October 1953 'Stranger in a Village'

9 If they take you in the morning, they will be coming for us that night.

in *New York Review of Books* 7 January 1971 'Open Letter to my Sister, Angela Davis'

Stanley Baldwin 1867–1947

British Conservative statesman; Prime Minister, 1923–4, 1924–9, 1935–7

on Baldwin: see **Beaverbrook** 34:2, **Churchill** 92:13, 93:3, **Curzon** 108:4, **Trevelyan** 368:3; cf. **Kipling** 214:1

1 They [parliament] are a lot of hard-faced men who look as if they had done very well out of the war.
J. M. Keynes *Economic Consequences of the Peace* (1919)

2 A platitude is simply a truth repeated until people get tired of hearing it.
in the House of Commons, 29 May 1924

3 There are three classes which need sanctuary more than others—birds, wild flowers, and Prime Ministers.
in *Observer* 24 May 1925

4 'Safety first' does not mean a smug self-satisfaction with everything as it is. It is a warning to all persons who are going to cross a road in dangerous circumstances.
in *The Times* 21 May 1929

5 Had the employers of past generations all of them dealt fairly with their men there would have been no unions.
speech in Birmingham, 14 January 1931

6 I think it is well also for the man in the street to realize that there is no power on earth that can protect him from being bombed. Whatever people may tell him, the bomber will always get through. The only defence is in offence, which means that you have to kill more women and children more quickly than the enemy if you want to save yourselves.
in the House of Commons, 10 November 1932

7 Since the day of the air, the old frontiers are gone. When you think of the defence of England you no longer think of the chalk cliffs of Dover; you think of the Rhine. That is where our frontier lies.
in the House of Commons, 30 July 1934

of his reasons for excluding **Churchill** *from the Cabinet:*

8 If there is going to be a war—and no one can say that there is not—we must keep him fresh to be our war Prime Minister.
letter 17 November 1935

9 I shall be but a short time tonight. I have seldom spoken with greater regret, for my lips are not yet unsealed. Were these troubles over I would make a case, and I guarantee that not a man would go into the lobby against us.
in the House of Commons on the Abyssinian crisis, 10 December 1935

usually quoted as 'My lips are sealed'

10 Supposing I had gone to the country and said that Germany was rearming and that we must rearm, does anybody think that this pacific democracy would have rallied to that cry at that moment? I cannot think of anything that would have made the loss of the election from my point of view more certain.
in the House of Commons, 12 November 1936

11 You will find in politics that you are much exposed to the attribution of false motive. Never complain and never explain.
Harold Nicolson *Diary* 21 July 1943

12 Do not run up your nose dead against the Pope or the NUM!
Lord Butler *The Art of Memory* (1982); cf. **Macmillan** 245:9

1 He spent his whole life in plastering together the true and the false and therefrom manufacturing the plausible.
of **Lloyd George**
attributed

2 The intelligent are to the intelligentsia what a gentleman is to a gent.
G. M. Young *Stanley Baldwin* (1952)

3 Then comes Winston with his hundred-horse-power mind and what can I do?
G. M. Young *Stanley Baldwin* (1952)

Arthur James Balfour 1848–1930

British Conservative statesman; Prime Minister, 1902–5; in 1917, as Foreign Secretary, Balfour issued the declaration in favour of a Jewish National Home in Palestine that came to be known as the Balfour Declaration.
on Balfour: see **Churchill** 88:2, 88:3, **Housman** 183:7, **Lloyd George** 229:1, 230:2

4 It is unfortunate, considering that enthusiasm moves the world, that so few enthusiasts can be trusted to speak the truth.
letter to Mrs Drew, 19 May 1891

5 Campbell-Bannerman is a mere cork, dancing on a torrent he cannot control.
of the election of 1906, which had produced a Liberal landslide and 50 Labour MPs, and in which Balfour, the former Tory Prime Minister, and six of his Cabinet colleagues had lost their seats
letter to Lady Salisbury, 1906; Blanche Dugdale *Arthur James Balfour* (1939)

6 His Majesty's Government view with favour the establishment in Palestine of a national home for the Jewish people, and will use their best endeavours to facilitate the achievement of this object, it being clearly understood that nothing shall be done which may prejudice the civil and religious rights of existing non-Jewish communities in Palestine, or the rights and political status enjoyed by Jews in any other country.
letter to Lord Rothschild, 2 November 1917

7 Zionism, be it right or wrong, good or bad, is rooted in age-long traditions, in present need, in future hopes, of far profounder import than the desires and prejudices of the seven hundred thousand Arabs who now inhabit that ancient land.
in August 1919; Max Egremont *Balfour* (1980)

on being asked what he thought of the behaviour of the German delegation at the signing of the Treaty of Versailles:
8 I make it a rule never to stare at people when they are in obvious distress.
Max Egremont *Balfour* (1980)

replying to Frank Harris, who had claimed that 'all the faults of the age come from Christianity and journalism':
9 Christianity, of course... but why journalism?
Margot Asquith *Autobiography* (1920) vol. 1

on the continuing financial dependence of **Curzon**, *who had failed to become Prime Minister in succession to* **Bonar Law**, *on his second wife Grace Duggan:*
10 He may have lost the hope of glory, but he still retains the means of Grace.
attributed

1 Biography should be written by an acute enemy.

in *Observer* 30 January 1927

2 [Our] whole political machinery pre-supposes a people so fundamentally at one that they can safely afford to bicker.

introduction to Walter Bagehot *The English Constitution* (World Classics ed., 1928)

of an unwelcome supporter:

3 He pursues us with malignant fidelity.

Winston Churchill *Great Contemporaries* (1937)

4 I am more or less happy when being praised, not very uncomfortable when being abused, but I have moments of uneasiness when being explained.

K. Young *A. J. Balfour* (1963)

5 I never forgive but I always forget.

R. Blake *Conservative Party* (1970)

6 I thought he was a young man of promise, but it appears he is a young man of promises.

describing Churchill

Winston Churchill *My Early Life* (1930)

Lord Balogh 1905–85

Hungarian-born political economist and adviser to Harold **Wilson**'s Government

7 Blatant fallacies leading to inappropriate, indeed catastrophic, policies can survive if a sufficient part of the profession [of economists] is committed to them.

The Irrelevance of Conventional Economics (1982)

8 Some people would believe anything, especially if it eliminates awkward social and political problems.

The Irrelevance of Conventional Economics (1982)

E. Digby Baltzell 1915–

9 There is a crisis in American leadership in the middle of the twentieth century that is partly due, I think, to the declining authority of an establishment which is now based on an increasingly castelike White-Anglo Saxon-Protestant (WASP) upper class.

The Protestant Establishment (1964)

Honoré de Balzac 1799–1850

French novelist

10 Despotism accomplishes great things illegally; liberty doesn't even go to the trouble of accomplishing small things legally.

La Peau de Chagrin (1831)

George Bancroft 1800–91

American historian and politician

11 Calvinism [in Switzerland]... established a religion without a prelate, a government without a king.

History of the United States (1855 ed.) vol. 3

Lord Bancroft 1922–

British civil servant; Head of the Civil Service 1978–81

1 Conviction politicians, certainly: conviction civil servants, no.

'Whitehall: Some Personal Reflections', lecture at the London School of Economics 1 December 1983

Imamu Amiri Baraka 1934–

American poet and playwright

2 A man is either free or he is not. There cannot be any apprenticeship for freedom.

in *Kulchur* Spring 1962 'Tokenism'

Ernest Barker 1874–1960

British political scientist

3 Sovereignty is unlimited—unlimited and illimitable.

Principles of Social and Political Theory (1951)

Bernard Baruch 1870–1965

American financier and presidential adviser

4 Behind the black portent of a new atomic age lies a hope which, seized upon with faith, can work out salvation... Let us not deceive ourselves: we must elect world peace or world destruction.

address to the United Nations Atomic Energy Commission, 14 June 1946

5 Let us not be deceived—we are today in the midst of a cold war.

speech to South Carolina Legislature 16 April 1947; the expression 'cold war' was suggested to him by H. B. Swope, former editor of the *New York World*

6 We are in the midst of a cold war which is getting warmer.

speech before the Senate Committee, 1948

7 Vote for the man who promises least; he'll be the least disappointing.

Meyer Berger *New York* (1960)

8 You can talk about capitalism and communism and all that sort of thing, but the important thing is the struggle everybody is engaged in to get better living conditions, and they are not interested too much in government.

in *The Times* 20 August 1964

9 A political leader must keep looking over his shoulder all the time to see if the boys are still there. If they aren't still there, he's no longer a political leader.

in *New York Times* 21 June 1965

Lord Bauer 1915–

British economist

1 Foreign aid is a system of taking money from poor people in rich countries and giving it to rich people in poor countries.
attributed; not recollected by Lord Bauer but not repudiated by him

Beverley Baxter 1891–1964

British journalist and Conservative politician

2 Beaverbrook is so pleased to be in the Government that he is like the town tart who has finally married the Mayor!
Henry ('Chips') Channon diary 12 June 1940

Charles Austin Beard 1874–1948 and **Mary Ritter Beard** 1876–1958

3 At no time, at no place, in solemn convention assembled, through no chosen agents, had the American people officially proclaimed the United States to be a democracy...When the Constitution was framed no respectable person called himself or herself a democrat.
America in Midpassage (1939)

Lord Beaverbrook 1879–1964

Canadian-born British newspaper proprietor and Conservative politician

on Beaverbrook: see **Baxter** 33:2, **Lloyd George** 230:12, **Wells** 385:6; cf. also **Kipling** 214:1

4 I hope you will give up the New Party. If you must burn your fingers in public life, go to a bright and big blaze.
to Harold **Nicolson**
letter 25 June 1931 in *Harold Nicolson Diaries* (1980)

5 Churchill on top of the wave has in him the stuff of which tyrants are made.
Politicians and the War (1932)

6 Our cock won't fight.
said to Winston **Churchill**, *of* **Edward VIII**, *during the abdication crisis of 1936*
Frances Donaldson *Edward VIII* (1974)

7 The Daily Express declares that Great Britain will not be involved in a European war this year or next year either.
in *Daily Express* 19 September 1938

8 Now who is responsible for this work of development on which so much depends? To whom must the praise be given? To the boys in the back rooms. They do not sit in the limelight. But they are the men who do the work.
in *Listener* 27 March 1941

9 I ran the paper [the *Daily Express*] purely for propaganda and with no other purpose.
evidence to the Royal Commission on the Press, 18 March 1948
A. J. P. Taylor *Beaverbrook* (1972)

10 Always threatening resignation, he never signed off.
of Lord **Derby**
Men and Power (1956)

of Lord **Curzon**, *who had been created Viceroy of India at the age of thirty-nine:*

1 For all the rest of his life Curzon was influenced by his sudden journey to heaven at the age of thirty-nine, and then by his return seven years later to earth, for the remainder of his mortal existence.

Men and Power (1956)

2 His conversation turned on the beauty of the mountain rose, and the splendour of hawthorn buds in spring.
of Stanley **Baldwin**

Men and Power (1956)

3 Often undecided whether to desert a sinking ship for one that might not float, he would make up his mind to sit on the wharf for a day.
of Lord **Curzon**

Men and Power (1956)

4 With the publication of his Private Papers in 1952, he [Earl Haig] committed suicide 25 years after his death.
of Earl **Haig**

Men and Power (1956)

5 [Lloyd George] did not seem to care which way he travelled providing he was in the driver's seat.

The Decline and Fall of Lloyd George (1963)

6 The British electors will not vote for a man who does not wear a hat.
advice to Tom Driberg

Alan Watkins *Brief Lives* (1982)

of **Bonar Law** *and* **Churchill**:

7 I have had two masters and one of them betrayed me.

A. J. P. Taylor letter 16 December 1973; *Letters to Eva* (1991)

Henry Becque 1837–99

French dramatist and critic

8 What makes equality such a difficult business is that we only want it with our superiors.

Querelles littéraires (1890)

Brendan Behan 1923–64

Irish playwright

9 PAT: He was an Anglo-Irishman.
MEG: In the blessed name of God what's that?
PAT: A Protestant with a horse.

The Hostage (1958)

10 When I came back to Dublin, I was courtmartialled in my absence and sentenced to death in my absence, so I said they could shoot me in my absence.

The Hostage (1958)

Francis Bellamy 1856–1931

American clergyman and editor

11 I pledge allegiance to the flag of the United States of America and to the republic for which it stands, one nation under God, indivisible, with liberty and justice for all.

The Pledge of Allegiance to the Flag (1892)

Hilaire Belloc 1870–1953

British poet, essayist, historian, novelist, and Liberal politician

1 Whatever happens we have got
The Maxim Gun, and they have not.

The Modern Traveller (1898)

2 Gentlemen, I am a Catholic... If you reject me on account of my religion, I shall thank God that He has spared me the indignity of being your representative.

speech to voters of South Salford, 1906; Speaight *Life of Hilaire Belloc* (1957)

3 Sir! you have disappointed us!
We had intended you to be
The next Prime Minister but three:
The stocks were sold; the Press was squared;
The Middle Class was quite prepared.
But as it is!... My language fails!
Go out and govern New South Wales!

Cautionary Tales (1907) 'Lord Lundy'

of the House of Commons:

4 A man can no more make a good speech in such a place than sing a song in it.

Hugh Dalton *Political Diary* (1986) 29 July 1930

5 Here richly, with ridiculous display,
The Politician's corpse was laid away.
While all of his acquaintance sneered and slanged
I wept: for I had longed to see him hanged.

'Epitaph on the Politician Himself' (1923)

Julien Benda 1867–1956

French philosopher and novelist

6 *La trahison des clercs.*
The treachery of the intellectuals.

title of book, 1927

Ruth Fulton Benedict 1887–1948

American anthropologist

7 The tough-minded... respect difference. Their goal is a world made safe for differences, where the United States may be American to the hilt without threatening the peace of the world, and France may be France, and Japan may be Japan on the same conditions.

The Chrysanthemum and the Sword (1946)

Ernest Benn 1875–1954

English publisher and economist

8 Politics is the art of looking for trouble, finding it whether it exists or not, diagnosing it incorrectly, and applying the wrong remedy.

attributed

Tony Benn 1925–

British Labour politician and sometime Viscount Stansgate, who campaigned for the change in the law that made it possible to renounce a hereditary peerage
on Benn: see **Levin** 222:4, **Wilson** 391:8

1 Not a reluctant peer but a persistent commoner.
at a Press Conference, 23 November 1960

2 Broadcasting is really too important to be left to the broadcasters.
as Minister of Technology in 1968
Anthony Sampson *The New Anatomy of Britain* (1971)

3 Some of the jam we thought was for tomorrow, we've already eaten.
attributed, 1969; cf. **Carroll** 77:2

4 The crisis that we inherit when we come to power will be the occasion for fundamental change and not the excuse for postponing it.
at the Labour Party Conference, 1973

5 In developing our industrial strategy for the period ahead, we have the benefit of much experience. Almost everything has been tried at least once.
speech in House of Commons, 13 March 1974

on seeing Harold **Wilson***, who had resigned as Prime Minister in March, looking 'absolutely shrunk':*
6 Office is something that builds up a man only if he is somebody in his own right.
diary 12 April 1976

7 Marxism is now a world faith and must be allowed to enter into a continuous dialogue with other world faiths, including religious faiths.
Karl Marx lecture, 16 March 1982

of the influence of Parliament:
8 Through talk, we tamed kings, restrained tyrants, averted revolution.
Anthony Sampson *The Changing Anatomy of Britain* (1982)

9 I did not enter the Labour Party forty-seven years ago to have our manifesto written by Dr Mori, Dr Gallup and Mr Harris.
in *Guardian* 13 June 1988

10 A faith is something you die for; a doctrine is something you kill for: there is all the difference in the world.
in *Observer* 16 April 1989 'Sayings of the Week'

questions habitually asked by Tony Benn on meeting somebody in power:
11 What power have you got? Where did you get it from? In whose interests do you exercise it? To whom are you accountable? How do we get rid of you?
'The Independent Mind', lecture at Nottingham, 18 June 1993

12 To understand how we're governed, and hence the power of the Prime Minister, you have to understand the power of the Crown. It's like the Trinity: God the Father is the Queen—she's just there and nobody knows very much about her; God the Son is the Prime Minister—who exercises all the patronage and has all the real power; and God the Holy Ghost is the Crown—the Royal Prerogative—and the Crown in a state-within-a-state, surrounded by barbed wire and covered in secrecy.
briefing for a 'Cabinet and Premiership' course at Queen Mary and Westfield College, 26 April 1994

1 The Civil Service is a bit like a rusty weathercock. It moves with opinion then it stays where it is until another wind moves it in a different direction.

briefing for 'Cabinet and Premiership' course (Queen Mary and Westfield College), held at the House of Commons 1 March 1995

2 When you get to No. 10, you've climbed there on a little ladder called 'the status quo'. And, when you're there, the status quo looks very good.

at the House of Commons 1 March 1995

Arnold Bennett 1867–1931

English novelist

3 Examine the Honours List and you can instantly tell how the Government feels in its inside. When the Honours List is full of rascals, millionaires, and—er—chumps, you may be quite sure that the Government is dangerously ill.

The Title (1918)

4 Literature's always a good card to play for Honours. It makes people think that Cabinet ministers are educated.

The Title (1918)

5 Seventy minutes had passed before Mr Lloyd George arrived at his proper theme. He spoke for a hundred and seventeen minutes, in which period he was detected only once in the use of an argument.

Things that have Interested Me (1921) 'After the March Offensive'

A. C. Benson 1862–1925

English writer

6 Land of Hope and Glory, Mother of the Free,
How shall we extol thee who are born of thee?
Wider still and wider shall thy bounds be set;
God who made thee mighty, make thee mightier yet.

'Land of Hope and Glory' written to be sung as the Finale to Elgar's *Coronation Ode* (1902)

Jeremy Bentham 1748–1832

English philosopher

7 Right...is the child of law: from real laws come real rights; but from imaginary laws, from laws of nature, fancied and invented by poets, rhetoricians, and dealers in moral and intellectual poisons, come imaginary rights, a bastard brood of monsters.

Anarchical Fallacies (1843)

8 Natural rights is simple nonsense: natural and imprescriptible rights, rhetorical nonsense—nonsense upon stilts.

Anarchical Fallacies (1843)

9 The greatest happiness of the greatest number is the foundation of morals and legislation.

Bentham claims to have acquired the 'sacred truth' either from Joseph Priestley (1733–1804) or Cesare Beccaria (1738–94)

The Commonplace Book (1843)

10 Every law is contrary to liberty.

Principles of the Civil Code (1843)

11 He rather hated the ruling few than loved the suffering many.

of James Mill

H. N. Pym (ed.) *Memories of Old Friends, being Extracts from the Journals and Letters of Caroline Fox* (1882)

Edmund Clerihew Bentley 1875–1956

English writer

1 When their lordships asked Bacon
How many bribes he had taken
He had at least the grace
To get very red in the face.

Baseless Biography (1939) 'Bacon'

2 George the Third
Ought never to have occurred.
One can only wonder
At so grotesque a blunder.

More Biography (1929) 'George the Third'

Lloyd Bentsen 1921–

American Democratic politician

responding to Dan Quayle's claim to have 'as much experience in the Congress as Jack **Kennedy** *had when he sought the presidency':*

3 Senator, I served with Jack Kennedy. I knew Jack Kennedy. Jack Kennedy was a friend of mine. Senator, you're no Jack Kennedy.

in the vice-presidential debate, 5 October 1988

George Berkeley 1685–1753

Irish philosopher and Anglican bishop

4 Westward the course of empire takes its way;
The first four acts already past,
A fifth shall close the drama with the day:
Time's noblest offspring is the last.

'On the Prospect of Planting Arts and Learning in America' (1752); cf. John Quincy Adams *Oration at Plymouth* (1802): 'Westward the star of empire takes its way'

Peter Berger

political scientist

5 Capitalism, as an institutional arrangement, has been singularly devoid of plausible myths. By contrast, socialism, its major alternative under modern conditions, has been singularly blessed with myth-generating potency.

in 1986; Anthony Sampson *The Company Man* (1995)

Irving Berlin 1888–1989

American songwriter

6 God bless America,
Land that I love,
Stand beside her and guide her
Thru the night with a light from above.
From the mountains to the prairies,
To the oceans white with foam,
God bless America,
My home sweet home.

'God Bless America' (1939)

Isaiah Berlin 1909–

British philosopher

1 Liberty is liberty, not equality or fairness or justice or human happiness or a quiet conscience.
Two Concepts of Liberty (1958)

2 It is this—the 'positive' conception of liberty: not freedom from, but freedom to—which the adherents of the 'negative' notion represent as being, at times, no better than a specious disguise for brutal tyranny.
Two Concepts of Liberty (1958)

3 The fundamental sense of freedom is freedom from chains, from imprisonment, from enslavement by others. The rest is extension of this sense, or else metaphor.
Four Essays on Liberty (1969); introduction

4 Injustice, poverty, slavery, ignorance—these may be cured by reform or revolution. But men do not live only by fighting evils. They live by positive goals, individual and collective, a vast variety of them, seldom predictable, at times incompatible.
Four Essays on Liberty (1969)

5 Those who have ever valued liberty for its own sake believed that to be free to choose, and not be chosen for, is an inalienable ingredient in what makes human beings human.
Four Essays on Liberty (1969)

6 Few new truths have ever won their way against the resistance of established ideas save by being overstated.
Vico and Herder (1976)

Daniel Berrigan

US anti-Vietnam War activist

7 This is a war run to show the world, and particularly the Third World, where exactly it stands in relation to our technology.
attributed, 1973

Theobald von Bethmann Hollweg 1856–1921

Chancellor of Germany, 1909–17

8 Just for a word 'neutrality'—a word which in wartime has so often been disregarded—just for a scrap of paper, Great Britain is going to make war on a kindred nation who desires nothing better than to be friends with her.
summary of a report by E. Goschen to Edward Grey in *British Documents on Origins of the War 1898–1914* (1926) vol. 11

Mary McLeod Bethune 1875–1955

American educator

9 If we accept and acquiesce in the face of discrimination, we accept the responsibility ourselves and allow those responsible to salve their conscience by believing that they have our acceptance and concurrence.
Rayford W. Logan (ed.) *What the Negro Wants* (1944) 'Certain Inalienable Rights'

John Betjeman 1906–84

English poet

1 Think of what our Nation stands for,
Books from Boots' and country lanes,
Free speech, free passes, class distinction,
Democracy and proper drains.
Lord, put beneath Thy special care
One-eighty-nine Cadogan Square.

'In Westminster Abbey' (1940)

Aneurin Bevan 1897–1960

British Labour politician

2 The worst thing I can say about democracy is that it has tolerated the Right Honourable Gentleman for four and a half years.
of Neville **Chamberlain**

in the House of Commons, 23 July 1929

3 Listening to a speech by Chamberlain is like paying a visit to Woolworth's: everything in its place and nothing above sixpence.

Michael Foot *Aneurin Bevan* vol. 1 (1962)

taking over as Minister of Health in 1945, Bevan immediately banished a well-upholstered leather armchair:

4 This won't do. It drains all the blood from the head and explains a lot about my predecessors.

Michael Foot *Aneurin Bevan* vol. 2 (1973)

5 This island is made mainly of coal and surrounded by fish. Only an organizing genius could produce a shortage of coal and fish at the same time.

speech at Blackpool 24 May 1945

6 No amount of cajolery, and no attempts at ethical or social seduction, can eradicate from my heart a deep burning hatred for the Tory Party...So far as I am concerned they are lower than vermin.

speech at Manchester, 4 July 1948, in *The Times* 5 July 1948

7 The language of priorities is the religion of Socialism.

speech at Labour Party Conference in Blackpool, 8 June 1949

8 Why read the crystal when he can read the book?
referring to Robert **Boothby** *during a debate on the Sterling Exchange Rate*

in the House of Commons, 29 September 1949

9 The Tories, every election, must have a bogy man. If you haven't got a programme, a bogy man will do. In 1945 it was Harold Laski, in 1951 it is me.

speech in the general election campaign at Stonehouse, Gloucester, 13 October 1951

10 [Winston Churchill] does not talk the language of the 20th century but that of the 18th. He is still fighting Blenheim all over again. His only answer to a difficult situation is send a gun-boat.

speech at Labour Party Conference, Scarborough, 2 October 1951

11 Discontent arises from a knowledge of the possible, as contrasted with the actual.

In Place of Fear (1952)

12 He is a man suffering from petrified adolescence.
of Winston **Churchill**

Vincent Brome *Aneurin Bevan* (1953)

13 We know what happens to people who stay in the middle of the road. They get run down.

in *Observer* 6 December 1953

1 Damn it all, you can't have the crown of thorns *and* the thirty pieces of silver.
on his position in the Labour Party, c.1956
Michael Foot *Aneurin Bevan* vol. 2 (1973)

2 I am not going to spend any time whatsoever in attacking the Foreign Secretary... If we complain about the tune, there is no reason to attack the monkey when the organ grinder is present.
during a debate on the Suez crisis
in the House of Commons, 16 May 1957

3 If you carry this resolution you will send Britain's Foreign Secretary naked into the conference chamber.
speaking against a motion proposing unilateral nuclear disarmament by the United Kingdom
speech at Labour Party Conference in Brighton, 3 October 1957

4 You call that statesmanship? I call it an emotional spasm.
speaking against a motion proposing unilateral nuclear disarmament by the United Kingdom
speech at Labour Party Conference in Brighton, 3 October 1957

5 I know that the right kind of leader for the Labour Party is a desiccated calculating machine who must not in any way permit himself to be swayed by indignation. If he sees suffering, privation or injustice he must not allow it to move him, for that would be evidence of the lack of proper education or of absence of self-control. He must speak in calm and objective accents and talk about a dying child in the same way as he would about the pieces inside an internal combustion engine.
frequently taken as referring to Hugh **Gaitskell**, *although Bevan specifically denied it in an interview with Robin Day on 28 April 1959*
Michael Foot *Aneurin Bevan* vol. 2 (1973)

6 The conquest of the commanding heights of the economy.
recalling his own earlier use of the phrase (possibly originated by Lenin)
at the Labour Party Conference, November 1959

7 The Prime Minister has an absolute genius for putting flamboyant labels on empty luggage.
of Harold **Macmillan**
in the House of Commons, 3 November 1959

8 Tory shame was only slightly alleviated by Walter Monckton—and then they didn't know whether to wear him as a gas-mask or a jock strap.
of Walter **Monckton** *at the time of Suez*
Andrew Roberts *Eminent Churchillians* (1994)

9 I read the newspapers avidly. It is my one form of continuous fiction.
in *The Times* 29 March 1960

of his handling of the consultants during the establishment of the National Health Service:

10 I stuffed their mouths with gold.
Brian Abel-Smith *The Hospitals 1800–1948* (1964)

11 There are only two ways of getting into the Cabinet. One way is to crawl up the staircase of preferment on your belly; the other way is to kick them in the teeth.
Richard Crossman *Inside View* (1972)

Albert Jeremiah Beveridge 1862–1927

American Republican politician and member of the Senate, who in 1912 chaired the convention that organized the Progressive party and nominated Theodore **Roosevelt** for President

1 This party comes from the grass roots. It has grown from the soil of the people's hard necessities.
address at the Bull Moose Convention in Chicago, 5 August 1912

William Henry Beveridge 1879–1963

British economist

2 The object of government in peace and in war is not the glory of rulers or of races, but the happiness of the common man.
Social Insurance and Allied Services (1942)

3 Want is one only of five giants on the road of reconstruction... the others are Disease, Ignorance, Squalor and Idleness.
Social Insurance and Allied Services (1942)

4 Ignorance is an evil weed, which dictators may cultivate among their dupes, but which no democracy can afford among its citizens.
Full Employment in a Free Society (1944)

5 The state is or can be master of money, but in a free society it is master of very little else.
Voluntary Action (1948)

Ernest Bevin 1881–1951

British Labour politician and trade unionist

6 The most conservative man in this world is the British Trade Unionist when you want to change him.
speech, 8 September 1927

7 I hope you will carry no resolution of an emergency character telling a man with a conscience like Lansbury what he ought to do... It is placing the Executive in an absolutely wrong position to be taking your conscience round from body to body to be told what you ought to do with it.
often quoted as 'hawking his conscience round the Chancellories of Europe'
in *Labour Party Conference Report* (1935)

the scientist Patrick Blackett had questioned the wisdom of trying to manufacture a British atomic bomb:

8 Stick to science.
Henry Pelling *The Labour Governments, 1945–51* (1984)

9 I am not one of those who decry Eton and Harrow. I was very glad of them in the Battle of Britain.
speech at Blackpool, 1945; D. Healey *The Time of My Life* (1989)

10 There never has been a war yet which, if the facts had been put calmly before the ordinary folk, could not have been prevented... The common man, I think, is the great protection against war.
in the House of Commons, 23 November 1945

as Minister of Labour to his Civil Servants:

1 You've just given me twenty reasons why I can't do this; I'm sure that clever chaps like you can go away and produce twenty good reasons why I can. — oral tradition; Peter Hennessy *Whitehall* (1990)

on being told, at the ending of the British Mandate, that the Air Staff wanted to stay in Palestine:

2 If they want to stay, they'll have to stay up in helicopters. — Hugh Dalton diary *Political Diary* (1986) 20 September 1947

someone had remarked that Aneurin **Bevan** *was his own worst enemy:*

3 Not while I'm alive 'e ain't.
also attributed to Bevin of Herbert **Morrison** — Roderick Barclay *Ernest Bevin and the Foreign Office* (1975)

4 My [foreign] policy is to be able to take a ticket at Victoria Station and go anywhere I damn well please. — in *Spectator* 20 April 1951

5 If you open that Pandora's Box, you never know what Trojan 'orses will jump out.
on the Council of Europe — Roderick Barclay *Ernest Bevin and the Foreign Office* (1975)

6 I didn't ought never to have done it. It was you, Willie, what put me up to it.
to Lord Strang, after officially recognizing Communist China — C. Parrott *Serpent and Nightingale* (1977)

The Bible (Authorized Version)

7 Let my people go. — Exodus

8 Let them live; but let them be hewers of wood and drawers of water unto all the congregation. — Joshua

9 He smote them hip and thigh. — Judges

10 And she named the child I-chabod, saying, The glory is departed from Israel. — I Samuel

11 And Saul said, God hath delivered him into mine hand. — I Samuel

12 He shall know that there is a prophet in Israel. — II Kings

13 Thus shall it be done to the man whom the king delighteth to honour. — Esther

14 Great men are not always wise. — Job

15 Where there is no vision, the people perish. — Proverbs

16 The race is not to the swift, nor the battle to the strong. — Ecclesiastes

17 Woe to thee, O land, when thy king is a child. — Ecclesiastes

18 They shall beat their swords into plowshares, and their spears into pruninghooks: nation shall not lift up sword against nation, neither shall they learn war any more. — Isaiah; cf. **Rendall** 303:1

19 Of the increase of his government and peace there shall be no end. — Isaiah

20 Now, O king, establish the decree, and sign the writing, that it be not changed, according to the law of the Medes and Persians, which altereth not. — Daniel

1 They have sown the wind, and they shall reap the whirlwind. — Hosea

2 Let us now praise famous men, and our fathers that begat us. — Ecclesiasticus

3 Such as did bear rule in their kingdoms. — Ecclesiasticus

4 Judge not, that ye be not judged. — St Matthew

5 I came not to send peace, but a sword. — St Matthew

6 He that is not with me is against me. — St Matthew; St Luke

7 Render therefore unto Caesar the things which are Caesar's; and unto God the things that are God's. — St Matthew

8 Ye shall hear of wars and rumours of wars: see that ye be not troubled: for all these things must come to pass but the end is not yet. — St Matthew

9 For nation shall rise against nation, and kingdom against kingdom. — St Matthew, St John

10 Those that have turned the world upside down are come hither also. — Acts of the Apostles

11 But Paul said, I am a man which am a Jew of Tarsus, a city in Cilicia, a citizen of no mean city. — Acts of the Apostles

12 Hast thou appealed unto Caesar? unto Caesar shalt thou go. — Acts of the Apostles

13 For where no law is, there is no transgression. — Romans

Georges Bidault 1899–1983

French statesman; Prime Minister, 1946, 1949–50

14 The weak have one weapon: the errors of those who think they are strong. — in *Observer* 15 July 1962 'Sayings of the Week'

Ambrose Bierce 1842–*c.*1914

American writer

15 BATTLE, *n.* A method of untying with the teeth a political knot that would not yield to the tongue. — *The Cynic's Word Book* (1906)

16 CONSERVATIVE, *n.* A statesman who is enamoured of existing evils, as distinguished from the Liberal, who wishes to replace them with others. — *The Cynic's Word Book* (1906)

17 PEACE, *n.* In international affairs, a period of cheating between two periods of fighting. — *The Devil's Dictionary* (1911)

John Biffen 1930–

British Conservative politician

commenting on a critical remark from the Downing Street Press Secretary, Bernard **Ingham**:

18 He was the sewer and not the sewage. — recorded for a television interview, *c.*1988, but not broadcast

of Margaret **Thatcher** *as Prime Minister:*

1 She was a tigress surrounded by hamsters. — in *Observer* 9 December 1990

2 In politics I think it is wiser to leave five minutes too soon than to continue for five years too long. — in *Daily Telegraph* 5 January 1995
resignation letter

John Biggs-Davison 1918–88

British Conservative politician

3 I have never conceived it my duty as a Member of Parliament to seek to amend the Ten Commandments. — speech at Chelmsford, 7 November 1976

Steve Biko 1946–77

South African anti-apartheid campaigner

4 The most potent weapon in the hands of the oppressor is the mind of the oppressed. — statement as witness, 3 May 1976

Josh Billings 1818–85

American humorist

5 It is better to know nothing than to know what ain't so. — *Proverb* (1874)

Nigel Birch 1906–81

British Conservative politician

on hearing of the resignation of Hugh **Dalton**, *Chancellor of the Exchequer in the Labour Government, 13 November 1947:*

6 My God! They've shot our fox! — Harold Macmillan *Tides of Fortune* (1969)

as Minister of Works in 1951, Birch said that he had enjoyed:

7 Gardening with a staff of three thousand. — in *Dictionary of National Biography*

8 For the second time the Prime Minister has got rid of a Chancellor of the Exchequer who tried to get expenditure under control. Once is more than enough. — letter to *The Times*, 14 July 1962
after Harold **Macmillan***'s dismissal of Selwyn* **Lloyd** *in favour of Reginald Maudling*

9 I must say that he never struck me as a man at all like a cloistered monk; and Miss Keeler was a professional prostitute... There seems to me to be a certain basic improbability about the proposition that their relationship was purely platonic. — in the House of Commons, 17 June 1963
of John Profumo, during the Profumo debate

10 On the question of competence and good sense I cannot think that the verdict can be favourable. — in the House of Commons, 17 June 1963
of Harold **Macmillan** *and his handling of the Profumo affair; Birch's peroration for this speech was from Browning's 'The Lost Leader': 'Let him never come back to us... never glad confident morning again'*

1 No one could accuse himself of courage more often than the Prime Minister.
of Harold **Wilson**

in the House of Commons, 2 August 1965

Lord Birkenhead see F. E. Smith

Augustine Birrell 1850–1933

British essayist and politician

at a dinner in Trinity College, Cambridge, in 1902, the Master in proposing the health of the college pointed out that at that moment the Sovereign and the Prime Minister were both Trinity men:

2 The Master should have added that he can go further, for it is obvious that the affairs of the world are built upon the momentous fact that God also is a Trinity man.

Harold Laski letter to Oliver Wendell Holmes 4 December 1926

Otto von Bismarck 1815–98

German statesman, and the driving force behind the unification of Germany; Chancellor of the new German Empire 1871–90
on Bismarck: see **Taylor** 356:9, **Tenniel** 359:6

3 The secret of politics? Make a good treaty with Russia.
in 1863, when first in power

A. J. P. Taylor *Bismarck* (1955)

4 Politics is not an exact science.

speech to the Prussian legislature, 18 December 1863

after the Austro-Prussian war of 1866, there were calls in Prussia for punishment of the defeated Austrians:

5 Austria was no more in the wrong in opposing our claims than we were in making them.

A. J. P. Taylor *Bismarck* (1955)

6 Politics is the art of the possible.

in conversation with Meyer von Waldeck, 11 August 1867

7 The politician has not to revenge what has happened but to ensure that it does not happen again.
in 1867, following public criticism of courtesy shown to the defeated Napoleon III after the battle of Sedan

A. J. P. Taylor *Bismarck* (1955)

8 Let us...put Germany in the saddle! She will know well enough how to ride!

in 1867; Alan Palmer *Bismarck* (1976)

9 Whoever speaks of Europe is wrong, [it is] a geographical concept.

marginal note on a letter from the Russian Chancellor Gorchakov, November 1876; cf. **Metternich** 257:7

10 I have always found the word Europe on the lips of those politicians who wanted something from other Powers which they dared not demand in their own names.
to the Russian Chancellor Gorchakov, who had urged that a rising in Bosnia in 1878 was a European, rather than a German or Russian, question

A. J. P. Taylor *Bismarck* (1955)

1 I do not regard the procuring of peace as a matter in which we should play the role of arbiter between different opinions…more that of an honest broker who really wants to press the business forward.
before the Congress of Berlin
speech to the Reichstag, 19 February 1878

2 A lath of wood painted to look like iron.
of Lord **Salisbury** *at the Congress of Berlin in 1878*
attributed, but vigorously denied by Sidney Whitman in *Personal Reminiscences of Prince Bismarck* (1902)

3 The old Jew! That is the man.
of **Disraeli** *at the Congress of Berlin*
attributed

4 Place in the hands of the King of Prussia the strongest possible military power, then he will be able to carry out the policy you wish; this policy cannot succeed through speeches, and shooting-matches, and songs; it can only be carried out through blood and iron.
in the Prussian House of Deputies, 28 January 1886; in a speech on 30 September 1862, Bismarck had used the form 'iron and blood'

5 I am bored; the great things are done. The German *Reich* is made.
A. J. P. Taylor *Bismarck* (1955)

6 Jena came twenty years after the death of Frederick the Great; the crash will come twenty years after my departure if things go on like this.
to Kaiser **Wilhelm II** *at their last meeting in 1895*
A. J. P. Taylor *Bismarck* (1955)

of the English political system:

7 If reactionary measures are to be carried, the Liberal party takes the rudder, from the correct assumption that it will not overstep the necessary limits; if liberal measures are to be carried, the Conservative party takes office in its turn for the same consideration.
A. J. P. Taylor *Bismarck* (1955)

8 If there is ever another war in Europe, it will come out of some damned silly thing in the Balkans.
reported by the shipping magnate Herr Ballen as being said by Bismarck in his later years; quoted in the House of Commons, 16 August 1945

9 Man cannot create the current of events. He can only float with it and steer.
A. J. P. Taylor *Bismarck* (1955)

of possible German involvement in the Balkans:

10 Not worth the healthy bones of a single Pomeranian grenadier.
George O. Kent *Bismarck and his Times* (1978)

11 A statesman…must wait until he hears the steps of God sounding through events; then leap up and grasp the hem of his garment.
A. J. P. Taylor *Bismarck* (1955)

12 There is a providence that protects idiots, drunkards, children, and the United States of America.
attributed, perhaps apocryphal

13 The tongue in the balance.
of Germany's position in relation to other European states
A. J. P. Taylor *Bismarck* (1955)

14 What is an opportunist? He is a man who uses the most favourable opportunity to carry through what he regards as useful and appropriate.
A. J. P. Taylor *Bismarck* (1955)

1 When a man says he approves of something in principle, it means he hasn't the slightest intention of putting it into practice.

attributed

Hugo La Fayette Black 1886–1971

American judge

2 The First Amendment has erected a wall between church and state. That wall must be kept high and impregnable. We could not approve the slightest breach.

in *Emerson v. Board of Education* 1947

3 It is my belief that there *are* absolutes in our Bill of Rights, and that they were put there on purpose by men who knew what words meant and meant their prohibitions to be 'absolutes'.

interview before the American Jewish Congress, 14 April 1962

4 An unconditional right to say what one pleases about public affairs is what I consider to be the minimum guarantee of the First Amendment.

in *New York Times Company v. Sullivan* 1964

5 In revealing the workings of government that led to the Vietnam War, the newspapers nobly did precisely that which the Founders hoped and trusted they would do.

concurring opinion on the publication of the Pentagon Papers, 1971

William Blackstone 1723–80

English jurist

6 The king never dies.

Commentaries on the Laws of England (1765)

7 The royal navy of England hath ever been its greatest defence and ornament; it is its ancient and natural strength; the floating bulwark of the island.

Commentaries on the Laws of England (1765)

8 That the king can do no wrong, is a necessary and fundamental principle of the English constitution.

Commentaries on the Laws of England (1765)

9 In all tyrannical governments the supreme magistracy, or the right both of making and of enforcing the laws, is vested in one and the same man, or one and the same body of men; and wherever these two powers are united together, there can be no public liberty.

Commentaries on the Laws of England (1765)

10 Herein indeed consists the excellence of the English government, that all parts of it form a mutual check upon each other.

Commentaries on the Laws of England (1765)

Tony Blair 1953–

British Labour politician; Leader of the Labour Party since 1994

11 Labour is the party of law and order in Britain today. Tough on crime and tough on the causes of crime.
as Shadow Home Secretary

speech at the Labour Party Conference, 30 September 1993

12 The art of leadership is saying no, not yes. It is very easy to say yes.

in *Mail on Sunday* 2 October 1994

1 It has surely come to something when a government can only secure the passage of its own legislative programme by threatening its own demise.
of John **Major***'s warning to Conservative rebels*
in *Independent* 17 November 1994

2 Those who seriously believe we cannot improve on words written for the world of 1918 when we are now in 1995 are not learning from our history but living it.
on the proposed revision of Clause IV
in *Independent* 11 January 1995; cf. **Anonymous** 14:3

William Blake 1757–1827

English poet

3 The strongest poison ever known
Came from Caesar's laurel crown.
'Auguries of Innocence' (*c.*1803)

4 The whore and gambler by the State
Licensed build that nation's fate
The harlot's cry from street to street
Shall weave old England's winding sheet.
'Auguries of Innocence' (*c.*1803)

5 And was Jerusalem builded here
Among these dark Satanic mills?
Milton (1804–10) preface 'And did those feet in ancient time'

6 I will not cease from mental fight,
Nor shall my sword sleep in my hand,
Till we have built Jerusalem,
In England's green and pleasant land.
Milton (1804–10) preface 'And did those feet in ancient time'

Alfred Blunt, Bishop of Bradford 1879–1957

English clergyman

7 The benefit of the King's Coronation depends, under God, upon two elements: First on the faith, prayer, and self-dedication of the King himself, and on that it would be improper for me to say anything except to commend him, and ask you to commend him, to God's grace, which he will so abundantly need...if he is to do his duty faithfully. We hope that he is aware of his need. Some of us wish that he gave more positive signs of his awareness.
it was this speech that broke the story of **Edward VIII** *and Mrs Simpson which the media had been voluntarily suppressing until then*
speech to Bradford Diocesan Conference, 1 December 1936

William Joseph Blyton 1887–1944

English journalist and author

8 Winston [Churchill] is so wonderfully eloquent, impressive and wrong.
letter to his publisher on his book Arrows of Desire
Andrew Roberts *Eminent Churchillians* (1994)

David Boaz 1953–

American foundation executive

1 Alcohol didn't cause the high crime rates of the '20s and '30s, Prohibition did. Drugs don't cause today's alarming crime rates, but drug prohibition does.

'The Legalization of Drugs' 27 April 1988

2 Trying to wage war on 23 million Americans who are obviously very committed to certain recreational activities is not going to be any more successful than Prohibition was.

'The Legalization of Drugs' 27 April 1988

Allan Boesak 1945–

South African politician and clergyman, anti-apartheid campaigner

3 My humanity is not dependent on the acceptance of white people.

after losing in Western Cape, April 1994, as an African National Congress candidate

in *The New York Review of Books* 20 October 1994 'The Election Mandela Lost'

Ivan Boesky 1937–

American financier, imprisoned in 1987 for insider dealing

4 Greed is all right... Greed is healthy. You can be greedy and still feel good about yourself.

commencement address at the University of California, Berkeley, 18 May 1986; cf. **Weiser** 383:6

Curtis Bok 1897–1962

American federal judge

5 It has been said that a judge is a member of the Bar who once knew a Governor.

The Backbone of the Herring (1941)

Henry St John, Lord Bolingbroke 1678–1751

English statesman

6 The great mistake is that of looking upon men as virtuous, or thinking that they can be made so by laws.

comment (*c.*1728) in Joseph Spence *Observations, Anecdotes, and Characters* (1820)

7 The greatest art of a politician is to render vice serviceable to the cause of virtue.

comment (*c.*1728) in Joseph Spence *Observations, Anecdotes, and Characters* (1820)

8 Nations, like men, have their infancy.

On the Study of History letter 5, in *Works* (1809) vol. 3

Simón Bolívar 1783–1830

Venezuelan patriot and statesman

1 A state too extensive in itself, or by virtue of its dependencies, ultimately falls into decay; its free government is transformed into a tyranny; it disregards the principles which it should preserve, and finally degenerates into despotism. The distinguishing characteristic of small republics is stability: the character of large republics is mutability. — *Letter from Jamaica* Summer 1815

2 Those who have served the cause of the revolution have ploughed the sea. — attributed

Robert Bolt 1924–95

English playwright

3 THOMAS MORE: This country's planted thick with laws from coast to coast—Man's laws, not God's—and if you cut them down—and you're just the man to do it—d'you really think you could stand upright in the winds that would blow then? — *A Man for All Seasons* (1960)

Andrew Bonar Law 1858–1923

Canadian-born British Conservative statesman, Prime Minister 1922–3

4 If, therefore, war should ever come between these two countries [Great Britain and Germany], which Heaven forbid! it will not, I think, be due to irresistible natural laws, it will be due to want of human wisdom. — in the House of Commons, 27 November 1911

5 If I am a great man, then all great men are frauds. — Lord Beaverbrook *Politicians and the War* (1932)

The Book of Common Prayer 1662

6 The Bishop of Rome hath no jurisdiction in this Realm of England. — *Articles of Religion* (1562) no. 37

Christopher Booker 1937–

English author and journalist

7 In the life of any government, however safe its majority, there comes a moment when the social movements of which it had once been the expression turn inexorably against it. Up to that moment, however many mistakes it makes, however damning the criticisms that may be levelled against it, however unpopular it may become, it can sail on serenely...But after that moment, every mistake it makes becomes magnified; indeed blunders multiply as if feeding on themselves; and both outwardly — *The Neophiliacs* (1969) and inwardly the Government appears to be at the mercy of every wind.

1 It is a familiar pattern of history that, on the eve of revolutionary crises, the established order veers erratically between liberal concessions and recklessly reactionary steps which seem calculated to cast it in the most unfavourable light and to hasten its own destruction.
The Neophiliacs (1969)

2 Our government has recently unleashed the greatest avalanche of regulations in peacetime history; and wherever we examine their working we see that they are using a sledgehammer to miss a nut.
speech, 1995

John Wilkes Booth 1838–65

American assassin

3 *Sic semper tyrannis!* The South is avenged.
having shot President **Lincoln,** *14 April 1865* ('Sic semper tyrannis [*Thus always to tyrants*]' *— motto of the State of Virginia; the second part of the statement is possibly apocryphal)*
in *New York Times* 15 April 1865

Robert Boothby 1900–86

British Conservative politician

4 *You* speak for Britain!
to Arthur Greenwood, acting Leader of the Labour Party, after Neville **Chamberlain** *had failed to announce an ultimatum to Germany; perhaps taking up an appeal already voiced by Leo* **Amery**
Harold Nicolson diary 2 September 1939; cf. **Amery** 7:7

Betty Boothroyd 1929–

Labour politician; Speaker of the House of Commons since 1992

5 My desire to get here [Parliament] was like miners' coal dust, it was under my fingers and I couldn't scrub it out.
Glenys Kinnock and Fiona Millar (eds.) *By Faith and Daring* (1993)

James H. Boren 1925–

American bureaucrat

6 Guidelines for bureaucrats: (1) When in charge, ponder. (2) When in trouble, delegate. (3) When in doubt, mumble.
in *New York Times* 8 November 1970

Jorge Luis Borges 1899–1986

Argentinian writer

7 The Falklands thing was a fight between two bald men over a comb.
application of a proverbial phrase; in *Time* 14 February 1983

Cesare Borgia 1476–1507

Italian statesman

1 *Aut Caesar, aut nihil.*
Caesar or nothing.
motto inscribed on his sword

John Leslie Garner *Caesar Borgia* (1912)

Robert H. Bork 1927–

American judge and educationalist

2 One of the uses of history is to free us of a falsely imagined past. The less we know of how ideas actually took root and grew, the more apt we are to accept them unquestioningly, as inevitable features of the world in which we move.

The Antitrust Paradox (1978)

George Borrow 1803–81

English writer

3 I am invariably of the politics of the people at whose table I sit, or beneath whose roof I sleep.

The Bible in Spain (1843)

James Boswell 1740–95

Scottish lawyer; biographer of Samuel Johnson

4 We [Boswell and Johnson] are both *Tories*; both convinced of the utility of monarchical power, and both lovers of that reverence and affection for a sovereign which constitute loyalty, a principle which I take to be absolutely extinguished in Britain.

Journal of a Tour to the Hebrides 13 September 1773

Antoine Boulay de la Meurthe 1761–1840

French statesman

on hearing of the execution of the Duc d'Enghien, 1804:

5 It is worse than a crime, it is a blunder.

C.-A. Sainte-Beuve *Nouveaux Lundis* (1870) vol. 12

Pierre Boulez 1925–

French conductor and composer

6 Revolutions are celebrated when they are no longer dangerous.

in *Guardian* 13 January 1989

Randolph Silliman Bourne 1886–1918

7 War is the health of the state. It automatically sets in motion throughout society those irresistible forces for uniformity, for passionate cooperation with the Government in coercing into obedience the minority groups and individuals which lack the larger herd sense.

The State (1918)

Lord Bowen 1835–94

British judge

1 The man on the Clapham omnibus. — in *Law Reports* (1903); attributed
the average man

Edward Boyle 1923–81

British Conservative politician

2 Nothing in politics is ever as good or as bad as it first appears. — William Whitelaw *Memoirs* (1989)

Omar Bradley 1893–1981

American general

3 The way to win an atomic war is to make certain it never starts. — speech to Boston Chamber of Commerce, 10 November 1948

4 We have grasped the mystery of the atom and rejected the Sermon on the Mount. — speech on Armistice Day, 1948

5 The world has achieved brilliance without wisdom, power without conscience. Ours is a world of nuclear giants and ethical infants. — speech on Armistice Day, 1948

6 In war there is no second prize for the runner-up. — in *Military Review* February 1950

7 This strategy would involve us in the wrong war, at the wrong place, at the wrong time, and with the wrong enemy. — in *US Congressional Senate Committee on Armed Service* (1951) vol. 2
on General Macarthur's wish to extend the Korean War into China

John Bradshaw 1602–59

English judge at the trial of Charles I

8 Rebellion to tyrants is obedience to God. — suppositious epitaph; Henry S. Randall *Life of Thomas Jefferson* (1865) vol. 3

Edward Stuyvesant Bragg 1827–1912

American politician

9 They love him most for the enemies he has made. — speech 9 July 1884
seconding the presidential nomination of Grover **Cleveland**

Louis D. Brandeis 1856–1941

Justice of the US Supreme Court

10 Those who won our independence believed that the final end of the State was to make men free to develop their faculties; and that in its government the deliberative forces should prevail over the arbitrary. They valued liberty both as an end and as a means. They believed — in *Whitney v. California* (1927)

liberty to be the secret of happiness and courage to be the secret of liberty.

1 Fear of serious injury cannot alone justify suppression of free speech and assembly. Men feared witches and burned women. It is the function of speech to free men from the bondage of irrational fears.

in *Whitney v. California* (1927)

2 They [the makers of the Constitution] conferred, as against the Government, the right to be let alone—the most comprehensive of rights and the right most valued by civilized men.

in *Olmstead v. United States* (1928)

3 Experience should teach us to be most on our guard to protect liberty when the government's purposes are beneficent…the greatest dangers to liberty lurk in insidious encroachment by men of zeal, well-meaning but without understanding.

dissenting opinion in *Olmstead v. United States* (1928)

4 There is in most Americans some spark of idealism, which can be fanned into a flame. It takes sometimes a divining rod to find what it is; but when found, and that means often, when disclosed to the owners, the results are often most extraordinary.

The Words of Justice Brandeis (1951)

William Cowper Brann 1855–98

5 No man can be a patriot on an empty stomach.

The Iconoclast, Old Glory 4 July 1893

Bertolt Brecht 1898–1956

German playwright

6 ANDREA: Unhappy the land that has no heroes!…
GALILEO: No. Unhappy the land that needs heroes.

Life of Galileo (1939)

7 One observes, they have gone too long without a war here. Where is morality to come from in such a case, I ask? Peace is nothing but slovenliness, only war creates order.

Mother Courage (1939)

8 The finest plans are always ruined by the littleness of those who ought to carry them out, for the Emperors can actually do nothing.

Mother Courage (1939)

9 War always finds a way.

Mother Courage (1939)

10 Don't tell me peace has broken out, when I've just bought some new supplies.

Mother Courage (1939)

William Joseph Brennan Jr. 1906–

American judge

11 Debate on public issues should be uninhibited, robust, and wide open, and that…may well include vehement, caustic, and sometimes unpleasantly sharp attacks on government and public officials.

in *New York Times Co. v. Sullivan* (1964)

1 If the right of privacy means anything, it is the right of the individual, married or single, to be free from unwarranted governmental intrusion into matters so fundamentally affecting a person as the decision whether to bear or beget a child.

in *Eisenstadt v. Baird* (1972)

Aristide Briand 1862–1932

French statesman

2 The high contracting powers solemnly declare...that they condemn recourse to war and renounce it...as an instrument of their national policy towards each other... The settlement or the solution of all disputes or conflicts of whatever nature or of whatever origin they may be which may arise...shall never be sought by either side except by pacific means.

draft, 20 June 1927, later incorporated into the Kellogg Pact, 1928, in *Le Temps* 13 April 1928

Edward Bridges 1892–1969

British Cabinet Secretary and Head of the Civil Service

3 I confidently expect that we [civil servants] shall continue to be grouped with mothers-in-law and Wigan Pier as one of the recognized objects of ridicule.

Portrait of a Profession (1950)

John Bright 1811–89

English Liberal politician and reformer

4 The angel of death has been abroad throughout the land; you may almost hear the beating of his wings.
on the effects of the war in the Crimea

in the House of Commons, 23 February 1855

5 I am for 'Peace, retrenchment, and reform', the watchword of the great Liberal party 30 years ago.

speech at Birmingham, 28 April 1859, in *The Times* 29 April 1859; the phrase quoted may be found in Samuel Warren's novel *Ten Thousand a Year* (1841)

6 My opinion is that the Northern States will manage somehow to muddle through.
said during the American Civil War

Justin McCarthy *Reminiscences* (1899) vol. 1

7 England is the mother of Parliaments.

speech at Birmingham, 18 January 1865

of Robert Lowe, leader of the dissident Whigs opposed to the Reform Bill of 1866:

8 The right hon Gentleman...has retired into what may be called his political Cave of Adullam—and he has called about him every one that was in distress and every one that was discontented.

in the House of Commons, 13 March 1866; cf. I Samuel ch. 22

of Robert Lowe and Edward Horsman:

9 This party of two is like the Scotch terrier that was so covered with hair that you could not tell which was the head and which was the tail.

in the House of Commons, 13 March 1866

1 Force is not a remedy.

speech to the Birmingham Junior Liberal Club, 16 November 1880, in *The Times* 17 November 1880

of British foreign policy:

2 A gigantic system of outdoor relief for the aristocracy of Great Britain.

speech at Birmingham, 29 October 1858

Vera Brittain 1893–1970

English writer

3 Politics are usually the executive expression of human immaturity.

Rebel Passion (1964)

David Broder 1929–

American columnist

4 Anybody that wants the presidency so much that he'll spend two years organizing and campaigning for it is not to be trusted with the office.

in *Washington Post* 18 July 1973

D. W. Brogan 1900–74

Scottish historian

5 A people that has licked a more formidable enemy than Germany or Japan, primitive North America . . . a country whose national motto has been 'root, hog, or die.'

The American Character (1944)

6 Any well-established village in New England or the northern Middle West could afford a town drunkard, a town atheist, and a few Democrats.

The American Character (1944)

Henry Brooke 1703–83

Irish poet and playwright

7 For righteous monarchs,
Justly to judge, with their own eyes should see;
To rule o'er freemen, should themselves be free.

Earl of Essex (performed 1750, published 1761)

Robert Barnabas Brough 1828–60

English satirical writer

8 My Lord Tomnoddy is thirty-four;
The Earl can last but a few years more.
My Lord in the Peers will take his place:
Her Majesty's councils his words will grace.
Office he'll hold and patronage sway;
Fortunes and lives he will vote away;
And what are his qualifications?—ONE!
He's the Earl of Fitzdotterel's eldest son.

Songs of the Governing Classes (1855) 'My Lord Tomnoddy'

Lord Brougham 1778–1868

Scottish lawyer and politician; Lord Chancellor 1830–4
on Brougham: see **Melbourne** 255:6, 255:7

1 In my mind, he was guilty of no error—he was chargeable with no exaggeration—he was betrayed by his fancy into no metaphor, who once said, that all we see about us, King, Lords, and Commons, the whole machinery of the State, all the apparatus of the system, and its varied workings, end in simply bringing twelve good men into a box.
in the House of Commons, 7 February 1828

2 Education makes a people easy to lead, but difficult to drive; easy to govern, but impossible to enslave.
attributed

Heywood Broun 1888–1939

American journalist

3 Just as every conviction begins as a whim so does every emancipator serve his apprenticeship as a crank. A fanatic is a great leader who is just entering the room.
in *New York World* 6 February 1928

4 Appeasers believe that if you keep on throwing steaks to a tiger, the tiger will turn vegetarian.
attributed

George Brown 1914–85

British Labour politician

5 I've seen MPs on both sides of the House obviously having to create a sensation on Thursday in order to have a peg on which to hang an article for Sunday.
on Members of Parliament who were also journalists
In My Way (1971)

Gordon Brown 1951–

British Labour politician

6 Ideas which stress the growing importance of international cooperation and new theories of economic sovereignty across a wide range of areas—macroeconomics, the environment, the growth of post neo-classical endogenous growth theory and the symbiotic relationships between growth and investment in people and infrastructure.
New Labour Economics speech, September 1994, 'winner' of the ironic Plain English No Nonsense Award for 1994

H. Rap Brown 1943–

American Black Power leader

7 I say violence is necessary. It is as American as cherry pie.
speech at Washington, 27 July 1967, in *Washington Post* 28 July 1967

John Brown 1800–59

American abolitionist

1 Had I so interfered in behalf of the rich, the powerful, the intelligent, the so-called great, or in behalf of any of their friends... every man in this court would have deemed it an act worthy of reward rather than punishment.
last speech to the court at his trial
on 2 November 1859

2 I am yet too young to understand that God is any respecter of persons.
last speech to the court at his trial
on 2 November 1859

3 If it is deemed necessary that I should forfeit my life for the furtherance of the ends of justice, and mingle my blood further with the blood of my children, and with the blood of millions in this slave country whose rights are disregarded by wicked, cruel, and most unjust enactments, I submit: so let it be done!
last speech to the court at his trial
on 2 November 1859

4 This *is* a beautiful country!
as he rode to the gallows, seated on his coffin
at his execution on 2 December 1859

Joseph Brown 1821–94

American politician; Confederate Governor of Georgia during the Civil War

refusing to accept the Confederate President Jefferson **Davis**'*s call for a day of national fasting:*

5 I entered into this Revolution to contribute my mite to sustain the rights of states and prevent the consolidation of the Government, and I am *still* a rebel... no matter who may be in power.
in 1863; Geoffrey C. Ward *The Civil War* (1991)

William Browne 1692–1774

English physician and writer

6 The King to Oxford sent a troop of horse,
For Tories own no argument but force:
With equal skill to Cambridge books he sent,
For Whigs admit no force but argument.
reply to Trapp's epigram, in J. Nichols *Literary Anecdotes* vol. 3; cf. **Trapp** 367:6

Frederick 'Boy' Browning 1896–1965

British soldier and courtier; husband of Daphne du Maurier

expressing reservations about the Arnhem 'Market Garden' operation to Field Marshal Montgomery on 10 September 1944:

7 I think we might be going a bridge too far.
R. E. Urquhart *Arnhem* (1958)

Robert Browning 1812–89

English poet

1 Just for a handful of silver he left us,
Just for a riband to stick in his coat.

of **Wordsworth***'s implied abandonment of radical principles by his acceptance of the Laureateship*

'The Lost Leader' (1845)

2 Life's night begins: let him never come back to us!
There would be doubt, hesitation and pain,
Forced praise on our part—the glimmer of twilight,
Never glad confident morning again!

'The Lost Leader' (1845); cf. **Birch** 45:10

Louis Brownlow 1879–1963

of presidential aides (from advice given by Stanley **Baldwin***'s private secretary Tom Jones):*

3 They should be possessed of high competence, great physical vigour, and a passion for anonymity.

in *Administrative Management in the Government of the United States: Report of the President's Committee on Administrative Management* January 1937

William Jennings Bryan 1860–1925

American Democratic politician; a fervent proponent of bimetallism as an alternative to the gold standard

4 The humblest citizen of all the land, when clad in the armour of a righteous cause, is stronger than all the hosts of error.

speech at the Democratic National Convention, Chicago, 1896

5 Destroy our farms and the grass will grow in the streets of every city in the country.

speech at the Democratic National Convention, Chicago 1896; cf. **Hoover** 182:10

6 You shall not press down upon the brow of labour this crown of thorns, you shall not crucify mankind upon a cross of gold.

speech at the Democratic National Convention, Chicago, 1896

Arthur Bryant 1899–1985

English historical writer

7 The great German whom fate has raised up to rescue his people.

of Adolf **Hitler**

Andrew Roberts *Eminent Churchillians* (1994)

8 Liberty does not consist merely of denouncing Tyranny, any more than horticulture does of deploring and abusing weeds, or even pulling them out.

in *Illustrated London News* 24 June 1939

of England in 1699:

9 A world of hedges, squires and parsons, of yeomen, cottages and ragged squatters, making their wares and pleasures after the manner of their forefathers.

Protestant Island (1967)

James Bryce 1838–1922

British historian and diplomat

1 Europeans often ask, and Americans do not often explain, how it happens that this great office [the presidency], the greatest in the world, unless we except the Papacy, to which any man can rise by his own merits, is not more frequently filled by great and striking men.

The American Commonwealth (1888) vol. 1

2 The government of cities is the one conspicuous failure of the United States.

The American Commonwealth (1888) vol. 1

Zbigniew Brzezinski 1928–

US Secretary of State and National Security Advisor

3 Russia can be an empire or a democracy, but it cannot be both.

in *Foreign Affairs* March/April 1994 'The Premature Partnership'

Frank Buchman 1878–1961

American evangelist; founder of the Moral Re-Armament movement

4 I thank heaven for a man like Adolf Hitler, who built a front line of defence against the anti-Christ of Communism.

in *New York World-Telegram* 26 August 1936

Gerald Bullett

British writer

5 My Lord Archbishop, what a scold you are!
And when your man is down how bold you are!
Of charity how oddly scant you are!
How Lang, O Lord, how full of Cantuar!

on the role of Cosmo Gordon Lang, Archbishop of Canterbury, in the abdication of Edward VIII

in 1936

Ivor Bulmer-Thomas 1905–93

British Conservative politician

of Harold **Wilson**:

6 If he ever went to school without any boots it was because he was too big for them.

speech at the Conservative Party Conference, in *Manchester Guardian* 13 October 1949

Prince Bernhard von Bülow 1849–1929

Chancellor of Germany, 1900–9

7 In a word, we desire to throw no one into the shade [in East Asia], but we also demand our own place in the sun.

speech in the Reichstag, 6 December 1897; cf. **Wilhelm II** 388:9

Edward George Bulwer-Lytton 1803–73

British novelist and politician

1 Here Stanley meets,—how Stanley scorns, the glance!
The brilliant chief, irregularly great,
Frank, haughty, rash,—the Rupert of Debate!
on Edward Stanley, 14th Earl of **Derby**

The New Timon (1846); cf. **Disraeli** 117:14

Samuel Dickinson Burchard 1812–91

American Presbyterian minister

2 We are Republicans and don't propose to leave our party and identify ourselves with the party whose antecedents are rum, Romanism, and rebellion.

speech at the Fifth Avenue Hotel, New York, 29 October 1884

Edmund Burke 1729–97

Irish-born Whig politician and man of letters
on Burke: see **Gibbon** 151:14, **Johnson** 198:11, **O'Brien** 276:5, **Paine** 282:4, 283:4

3 No passion so effectually robs the mind of all its powers of acting and reasoning as fear.

On the Sublime and Beautiful (1757)

4 In all forms of Government the people is the true legislator.

A Tract on the Popery Laws (planned *c.*1765)

5 Laws, like houses, lean on one another.

A Tract on the Popery Laws (planned *c.*1765)

6 People must be governed in a manner agreeable to their temper and disposition; and men of free character and spirit must be ruled with, at least, some condescension to this spirit and this character.

Observation on a Late Publication entitled 'The Present State of the Nation' (1769)

7 It is a general popular error to imagine the loudest complainers for the public to be the most anxious for its welfare.

Observations on a late Publication on the Present State of the Nation (2nd ed., 1769)

8 There is, however, a limit at which forbearance ceases to be a virtue.

Observations on a late Publication on the Present State of the Nation (2nd ed., 1769)

9 If ever there was in all the proceedings of government a rule that is fundamental, universal, invariable it is this: that you ought never to attempt a measure of authority you are not morally sure you can go through with.

in the House of Commons, 9 May 1770

10 To complain of the age we live in, to murmur at the present possessors of power, to lament the past, to conceive extravagant hopes of the future, are the common dispositions of the greatest part of mankind.

Thoughts on the Cause of the Present Discontents (1770)

11 I am not one of those who think that the people are never in the wrong. They have been so, frequently and outrageously, both in other countries and in this. But I do say, that in all disputes between them and their rulers, the presumption is at least upon a par in favour of the people.

Thoughts on the Cause of the Present Discontents (1770)

1 The power of the crown, almost dead and rotten as Prerogative, has grown up anew, with much more strength, and far less odium, under the name of Influence.
Thoughts on the Cause of the Present Discontents (1770)

2 We must soften into a credulity below the milkiness of infancy to think all men virtuous. We must be tainted with a malignity truly diabolical, to believe all the world to be equally wicked and corrupt.
Thoughts on the Cause of the Present Discontents (1770)

3 When...[people] imagine that their food is only a cover for poison, and when they neither love nor trust the hand that serves it, it is not the name of the roast beef of old England that will persuade them to sit down to the table that is spread for them.
Thoughts on the Cause of the Present Discontents (1770)

4 When bad men combine, the good must associate; else they will fall, one by one, an unpitied sacrifice in a contemptible struggle.
Thoughts on the Cause of the Present Discontents (1770)

5 Of this stamp is the cant of *Not men, but measures*; a sort of charm by which many people get loose from every honourable engagement.
Thoughts on the Cause of the Present Discontents (1770); cf. **Canning** 74:9

6 It is therefore our business carefully to cultivate in our minds, to rear to the most perfect vigour and maturity, every sort of generous and honest feeling that belongs to our nature. To bring the dispositions that are lovely in private life into the service and conduct of the commonwealth; so to be patriots, as not to forget we are gentlemen.
Thoughts on the Cause of the Present Discontents (1770)

7 The greater the power, the more dangerous the abuse.
speech on the Middlesex Election, 7 February 1771

8 Your representative owes you, not his industry only, but his judgement; and he betrays, instead of serving you, if he sacrifices it to your opinion.
speech, 3 November 1774, in *Speeches at his Arrival at Bristol* (1774)

9 Abstract liberty, like other mere abstractions, is not to be found.
On Conciliation with America (1775)

10 All Protestantism, even the most cold and passive, is a sort of dissent. But the religion most prevalent in our northern colonies is a refinement on the principle of resistance; it is the dissidence of dissent, and the Protestantism of the Protestant religion.
On Conciliation with America (1775)

11 By adverting to the dignity of this high calling, our ancestors have turned a savage wilderness into a glorious empire: and have made the most extensive, and the only honourable conquests; not by destroying, but by promoting the wealth, the number, the happiness of the human race.
On Conciliation with America (1775)

12 Deny them this participation of freedom, and you break that sole bond, which originally made, and must still preserve the unity of the empire.
On Conciliation with America (1775)

1 Freedom and not servitude is the cure of anarchy; as religion, and not atheism, is the true remedy for superstition. — *On Conciliation with America* (1775)

2 I do not know the method of drawing up an indictment against an whole people. — *On Conciliation with America* (1775)

3 I have in general no very exalted opinion of the virtue of paper government. — *On Conciliation with America* (1775)

4 Instead of a standing revenue, you will have therefore a perpetual quarrel. — *On Conciliation with America* (1775)

5 It is not, what a lawyer tells me I *may* do; but what humanity, reason, and justice, tells me I ought to do. — *On Conciliation with America* (1775)

6 It is the love of the people; it is their attachment to their government, from the sense of the deep stake they have in such a glorious institution, which gives you your army and your navy, and infuses into both that liberal obedience, without which your army would be a base rabble, and your navy nothing but rotten timber. — *On Conciliation with America* (1775)

7 Magnanimity in politics is not seldom the truest wisdom; and a great empire and little minds go ill together. — *On Conciliation with America* (1775)

8 Nothing less will content me, than *whole America.* — *On Conciliation with America* (1775)

9 Parties must ever exist in a free country. — *On Conciliation with America* (1775)

10 Slavery they can have anywhere. It is a weed that grows in every soil. — *On Conciliation with America* (1775)

11 The concessions of the weak are the concessions of fear. — *On Conciliation with America* (1775)

12 The use of force alone is but *temporary*. It may subdue for a moment; but it does not remove the necessity of subduing again; and a nation is not governed, which is perpetually to be conquered. — *On Conciliation with America* (1775)

13 When we speak of the commerce with our colonies, fiction lags after truth; invention is unfruitful, and imagination cold and barren. — *On Conciliation with America* (1775)

14 It is the nature of all greatness not to be exact; and great trade will always be attended with considerable abuses. — *On American Taxation* (1775)

15 To tax and to please, no more than to love and to be wise, is not given to men. — *On American Taxation* (1775)

16 Bodies tied together by so unnatural a bond of union as mutual hatred are only connected to their ruin. — *Letter to the Sheriffs of Bristol* (1777)

17 I was persuaded that government was a practical thing made for the happiness of mankind, and not to furnish out a spectacle of uniformity to gratify the schemes of visionary politicians. — *Letter to the Sheriffs of Bristol* (1777)

18 Among a people generally corrupt, liberty cannot long exist. — *Letter to the Sheriffs of Bristol* (1777)

1 Liberty too must be limited in order to be possessed. *Letter to the Sheriffs of Bristol* (1777)

2 Nothing in progression can rest on its original plan. We may as well think of rocking a grown man in the cradle of an infant. *Letter to the Sheriffs of Bristol* (1777)

3 People crushed by law have no hopes but from power. If laws are their enemies, they will be enemies to laws; and those, who have much to hope and nothing to lose, will always be dangerous, more or less. letter to Charles James Fox, 8 October 1777

4 Bad laws are the worst sort of tyranny. *Speech at Bristol, previous to the Late Election* (1780)

5 The people are the masters. in the House of Commons, 11 February 1780

of the younger **Pitt***'s maiden speech, February 1781:*

6 Not merely a chip of the old 'block', but the old block itself. N. W. Wraxall *Historical Memoirs of My Own Time* (1904 ed.)

7 I feel an insuperable reluctance in giving my hand to destroy any established institution of government, upon a theory, however plausible it may be. in the House of Commons on Fox's East India Bill, 1 December 1783

8 Men will not look to acts of parliament, to regulations, to declarations, to votes, and resolutions. No, they are not such fools. They will ask, what is the road to power, credit, wealth, and honours. They will ask, what conduct ends in neglect, disgrace, poverty, exile, prison, and gibbet? These will teach them the course which they are to follow. It is your distribution of these that will give the character and tone to your government. All the rest is miserable grimace. in the House of Commons on Fox's East India Bill, 1 December 1783

9 Every other conqueror of every other description has left some monument, either of state or beneficence, behind him. Were we to be driven out of India this day, nothing would remain to tell that it had been possessed, during the inglorious period of our dominion, by anything better than the orang-outang or the tiger. in the House of Commons, 1 December 1783

speech on Fox's East India Bill

10 The people never give up their liberties but under some delusion. speech at County Meeting of Buckinghamshire, 1784, attributed in E. Latham *Famous Sayings* (1904), with 'except' substituted for 'but'

11 The laws of morality are the same everywhere, and... there is no action which would pass for an act of extortion, of peculation, of bribery, and of oppression in England, that is not an act of extortion, of peculation, of bribery and oppression in Europe, Asia, Africa, and all the world over. opening speech at impeachment of Warren Hastings, 16 February 1788

12 Where two motives, neither of them perfectly justifiable, may be assigned, the worst has the chance of being preferred. opening speech, impeachment of Warren Hastings, House of Commons 13 February 1788

1 You strike at the whole corps, if you strike at the head. — opening speech, impeachment of Warren Hastings, House of Commons 13 February 1788

2 Never wholly separate in your mind the merits of any political question from the men who are concerned in it. You will be told, that if a measure is good, what have you [to] do with the character and views of those who bring it forward. But designing men never separate their plans from their interests. — letter to Charles-Jean-François Depont, November 1789

3 There is a mob of their constituents ready to hang them if they should deviate into moderation. — letter 27 September 1789

4 An event has happened, upon which it is difficult to speak, and impossible to be silent. — speech, 5 May 1789; E. A. Bond (ed.) *Speeches... in the Trial of Warren Hastings* (1859) vol. 2

5 At last dying in the last dyke of prevarication. — speech, 7 May 1789; E. A. Bond (ed.) *Speeches... in the Trial of Warren Hastings* (1859) vol. 2

6 I flatter myself that I love a manly, moral, regulated liberty as well as any gentleman. — *Reflections on the Revolution in France* (1790)

7 Whenever our neighbour's house is on fire, it cannot be amiss for the engines to play a little on our own. — *Reflections on the Revolution in France* (1790)

8 A state without the means of some change is without the means of its conservation. — *Reflections on the Revolution in France* (1790)

9 Make the Revolution a parent of settlement, and not a nursery of future revolutions. — *Reflections on the Revolution in France* (1790)

10 People will not look forward to posterity, who never look backward to their ancestors. — *Reflections on the Revolution in France* (1790)

11 Those who attempt to level never equalize. — *Reflections on the Revolution in France* (1790)

12 Government is a contrivance of human wisdom to provide for human *wants*. Men have a right that these wants should be provided for by this wisdom. — *Reflections on the Revolution in France* (1790)

13 Flattery corrupts both the receiver and the giver. — *Reflections on the Revolution in France* (1790)

14 This sort of people are so taken up with their theories about the rights of man, that they have totally forgotten his nature. — *Reflections on the Revolution in France* 1790

of **Marie-Antoinette**:

15 I thought ten thousand swords must have leapt from their scabbards to avenge even a look that threatened her with insult. — *Reflections on the Revolution in France* (1790)

16 The age of chivalry is gone.—That of sophisters, economists, and calculators, has succeeded; and the glory of Europe is extinguished for ever. — *Reflections on the Revolution in France* (1790)

17 This barbarous philosophy, which is the offspring of cold hearts and muddy understandings. — *Reflections on the Revolution in France* (1790)

1 In the groves of *their* academy, at the end of every vista, you see nothing but the gallows. — *Reflections on the Revolution in France* (1790)

2 Kings will be tyrants from policy when subjects are rebels from principle. — *Reflections on the Revolution in France* (1790)

3 Because half a dozen grasshoppers under a fern make the field ring with their importunate chink, whilst thousands of great cattle, reposed beneath the shadow of the British oak, chew the cud and are silent, pray do not imagine that those who make the noise are the only inhabitants of the field. — *Reflections on the Revolution in France* 1790

4 A perfect democracy is therefore the most shameless thing in the world. — *Reflections on the Revolution in France* (1790)

5 Society is indeed a contract...it becomes a partnership not only between those who are living, but between those who are living, those who are dead, and those who are to be born. — *Reflections on the Revolution in France* (1790)

6 Nobility is a graceful ornament to the civil order. It is the Corinthian capital of polished society. — *Reflections on the Revolution in France* (1790)

7 History consists, for the greater part, of the miseries brought upon the world by pride, ambition, avarice, revenge, lust, sedition, hypocrisy, ungoverned zeal, and all the train of disorderly appetites...these vices are the *causes* of those storms. Religion, morals, laws, prerogatives, privileges, liberties, rights of men, are the *pretexts*. — *Reflections on the Revolution in France* (1790)

8 By hating vices too much, they come to love men too little. — *Reflections on the Revolution in France* (1790)

9 We begin our public affections in our families. No cold relation is a zealous citizen. — *Reflections on the Revolution in France* (1790)

10 Good order is the foundation of all good things. — *Reflections on the Revolution in France* (1790)

11 Every politician ought to sacrifice to the graces; and to join compliance with reason. — *Reflections on the Revolution in France* (1790)

12 Nothing turns out to be so oppressive and unjust as a feeble government. — *Reflections on the Revolution in France* (1790)

13 The conduct of a losing party never appears right: at least it never can possess the only infallible criterion of wisdom to vulgar judgements—success. — *Letter to a Member of the National Assembly* (1791)

14 Those who have been once intoxicated with power, and have derived any kind of emolument from it, even though for but one year, can never willingly abandon it. — *Letter to a Member of the National Assembly* (1791)

15 Tyrants seldom want pretexts. — *Letter to a Member of the National Assembly* (1791)

16 You can never plan the future by the past. — *Letter to a Member of the National Assembly* (1791)

17 Somebody has said, that a king may make a nobleman but he cannot make a gentleman. — letter to William Smith, 29 January 1795

1 All men that are ruined are ruined on the side of their natural propensities.
Two Letters on the Proposals for Peace with the Regicide Directory (9th ed., 1796)

2 Falsehood and delusion are allowed in no case whatsoever: But, as in the exercise of all the virtues, there is an economy of truth.
Two Letters on the Proposals for Peace with the Regicide Directory (9th ed., 1796); cf. **Armstrong** 16:12

3 The king, and his faithful subjects, the lords and commons of this realm,—the triple cord, which no man can break.
A Letter to a Noble Lord (1796)

4 To innovate is not to reform.
A Letter to a Noble Lord (1796)

5 Well is it known that ambition can creep as well as soar.
Third Letter... on the Proposals for Peace with the Regicide Directory (1797)

6 And having looked to government for bread, on the very first scarcity they will turn and bite the hand that fed them.
Thoughts and Details on Scarcity (1800)

7 It is necessary only for the good man to do nothing for evil to triumph.
attributed (in a number of forms) to Burke, but not found in his writings.

8 It is the interest of the commercial world that wealth should be found everywhere.
The Correspondence of Edmund Burke (1958–78) vol. 3

John Burns 1858–1943

British Labour politician

9 I have seen the Mississippi. That is muddy water. I have seen the St Lawrence. That is crystal water. But the Thames is liquid history.
in *Daily Mail* 25 January 1943

Robert Burns 1759–96

Scottish poet

10 The rank is but the guinea's stamp,
The man's the gowd for a' that!
'For a' that and a' that' (1790)

11 A fig for those by law protected!
LIBERTY's a glorious feast!
Courts for cowards were erected,
Churches built to please the PRIEST.
'The Jolly Beggars' (1799)

12 Liberty's in every blow!
Let us do—or die!!!
'Robert Bruce's March to Bannockburn' (1799)

13 We labour soon, we labour late,
To feed the titled knave, man;
And a' the comfort we're to get,
Is that ayont the grave, man.
'The Tree of Liberty' (1838)

Aaron Burr 1756–1836

American politician

1 Law is whatever is boldly asserted and plausibly maintained.
attributed

Ian Buruma 1951–

2 She did much to replace birth as a mark of distinction with money.
of Margaret **Thatcher**
in *The New York Review of Books* 20 October 1994 'Action Anglaise'

Barbara Bush 1925–

wife of George **Bush**; First Lady 1989–93

3 Somewhere out in this audience may even be someone who will one day follow in my footsteps, and preside over the White House as the President's spouse. I wish him well!
at Wellesley College Commencement, 1 June 1990

asked why she thought she was a popular First Lady:

4 It was because I threatened no one. I was old, white-headed and large.
in *Independent on Sunday* 4 December 1994 'Quotes of the Week'

George Bush 1924–

American Republican statesman; 41st President of the US, 1989–93

on Bush: see **Richards** 305:2

5 Oh, the vision thing.
responding to the suggestion that he turn his attention from short-term campaign objectives and look to the longer term.
in *Time* 26 January 1987

6 We are a nation of communities, of tens and tens of thousands of ethnic, religious, social, business, labour union, neighbourhood, regional and other organizations, all of them varied, voluntary, and unique...a brilliant diversity spread like stars, like a thousand points of light in a broad and peaceful sky.
acceptance speech at the Republican National Convention in New Orleans, 18 August 1988

7 Read my lips: no new taxes.
accepting the Republican nomination
in *New York Times* 19 August 1988

8 Giving peace a chance does not mean taking a chance on peace.
to the Veterans of Foreign Wars Convention in Baltimore, 20 August 1990
in *Guardian* 21 August 1990

9 The continent, frozen in hostility for so long, has become a continent of revolutionary change.
in *Guardian* 23 November 1990

David Butler 1924–

British political scientist

1 Has he got a resignation in him?
of James **Callaghan,** *to Hugh* **Dalton**
Hugh Dalton *Political Diary* (1986) 13 July 1960

R. A. ('Rab') Butler 1902–82

British Conservative politician
on Butler: see **Hennessy** 175:1, **Macmillan** 245:12

on hearing of the appointment of Winston **Churchill** *as Prime Minister in succession to Neville* **Chamberlain**:

2 The good clean tradition of English politics, that of Pitt as opposed to Fox, has been sold to the greatest adventurer of modern political history.
John Colville *The Fringes of Power, Downing Street Diaries 1939–1955* (1985) 10 May 1940

3 REPORTER: Mr Butler, would you say that this [Anthony Eden] is the best Prime Minister we have?
R A BUTLER: Yes.
interview at London Airport, 8 January 1956
R. A. Butler *The Art of the Possible* (1971)

4 The Civil Service is a bit like a Rolls-Royce—you know it's the best machine in the world, but you're not quite sure what to do with it.
Anthony Sampson *Anatomy of Britain* (1962)

5 I think a Prime Minister has to be a butcher and know the joints. That is perhaps where I have not been quite competent, in knowing all the ways that you can cut up a carcass.
in *Listener* 28 June 1966

6 I cannot help feeling that a man who always held all the bridge scores in his head, who seemed to know all the numbers, and played *vingt et un* so successfully would have been useful.
on Iain **Macleod***'s likely success as Chancellor*
The Art of Memory (1982)

7 I especially like Gibbon on the Christians. They really had nothing to offer except bishops and the after-life, but they pushed on and came through rather well.
John Mortimer *In Character* 'Remember Compassion'

8 Politics is largely a matter of heart.
Peter Hennessy in *Independent* 8 May 1987

9 In politics you must always keep running with the pack. The moment that you falter and they sense that you are injured, the rest will turn on you like wolves.
Dennis Walters *Not Always with the Pack* (1989)

John Byrom 1692–1763

English poet

10 God bless the King, I mean the Faith's Defender;
God bless—no harm in blessing—the Pretender;
But who Pretender is, or who is King,
God bless us all—that's quite another thing.
'To an Officer in the Army, Extempore, Intended to allay the Violence of Party-Spirit' (1773)

Lord Byron 1788–1824

English poet

1 I have no consistency, except in politics; and *that* probably arises from my indifference on the subject altogether.
letter 16 January 1814

2 The Cincinnatus of the West.
of George **Washington**
'Ode to Napoleon Bonaparte' (1814)

3 The arbiter of others' fate
A suppliant for his own!
'Ode to Napoleon Bonaparte' (1814)

4 So he has cut his throat at last!—He! Who?
The man who cut his country's long ago.
on Castlereagh's suicide, c.1822
'Epigram on Lord Castlereagh'

5 For what were all these country patriots born?
To hunt, and vote, and raise the price of corn?
'The Age of Bronze' (1823)

6 Year after year they voted cent per cent
Blood, sweat, and tear-wrung millions—why? for rent!
'The Age of Bronze' (1823)

Julius Caesar 100–44 BC

Roman general and statesman

7 *Gallia est omnis divisa in partes tres.*
Gaul as a whole is divided into three parts.
De Bello Gallico

8 Men are nearly always willing to believe what they wish.
De Bello Gallico

9 Caesar's wife must be above suspicion.
oral tradition, based on Plutarch *Parallel Lives* 'Julius Caesar'

10 Caesar, when he first went into Gaul, made no scruple to profess 'That he had rather be first in a village than second at Rome'.
Francis Bacon *The Advancement of Learning* (based on Plutarch *Parallel Lives* 'Julius Caesar')

11 The die is cast.
at the crossing of the Rubicon
Suetonius *Lives of the Caesars* 'Divus Julius' (often quoted in Latin *'Iacta alea est'* but originally spoken in Greek)

12 *Veni, vidi, vici.*
I came, I saw, I conquered.
inscription displayed in Caesar's Pontic triumph, according to Suetonius *Lives of the Caesars* 'Divus Julius'; or, according to Plutarch *Parallel Lives* 'Julius Caesar', written in a letter by Caesar, announcing the victory of Zela which concluded the Pontic campaign

13 *Et tu, Brute?*
You too, Brutus?
traditional rendering of Suetonius *Lives of the Caesars* 'Divus Julius': 'Some have written that when Marcus Brutus rushed at him, he said in Greek, "You too, my child?" '

Joseph Cairns 1920–

British industrialist and politician

1 The betrayal of Ulster, the cynical and entirely undemocratic banishment of its properly elected Parliament and a relegation to the status of a fuzzy wuzzy colony is, I hope, a last betrayal contemplated by Downing Street because it is the last that Ulster will countenance.
speech on retiring as Lord Mayor of Belfast, 31 May 1972
in *Daily Telegraph* 1 June 1972

John Caldwell Calhoun 1782–1850

American politician
on Calhoun: see **Jackson** 189:5

2 The very essence of a free government consists in considering offices as public trusts, bestowed for the good of the country, and not for the benefit of an individual or party.
speech 13 February 1835

3 A power has risen up in the government greater than the people themselves, consisting of many and various and powerful interests, combined into one mass, and held together by the cohesive power of the vast surplus in the banks.
speech 27 May 1836

4 The surrender of life is nothing to sinking down into acknowledgement of inferiority.
speech in the Senate, 19 February 1847

Caligula (Gaius Julius Caesar Germanicus) AD 12–41

Roman emperor from AD 37

5 Would that the Roman people had but one neck!
Suetonius *Lives of the Caesars* 'Gaius Caligula'

James Callaghan 1912–

British Labour statesman; Prime Minister 1976–9
on Callaghan: see **Butler** 70:1, **Jenkins** 194:2; cf. also **Anonymous** 9:10

6 Leaking is what you do; briefing is what *I* do.
when giving evidence to the Franks Committee on Official Secrecy in 1971
Franks Report (1972); oral evidence

7 We say that what Britain needs is a new social contract. That is what this document [*Labour's Programme for Britain*] is about.
speech at Labour Party Annual Conference, 2 October 1972

8 You cannot now, if you ever could, spend your way out of a recession.
speech at Labour Party Conference, 28 September 1976

9 You never reach the promised land. You can march towards it.
in a television interview, 20 July 1978

1 It's the first time in recorded history that turkeys have been known to vote for an early Christmas.
in the debate resulting in the fall of the Labour government, when the pact between Labour and the Liberals had collapsed, and the Nationalists also withdrew their support in the wake of the failure of the devolution bills

in the House of Commons, 28 March 1979

of the popularity of Mrs **Thatcher**:

2 The further you got from Britain, the more admired you found she was.

in *Spectator* 1 December 1990

3 Well, it works, doesn't it? So I think that's the answer, even if it is on the back of an envelope and doesn't have a written constitution with every comma and every semi-colon in place. Because sometimes they can make for difficulties that common sense can overcome.

Peter Hennessy and Simon Coates *The Back of the Envelope* (1991)

Italo Calvino 1923–85

Italian novelist and short-story writer

4 Revolutionaries are more formalistic than conservatives.

Il Barone Rampante (1957)

Lord Camden 1714–94

British Whig politician; Lord Chancellor, 1766–70

5 Taxation and representation are inseparable . . . whatever is a man's own, is absolutely his own; no man hath a right to take it from him without his consent either expressed by himself or representative; whoever attempts to do it, attempts an injury; whoever does it, commits a robbery; he throws down and destroys the distinction between liberty and slavery.
on the taxation of Americans by the British parliament

in the House of Lords, 10 February 1766

Simon Cameron 1799–1889

American politician

6 An honest politician is one who when he's bought stays bought.

attributed

Lord Campbell of Eskan 1912–

British industrialist

7 The only justification of the [House of] Lords is its irrationality: once you try to make it rational, you satisfy no one.

Anthony Sampson *The Changing Anatomy of Britain* (1982)

Thomas Campbell 1777–1844

Scottish poet

8 What millions died—that Caesar might be great!

Pleasures of Hope (1799)

Timothy Campbell 1840–1904

American politician

1 What's the Constitution between friends?
reported response to President **Cleveland***'s refusing to support a bill on the grounds of its being unconstitutional*
attributed, *c.*1885

Henry Campbell-Bannerman 1836–1908

British Liberal statesman, Prime Minister 1905–8
on Campbell-Bannerman: see **Asquith** 18:9, **Balfour** 30:5

2 There is a phrase which seems in itself somewhat self-evident, which is often used to account for a good deal—that 'war is war' But when you come to ask about it, then you are told that the war now going on is not war. [Laughter] When is a war not a war? When it is carried on by methods of barbarism in South Africa.
speech to National Reform Union, 14 June 1901

3 Good government could never be a substitute for government by the people themselves.
speech at Stirling, 23 November 1905

4 No more tact than a hippopotamus...Haldane always prefers the backstairs. But it does not matter. The clatter can be heard all over the house.
of R. B. **Haldane**
attributed

Albert Camus 1913–60

French novelist, playwright, and essayist

5 Politics and the fate of mankind are formed by men without ideals and without greatness. Those who have greatness within them do not go in for politics.
Carnets, 1935–42 (1962)

6 What is a rebel? A man who says no.
L'Homme révolté (1951)

7 All modern revolutions have ended in a reinforcement of the State.
L'Homme révolté (1951)

8 Every revolutionary ends as an oppressor or a heretic.
L'Homme révolté (1951)

George Canning 1770–1827

British Tory statesman; Prime Minister, 1827

9 Away with the cant of 'Measures not men'!—the idle supposition that it is the harness and not the horses that draw the chariot along. If the comparison must be made, if the distinction must be taken, men are everything, measures comparatively nothing.
speech on the Army estimates, 8 December 1802
Speeches of... Canning (1828) vol. 2; the phrase 'measures not men' may be found as early as 1742 (in a letter from Chesterfield to Dr Chevenix, 6 March); also in Goldsmith *The Good Natured Man* (1768), 'Measures not men, have always been my mark'; cf. **Burke** 63:5

10 Pitt is to Addington
As London is to Paddington.
'The Oracle' (*c.*1803)

1 A steady patriot of the world alone,
The friend of every country but his own.
on the Jacobin
'New Morality' (1821)

2 And finds, with keen discriminating sight,
Black's not so black;—nor white so very white.
'New Morality' (1821)

3 In matters of commerce the fault of the Dutch
Is offering too little and asking too much.
The French are with equal advantage content,
So we clap on Dutch bottoms just twenty per cent.
dispatch, in cipher, to the English ambassador at the Hague, 31 January 1826; Harry Poland *Mr Canning's Rhyming 'Dispatch' to Sir Charles Bagot* (1905)

4 I called the New World into existence, to redress the balance of the Old.
speech on the affairs of Portugal
in the House of Commons, 12 December 1826

5 [The Whip's duty is] to make a House, and keep a House, and cheer the minister.
J. E. Ritchie *Modern Statesmen* (1861)

Al Capone 1899–1947

Italian-born American gangster, notorious for his domination of organized crime in Chicago in the 1920s

6 Don't you get the idea I'm one of these goddam radicals. Don't get the idea I'm knocking the American system.
interview, *c.*1929; Claud Cockburn *In Time of Trouble* (1956)

Benjamin Nathan Cardozo 1870–1938

American judge

7 [The Constitution] was framed upon the theory that the peoples of the several states must sink or swim together, and that in the long run prosperity and salvation are in union and not division.
in *Baldwin v. Seelig* (1935)

Thomas Carlyle 1795–1881

Scottish historian and political philosopher

8 Two centuries; hardly less; before Democracy go through its due, most baleful, stages of *Quackocracy*.
History of the French Revolution (1837) vol. 1

9 The seagreen Incorruptible.
describing **Robespierre**
History of the French Revolution (1837) vol. 2

10 Aristocracy of the Moneybag.
History of the French Revolution (1837) vol. 3

11 France was long a despotism tempered by epigrams.
History of the French Revolution (1837) vol. 3

12 The three great elements of modern civilization, Gunpowder, Printing, and the Protestant Religion.
Critical and Miscellaneous Essays (1838) 'The State of German Literature'

13 To the very last he [Napoleon] had a kind of idea; that, namely, of *La carrière ouverte aux talents*, The tools to him that can handle them.
Critical and Miscellaneous Essays (1838) 'Sir Walter Scott'

1 A witty statesman said, you might prove anything by figures. — *Chartism* (1839)

2 In epochs when cash payment has become the sole nexus of man to man. — *Chartism* (1839)

3 Surely of all 'rights of man', this right of the ignorant man to be guided by the wiser, to be, gently or forcibly, held in the true course by him, is the indisputablest. — *Chartism* (1839)

4 A Hell in England—the Hell of not making money. — *Past and Present* (1843)

on parliamentarians:

5 Windbag, weak in the faith of a God, which he believes only at church on Sundays, if even then; strong only in the faith that paragraphs and plausibilities bring votes; that force of public opinion, as he calls it, is the primal necessity of things, and highest God we have. — *Past and Present* (1843)

6 Despotism is essential in most enterprises. — *Past and Present* (1843)

7 A Parliament speaking through reporters to Buncombe and the twenty-seven millions mostly fools. — *Latter-Day Pamphlets* (1850) 'Parliaments'; cf. **Walker** 376:8

of himself:

8 Little other than a redtape talking-machine, and unhappy bag of parliamentary eloquence. — *Latter-Day Pamphlets* (1850) 'The Present Time'

of political economy:

9 The Dismal Science. — *Latter-Day Pamphlets* (1850) 'The Present Time'

10 Councillors of state sit plotting, and playing their high chess-game, whereof the pawns are men. — *Sartor Resartus* (1858)

11 These ballot-boxing, Nigger-emancipating, empty, dirt-eclipsed days. — *Shooting Niagara: and After?* (1867)

in an anti-liberal polemic which caused great offence by its mode of expression

of **Disraeli**:

12 A superlative Hebrew conjuror. — *Shooting Niagara: and After?* (1867)

13 Cobden is an inspired bagman, who believes in a calico millenium. — T. W. Reid *Life, Letters and Friendships of Richard Monckton* (1890) vol. 1

14 Democracy, which means despair of finding any heroes to govern you. — attributed

15 Vote by ballot is the dyspepsia of the society. — Simon Heffer *Moral Desperado* (1995)

Stokely Carmichael 1941– and **Charles Vernon Hamilton** 1929–

16 Black power...is a call for black people in this country to unite, to recognize their heritage, to build a sense of community. — *Black Power* (1967)

17 Before a group can enter the open society, it must first close ranks. — *Black Power* (1967)

Lewis Carroll 1832–98

English writer and logician

1 'When *I* use a word,' Humpty Dumpty said in a rather scornful tone, 'it means just what I choose it to mean—neither more nor less.'

Through the Looking-Glass (1872); cf. **Shawcross** 337:4

2 The rule is, jam to-morrow and jam yesterday—but never jam today.

Through the Looking-Glass (1872); cf. **Benn** 36:3

Edward Carson 1854–1935

British lawyer and politician, Ulster leader and Unionist

3 My only great qualification for being put at the head of the Navy is that I am very much at sea.

Ian Colvin *Life of Lord Carson* (1936) vol. 3

4 From the day I first entered parliament up to the present, devotion to the union has been the guiding star of my political life.

in *Dictionary of National Biography*

Jimmy Carter 1924–

American Democratic statesman, 39th President of the US, 1977–81

5 We should live our lives as though Christ were coming this afternoon.

to a Bible class at Plains, Georgia, March 1976

in *Boston Sunday Herald Advertiser* 11 April 1976

6 We are of course a nation of differences. Those differences don't make us weak. They're the source of our strength... The question is not when we came here... but why our families came here. And what we did after we arrived.

speech at Al Smith dinner in New York City, 21 October 1976

7 I've looked on a lot of women with lust. I've committed adultery in my heart many times. This is something that God recognizes I will do—and I have done it—and God forgives me for it.

in *Playboy* November 1976

8 Two problems of our country—energy and malaise.

at town meeting in Bardstown, Kentucky, 31 July 1979

John Cartwright 1740–1824

English political reformer

9 One man shall have one vote.

The People's Barrier Against Undue Influence (1780) 'Principles, maxims, and primary rules of politics' no. 68

Thomas Nixon Carver

American conservative, who had previously given the course in agricultural economics at Harvard taken over by Galbraith in 1934

1 The trouble with radicals is that they only read radical literature, and the trouble with conservatives is that they don't read anything.

'Carver's Law'; J. K. Galbraith *A Life in Our Times* (1981)

Roger Casement 1864–1916

Irish nationalist; executed for treason in 1916

2 Where all your rights become only an accumulated wrong; where men must beg with bated breath for leave to subsist in their own land, to think their own thoughts, to sing their own songs, to garner the fruits of their own labours... then surely it is a braver, a saner and truer thing, to be a rebel in act and deed against such circumstances as these than tamely to accept it as the natural lot of men.

statement from prison, 29 June 1916

Ted Castle 1907–79

British journalist

3 In place of strife.

title of Labour Government White Paper, 17 January 1969; suggested by Castle to his wife, Barbara Castle, then Secretary of State for Employment

Catherine the Great 1729–96

Empress of Russia from 1762

4 I shall be an autocrat: that's my trade. And the good Lord will forgive me: that's his.

attributed

Wyn Catlin

5 Diplomacy is saying 'Nice doggie' until you find a rock.

Laurence J. Peter (ed.) *Quotations for our Time* (1977)

Carrie Chapman Catt 1859–1947

American feminist

6 No written law has ever been more binding than unwritten custom supported by popular opinion.

speech at Senate hearing on woman's suffrage, 13 February 1900

Why We Ask for the Submission of an Amendment (1900)

7 When a just cause reaches its flood-tide... whatever stands in the way must fall before its overwhelming power.

speech at Stockholm, *Is Woman Suffrage Progressing?* (1911)

Cato the Elder (or 'the Censor') 234–149 BC

Roman statesman, orator, and writer

1 *Delenda est Carthago.*
Carthage must be destroyed.
Pliny the Elder *Naturalis Historia*

Constantine Cavafy 1863–1933

Greek poet

2 What are we waiting for, gathered in the market-place?
The barbarians are to arrive today.
'Waiting for the Barbarians' (1904)

3 And now, what will become of us without the barbarians?
Those people were a kind of solution.
'Waiting for the Barbarians' (1904)

Count Cavour 1810–61

Italian statesman

4 We are ready to proclaim throughout Italy this great principle: a free church in a free state.
speech, 27 March 1861

Lord Edward Cecil 1867–1918

British soldier and civil servant; chief British adviser in the Egyptian government

definition of a compromise:

5 An agreement between two men to do what both agree is wrong.
letter 3 September 1911

Lord Hugh Cecil 1869–1956

British Conservative politician and Provost of Eton

6 There is no more ungraceful figure than that of a humanitarian with an eye to the main chance.
dismissal of a manoeuvre by **Campbell-Bannerman**
in *The Times* 24 June 1901

7 The socialist believes that it is better to be rich than poor, the Christian that it is better to be poor than rich.
Conservatism (1912)

8 Losses to a nation may be so great that they change the character of the nation itself. It would be so with us if we lost our dominions beyond the sea.
Conservatism (1912)

Robert Cecil 1563–1612

English courtier and statesman, son of William Cecil, Lord Burghley

9 Rest content, and give heed to one that hath sorrowed in the bright lustre of a court, and gone heavily even on the best-seeming fair ground...I know it bringeth little comfort on earth; and he is, I reckon, no wise man that looketh this way to Heaven.
letter to Sir John Harington; Algernon Cecil *A Life of Robert Cecil* (1915)

Joseph Chamberlain 1836–1914

British Liberal politician; father of Neville **Chamberlain**
on Chamberlain: see **Housman** 183:7

1 In politics, there is no use looking beyond the next fortnight.
A. J. Balfour letter to Lord Salisbury, 24 March 1886; cf. **Wilson** 390:8

2 It is not to your interest to arouse the prejudices of the society in which you hope one day again to take your place... Therefore my advice is: Be as Radical as you like. Be Home Ruler if you must. But be a little Jingo if you can.
to his friend Charles Dilke, who was hoping to make a political comeback
Roy Jenkins *Sir Charles Dilke* (1958)

3 It is no use blowing the trumpet for the charge, and then looking around to find nobody following.
discussing negotiations with President **Kruger** *prior to the Second Boer War*
Winston Churchill *Great Contemporaries* (1937)

4 Provided that the City of London remains, as it is at present, the clearing-house of the world, any other nation may be its workshop.
speech at the Guildhall, 19 January 1904

5 Learn to think Imperially.
with reference to Alexander **Hamilton***'s advice to the newly independent United States*
speech at the Guildhall, 19 January 1904; cf. **Hamilton** 167:7

6 The day of small nations has long passed away. The day of Empires has come.
speech at Birmingham, 12 May 1904

7 We are not downhearted. The only trouble is we cannot understand what is happening to our neighbours.
referring to a constituency which had remained unaffected by an electoral landslide
speech at Smethwick, 18 January 1906

Neville Chamberlain 1869–1940

British Conservative statesman; Prime Minister, 1937–40; son of Joseph **Chamberlain**
on Chamberlain: see **Bevan** 40:2, **Channon** 81:7, **Churchill** 90:2, **Lloyd George** 230:7, **Nicolson** 272:1, 272:2

8 In war, whichever side may call itself the victor, there are no winners, but all are losers.
speech at Kettering, 3 July 1938

9 How horrible, fantastic, incredible it is that we should be digging trenches and trying on gas-masks here because of a quarrel in a far away country between people of whom we know nothing.
on Germany's annexation of the Sudetenland
radio broadcast, 27 September 1938

10 This morning I had another talk with the German Chancellor, Herr Hitler, and here is the paper which bears his name upon it as well as mine... 'We regard the agreeement signed last night and the Anglo-German Naval Agreement, as symbolic of the desire of our two peoples never to go to war with one another again.'
speech at Heston Airport, 30 September 1938

1 This is the second time in our history that there has come back from Germany to Downing Street peace with honour. I believe it is peace for our time.
speech from the window of 10 Downing Street, 30 September 1938
in *The Times* 1 October 1938

2 It's no part of a Prime Minister's duty to take a country into a war which he thinks you can't win.
shortly before Munich, as recalled by Lord **Home**
attributed

the British Ambassador in Berlin had handed the German government a final note stating that unless the British government had heard by eleven o'clock that Germany was prepared to withdraw her troops from Poland, a state of war would exist between the two countries:

3 I have to tell you now that no such undertaking has been received, and that consequently this country is at war with Germany.
radio broadcast, 3 September 1939

4 Whatever may be the reason—whether it was that Hitler thought he might get away with what he had got without fighting for it, or whether it was that after all the preparations were not sufficiently complete—however, one thing is certain—he missed the bus.
speech at Central Hall, Westminster, 4 April 1940

Henry ('Chips') Channon 1897–1958

American-born British Conservative MP and diarist

5 I personally think... that there will be an unheaval, that the Throne will sway a little, but that it will survive and that the King will get away with it. We are working up to something terrific. What is history unfolding?
during the Abdication crisis of 1936
diary 22 November 1936

6 There is nowhere in the world where sleep is so deep as in the libraries of the House of Commons.
diary 17 December 1937

7 He is winning through and will probably be Premier for years to come.
of Neville **Chamberlain**
diary 15 January 1939

8 I gather it has now been decided not to embrace the Russian bear, but to hold out a hand and accept its paw gingerly. No more. The worst of both worlds.
diary 16 May 1939

Rab **Butler** *had asked whether he and Ivan Maisky could use Channon's house in Belgrave Square for a secret meeting:*

9 I never thought that the Russian Ambassador would ever cross my threshold; I checked up on the snuff-boxes on my return but did not notice anything missing.
diary 28 November 1939

on hearing Lady Mountbatten expounding her anti-monarchical views:

10 How easy it seems for a semi-royal millionairess, who has exhausted all the pleasures of money and position, to turn almost Communist!
diary 19 September 1944

John Jay Chapman 1862–1933

1 Everybody in America is soft, and hates conflict. The cure for this, both in politics and social life, is the same—hardihood. Give them raw truth.
Practical Agitation (1898)

Charles I 1600–49

King of England, Scotland, and Ireland from 1625
on Charles I: see **Marvell** 251:7

2 Never make a defence or apology before you be accused.
letter to Lord Wentworth, 3 September 1636

3 I see all the birds are flown.
after attempting to arrest the Five Members
in the House of Commons, 4 January 1642

4 You manifestly wrong even the poorest ploughman, if you demand not his free consent.
rejecting the jurisdiction of the High Court of Justice, 21 January 1649
S. R. Gardiner *Constitutional Documents of the Puritan Revolution* (1906 ed.)

5 Sweet-heart, now they will cut off thy father's head. Mark, child, what I say: they will cut off my head, and perhaps make thee a king. But mark what I say: you must not be a king, so long as your brothers Charles and James do live.
said to Prince Henry
in *Reliquiae Sacrae Carolinae* (1650)

6 As to the King, the laws of the land will clearly instruct you for that...For the people; and truly I desire their liberty and freedom, as much as any body: but I must tell you, that their liberty and freedom consists in having the government of those laws, by which their life and their goods may be most their own; 'tis not for having share in government [sirs] that is nothing pertaining to 'em. A subject and a sovereign are clean different things...If I would have given way to an arbitrary way, for to have all laws changed according to the power of the sword, I needed not to have come here; and therefore I tell you (and I pray God it be not laid to your charge) that I am the martyr of the people.
speech on the scaffold, 30 January 1649
J. Rushworth *Historical Collections* vol. 2 (1701)

7 I die a Christian, according to the profession of the Church of England, as I found it left me by my father.
J. Rushworth *Historical Collections* vol. 2 (1701)

Charles II 1630–85

King of England, Scotland and Ireland from 1660
on Charles II: see **Rochester** 307:5

8 It is upon the navy under the good Providence of God that the safety, honour, and welfare of this realm do chiefly depend.
'Articles of War' preamble (probably a popular paraphrase); Geoffrey Callender *The Naval Side of British History* (1952)

1 This is very true: for my words are my own, and my actions are my ministers'.
reply to Lord **Rochester**'*s epitaph on him*
in *Thomas Hearne: Remarks and Collections* (1885–1921) 17 November 1706; cf. **Rochester** 307:5

2 Better than a play.
on the debates in the House of Lords on Lord Ross's Divorce Bill
A. Bryant *King Charles II* (1931)

3 I am sure no man in England will take away my life to make you King.
to his brother James, afterwards James II
William King *Political & Literary Anecdotes* (1818)

4 I am weary of travelling and am resolved to go abroad no more. But when I am dead and gone I know not what my brother will do: I am much afraid that when he comes to wear the crown he will be obliged to travel again.
on the difference between himself and his brother
attributed

5 I, who will never use arbitrary government myself, am resolved not to suffer it in others.
to the Whigs
attributed

6 He had been, he said, an unconscionable time dying; but he hoped that they would excuse it.
Lord Macaulay *History of England* (1849) vol. 1

Salmon Portland Chase 1808–73

American lawyer and politician

7 The Constitution, in all its provisions, looks to an indestructible Union composed of indestructible States.
decision in Texas v. White, 1868

Mary Chesnut 1823–86

American diarist and Confederate supporter

8 The Confederacy has been done to death by politicians.
in 1863; Ken Burns *The Civil War* (documentary, 1989) episode 4

9 Atlanta is gone. That agony is over. There is no hope but we will try to have no fear.
after the fall of Atlanta to Sherman's army in 1864
Geoffrey C. Ward *The Civil War* (1991)

Lord Chesterfield 1694–1773

English writer and politician
on Chesterfield: see **Johnson** 197:1, **Walpole** 377:6

10 Women, then, are only children of a larger growth: they have an entertaining tattle, and sometimes wit; but for solid, reasoning good sense, I never knew in my life one that had it, or who reasoned or acted consequentially for four and twenty hours together.
letter 5 September 1748

11 Politicians neither love nor hate. Interest, not sentiment, directs them.
Letters 1748

12 I...could not help reflecting in my way upon the singular ill-luck of this my dear country, which, as long
in *The World* 7 October 1756

as ever I remember it, and as far back as I have read, has always been governed by the only two or three people, out of two or three millions, totally incapable of governing, and unfit to be trusted.

G. K. Chesterton 1874–1936

English essayist, novelist, and poet

1 'My country, right or wrong' is a thing no patriot would ever think of saying except in a desperate case. It is like saying, 'My mother, drunk or sober.' *The Defendant* (1901)

2 Tradition means giving votes to the most obscure of all classes, our ancestors. It is the democracy of the dead. *Orthodoxy* (1908)

3 Democrats object to men being disqualified by the accident of birth; tradition objects to their being disqualified by the accident of death. Tradition refuses to submit to the small and arrogant oligarchy of those who merely happen to be walking around. *Orthodoxy* (1908)

4 All conservatism is based upon the idea that if you leave things alone you leave them as they are. But you do not. If you leave a thing alone you leave it to a torrent of change. *Orthodoxy* (1908)

5 Are they clinging to their crosses, F. E. Smith? 'Antichrist' (1912)
satirizing F. E. **Smith***'s response to the Welsh Disestablishment Bill*

6 Talk about the pews and steeples 'Antichrist' (1912)
And the Cash that goes therewith!
But the souls of Christian peoples...
Chuck it, Smith!

7 Smile at us, pay us, pass us; but do not quite forget. 'The Secret People' (1915)
For we are the people of England, that never have spoken yet.

8 We only know the last sad squires ride slowly towards the sea, 'The Secret People' (1915)
And a new people takes the land: and still it is not we.

9 They have given us into the hand of new unhappy lords, 'The Secret People' (1915)
Lords without anger and honour, who dare not carry their swords.
They fight us by shuffling papers; they have bright dead alien eyes;
And they look at our labour and laughter as a tired man looks at flies.
And the load of their loveless pity is worse than the ancient wrongs,
Their doors are shut in the evening; And they know no songs.

10 They died to save their country and they only saved the world. 'English Graves' (1922)

11 Lancashire merchants whenever they like 'Songs of Education: II Geography' (1922)
Can water the beer of a man in Klondike

Or poison the meat of a man in Bombay;
And that is the meaning of Empire Day.

1 Democracy means government by the uneducated, while aristocracy means government by the badly educated. — in *New York Times* 1 February 1931

Lydia Maria Child 1802–80

American abolitionist and suffragist

2 We first crush people to the earth, and then claim the right of trampling on them forever, because they are prostrate. — *An Appeal on Behalf of That Class of Americans Called Africans* (1833)

3 Woman stock is rising in the market. I shall not live to see women vote, but I'll come and rap at the ballot box. — letter to Sarah Shaw, 3 August 1856

Erskine Childers 1870–1922

Anglo-Irish writer and political activist

to the firing squad at his execution:

4 Come closer, boys. It will be easier for you. — Burke Wilkinson *The Zeal of the Convert* (1976)

Lawton Chiles 1930–

American politician

5 You are misunderstood, maligned, viewed by the press as a Pulitzer Prize ready to be won.
on the problems of investigative journalism for politicians — in *St Petersburg (Florida) Times* 6 March 1991

Rufus Choate 1799–1859

American lawyer and politician

6 The courage of New England was the 'courage of conscience'. It did not rise to that insane and awful passion, the love of war for itself. — address at Ipswich, Massachusetts, Centennial, 1834

7 We join ourselves to no party that does not carry the flag and keep step to the music of the Union. — letter to the Whig Convention, Worcester, Massachusetts, 1 October 1855

8 Its constitution the glittering and sounding generalities of natural right which make up the Declaration of Independence. — letter to the Maine Whig State Central Committee, 9 August 1856

Frank Chodorov 1887–1966

American economist and writer

9 [When people] say 'let's do something about it,' they mean 'let's get hold of the political machinery so that we can do something to somebody else.' And that somebody is invariably you. — 'Freedom is Better' (1949)

10 The only way to a world society is through free trade. — 'One Worldism' (1950)

David Christy 1802–c.68

1 Cotton is King; or, the economical relations of slavery. — title of book, 1855

Clementine Churchill 1885–1977

wife of Winston **Churchill**

2 Winston...has the supreme quality which I venture to say very few of your present or future Cabinet possess, the power, the imagination, the deadliness to fight Germany.

letter to **Asquith** *on Winston* **Churchill***'s dismissal from the Admiralty, May 1915*

Martin Gilbert *In Search of Churchill* (1994)

Lord Randolph Churchill 1849–94

British Conservative politician; father of Winston **Churchill**

on Churchill: see **Gladstone** 155:2; **Rosebery** 312:6

3 To tell the truth I don't know myself what Tory Democracy is. But I believe it is principally opportunism.

having urged Wilfrid Scawen Blunt in 1885 to stand for Parliament as a Tory Democrat

Elizabeth Longford *A Pilgrimage of Passion* (1979)

4 For the purposes of recreation he [Gladstone] has selected the felling of trees, and we may usefully remark that his amusements, like his politics, are essentially destructive...The forest laments in order that Mr Gladstone may perspire. — speech on Financial Reform, delivered in Blackpool, 24 January 1884

5 He [Gladstone] told them that he would give them and all other subjects of the Queen much legislation, great prosperity, and universal peace, and he has given them nothing but chips. Chips to the faithful allies in Afghanistan, chips to the trusting native races of South Africa, chips to the Egyptian fellah, chips to the British farmer, chips to the manufacturer and the artisan, chips to the agricultural labourer, chips to the House of Commons itself. — speech on Financial Reform, delivered in Blackpool, 24 January 1884

6 Ulster will fight; Ulster will be right. — public letter, 7 May 1886

7 An old man in a hurry.

of **Gladstone**

in an address to the electors of South Paddington, 19 June 1886

8 I decided some time ago that if the G.O.M. [Gladstone] went for Home Rule, the Orange card would be the one to play. Please God it may turn out the ace of trumps and not the two.

often quoted as 'Play the Orange card'; cf. **Shapiro** 335:12

letter to Lord Justice FitzGibbon, 16 February 1886

9 All great men make mistakes. Napoleon forgot Blücher, I forgot Goschen.

when Lord Randolph suddenly resigned the position of Chancellor of the Exchequer in 1886, **Goschen** *had been appointed in his place*

in *Leaves from the Notebooks of Lady Dorothy Nevill* (1907)

1 I never could make out what those damned dots meant.
of decimal points
Winston Churchill *Lord Randolph Churchill* (1906) vol. 2

Winston Churchill 1874–1965

British Conservative statesman; Prime Minister, 1940–5, 1951–5
on Churchill: see **Asquith** 18:8, **Baldwin** 29:8, **Bevan** 40:10, 40:12, **Butler** 70:2, **Headlam** 172:1, **Laski** 218:4, **Lloyd George** 230:9, 230:16, **Morton** 266:8, **Nicolson** 272:5, **Webb** 381:2, **Wilson** 391:10

2 It may be that vengeance is sweet, and that the gods forbade vengeance to men because they reserved for themselves so delicious and intoxicating a drink. But no one should drain the cup to the bottom. The dregs are often filthy-tasting.
The River War (1899)

3 Corruption at home, aggression abroad to cover it up... Sentiment by the bucketful, patriotism by the imperial pint; the open hand at the public exchequer, the open door at the public house; dear food for the millions, cheap labour for the millionaire.
of the Conservatives in 1904 as the Party of great vested interests
Andrew Roberts *Eminent Churchillians* (1994)

4 A labour contract into which men enter voluntarily for a limited and for a brief period, under which they are paid wages which they consider adequate, under which they are not bought or sold and from which they can obtain relief...on payment of £17.10s, the cost of their passage, may not be a healthy or proper contract, but it cannot in the opinion of His Majesty's Government be classified as slavery in the extreme acceptance of the word without some risk of terminological inexactitude.
in the House of Commons, 22 February 1906

5 He [Lord Charles Beresford] is one of those orators of whom it was well said, 'Before they get up, they do not know what they are going to say; when they are speaking, they do not know what they are saying; and when they have sat down, they do not know what they have said.'
in the House of Commons, 20 December 1912

6 Business carried on as usual during alterations on the map of Europe.
on the self-adopted 'motto' of the British people
speech at Guildhall, 9 November 1914

7 I am never going to have anything more to do with politics or politicians. When this war is over I shall confine myself entirely to writing and painting.
to a fellow officer on the Western Front, 1915
Martin Gilbert *In Search of Churchill* (1994)

8 We live very simply—but with all the essentials of life well understood and well provided for—hot baths, cold champagne, new peas, and old brandy.
of life at his country bolthole, Hoe Farm, after his dismissal from the Admiralty in 1915
Martin Gilbert *In Search of Churchill* (1994)

1 A drizzle of Empires . . . falling through the air.
of the Austro-Hungarian and Ottoman empires in 1918
Martin Gilbert *In Search of Churchill* (1994)

comparing H. H. **Asquith** *with Arthur* **Balfour**:

2 The difference between him and Arthur is that Arthur is wicked and moral, Asquith is good and immoral.
E. T. Raymond *Mr Balfour* (1920)

of **Balfour***'s moving from* **Asquith***'s Cabinet to that of* **Lloyd George**:

3 Like a powerful graceful cat walking delicately and unsoiled across a rather muddy street.
Great Contemporaries (1937)

4 The whole map of Europe has been changed . . . but as the deluge subsides and the waters fall short we see the dreary steeples of Fermanagh and Tyrone emerging once again.
in the House of Commons, 16 February 1922

5 Anyone can rat, but it takes a certain amount of ingenuity to re-rat.
on rejoining the Conservatives twenty years after leaving them for the Liberals, c.1924
Kay Halle *Irrepressible Churchill* (1966)

of a meeting in 1926 with **LLoyd George**, *by then out of office:*

6 Within five minutes the old relationship between us was completely re-established. The relationship between Master and Servant. And I was the Servant.
Lord Boothby *Recollections of a Rebel* (1978)

7 I decline utterly to be impartial as between the fire brigade and the fire.
replying to complaints of his bias in editing the British Gazette *during the General Strike*
in the House of Commons, 7 July 1926

8 If you strike at savings you at once propagate the idea of 'Let us eat, drink and be merry, for tomorrow we die.' That is at once the inspiration and the mortal disease by which the Socialist philosophy is affected.
in the House of Commons, 19 May 1927

9 Cultured people are merely the glittering scum which floats upon the deep river of production.
on hearing his son Randolph criticize the lack of culture of the Calgary oil magnates, probably c.1929
Martin Gilbert *In Search of Churchill* (1994)

when taking the entrance examination for Harrow, Churchill's answer paper consisted of his own name and a bracketed figure 1 for the first question:

10 It was from these slender indications of scholarship that Mr Welldon drew the conclusion that I was worthy to pass into Harrow. It is very much to his credit.
My Early Life (1930)

11 Headmasters have powers at their disposal with which Prime Ministers have never yet been invested.
My Early Life (1930)

12 I am biased in favour of boys learning English. I would make them all learn English: and then I would let the clever ones learn Latin as an honour, and Greek as a treat.
My Early Life (1930)

13 Mr Gladstone read Homer for fun, which I thought served him right.
My Early Life (1930)

14 I had no idea [in 1894] of the enormous and unquestionably helpful part that humbug plays in the
My Early Life (1930)

social life of great peoples dwelling in a state of democratic freedom.

1 I remember, when I was a child, being taken to the celebrated Barnum's circus, which contained an exhibition of freaks and monstrosities, but the exhibit on the programme which I most desired to see was the one described as 'The Boneless Wonder'. My parents judged that that spectacle would be too revolting and demoralizing for my youthful eyes, and I have waited 50 years to see the boneless wonder sitting on the Treasury Bench.
of Ramsay **MacDonald**
in the House of Commons, 28 January 1931

2 I do not like elections, but it is in my many elections that I have learnt to know and honour the people of this island. They are good through and through.
Thoughts and Adventures (1932)

of the General Election of 1922:
3 In the twinkling of an eye I found myself without an office, without a seat, without a party, and without an appendix.
Thoughts and Adventures (1932)

4 Tell your boss from me that anti-Semitism may be a good starter, but it is a bad sticker.
in 1932, having been asked by a German friend of his son Randolph whether he would be willing to meet **Hitler**
Martin Gilbert *In Search of Churchill* (1994)

5 A gigantic quilt of jumbled crochet work, a monstrous monument of shame built by pigmies.
on the Government of India Bill, 1935
Kenneth Rose *The Later Cecils* (1975)

6 There is not much collective security in a flock of sheep on the way to the butcher.
speech at the New Commonwealth Society luncheon, Dorchester Hotel, 25 November 1936

7 So they [the Government] go on in strange paradox, decided only to be undecided, resolved to be irresolute, adamant for drift, solid for fluidity, all-powerful to be impotent.
in the House of Commons, 12 November 1936

8 Dictators ride to and fro upon tigers which they dare not dismount. And the tigers are getting hungry.
letter, 11 November 1937

of the career of Lord **Curzon**:
9 The morning had been golden; the noontide was bronze; and the evening lead. But all were solid, and each was polished till it shone after its fashion.
Great Contemporaries (1937)

10 No part of the education of a politician is more indispensable than the fighting of elections.
Great Contemporaries (1937)

11 The utmost he [Neville Chamberlain] has been able to gain for Czechoslovakia and in the matters which were in dispute has been that the German dictator, instead of snatching his victuals from the table, has been content to have them served to him course by course.
in the House of Commons, 5 October 1938

1 I cannot forecast to you the action of Russia. It is a riddle wrapped in a mystery inside an enigma. — radio broadcast, 1 October 1939

on being asked where to set the podium from which Neville **Chamberlain** *was to give an address to local Conservatives:*

2 It doesn't matter where you put it as long as he has the sun in his eyes and the wind in his teeth. — Martin Gilbert *In Search of Churchill* (1994)

3 An appeaser is one who feeds a crocodile hoping it will eat him last. — in the House of Commons, January 1940

as Prime Minister:

4 [I was] conscious of a profound source of relief. I felt as if I was walking with destiny, and that all my past life had been but a preparation for this hour and this trial. — on 10 May 1940

5 I have nothing to offer but blood, toil, tears and sweat. — in the House of Commons, 13 May 1940

6 What is our policy?...to wage war against a monstrous tyranny, never surpassed in the dark, lamentable catalogue of human crime. — in the House of Commons, 13 May 1940

7 We shall not flag or fail. We shall go on to the end. We shall fight in France, we shall fight on the seas and oceans, we shall fight with growing confidence and growing strength in the air, we shall defend our island, whatever the cost may be. We shall fight on the beaches, we shall fight on the landing grounds, we shall fight in the fields and in the streets, we shall fight in the hills; we shall never surrender. — in the House of Commons, 4 June 1940

8 Let us therefore brace ourselves to our duty, and so bear ourselves that, if the British Commonwealth and its Empire lasts for a thousand years, men will still say, 'This was their finest hour.' — in the House of Commons, 18 June 1940

on being bombed:

9 Learn to get used to it. Eels get used to skinning. — notes for a speech, 20 June 1940

10 Never in the field of human conflict was so much owed by so many to so few. — in the House of Commons, 20 August 1940

on the skill and courage of British airmen

11 Death and sorrow will be the companions of our journey; hardship our garment; constancy and valour our only shield. We must be united, we must be undaunted, we must be inflexible. — in the House of Commons, 8 October 1940

comment allegedly made on a long-winded report submitted by Anthony **Eden** *on his tour of the Near East:*

12 As far as I can see you have used every cliché except 'God is Love' and 'Please adjust your dress before leaving.' — in *Life* December 1940

13 I well appreciate the necessity of preserving the piebald complexion of my pony. — Andrew Roberts *Eminent Churchillians* (1994)

on a proposed appointment likely to upset the balance of his coalition

14 What I want is for you to keep the flies off the meat. It becomes bad if they are allowed to settle even for — Andrew Roberts *Eminent Churchillians* (1994)

a moment. I am the meat and you must show me the warning light when troubles arise in the Parliamentary and political scene.
to his newly appointed Parliamentary Private Secretary, c.1941

1 What could you hope to achieve except to be sunk in a bigger and more expensive ship this time?
to **Mountbatten** *in November 1941, overriding his protests at being appointed to a desk job as Adviser on Combined Operations rather than being allowed to remain on active service in the Navy*
Andrew Roberts *Eminent Churchillians* (1994)

2 A medal glitters, but it also casts a shadow.
a reference to the envy caused by the award of honours
in 1941; Kenneth Rose *King George V* (1983)

3 It becomes still more difficult to reconcile Japanese action with prudence or even with sanity. What kind of a people do they think we are?
speech to US Congress, 26 December 1941

4 The British nation is unique in this respect. They are the only people who like to be told how bad things are, who like to be told the worst.
in the House of Commons, 10 June 1941

5 The people of London with one voice would say to Hitler: 'You have committed every crime under the sun...We will have no truce or parley with you, or the grisly gang who work your wicked will. You do your worst—and we will do our best.
speech at County Hall, London, 14 July 1941

6 Here is the answer which I will give to President Roosevelt...Give us the tools and we will finish the job.
radio broadcast 9 February 1941

7 When I warned them [the French Government] that Britain would fight on alone whatever they did, their generals told their Prime Minister and his divided Cabinet, 'In three weeks England will have her neck wrung like a chicken.' Some chicken! Some neck!
speech to Canadian Parliament, 30 December 1941

8 There you are, fixed, old cock.
note sent to the Minister of Education, Rab **Butler***, who was working on the Education Act in 1942 when the Cardinal Archbishop of Westminster publicly asserted the independence of Roman Catholic education*
R. A. Butler *The Art of Memory* (1982)

9 I have not become the King's First Minister in order to preside over the liquidation of the British Empire.
speech in London, 10 November 1942

10 Now this is not the end. It is not even the beginning of the end. But it is, perhaps, the end of the beginning.
on British success in the North African campaign
speech at the Mansion House, London, 10 November 1942

11 We make this wide encircling movement in the Mediterranean, having for its primary object the recovery of the command of that vital sea, but also having for its object the exposure of the under-belly of the Axis, especially Italy, to heavy attack.
often misquoted as 'the soft under-belly of the Axis'
in the House of Commons, 11 November 1942

12 National compulsory insurance for all classes for all purposes from the cradle to the grave.
radio broadcast 21 March 1943

1 There is no finer investment for any community than putting milk into babies. — radio broadcast, 21 March 1943

2 The empires of the future are the empires of the mind. — speech at Harvard, 6 September 1943

on rebuilding the Houses of Parliament:
3 We shape our dwellings, and afterwards our dwellings shape us. — in the House of Commons, 28 October 1944

4 I do not see any other way of realizing our hopes about World Organization in five or six days. Even the Almighty took seven.
to Franklin **Roosevelt** *on the likely duration of the Yalta conference with* **Stalin** *in 1945* — *The Second World War* (1954) vol. 6

5 He devised the extraordinary measure of assistance called Lend-Lease, which will stand forth as the most unselfish and unsordid financial act of any country in all history.
of President **Roosevelt** — in the House of Commons, 17 April 1945

6 One day President Roosevelt told me that he was asking publicly for suggestions about what the war should be called. I said at once, 'The Unnecessary War'. — *The Second World War* (1948) vol. 1

after the General Election of 1945:
7 Why should I accept the Order of the Garter from His Majesty when the people have just given me the order of the boot? — D. Bardens *Churchill in Parliament* (1967)

of Aneurin **Bevan**:
8 Unless the right hon. gentleman changes his policy and methods and moves without the slightest delay, he will be as great a curse to this country in time of peace, as he was a squalid nuisance in time of war. — in the House of Commons, 6 December 1945

9 The Prime Minister has nothing to hide from the President of the United States
on stepping from his bath in the presence of a startled President **Roosevelt** — as recalled by Roosevelt's son in *Churchill* (BBC television series presented by Martin Gilbert, 1992) pt. 3

10 From Stettin in the Baltic to Trieste in the Adriatic an iron curtain has descended across the Continent.
the expression 'iron curtain' previously had been applied by others to the Soviet Union or her sphere of influence, e.g. Ethel Snowden Through Bolshevik Russia *(1920), Dr Goebbels* Das Reich, *25 February 1945, and by Churchill himself in a cable to President Truman, 4 June 1945* — speech at Westminster College, Fulton, Missouri, 5 March 1946

11 We must build a kind of United States of Europe. — in Zurich, 19 September 1946

after the Nuremberg war trials:
12 From now on I shall have to take care not to lose wars. — attributed

13 I wish Stanley Baldwin no ill, but it would have been much better if he had never lived.
on being asked to send **Baldwin** *an 80th birthday tribute* — Martin Gilbert *In Search of Churchill* (1994)

14 It would be a great reform in politics if wisdom could be made to spread as easily and as rapidly as folly. — speech at the Guildhall, London, 10 September 1947

1 No one pretends that democracy is perfect or all-wise. Indeed, it has been said that democracy is the worst form of Government except all those other forms that have been tried from time to time.
in the House of Commons, 11 November 1947

2 When I am abroad I always make it a rule never to criticize or attack the Government of my country. I make up for lost time when I am at home.
in the House of Commons, 18 April 1947

3 The candle in that great turnip has gone out.
on Stanley **Baldwin** *in his last years*
Harold Nicolson diary 17 August 1950

4 This is the sort of English up with which I will not put.
after an official had gone through one of his papers moving prepositions away from the ends of sentences
Ernest Gowers *Plain Words* (1948) 'Troubles with Prepositions'

5 In war: resolution. In defeat: defiance. In victory: magnanimity. In peace: goodwill.
The Second World War vol. 1 (1948) epigraph, which according to Edward Marsh in *A Number of People* (1939), occurred to Churchill shortly after the conclusion of the First World War

6 The loyalties which centre upon number one are enormous. If he trips he must be sustained. If he makes mistakes they must be covered. If he sleeps he must not be wantonly disturbed. If he is no good he must be pole-axed. But this last extreme process cannot be carried out every day; and certainly not in the days just after he has been chosen.
The Second World War vol. 2 (1949)

7 Naval tradition? Monstrous. Nothing but rum, sodomy, prayers, and the lash.
often quoted as, 'rum, sodomy, and the lash', as in Peter Gretton Former Naval Person *(1968)*
Harold Nicolson diary 17 August 1950

8 When the English history of the first quarter of the twentieth century is written, it will be seen that the greater part of our fortunes in peace and in war were shaped by this one man.
of **Lloyd George**
in *Evening Standard* 4 October 1951

9 It is an error to believe that the world began when any particular party or statesman got into office. It has all been going on quite a long time.
speech at the Guildhall, London, 9 November 1951

10 It may almost be said, 'Before Alamein we never had a victory. After Alamein we never had a defeat.'
The Second World War (1951) vol. 4

11 I did not suffer from any desire to be relieved of my responsibilities. All I wanted was compliance with my wishes after reasonable discussion.
The Second World War vol. 4 (1951)

12 There but for the grace of God, goes God.
of Stafford Cripps
P. Brendon *Churchill* (1984)

13 A modest man who has much to be modest about.
of Clement **Attlee**
in *Chicago Sunday Tribune Magazine of Books* 27 June 1954

14 I am prepared to meet my Maker. Whether my Maker is prepared for the great ordeal of meeting me is another matter.
at a news conference in Washington in 1954

1 It was the nation and the race dwelling all round the globe that had the lion's heart. I had the luck to be called upon to give the roar. — speech at Westminster Hall, 30 November 1954

2 To jaw-jaw is always better than to war-war. — speech at the White House, 26 June 1954

to Hugh Foot, Governor of Jamaica, in the early 1950s, on the prospect of immigration continuing unabated:

3 We would have a magpie society: that would never do. — Andrew Roberts *Eminent Churchillians* (1994)

4 I still have the ideas, Walter, but I can't find the words to clothe them. — Tony Benn diary 15 December 1956

to Walter **Monckton**

of Lord **Montgomery**:

5 In defeat unbeatable: in victory unbearable. — Edward Marsh *Ambrosia and Small Beer* (1964)

of the qualifications desirable in a prospective politician:

6 The ability to foretell what is going to happen tomorrow, next week, next month, and next year. And to have the ability afterwards to explain why it didn't happen. — B. Adler *Churchill Wit* (1965)

7 As to freedom of the press, why should any man be allowed to buy a printing press and disseminate pernicious opinions calculated to embarrass the government? — Piers Brendon *Winston Churchill* (1984)

of his recurring depression:

8 Black dog is back again. — attributed

9 An empty taxi arrived at 10 Downing Street, and when the door was opened Attlee got out. — Kenneth Harris *Attlee* (1982)

attributed to Churchill, but strongly repudiated by him

of Stanley **Baldwin**:

10 He occasionally stumbled over the truth, but hastily picked himself up and hurried on as if nothing had happened. — attributed

11 I am fond of pigs. Dogs look up to us. Cats look down on us. Pigs treat us as equals. — Martin Gilbert *Never Despair* (1988); attributed

12 I have taken more out of alcohol than alcohol has taken out of me. — Quentin Reynolds *By Quentin Reynolds* (1964)

13 I know of no case where a man added to his dignity by standing on it. — attributed

14 If you have ten thousand regulations you destroy all respect for the law. — attributed

15 In the course of my life I have often had to eat my words, and I must confess that I have always found it a wholesome diet. — W. Manchester *The Caged Lion* (1988)

16 Most wars in history have been avoided simply by postponing them. — J. K. Galbraith *A Life in Our Times* (1981)

17 A sheep in sheep's clothing. — Lord Home *The Way the Wind Blows* (1976)

of Clement **Attlee**

1 Take away that pudding—it has no theme. — Lord Home *The Way the Wind Blows* (1976)

2 There he stalks, that Wuthering Height.
of John Reith — Andrew Boyle *Only the Wind Will Listen*

of Alfred Bossom:
3 Who is this man whose name is neither one thing nor the other? — attributed

Count Galeazzo Ciano 1903–44

Italian fascist politician; son-in-law of Mussolini

4 Victory has a hundred fathers, but defeat is an orphan. — *Diary* (1946) vol. 2, 9 September 1942 (literally 'no-one wants to recognise defeat as his own')

Cicero (Marcus Tullius Cicero) 106–43 BC

Roman orator and statesman
on Cicero: see **Plutarch** 294:9, **Stevenson** 350:13

5 For he delivers his opinions as though he were living in Plato's Republic rather than among the dregs of Romulus.
of M. Porcius Cato, the Younger — *Ad Atticum*

6 *Salus populi suprema est lex.*
The good of the people is the chief law. — *De Legibus*

7 Let war yield to peace, laurels to paeans. — *De Officiis*

8 In men of the highest character and noblest genius there is to be found an insatiable desire for honour, command, power, and glory. — *De Officis*

9 *O tempora, O mores!*
Oh, the times! Oh, the manners! — *In Catilinam*

10 *Civis Romanus sum.*
I am a Roman citizen. — *In Verrem*

11 The sinews of war, unlimited money. — *Fifth Philippic*

12 Laws are silent in time of war. — *Pro Milone*

13 The young man should be praised, decorated, and got rid of.
of Octavian, the future Emperor **Augustus** — referred to in a letter from Decimus Brutus to Cicero; *Epistulae ad Familiares*

Lord Clare 1749–1802

Lord Chancellor of Ireland from 1789

14 Make him a bishop, or even an archbishop, but not a Chief Justice.
an Irish Lord Chancellor's view of the proposed appointment of Lord Norbury as Lord Chief Justice — in *Dictionary of National Biography*

Edward Hyde, Lord Clarendon 1609–74

English statesman and historian

1 Without question, when he first drew the sword, he threw away the scabbard.
of John Hampden
The History of the Rebellion (1703) vol. 3

2 He had a head to contrive, a tongue to persuade, and a hand to execute any mischief.
of Hampden
The History of the Rebellion (1703) vol. 3

3 He...would, with a shrill and sad accent, ingeminate the word *Peace, Peace.*
of **Falkland**
The History of the Rebellion (1703) vol. 3

4 So enamoured on peace that he would have been glad the King should have bought it at any price.
of **Falkland**
The History of the Rebellion (1703) vol. 3

5 He will be looked upon by posterity as a brave bad man.
of **Cromwell**
The History of the Rebellion (1703) vol. 6

Alan Clark 1928–

British Conservative politician

6 In the end we are all sacked and it's always awful. It is as inevitable as death following life. If you are elevated there comes a day when you are demoted. Even Prime Ministers.
diary 21 June 1983

7 Give a civil servant a good case and he'll wreck it with clichés, bad punctuation, double negatives and convoluted apology.
diary 22 July 1983

8 Like most Chief Whips he knew who the shits were.
of Michael Jopling
diary 17 June 1987

9 There's nothing so improves the mood of the Party as the imminent execution of a senior colleague.
diary 13 July 1990

10 There are no true friends in politics. We are all sharks circling, and waiting, for traces of blood to appear in the water.
diary 30 November 1990

Karl von Clausewitz 1780–1831

Prussian soldier and military theorist

11 War is nothing but a continuation of politics with the admixture of other means.
commonly rendered 'War is the continuation of politics by other means'
On War (1832–4)

Henry Clay 1777–1852

American politician

on Clay: see **Glascock** 156:4, **Jackson** 189:5

1 I am for resistance by the *sword*. No man in the nation desires peace more than I. But I prefer the troubled ocean of war...to the tranquil, putrescent pool of ignominious peace.
speech in the US Senate on the Macon Bill, 22 February 1810

2 If you wish to avoid foreign collision, you had better abandon the ocean.
in the House of Representatives, 22 January 1812

3 The gentleman [Josiah Quincy] can not have forgotten his own sentiment, uttered even on the floor of this House, 'peaceably if we can, forcibly if we must'.
speech in Congress, 8 January 1813

Clay had been shown a letter from **Canning** *to Christopher Hughes, US minister to Sweden:*

4 I should fall in love with Mr Canning, if I were to read many more of such letters from him...Under his ministry...Mr Canning is placing England in her natural attitude, that of being the head of European liberal principles, political and commercial.
letter to Samuel Smith, 4 May 1825

of the Native American peoples:

5 Their disappearance from the human family will be no great loss to the world.
at a cabinet meeting in 1825; Robert V. Remini *Henry Clay*

6 [Andrew Jackson] is ignorant, passionate, hypocritical, corrupt, and easily swayed by the basest men who surround him.
letter to Francis T. Brooke, 2 August 1833

7 The arts of power and its minions are the same in all countries and in all ages. It marks a victim; denounces it; and excites the public odium and the public hatred, to conceal its own abuses and encroachments.
speech in the Senate, 14 March 1834

8 I had rather be right than be President.
to Senator Preston of South Carolina, 1839; S. W. McCall *Life of Thomas Brackett Reed* (1914)

9 It has been my invariable rule to do all for the Union. If any man wants the key of my heart, let him take the key of the Union, and that is the key to my heart.
speech in Norfolk, 22 April 1844

when Speaker of the US Senate, Clay was seen leaving a party at sunrise, and asked how he could expect to preside over the House that day:

10 Come up, and you shall see how I will throw the reins over their necks.
Robert V. Remini *Henry Clay* (1991)

to Madame de Stäel, expressing his regret that the British forces in America had not been commanded by **Wellington***:*

11 Had we beaten the Duke, we should have gained immortal honour, whilst we should have lost none, had we been defeated by the Conqueror of Napoleon.
Robert V. Remini *Henry Clay* (1991)

12 I have heard something said about allegiance to the South. I know no South, no North, no East, no West, to
speech in the US Senate, 1848

which I owe any allegiance...The Union, sir, is my country.

1 The Constitution of the United States was made not merely for the generation that then existed, but for posterity—unlimited, undefined, endless, perpetual posterity.

speech in the US Senate, 1850

Eldridge Cleaver 1935–

American political activist

2 What we're saying today is that you're either part of the solution or you're part of the problem.

speech in San Francisco, 1968; R. Scheer *Eldridge Cleaver, Post Prison Writings and Speeches* (1969)

Sarah Norcliffe Cleghorn 1876–1959

3 The golf-links lie so near the mill
That almost every day
The labouring children can look out
And watch the men at play.

'For Some Must Watch, While —' (1914)

Georges Clemenceau 1841–1929

French statesman; Prime Minister of France, 1906–9, 1917–20

on Clemenceau: see **Keynes** 207:3, **Lloyd George** 229:10

4 My home policy: I wage war; my foreign policy: I wage war. All the time I wage war.

speech to French Chamber of Deputies, 8 March 1918

to André Tardieu, on being asked why he always gave in to **Lloyd George** *at the Paris Peace Conference, 1918*

5 What do you expect when I'm between two men of whom one [Lloyd George] thinks he is Napoleon and the other [Woodrow Wilson] thinks he is Jesus Christ?

James Lees-Milne *Harold Nicolson* (1980) vol. 1, letter from Nicolson to his wife, 20 May 1919

6 It is easier to make war than to make peace.

speech at Verdun, 20 July 1919

7 War is too serious a matter to entrust to military men.

attributed to Clemenceau, e.g. in Hampden Jackson *Clemenceau and the Third Republic* (1946), but also to Briand and Talleyrand

on seeing a pretty girl on his eightieth birthday:

8 Oh, to be seventy again!

James Agate diary 19 April 1938; has also been attributed to Oliver Wendell **Holmes** Jr.

Grover Cleveland 1837–1908

American Democratic statesman, 22nd and 24th President of the US, 1885–9 and 1893–7
on Cleveland: see **Bragg** 54:9

1 Your every voter, as surely as your chief magistrate, exercises a public trust.
'public office is a public trust' was used as the motto of the Cleveland administration
inaugural address, 4 March 1885

2 I have considered the pension list of the republic a roll of honour.
veto of Dependent Pension Bill, 5 July 1888

3 The lessons of paternalism ought to be unlearned and the better lesson taught that, while the people should patriotically and cheerfully support their government, its functions do not include the support of the people.
inaugural address, 4 March 1893

Harlan Cleveland 1918–

American government official

4 The revolution of rising expectations.
phrase coined, 1950; see Arthur Schlesinger *A Thousand Days* (1965)

William Jefferson ('Bill') Clinton 1946–

American Democratic statesman; 42nd President of the US from 1993
on Clinton: see **Jackson** 189:8

5 I experimented with marijuana a time or two. And I didn't like it, and I didn't inhale.
in *Washington Post* 30 March 1992

6 The comeback kid!
description of himself after coming second in the New Hampshire primary in the 1992 presidential election (since 1952, no presidential candidate had won the election without first winning in New Hampshire)
Michael Barone and Grant Ujifusa *The Almanac of American Politics 1994*

7 The urgent question of our time is whether we can make change our friend and not our enemy.
inaugural address, 1993

Lord Clive 1725–74

British general; Governor of Bengal

while attempting to take his own life, his pistol twice failed to fire:

8 I feel that I am reserved for some end or other.
G. R. Gleig *The Life of Robert, First Lord Clive* (1848)

9 By God, Mr Chairman, at this moment I stand astonished at my own moderation!
reply during Parliamentary cross-examination, 1773
G. R. Gleig *The Life of Robert, First Lord Clive* (1848)

Thomas W. Cobb

American politician

1 If you persist, the Union will be dissolved. You have kindled a fire which all the waters of the ocean cannot put out, which seas of blood can only extinguish.
to James Tallmadge, on his amendment to the bill to admit Missouri to the Union as a slave state in 1820
Robert V. Remini *Henry Clay* (1991)

William Cobbett 1762–1835

English political reformer and radical journalist

2 Nouns of number, or multitude, such as Mob, Parliament, Rabble, House of Commons, Regiment, Court of King's Bench, Den of Thieves, and the like.
English Grammar (1817)

3 But what is to be the fate of the great wen of all? The monster, called… 'the metropolis of the empire'?
of London
Rural Rides: The Kentish Journal 5 January 1822

4 From a very early age, I had imbibed the opinion, that it was every man's duty to do all that lay in his power to leave his country as good as he had found it.
Political Register 22 December 1832

Lord Cobbold 1904–87

Lord Chamberlain, 1963–71

5 All ceremonial is ridiculous unless it is perfect.
attributed

Claud Cockburn 1904–81

British left-wing journalist

6 Believe nothing until it has been officially denied.
advice frequently given to the young Claud Cockburn
In Time of Trouble (1956)

7 I am prepared to believe that a lot of the people I had cast as principal figures were really mere cat's-paws. But then a cat's-paw is a cat's-paw and must expect to be treated as part of the cat.
of his writing about the 'Cliveden Set'
Crossing the Line (1958)

8 Discipline, unless operated by very remote control, gives me claustrophobia.
of his membership of the Communist Party
Crossing the Line (1958)

9 A war-time Minister of Information is compelled, in the national interest, to such continuous acts of duplicity that even his natural hair must grow to resemble a wig.
of Brendan **Bracken**
Crossing the Line (1958)

Edward Coke 1552–1634

English jurist

1 Magna Charta is such a fellow, that he will have no sovereign.
on the Lords' Amendment to the Petition of Right, 17 May 1628

J. Rushworth *Historical Collections* (1659) vol. 1

Samuel Taylor Coleridge 1772–1834

English poet, critic, and philosopher

2 In politics, what begins in fear usually ends in folly.

Table Talk (1835) 5 October 1830

3 State policy, a cyclops with one eye, and that in the back of the head!

On the Constitution of the Church and State (1839)

Michael Collins 1890–1922

Irish nationalist leader and politician; on the death of Arthur Griffith in 1922, he became head of state, but was shot in an ambush ten days later

4 I tell you—early this morning I signed my death warrant.
on signing the Anglo-Irish Treaty of 1921

letter 6 December 1921

on arriving at Dublin Castle for the handover by British forces on 16 January 1922, and being told that he was seven minutes late:

5 We've been waiting 700 years, you can have the seven minutes.

Tim Pat Coogan *Michael Collins* (1990); attributed

Barber B. Conable Jr. 1922–

American Republican politician and banker

6 I guess we have found the smoking pistol, haven't we?
on hearing a tape of President **Nixon***'s discussion with H. R.* **Haldeman***, on 23 June 1972, as to how the FBI's investigation of the Watergate burglary could be limited*

Nigel Rees *Brewer's Quotations* (1994)

James M. Connell 1852–1929

Irish socialist songwriter

7 The people's flag is deepest red;
It shrouded oft our martyred dead,
And ere their limbs grew stiff and cold,
Their heart's blood dyed its every fold.
Then raise the scarlet standard high!
Within its shade we'll live or die.
Tho' cowards flinch and traitors sneer,
We'll keep the red flag flying here.

'The Red Flag' (1889)

Cyril Connolly 1903–74

English writer

1 M is for Marx
And Movement of Masses
And Massing of Arses.
And Clashing of Classes.
'Where Engels Fears to Tread'

James Connolly 1868–1916

Irish labour leader; executed after the Easter Rising, 1916

2 The worker is the slave of capitalist society, the female worker is the slave of that slave. *The Re-conquest of Ireland* (1915)

Joseph Conrad 1857–1924

Polish-born English novelist

3 The terrorist and the policeman both come from the same basket. *The Secret Agent* (1907)

4 The scrupulous and the just, the noble, humane, and devoted natures; the unselfish and the intelligent may begin a movement—but it passes away from them. They are not the leaders of a revolution. They are its victims. *Under Western Eyes* (1911)

A. J. Cook 1885–1931

English labour leader; Secretary of the Miners' Federation of Great Britain, 1924–31

5 Not a penny off the pay, not a second on the day. speech at York, 3 April 1926
often quoted with 'minute' substituted for 'second'

Peter Cook 1937–95

British satirist and performer

6 I have recently been travelling round the world—on your behalf, and at your expense—visiting some of the chaps with whom I hope to be shaping your future. I went first to Germany, and there I spoke with the German Foreign Minister, Herr... Herr and there, and we exchanged many frank words in our respective languages. *Beyond the Fringe* (1961)
sketch satirizing the Prime Minister, Harold **Macmillan**

7 The people who went into politics were those who couldn't get in the Footlights or were no good at journalism. in *Guardian* 10 January 1995
of his Cambridge contemporaries

Calvin Coolidge 1872–1933

American Republican statesman, 30th President of the US 1923–9
on Coolidge: see **Anonymous** 13:12, **Mencken** 256:13, **Parker** 285:3

1 There is no right to strike against the public safety by anybody, anywhere, any time.
telegram to Samuel Gompers, 14 September 1919

2 Civilization and profits go hand in hand.
speech in New York, 27 November 1920

3 The chief business of the American people is business.
speech in Washington, 17 January 1925

4 They hired the money, didn't they?
on the subject of war debts incurred by England and others
John H. McKee *Coolidge: Wit and Wisdom* (1933)

account (probably apocryphal) supposedly given by Coolidge to his wife of what a preacher had said about sin:
5 He was against it.
John H. McKee *Coolidge: Wit and Wisdom* (1933)

6 Nothing is easier than spending the public money. It does not appear to belong to anybody. The temptation is overwhelming to bestow it on somebody.
attributed

7 When a great many people are unable to find work, unemployment results.
attributed

Francis M. Cornford 1874–1943

English classical scholar

8 Every public action, which is not customary, either is wrong, or, if it is right, is a dangerous precedent. It follows that nothing should ever be done for the first time.
Microcosmographia Academica (1908)

of propaganda:
9 That branch of the art of lying which consists in very nearly deceiving your friends without quite deceiving your enemies.
Microcosmographia Academica (1922 ed.)

Coronation Service

10 We present you with this Book, the most valuable thing that this world affords. Here is wisdom; this is the royal Law; these are the lively Oracles of God.
'The Presenting of the Holy Bible'; L. G. Wickham Legge *English Coronation Records* (1901)

Thomas Coventry 1578–1640

English judge

11 The dominion of the sea, as it is an ancient and undoubted right of the crown of England, so it is the best security of the land... The wooden walls are the best walls of this kingdom.
speech to the Judges, 17 June 1635

Michel Guillaume Jean de Crèvecoeur

1735–1813

French-born immigrant to America

1 What then is the American, this new man? He is either a European, or the descendant of a European, hence that strange mixture of blood, which you will find in no other country...Here individuals of all nations are melted into a new race of men, whose labours and posterity will one day cause great changes in the world. — *Letters from an American Farmer* (1782)

Ivor Crewe 1945–

British political scientist

2 The British public has always displayed a healthy cynicism of MPs. They have taken it for granted that MPs are self-serving impostors and hypocrites who put party before country and self before party. — in *Guardian* 18 January 1995

addressing the Nolan inquiry into standards in public life

George Washington Crile 1864–1943

American surgeon and physiologist

3 France...a nation of forty millions with a deep-rooted grievance and an iron curtain at its frontier. — *A Mechanistic View of War and Peace* (1915)

Julian Critchley 1930–

British Conservative politician and journalist

4 The only safe pleasure for a parliamentarian is a bag of boiled sweets. — in *Listener* 10 June 1982

5 She cannot see an institution without hitting it with her handbag. — in *The Times* 21 June 1982

of Margaret **Thatcher**

6 Humming, Hawing and Hesitation are the three Graces of contemporary Parliamentary oratory. — *Westminster Blues* (1985)

7 He could not see a parapet without ducking beneath it. — *Heseltine* (1987)

of Michael **Heseltine**

8 Like Marxism, Thatcherism is, in fact, riddled with contradictions. Mrs Thatcher, on the other hand, is free of doubt, she is the label on the can of worms. — *Palace of Varieties* (1989)

9 Disloyalty is the secret weapon of the Tory Party. — in *Observer* 11 November 1990

Oliver Cromwell 1599–1658

English soldier, politician, and general; Lord Protector from 1653

on being asked by **Lord Falkland** *what he would have done if the Grand Remonstrance of 1641 against the King had not passed:*

1 I would have sold all I had the next morning, and never have seen England more. — Clarendon *History of the Rebellion* (1826)

2 A few honest men are better than numbers. — letter to William Spring, September 1643

3 I would rather have a plain russet-coated captain that knows what he fights for, and loves what he knows, than that which you call 'a gentleman' and is nothing else. — letter to William Spring, September 1643

4 Cruel necessity.
on the execution of **Charles I** — Joseph Spence *Anecdotes* (1820)

5 For that which you mention concerning liberty of conscience, I meddle not with any man's conscience.
letter to the Governor of Ross in Ireland, 19 October 1649 — W. C. Abbott *Writings and Speeches of Oliver Cromwell* (1939) vol. 3

6 I beseech you, in the bowels of Christ, think it possible you may be mistaken. — letter to the General Assembly of the Kirk of Scotland, 3 August 1650

7 The dimensions of this mercy are above my thoughts. It is, for aught I know, a crowning mercy. — letter to William **Lenthall**, Speaker of the Parliament of England, 4 September 1651

8 You have sat too long here for any good you have been doing. Depart, I say, and let us have done with you. In the name of God, go!
addressing the Rump Parliament, 20 April 1653 (oral tradition; quoted by Leo **Amery** *to Neville* **Chamberlain** *in the House of Commons, 7 May 1940)* — Bulstrode Whitelock *Memorials of the English Affairs* (1732 ed.)

9 Take away that fool's bauble, the mace.
at the dismissal of the Rump Parliament, 20 April 1653; often quoted as 'Take away these baubles' — Bulstrode Whitelock *Memorials of the English Affairs* (1732 ed.)

10 It's a maxim not to be despised, 'Though peace be made, yet it's interest that keeps peace.' — speech to Parliament, 4 September 1654

11 Necessity hath no law. Feigned necessities, imaginary necessities... are the greatest cozenage that men can put upon the Providence of God, and make pretences to break known rules by. — speech to Parliament, 12 September 1654

12 Your poor army, those poor contemptible men, came up hither. — speech to Parliament, 21 April 1657

13 You have accounted yourselves happy on being environed with a great ditch from all the world besides. — speech to Parliament, 25 January 1658

14 Mr Lely, I desire you would use all your skill to paint my picture truly like me, and not flatter me at all; but remark all these roughnesses, pimples, warts, and everything as you see me; otherwise I will never pay — Horace Walpole *Anecdotes of Painting in England* vol. 3 (1763)

a farthing for it.
commonly quoted as 'warts and all'

1 None climbs so high as he who knows not whither he is going. — attributed

2 There is no one I am more at a loss how to manage than that Marcus Tullius Cicero, the little man with three names.
of Anthony Ashley Cooper, Lord **Shaftesbury** — B. Martyn and Dr Kippis *The Life of the First Earl of Shaftesbury* (1836)

3 My design is to make what haste I can to be gone.
last words — John Morley *Oliver Cromwell* (1900)

Anthony Crosland 1918–77

British Labour politician; Foreign Secretary 1976–7

4 Total abstinence and a good filing system are not now the right signposts to the socialist Utopia; or at least, if they are, some of us will fall by the wayside. — *The Future of Socialism* (1956)

5 If it's the last thing I do, I'm going to destroy every fucking grammar school in England. And Wales, and Northern Ireland.
c.1965, while Secretary of State for Education and Science — Susan Crosland *Tony Crosland* (1982)

6 The party's over.
cutting back central government's support for rates, as Minister of the Environment in the 1970's — Anthony Sampson *The Changing Anatomy of Britain* (1982)

7 In the blood of the socialist there should always run a trace of the anarchist and the libertarian, and not too much of the prig and the prude. — Susan Crosland *Tony Crosland* (1982)

Lord Cross 1823–1914

British Conservative politician

8 I hear a smile.
when the House of Lords laughed at his speech in favour of Spiritual Peers — G. W. E. Russell *Collections and Recollections* (1898)

Richard Crossman 1907–74

British Labour politician
on Crossman: see **Dalton** 109:2

9 While there is death there is hope.
on the death of Hugh **Gaitskell** *in 1963* — Tam Dalyell *Dick Crossman* (1989)

10 The Civil Service is profoundly deferential—'Yes, Minister! No, Minister! If you wish it, Minister!' — *Diaries of a Cabinet Minister* vol. 1 (1975) 22 October 1964

11 There is a cracking sound in the political atmosphere: the sound of the consensus breaking up. — in 1970; Anthony Sampson *The Changing Anatomy of Britain* (1982)

12 [To strip away] the thick masses of foliage which we call the myth of democracy. — introduction to *Diaries of a Cabinet Minister* vol. 1 (1975)

Robert Crouch

British Conservative politician

criticizing the conduct of Ministry of Agriculture officials in the Crichel Down affair, when landowners were not permitted to buy back land compulsorily purchased for a wartime airfield:

1 Charles I lost his head for no less than this. — in the House of Commons, 20 July 1954

E. E. Cummings 1894–1962

American poet

2 a politician is an arse upon
which everyone has sat except a man. — *1 x 1* (1944) no. 10

Mario Cuomo 1932–

American Democratic politician, former Governor of New York

3 You campaign in poetry. You govern in prose. — in *New Republic*, Washington, DC, 8 April 1985

John Philpot Curran 1750–1817

Irish judge

4 The condition upon which God hath given liberty to man is eternal vigilance; which condition if he break, servitude is at once the consequence of his crime, and the punishment of his guilt. — speech on the right of election of the Lord Mayor of Dublin, 10 July 1790

of Robert **Peel***'s smile:*

5 Like the silver plate on a coffin. — quoted by Daniel **O'Connell** in the House of Commons, 26 February 1835

Edwina Currie 1946–

British Conservative politician

6 I honestly don't think that problem has anything to do with poverty... The problem very often for people is, I think, just ignorance.
on problems of high smoking and alcoholism — speech at Newcastle upon Tyne, 23 September 1986

7 My message to the businessmen of this country when they go abroad on business is that there is one thing above all they can take with them to stop them catching Aids—and that is the wife. — speech at Runcorn, 12 February 1987

Lord Curzon 1859–1925

British Conservative politician; Viceroy of India 1898–1905
on Curzon: **Beaverbrook** 34:1, 34:3; **Churchill** 89:9, **Nehru** 270:12

1 Other countries have but one capital—Paris, Berlin, Madrid. Great Britain has a series of capitals all over the world, from Ottawa to Shanghai.
notebook, 1887; Kenneth Rose *Superior Person* (1969)

2 I never knew that the lower classes had such white skins.
supposedly said when watching troops bathing during the First World War
Kenneth Rose *Superior Person* (1969)

3 When a group of Cabinet Ministers begins to meet separately and to discuss independent action, the death-tick is audible in the rafters.
in November 1922, shortly before the fall of **Lloyd George***'s Coalition Government*
David Gilmour *Curzon* (1994)

4 Not even a public figure. A man of no experience. And of the utmost insignificance.
of Stanley **Baldwin***, appointed Prime Minister in 1923 in succession to* **Bonar Law**
Harold Nicolson *Curzon: the Last Phase* (1934)

5 Gentlemen do not take soup at luncheon.
E. L. Woodward *Short Journey* (1942)

Astolphe Louis Léonard, Marquis de Custine 1790–1857

French author and traveller

6 This empire, vast as it is, is only a prison to which the emperor holds the key.
of Russia
La Russie en 1839; at Peterhof, 23 July 1839

7 Whoever has really seen Russia will find himself content to live anywhere else. It is always good to know that a society exists where no happiness is possible because, by a law of nature, man cannot be happy unless he is free.
La Russie en 1839; at Peterhof, 23 July 1839; conclusion

Richard J. Daley 1902–76

American Democratic politician and Mayor of Chicago

8 The policeman isn't there to create disorder; the policeman is there to preserve disorder.
to the press, on the riots during the Democratic Convention in 1968
Milton N. Rakove *Don't Make No Waves: Don't Back No Losers* (1975)

Hugh Dalton 1887–1962

British Labour politician
on Dalton: see **Anonymous** 13:10; **Attlee** 20:3; **Birch** 45:6

9 It is very difficult for anybody outside the cage of the Parliamentary Labour Party to measure up the
Political Diary (1986) 15 June 1938

inclinations of the inmates.
on support for a challenge by Herbert **Morrison** *to* **Attlee***'s leadership*

1 The King says that he has to remind Winston that he is only PM in England and not in France as well.
diary 31 May 1940

2 I view this able and energetic man with some detachment. He is loyal to his own career but only incidentally to anything or anyone else.
of Richard **Crossman**
diary 17 September 1941

3 How I love a colleague-free day! Then I can really get on with the job.
as Chancellor of the Exchequer
Political Diary (1986) 15 May 1946

George Dangerfield

4 To reform the House of Lords [in 1910] meant to set down in writing a Constitution which for centuries had remained happily unwritten, to conjure a great ghost into the narrow and corruptible flesh of a code.
The Strange Death of Liberal England (1936)

Samuel Daniel 1563–1619

English poet and playwright

5 Princes in this case
Do hate the traitor, though they love the treason.
The Tragedy of Cleopatra (1594)

Georges Jacques Danton 1759–94

French revolutionary

6 *De l'audace, et encore de l'audace, et toujours de l'audace!*
Boldness, and again boldness, and always boldness!
speech to the Legislative Committee of General Defence, 2 September 1792

7 Thou wilt show my head to the people: it is worth showing.
to his executioner, 5 April 1794
Thomas Carlyle *History of the French Revolution* (1837) vol. 3

Clarence Darrow 1857–1938

American lawyer

8 When I was a boy I was told that anybody could become President. I'm beginning to believe it.
Irving Stone *Clarence Darrow for the Defence* (1941)

Harry Daugherty 1860–1941

American Republican supporter

9 Some twelve or fifteen men, worn out and bleary-eyed for lack of sleep, will sit down about two o'clock in the morning around a table in a smoke-filled room in some hotel and decide the nomination.
the way in which the Republican Party's presidential candidate
attributed (although subsequently denied by Daugherty); William Safire *The New Language of Politics* (1968)

for 1920 would be selected if (as in fact happened) no clear nomination emerged from the convention; cf. **Simpson** 340:7

Charles D'Avenant 1656–1714

English playwright and political economist

1 Custom, that unwritten law,
By which the people keep even kings in awe.

Circe (1677)

David Davis 1815–86

American judge

2 The Constitution of the United States is a law for rulers and people, equally in war and in peace, and covers with the shield of its protection all classes of men, at all times, and under all circumstances. No doctrine, involving more pernicious consequences, was ever invented by the wit of man than that any of its provisions can be suspended during any of the great exigencies of government.

in *Ex Parte Milligan* (1866)

Jefferson Davis 1808–89

American statesman; President of the Confederate states 1861–5
on Davis: see **Yancey** 395:3

3 If the Confederacy fails, there should be written on its tombstone: *Died of a Theory*.

in 1865; Geoffrey C. Ward *The Civil War* (1991)

Christopher Dawson 1889–1970

4 As soon as men decide that all means are permitted to fight an evil, then their good becomes indistinguishable from the evil that they set out to destroy.

The Judgment of the Nations (1942)

Lord Dawson of Penn 1864–1945

British doctor; physician to King **George V**

5 The King's life is moving peacefully towards its close.
bulletin, drafted on a menu card at Buckingham Palace on the eve of the king's death, 20 January 1936

Kenneth Rose *King George V* (1983)

John Dean 1938–

American lawyer and White House counsel during the Watergate affair

6 We have a cancer within, close to the Presidency, that is growing.

from the [Nixon] Presidential Transcripts, 21 March 1973

Régis Debray 1940–

French Marxist theorist

1 International life is right-wing, like nature. The social contract is left-wing, like humanity. — *Charles de Gaulle* (1994)

Eugene Victor Debs 1855–1926

founder of the Socialist Party of America

2 When great changes occur in history, when great principles are involved, as a rule the majority are wrong. The minority are right. — *Speeches* (1928)

speech at his trial for sedition in Cleveland, Ohio, 11 September 1918

3 While there is a lower class, I am in it; while there is a criminal element, I am of it; while there is a soul in prison, I am not free. — in *Liberator* November 1918

speech at his trial for sedition in Cleveland, Ohio, 11 September 1918

Stephen Decatur 1779–1820

American naval officer

4 Our country! In her intercourse with foreign nations, may she always be in the right; but our country, right or wrong. — A. S. Mackenzie *Life of Stephen Decatur* (1846); cf. **Adams** 4:6

Decatur's toast at Norfolk, Virginia, April 1816

Daniel Defoe 1660–1731

English novelist and journalist

5 Fools out of favour grudge at knaves in place. — *The True-Born Englishman* (1701) introduction

6 From this amphibious ill-born mob began
That vain, ill-natured thing, an Englishman. — *The True-Born Englishman* (1701)

7 Your Roman-Saxon-Danish-Norman English. — *The True-Born Englishman* (1701)

8 His lazy, long, lascivious reign. — *The True-Born Englishman* (1701)

of **Charles II**

9 Great families of yesterday we show,
And lords whose parents were the Lord knows who. — *The True-Born Englishman* (1701)

10 And of all plagues with which mankind are curst,
Ecclesiastic tyranny's the worst. — *The True-Born Englishman* (1701)

11 When kings the sword of justice first lay down,
They are no kings, though they possess the crown.
Titles are shadows, crowns are empty things,
The good of subjects is the end of kings. — *The True-Born Englishman* (1701)

12 Nature has left this tincture in the blood,
That all men would be tyrants if they could. — *The History of the Kentish Petition* (1712–13)

Charles de Gaulle 1890–1970

French general; President of France, 1959–69

1 Authority doesn't work without prestige, or prestige without distance. — *Le Fil de l'épée* (1932) 'Du caractère'

2 The sword is the axis of the world and its power is absolute. — *Vers l'armée de métier* (1934) 'Comment?' Commandement 3

3 France has lost a battle. But France has not lost the war! — proclamation, 18 June 1940

4 Since they whose duty it was to wield the sword of France have let it fall shattered to the ground, I have taken up the broken blade. — speech, 13 July 1940

5 When I am right, I get angry. Churchill gets angry when he is wrong. We are angry at each other much of the time. — attributed

on the death of his daughter, who had been born with Down's Syndrome:

6 And now she is like everyone else. — in 1948; Jean Lacouture *De Gaulle* (1965)

7 Is it credible that at the age of sixty-seven I am going to begin a career as a dictator? — attibuted, 1958

8 Yes, it is Europe, from the Atlantic to the Urals, it is Europe, it is the whole of Europe, that will decide the fate of the world. — speech to the people of Strasbourg, 23 November 1959

9 Politics are too serious a matter to be left to the politicians. — Clement Attlee *A Prime Minister Remembers* (1961)

replying to Clement **Attlee***'s remark that 'De Gaulle is a very good soldier and a very bad politician'*

10 *Europe des patries.*
A Europe of nations. — widely associated with De Gaulle and taken as encapsulating his views, although perhaps not coined by him; J. Lacouture *De Gaulle: the Ruler* (1991)

11 How can you govern a country which has 246 varieties of cheese? — Ernest Mignon *Les Mots du Général* (1962)

12 Since a politician never believes what he says, he is quite surprised to be taken at his word. — Ernest Mignon *Les Mots du Général* (1962)

13 Treaties, you see, are like girls and roses: they last while they last. — speech at Elysée Palace, 2 July 1963

14 *Vive Le Québec Libre.*
Long Live Free Quebec. — speech in Montreal, 24 July 1967

quoting the slogan of the separatist movement for an independent Quebec

Vine Victor Deloria Jr. 1933–

Standing Rock Sioux

15 Tribalism is the strongest force at work in the world today. — *Custer Died for Your Sins* (1969)

1 This country was a lot better off when the Indians were running it.

in *New York Times Magazine* 3 March 1970

Demosthenes *c.*384–*c.*322 BC

Athenian orator and statesman

2 There is one safeguard known generally to the wise, which is an advantage and security to all, but especially to democracies against despots—suspicion.

Philippic

Jack Dempsey 1895–1983

American boxer

3 Honey, I just forgot to duck.

to his wife, on losing the World Heavyweight title, 23 September 1926; after a failed attempt on his life in 1981, Ronald **Reagan** *quipped to his wife 'Honey, I forgot to duck'*

J. and B. P. Dempsey *Dempsey* (1977)

Deng Xiaoping 1904–

Chinese Communist statesman, Vice-Premier 1973–6 and 1977–80; Vice-Chairman of the Central Committee of the Chinese Communist Party 1977–80; still regarded as the effective leader of China

4 The colour of the cat doesn't matter as long as it catches the mice.

proverbial expression; in *Financial Times* 18 December 1986

Lord Denning 1899–

British judge

5 The Treaty [of Rome] is like an incoming tide. It flows into the estuaries and up the rivers. It cannot be held back.

in 1975; Anthony Sampson *The Essential Anatomy of Britain* (1992)

6 To every subject of this land, however powerful, I would use Thomas Fuller's words over three hundred years ago, 'Be ye never so high, the law is above you.'

in a High Court ruling against the Attorney-General, January 1977; cf. **Fuller** 144:6

7 The keystone of the rule of law in England has been the independence of judges. It is the only respect in which we make any real separation of powers.

The Family Story (1981)

8 Properly exercised the new powers of the executive lead to the welfare state; but abused they lead to the totalitarian state.

Anthony Sampson *The Changing Anatomy of Britain* (1982)

Edward Stanley, 14th Earl of Derby

1799–1869

British Conservative statesman; Prime Minister, 1852, 1858–9, 1866–8

on Derby: see **Bulwer-Lytton** 62:1; **Disraeli** 117:14

1 The duty of an Opposition [is] very simple...to oppose everything, and propose nothing.
quoting 'Mr Tierney, a great Whig authority', in the House of Commons, 4 June 1841

2 Meddle and muddle.
summarizing Lord John **Russell***'s foreign policy*
speech on the Address, in the House of Lords 4 February 1864

Edward Stanley, 15th Earl of Derby

1826–93

British Conservative politician

3 She is civil to persons in power under her, whose good will contributes to her comfort (and not always to them): but sees no reason for wasting civility on those who can no longer be of use to her.
of Queen **Victoria***, as seen in her relations with her former Prime Minister, the fourteenth earl of* **Derby***, in his last illness*
Political Journals of Lord Stanley 1849–69

Camille Desmoulins 1760–94

French revolutionary

4 My age is that of the *bon Sansculotte Jésus*; an age fatal to Revolutionists.
reply given at his trial
Thomas Carlyle *History of the French Revolution* (1837)

Thomas E. Dewey 1902–71

American politician and presidential candidate

5 That's why it's time for a change!
phrase used extensively in campaigns of 1944, 1948, and 1952
campaign speech in San Francisco, 21 September 1944

Porfirio Diaz 1830–1915

President of Mexico, 1877–80, 1884–1911

6 Poor Mexico, so far from God and so close to the United States.
attributed

A. V. Dicey 1835–1922

British jurist

7 The beneficial effect of state intervention, especially in the form of legislation, is direct, immediate, and, so to speak, visible, while its evil effects are gradual and indirect, and lie out of sight...Hence the majority of mankind must
Lectures on the Relation between Law and Public Opinion (1914)

almost of necessity look with undue favour upon government intervention.

Charles Dickens 1812–70

English novelist

1 'It's always best on these occasions to do what the mob do.' 'But suppose there are two mobs?' suggested Mr Snodgrass. 'Shout with the largest,' replied Mr Pickwick.

Pickwick Papers (1837)

2 O let us love our occupations,
Bless the squire and his relations,
Live upon our daily rations,
And always know our proper stations.

The Chimes (1844) 'The Second Quarter'

3 Annual income twenty pounds, annual expenditure nineteen nineteen six, result happiness. Annual income twenty pounds, annual expenditure twenty pounds ought and six, result misery.

David Copperfield (1850)

4 It was the best of times, it was the worst of times, it was the age of wisdom, it was the age of foolishness, it was the epoch of belief, it was the epoch of incredulity, it was the season of Light, it was the season of Darkness, it was the spring of hope, it was the winter of despair, we had everything before us, we had nothing before us, we were all going direct to Heaven, we were all going direct the other way.

of the French Revolution

A Tale of Two Cities (1859)

5 'It is possible—that it may not come, during our lives... We shall not see the triumph.' 'We shall have helped it,' returned madame.

A Tale of Two Cities (1859)

6 Detestation of the high is the involuntary homage of the low.

A Tale of Two Cities (1859)

7 My faith in the people governing is, on the whole, infinitesimal; my faith in The People governed is, on the whole, illimitable.

speech at Birmingham and Midland Institute, 27 September 1869

John Dickinson 1732–1808

American politician

8 Then join hand in hand, brave Americans all,—
By uniting we stand, by dividing we fall.

'The Liberty Song' (1768)

9 We have counted the cost of this contest, and find nothing so dreadful as voluntary slavery... Our cause is just, our union is perfect.

declaration of reasons for taking up arms against England, presented to Congress, 8 July 1775

C. J. Stillé *The Life and Times of John Dickinson* (1891)

Denis Diderot 1713–84

French philosopher and man of letters

1 And [with] the guts of the last priest
Let's shake the neck of the last king.
Dithrambe sur fete de rois; cf. **Meslier** 257:6

Joan Didion 1934–

American writer

2 When we start deceiving ourselves into thinking not that we want something or need something, not that it is a pragmatic necessity for us to have it, but that it is a *moral imperative* that we have it, then is when we join the fashionable madmen, and then is when the thin whine of hysteria is heard in the land, and then is when we are in bad trouble.
Slouching towards Bethlehem (1968) 'On Morality'

Benjamin Disraeli 1804–81

British Tory statesman, Prime Minister 1868 and 1874–80
on Disraeli: see **Bismarck** 47:3, **Carlyle** 76:12, **Foot** 138:6, **Palmerston** 284:3

3 I repeat...that all power is a trust—that we are accountable for its exercise—that, from the people, and for the people, all springs, and all must exist.
Vivian Grey (1826)

4 Experience is the child of thought and thought is the child of action. We cannot learn men from books.
Vivian Grey (1826)

5 There is no act of treachery or meanness of which a political party is not capable; for in politics there is no honour.
Vivian Grey (1826)

6 The Lords do not encourage wit, and so are obliged to put up with pertness.
The Young Duke (1831)

7 Read no history: nothing but biography, for that is life without theory.
Contarini Fleming (1832)

8 The practice of politics in the East may be defined by one word—dissimulation.
Contarini Fleming (1832)

9 Between ourselves I could floor them all. This *entre nous*. I was never more confident of anything than that I could carry everything before me in that House. The time will come.
four years before he entered Parliament
letter 7 February 1833

10 In the 'Town' yesterday, I am told 'some one asked Disraeli, in offering himself for Marylebone, on what he intended *to stand*. "On my head," was the reply.'
letter 8 April 1833

11 What we anticipate seldom occurs; what we least expected generally happens.
Henrietta Temple (1837)

12 Though I sit down now, the time will come when you will hear me.
maiden speech
in the House of Commons, 7 December 1837

1 The Continent will [not] suffer England to be the workshop of the world. — in the House of Commons, 15 March 1838

2 The House of Commons is absolute. It is the State. 'L'État c'est moi.' — *Coningsby* (1844)

3 What by way of jest they call the Lower House.
of the House of Commons — *Coningsby* (1844)

4 A government of statesmen or of clerks? Of Humbug or Humdrum? — *Coningsby* (1844)

5 We owe the English peerage to three sources: the spoliation of the Church; the open and flagrant sale of honours by the elder Stuarts; and the borough-mongering of our own time. — *Coningsby* (1844)

6 Conservatism discards Prescription, shrinks from Principle, disavows Progress; having rejected all respect for antiquity, it offers no redress for the present, and makes no preparation for the future. — *Coningsby* (1844)

7 'A sound Conservative government,' said Taper, musingly. 'I understand: Tory men and Whig measures.' — *Coningsby* (1844)

8 Youth is a blunder; Manhood a struggle; Old Age a regret. — *Coningsby* (1844)

9 It seems to me a barren thing this Conservatism—an unhappy cross-breed, the mule of politics that engenders nothing. — *Coningsby* (1844); cf. **Donnelly** 122:7, **Power** 298:1

10 The depositary of power is always unpopular. — *Coningsby* (1844)

11 Where can we find faith in a nation of sectaries? — *Coningsby* (1844)

12 No Government can be long secure without a formidable Opposition. — *Coningsby* (1844)

13 Thus you have a starving population, an absentee aristocracy, and an alien Church, and in addition the weakest executive in the world. That is the Irish Question. — in the House of Commons, 16 February 1844

14 The noble Lord is the Prince Rupert of Parliamentary discussion.
of Lord Stanley, later the 14th Earl of **Derby** — in the House of Commons, 24 April 1844; cf. **Bulwer-Lytton** 62:1

15 The right hon. Gentleman caught the Whigs bathing, and walked away with their clothes.
on Robert **Peel***'s abandoning protection in favour of free trade, traditionally the policy of the* [*Whig*] *Opposition* — in the House of Commons, 28 February 1845

16 Protection is not a principle, but an expedient. — in the House of Commons, 17 March 1845

17 A Conservative Government is an organized hypocrisy. — in the House of Commons, 17 March 1845, (Bagehot, quoting Disraeli in *The English Constitution* (1867) 'The House of Lords', elaborated on the theme with the words 'so much did the ideas of its "head" differ from the sensations of its "tail" ')

1 He traces the steam-engine always back to the tea-kettle. — in the House of Commons, 11 April 1845
of Robert **Peel**

2 'Two nations; between whom there is no intercourse and no sympathy; who are as ignorant of each other's habits, thoughts, and feelings, as if they were dwellers in different zones, or inhabitants of different planets; who are formed by a different breeding, are fed by a different food, are ordered by different manners, and are not governed by the same laws.' 'You speak of—' said Egremont, hesitatingly, 'THE RICH AND THE POOR' — *Sybil* (1845)

3 I was told that the Privileged and the People formed Two Nations. — *Sybil* (1845)

4 Pretending that people can be better off than they are is radicalism and nothing else. — *Sybil* (1845)

5 'Frank and explicit'—that is the right line to take when you wish to conceal your own mind and to confuse the minds of others. — *Sybil* (1845)

6 The Youth of a Nation are the trustees of Posterity. — *Sybil* (1845)

7 That fatal drollery called a representative government. — *Tancred* (1847)

8 A majority is always the best repartee. — *Tancred* (1847)

9 Progress to what and from where... The European talks of progress because by an ingenious application of some scientific acquirements he has established a society which has mistaken comfort for civilization. — *Tancred* (1847)

10 London is a modern Babylon. — *Tancred* (1847)

11 We should never lose an occasion. Opportunity is more powerful even than conquerors and prophets. — *Tancred* (1847)

12 The grovelling tyranny of self-government. — *Tancred* (1847)

of Robert **Peel**:

13 He is a burglar of others' intellect... There is no statesman who has committed political petty larceny on so great a scale. — W. Monypenny and G. Buckle *Life of Benjamin Disraeli* vol. 2 (1912)

14 Justice is truth in action. — in the House of Commons, 11 February 1851

15 I read this morning an awful, though monotonous, manifesto in the great organ of public opinion, which always makes me tremble: Olympian bolts; and yet I could not help fancying amid their rumbling terrors I heard the plaintive treble of the Treasury Bench. — in the House of Commons, 13 February 1851

16 He has to learn that petulance is not sarcasm, and that insolence is not invective. — in the House of Commons, 16 December 1852
of Charles Wood

17 England does not love coalitions. — in the House of Commons, 16 December 1852

18 An aristocracy is rather apt to exaggerate the qualities and magnify the importance of a plebeian leader. — *Lord George Bentinck* (1852)

of Robert **Peel**:

1 Wanting imagination he lacked prescience...His judgement was faultless provided he had not to deal with the future. — *Lord George Bentinck* (1852)

2 These wretched colonies will all be independent, too, in a few years, and are a millstone round our necks. — letter to Lord Malmesbury, 13 August 1852

3 Finality is not the language of politics. — in the House of Commons, 28 February 1859

4 He seems to think that posterity is a pack-horse, always ready to be loaded. — speech, 3 June 1862; attributed

5 It is, I say, in the noble Lord's power to come to some really cordial understanding...between this country and France...and to put an end to these bloated armaments which only involve states in financial embarrassment. — in the House of Commons, 8 May 1862

6 Colonies do not cease to be colonies because they are independent. — in the House of Commons, 5 February 1863

7 You are not going, I hope, to leave the destinies of the British Empire to prigs and pedants. — in the House of Commons, 5 February 1863

8 I hold that the characteristic of the present age is craving credulity. — speech at Oxford, 25 November 1864

9 Party is organized opinion. — speech at Oxford, 25 November 1864

10 Is man an ape or an angel? Now I am on the side of the angels. — speech at Oxford, 25 November 1864

11 Assassination has never changed the history of the world. — in the House of Commons, 1 May 1865

12 I had to prepare the mind of the country, and...to educate our party. — speech at Edinburgh, 29 October 1867

13 Change is inevitable in a progressive country. Change is constant. — speech at Edinburgh, 29 October 1867

14 There can be no economy where there is no efficiency. — address to his Constituents, 1 October 1868

to Queen Victoria after the publication of Leaves from the Journal of our Life in the Highlands *in 1868:*

15 We authors, Ma'am. — Elizabeth Longford *Victoria R.I.* (1964)

16 We have legalized confiscation, consecrated sacrilege, and condoned high treason. — in the House of Commons, 27 February 1871

on **Gladstone***'s Irish policy*

17 I look upon Parliamentary Government as the noblest government in the world. — speech at Manchester, 3 April 1872

18 I believe that without party Parliamentary government is impossible. — speech at Manchester, 3 April 1872

19 You behold a range of exhausted volcanoes. — speech at Manchester, 3 April 1872

of the Liberal Government

20 Increased means and increased leisure are the two civilizers of man. — speech at Manchester, 3 April 1872

1 The very phrase 'foreign affairs' makes an Englishman convinced that I am about to treat of subjects with which he has no concern.
speech at Manchester, 3 April 1872

2 A University should be a place of light, of liberty, and of learning.
in the House of Commons, 11 March 1873

3 An author who speaks about his own books is almost as bad as a mother who talks about her own children.
at a banquet given in Glasgow on his installation as Lord Rector, 19 November 1873
in *The Times* 20 November 1873

4 King Louis Philippe once said to me that he attributed the great success of the British nation in political life to their talking politics after dinner.
in Glasgow, 19 November 1873

5 He is a great master of gibes and flouts and jeers.
of Lord **Salisbury**
in the House of Commons, 5 August 1874

6 Upon the education of the people of this country the fate of this country depends.
in the House of Commons, 15 June 1874

7 Coffee house babble.
on the Bulgarian Atrocities, 1876
R. W. Seton-Watson *Britain in Europe 1789–1914* (1955)

8 Cosmopolitan critics, men who are the friends of every country save their own.
speech at Guildhall, 9 November 1877

9 Lord Salisbury and myself have brought you back peace—but a peace I hope with honour.
speech on returning from the Congress of Berlin, 16 July 1878
in *The Times* 17 July 1878

10 A series of congratulatory regrets.
of Lord Harrington's Resolution on the Berlin Treaty
at a banquet, Knightsbridge, 27 July 1878

11 A sophistical rhetorician, inebriated with the exuberance of his own verbosity.
of **Gladstone**
in *The Times* 29 July 1878

12 I admit that there is gossip...But the government of the world is carried on by sovereigns and statesmen, and not by anonymous paragraph writers...or by the hare-brained chatter of irresponsible frivolity.
speech at Guildhall, London, 9 November 1878

13 One of the greatest of Romans, when asked what were his politics, replied, *Imperium et Libertas*. That would not make a bad programme for a British Ministry.
speech at Mansion House, London, 10 November 1879, paraphrasing Tacitus *Agricola*

14 the transient and embarrassed phantom of Lord Goderich.
of Lord Goderich as Prime Minister
Endymion (1880)

15 An insular country, subject to fogs, and with a powerful middle class, requires grave statesmen.
Endymion (1880)

16 I look upon the House of Commons as a mere vestry. Reform has dished it.
Endymion (1880)

17 As for our majority...one is enough.
Endymion (1880)

18 The greatest opportunity that can be offered to an Englishman—a seat in the House of Commons.
Endymion (1880)

19 The sweet simplicity of the three per cents.
Endymion (1880); cf. **Stowell** 352:2

1 I believe they went out, like all good things, with the Stuarts.
Endymion (1880)

2 The key of India is London.
in the House of Commons, 4 March 1881

3 Damn your principles! Stick to your party.
attributed to Disraeli and believed to have been said to Edward **Bulwer-Lytton**; E. Latham *Famous Sayings and their Authors* (1904)

4 Everyone likes flattery; and when you come to Royalty you should lay it on with a trowel.
to Matthew **Arnold**, in G. W. E. Russell *Collections and Recollections* (1898) ch. 23

5 I have climbed to the top of the greasy pole.
on becoming Prime Minister
W. Monypenny and G. Buckle *Life of Benjamin Disraeli* vol. 4 (1916)

6 I am dead; dead, but in the Elysian fields.
to a peer, on his elevation to the House of Lords
W. Monypenny and G. Buckle *Life of Benjamin Disraeli* vol. 5 (1920)

7 I never deny; I never contradict; I sometimes forget.
said to Lord Esher of his relations with Queen Victoria
Elizabeth Longford *Victoria R. I* (1964)

8 Never complain and never explain.
J. Morley *Life of William Ewart Gladstone* (1903) vol. 1; cf. **Fisher** 137:4

9 Posterity will do justice to that unprincipled maniac Gladstone—extraordinary mixture of envy, vindictiveness, hypocrisy and superstition; and with one commanding characteristic—whether Prime Minister or Leader of the Opposition, whether preaching, praying, speechifying or scribbling—never a gentleman.
W. Monypenny and G. Buckle *Life of Benjamin Disraeli* vol. 6 (1920)

10 Pray remember, Mr Dean, no dogma, no Dean.
W. Monypenny and G. Buckle *Life of Benjamin Disraeli* vol. 4 (1916)

11 Protection is not only dead, but damned.
W. Monypenny and G. Buckle *Life of Benjamin Disraeli* vol. 3 (1914)

on being offered an air cushion to sit on:
12 Take away that emblem of mortality.
Robert Blake *Disraeli* (1966)

13 The palace is not safe when the cottage is not happy.
Robert Blake *Disraeli* (1966)

14 The school of Manchester.
of the free trade politics of Cobden and **Bright**
Robert Blake *Disraeli* (1966)

15 There are three kinds of lies: lies, damned lies and statistics.
attributed to Disraeli in Mark Twain *Autobiography* (1924) vol. 1

16 We came here for fame.
to John **Bright***, in the House of Commons*
Robert Blake *Disraeli* (1966)

17 When Gentlemen cease to be returned to Parliament this Empire will perish.
W. Fraser *Disraeli and His Day* (1891)

18 When I want to read a novel, I write one.
W. Monypenny and G. Buckle *Life of Benjamin Disraeli* vol. 6 (1920)

19 You will find as you grow older that courage is the rarest of all qualities to be found in public life.
to Lady Gwendolen Cecil, telling her that her father Lord
Lady Gwendolen Cecil *Life of Robert Marquis of Salisbury* (1931)

Salisbury *was the only man of real courage with whom Disraeli had worked*

1 I will not go down to posterity talking bad grammar. — Robert Blake *Disraeli* (1966)
while correcting proofs of his last Parliamentary speech, 31 March 1881

on his death-bed, declining a proposed visit from Queen Victoria:

2 No it is better not. She would only ask me to take a message to Albert. — Robert Blake *Disraeli* (1966)

Milovan Djilas 1911–

political writer and former member of the Yugoslav Communist Party (from which he resigned in April 1954)

3 The Party line is that there is no Party line. — Fitzroy Maclean *Disputed Barricade* (1957)
comment on reforms of the Yugoslavian Communist Party, November 1952

Michael Dobbs 1948–

British writer

4 You might very well think that. I couldn't possibly comment. — *House of Cards* (as dramatized for television, 1990)
the Chief Whip's habitual response to questioning

Bubb Dodington 1691–1762

English politician

5 Love thy country, wish it well,
Not with too intense a care,
'Tis enough, that when it fell,
Thou its ruin didst not share.
— 'Ode' (written 1761) in Joseph Spence *Anecdotes* (1820)

Robert Dole 1923–

American Republican politician
on Dole: see **Gingrich** 153:2

6 A little gridlock might be good from time to time. — Michael Barone and Grant Ujifusa *The American Political Almanac 1994*
as Senate Republican leader, immediately after the election of President Clinton ('gridlock', a traffic jam affecting a network of streets, being the term used in Washington for the situation in which legislation makes no progress because of conflicts between Congress and the Administration)

Ignatius Donnelly 1831–1901

American politician

7 The Democratic Party is like a mule—without pride of ancestry or hope of posterity. — attributed; cf. **Disraeli** 117:9, **Power** 298:1

Reginald Dorman-Smith 1899–1977

British politician; Minister of Agriculture and Fisheries, 1939–40

1 Let 'Dig for Victory' be the motto of every one with a garden and of every able-bodied man and woman capable of digging an allotment in their spare time.

radio broadcast, 3 October 1939, in *The Times* 4 October 1939

John Dos Passos 1896–1970

American novelist, noted for his collage-like portrayal of the energy and diversity of American life in the first decades of the 20th century

2 America our nation has been beaten by strangers who have bought the laws and fenced off the meadows and cut down the woods for pulp and turned our pleasant cities into slums and sweated the wealth out of our people and when they want to they hire the executioner to throw the switch.

The Big Money (1936)

William O. Douglas 1898–1980

US Justice of the Supreme Court

3 The Fifth Amendment is an old friend and a good friend. It is one of the great landmarks in man's struggle to be free of tyranny, to be decent and civilized.

An Almanac of Liberty (1954)

4 The search...for ways and means to make the machine—and the vast bureaucracy of the corporation state and of government that runs that machine—the servant of man. That is the revolution that is coming.

in 1970; Anthony Sampson *The Company Man* (1995)

Alec Douglas-Home see **Home**

Caroline Douglas-Home 1937–

daughter of Lord **Home**

5 He is used to dealing with estate workers. I cannot see how anyone can say he is out of touch.

on Lord **Home***'s becoming Prime Minister in succession to Harold* **Macmillan**

in *Daily Herald* 21 October 1963

Frederick Douglass *c.*1818–95

American former slave and Civil Rights campaigner

6 What, to the American slave, is your Fourth of July? I answer: A day that reveals to him, more than all other days in the year, the gross injustice and cruelty to which he is the constant victim. To him your celebration is a sham.

speech at Rochester, New York, 4 July 1852

1 The ground which a coloured man occupies in this country is, every inch of it, sternly disputed.

speech at the American and Foreign Anti-Slavery Society annual meeting in New York City, May 1853

2 In all the relations of life and death, we are met by the colour line.

speech at the Convention of Coloured Men, Louisville, Kentucky, 24 September 1883

3 No man can put a chain about the ankle of his fellow man without at last finding the other end fastened about his own neck.

speech at Civil Rights Mass Meeting, Washington, DC, 22 October 1883

4 Where justice is denied, where poverty is enforced, where ignorance prevails, and where any one class is made to feel that society is in an organized conspiracy to oppress, rob, and degrade them, neither persons nor property will be safe.

speech on the twenty-fourth anniversary of Emancipation in the District of Columbia, Washington, DC, April 1886

Margaret Drabble 1939–

English novelist

5 England's not a bad country... It's just a mean, cold, ugly, divided, tired, clapped-out, post-imperial, post-industrial slag-heap covered in polystyrene hamburger cartons.

A Natural Curiosity (1989)

Francis Drake c.1540–96

English sailor and explorer

6 The singeing of the King of Spain's Beard.
on the expedition to Cadiz, 1587

Francis Bacon *Considerations touching a War with Spain* (1629)

7 There is plenty of time to win this game, and to thrash the Spaniards too.

attributed, in *Dictionary of National Biography* (1917–) vol. 5

Joseph Rodman Drake 1795–1820

American poet

8 Forever float that standard sheet!
Where breathes the foe but falls before us,
With Freedom's soil beneath our feet,
And Freedom's banner streaming o'er us?

'The American Flag' in *New York Evening Post*, 29 May 1819 (also attributed to Fitz-Greene Halleck)

William Driver 1803–86

9 I name thee Old Glory.
as the flag was hoisted to the masthead of his ship (Driver was captain of the Charles Doggett, *the ship on which the Bounty mutineers were returned from Tahiti to Pitcairn, and was presented with a large American flag by a band of women in recognition of this)*

attributed

John Dryden 1631–1700

English poet, critic, and playwright

1 If by the people you understand the multitude, the *hoi polloi*, 'tis no matter what they think; they are sometimes in the right, sometimes in the wrong: their judgement is a mere lottery.

An Essay of Dramatic Poesy (1668)

2 But 'tis the talent of our English nation,
Still to be plotting some new reformation.

'The Prologue at Oxford, 1680' (prologue to Nathaniel Lee *Sophonisba*, 2nd ed., 1681)

3 Plots, true or false, are necessary things,
To raise up commonwealths and ruin kings.

Absalom and Achitophel (1681)

4 Of these the false Achitophel was first,
A name to all succeeding ages curst.
For close designs and crooked counsels fit,
Sagacious, bold, and turbulent of wit,
Restless, unfixed in principles and place,
In power unpleased, impatient of disgrace.

in Dryden's political satire relating to the Protestant succession 'Achitophel' represented **Shaftesbury**, *and 'Absalom' the Duke of* **Monmouth**

Absalom and Achitophel (1681)

5 A daring pilot in extremity;
Pleased with the danger, when the waves went high
He sought the storms; but for a calm unfit,
Would steer too nigh the sands to boast his wit.

Absalom and Achitophel (1681)

6 In friendship false, implacable in hate:
Resolved to ruin or to rule the state.

Absalom and Achitophel (1681)

7 The people's prayer, the glad diviner's theme,
The young men's vision and the old men's dream!

Absalom and Achitophel (1681)

8 All empire is no more than power in trust.

Absalom and Achitophel (1681)

9 Better one suffer, than a nation grieve.

Absalom and Achitophel (1681)

10 Youth, beauty, graceful action seldom fail:
But common interest always will prevail:
And pity never ceases to be shown
To him, who makes the people's wrongs his own.

Absalom and Achitophel (1681)

11 For who can be secure of private right,
If sovereign sway may be dissolved by might?
Nor is the people's judgement always true:
The most may err as grossly as the few.

Absalom and Achitophel (1681)

12 Never was patriot yet, but was a fool.

Absalom and Achitophel (1681)

13 But treason is not owned when 'tis descried;
Successful crimes alone are justified.

The Medal (1682)

14 Freedom which in no other land will thrive,
Freedom an English subject's sole prerogative.

Threnodia Augustalis (1685)

15 Reason to rule, but mercy to forgive:
The first is law, the last prerogative.

The Hind and the Panther (1687)

16 Either be wholly slaves or wholly free.

The Hind and the Panther (1687)

1 T'abhor the makers, and their laws approve,
Is to hate traitors and the treason love.

The Hind and the Panther (1687)

2 War is the trade of kings.

King Arthur (1691)

Alexander Dubček 1921–92

Czechoslovak statesman, First Secretary of the Czechoslovak Communist Party 1968–9

3 In the service of the people we followed such a policy that socialism would not lose its human face.

in *Rudé Právo* 19 July 1968

Joachim Du Bellay 1522–60

French poet

4 France, mother of arts, of warfare, and of laws.

Les Regrets (1558) Sonnet no. 9

W. E. B. Du Bois 1868–1963

American social reformer and political activist

5 The problem of the twentieth century is the problem of the colour line—the relation of the darker to the lighter races of men in Asia and Africa, in America and the islands of the sea.

The Souls of Black Folk (1905)

6 Herein lies the tragedy of the age: not that men are poor...not that men are wicked...but that men know so little of men.

The Souls of Black Folk (1905)

7 The cost of liberty is less than the price of repression.

John Brown (1909)

John Foster Dulles 1888–1959

American international lawyer and politician

8 If...the European Defence Community should not become effective; if France and Germany remain apart...That would compel an agonizing reappraisal of basic United States policy.

speech to NATO Council in Paris, 14 December 1953

9 You have to take chances for peace, just as you must take chances in war. Some say that we were brought to the verge of war. Of course we were brought to the verge of war. The ability to get to the verge without getting into the war is the necessary art. If you cannot master it, you inevitably get into war. If you try to run away from it, if you are scared to go to the brink, you are lost. We've had to look it square in the face—on the question of enlarging the Korean war, on the question of getting into the Indochina war, on the question of Formosa. We walked to the brink and we looked it in the face.

this policy became known as 'brinkmanship'

in *Life* 16 January 1956; cf. **Stevenson** 350:10

John Dunning, Lord Ashburton 1731–83

English lawyer and politician

1 The influence of the Crown has increased, is increasing, and ought to be diminished. — resolution passed in the House of Commons, 6 April 1780

Eric Dupin

journalist

2 His inconstancy is his great constant.
of François **Mitterrand** — in *The New York Review of Books* 3 November 1994

Lillian K. Dykstra

3 He is just about the nastiest little man I've ever known. He struts sitting down.
of Thomas **Dewey** — letter to Franz Dykstra, 8 July 1952; James T. Patterson *Mr Republican* (1972)

Stephen T. Early 1889–1951

4 Don't Worry Me—I am an 8 Ulcer Man on 4 Ulcer Pay.
card received by Harry Truman — William Hillman *Mr President: the First Publication from the Personal Diaries, Private Letters, Papers and Revealing Interviews of Harry S. Truman* (1952)

Abba Eban 1915–

Israeli diplomat

5 History teaches us that men and nations behave wisely once they have exhausted all other alternatives. — speech in London, 16 December 1970

of the British Foreign Office:
6 A hotbed of cold feet. — in conversation with Antony Jay

Anthony Eden 1897–1977

British Conservative statesman, Prime Minister 1955–7
on Eden: see **Butler** 70:3, **McLachlan** 242:5, **Monkton** 261:11, **Muggeridge** 268:1

7 We are in an armed conflict; that is the phrase I have used. There has been no declaration of war.
on the Suez crisis — in the House of Commons, 1 November 1956

8 Everyone is always in favour of general economy and particular expenditure. — in *Observer* 17 June 1956

Clarissa Eden 1920–

wife of Anthony **Eden**

1 For the past few weeks I have really felt as if the Suez Canal was flowing through my drawing room.

speech at Gateshead, 20 November 1956

Edward VII 1841–1910

King of the United Kingdom from 1901

2 Because a man has a black face and a different religion from our own, there is no reason why he should be treated as a brute.

letter to Lord Granville, 30 November 1875

3 The last King of England.
introducing his son, the future George V, to Lord Haldane, expressing his pessimism for the survival of the British monarchy

Andrew Roberts *Eminent Churchillians* (1994)

Edward VIII 1894–1972

King of the United Kingdom, 1936; afterwards Duke of Windsor
on Edward VIII: see **George V** 149:10, **Thomas** 363:5

4 These works brought all these people here. Something should be done to get them at work again.
speaking at the derelict Dowlais Iron and Steel Works, 18 November 1936 (generally quoted 'Something must be done')

in *Western Mail* 19 November 1936

5 At long last I am able to say a few words of my own... you must believe me when I tell you that I have found it impossible to carry the heavy burden of responsibility and to discharge my duties as King as I would wish to do without the help and support of the woman I love.
radio broadcast following his abdication, 11 December 1936

in *The Times* 12 December 1936

John Ehrlichman 1925–

Presidential assistant to Richard Nixon

6 I think we ought to let him hang there. Let him twist slowly, slowly in the wind.
speaking of Patrick Gray (regarding his nomination as director of the FBI) in a telephone conversation with John Dean

in *Washington Post* 27 July 1973

Albert Einstein 1879–1955

German-born American theoretical physicist, founder of the theory of relativity

7 The prestige of government has undoubtedly been lowered considerably by the Prohibition laws. For nothing is more destructive of respect for the government and the law of the land than passing laws which cannot be enforced. It is an open secret that the dangerous increase of crime in this country is closely connected with this.

after visiting America in 1921; *The World As I See It* (1935)

1 Nationalism is an infantile sickness. It is the measles of the human race.
Helen Dukas and Banesh Hoffman *Albert Einstein, the Human Side* (1979)

explaining why equations mattered more to him than politics:
2 Politics is for the present, but an equation is something for eternity.
Stephen Hawking *A Brief History of Time* (1988)

Dwight D. Eisenhower 1890–1969

American general and Republican statesman, 34th President of the US, 1953–61
on Eisenhower: see **Acheson** 1:8

3 People of Western Europe: A landing was made this morning on the coast of France by troops of the Allied Expeditionary Force. This landing is part of the concerted United Nations plan for the liberation of Europe, made in conjunction with our great Russian allies...I call upon all who love freedom to stand with us now. Together we shall achieve victory.
broadcast on D-Day, 6 June 1944

4 Every gun that is made, every warship launched, every rocket fired signifies, in the final sense, a theft from those who hunger and are not fed, those who are cold and are not clothed. This world in arms is not spending money alone. It is spending the sweat of its labourers, the genius of its scientists, the hopes of its children.
speech in Washington, 16 April 1953

5 You have broader considerations that might follow what you might call the 'falling domino' principle. You have a row of dominoes set up. You knock over the first one, and what will happen to the last one is that it will go over very quickly. So you have the beginning of a disintegration that would have the most profound influences.
speech at press conference, 7 April 1954

6 Governments are far more stupid than their people.
attributed, 1958

7 I think that people want peace so much that one of these days governments had better get out of the way and let them have it.
broadcast discussion, 31 August 1959

8 In the councils of government, we must guard against the acquisition of unwarranted influence, whether sought or unsought, by the military-industrial complex. The potential for the disastrous rise of misplaced power exists and will persist.
farewell broadcast, 17 January 1961
in *New York Times* 18 January 1961

9 Biggest damfool mistake I ever made.
of his appointment, in 1953, of Earl **Warren** *as Chief Justice of the United States*
attributed

George Eliot 1819–80

English novelist

1 An election is coming. Universal peace is declared, and the foxes have a sincere interest in prolonging the lives of the poultry.
Felix Holt (1866)

T. S. Eliot 1888–1965

Anglo-American poet, critic, and playwright

2 This is the way the world ends
Not with a bang but a whimper.
'The Hollow Men' (1925)

Queen Elisabeth of Belgium 1876–1965

German-born consort of King Albert of the Belgians

3 Between them [Germany] and me there is now a bloody curtain which has descended forever.
on Germany's invasion of Belgium in 1914
attributed

Elizabeth I 1533–1603

Queen of England and Ireland from 1558

4 I am your anointed Queen. I will never be by violence constrained to do anything. I thank God that I am endued with such qualities that if I were turned out of the Realm in my petticoat, I were able to live in any place in Christome.
speech to Members of Parliament, 5 November 1566

5 The queen of Scots is this day leichter of a fair son, and I am but a barren stock.
Sir James Melville *Memoirs of His Own Life* (1827 ed.)

6 As for me, I assure you I find no great cause I should be fond to live. I take no such pleasure in it that I should much wish it, nor conceive such terror in death that I should greatly fear it…I have had good experience and trial of this world. I know what it is to be a subject, what to be a Sovereign, what to have good neighbours, and sometimes meet evil-willers.
speech to a Parliamentary deputation at Richmond, 12 November 1586; the traditional version concludes: 'In trust I have found treason'
J. E. Neale *Elizabeth I and her Parliaments 1584–1601* (1957), from a report 'which the Queen herself heavily amended in her own hand'

7 I will make you shorter by the head.
to the leaders of her Council, who were opposing her course towards Mary Queen of Scots
F. Chamberlin *Sayings of Queen Elizabeth* (1923)

8 The daughter of debate, that eke discord doth sow.
on Mary Queen of Scots
George Puttenham (ed.) *The Art of English Poesie* (1589)

9 I know I have the body of a weak and feeble woman, but I have the heart and stomach of a king, and of a king of England too; and think foul scorn that Parma or Spain, or any prince of Europe, should dare to invade the borders of my realm.
Lord Somers *A Third Collection of Scarce and Valuable Tracts* (1751)

speech to the troops at Tilbury on the approach of the Armada, 1588

1 I will have here but one Mistress, and no Master.
reproving the presumption of the Earl of Leicester
Robert Naunton *Fragmenta Regalia* (1641)

2 I do entreat heaven daily for your longer life, else will my people and myself stand in need of cordials too. My comfort hath been in my people's happiness and their happiness in thy discretion.
to William Cecil on his death-bed
F. Chamberlin *Sayings of Queen Elizabeth* (1923)

3 My lord, we make use of you, not for your bad legs, but for your good head.
to William Cecil, who suffered from gout
F. Chamberlin *Sayings of Queen Elizabeth* (1923)

on being asked her opinion of Christ's presence in the Sacrament:

4 'Twas God the word that spake it,
He took the bread and brake it;
And what the word did make it;
That I believe, and take it.
S. Clarke *The Marrow of Ecclesiastical History* (1675) 'The Life of Queen Elizabeth'

5 God may pardon you, but I never can.
to the dying Countess of Nottingham, who was said to have prevented a last appeal by the Earl of Essex from reaching the Queen
David Hume *The History of England under the House of Tudor* (1759) vol. 2

6 I think that, at the worst, God has not yet ordained that England shall perish.
F. Chamberlin *Sayings of Queen Elizabeth* (1923)

7 I would not open windows into men's souls.
oral tradition, in J. B. Black *Reign of Elizabeth 1558–1603* (1936) (the words very possibly originating in a letter drafted by Bacon)

8 If thy heart fails thee, climb not at all.
lines after Walter **Ralegh**, *written on a window-pane*
Thomas Fuller *Worthies of England* vol. 1; cf. **Ralegh** 300:3

9 Like strawberry wives, that laid two or three great strawberries at the mouth of their pot, and all the rest were little ones.
describing the tactics of the Commission of Sales, in their dealings with her
Francis Bacon *Apophthegms New and Old* (1625)

10 Madam I may not call you; mistress I am ashamed to call you; and so I know not what to call you; but howsoever, I thank you.
to the wife of the Archbishop of Canterbury, the Queen disapproving of marriage among the clergy
John Harington *A Brief View of the State of the Church of England* (1653)

welcoming Edward de Vere, Earl of Oxford, on his return from seven years self-imposed exile, occasioned by the acute embarrassment to himself of breaking wind in the presence of the Queen:

11 My Lord, I had forgot the fart.
John Aubrey *Brief Lives* 'Edward de Vere'

1 Though God hath raised me high, yet this I count the glory of my crown: that I have reigned with your loves.
the Golden Speech, 1601

in *The Journals of All the Parliaments*... Collected by Sir Simonds D'Ewes (1682)

2 Must! Is *must* a word to be addressed to princes? Little man, little man! thy father, if he had been alive, durst not have used that word.
to Robert **Cecil**, *on his saying in her last illness that she must go to bed*

J. R. Green *A Short History of the English People* (1874); *Dodd's Church History of England* vol. 3 (ed. M. A. Tierney, 1840) adds, 'but thou knowest I must die, and that maketh thee so presumptuous'

3 All my possessions for a moment of time.
last words

attributed, but almost certainly apocryphal

Elizabeth II 1926–

Queen of the United Kingdom from 1952

4 I declare before you all that my whole life, whether it be long or short, shall be devoted to your service and the service of our great Imperial family to which we all belong.
broadcast speech, as Princess Elizabeth, to the Commonwealth from Cape Town, 21 April 1947

in *The Times* 22 April 1947

speech at Guildhall, London, on her 25th wedding anniversary:

5 I think everybody really will concede that on this, of all days, I should begin my speech with the words 'My husband and I'.

in *The Times* 21 November 1972

6 In the words of one of my more sympathetic correspondents, it has turned out to be an 'annus horribilis'.

speech at Guildhall, London, 24 November 1992

7 The British Constitution has always been puzzling and always will be.

Peter Hennessy *The Hidden Wiring* (1995)

Queen Elizabeth, the Queen Mother 1900–

Queen Consort of **George VI** and mother of **Elizabeth II**

8 I'm glad we've been bombed. It makes me feel I can look the East End in the face.
to a London policeman, 13 September 1940

John Wheeler-Bennett *King George VI* (1958)

on the suggestion that the royal family be evacuated during the Blitz:

9 The Princesses would never leave without me and I couldn't leave without the King, and the King will never leave.

Penelope Mortimer *Queen Elizabeth* (1986)

Alf Ellerton

10 Belgium put the kibosh on the Kaiser.

title of song

Ebenezer Elliott 1781–1849

English poet known as the 'Corn Law Rhymer'

1 What is a communist? One who hath yearnings
For equal division of unequal earnings.
'Epigram' (1850)

Ralph Waldo Emerson 1803–82

American philosopher and poet

2 The two parties which divide the state, the party of Conservatism and that of Innovation, are very old, and have disputed the possession of the world ever since it was made.
'The Conservative' (lecture, 1841)

3 There is always a certain meanness in the argument of conservatism, joined with a certain superiority in its fact.
The Conservative (1842)

4 The louder he talked of his honour, the faster we counted our spoons.
The Conduct of Life (1860) 'Worship'

5 When you strike at a king, you must kill him.
attributed to Emerson by Oliver Wendell **Holmes** Jr.; Max Lerner *The Mind and Faith of Justice Holmes* (1943)

Friedrich Engels 1820–95

German socialist; founder, with Karl Marx, of modern Communism

6 The State is not 'abolished', *it withers away.*
Anti-Dühring (1878)

7 Naturally, the workers are perfectly free; the manufacturer does not force them to take his materials and his cards, but he says to them... 'If you don't like to be frizzled in my frying-pan, you can take a walk into the fire'.
The Condition of the Working Class in England in 1844 (1892)

Friedrich Engels see also **Marx** and **Engels**

Ennius 239–169 BC

Roman writer

8 The Roman state survives by its ancient customs and its manhood.
Annals

9 One man by delaying put the state to rights for us.
referring to the Roman general Fabius Cunctator ('The Delayer')
Annals

Erasmus *c.*1469–1536

Dutch Christian humanist

10 In the country of the blind the one-eyed man is king.
Adages

Dudley Erwin 1917–84

Australian politician

Claiming that the 'political manoeuvre' which had cost him his job in the reshuffled Government was actually the Prime Minister's secretary:

1 It wiggles, it's shapely and its name is Ainsley Gotto

in *The Times* 14 November 1969

Robert Devereux, Lord Essex 1566–1601

English soldier and courtier, executed for treason

2 Reasons are not like garments, the worse for wearing.

letter to Lord Willoughby, 4 January 1599

William Maxwell Evarts 1818–83

American politician and lawyer

3 The pious ones of Plymouth, who, reaching the Rock, first fell upon their own knees and then upon the aborigines.

in *Louisville Courier-Journal* 4 July 1913; a pun which has been variously attributed

Edward Everett 1794–1865

American orator and politician

4 I should be glad if I could flatter myself that I came as near the central idea of the occasion in two hours as you did in two minutes.

to Abraham **Lincoln** *on the Gettysburg address, which had been publicly criticized while Everett's two hour speech had received adulatory attention in the press*

letter to Lincoln, 20 November 1863; cf. **Anonymous** 13:6

William Norman Ewer 1885–1976

British writer

5 I gave my life for freedom—This I know:
For those who bade me fight had told me so.

'Five Souls' (1917)

Quintus Fabius Maximus *c.*275–203 BC

Roman politician and general

6 To be turned from one's course by men's opinions, by blame, and by misrepresentation shows a man unfit to hold an office.

Plutarch *Parallel Lives* 'Fabius Maximus'

Émile Faguet 1847–1916

French writer and critic

commenting on Rousseau's 'Man is born free, but everywhere is found enslaved and in chains':

1 It would be equally correct to say that sheep are born carnivorous, and everywhere they nibble grass.

paraphrasing Joseph de Maistre; *Politiques et Moralistes du Dix-Neuvième Siècle* (1899)

Thomas Fairfax 1621–71

English Parliamentary general, appointed commander of the New Model Army in 1645, and replaced in 1650 by Oliver **Cromwell** for refusing to march against the Scots, who had proclaimed the future **Charles II** king

2 Human probabilities are not sufficient grounds to make war upon a neighbour nation.

to the proposal in 1650 that the expected attack by the Scots should be anticipated by the invasion of Scotland

in *Dictionary of National Biography*

Lucius Cary, Lord Falkland 1610–43

English royalist politician

3 When it is not necessary to change, it is necessary not to change.

Discourses of Infallibility (1660) 'A Speech concerning Episcopacy' delivered in 1641

Michael Faraday 1791–1867

English chemist and physicist

to **Gladstone**, *when asked about the usefulness of electricity:*

4 Why sir, there is every possibility that you will soon be able to tax it!

W. E. H. Lecky *Democracy and Liberty* (1899 ed.)

James A. Farley 1888–1976

American Democratic politician

5 As Maine goes, so goes Vermont.

after predicting correctly that Franklin **Roosevelt** *would carry all but two states in the election of 1936 (reworking an American political maxim of c.1888, 'as Maine goes, so goes the nation')*

statement to the press, 4 November 1936

Farouk 1920–65

King of Egypt, 1936–52

6 The whole world is in revolt. Soon there will be only five Kings left—the King of England, the King of Spades, the King of Clubs, the King of Hearts and the King of Diamonds.

Lord Boyd-Orr *As I Recall* (1966), addressed to the author at a conference in Cairo, 1948

Guy Fawkes 1570–1606

conspirator in the Gunpowder Plot, 1605

1 A desperate disease requires a dangerous remedy.
on 6 November 1605, in *Dictionary of National Biography* (1917–) vol. 6

Dianne Feinstein 1933–

American Democratic politician, Mayor of San Francisco

2 Toughness doesn't have to come in a pinstripe suit.
in *Time* 4 June 1984

3 There was a time when you could say the least government was the best—but not in the nation's most populous state.
campaign speech, 15 March 1990

Ferdinand I 1503–64

Holy Roman Emperor from 1558

4 *Fiat justitia et pereat mundus.*
Let justice be done, though the world perish.
motto; see Johannes Manlius *Locorum Communium Collectanea* (1563) vol. 2 'De Lege: Octatum Praeceptum'

Eric Field

5 Your King and Country need you.
First World War recruiting poster
Advertising (1959)

Frank Field 1942–

British Labour politician

6 Democracy no longer works for the poor if politicians treat them as a separate race.
in *Independent* 29 October 1994

L'Abbé Edgeworth de Firmont 1745–1807

Irish-born confessor to Louis XVI

7 Son of Saint Louis, ascend to heaven.
to Louis XVI as he mounted the steps of the guillotine, 1793
attributed

H. A. L. Fisher 1856–1940

English historian

8 Men wiser and more learned than I have discerned in history a plot, a rhythm, a predetermined pattern. These harmonies are concealed from me. I can see only one emergency following upon another as wave follows upon wave, only one great fact with respect to which, since it is unique, there can be no generalizations, only one safe rule for the historian: that he should recognize in the
A History of Europe (1935)

development of human destinies the play of the contingent and the unforeseen.

1 Purity of race does not exist. Europe is a continent of energetic mongrels.
A History of Europe (1935)

2 Nothing commends a radical change to an Englishman more than the belief that it is really conservative.
A History of Europe (1935)

John Arbuthnot Fisher 1841–1920

British admiral

3 Sack the lot!
on overmanning and overspending within government departments
letter to *The Times*, 2 September 1919

4 Never contradict
Never explain
Never apologize.
letter to *The Times*, 5 September 1919; cf. **Disraeli** 121:8

John Fiske 1842–1901

5 The United States—bounded on the north by the Aurora Borealis, on the south by the precession of the equinoxes, on the east by the primeval chaos, and on the west by the Day of Judgement.
Bounding the United States

Gerry Fitt 1926–

Northern Irish politician

6 People [in Northern Ireland] don't march as an alternative to jogging. They do it to assert their supremacy. It is pure tribalism, the cause of troubles all over the world.
in *The Times* 5 August 1994

Robert, Marquis de Flers 1872–1927 and Arman de Caillavet 1869–1915

French playwrights

7 Democracy is the name we give the people whenever we need them.
L'habit vert, in *La petite illustration série théâtre* 31 May 1913

Andrew Fletcher of Saltoun 1655–1716

Scottish patriot and anti-Unionist

8 I knew a very wise man so much of Sir Chr—'s sentiment, that he believed if a man were permitted to make all the ballads, he need not care who should make the laws of a nation.
'An Account of a Conversation concerning a Right Regulation of Government for the Good of Mankind. In a Letter to the Marquis of Montrose' (1704) in *Political Works* (1732)

Ferdinand Foch 1851–1929

French general

1 My centre is giving way, my right is retreating, situation excellent, I am attacking.
message sent during the first Battle of the Marne, September 1914
R. Recouly *Foch* (1919)

2 This is not a peace treaty, it is an armistice for twenty years.
at the signing of the Treaty of Versailles, 1919
Paul Reynaud *Mémoires* (1963) vol. 2

Michael Foot 1913–

British Labour politician

of Iain **Macleod**:

3 A perspiration of firm confidence exudes from every political pore.
in *Daily Herald* 8 October 1962

4 A speech from Ernest Bevin on a major occasion had all the horrific fascination of a public execution. If the mind was left immune, eyes and ears and emotions were riveted.
Aneurin Bevan (1962) vol. 1

5 Think of it! A second Chamber selected by the Whips. A seraglio of eunuchs.
in the House of Commons, 3 February 1969

6 Disraeli was my favourite Tory. He was an adventurer pure and simple, or impure and complex. I'm glad to say Gladstone got the better of him.
in *Observer* 16 March 1975 'Sayings of the Week'

7 It is not necessary that every time he rises he should give his famous imitation of a semi-house-trained polecat.
of Norman **Tebbit**
in the House of Commons, 2 March 1978

of David **Steel**, *Leader of the Liberal Party:*

8 He's passed from rising hope to elder statesman without any intervening period whatsoever.
in the House of Commons, 28 March 1979

9 If democratic socialism cannot secure the right answer at the next parliamentary opportunity, we may not be asked again, or rather this old famous socialist stream could perish in sectarian bogs and sands.
Anthony Sampson *The Changing Anatomy of Britain* (1982)

Gerald Ford 1909–

American Republican statesman, 38th President of the US 1974–7
on Ford: see **Abzug** 1:2, **Johnson** 196:10, **Morton** 267:1

10 If the Government is big enough to give you everything you want, it is big enough to take away everything you have.
John F. Parker *If Elected* (1960); a similar remark has been attributed to Barry **Goldwater**

11 I am a Ford, not a Lincoln.
on taking the vice-presidential oath, 6 December 1973
in *Washington Post* 7 December 1973

12 Our long national nightmare is over. Our Constitution works; our great Republic is a Government of laws and
speech on 9 August 1974

not of men.
on being sworn in as President in succession to Richard **Nixon**

1 I believe that truth is the glue that holds Government together, not only our Government, but civilization itself.
on being sworn in as President
speech on 9 August 1974

2 There is no Soviet domination of Eastern Europe and there never will be under a Ford administration.
in a television debate with Jimmy Carter, 6 October 1976
S. Kraus *Great Debates* (1979)

Howell Forgy 1908–83

American naval chaplain

3 Praise the Lord and pass the ammunition.
at Pearl Harbor, 7 December 1941, as Forgy moved along a line of sailors passing ammunition by hand to the deck (later the title of a song by Frank Loesser, 1942)
in *New York Times* 1 November 1942

E. M. Forster 1879–1970

English novelist

4 If I had to choose between betraying my country and betraying my friend, I hope I should have the guts to betray my country.
Two Cheers for Democracy (1951) 'What I Believe'

5 So Two cheers for Democracy: one because it admits variety and two because it permits criticism. Two cheers are quite enough: there is no occasion to give three. Only Love the Beloved Republic deserves that.
Two Cheers for Democracy (1951) 'What I Believe' ('Love, the beloved republic' borrowed from Swinburne's poem 'Hertha')

Harry Emerson Fosdick 1878–1969

American Baptist minister

6 I renounce war for its consequences, for the lies it lives on and propagates, for the undying hatred it arouses, for the dictatorships it puts in the place of democracy, for the starvation that stalks after it.
Armistice Day Sermon in New York, 1933, in *The Secret of Victorious Living* (1934)

Charles Foster 1828–1904

American politician

7 Isn't this a billion dollar country?
at the 51st Congress, responding to a Democratic gibe about a 'million dollar Congress'
also attributed to Thomas B. Reed, who reported the exchange in *North American Review* March 1892, vol. 154

George Foster 1847–1931

Canadian politician

1 In these somewhat troublesome days when the great Mother Empire stands splendidly isolated in Europe.

in *Official Report of the Debates of the House of Commons of the Dominion of Canada* (1896) vol. 41, for 16 January 1896; on 22 January 1896, *The Times* referred to this speech under the heading 'Splendid Isolation'

Charles Fourier 1772–1837

French social theorist

2 The extension of women's rights is the basic principle of all social progress.

Théorie des Quatre Mouvements (1808) vol. 2

Norman Fowler 1938–

British Conservative politician

3 I have a young family and for the next few years I should like to devote more time to them.
often quoted as 'spend more time with my family'

resignation letter to the Prime Minister, in *Guardian* 4 January 1990; cf. **Thatcher** 362:8

Caroline Fox d. 1774

wife of Henry Fox, Lord **Holland**, and mother of Charles James **Fox**

4 That little boy will be a thorn in Charles's side as long as he lives.
seeing in the young William **Pitt** *a prospective rival for her son Charles James* **Fox**

attributed

Charles James Fox 1749–1806

English Whig politician, son of Henry Fox, Lord **Holland** and Caroline **Fox**

on Fox: see **Gibbon** 152:1, **Holland** 181:4, **Johnson** 198:12, **Shaw-Lefevre** 337:5

5 He [Pitt the Younger] was uniformly of an opinion which, though not a popular one, he was ready to aver, that the right of governing was not property but a trust.
on **Pitt***'s scheme of Parliamentary Reform, 1785*

J. L. Hammond *Charles James Fox* (1903)

6 How much the greatest event it is that ever happened in the world! and how much the best!
on the fall of the Bastille

letter to Richard Fitzpatrick, 30 July 1789

In the last year of his life Fox's friends suggested that he should accept a peerage:

7 I will not close my politics in that foolish way.

in *Dictionary of National Biography*

1 I die happy.
last words
Lord John Russell *Life and Times of C. J. Fox* vol. 3 (1860)

Henry Fox see **Holland**

Anatole France 1844–1924

French novelist and man of letters

2 They [the poor] have to labour in the face of the majestic equality of the law, which forbids the rich as well as the poor to sleep under bridges, to beg in the streets, and to steal bread.
Le Lys rouge (1894)

3 In every well-governed state, wealth is a sacred thing; in democracies it is the only sacred thing.
L'Île des pingouins (1908)

Francis I 1494–1547

King of France from 1515

4 Of all I had, only honour and life have been spared.
letter to his mother following his defeat at Pavia, 1525, usually quoted as 'All is lost, save honour'
in *Collection des Documents Inédits sur l'Histoire de France* (1847) vol. 1

Barney Frank

American Democratic politician

5 He doesn't have ideas. He has ideas about how nice it would be to have ideas...He's operating on the level of abstraction and generality.
of the new Republican Speaker, Newton **Gingrich**
in *Daily Telegraph* 5 January 1995

Felix Frankfurter 1882–1965

American judge

6 The history of liberty has largely been the history of the observance of procedural standards.
in *McNabb v. the United States* (1943)

7 One who belongs to the most vilified and persecuted minority in history is not likely to be insensitive to the freedoms guaranteed by our Constitution...But as judges we are neither Jew nor Gentile, neither Catholic nor agnostic.
in *Flag Salute Cases* (1943)

8 It is a fair summary of history to say that the safeguards of liberty have been forged in controversies involving not very nice people.
dissenting opinion in *United States v. Rabinowitz* (1950)

Benjamin Franklin 1706–90

American politician, inventor, and scientist
on Franklin: see **Turgot** 372:7

9 They that can give up essential liberty to obtain a little temporary safety deserve neither liberty nor safety.
Historical Review of Pennsylvania (1759)

1 Idleness and pride tax with a heavier hand than kings and parliaments. If we can get rid of the former, we may easily bear the latter.
on the Stamp Act
letter 11 July 1765

2 We must indeed all hang together, or, most assuredly, we shall all hang separately.
at the signing of the Declaration of Independence, 4 July 1776 (possibly not original)
P. M. Zall *Ben Franklin* (1980)

3 Here [in France] you would know and enjoy what posterity will say of Washington. For a thousand leagues have nearly the same effect with a thousand years.
letter to Washington, 5 March 1780

4 There never was a good war, or a bad peace.
letter to Josiah Quincy, 11 September 1783

5 George Washington, Commander of the American Armies, who, like Joshua of old, commanded the sun and the moon to stand still, and they obeyed him.
toast given at a dinner at Versailles, when the British minister had proposed a toast to **George III**, *likening him to the sun, and the French minister had likened* **Louis XVI** *to the moon*
attributed

6 No nation was ever ruined by trade.
Thoughts on Commercial Subjects

7 I wish the bald eagle had not been chosen as the representative of our country; he is a bird of bad moral character... like those among men who live by sharping and robbing, he is generally poor, and often very lousy.
The turkey... is a much more respectable bird, and withal a true original native of America.
letter to Sarah Bache, 26 January 1784

on being asked, 'have we got a republic or a monarchy?':
8 A republic, if you can keep it.
in conversation, 18 September 1787

9 In this world nothing can be said to be certain, except death and taxes.
letter to Jean Baptiste Le Roy, 13 November 1789; cf. Daniel Defoe *History of the Devil* (1726) 'Things as certain as death and taxes, can be more firmly believed'

Lord Franks 1905–92

British philosopher and administrator

10 The Pentagon, that immense monument to modern man's subservience to the desk.
in *Observer* 30 November 1952

11 A secret in the Oxford sense: you may tell it to only one person at a time.
in *Sunday Telegraph* 30 January 1977

on the composition of such bodies as royal commissions and committees of inquiry:
12 There is a fashion in these things and when you are in fashion you are asked to do a lot.
in conversation, 24 January 1977; Peter Hennessy *Whitehall* (1990)

Michael Frayn 1933–

British writer

1 To be absolutely honest, what I feel really bad about is that I don't feel worse. That's the ineffectual liberal's problem in a nutshell.
in *Observer* 8 August 1965

Frederick the Great 1712–86

King of Prussia from 1740

2 Rascals, would you live for ever?
to hesitant Guards at Kolin, 18 June 1757
attributed

3 Drive out prejudices through the door, and they will return through the window.
letter to Voltaire, 19 March 1771

4 My people and I have come to an agreement which satisfies us both. They are to say what they please, and I am to do what I please.
his interpretation of benevolent despotism
attributed

E. A. Freeman 1823–92

English historian

5 History is past politics, and politics is present history.
Methods of Historical Study (1886)

John Freeth c.1731–1808

English poet

6 The loss of America what can repay?
New colonies seek for at Botany Bay.
'Botany Bay' in *New London Magazine* (1786)

Milton Friedman 1912–

American economist and exponent of monetarism; policy adviser to President Reagan 1981–9

7 Few trends could so thoroughly undermine the very foundations of our free society as the acceptance by corporate officials of a social responsibility other than to make as much money for their stockholders as possible.
Capitalism and Freedom (1962)

8 Economists may not know how to run the economy, but they do know how to create shortages or gluts simply by regulating prices below the market, or artificially supporting them from above.
in 1962, attributed

9 There's only one place where inflation is made: that's in Washington.
in 1977; attributed

10 A society that puts equality—in the sense of equality of outcome—ahead of freedom will end up with neither equality nor freedom.
Free to Choose (1980)

11 The high rate of unemployment among teenagers, and especially black teenagers, is both a scandal and a serious
Free to Choose (1980)

source of social unrest. Yet it is largely a result of minimum wage laws... We regard the minimum wage law as one of the most, if not the most, antiblack laws on the statute books.

1 There is an invisible hand in politics that operates in the opposite direction to the invisible hand in the market. In politics, individuals who seek to promote only the public good are led by an invisible hand to promote special interests that it was no part of their intention to promote.

Bright Promises, Dismal Performance: An Economist's Protest (1983)

2 Thank heavens we do not get all of the government that we are made to pay for.

attributed; quoted by Lord Harris in the House of Lords, 24 November 1994

Robert Frost 1874–1963

American poet

3 I never dared be radical when young
For fear it would make me conservative when old.

'Desert Places' (1936)

J. William Fulbright 1905–95

American Senator

4 A policy that can be accurately, though perhaps not prudently, defined as one of 'peaceful coexistence'.

speech in the US Senate, 27 March 1964

5 We must dare to think 'unthinkable' thoughts. We must learn to explore all the options and possibilities that confront us in a complex and rapidly changing world. We must learn to welcome and not to fear the voices of dissent. We must dare to think about 'unthinkable things' because when things become unthinkable, thinking stops and action becomes mindless.

speech in the US Senate, 27 March 1964

Thomas Fuller 1654–1734

English writer and physician

6 Be you never so high, the law is above you.

Gnomologia (1732); cf. **Denning** 113:6

Alfred Funke b. 1869

German writer

7 *Gott strafe England!*
God punish England!

Sword and Myrtle (1914)

David Maxwell Fyfe see **Kilmuir**

Hugh Gaitskell 1906–63

British Labour politician; Leader of the Labour Party from 1955
on Gaitskell: see **Bevan** 41:5, **Crossman** 106:9

1 There are some of us...who will fight and fight and fight again to save the Party we love.
opposing the vote in favour of unilateral disarmament
speech at Labour Party Conference, 5 October 1960

2 It means the end of a thousand years of history.
on a European federation
speech at Labour Party Conference, 3 October 1962

John Kenneth Galbraith 1908–

Canadian-born American economist, noted for his criticism of a perceived preoccupation in Western society with economic growth for its own sake; US Ambassador to India 1961–3

of the defeat of Germany in World War Two:

3 That they were defeated is conclusive testimony to the inherent inefficiencies of dictatorship, the inherent efficiencies of freedom.
in *Fortune* December 1945

4 It is not necessary to advertise food to hungry people, fuel to cold people, or houses to the homeless.
American Capitalism (1952)

5 [Intellectual torpor is] the disease of opposition parties, for initiative and imagination ordinarily lie with responsibility for action.
letter to Adlai Stevenson, September 1953

6 The affluent society.
title of book (1958)

7 The conventional wisdom.
ironic term for 'the beliefs that are at any time assiduously, solemnly and mindlessly traded between the conventionally wise'
The Affluent Society (1958)

8 These are the days when men of all social disciplines and all political faiths seek the comfortable and the accepted; when the man of controversy is looked upon as a disturbing influence; when originality is taken to be a mark of instability; and when, in minor modification of the scriptural parable, the bland lead the bland.
The Affluent Society (1958)

9 It is a far, far better thing to have a firm anchor in nonsense than to put out on the troubled seas of thought.
The Affluent Society (1958)

10 In a community where public services have failed to keep abreast of private consumption things are very different. Here, in an atmosphere of private opulence and public squalor, the private goods have full sway.
The Affluent Society (1958)

11 The greater the wealth, the thicker will be the dirt.
The Affluent Society (1958)

12 Politics is not the art of the possible. It consists in choosing between the disastrous and the unpalatable.
letter to President **Kennedy**, 2 March 1962; cf. **Bismarck** 46:6

13 You cannot know the intentions of a government that doesn't know them itself.
'Galbraith's First Law of Intelligence', formulated in early 1960s
J. K. Galbraith *A Life in Our Times* (1981)

1 There are times in politics when you must be on the right side and lose. — attributed, 1968

2 Galbraith's law states that anyone who says he won't resign four times, will. — attributed, 1973

3 I have never understood why one's affections must be confined, as once with women, to a single country. — *A Life in Our Times* (1981)

4 The reduction of politics to a spectator sport... has been one of the more malign accomplishments of television. Television newsmen are breathless on how the game is being played, largely silent on what the game is all about. — *A Life in Our Times* (1981)

5 The experience of being disastrously wrong is salutary; no economist should be denied it, and not many are. — *A Life in Our Times* (1981)

6 In public administration good sense would seem to require the public expectation be kept at the lowest possible level in order to minimize eventual disappointment. — *A Life in Our Times* (1981)

7 After a lifetime in public office, self-censorship becomes not only automatic but a part of one's personality. — *A Life in Our Times* (1981)

8 Nothing is so firmly established in Puritan and Presbyterian belief as that people cannot be suffering very much if they are out in healthy fresh air—and also safely out of sight. — *A Life in Our Times* (1981)

of the public view of rural as opposed to urban poverty

9 Of all the races on earth, the Indians have the most nearly inexhaustible appetite for oratory. — *A Life in Our Times* (1981)

10 From the fact of general well-being came the new position of the poor. They were now in most communities a minority. The voice of the people was now the voice of relative affluence. Politicians in pursuit of votes could be expected to have a diminishing concern for the very poor. Compassion would have to serve instead—an uncertain substitute. — *A Life in Our Times* (1981)

11 Civilian administration is by discussion and consensus; military action is by information and command. The latter has a rewarding simplicity for all civilians and especially for anyone from the discursive tradition of academic life. This is why few men become as dangerously warlike as the academic figure who is plunged into military affairs. — *A Life in Our Times* (1981)

12 One of the recurrent and dangerous influences on our foreign policy—fear of the political consequences of doing the sensible thing, which in many cases is nothing much at all. — *A Life in Our Times* (1981)

13 One of the little-celebrated powers of Presidents (and other high government officials) is to listen to their critics with just enough sympathy to ensure their silence. — *A Life in Our Times* (1981)

1 Trickle-down theory—the less than elegant metaphor that if one feeds the horse enough oats, some will pass through to the road for the sparrows. — *The Culture of Contentment* (1992)

Indira Gandhi 1917–84

Indian stateswoman and daughter of Jawaharlal **Nehru**, Prime Minister of India 1966–77 and 1980–4

2 Politics is the art of acquiring, holding, and wielding power. — attributed, 1975

Mahatma Gandhi 1869–1948

Indian nationalist and spiritual leader
on Gandhi: see **Naidu** 268:9, **Nehru** 270:8

3 Non-violence is the first article of my faith. It is also the last article of my creed. — in *Young India* 23 March 1922
speech at Shahi Bag, 18 March 1922, on a charge of sedition

on being asked what he thought of modern civilization:
4 That would be a good idea. — E. F. Schumacher *Good Work* (1979)
while visiting England in 1930

5 What difference does it make to the dead, the orphans and the homeless, whether the mad destruction is wrought under the name of totalitarianism or the holy name of liberty or democracy? — *Non-Violence in Peace and War* (1942) vol. 1

6 Please go on. It is my day of silence. — Peter Hennessy *Never Again* (1992)
note passed to the British Cabinet Mission at a meeting in 1942

7 The moment the slave resolves that he will no longer be a slave, his fetters fall. He frees himself and shows the way to others. Freedom and slavery are mental states. — *Non-Violence in Peace and War* (1949) vol. 2

James A. Garfield 1831–81

American Republican statesman, 20th President of the US, who was assassinated within months of taking presidential office

8 Fellow-citizens: God reigns, and the Government at Washington lives! — in *Death of President Garfield* (1881)
speech on the assassination of President **Lincoln**, *1865*

9 I am not willing that this discussion should close without any mention of the value of a true teacher. Give me a log hut, with only a simple bench, Mark Hopkins [president of Williams College] on one end and I on the other, and you may have all the buildings, apparatus and libraries without him. — address to Williams College Alumni, New York, 28 December 1871

Giuseppe Garibaldi 1807–82

Italian patriot and military leader

1 Men, I'm getting out of Rome. Anyone who wants to carry on the war against the outsiders, come with me. I can offer you neither honours nor wages; I offer you hunger, thirst, forced marches, battles and death. Anyone who loves his country, follow me.

Giuseppe Guerzoni *Garibaldi* (1882) vol. 1 (not a verbatim record)

John Nance Garner 1868–1967

American politician

2 The vice-presidency isn't worth a pitcher of warm piss.

O. C. Fisher *Cactus Jack* (1978)

William Lloyd Garrison 1805–79

American anti-slavery campaigner

3 I am in earnest—I will not equivocate—I will not excuse—I will not retreat a single inch—and I will be heard!

in *The Liberator* 1 January 1831 'Salutatory Address'

4 The compact which exists between the North and the South is 'a covenant with death and an agreement with hell'.

resolution adopted by the Massachusetts Anti-Slavery Society, 27 January 1843

5 With reasonable men, I will reason; with humane men I will plead; but to tyrants I will give no quarter, nor waste arguments where they will certainly be lost.

W. P. and F. J. T. Garrison *William Lloyd Garrison* (1885–89) vol. 1

James Louis Garvin 1868–1947

British journalist and editor of the *Observer*

6 He spoke for an hour and put the house in his pocket.

of F. E. **Smith***'s maiden speech in the House of Commons, 12 May 1906*

attributed

Eric Geddes 1875–1937

British politician and administrator

7 The Germans, if this Government is returned, are going to pay every penny; they are going to be squeezed as a lemon is squeezed—until the pips squeak.

speech at Cambridge, 10 December 1918

George II 1683–1760

King of Great Britain and Ireland from 1727

8 We are come for your good, for all your goods.

speech at Portsmouth, probably 1716, in Joseph Spence *Anecdotes* (ed. J. M. Osborn, 1966)

George III 1738–1820

King of Great Britain and Ireland from 1760
on George III: see **Walpole** 377:13

1 Born and educated in this country, I glory in the name of Briton. — *The King's Speech on Opening the Session* 18 November 1760

2 When he has wearied me for two hours he looks at his watch, to see if he may not tire me for an hour more. — in 1765; Horace Walpole *The Reign of George III* (1845)
of George **Grenville**

3 I would sooner meet Grenville at the point of the sword than let him into my closet. — Lord Hardwicke letter 10 July 1767
of George **Grenville**

of America:
4 Knavery seems to be so much the striking feature of its inhabitants that it may not in the end be an evil that they become aliens to this kingdom. — draft of letter to Lord Shelburne, 10 November 1782

George V 1865–1936

King of Great Britain and Ireland from 1910

5 I venture to allude to the impression which seemed generally to prevail among their brethren across the seas, that the Old Country must wake up if she intends to maintain her old position of pre-eminence in her Colonial trade against foreign competitors. — speech at Guildhall, 5 December 1901 (the speech was reprinted in 1911 with the title 'Wake up, England')

6 I have many times asked myself whether there can be more potent advocates of peace upon earth through the years to come than this massed multitude of silent witnesses to the desolation of war. — in *The Times* 15 May 1922
message read at Terlincthun Cemetery, Boulogne, 13 May 1922

7 You have kept up the dignity of the office without using it to give you dignity. — Ramsay MacDonald diary 7 June 1934
to the outgoing Prime Minister, **Ramsay MacDonald**

8 I will not have another war. *I will not.* The last one was none of my doing and if there is another one and we are threatened with being brought into it, I will go to Trafalgar Square and wave a red flag myself sooner than allow this country to be brought in. — Andrew Roberts *Eminent Churchillians* (1994)

in conversation with Anthony **Eden**, *23 December 1935, following Samuel Hoare's resignation as Foreign Secretary:*
9 I said to your predecessor: 'You know what they're all saying, no more coals to Newcastle, no more Hoares to Paris.' The fellow didn't even laugh. — Earl of Avon *Facing the Dictators* (1962)

10 After I am dead, the boy will ruin himself in twelve months. — Keith Middlemas and John Barnes *Baldwin* (1969)
on his son, the future **Edward VIII**

11 Bugger Bognor. — Kenneth Rose *King George V* (1983)
comment made either in 1929, when it was proposed that the town be named Bognor Regis on account of the king's convalescence there after a serious illness; or on his deathbed in

1936, when someone remarked 'Cheer up, your Majesty, you will soon be at Bognor again.'

1 How's the Empire? — Kenneth Rose *King George V* (1983)
to his private secretary on the morning of his death, probably prompted by an article in The Times, *which he held open at the imperial and foreign page*

2 Gentlemen, I am so sorry for keeping you waiting like this. I am unable to concentrate. — Lord Wigram memorandum 20 January 1936
on his deathbed

George VI 1895–1952

King of Great Britain and Northern Ireland from 1936

3 It [is] utterly damnable that that villain Hitler has upset everything. — Andrew Roberts *Eminent Churchillians* (1994)
on hearing of the Nazi-Soviet pact of 1940

4 Personally I feel happier now that we have no allies to be polite to and to pamper. — John Wheeler-Bennett *King George VI* (1958)
to Queen Mary, 27 June 1940

5 ATTLEE: I've won the election.
GEORGE VI: I know. I heard it on the Six O'Clock News. — Peter Hennessy *Never Again* (1992)
first exchange between the King and his newly elected Labour Prime Minister, 26 July 1945; perhaps apocryphal

6 Well the Prime Minister has had a very difficult time, I'm sure. What I say is 'Thank God for the Civil Service.' — Hugh Dalton *Political Diary* (1986) 28 July 1945
shortly after Labour's election victory

7 HARRY TRUMAN: You've had a revolution.
GEORGE VI: Oh no! we don't have those here. — Hugh Dalton *Political Diary* (1986) 28 July 1945
during President **Truman**'*s visit to Britain just after Labour's election victory.*

8 Everything is going nowadays. Before long, I shall have to go myself. — Andrew Roberts *Eminent Churchillians* (1994)
on hearing, c.1949, that the Sackville-West family home, Knole Park, was to be sold to the National Trust

Daniel George

English writer

9 O Freedom, what liberties are taken in thy name! — *The Perpetual Pessimist* (1963)

Henry George 1839–97

American economist and social reformer

10 So long as all the increased wealth which modern progress brings goes to build up great fortunes, to increase luxury and make sharper the contrast between the House of Have and the House of Want, progress is not real and cannot be permanent. — *Progress and Poverty* (1879); introduction

Edward Gibbon 1737–94

English historian

1 In elective monarchies, the vacancy of the throne is a moment big with danger and mischief. — *The Decline and Fall of the Roman Empire* (1776–88)

2 The division of Europe into a number of independent states connected, however, with each other, by the general resemblance of religion, language, and manners, is productive of the most beneficial consequences to the liberty of mankind. — *The Decline and Fall of the Roman Empire* (1776–88)

3 The various modes of worship, which prevailed in the Roman world, were all considered by the people as equally true; by the philosopher, as equally false; and by the magistrate, as equally useful. And thus toleration produced not only mutual indulgence, but even religious concord. — *The Decline and Fall of the Roman Empire* (1776–88)

4 The principles of a free constitution are irrecoverably lost, when the legislative power is nominated by the executive. — *The Decline and Fall of the Roman Empire* (1776–88)

5 The ascent to greatness, however steep and dangerous, may entertain an active spirit with the consciousness and exercise of its own powers; but the possession of a throne could never yet afford a lasting satisfaction to an ambitious mind. — *The Decline and Fall of the Roman Empire* (1776–88)

6 History...is, indeed, little more than the register of the crimes, follies, and misfortunes of mankind. — *The Decline and Fall of the Roman Empire* (1776–88)

7 In every age and country, the wiser, or at least the stronger, of the two sexes, has usurped the powers of the state, and confined the other to the cares and pleasures of domestic life. — *The Decline and Fall of the Roman Empire* (1776–88)

8 According to the reasoning of tyrants, those who have been esteemed worthy of the throne deserve death, and those who deliberate have already rebelled. — *The Decline and Fall of the Roman Empire* (1776–88)

9 Corruption, the most infallible symptom of constitutional liberty. — *The Decline and Fall of the Roman Empire* (1776–88)

10 In every deed of mischief he had a heart to resolve, a head to contrive, and a hand to execute.
of Comnenus — *The Decline and Fall of the Roman Empire* (1776–88)

11 Our sympathy is cold to the relation of distant misery. — *The Decline and Fall of the Roman Empire* (1776–88)

12 Persuasion is the resource of the feeble; and the feeble can seldom persuade. — *The Decline and Fall of the Roman Empire* (1776–88)

13 All that is human must retrograde if it does not advance. — *The Decline and Fall of the Roman Empire* (1776–88)

14 I admire his eloquence, I approve his politics, I adore his chivalry, and I can even forgive his superstition.
of Edmund **Burke** — letter to Lord Sheffield, 5 February 1791

1 Let him do what he will I must love the dog.
of Charles James **Fox**

letter to Lord Sheffield, 6 January 1793

2 The satirist may laugh, the philosopher may preach, but Reason herself will respect the prejudices and habits which have been consecrated by the experience of mankind.

Memoirs of My Life (1796)

Kahlil Gibran 1883–1931

Syrian writer and painter

3 Are you a politician who says to himself: 'I will use my country for my own benefit'?...Or are you a devoted patriot, who whispers in the ear of his inner self: 'I love to serve my country as a faithful servant.'

The New Frontier (1931)

W. S. Gilbert 1836–1911

English writer of comic and satirical verse

4 I always voted at my party's call,
And I never thought of thinking for myself at all.

HMS Pinafore (1878)

5 No Englishman unmoved that statement hears,
Because, with all our faults, we love our House of Peers.

The Pirates of Penzance (1879)

6 I often think it's comical
How Nature always does contrive
That every boy and every gal,
That's born into the world alive,
Is either a little Liberal,
Or else a little Conservative!

Iolanthe (1882)

7 The House of Peers, throughout the war,
Did nothing in particular,
And did it very well.

Iolanthe (1882)

8 When in that House MPs divide,
If they've a brain and cerebellum too,
They have to leave that brain outside,
And vote just as their leaders tell 'em to.

Iolanthe (1882)

9 The prospect of a lot
Of dull MPs in close proximity,
All thinking for themselves is what
No man can face with equanimity.

Iolanthe (1882)

10 The idiot who praises, with enthusiastic tone,
All centuries but this, and every country but his own.

Mikado (1885)

11 All shall equal be.
The Earl, the Marquis, and the Dook,
The Groom, the Butler, and the Cook,
The Aristocrat who banks with Coutts,
The Aristocrat who cleans the boots.

The Gondoliers (1889)

Ian Gilmour 1926–

British Conservative politician

1 Unfortunately monetarism, like Marxism, suffered the only fate that for a theory is worse than death: it was put into practice.
Dancing with Dogma (1992)

Newton Gingrich 1943–

American Republican politician; Speaker of the House of Representatives from 1995
on Gingrich: see **Frank** 141:5

of Senator Robert **Dole**:
2 The tax collector for the welfare state.
in *New York Times* 9 September 1984

3 One of the greatest intellectual failures of the welfare state is the penchant for sacrifice, so long as the only people being asked to sacrifice are working, tax-paying Americans.
in *USA Today* 16 January 1995

4 No society can survive, no civilization can survive, with 12-year-olds having babies, with 15-year-olds killing each other, with 17-year-olds dying of Aids, with 18-year-olds getting diplomas they can't read.
in December 1994, after the Republican electoral victory
in *The Times* 9 February 1995

George Gipp d. 1920

American footballer

5 Win just one for the Gipper.
catch-phrase later associated with Ronald **Reagan**, who uttered the immortal words in the 1940 film *Knute Rockne, All American*

Valéry Giscard d'Estaing 1926–

French statesman, President 1974–81

explaining why he should not stand again for the presidency:
6 Too old, too bourgeois, too distant from the average man, not supported by my political friends, too low in the opinion polls, and having already been sampled nobody wants to repeat the experience.
in *Independent on Sunday* 5 March 1995 'Quotes of the Week'

William Ewart Gladstone 1809–98

British Liberal statesman; Prime Minister, 1868–74, 1880–5, 1886, 1892–4

on Gladstone: see **Bagehot** 24:5, **Churchill** 86:4, 86:7, **Churchill** 88:13, **Disraeli** 120:11, 121:9, **Foot** 138:6, **Hennessy** 175:2, **King** 210:1, **Labouchere** 216:1, **Macaulay** 238:1, **Salisbury** 318:9, **Victoria** 374:6, 374:8

1 Ireland, Ireland! that cloud in the west, that coming storm.
letter to his wife, 12 October 1845

2 This is the negation of God erected into a system of Government.
A Letter to the Earl of Aberdeen on the State Prosecutions of the Neapolitan Government (1851)

3 Finance is, as it were, the stomach of the country, from which all the other organs take their tone.
article on finance, 1858
H. C. G. Matthew *Gladstone 1809–1874* (1986)

4 Your business is not to govern the country but it is, if you think fit, to call to account those who do govern it.
speech to the House of Commons, 29 January 1869

5 I am come among you 'unmuzzled'.
speech in Manchester, 18 July 1865, after his parliamentary defeat at Oxford University
John Morley *Life of Gladstone* (1903) vol. 2

6 You cannot fight against the future. Time is on our side.
speech on the Reform Bill
in the House of Commons, 27 April 1866

7 My mission is to pacify Ireland.
on receiving the news that he was to form his first cabinet, 1st December 1868
H. C. G. Matthew *Gladstone 1809–1874* (1986)

8 Swimming for his life, a man does not see much of the country through which the river winds.
diary 31 December 1868

9 We have been borne down in a torrent of gin and beer.
letter to his brother, 6 February 1874

10 Human justice is ever lagging after wrong, as the prayers in Homer came limping after sin.
in *Contemporary Review* December 1876

11 The love of freedom itself is hardly stronger in England than the love of aristocracy.
in *Nineteenth Century* 1877

12 Let the Turks now carry away their abuses in the only possible manner, namely by carrying off themselves… one and all, bag and baggage, shall I hope clear out from the province they have desolated and profaned.
Bulgarian Horrors and the Question of the East (1876)

13 [The British Constitution] presumes more boldly than any other the good sense and the good faith of those who work it.
Gleanings of Past Years (1879) vol. 1

14 [An] Established Clergy will always be a Tory Corps d'Armée.
letter to Bishop Goodwin, 8 September 1881

15 The resources of civilization against its enemies are not yet exhausted.
on the Irish Land League
speech at Leeds, 7 October 1881

16 It is perfectly true that these gentlemen wish to march through rapine to disintegration and dismemberment of
speech at Knowsley, 27 October 1881

the Empire, and, I am sorry to say, even to the placing of different parts of the Empire in direct hostility one with the other.
on the Irish Land League

1 To the actual, as distinct from the reported, strength of the Empire, India adds nothing. She immensely adds to the responsibility of Government.
H. C. G. Matthew *Gladstone 1875–1898* (1995)

2 There never was a Churchill from John of Marlborough down that had either morals or principles.
in conversation in 1882, recorded by Captain R. V. Briscoe; R. F. Foster *Lord Randolph Churchill* (1981)

3 Ideal perfection is not the true basis of English legislation. We look at the attainable; we look at the practical, and we have too much English sense to be drawn away by those sanguine delineations of what might possibly be attained in Utopia, from a path which promises to enable us to effect great good for the people of England.
on the Reform Bill
in the House of Commons, 28 February 1884

4 Our first site in Egypt, be it by larceny or be it by emption, will be the almost certain egg of a North African Empire, that will grow and grow... till we finally join hands across the Equator with Natal and Cape Town, to say nothing of the Transvaal and the Orange River on the south, or of Abyssinia or Zanzibar to be swallowed by way of *viaticum* on our journey.
Aggression on Egypt and Freedom in the East (1884)

5 I will venture to say, that upon the one great class of subjects, the largest and the most weighty of them all, where the leading and determining considerations that ought to lead to a conclusion are truth, justice, and humanity—upon these, gentlemen, all the world over, I will back the masses against the classes.
speech in Liverpool, 28 June 1886

6 I would tell them of my own intention to keep my counsel... and I will venture to recommend them, as an old Parliamentary hand, to do the same.
in the House of Commons, 21 January 1886

7 This, if I understand it, is one of those golden moments of our history, one of those opportunities which may come and may go, but which rarely returns.
on the Second Reading of the Home Rule Bill
in the House of Commons, 7 June 1886

8 One prayer absorbs all others: Ireland, Ireland, Ireland.
diary 10 April 1887

9 The blubbering Cabinet.
of the colleagues who wept at his final Cabinet meeting
diary 1 March 1894; note

10 What that Sicilian mule was to me, I have been to the Queen.
memorandum on relations with Queen **Victoria**, *20 March 1894*
Autobiographical Memoranda 1868–94 (1981)

11 I absorb the vapour and return it as a flood.
on public speaking
Lord Riddell *Some Things That Matter* (1927 ed.)

12 It is not a Life at all. It is a Reticence, in three volumes.
on J. W. Cross's Life of George Eliot
E. F. Benson *As We Were* (1930)

1 We are bound to lose Ireland in consequence of years of cruelty, stupidity and misgovernment and I would rather lose her as a friend than as a foe.

Margot Asquith *More Memories* (1933)

2 [Money should] fructify in the pockets of the people.

H. C. G. Matthew *Gladstone 1809–1874* (1986)

3 There is scarcely a single moral action of a single man of which other men can have such a knowledge, in its ultimate grounds, its surrounding incidents, and the real determining cause of its merits, as to warrant their pronouncing a conclusive judgement upon it.

H. C. G. Matthew *Gladstone 1875–1898* (1995)

Thomas Glascock

US Senator

when General Thomas Glascock of Georgia took his seat in the US Senate, a mutual friend expressed the wish to introduce him to Henry **Clay** *of Virginia:*

4 No, sir! I am his adversary, and choose not to subject myself to his fascination.

Robert V. Remini *Henry Clay* (1991)

Joseph Goebbels 1897–1945

German Nazi leader

5 We can manage without butter but not, for example, without guns. If we are attacked we can only defend ourselves with guns not with butter.

speech in Berlin, 17 January 1936; cf. **Goering** 156:6

Hermann Goering 1893–1946

German Nazi leader

6 We have no butter...but I ask you—would you rather have butter or guns?...preparedness makes us powerful. Butter merely makes us fat.

speech at Hamburg, 1936; W. Frischauer *Goering* (1951); cf. **Goebbels** 156:5

7 I herewith commission you to carry out all preparations with regard to...a *total solution* of the Jewish question in those territories of Europe which are under German influence.

instructions to Heydrich, 31 July 1941

W. L. Shirer *The Rise and Fall of the Third Reich* (1962)

Nikolai Gogol 1809–52

Russian writer

8 [Are not] you too, Russia, speeding along like a spirited *troika* that nothing can overtake?...Everything on earth is flying past, and looking askance, other nations and states draw aside and make way.

Dead Souls (1842)

Isaac Goldberg 1887–1938

9 Diplomacy is to do and say
The nastiest thing in the nicest way.

The Reflex October 1927

Ludwig Max Goldberger 1848–1913

1 America, the land of unlimited possibilities. — *Land of Unlimited Possibilities: Observations on Economic Life in the United States of America* (1903)

Emma Goldman 1869–1940

American anarchist

2 Anarchism, then, really, stands for the liberation of the human mind from the dominion of religion; the liberation of the human body from the dominion of property; liberation from the shackles and restraints of government. — *Anarchism and Other Essays* (1910)

Oliver Goldsmith 1730–74

Anglo-Irish writer, poet, and playwright

3 Such is the patriot's boast, where'er we roam,
His first, best country ever is, at home. — *The Traveller* (1764)

4 Laws grind the poor, and rich men rule the law. — *The Traveller* (1764)

5 How small, of all that human hearts endure,
That part which laws or kings can cause or cure! — *The Traveller* (1764); cf. **Johnson** 197:7

6 Ill fares the land, to hast'ning ills a prey,
Where wealth accumulates, and men decay;
Princes and lords may flourish, or may fade;
A breath can make them, as a breath has made;
But a bold peasantry, their country's pride,
When once destroyed, can never be supplied.
A time there was, ere England's griefs began,
When every rood of ground maintained its man;
For him light labour spread her wholesome store,
Just gave what life required, but gave no more;
His best companions, innocence and health;
And his best riches, ignorance of wealth. — *The Deserted Village* (1770)

7 How wide the limits stand
Between a splendid and a happy land. — *The Deserted Village* (1770)

Barry Goldwater 1909–

American Republican politician

8 I would remind you that extremism in the defence of liberty is no vice! And let me remind you also that moderation in the pursuit of justice is no virtue!
speech accepting the presidential nomination, 16 July 1964 — in *New York Times* 17 July 1964

Richard Goodwin

1 People come to Washington believing it's the centre of power. I know I did. It was only much later that I learned that Washington is a steering wheel that's not connected to the engine.

Peter McWilliams *Ain't Nobody's Business If You Do* (1993)

Mikhail Sergeevich Gorbachev 1931–

Soviet statesman, General Secretary of the Communist Party of the USSR 1985–91 and President 1988–91
on Gorbachev: see **Gromyko** 162:4, **Thatcher** 361:11

2 The guilt of Stalin and his immediate entourage before the Party and the people for the mass repressions and lawlessness they committed is enormous and unforgivable.

speech on the seventieth anniversary of the Russian Revolution, 2 November 1987

3 The idea of restructuring [*perestroika*]...combines continuity and innovation, the historical experience of Bolshevism and the contemporaneity of socialism.

speech on the seventieth anniversary of the Russian Revolution, 2 November 1987

George Joachim, Lord Goschen
1831–1907

British Liberal Unionist politician, appointed Chancellor of the Exchequer in 1886 on the sudden resignation of Lord Randolph **Churchill**
on Goschen: see **Churchill** 86:9

4 I have the courage of my opinions, but I have not the temerity to give a political blank cheque to Lord Salisbury.

in the House of Commons, 19 February 1884

Ernest Gowers 1880–1966

British public servant

5 It is not easy nowadays to remember anything so contrary to all appearances as that officials are the servants of the public; and the official must try not to foster the illusion that it is the other way round.

Plain Words (1948)

D. M. Graham 1911–

6 That this House will in no circumstances fight for its King and Country.
motion for a debate at the Oxford Union, 9 February 1933 (passed by 275 votes to 153)

motion worded by Graham when Librarian of the Oxford Union

James Graham, Marquess of Montrose
1612–50

Scottish royalist general and poet

1 Great, Good and Just, could I but rate
My grief to thy too rigid fate!

'Epitaph on King Charles I'

2 Let them bestow on every airth a limb;
Then open all my veins, that I may swim
To thee, my Maker! in that crimson lake;
Then place my parboiled head upon a stake—
Scatter my ashes—strew them in the air;—
Lord! since thou know'st where all these atoms are,
I'm hopeful thou'lt recover once my dust,
And confident thou'lt raise me with the just.

'Lines written on the Window of his Jail the Night before his Execution'

Phil Gramm 1942–

American Republican politician

3 Balancing the budget is like going to heaven. Everybody wants to do it, but nobody wants to do what you have to do to get there.

in a television interview, 16 September 1990

4 I did not come to Washington to be loved, and I have not been disappointed.

Michael Barone and Grant Ujifusa *The American Political Almanac 1994*

Bernie Grant 1944–

British Labour politician

5 The police were to blame for what happened on Sunday night and what they got was a bloody good hiding.
after the Broadwater Farm riots in which a policeman was killed

as leader of Haringey Council outside Tottenham Town Hall, 8 October 1985

Ulysses S. Grant 1822–85

American Union general and 18th President of the US
on Grant: see **Sherman** 339:2

6 No terms except unconditional and immediate surrender can be accepted. I propose to move immediately upon your works.
to Simon Bolivar Buckner, under siege at Fort Donelson, 16 February 1862

P. C. Headley *The Life and Campaigns of General U. S. Grant* (1869)

7 I purpose to fight it out on this line, if it takes all summer.
dispatch to Washington, from headquarters in the field, 11 May 1864

P. C. Headley *The Life and Campaigns of General U. S. Grant* (1869)

8 The war is over—the rebels are our countrymen again.
preventing his men from cheering after **Lee**'*s surrender at Appomattox*

on 9 April, 1865

1 Let us have peace.
letter to General Joseph R. Hawkey, 29 May 1868, accepting the presidential nomination
P. C. Headley *The Life and Campaigns of General U. S. Grant* (1869)

2 I know no method to secure the repeal of bad or obnoxious laws so effective as their stringent execution.
inaugural address, 4 March 1869

3 Leave the matter of religion to the family altar, the church, and the private school, supported entirely by private contributions. Keep the church and state forever separate.
speech at Des Moines, Iowa, 1875

4 Labour disgraces no man; unfortunately you occasionally find men disgrace labour.
speech at Midland International Arbitration Union, Birmingham, England, 1877

Henry Grattan 1746–1820

Irish nationalist leader

5 The thing he proposes to buy is what cannot be sold—liberty.
speech in the Irish Parliament against the proposed union, 16 January 1800
in *Dictionary of National Biography*

John Chipman Gray 1839–1915

American lawyer

6 Dirt is only matter out of place; and what is a blot on the escutcheon of the Common Law may be a jewel in the crown of the Social Republic.
Restraints on the Alienation of Property (2nd ed., 1895) preface

Patrick, Lord Gray d. 1612

7 A dead woman bites not.
oral tradition, Gray being said to have pressed hard for the execution of **Mary** *Queen of Scots in 1587, with the words* 'Mortua non mordet [*Being dead, she will bite no more*]'
A. Darcy's 1625 translation of William Camden's *Annals of the Reign of Queen Elizabeth* (1615) vol. 1

Thomas Gray 1716–71

English poet

8 Some village-Hampden, that with dauntless breast
The little tyrant of his fields withstood;
Some mute inglorious Milton here may rest,
Some Cromwell guiltless of his country's blood.

Th'applause of list'ning senates to command
The threats of pain and ruin to despise,
To scatter plenty o'er a smiling land,
And read their history in a nations eyes,

Their lot forbad: nor circumscribed alone
Their growing virtues, but their crimes confined;
Forbad to wade through slaughter to a throne,
And shut the gates of mercy on mankind.

Elegy Written in a Country Churchyard (1751)

Horace Greeley 1811–72

American editor and politician

1 The illusion that times that were are better than those that are, has probably pervaded all ages. — *The American Conflict* (1864-6)

2 I never said all Democrats were saloon keepers. What I said was that all saloon keepers were Democrats. — attributed

Gregory VII *c.*1020–85

Pope from 1073

3 I have loved justice and hated iniquity: therefore I die in exile.
last words — J. W. Bowden *The Life and Pontificate of Gregory VII* (1840) vol. 2

George Grenville 1712–70

British Whig statesman; Prime Minister 1763–5
on Grenville: see **George III** 149:2, 149:3, **Walpole** 377:12

4 A wise government knows how to enforce with temper, or to conciliate with dignity.
speaking against the expulsion of John **Wilkes** — in the House of Commons, 3 February 1769

Lord Grey of Fallodon 1862–1933

British Liberal politician

5 The lamps are going out all over Europe; we shall not see them lit again in our lifetime.
on the eve of the First World War — *25 Years* (1925) vol. 2

John Grey Griffith 1918–

British lawyer and academic

6 The Constitution is what happens. — to Peter Hennessy during the Westland affair, 5 February 1986; Peter Hennessy *Whitehall* (1990)

Roy Griffiths

7 If Florence Nightingale were carrying her lamp through the corridors of the NHS today she would almost certainly be searching for the people in charge. — in *Report of the NHS Management Inquiry*, DHSS, 1983

John Grigg 1924–

British writer and journalist

8 Lloyd George would have a better rating in British mythology if he had shared the fate of Abraham Lincoln. — attributed, 1963

9 Politicians are exiles from the normal, private world. — attributed, 1964

Joseph ('Jo') Grimond 1913–93

British Liberal politician, Leader of the Liberal Party 1956–67

1 In bygone days, commanders were taught that when in doubt, they should march their troops towards the sound of gunfire. I intend to march my troops towards the sound of gunfire.
speech to the Liberal Party Assembly, 14 September 1963

on the chance of a pact with the Labour Government:
2 Our teeth are in the real meat.
speech to the Liberal Party Assembly, 1965

3 The trouble with the Labour Party is that they don't really believe in Socialism, but they cannot wholeheartedly approve of private enterprise either.
attributed, 1965

Andrei Gromyko 1909–89

Soviet statesman, President of the USSR 1985–8

4 Comrades, this man has a nice smile, but he's got iron teeth.
of Mikhail **Gorbachev**
speech to Soviet Communist Party Central Committee, 11 March 1985

Philip Guedalla 1889–1944

British historian and biographer

of the Admiralty committee to examine inventions:
5 There they sit, like inverted Micawbers, waiting for something to turn down.
in a speech at the Oxford Union, 1912; a similar comment has also been attributed to Winston Churchill of Treasury staff (Anthony Sampson *The Anatomy of Britain Today*)

Henry Gurney 1898–1951

Colonial civil servant and last Chief Secretary of the British Administration in Palestine

on the last day of the British Mandate, Gurney was allegedly asked to whom he intended to give the keys of his office:
6 To Nobody. I shall put them under the mat.
apocryphal; Gurney's diary records that having had the stores locked up he informed the initially unwilling United Nations that if they did not accept the keys, the British would 'leave the keys on their doorstep'
Peter Hennessy *Never Again* (1992)

Nell Gwyn 1650–87

English actress and courtesan

7 Pray, good people, be civil. I am the Protestant whore.
at Oxford, during the Popish Terror, 1681
B. Bevan *Nell Gwyn* (1969)

Earl Haig 1861–1928

Commander of British armies in France, 1915–18

1 A very weak-minded fellow I am afraid, and, like the feather pillow, bears the marks of the last person who has sat on him!
describing the 17th Earl of Derby, in a letter to Lady Haig, 14 January 1918
R. Blake *Private Papers of Douglas Haig* (1952)

2 Every position must be held to the last man: there must be no retirement. With our backs to the wall, and believing in the justice of our cause, each one of us must fight on to the end.
order to British troops, 12 April 1918
A. Duff Cooper *Haig* (1936) vol. 2

Lord Hailsham 1907–

British Conservative politician

3 Conservatives do not believe that the political struggle is the most important thing in life ... The simplest of them prefer fox-hunting—the wisest religion.
The Case for Conservatism (1947)

4 The responsibility of a political party is in inverse proportion to its chances of getting office.
in the House of Lords, 13 February 1961

5 A great party is not to be brought down because of a squalid affair between a woman of easy virtue and a proved liar.
on the Profumo affair
in a television interview, 13 June 1963

6 If the British public falls for this, I think it will be stark, raving bonkers.
on the Labour Party programme
at a press conference at Conservative Central Office, 12 October 1964

7 I believe there is a golden thread which alone gives meaning to the political history of the West, from Marathon to Alamein, from Solon to Winston Churchill and after. This I chose to call the doctrine of liberty under the law.
in 1975; Anthony Sampson *The Changing Anatomy of Britain* (1982)

8 The elective dictatorship.
title of the Dimbleby Lecture, 19 October 1976

9 In a confrontation with the politics of power, the soft centre has always melted away.
in October 1981; Anthony Sampson *The Changing Anatomy of Britain* (1982)

of Denis **Healey**:

10 A piratical old bruiser with a first-class mind and very bad manners.
interview in *The Times* 2 June 1987

11 Nations begin by forming their institutions, but in the end, are continuously formed by them or under their influence.
'The Granada Guildhall Lecture 1987' 10 November 1987

12 The English and, more latterly, the British, have the habit of acquiring their institutions by chance or inadvertence, and shedding them in a fit of absent-mindedness.
'The Granada Guildhall Lecture 1987' 10 November 1987; cf. **Seeley** 322:6

1 We are a democratically governed republic with a wholly admirable head of state.

Values: Collapse and Cure (1994)

Richard Burdon Haldane 1856–1928

British politician, lawyer, and philosopher
on Haldane: see **Asquith** 18:9, **Campbell-Bannerman** 74:4

2 We have come to the conclusion...that in the sphere of civil government the duty of investigation and thought, as preliminary to action, might with great advantage be more definitely added.

Peter Hennessy *Whitehall* (1990)

H. R. Haldeman 1929–93

Presidential assistant to Richard **Nixon**

3 Once the toothpaste is out of the tube, it is awfully hard to get it back in.
on the Watergate affair, to John Dean, 8 April 1973

in *Hearings Before the Select Committee on Presidential Campaign Activities of US Senate: Watergate and Related Activities* (1973) vol. 4

Edward Everett Hale 1822–1909

American clergyman

4 'Do you pray for the senators, Dr Hale?' 'No, I look at the senators and I pray for the country.'

Van Wyck Brooks *New England Indian Summer* (1940)

Matthew Hale 1609–76

English judge

5 Christianity is part of the laws of England.

William Blackstone's summary of Hale's words (Taylor's case, 1676) in *Commentaries* (1769) vol. 4; the origin of the expression has been traced to Sir John Prisot (d. 1460)

Nathan Hale 1755–76

American revolutionary

6 I only regret that I have but one life to lose for my country.
prior to his execution by the British for spying, 22 September 1776

Henry Phelps Johnston *Nathan Hale, 1776* (1914)

William Haley 1901–87

British journalist

7 It *is* a moral issue.
heading of leading article on the Profumo affair

in *The Times* 11 June 1963

Lord Halifax ('the Trimmer') 1633–95

English politician and essayist

1 Lord Rochester was made Lord president: which being a post superior in rank, but much inferior both in advantage and credit to that he held formerly, drew a jest from Lord Halifax...he had heard of many kicked down stairs, but never of any that was kicked up stairs before.

Gilbert Burnet *History of My Own Time* (written 1683–6) vol. 1 (1724)

2 This innocent word *Trimmer* signifieth no more than this, that if men are together in a boat, and one part of the company would weigh it down on one side, another would make it lean as much to the contrary.

Character of a Trimmer (1685, printed 1688)

3 To the question, What shall we do to be saved in this World? there is no other answer but this, Look to your Moat.

A Rough Draft of a New Model at Sea (1694)

4 Men in business are in as much danger from those that work under them, as from those that work against them.

Political, Moral, and Miscellaneous Thoughts and Reflections (1750) 'Instruments of State Ministers'

5 The best way to suppose what may come, is to remember what is past.

Political, Moral, and Miscellaneous Thoughts and Reflections (1750) 'Miscellaneous: Experience'

6 A known liar should be outlawed in a well-ordered government.

Political, Moral, and Miscellaneous Thoughts and Reflections (1750) 'Miscellaneous: Lying'

7 Anger is never without an argument, but seldom with a good one.

Political, Moral, and Miscellaneous Thoughts and Reflections (1750) 'Of Anger'

8 After a revolution, you see the same men in the drawing-room, and within a week the same flatterers.

Political, Moral, and Miscellaneous Thoughts and Reflections (1750) 'Of Courts'

9 Most men make little other use of their speech than to give evidence against their own understanding.

Political, Moral, and Miscellaneous Thoughts and Reflections (1750) 'Of Folly and Fools'

10 There is...no fundamental, but that *every supreme power must be arbitrary*.

Political, Moral, and Miscellaneous Thoughts and Reflections (1750) 'Of Fundamentals'

11 The people are never so perfectly backed, but that they will kick and fling if not stroked at seasonable times.

Political, Moral, and Miscellaneous Thoughts and Reflections (1750) 'Of Fundamentals'

12 In corrupted governments the place is given for the sake of the man; in good ones the man is chosen for the sake of the place.

Political, Moral, and Miscellaneous Thoughts and Reflections (1750) 'Of Fundamentals'

13 It is in a disorderly government as in a river, the lightest things swim at the top.

Political, Moral, and Miscellaneous Thoughts and Reflections (1750) 'Of Government'

14 The best definition of the best government is, that it has no inconveniences but such as are supportable; but inconveniences there must be.

Political, Moral, and Miscellaneous Thoughts and Reflections (1750) 'Of Government'

1 If the laws could speak for themselves, they would complain of the lawyers in the first place.
Political, Moral, and Miscellaneous Thoughts and Reflections (1750) 'Of Laws'

2 Malice is of a low stature, but it hath very long arms.
Political, Moral, and Miscellaneous Thoughts and Reflections (1750) 'Of Malice and Envy'

3 In parliaments, men wrangle in behalf of liberty, that do as little care for it, as they deserve it.
Political, Moral, and Miscellaneous Thoughts and Reflections (1750) 'Of Parliaments'

4 The best party is but a kind of conspiracy against the rest of the nation.
Political, Moral, and Miscellaneous Thoughts and Reflections (1750) 'Of Parties'

5 There are men who shine in a faction, and make a figure by opposition, who would stand in a worse light, if they had the preferments they struggle for.
Political, Moral, and Miscellaneous Thoughts and Reflections (1750) 'Of Parties'

6 Party is little less than an inquisition, where men are under such a discipline in carrying on the common cause, as leaves no liberty of private opinion.
Political, Moral, and Miscellaneous Thoughts and Reflections (1750) 'Of Parties'

7 When the people contend for their liberty, they seldom get anything by their victory but new masters.
Political, Moral, and Miscellaneous Thoughts and Reflections (1750) 'Of Prerogative, Power and Liberty'

8 Power is so apt to be insolent and Liberty to be saucy, that they are very seldom upon good terms.
Political, Moral, and Miscellaneous Thoughts and Reflections (1750) 'Of Prerogative, Power and Liberty'

9 If none were to have liberty but those who understand what it is, there would not be many freed men in the world.
Political, Moral, and Miscellaneous Thoughts and Reflections (1750) 'Of Prerogative, Power and Liberty'

10 Men are not hanged for stealing horses, but that horses may not be stolen.
Political, Moral, and Miscellaneous Thoughts and Reflections (1750) 'Of Punishment'

11 Wherever a knave is not punished, an honest man is laughed at.
Political, Moral, and Miscellaneous Thoughts and Reflections (1750) 'Of Punishment'

12 State business is a cruel trade; good nature is a bungler in it.
Political, Moral, and Miscellaneous Thoughts and Reflections (1750) 'Wicked Ministers'

Lord Halifax 1881–1959

British Conservative politician and Foreign Secretary

On being asked immediately after the Munich crisis if he were not worn out by the late nights:

13 No, not exactly. But it spoils one's eye for the high birds.
attributed

Alexander Hamilton *c.*1755–1804

American Federalist politician, killed in a duel by Aaron **Burr**
on Hamilton: see **Webster** 382:6

1 A national debt, if it is not excessive, will be to us a national blessing.
letter to Robert Morris, 30 April 1781

2 I believe the British government forms the best model the world ever produced...This government has for its object public strength and individual security.
in *Debates of the Federal Convention* 18 June 1787

3 All communities divide themselves into the few and the many. The first are the rich and wellborn, the other the mass of the people...The people are turbulent and changing; they seldom judge or determine right. Give therefore to the first class a distinct, permanent share in the government. They will check the unsteadiness of the second, and as they cannot receive any advantage by a change, they therefore will ever maintain good government.
in *Debates of the Federal Convention* 18 June 1787

4 We are now forming a republican government. Real liberty is neither found in despotism or the extremes of democracy, but in moderate government.
in *Debates of the Federal Convention* 26 June 1787

5 Let Americans disdain to be the instruments of European greatness. Let the thirteen States, bound together in a strict and indissoluble Union, concur in erecting one great American system, superior to the control of all transatlantic force or influence, and able to dictate the terms of the connection between the old and the new world!
in *The Federalist* (1787–8) no. 11

6 Why has government been instituted at all? Because the passions of men will not conform to the dictates of reason and justice, without constraint.
in *The Federalist* (1787–8) no. 15

7 Learn to think continentally.
advice to the newly independent United States
attributed; cf. **Chamberlain** 80:5

8 To admit foreigners indiscriminately to the rights of citizens...would be nothing less than to admit the Grecian horse into the citadel of our liberty and sovereignty.
Works (1886) vol.7

Richard Hampden 1631–95

Parliamentary supporter, Chancellor of the Exchequer 1690–94

9 To tie a popish successor with laws for the preservation of the Protestant religion was binding Samson with withes.
moving a bill to exclude the Duke of York by name from the succession, 11 May 1679
in *Dictionary of National Biography*

Mark Hanna 1837–1904

American politician and businessman

on Theodore **Roosevelt***'s acceding to the Presidency on the assassination of William McKinley*

1 Now look, that damned cowboy is President of the United States. — in September 1901

William Harcourt 1827–1904

British Liberal politician; Chancellor of the Exchequer

2 We are all socialists now. — G. B. Shaw (ed.) *Fabian Essays in Socialism* (1889)

during the passage of Lord **Goschen***'s 1888 budget, noted for the reduction of the national debt*

3 The value of the political heads of departments is to tell the permanent officials what the public will not stand. — A. G. Gardiner *The Life of Sir William Harcourt* (1923) vol. 2

Keir Hardie 1856–1915

Scottish Labour politician

4 From his childhood onward this boy [the future Edward VIII] will be surrounded by sycophants and flatterers by the score—[*Cries of* 'Oh, oh!']—and will be taught to believe himself as of a superior creation. [*Cries of* 'Oh, oh!'] A line will be drawn between him and the people whom he is to be called upon some day to reign over. In due course, following the precedent which has already been set, he will be sent on a tour round the world, and probably rumours of a morganatic alliance will follow—[*Loud cries of* 'Oh, oh!' *and* 'Order!']—and the end of it all will be that the country will be called upon to pay the bill. [*Cries of* Divide!] — in the House of Commons, 28 June 1894

Warren G. Harding 1865–1923

American Republican statesman, 29th President of the US 1921–3

5 In the great fulfillment we must have a citizenship less concerned about what the government can do for it and more anxious about what it can do for the nation. — speech at the Republican National Convention, 7 June 1916; cf. **Kennedy** 204:7

6 America's present need is not heroics, but healing; not nostrums but normalcy; not revolution, but restoration. — speech at Boston, 14 May 1920

Thomas Hardy 1840–1928

English novelist and poet

7 The offhand decision of some commonplace mind high in office at a critical moment influences the course of events for a hundred years. — Florence Hardy *The Early Life of Thomas Hardy 1840–91* (1928)

John Harington 1561–1612

English writer and courtier

1 Treason doth never prosper, what's the reason?
For if it prosper, none dare call it treason.

Epigrams (1618)

John Marshall Harlan 1833–1911

American judge

2 Our Constitution is colour-blind, and neither knows nor tolerates classes among citizens. In respect of civil rights, all citizens are equal before the law. The humblest is the peer of the most powerful.

dissenting opinion in *Plessy v. Ferguson* (1896)

Lord Harlech 1918–85

British Ambassador to Washington, 1961–5

3 Britain will be honoured by historians more for the way she disposed of an empire than for the way in which she acquired it.

in *New York Times* 28 October 1962

Harold II *c.*1019–66

King of England, 1066

4 He will give him seven feet of English ground, or as much more as he may be taller than other men.
his offer to Harald Sigurdson, invading England

Snorri Sturluson *King Harald's Saga* (*c.*1260)

Robert Goodloe Harper 1765–1825

5 Millions for defence, but not one cent for tribute.

toast at a banquet for John **Marshall**, 18 June 1798

Michael Harrington 1928–89

American writer and sociologist

6 For the urban poor the police are those who arrest you. In almost any slum there is a vast conspiracy against the forces of law and order.

The Other America: Poverty in the United States (1962)

William Henry Harrison 1773–1841

American Whig statesman and soldier, noted for his victory at the battle of Tippecanoe in 1811, and 9th President of the US, 1841, who died of pneumonia one month after his inauguration
on Harrison: see **Morris** 266:4, **Ross** 313:3

7 We admit of no government by divine right ... the only legitimate right to govern is an express grant of power from the governed.

inaugural address, 4 March 1841

1 A decent and manly examination of the acts of government should be not only tolerated, but encouraged.
inaugural address, 4 March 1841

Minnie Louise Haskins 1875–1957

English teacher and writer

2 And I said to the man who stood at the gate of the year: 'Give me a light that I may tread safely into the unknown.'
And he replied:
'Go out into the darkness and put your hand into the Hand of God. That shall be to you better than light and safer than a known way.'
quoted by King **George VI** *in his Christmas broadcast, 25 December 1939*
Desert (1908) 'God Knows'

Roy Hattersley 1932–

British Labour politician

3 Opposition is four or five years' humiliation in which there is no escape from the indignity of no longer controlling events.
in *Independent* 25 March 1995 'Quote Unquote'

Václav Havel 1936–

Czech dramatist and statesman; President of Czechoslovakia 1989–92 and of the Czech Republic since 1993

4 A spectre is haunting eastern Europe: the spectre of what in the West is called 'dissent'.
The Power of the Powerless (1978)

5 I see a renewed focus of politics on real people as something far more profound than merely returning to the everyday mechanisms of western (or if you like bourgeois) democracy.
Václav Havel et al. *The Power of the Powerless* (1985)

6 To respond to evil by committing another evil does not eliminate evil but allows it to go on forever.
letter 5 November 1989

R. S. Hawker 1803–75

English clergyman and poet

7 And have they fixed the where and when?
And shall Trelawny die?
Here's twenty thousand Cornish men
Will know the reason why!
the last three lines are taken from a traditional rhyme dating from the imprisonment by James II, in 1688, of the seven Bishops, including Trelawny, Bishop of Bristol
'The Song of the Western Men'

John Milton Hay 1838–1905

American politician

1 It has been a splendid little war, begun with the highest motives, carried on with magnificent intelligence and spirit, favoured by that fortune which loves the brave.
on the Spanish-American War of 1898
letter to Theodore Roosevelt, 27 July 1898

2 The open door.
on the completion of the trade policy he had negotiated with China
letter to the Cabinet, 2 January 1900

Bill Hayden 1933–

Australian Labor politician

Hayden had resigned as Opposition leader in 1983 as Malcolm Fraser was in the process of calling the election, but remained convinced that he would have won:

3 I am not convinced the Labor Party could not win under my leadership. I believe a drover's dog could lead the Labor Party to victory the way the country is.
John Stubbs *Hayden* (1989)

Friedrich August von Hayek 1899–1992

Austrian-born economist

4 The system of private property is the most important guarantee of freedom, not only for those who own property, but scarcely less for those who do not.
The Road to Serfdom (1944)

5 Probably nothing has done so much harm to the liberal cause as the wooden insistence of some liberals on certain rough rules of thumb, above all the principle of *laissez-faire*.
The Road to Serfdom (1944)

6 Although the professed aims of planning would be that man should cease to be a mere means, in fact...the individual would more than ever become a mere means, to be used by the authority in the service of such abstractions as the 'social welfare' or the 'good of the community'
The Road to Serfdom (1944)

7 In any society freedom of thought will probably be of direct significance only for a small minority. But this does not mean that anyone is competent, or ought to have power, to select those to whom this freedom is to be reserved.
The Road to Serfdom (1944)

8 We need good principles rather than good people. We need fixed rules, not fixers.
Studies in Philosophy, Politics and Economics (1967)

9 I am certain that nothing has done so much to destroy the juridical safeguards of individual freedom as the striving after this miracle of social justice.
Economic Freedom and Representative Government (1973)

10 One cannot help a country to maintain its standard of life by assisting people to consume more than they produce.
in *Daily Telegraph* 26 August 1976

Cuthbert Morley Headlam 1876–1964

British Conservative politician

1 He is a terrible burden for any Govt. to carry—someone said of Randolph Churchill that he was the kind of man who would like to be the bride at a wedding, and the corpse at the funeral—the same applies to his more brilliant son.
of Winston **Churchill**

diary 20 July 1927

2 He is very clever and takes infinite pains to make himself well informed—but somehow I doubt whether he will ever make much political progress. He bores people too quickly and has little or no sense of humour. However, it is never safe to prophesy about anyone's political prospects and Harold may yet come out on top.
of Harold **Macmillan**

diary 31 January 1932

3 This Parliament is enough to discourage anyone from entering political life—a vast untutored majority with a helpless minority and an extremely uninteresting Government.

diary 27 March 1933

4 We ought to have made up more to the political leaders and their wives—the latter are an unattractive lot, but their influence is greater than one supposes.

diary 28 July 1933

5 In politics only one thing really counts and that is a power of decision: a policy is all that is required... Better to break your party on a matter of principle than to let it fall to pieces because you cannot yourself make up your mind what you want to do.

diary 2 April 1934

Denis Healey 1917–

British Labour politician

on Healey: see **Hailsham** 163:10

6 The Fabians...found socialism wandering aimlessly in Cloud-cuckoo-land and set it working on the gas and water problems of the nearest town or village.
of the parochialism of the Fabians

New Fabian Essays (1952)

7 There are going to be howls of anguish from the 80,000 people who are rich enough to pay over 75% [tax] on the last slice of their income.

speech at the Labour Party Conference, 1 October 1973

8 It's no good ceasing to become the world's policeman in order to become the world's parson instead.

at a meeting of the Cabinet at Chequers, 17 November 1974; Peter Hennessy *Whitehall* (1990)

9 We should not allow middle-class guilt to blind us to what's going on.
of the susceptibility of ministers, in the Labour Cabinet of 1974, to the charge that they did not understand the problems of the workers or the unemployed

Anthony Sampson *The Changing Anatomy of Britain*

of being criticized by Geoffrey **Howe** *in the House of Commons:*

10 Like being savaged by a dead sheep.

in the House of Commons, 14 June 1978

of Margaret **Thatcher**:

1 And who is the Mephistopheles behind this shabby Faust [the Foreign Secretary, Geoffrey Howe]?...To quote her own backbenchers, the Great She-elephant, She-Who-Must-Be-Obeyed, the Catherine the Great of Finchley, the Prime Minister herself.
in the House of Commons, 27 February 1984

2 La Passionaria of middle-class privilege.
of Margaret **Thatcher**
Kenneth Minogue and Michael Biddiss *Thatcherism* (1987)

3 Healey's first law of politics: when you're in a hole, stop digging.
attributed

4 While the rest of Europe is marching to confront the new challenges, the Prime Minister is shuffling along in the gutter in the opposite direction, like an old bag lady, muttering imprecations at anyone who catches her eye.
in the House of Commons, 22 February 1990

William Randolph Hearst 1863–1951

American newspaper publisher and tycoon

5 You furnish the pictures and I'll furnish the war.
message to the artist Frederic Remington in Havana, Cuba, during the Spanish-American War of 1898
attributed

Edward Heath 1916–

British Conservative statesman; Prime Minister 1970–4
on Heath: see **Hennessy** 175:2, **Jenkins** 194:8, **Thatcher** 360:9

6 This would, at a stroke, reduce the rise in prices, increase productivity and reduce unemployment.
press release, never actually spoken by Heath
from Conservative Central Office, 16 June 1970

7 I entered the House in 1950 having fought an election on Mr Churchill's theme that Conservatives were to set the people free. It was not a theme that we were to set the people free to do what we tell them.
speech at the Conservative Party Conference, October 1970

8 The unpleasant and unacceptable face of capitalism.
on the Lonrho affair
in the House of Commons, 15 May 1973

9 If politicians lived on praise and thanks they'd be forced into some other line of business.
attributed, 1973

10 I am not a product of privilege. I am a product of opportunity.
attributed, 1974

11 Out go the estate-owners, in come the estate agents.
in *Observer* 30 September 1990

G. W. F. Hegel 1770–1831

German idealist philosopher

12 What experience and history teach is this—that nations and governments have never learned anything from history, or acted upon any lessons they might have drawn from it.
Lectures on the Philosophy of World History: Introduction (1830)

Heinrich Heine 1797–1856

German poet

1 Wherever books will be burned, men also, in the end, are burned. — *Almansor* (1823)

Joseph Heller 1923–

American novelist

2 If I'm going to be trivial, inconsequential, and deceitful... then I might as well be in government. — *Closing Time* (1994)

Lillian Hellman 1905–84

American playwright

3 I cannot and will not cut my conscience to fit this year's fashions. — letter to John S. Wood, 19 May 1952

Leona Helmsley *c.*1920–

American hotelier

4 Only the little people pay taxes.
reported at her trial for tax evasion — to her housekeeper; in *New York Times* 12 July 1983

Arthur Henderson 1863–1935

British Labour politician and from 1931 Party Leader

to critics in his own party, when as adviser on labour matters he was made minister without portfolio in **Lloyd George***'s War Cabinet (December 1916):*

5 I am not here either to please myself or you; I am here to see the war through. — in *Dictionary of National Biography*

6 The first forty-eight hours decide whether a Minister is going to run his office or whether his office is going to run him. — Susan Crosland *Tony Crosland* (1982)

Leon Henderson 1895–1956

American economist; appointed by Roosevelt to the National Defense Advisory Commission in 1940

7 Having a little inflation is like being a little pregnant. — J. K. Galbraith *A Life in Our Times* (1981)

Peter Hennessy 1947–

English historian and writer

8 MI5 is a job creation scheme for muscular underachievers from the ancient universities. — in *The Times* 1981, profile of Roger Hollis

of Rab **Butler** *in his last years:*

1 He seemed like a benign and decent beached whale washed up on the harder shores of modern Conservatism.

in *Independent* 8 May 1987

2 The model of a modern Prime Minister would be a kind of grotesque composite freak—someone with the dedication to duty of a Peel, the physical energy of a Gladstone, the detachment of a Salisbury, the brains of an Asquith, the balls of a Lloyd George, the word-power of a Churchill, the administrative gifts of an Attlee, the style of a Macmillan, the managerialism of a Heath, and the sleep requirements of a Thatcher. Human beings do not come like that.

The Hidden Wiring (1995)

Henri IV (of Navarre) 1553–1610

King of France from 1589

3 Hang yourself, brave Crillon; we fought at Arques and you were not there.

traditional form given by Voltaire to a letter from Henri to Crillon, 20 September 1597; Henri's actual words were: 'My good man, Crillon, hang yourself for not having been at my side last Monday at the greatest event that's ever been seen and perhaps ever will be seen'

4 The wisest fool in Christendom.
of **James I** *of England*

attributed both to Henri IV and **Sully**

5 I want there to be no peasant in my kingdom so poor that he is unable to have a chicken in his pot every Sunday.

In Hardouin de Péréfixe *Histoire de Henry le Grand* (1681); cf. **Hoover** 182:9

6 Paris is well worth a mass.
when told that, though a Protestant, he must hear mass at Notre-Dame Cathedral to be consecrated king

attributed to Henri IV; alternatively to his minister Sully, in conversation with Henri

Henry II 1133–89

King of England from 1154

7 Will no one rid me of this turbulent priest?
of Thomas Becket, Archbishop of Canterbury, murdered in Canterbury Cathedral, December 1170

oral tradition, conflating a number of variant forms, including G. Lyttelton *History of the Life of King Henry the Second* (1769): 'so many cowardly and ungrateful men in his court, none of whom would revenge him of the injuries he sustained from one turbulent priest'

Henry VIII 1491–1547

King of England from 1509

1 The King found her [Anne of Cleves] so different from her picture ... that ... he swore they had brought him a Flanders mare.
Tobias Smollett *A Complete History of England* (3rd ed., 1759)

2 This man hath the right sow by the ear.
of Thomas Cranmer, June 1529
in *Acts and Monuments of John Foxe* ['Fox's Book of Martyrs'] (1570)

Patrick Henry 1736–99

American statesman

3 Caesar had his Brutus—Charles the First, his Cromwell—and George the Third—('Treason,' cried the Speaker) ... *may profit by their example.* If *this* be treason, make the most of it.
speech in the Virginia assembly, May 1765

4 I am not a Virginian, but an American.
in [John Adams's] Notes of Debates in the Continental Congress, Philadelphia, 6 September 1774

5 I know not what course others may take; but as for me, give me liberty, or give me death!
speech in Virginia Convention, 23 March 1775

6 I have but one lamp by which my feet are guided, and that is the lamp of experience. I know no way of judging the future but by the past.
speech in Virginia Convention, Richmond, 23 March 1775

7 We are not weak if we make a proper use of those means which the God of Nature has placed in our power ... The battle, sir, is not to the strong alone; it is to the vigilant, the active, the brave.
speech in Virginia Convention, Richmond, 23 March 1775

8 Guard with jealous attention the public liberty. Suspect everyone who approaches that jewel. Unfortunately, nothing will preserve it but downright force. Whenever you give up that force, you are inevitably ruined.
attributed

A. P. Herbert 1890–1971

English writer and humorist

9 This high official, all allow,
Is grossly overpaid;
There wasn't any Board, and now
There isn't any Trade.
'The President of the Board of Trade' (1922)

10 Testators would do well to provide some indication of the particular Liberal Party which they have in mind, such as a telephone number or a Christian name.
Misleading Cases (1935)

11 People must not do things for fun. We are not here for fun. There is no reference to fun in any Act of Parliament.
Uncommon Law (1935) 'Is it a Free Country?'

1 The Common Law of England has been laboriously built about a mythical figure—the figure of 'The Reasonable Man'. — *Uncommon Law* (1935) 'The Reasonable Man'

Frank Herbert 1920–86

American writer of science fiction

2 If you think of yourselves as helpless and ineffectual, it is certain that you will create a despotic government to be your master. The wise despot, therefore, maintains among his subjects a popular sense that they are helpless and ineffectual. — *The Dosadi Experiment* (1978)

Herodotus *c.*485–*c.*425 BC

Greek historian

3 In peace, children inter their parents; war violates the order of nature and causes parents to inter their children. — *Histories*

4 The most hateful torment for men is to have knowledge of everything but power over nothing. — *Histories*

Lord Hervey 1696–1743

English politician and writer

5 Whoever would lie usefully should lie seldom. — *Memoirs of the Reign of George II* (ed. J. W. Croker, 1848) vol. 1

6 I am fit for nothing but to carry candles and set chairs all my life. — letter to Sir Robert Walpole, 1737

Alexander Ivanovich Herzen 1812–70

Russian author and revolutionary

7 Communism is a Russian autocracy turned upside down. — *The Development of Revolutionary Ideas in Russia* (1851)

8 Russia's future will be a great danger for Europe and a great misfortune for Russia if there is no emancipation of the individual. One more century of present despotism will destroy all the good qualities of the Russian people. — *The Development of Revolutionary Ideas in Russia* (1851)

Michael Heseltine 1933–

British Conservative politician

on Heseltine: see **Critchley** 104:7

9 I knew that, 'He who wields the knife never wears the crown.' — in *New Society* 14 February 1986

10 There are those who never stretch out the hand for fear it will be bitten. But those who never stretch out the hand will never feel it clasped in friendship. — *Where There's a Will* (1987)

11 The market has no morality. — on *Panorama* BBC1 27 June 1988

1 The biggest headline is always the last headline. I don't want the last headline. You don't if you want a future in politics. Which I suppose I have.
on why he avoided criticism of Mrs **Thatcher***'s anti-Europeanism during the Euro Elections*

interview in *The Spectator* 16 September 1989

2 Polluted rivers, filthy streets, bodies bedded down in doorways are no advertisement for a prosperous or caring society.

speech at Conservative Party Conference 10 October 1989

3 The Tory recognizes the contrast between laissez-faire and noblesse oblige.

in *Observer* 18 March 1990 'Sayings of the Week'

4 If I have to intervene to help British companies . . . I'll intervene—before breakfast, before lunch, before tea and before dinner. And I'll get up the next morning and I'll start all over again.
of his role as President of the Board of Trade

to the Conservative Party Conference, 7 October 1992

Gordon Hewart 1870–1943

British lawyer and politician

5 A long line of cases shows that it is not merely of some importance, but is of fundamental importance that justice should not only be done, but should manifestly and undoubtedly be seen to be done.

in *Rex v Sussex Justices* 9 November 1923

J. R. Hicks 1904–89

British economist

6 The best of all monopoly profits is a quiet life.

Econometrica (1935) 'The Theory of Monopoly'

Charles Hill 1904–89

British Conservative politician, doctor, and broadcaster

7 It does not do to appear clever. Advancement in this man's party is due entirely to alcoholic stupidity.
advice given in 1959 to the newly elected MP, Julian **Critchley,** *whom he had seen reading in the Smoking Room of the House of Commons*

Julian Critchley *A Bag of Boiled Sweets* (1994)

Joe Hill 1879–1915

American labour leader and songwriter

8 You will eat, bye and bye,
In that glorious land above the sky;
Work and pray, live on hay,
You'll get pie in the sky when you die.

'Preacher and the Slave' in *Songs of the Workers* (Industrial Workers of the World, 1911)

9 I will die like a true-blue rebel. Don't waste any time in mourning—organize.
farewell telegram to Bill Haywood, 18 November 1915, prior to his death by firing squad

in *Salt Lake* (Utah) *Tribune* 19 November 1915

Emperor Hirohito 1901–89

Emperor of Japan 1926–89

1 The war situation has developed not necessarily to Japan's advantage. — on 15 August 1945

announcing Japan's surrender, in a broadcast to his people after atom bombs had destroyed Hiroshima and Nagasaki

2 Certainly things happened during the Second World War for which I feel personally sorry. — attributed, 1971

Adolf Hitler 1889–1945

German dictator

3 The broad mass of a nation... will more easily fall victim to a big lie than to a small one. — *Mein Kampf* (1925) vol. 1

4 The night of the long knives. — speech in the Reichstag, 13 July 1934

applied to the massacre of Ernst Roehm and his associates by Hitler on 29–30 June 1934, though taken from an early Nazi marching song; the phrase was subsequently associated with Harold **Macmillan***'s Cabinet dismissals of 13 July 1962*

5 I go the way that Providence dictates with the assurance of a sleepwalker. — speech in Munich, 15 March 1936

6 It is the last territorial claim which I have to make in Europe, but it is the claim from which I will not recede and which, God-willing, I will make good. — speech at Berlin Sportpalast, 26 September 1938

on the Sudetenland

7 With regard to the problem of the Sudeten Germans, my patience is now at an end! — speech at Berlin Sportpalast, 26 September 1938

to Mussolini, having spent nine hours intermittently in Franco's company:

8 Rather than go through that again, I would prefer to have three or four teeth taken out. — Paul Preston *Franco* (1993)

Thomas Hobbes 1588–1679

English philosopher

9 By art is created that great Leviathan, called a commonwealth or state, (in Latin *civitas*) which is but an artificial man... and in which, the sovereignty is an artificial soul. — *Leviathan* (1651); introduction

10 I put for a general inclination of all mankind, a perpetual and restless desire of power after power, that ceaseth only in death. — *Leviathan* (1651)

11 They that approve a private opinion, call it opinion; but they that mislike it, heresy: and yet heresy signifies no more than private opinion. — *Leviathan* (1651)

12 During the time men live without a common power to keep them all in awe, they are in that condition which is — *Leviathan* (1651)

called war; and such a war as is of every man against every man.

1 For as the nature of foul weather, lieth not in a shower or two of rain; but in an inclination thereto of many days together: so the nature of war consisteth not in actual fighting, but in the known disposition thereto during all the time there is no assurance to the contrary. *Leviathan* (1651)

2 No arts; no letters; no society; and which is worst of all, continual fear and danger of violent death; and the life of man, solitary, poor, nasty, brutish, and short. *Leviathan* (1651)

3 Force, and fraud, are in war the two cardinal virtues. *Leviathan* (1651)

4 There is written on the turrets of the city of Lucca...the word *libertas*: yet no man can thence infer, that a particular man has more liberty, or immunity from the service of the commonwealth there, than in Constantinople. Whether a commonwealth be monarchical or popular, the freedom is still the same. *Leviathan* (1651)

5 Liberties...depend on the silence of the law. *Leviathan* (1651)

6 The obligation of subjects to the sovereign, is understood to last as long, and no longer, than the power lasteth, by which he is able to protect them. *Leviathan* (1651)

7 I put down for one of the most effectual seeds of the death of any state, that the conquerors require not only a submission of men's actions to them for the future, but also an approbation of all their actions past. *Leviathan* (1651)

8 They that are discontented under *monarchy*, call it *tyranny*; and they that are displeased with *aristocracy*, call it *oligarchy*: so also, they which find themselves grieved under a *democracy*, call it *anarchy*, which signifies the want of government; and yet I think no man believes, that want of government, is any new kind of government. *Leviathan* (1651)

9 The papacy is not other than the ghost of the deceased Roman Empire, sitting crowned upon the grave thereof. *Leviathan* (1651)

John Cam Hobhouse 1786–1869

English politician

10 When I invented the phrase 'His Majesty's Opposition' [Canning] paid me a compliment on the fortunate hit. *Recollections of a Long Life* (1865) vol. 2; cf. **Bagehot** 24:14

August Heinrich Hoffman 1798–1874

German poet

11 *Deutschland über alles.*
Germany above all. Title of poem (1841)

Lancelot Hogben 1895–1975

English scientist

1 This is not the age of pamphleteers. It is the age of the engineers. The spark-gap is mightier than the pen. Democracy will not be salvaged by men who talk fluently, debate forcefully and quote aptly.

Science for the Citizen (1938) epilogue

James Hogg 1770–1835

Scottish poet

2 God bless our lord the king!
God save our lord the king!
God save the king!
Make him victorious,
Happy, and glorious,
Long to reign over us:
God save the king!

'The King's Anthem' in *Jacobite Relics of Scotland* Second Series (1821)

Sarah Hogg 1946–

former head of John Major's policy unit

3 So much of cabinet consists of reporting, rather than debating; congratulating, rather than arguing.
on leaving the Prime Minister's policy unit

in *Sunday Times* 9 April 1995

Henry Fox, Lord Holland 1705–74

English Whig politician, father of Charles James **Fox**
on Holland: see **Walpole** 377:8

4 Let nothing be done to break his spirit. The world will do that business fast enough.
of his son Charles James **Fox** *as a child*

attributed

5 If Mr Selwyn calls again, shew him up: if I am alive I shall be delighted to see him; and if I am dead he would like to see me.
during his last illness

J. H. Jesse *George Selwyn and his Contemporaries* (1844) vol. 3

Oliver Wendell Holmes Jr. 1841–1935

Justice of the US Supreme Court

6 Men must turn square corners when they deal with the Government.

in *Rock Island, Arkansas & Louisiana Ry. v. United States* (1920)

7 I pay my tax bills more readily than any others—for whether the money is well or ill spent I get civilized society for it.

letter to Harold Laski, 12 May 1930

8 A second-class intellect. But a first-class temperament!
of Franklin **Roosevelt**

on 8 March 1933

1 The mind of a bigot is like the pupil of the eye; the more light you pour upon it, the more it will contract. — attributed

Alec Douglas-Home, Lord Home 1903–95

British Conservative statesman; Prime Minister, 1963–4

2 When I have to read economic documents I have to have a box of matches and start moving them into position to simplify and illustrate the points to myself. — in *Observer* 16 September 1962

3 As far as the fourteenth earl is concerned, I suppose Mr Wilson, when you come to think of it, is the fourteenth Mr Wilson. — in *Daily Telegraph* 22 October 1963

replying to Harold **Wilson***'s remark (on Home's leading the Conservatives to victory in the 1963 election) that 'the whole* [*democratic*] *process has ground to a halt with a fourteenth Earl'*

4 There are two problems in my life. The political ones are insoluble and the economic ones are incomprehensible. — attributed, 1964

Richard Hooker *c.*1554–1600

English theologian

5 He that goeth about to persuade a multitude, that they are not so well governed as they ought to be, shall never want attentive and favourable hearers. — *Of the Laws of Ecclesiastical Polity* (1593)

6 Alteration though it be from worse to better hath in it inconveniences, and those weighty. — *Of the Laws of Ecclesiastical Polity* (1593)

Herbert Hoover 1874–1964

American Republican statesman; 31st President of the US 1929–33

7 Our country has deliberately undertaken a great social and economic experiment, noble in motive and far-reaching in purpose. — letter to Senator W. H. Borah, 23 February 1928

on the Eighteenth Amendment enacting Prohibition, often referred to as 'the noble experiment'

8 The American system of rugged individualism. — speech in New York City, 22 October 1928

9 The slogan of progress is changing from the full dinner pail to the full garage. — speech in New York, 22 October 1928; cf. **Henri IV** 175:5

sometimes paraphrased as, 'a car in every garage and a chicken in every pot'

10 The grass will grow in the streets of a hundred cities, a thousand towns. — speech, 31 October 1932; cf. **Bryan** 60:5

on proposals 'to reduce the protective tariff to a competitive tariff for revenue'

11 A good many things go around in the dark besides Santa Claus. — address to the John Marshall Republican Club, St Louis, Missouri, 16 December 1935

1 Older men declare war. But it is youth who must fight and die.

speech at the Republican National Convention, Chicago, 27 June 1944

Bob Hope 1903–

American comedian

2 I must say the Senator's victory in Wisconsin was a triumph for democracy. It proves that a millionaire has just as good a chance as anybody else.

of John Fitzgerald **Kennedy***'s electoral victory*

in 1960; William Robert Faith *Bob Hope* (1983)

Horace 65–8 BC

Roman poet

3 O citizens, first acquire wealth; you can practise virtue afterwards

Satires; cf. **Pope** 295:6

Samuel Horsley 1733–1806

English bishop

4 In this country...the individual subject...'has nothing to do with the laws but to obey them.'

defending a maxim he had used earlier in committee

in the House of Lords, 13 November 1795

John Hoskyns 1927–

British businessman; head of the Prime Minister's Policy Unit 1979–82

5 The House of Commons is the greatest closed shop of all...For the purposes of government, a country of 55 million people is forced to depend on a talent pool which could not sustain a single multinational company.

'Conservatism is Not Enough' (Institute of Directors Annual Lecture) 25 September 1983

6 The Tory party never panics, except in a crisis.

in *Sunday Times* 19 February 1989

A. E. Housman 1859–1936

English poet and classicist

7 To represent [Joseph] Chamberlain as an injured man, and Balfour as the man who injured him, is like saying that Christ crucified Pontius Pilate.

letter 7 December 1922

Samuel Houston 1793–1863

American politician and military leader who led the struggle to win control of Texas (1834–6) and make it part of the US

8 The North is determined to preserve this Union. They are not a fiery, impulsive people as you are, for they live in colder climates. But when they begin to move in a given direction...they move with the steady momentum and perseverance of a mighty avalanche.

in 1861, warning the people of Texas against secession

Geoffrey C. Ward *The Civil War* (1991)

Geoffrey Howe 1926–

British Conservative politician; Foreign Secretary 1983-9

on Howe: see **Healey** 172:10

1 It is rather like sending your opening batsmen to the crease only for them to find, the moment the first balls are bowled, that their bats have been broken before the game by the team captain.
resignation speech which precipitated the fall of Margaret **Thatcher**
in the House of Commons, 13 November 1990

2 The time has come for others to consider their own response to the tragic conflict of loyalties with which I have myself wrestled for perhaps too long.
resignation speech
in the House of Commons, 13 November 1990

Julia Ward Howe 1819–1910

American Unitarian lay preacher

3 Mine eyes have seen the glory of the coming of the Lord:
He is trampling out the vintage where the grapes of wrath are stored;
He hath loosed the fateful lightning of his terrible swift sword:
His truth is marching on.
'Battle Hymn of the Republic' (1862)

4 As He died to make men holy, let us die to make men free.
'Battle Hymn of the Republic' (1862)

Victor Hugo 1802–85

French poet, novelist, and playwright

5 A stand can be made against invasion by an army; no stand can be made against invasion by an idea.
Histoire d'un Crime (written 1851–2, published 1877)

6 Take away *time is money*, and what is left of England? take away *cotton is king*, and what is left of America?
Les Misérables (1862)

David Hume 1711–76

Scottish philosopher

7 Money...is none of the wheels of trade: it is the oil which renders the motion of the wheels more smooth and easy.
Essays: Moral and Political (1741–2) 'Of Money'

8 That policy is violent, which aggrandizes the public by the poverty of individuals.
Essays: Moral and Political (1741–2) 'Of Money'

9 Should it be said, that, by living under the dominion of a prince, which one might leave, every individual has given a tacit assent to his authority...We may as well assert, that a man by remaining in a vessel, freely consents to the dominion of the master; though he was carried on board while asleep, and must leap into the ocean, and perish, the moment he leaves her.
'Of the Original Contract' (1748)

1 In all ages of the world, priests have been enemies of liberty.

'Of the Parties of Great Britain' (1741–2)

2 It is a just political maxim, that every man must be supposed a knave.

Political Discourses (1751)

Hubert Humphrey 1911–78

American Democratic politician

3 There are not enough jails, not enough policemen, not enough courts to enforce a law not supported by the people.

speech at Williamsburg, 1 May 1965

4 The right to be heard does not automatically include the right to be taken seriously.

speech to National Student Association at Madison, 23 August 1965

5 Here we are the way politics ought to be in America, the politics of happiness, the politics of purpose and the politics of joy.

speech in Washington, 27 April 1968

6 Compassion is not weakness, and concern for the unfortunate is not socialism.

attributed

Lord Hunt of Tanworth 1919–

British civil servant; Secretary of the Cabinet 1973–9

of British Cabinet government, described as 'a shambles':

7 It has got to be, so far as possible, a democratic and accountable shambles.

at a seminar at the Institute of Historical Research, 20 October 1993

Douglas Hurd 1930–

British conservative politician; Foreign Secretary

8 Lord Rothschild roamed like a condottiere through Whitehall, laying an ambush here, there breaching some crumbling fortress which had outlived its usefulness… He respected persons occasionally but rarely policies.

of Lord **Rothschild** *as first Director of the Central Policy Review Staff*

An End to Promises (1979)

9 If President Clinton decides to accelerate the run-down in US forces in Europe—and by implication the priority Washington attaches to Nato—that wedge will be removed. With it will go one of the principal props which have allowed Britain to punch above its weight in the world.

speech at Chatham House; in *Financial Times* 4 February 1993

Saddam Hussein 1937–

President of Iraq from 1979

1 The mother of battles.
popular interpretation of his description of the approaching Gulf War, given in a speech in Baghdad, 6 January 1991

in *The Times* 7 January 1991 it was reported that Saddam had no intention of relinquishing Kuwait and was ready for the 'mother of all wars'

Robert Maynard Hutchins 1899–1977

2 The death of democracy is not likely to be an assassination from ambush. It will be a slow extinction from apathy, indifference, and undernourishment.

Great Books (1954)

Aldous Huxley 1894–1963

English novelist

3 So long as men worship the Caesars and Napoleons, Caesars and Napoleons will duly arise and make them miserable.

Ends and Means (1937)

4 Idealism is the noble toga that political gentlemen drape over their will to power.

in *New York Herald Tribune* 25 November 1963

5 The propagandist's purpose is to make one set of people forget that certain other sets of people are human.

attributed

Dolores Ibarruri ('La Pasionaria') 1895–1989

Spanish Communist leader

6 It is better to die on your feet than to live on your knees.

speech in Paris, 3 September 1936; also attributed to Emiliano Zapata; cf. **Roosevelt** 309:12

7 *No pasarán.*
They shall not pass.

radio broadcast, Madrid, 19 July 1936; cf. **Anonymous** 10:9

Henrik Ibsen 1828–1906

Norwegian playwright

8 The majority never has right on its side. Never I say! That is one of the social lies that a free, thinking man is bound to rebel against. Who makes up the majority in any given country? Is it the wise men or the fools? I think we must agree that the fools are in a terrible overwhelming majority, all the wide world over. But, damn it, it can surely never be right that the stupid should rule over the clever!

An Enemy of the People (1882)

9 You should never have your best trousers on when you go out to fight for freedom and truth.

An Enemy of the People (1882)

Harold L. Ickes 1874–1952

American lawyer and administrator

1 The trouble with Senator Long...is that he's suffering from halitosis of the intellect. That's presuming Emperor Long has an intellect.
speech, 1935; G. Wolfskill and J. A. Hudson *All But the People: Franklin D. Roosevelt and his Critics, 1933–39* (1969)

2 Dewey threw his diaper into the ring.
on the Republican candidate for the presidency
in *New York Times* 12 December 1939

3 I am against government by crony.
on resigning as secretary of the interior
in February 1946

Ivan Illich 1926–

American sociologist

4 In a consumer society there are inevitably two kinds of slaves: the prisoners of addiction and the prisoners of envy.
Tools for Conviviality (1973)

William Ralph Inge 1860–1954

English writer; Dean of St. Paul's, 1911–34

5 It takes in reality only one to make a quarrel. It is useless for the sheep to pass resolutions in favour of vegetarianism, while the wolf remains of a different opinion.
Outspoken Essays: First Series (1919)

6 The nations which have put mankind and posterity most in their debt have been small states—Israel, Athens, Florence, Elizabethan England.
Outspoken Essays: Second Series (1922) 'State, visible and invisible'

7 A man may build himself a throne of bayonets, but he cannot sit on it.
Philosophy of Plotinus (1923) vol. 2, quoted by Boris **Yeltsin** at the time of the failed military coup in Russia, August 1991

8 The enemies of Freedom do not argue; they shout and they shoot.
End of an Age (1948)

9 The effect of boredom on a large scale in history is underestimated. It is a main cause of revolutions, and would soon bring to an end all the static Utopias and the farmyard civilization of the Fabians.
End of an Age (1948)

Bernard Ingham 1932–

British journalist and public relations specialist, Chief Press Secretary to the Prime Minister, 1979–90
on Ingham: see **Biffen** 44:18

10 Blood sport is brought to its ultimate refinement in the gossip columns.
speech, 5 February 1986

1 The media, I tell pedants in the Government, is like an oil painting. Close up, it looks like nothing on earth. Stand back and you get the drift. — speech to the Parliamentary Press Gallery, February 1990

at a meeting of the Parliamentary Lobby, noticing that he had a spot of blood on his shirt:

2 My God, I've been stabbed in the front. — recalled in a letter to Antony Jay, January 1995

Eugène Ionesco 1912–94

French playwright

3 A civil servant doesn't make jokes. — *The Killer* (1958)

Hastings Lionel ('Pug') Ismay 1887–1965

British general and Secretary to the Committee of Imperial Defence; first Secretary-General of Nato

4 NATO exists for three reasons—to keep the Russians out, the Americans in and the Germans down.
to a group of British Conservative backbenchers in 1949 — Peter Hennessy *Never Again* (1992); oral tradition

Alija Izetbegović 1925–

Bosnian statesman; President of Bosnia and Herzegovina since 1990

5 And to my people I say, this may not be a just peace, but it is more just than a continuation of war.
after signing the Dayton accord with representatives of Serbia and Croatia — in Dayton, Ohio, 21 November 1995

Andrew Jackson 1767–1845

American general and Democratic statesman, 7th President of the US 1829–37
on Jackson: see **Clay** 97:6

6 The individual who refuses to defend his rights when called by his Government, deserves to be a slave, and must be punished as an enemy of his country and friend to her foe. — proclamation to the people of Louisiana from Mobile, 21 September 1814

7 The brave man inattentive to his duty, is worth little more to his country, than the coward who deserts her in the hour of danger.
to troops who had abandoned their lines during the battle of New Orleans, 8 January 1815 — attributed

8 Our Federal Union: it must be preserved.
toast given on the Jefferson Birthday Celebration, 13 April 1830 — Thomas Hart Benton *Thirty Years' View* (1856) vol. 1

9 Each public officer who takes an oath to support the constitution swears that he will support it as he understands it, and not as it is understood by others.
presidential message vetoing the bill to re-charter the Bank of the United States, 10 July 1832 — H. S. Commager (ed.) *Documents of American History* vol. 1 (1963)

1 Every man is equally entitled to protection by law; but when the laws undertake to add... artificial distinctions, to grant titles, gratuities, and exclusive privileges, to make the rich richer and the potent more powerful, the humble members of society—the farmers, mechanics, and labourers—who have neither the time nor the means of securing like favours to themselves, have a right to complain of the injustice of their government.
veto of the Bank Bill, 10 July 1832

2 There are no necessary evils in government. Its evils exist only in its abuses. If it would confine itself to equal protection, and, as Heaven does its rains, shower its favours alike on the high and the low, the rich and the poor, it would be an unqualified blessing.
veto of the Bank Bill, 10 July 1832

3 You are uneasy; you never sailed with *me* before, I see.
James Parton *Life of Jackson* (1860) vol. 3

4 One man with courage makes a majority.
attributed

shortly before his death, Jackson was asked if he had left anything undone:

5 I didn't shoot Henry Clay, and I didn't hang John C. Calhoun.
Robert V. Remini *Henry Clay* (1991); attributed

Jesse Jackson 1941–

American Democratic politician and clergyman

6 My right and my privilege to stand here before you has been won—won in my lifetime—by the blood and the sweat of the innocent.
speech at Democratic National Convention, Atlanta, 19 July 1988

7 When I look out at this convention, I see the face of America, red, yellow, brown, black, and white. We are all precious in God's sight—the real rainbow coalition.
speech at Democratic National Convention, Atlanta, 19 July 1988

8 You can't keep on running from labour, running from blacks, running from cities and expect to inspire them to vote.
on President **Clinton**, *after the results of the 1994 election*
in *Guardian* 28 November 1994

James I (James VI of Scotland) 1566–1625

King of Scotland from 1567 and of England from 1603

9 No bishop, no King.
to a deputation of Presbyterians from the Church of Scotland, seeking religious tolerance in England
W. Barlow *Sum and Substance of the Conference* (1604)

10 The king is truly *parens patriae*, the polite father of his people.
speech to Parliament, 21 March 1610

11 The state of monarchy is the supremest thing upon earth; for kings are not only God's lieutenants upon earth, and sit upon God's throne, but even by God himself they are called gods.
speech to Parliament, 21 March 1610

1 That which concerns the mystery of the king's power is not lawful to be disputed; for that is to wade into the weakness of Princes and to take away the mystical reverence, that belongs unto them that sit in the throne of God.

'A Speech in the Star Chamber' [speech to the judges] 20 June 1616

2 I will govern according to the common weal, but not according to the common will.

in December, 1621; J. R. Green *History of the English People* vol. 3 (1879)

James V 1512–42

King of Scotland from 1513

of the crown of Scotland (which had come to the Stuarts through the female line), on learning of the birth of **Mary** *Queen of Scots, December 1542:*

3 It came with a lass, and it will pass with a lass.

Robert Lindsay of Pitscottie (*c.*1500–65) *History of Scotland* (1728)

Antony Jay see **Lynn** and **Jay**

Douglas Jay 1907–96

British Labour politician

4 In the case of nutrition and health, just as in the case of education, the gentleman in Whitehall really does know better what is good for people than the people know themselves.

The Socialist Case (1939)

5 Fair shares for all, is Labour's call.
slogan devised for the North Battersea by-election, 1946

Change and Fortune (1980)

Thomas Jefferson 1743–1826

American Democratic Republican statesman, 3rd President of the US 1801–9
on Jefferson: see **Adams** 4:4, **Kennedy** 205:1

6 We must therefore...hold them [the British] as we hold the rest of mankind, enemies in war, in peace friends.

Declaration of Independence 4 July 1776

7 When in the course of human events, it becomes necessary for one people to dissolve the political bonds which have connected them with another, and to assume among the powers of the earth the separate and equal station to which the laws of nature and of Nature's God entitle them, a decent respect to the opinions of mankind requires that they should declare the causes which impel them to the separation.

American Declaration of Independence, 4 July 1776 (preamble)

1 We hold these truths to be sacred and undeniable; that all men are created equal and independent, that from that equal creation they derive rights inherent and inalienable, among which are the preservation of life, and liberty, and the pursuit of happiness.
'Rough Draft' of the American Declaration of Independence; J. P. Boyd et al. *Papers of Thomas Jefferson* vol. 1 (1950)

2 Millions of innocent men, women, and children, since the introduction of Christianity, have been burnt, tortured, fined, imprisoned; yet we have not advanced one inch towards uniformity [of opinion]. What has been the effect of coercion? To make one half the world fools, and the other half hypocrites.
Notes on the State of Virginia (1781–5)

3 Indeed I tremble for my country when I reflect that God is just.
Notes on the State of Virginia (1781–5)

4 The basis of our government being the opinion of the people, the very first object should be to keep that right; and were it left to me to decide whether we should have a government without newspapers or newspapers without a government, I should not hesitate for a moment to prefer the latter.
letter to Colonel Edward Carrington, 16 January 1787

5 Experience declares that man is the only animal which devours its own kind, for I can apply no milder term to the governments of Europe, and to the general prey of the rich on the poor.
letter to Colonel Edward Carrington, 16 January 1787

6 A little rebellion now and then is a good thing.
letter to James Madison, 30 January 1787

7 The tree of liberty must be refreshed from time to time with the blood of patriots and tyrants. It is its natural manure.
letter to W. S. Smith, 13 November 1787

8 The natural progress of things is for liberty to yield and governments to gain ground.
letter to Colonel Edward Carrington, 27 May 1788

9 If I could not go to Heaven but with a party, I would not go there at all.
letter to Francis Hopkinson, 13 March 1789

10 The republican is the only form of government which is not eternally at open or secret war with the rights of mankind.
letter to William Hunter, 11 March 1790

11 We are not to expect to be translated from despotism to liberty in a featherbed.
letter to Lafayette, 2 April 1790

12 No government ought to be without censors: and where the press is free, no one ever will.
letter to George Washington, 9 September 1792

13 The second office of government is honourable and easy, the first is but a splendid misery.
letter to Elbridge Gerry, 13 May 1797

14 Offices are acceptable here as elsewhere, and whenever a man has cast a longing eye on them [official positions], a rottenness begins in his conduct.
letter to Tench Coxe, 21 May 1799

15 To the press alone, chequered as it is with abuses, the world is indebted for all the triumphs which have been gained by reason and humanity over error and oppression.
Virginia and Kentucky Resolutions (1799)

1 What an augmentation of the field for jobbing, speculating, plundering, office-building and office-hunting would be produced by an assumption of all the state powers into the hands of the general government.
letter 13 August 1800

2 If the principle were to prevail, of a common law [i.e. a single government] being in force in the U.S.... it would become the most corrupt government on the earth.
letter to Gideon Granger, 13 August 1800

3 Still one thing more, fellow citizens—a wise and frugal government, which shall restrain men from injuring one another, which shall leave them otherwise free to regulate their own pursuits of industry and improvement, and shall not take from the mouth of labour the bread it has earned. This is the sum of good government, and this is necessary to close the circle of our felicities.
first inaugural address, 4 March 1801

4 We are all Republicans—we are all Federalists. If there be any among us who would wish to dissolve this Union or to change its republican form, let them stand undisturbed as monuments of the safety with which error of opinion may be tolerated where reason is left free to combat it.
first inaugural address, 4 March 1801

5 All, too, will bear in mind this sacred principle, that though the will of the majority is in all cases to prevail, that will to be rightful must be reasonable; that the minority possess their equal rights, which equal law must protect, and to violate would be oppression.
first inaugural address, 4 March 1801

6 Would the honest patriot, in the full tide of successful experiment, abandon a government which has so far kept us free and firm?
first inaugural address, 4 March 1801

7 Peace, commerce, and honest friendship with all nations—entangling alliances with none.
first inaugural address, 4 March 1801

8 Freedom of religion; freedom of the press, and freedom of person under the protection of *habeas corpus*, and trial by juries impartially selected. These principles form the bright constellation which has gone before us, and guided our steps through an age of revolution and reformation.
first inaugural address, 4 March 1801

9 If a due participation of office is a matter of right, how are vacancies to be obtained? Those by death are few; by resignation none.
usually quoted as: 'Few die and none resign'
letter to E. Shipman and others, 12 July 1801

10 If we can prevent the government from wasting the labours of the people, under the pretence of taking care of them, they must become happy.
letter to Thomas Cooper, 29 November 1802

11 Whensoever hostile aggressions...require a resort to war, we must meet our duty and convince the world that we are just friends and brave enemies.
letter to Andrew Jackson, 3 December 1806

12 When a man assumes a public trust, he should consider himself as public property.
to Baron von Humboldt, 1807
B. L. Rayner *Life of Jefferson* (1834)

1 The care of human life and happiness, and not their destruction, is the first and only legitimate object of good government.
to the Republican Citizens of Washington County, Maryland, 31 March 1809

2 A strict observance of the written law is doubtless one of the high duties of a good citizen, but it is not the highest. The laws of necessity, of self-preservation, of saving our country when in danger, are of higher obligation.
letter to John B. Colvin, 20 September 1810

3 Politics, like religion, hold up the torches of martyrdom to the reformers of error.
letter to James Ogilvie, 4 August 1811

4 I agree with you that there is a natural aristocracy among men. The grounds of this are virtue and talents.
letter to John Adams, 28 October 1813

5 Merchants have no country. The mere spot they stand on does not constitute so strong an attachment as that from which they draw their gains.
letter to Horatio G. Spafford, 17 March 1814

6 If a nation expects to be ignorant and free, in a state of civilization, it expects what never was and never will be.
letter to Colonel Charles Yancey, 6 January 1816

7 But this momentous question [the Missouri Compromise], like a firebell in the night awakened and filled me with terror. I considered it the knell of the Union.
letter to John Holmes, 22 April 1820

8 I know no safe depository of the ultimate powers of the society but the people themselves; and if we think them not enlightened enough to exercise their control with a wholesome discretion, the remedy is not to take it from them, but to inform their discretion by education.
letter to William Charles Jarvis, 28 September 1820

9 We have the wolf by the ears; and we can neither hold him, nor safely let him go. Justice is in one scale, and self-preservation in the other.
on slavery
letter to John Holmes, 22 April 1820

10 That one hundred and fifty lawyers should do business together ought not to be expected.
on the United States Congress
Autobiography 6 January 1821

11 To attain all this [universal republicanism], however, rivers of blood must yet flow, and years of desolation pass over; yet the object is worth rivers of blood, and years of desolation.
letter to John Adams, 4 September 1823

12 The good old Dominion, the blessed mother of us all.
Thoughts on Lotteries (1826)

13 The legitimate powers of government extend to such acts only as are injurious to others. But it does me no injury for my neighbour to say there are twenty gods, or no God. It neither picks my pocket nor breaks my leg.
attributed

14 No duty the Executive had to perform was so trying as to put the right man in the right place.
J. B. MacMaster *History of the People of the United States* (1883–1913) vol. 2

15 The policy of the American government is to leave their citizens free, neither restraining nor aiding them in their pursuits.
attributed

16 Were we directed from Washington when to sow, and when to reap, we should soon want bread.
Autobiography

1 This is the Fourth?
last words
on 4 July 1826

Roy Jenkins 1920–

British politician; co-founder of the Social Democratic Party, 1981

of James **Callaghan**:

2 There is nobody in politics I can remember and no case I can think of in history where a man combined such a powerful political personality with so little intelligence.
Richard Crossman diary 5 September 1969

3 He simply stopped the engine in its tracks, lifted it up, and put it back facing in the other direction.
of Ernest **Bevin** *changing the course of a Cabinet meeting*
Roy Jenkins *Nine Men of Power* (1974)

4 The politics of the left and centre of this country are frozen in an out-of-date mould which is bad for the political and economic health of Britain and increasingly inhibiting for those who live within the mould. Can it be broken?
speech to Parliamentary Press Gallery, 9 June 1980

of the Labour Party:

5 A dead or dying beast lying across a railway line and preventing other trains from getting through.
in *Guardian* 16 May 1987

of Margaret **Thatcher**:

6 A First Minister whose self-righteous stubbornness has not been equalled, save briefly by Neville Chamberlain, since Lord North.
in *Observer* 11 March 1990

7 The record does not provide much sustenance for the view that limpet-like Prime Ministers can be easily disposed of by their parties.
in *Guardian* 14 April 1990

of Edward **Heath**:

8 A great lighthouse which stands there, flashing out beams of light, indifferent to the waves which beat against him.
in *Independent* 22 September 1990

Simon Jenkins 1943–

British political journalist

9 A belief in ever-rising crime seems to answer a deep social need: spurious proof that all bad news must be true. It is statistics as pornography.
in *Sunday Times* 22 March 1987

10 A truth not universally acknowledged is that every politician not in Government must needs be in Opposition.
interview with Margaret **Thatcher** in *The Times* 29 June 1991

W. Stanley Jevons 1835–82

English economist

11 All classes of society are trades unionists at heart, and differ chiefly in the boldness, ability, and secrecy with which they pursue their respective interests.
The State in Relation to Labour (1882)

John XXIII 1881–1963

Pope from 1958

1 If civil authorities legislate for or allow anything that is contrary to that order and therefore contrary to the will of God, neither the laws made or the authorizations granted can be binding on the consciences of the citizens, since God has more right to be obeyed than man.
Pacem in Terris (1963)

2 The social progress, order, security and peace of each country are necessarily connected with the social progress, order, security and peace of all other countries.
Pacem in Terris (1963)

3 [In the universal *Declaration of Human Rights* (December, 1948)] in most solemn form, the dignity of a person is acknowledged to all human beings; and as a consequence there is proclaimed, as a fundamental right, the right of free movement in search for truth and in the attainment of moral good and of justice, and also the right to a dignified life.
Pacem in Terris (1963)

Lyndon Baines Johnson 1908–73

American Democratic statesman, 36th President of the US 1963–9

on Johnson: see **White** 387:1

to a reporter who had queried his embracing Richard **Nixon** *on the vice-president's return from a controversial tour of South America in 1958:*

4 Son, in politics you've got to learn that overnight chicken shit can turn to chicken salad.
Fawn Brodie *Richard Nixon* (1983)

5 I am a free man, an American, a United States Senator, and a Democrat, in that order.
in *Texas Quarterly* Winter 1958

6 I'll tell you what's at the bottom of it. If you can convince the lowest white man that he's better than the best coloured man, he won't notice you're picking his pocket. Hell, give him someone to look down on and he'll empty his pockets for you.
during the 1960 Presidential campaign, to Bill Moyers
Robert Dallek *Lone Star Rising* (1991)

7 All I have I would have given gladly not to be standing here today.
following the assassination of J. F. **Kennedy**
first speech to Congress as President, 27 November 1963

8 We have talked long enough in this country about equal rights. We have talked for a hundred years or more. It is time now to write the next chapter, and to write it in the books of law.
speech to Congress, 27 November 1963

9 We hope that the world will not narrow into a neighbourhood before it has broadened into a brotherhood.
speech at the lighting of the Nation's Christmas Tree
on 22 December 1963

10 This administration, here and now declares unconditional war on poverty in America.
State of the Union address to Congress, 8 January 1964

1 For the first time in our history, it is possible to conquer poverty.
speech to Congress, 16 March 1964

2 In your time we have the opportunity to move not only toward the rich society and the powerful society, but upward to the Great Society.
speech at University of Michigan, 22 May 1964

3 We Americans know, although others appear to forget, the risks of spreading conflict. We still seek no wider war.
speech on radio and television, 4 August 1964

4 We are not about to send American boys 9 or 10,000 miles away from home to do what Asian boys ought to be doing for themselves.
speech at Akron University, 21 October 1964

5 Extremism in the pursuit of the Presidency is an unpardonable vice. Moderation in the affairs of the nation is the highest virtue.
speech in New York, 31 October 1964

6 A President's hardest task is not to *do* what is right, but to *know* what is right.
State of the Union address to Congress, 4 January 1965

7 It is not enough to open the gates of opportunity. All of our citizens must have the ability to walk through those gates.
speech at Harvard in 1965
Paul L. Fisher and Ralph L. Lavenstein (eds.) *Race and the News Media* (1967)

8 I don't want loyalty. I want *loyalty*. I want him to kiss my ass in Macy's window at high noon and tell me it smells like roses. I want his pecker in my pocket.
discussing a prospective assistant
David Halberstam *The Best and the Brightest* (1972)

9 Better to have him inside the tent pissing out, than outside pissing in.
of J. Edgar Hoover
David Halberstam *The Best and the Brightest* (1972)

10 So dumb he can't fart and chew gum at the same time.
of Gerald **Ford**
Richard Reeves *A Ford, not a Lincoln* (1975)

11 Come now, let us reason together.
habitual saying

12 Did you ever think that making a speech on economics is a lot like pissing down your leg? It seems hot to you, but it never does to anyone else.
to J. K. **Galbraith**
J. K. Galbraith *A Life in Our Times* (1981)

Paul Johnson 1928–

British journalist

13 Tories, in short, are atrophied Englishmen, lacking certain moral and intellectual reflexes. They are recognizable, homely—even, on occasions, endearing—but liable to turn very nasty at short notice.
in *New Statesman* 18 October 1958 'Rule Like Pigs'

Samuel Johnson 1709–84

English poet, critic, and lexicographer

14 Superfluous lags the vet'ran on the stage.
The Vanity of Human Wishes (1749)

1 This man [Lord Chesterfield] I thought had been a Lord among wits; but, I find, he is only a wit among Lords.

James Boswell *Life of Samuel Johnson* (1791) 1754

2 If the changes we fear be thus irresistible, what remains but to acquiesce with silence, as in the other insurmountable distresses of humanity? It remains that we retard what we cannot repel, that we palliate what we cannot cure.

A Dictionary of the English Language (1755) preface

3 *Pension*. Pay given to a state hireling for treason to his country.

A Dictionary of the English Language (1755)

4 Among the calamities of war may be jointly numbered the diminution of the love of truth, by the falsehoods which interest dictates and credulity encourages.

The Idler 11 November 1758; possibly the source, in essence, of 'When war is declared, Truth is the first casualty', epigraph to Arthur Ponsonby's *Falsehood in Wartime* (1928) (in this form, it has been attributed also to Hiram Johnson, speaking in the US Senate, 1918, but is not recorded in his speech)

5 In all pointed sentences, some degree of accuracy must be sacrificed to conciseness.

'The Bravery of the English Common Soldier' in *The British Magazine* January 1760

6 Liberty is, to the lowest rank of every nation, little more than the choice of working or starving.

'The Bravery of the English Common Soldier' in *The British Magazine* January 1760

7 How small of all that human hearts endure,
That part which laws or kings can cause or cure.

lines added to Oliver Goldsmith's *The Traveller* (1764); cf. **Goldsmith** 157:5

8 Your levellers wish to level *down* as far as themselves; but they cannot bear levelling *up* to themselves.

James Boswell *Life of Samuel Johnson* (1791) 21 July 1763

9 A woman's preaching is like a dog's walking on his hinder legs. It is not done well; but you are surprised to find it done at all.

James Boswell *Life of Samuel Johnson* (1791) 31 July 1763

10 BOSWELL: So, Sir, you laugh at schemes of political improvement.
JOHNSON: Why, Sir, most schemes of political improvement are very laughable things.

James Boswell *Life of Samuel Johnson* (1791) 26 October 1769

11 So many objections may be made to everything, that nothing can overcome them but the necessity of doing something.

James Boswell *Life of Samuel Johnson* (1791) 1770

12 A decent provision for the poor, is the true test of civilization.

James Boswell *Life of Samuel Johnson* (1791) 1770

13 I would not give half a guinea to live under one form of government rather than another. It is of no moment to the happiness of an individual.

James Boswell *Life of Samuel Johnson* (1791) 31 March 1772

14 I do not much like to see a Whig in any dress; but I hate to see a Whig in a parson's gown.

James Boswell *Journal of a Tour to the Hebrides* (1785) 24 September 1773

1 There are few ways in which a man can be more innocently employed than in getting money.
James Boswell *Life of Samuel Johnson* (1791) 27 March 1775

2 George the First knew nothing, and desired to know nothing; did nothing, and desired to do nothing; and the only good thing that is told of him is, that he wished to restore the crown to its hereditary successor.
James Boswell *Life of Samuel Johnson* (1791) 6 April 1775

3 Patriotism is the last refuge of a scoundrel.
James Boswell *Life of Samuel Johnson* (1791) 7 April 1775

4 Politics are now nothing more than means of rising in the world.
James Boswell *Life of Samuel Johnson* (1791) 18 April 1775

5 Every man who attacks my belief, diminishes in some degree my confidence in it, and therefore makes me uneasy; and I am angry with him who makes me uneasy.
James Boswell *Life of Samuel Johnson* (1791) 3 April 1776

6 It is better that some should be unhappy than that none should be happy, which would be the case in a general state of equality.
James Boswell *Life of Samuel Johnson* (1791) 7 April 1776

7 Though we cannot out-vote them we will out-argue them.
James Boswell *Life of Samuel Johnson* (1791) 3 April 1778

8 I have always said, the first Whig was the Devil.
James Boswell *Life of Samuel Johnson* (1791) 28 April 1778

9 How is it that we hear the loudest yelps for liberty among the drivers of negroes?
Taxation No Tyranny (1775)

10 A wise Tory and a wise Whig, I believe, will agree. Their principles are the same, though their modes of thinking are different.
James Boswell *Life of Samuel Johnson* (1791) May 1781; written statement given to Boswell

11 If a man were to go by chance at the same time with Burke under a shed, to shun a shower, he would say—'this is an extraordinary man.'
on Edmund **Burke**
James Boswell *Life of Samuel Johnson* (1791) 15 May 1784

12 Fox divided the kingdom with Caesar; so that it was a doubt whether the nation should be ruled by the sceptre of George III or the tongue of Fox.
on the Parliamentary defeat of Charles James **Fox**, *and the subsequent dissolution, in 1784*
in *Dictionary of National Biography*

13 Mankind are happier in a state of inequality and subordination. Were they to be in this pretty state of equality, they would soon degenerate into brutes.
attributed

Hanns Johst 1890–1978

German playwright

14 Whenever I hear the word culture... I release the safety-catch of my Browning!
often quoted as: 'Whenever I hear the word culture, I reach for my pistol!', and attributed to Hermann **Goering**
Schlageter (1933)

John Paul Jones 1747–92

American admiral

1 I have not yet begun to fight.
as his ship was sinking, 23 September 1779, having been asked whether he had lowered his flag
Mrs Reginald De Koven *Life and Letters of John Paul Jones* (1914) vol. 1

William Jones 1746–94

English jurist

2 My opinion is, that power should always be distrusted, in whatever hands it is placed.
letter to Lord Althorpe, 5 October 1782

Ben Jonson *c.*1573–1637

English playwright and poet

3 PEOPLE: The Voice of Cato is the voice of Rome.
CATO: The voice of Rome is the consent of heaven!
Catiline his Conspiracy (1611)

Barbara Jordan

American Democratic politician

4 The Bill of Rights was not ordained by nature or God. It's very human, very fragile.
in *New York Times Magazine* 21 October 1990

Thomas Jordan *c.*1612–85

English poet and playwright

5 They plucked communion tables down
And broke our painted glasses;
They threw our altars to the ground
And tumbled down the crosses.
They set up Cromwell and his heir—
The Lord and Lady Claypole—
Because they hated Common Prayer,
The organ and the maypole.
'How the War began' (1664)

Keith Joseph 1918–94

British Conservative politician

6 Problems reproduce themselves from generation to generation . . . I refer to this as a 'cycle of deprivation'.
speech in London to the Pre-School Playgroups Association, 29 June 1972

7 We [the Conservative Party] found it hard to avoid the feeling that somehow the lean and tight-lipped mufflered men in the 1930s dole queue were at least partly our fault.
reflection occasioned by the national euphoria in 1945 on the outcome of the Second World War
Peter Jenkins *Mrs Thatcher's Revolution* (1987)

1 People who could not tell a lathe from a lawn mower and have never carried the responsibilities of management never tire of telling British management off for its alleged inefficiency.
in *The Times* 9 August 1974

2 Incomes policy alone as a way to abate inflation caused by excessive money supply is like trying to stop water coming out of a leaky hose without turning off the tap.
speech at Preston, 5 September 1974

3 The balance of our population, our human stock, is threatened... a high and rising proportion of children are being born to mothers least fitted to bring children into the world and bring them up.
speech in Birmingham, 19 October 1974

4 If we are to be prosperous we need more millionaires and more bankrupts.
maiden speech in the House of Lords, 19 February 1988

5 There are no illegitimate children, only illegitimate parents.
in Kiss Hollywood Good-Bye *(1978), Anita Loos attributes an earlier coinage of this statement to the American philanthropist Edna Gladney*
speech to National Children's Home, 6 November 1991

Joseph Joubert 1754–1824

French essayist and moralist

6 One of the surest ways of killing a tree is to lay bare its roots. It is the same with institutions. We must not be too ready to disinter the origins of those we wish to preserve. All beginnings are small.
Pensées (1842)

7 It's better to debate a question without settling it than to settle a question without debating it.
attributed

William Joyce ('Lord Haw-Haw') 1906–46

Fascist supporter and wartime broadcaster from Nazi Germany; executed for treason in 1946

8 Germany calling! Germany calling!
habitual introduction to propaganda broadcast
broadcasts from Germany to Britain during the Second World War

'Junius'

18th-century pseudonymous writer, probably Philip Francis (1740–1818)

9 The right of election is the very essence of the constitution.
in *Public Advertiser* 24 April 1769, letter 11

10 Is this the wisdom of a great minister? or is it the ominous vibration of a pendulum?
in *Public Advertiser* 30 May 1769, letter 12

11 There is a holy mistaken zeal in politics as well as in religion. By persuading others, we convince ourselves.
in *Public Advertiser* 19 December 1769, letter 35

12 However distinguished by rank or property, in the rights of freedom we are all equal.
in *Public Advertiser* 19 March 1770, letter 37

1 The injustice done to an individual is sometimes of service to the public.
in *Public Advertiser* 14 November 1770, letter 41

2 As for Mr Wedderburne, there is something about him, which even treachery cannot trust.
in *Public Advertiser* 22 June 1771, letter 49

3 The liberty of the press is the *Palladium* of all the civil, political, and religious rights of an Englishman.
The Letters of Junius (1772 ed.) 'Dedication to the English Nation'

John Junor 1919–

British journalist

4 Such a graceful exit. And then he had to go and do this on the doorstep.
on Harold **Wilson***'s 'Lavender List', the honours list he drew up on resigning the British premiership in 1976*
in *Observer* 23 January 1990

Juvenal AD 483–565

Roman satirist

5 Who would put up with the Gracchi complaining about subversion?
referring to the Roman tribune Tiberius Sempronius Gracchus (163–133 BC) and his brother Gaius Sempronius Gracchus (c.153–121 BC), who were responsible for radical social and economic legislation, passed against the wishes of the senatorial class
Satires

6 *Sed quis custodiet ipsos*
Custodes?
But who is to guard the guards themselves?
Satires

7 A huge wordy letter came from Capri.
on the Emperor Tiberius's letter to the Senate, which caused the downfall of Sejanus in AD 31
Satires

8 Only two things does he [the modern citizen] anxiously wish for—bread and circuses.
Satires

Franz Kafka 1883–1924

Czech novelist

9 It's often better to be in chains than to be free.
The Trial (1925)

Nicholas Kaldor 1908–86

British economist

10 There is no need for the economist to prove...that as a result of the adoption of a certain measure nobody is going to suffer. In order to establish his case, it is quite sufficient for him to show that even if all those who suffer as a result are fully compensated for their loss, the rest of the community will still be better off than before.
'Welfare Propositions of Economics' in *Economic Journal* September 1939

Immanuel Kant 1724–1804

German philosopher

1 Out of the crooked timber of humanity no straight thing was ever made.

Idee zu einer allgemeinen Geschichte in weltbürgerliche Absicht (1784)

2 There is, therefore, only one categorical imperative. It is: Act only according to that maxim by which you can at the same time will that it should become a universal law.

Fundamental Principles of the Metaphysics of Ethics (1785)

Gerald Kaufman 1930–

British Labour politician

3 Cabinet minutes are studied in Government Departments with the reverence generally reserved for sacred texts, and can be triumphantly produced conclusively to settle any arguments.

How to be a Minister (1980)

4 The longest suicide note in history.

on the Labour Party's New Hope for Britain *(1983)*

Denis Healey *The Time of My Life* (1989)

John Keane 1949–

Australian political scientist

5 Sovereign state power is an indispensable condition of the democratization of civil society... a more democratic order cannot be built *through* state power, it cannot be built *without* state power.

Democracy and Civil Society (1988)

Paul Keating 1944–

Australian Labor statesman; Prime Minister 1991–6

6 You look like an Easter Island statue with an arse full of razor blades.

in the Australian Parliament to the then Prime Minister, Malcolm Fraser

Michael Gordon *A Question of Leadership* (1993)

7 Even as it [Great Britain] walked out on you and joined the Common Market, you were still looking for your MBEs and your knighthoods, and all the rest of the regalia that comes with it. You would take Australia right back down the time tunnel to the cultural cringe where you have always come from.

addressing Australian Conservative supporters of Great Britain in the Australian Parliament, 27 February 1992

in *House of Representatives Weekly Hansard* [Australia] (1992) no. 1

8 These are the same old fogies who doffed their lids and tugged the forelock to the British establishment.

of Australian Conservative supporters of Great Britain, 27 February 1992

in *House of Representatives Weekly Hansard* [Australia] (1992) no. 1

9 This little flower, this delicate little beauty, this cream puff, is supposed to be beyond personal criticism... He is

attributed

simply a shiver looking for a spine to run up.
of the then Australian Liberal leader, John Hewson

1 I'm a bastard. But I'm a bastard who gets the mail through. And they appreciate that.
in 1994, to a senior colleague
in *Sunday Telegraph* 20 November 1994

2 Leadership is not about being nice. It's about being right and being strong.
in *Time* 9 January 1995

Garrison Keillor 1942–

American writer

3 Ronald Reagan, the President who never told bad news to the American people.
We Are Still Married (1989), introduction

4 My ancestors were Puritans from England. They arrived here in 1648 in the hope of finding greater restrictions than were permissible under English law at that time.
attributed, 1993

George F. Kennan 1904–

American diplomat and historian

5 There is no political or ideological difference between the Soviet Union and the United States—nothing which either side would like, or would hope, to achieve at the expense of the other—that would be worth the risks and sacrifices of a military encounter.
The Cloud of Danger (1977)

6 A war regarded as inevitable or even probable, and therefore much prepared for, has a very good chance of being eventually fought.
The Cloud of Danger (1977)

7 Government...is simply not the channel through which men's noblest impulses are to be realized. Its task, on the contrary, is largely to see to it that the ignoble ones are kept under restraint and not permitted to go too far.
Around the Cragged Hill (1993)

John F. Kennedy 1917–63

American Democratic statesman, 35th President of the US 1961–3, son of Joseph and Rose **Kennedy** and brother of Robert **Kennedy**

on Kennedy: see **Bentsen** 38:3, **Hope** 183:2, **Kennedy** 206:1, **Stevenson** 350:13

8 Don't buy a single vote more than necessary. I'll be damned if I'm going to pay for a landslide.
telegraphed message from his father, read at a Gridiron dinner in Washington, 15 March 1958, and almost certainly JFK's invention
J. F. Cutler *Honey Fitz* (1962)

9 We stand today on the edge of a new frontier...But the New Frontier of which I speak is not a set of promises—it is a set of challenges. It sums up not what I intend to offer the American people, but what I intend to ask of
speech in Los Angeles, 15 July 1960

them.
accepting the Democratic nomination

1 I am not the Catholic candidate for President. I am the Democratic Party's candidate for President, who happens also to be a Catholic.
speech to Greater Houston Ministerial Association, 12 September 1960

2 Let the word go forth from this time and place, to friend and foe alike, that the torch has been passed to a new generation of Americans—born in this century, tempered by war, disciplined by a hard and bitter peace, proud of our ancient heritage—and unwilling to witness or permit the slow undoing of those human rights to which this nation has always been committed, and to which we are committed today at home and around the world.
Let every nation know, whether it wishes us well or ill, that we shall pay any price, bear any burden, meet any hardship, support any friend, oppose any foe to assure the survival and the success of liberty.
inaugural address, 20 January 1961

3 If a free society cannot help the many who are poor, it cannot save the few who are rich.
inaugural address, 20 January 1961

4 Let us never negotiate out of fear. But let us never fear to negotiate.
inaugural address, 20 January 1961

5 All this will not be finished in the first 100 days. Nor will it be finished in the first 1,000 days, nor in the life of this Administration, nor even perhaps in our lifetime on this planet. But let us begin.
inaugural address, 20 January 1961

6 Now the trumpet summons us again—not as a call to bear arms, though arms we need—not as a call to battle, though embattled we are—but a call to bear the burden of a long twilight struggle, year in and year out, 'rejoicing in hope, patient in tribulation'—a struggle against the common enemies of man: tyranny, poverty, disease and war itself.
inaugural address, 20 January 1961

7 And so, my fellow Americans: ask not what your country can do for you—ask what you can do for your country. My fellow citizens of the world: ask not what America will do for you, but what together we can do for the freedom of man.
inaugural address, 20 January 1961; Oliver Wendell **Holmes** Jr., speaking at Keene, New Hampshire, 30 May 1884 said: 'We pause to . . . recall what our country has done for each of us and to ask ourselves what we can do for our country in return'

8 I believe that this Nation should commit itself to achieving the goal, before this decade is out, of landing a man on the Moon and returning him safely to earth.
supplementary State of the Union message to Congress, 25 May 1961

9 When we got into office, the thing that surprised me most was to find that things were just as bad as we'd been saying they were.
speech at the White House, 27 May 1961

10 Mankind must put an end to war or war will put an end to mankind.
speech to United Nations General Assembly, 25 September 1961

11 Those who make peaceful revolution impossible will make violent revolution inevitable.
speech at the White House, 13 March 1962

1 Probably the greatest concentration of talent and genius in this house except for perhaps those times when Thomas Jefferson ate alone.
of a dinner for the Nobel prizewinners at the White House
in *New York Times* 30 April 1962

2 My father always told me that all businessmen were sons of bitches, but I never believed it till now.
on the price increases proposed by US Steel
in April 1962

3 Liberty without learning is always in peril and learning without liberty is always in vain.
said on the ninetieth anniversary of Vanderbilt University, 18 March 1963

4 If we cannot end now our differences, at least we can help make the world safe for diversity.
address at American University, Washington, DC, 10 June 1963

5 No one has been barred on account of his race from fighting or dying for America—there are no 'white' or 'coloured' signs on the foxholes or graveyards of battle.
message to Congress on proposed Civil Rights Bill, 19 June 1963

speaking in the then newly divided city of West Berlin:
6 All free men, wherever they may live, are citizens of Berlin, and therefore, as a free man, I take pride in the words *Ich bin ein Berliner* [I am a Berliner].
in 1963, expressing the USA's commitment to the support and defence of West Berlin (it was later the cause of some hilarity, as ein Berliner *is the German name for a doughnut)*
speech in West Berlin, 26 June 1963

7 Yesterday, a shaft of light cut into the darkness... For the first time, an agreement has been reached on bringing the forces of nuclear destruction under international control.
television address in Washington, 26 July 1963

8 When power leads man toward arrogance, poetry reminds him of his limitations. When power narrows the areas of man's concern, poetry reminds him of the richness and diversity of his existence. When power corrupts, poetry cleanses. For art establishes the basic human truths which must serve as the touchstone of our judgement.
speech at Amherst College, Massachusetts, 26 October 1963

9 In free society art is not a weapon... Artists are not engineers of the soul.
speech at Amherst College, Massachusetts, 26 October 1963

10 I'm an idealist without illusions.
attributed; cf. **Macleod** 243:4

on being asked how he became a war hero:
11 It was involuntary. They sank my boat.
Arthur M. Schlesinger Jr. *A Thousand Days* (1965)

12 Washington is a city of southern efficiency and northern charm.
Arthur M. Schlesinger Jr. *A Thousand Days* (1965)

Joseph P. Kennedy 1888–1969

American financier and diplomat; father of John Fitzgerald **Kennedy** and Robert **Kennedy**; husband of Rose **Kennedy**

13 This is a hell of a long way from East Boston.
to his wife Rose, on a visit to Windsor Castle two weeks after his arrival as Ambassador
in *The Times* 24 January 1995 (obituary of Rose **Kennedy**)

1 We're going to sell Jack like soapflakes.
when his son John F. **Kennedy** *made his bid for the Presidency*
John H. Davis *The Kennedy Clan* (1984)

2 When the going gets tough, the tough get going.
J. H. Cutler *Honey Fitz* (1962); also attributed to Knute Rockne

Robert F. Kennedy 1925–68

American democratic politician; son of Joseph and Rose **Kennedy** and brother of John Fitzgerald **Kennedy**

3 About one-fifth of the people are against everything all the time.
speech at University of Pennsylvania, 6 May 1964

Rose Kennedy 1890–1995

wife of Joseph **Kennedy**, mother of John Fitzgerald and Robert **Kennedy**

4 It's our money, and we're free to spend it any way we please...If you have money you spend it, and win.
in response to criticism of overlavish funding of her son Robert **Kennedy***'s 1968 presidential campaign*
in *Daily Telegraph* 24 January 1995 (obituary)

5 Now Teddy must run.
to her daughter, on hearing of the assassination of Robert **Kennedy**
in *The Times* 24 January 1995 (obituary); attributed, perhaps apocryphal

Jomo Kenyatta 1891–1978

Kenyan statesman, Prime Minister of Kenya 1963 and President 1964–78

6 The African is conditioned, by the cultural and social institutions of centuries, to a freedom of which Europe has little conception, and it is not in his nature to accept serfdom forever. He realizes that he must fight unceasingly for his own emancipation; for without this he is doomed to remain the prey of rival imperialisms.
Facing Mount Kenya (1938); conclusion

Philip Henry Kerr, Lord Lothian

1882–1940

British journalist and politician, ambassador to the United States from 1939

of German troops re-entering the Rhineland in 1936:

7 After all, they are only going into their own back garden.
A. Lentin *Lloyd George, Woodrow Wilson and the Guilt of Germany* (1984)

8 If you back us you won't be backing a quitter.
address to the American people, read for him on the day before his death
in *Dictionary of National Biography*

Francis Scott Key 1779–1843

American lawyer and verse-writer

1 'Tis the star-spangled banner; O long may it wave
O'er the land of the free, and the home of the brave!
'The Star-Spangled Banner' (1814)

John Maynard Keynes 1883–1946

English economist

2 I work for a Government I despise for ends I think criminal.
letter to Duncan Grant, 15 December 1917

of **Clemenceau**:

3 He felt about France what Pericles felt of Athens—unique value in her, nothing else mattering; but his theory of politics was Bismarck's. He had one illusion—France; and one disillusion—mankind, including Frenchmen, and his colleagues not least.
The Economic Consequences of the Peace (1919)

4 Like Odysseus, the President looked wiser when he was seated.
of Woodrow **Wilson**
The Economic Consequences of the Peace (1919)

5 Lenin was right. There is no subtler, no surer means of overturning the existing basis of society than to debauch the currency. The process engages all the hidden forces of economic law on the side of destruction, and does it in a manner which not one man in a million is able to diagnose.
The Economic Consequences of the Peace (1919)

6 But this *long run* is a misleading guide to current affairs. *In the long run* we are all dead.
A Tract on Monetary Reform (1923)

7 Capitalism, wisely managed, can probably be made more efficient for attaining economic ends than any alternative system yet in sight, but...in itself it is in many ways extremely objectionable.
The End of Laissez-Faire (1926)

8 Marxian Socialism must always remain a portent to the historians of Opinion—how a doctrine so illogical and so dull can have exercised so powerful and enduring an influence over the minds of men, and, through them, the events of history.
The End of Laissez-Faire (1926)

9 I do not know which makes a man more conservative—to know nothing but the present, or nothing but the past.
The End of Laissez-Faire (1926)

10 The important thing for Government is not to do things which individuals are doing already, and to do them a little better or a little worse; but to do those things which at present are not done at all.
The End of Laissez-Faire (1926)

of **Lloyd George**:

11 This extraordinary figure of our time, this syren, this goat-footed bard, this half-human visitor to our age from the hag-ridden magic and enchanted woods of Celtic antiquity.
Essays in Biography (1933) 'Mr Lloyd George'

of **Lloyd George**:

1 Who shall paint the chameleon, who can tether a broomstick?

Essays and Biography (1933) 'Mr Lloyd George'

2 It is better that a man should tyrannize over his bank balance than over his fellow-citizens.

General Theory (1936)

3 We take it as a fundamental psychological rule of any modern community that, when its real income is increased, it will not increase its consumption by an equal *absolute* amount.

General Theory (1936)

4 If the Treasury were to fill old bottles with banknotes, bury them at suitable depths in disused coalmines which are then filled up to the surface with town rubbish, and leave it to private enterprise on well-tried principles of *laissez-faire* to dig the notes up again (the right to do so being obtained, of course, by tendering for leases of the note-bearing territory) there need be no more unemployment and, with the help of the repercussions, the real income of the community, and its capital wealth also, would probably become a good deal greater than it actually is. It would, indeed, be more sensible to build houses and the like; but as there are political and practical difficulties in the way of this, the above would be better than nothing.

General Theory (1936)

5 I evidently knew more about economics than my examiners.

explaining why he performed badly in the Civil Service examinations

Roy Harrod *Life of John Maynard Keynes* (1951)

6 The ideas of economists and political philosophers, both when they are right and when they are wrong, are more powerful than is commonly understood... Practical men, who believe themselves to be quite exempt from any intellectual influences, are usually the slaves of some defunct economist. Madmen in authority, who hear voices in the air, are distilling their frenzy from some academic scribbler of a few years back.

General Theory (1947 ed.)

7 We threw good housekeeping to the winds. But we saved ourselves and helped save the world.

of Britain in the Second World War

A. J. P. Taylor *English History, 1914–1945* (1965)

8 LADY VIOLET BONHAM CARTER: What do you think happens to Mr Lloyd George when he is alone in the room?
MAYNARD KEYNES: When he is alone in the room there is nobody there.

Lady Violet Bonham Carter *The Impact of Personality in Politics* (Romanes Lecture, 1963)

Ayatollah Ruhollah Khomeini 1900–89

Iranian Shiite Muslim leader, who returned to Iran from exile in 1979 to lead an Islamic revolution which overthrew the Shah

9 If laws are needed, Islam has established them all.There is no need... after establishing a government, to sit down and draw up laws.

Islam and Revolution: Writings and Declarations of Imam Khomeini (1981) 'Islamic Government'

Nikita Khrushchev 1894–1971

Soviet statesman; Premier, 1958–64

1 If anyone believes that our smiles involve abandonment of the teaching of Marx, Engels and Lenin he deceives himself. Those who wait for that must wait until a shrimp learns to whistle.
speech in Moscow, 17 September 1955

2 We must abolish the cult of the individual decisively, once and for all.
speech to secret session of the 20th Congress of the Communist Party, 25 February 1956

3 We say this not only for the socialist states, who are more akin to us. We base ourselves on the idea that we must peacefully co-exist. About the capitalist States, it doesn't depend on you whether or not we exist. If you don't like us, don't accept our invitations and don't invite us to come to see you. Whether you like it or not, history is on our side. We will bury you.
in *The Times* 19 November 1956

speech to Western diplomats at reception in Moscow for Polish leader Mr Gomulka, 18 November 1956; 'We will bury you' in this context means 'we will outlive you'

4 If one cannot catch the bird of paradise, better take a wet hen.
in *Time* 6 January 1958

5 We are going to make the imperialists dance like fishes in a saucepan, even without war.
in Vienna, 2 July 1960

6 Politicians are the same all over. They promise to build a bridge where there is no river.
at a press conference in New York, October 1960

7 If you start throwing hedgehogs under me, I shall throw a couple of porcupines under you.
in *New York Times* 7 November 1963

8 Anyone who believes that the worker can be lulled by fine revolutionary phrases is mistaken...If no concern is shown for the growth of material and spiritual riches, the people will listen today, they will listen tomorrow, and then they may say: 'Why do you promise us everything for the future? You are talking, so to speak, about life beyond the grave. The priest has already told us about this.'
speech at World Youth Forum, 19 September 1964

David Maxwell Fyfe, Lord Kilmuir

1900–67

British Conservative politician and lawyer

on Kilmuir: see **Anonymous** 12:8

9 Loyalty is the Tory's secret weapon.
Anthony Sampson *Anatomy of Britain* (1962); cf. **Critchley** 104:9

10 Gratitude is not a normal feature of political life.
Political Adventure (1964)

Edward King 1829–1910

English clergyman, the first Professor of Pastoral Theology at Oxford

1 I have been voting against Gladstone all my life, and now he makes me a bishop.
view of a staunch Conservative on being appointed Bishop of Lincoln in 1885
in *Dictionary of National Biography*

Martin Luther King 1929–68

American civil rights leader

2 I want to be the white man's brother, not his brother-in-law.
in *New York Journal-American* 10 September 1962

3 If we assume that mankind has a right to survive, then we must find an alternative to war and destruction. In our day of space vehicles and guided ballistic missiles, the choice is either nonviolence or nonexistence.
Strength to Love (1963)

4 Jesus eloquently affirmed from the cross a higher law. He knew that the old eye-for-an-eye philosophy would leave everyone blind. He did not seek to overcome evil with evil. He overcame evil with good.
Strength to Love (1963)

5 Nothing in all the world is more dangerous than sincere ignorance and conscientious stupidity.
Strength to Love (1963)

6 The ultimate measure of a man is not where he stands in moments of comfort and convenience, but where he stands at times of challenge and controversy.
Strength to Love (1963)

7 Injustice anywhere is a threat to justice everywhere.
letter from Birmingham Jail, Alabama, 16 April 1963

8 The Negro's great stumbling block in the stride toward freedom is not the White Citizens Councillor or the Ku Klux Klanner but the white moderate who is more devoted to order than to justice; who prefers a negative peace which is the absence of tension to a positive peace which is the presence of justice.
letter from Birmingham Jail, Alabama, 16 April 1963

9 I submit to you that if a man hasn't discovered something he will die for, he isn't fit to live.
speech in Detroit, 23 June 1963

10 I have a dream that one day on the red hills of Georgia the sons of former slaves and the sons of former slave owners will be able to sit down together at the table of brotherhood...

I have a dream that my four little children will one day live in a nation where they will not be judged by the colour of their skin but by the content of their character.
speech at Civil Rights March in Washington, 28 August 1963

11 When we let freedom ring, when we let it ring from every village and every hamlet, from every state and every city, we will be able to speed up that day when all of God's children, black men and white men, Jews and Gentiles, Protestants and Catholics, will be able to join hands and sing in the words of the old Negro spiritual,
speech at Civil Rights March in Washington, 28 August 1963

'Free at last! Free at last! Thank God Almighty, we are free at last!'

1 The means by which we live have outdistanced the ends for which we live. Our scientific power has outrun our spiritual power. We have guided missiles and misguided men.

Strength to Love (1963)

2 We must learn to live together as brothers or perish together as fools.

speech at St Louis, 22 March 1964

3 A riot is at bottom the language of the unheard.

Where Do We Go From Here? (1967)

4 I just want to do God's will. And he's allowed me to go up to the mountain. And I've looked over, and I've seen the promised land...So I'm happy tonight. I'm not worried about anything. I'm not fearing any man.

speech in Memphis, 3 April 1968, the day before his assassination

in *New York Times* 4 April 1968

David Kingsley, Dennis Lyons, and Peter Lovell-Davis

5 Yesterday's men (they failed before!).

advertising slogan for the Labour Party, referring to the Conservatives

David Butler and Michael Pinto-Duschinsky *The British General Election of 1970* (1971)

Hugh Kingsmill 1889–1949

English man of letters

6 A nation is only at peace when it's at war.

attributed

Neil Kinnock 1942–

British Labour politician; Leader of the Labour Party 1983–92

7 Loyalty is a fine quality but in excess it fills political graveyards.

in June 1976, in opposition to Conference decisions on devolution

G. M. F. Drower *Neil Kinnock* (1984)

8 They want a kindly capitalism, a gentle market economy, an air-conditioned jungle.

of the Council for Social Democracy

in *Guardian* 6 February 1981

of servicemen in the Falklands War, when replying to a heckler who said that Mrs **Thatcher** *'showed guts':*

9 It's a pity others had to leave theirs on the ground at Goose Green to prove it.

television interview, 6 June 1983

10 If Margaret Thatcher wins on Thursday, I warn you not to be ordinary, I warn you not to be young, I warn you not to fall ill, and I warn you not to grow old.

on the prospect of a Conservative re-election

speech at Bridgend, 7 June 1983

11 The grotesque chaos of a Labour council hiring taxis to scuttle round the city handing out redundancy notices to

speech at the Labour Party Conference, 1 October 1985

its own workers.
of the actions of the Labour city council in Liverpool

1 I would die for my country but I could never let my country die for me. — speech at Labour Party Conference, 30 September 1986

2 Why am I the first Kinnock in a thousand generations to be able to get to university? — speech at Llandudno, 15 May 1987
later plagiarized by the American politician Joe Biden

3 There are lots of ways to get socialism, but I think trying to fracture the Labour party by incessant contest cannot be one of them. — in *Guardian* 29 January 1988

4 I don't think anyone could accuse someone who has been leader of the Labour party for more than seven years of being impulsive. — in *Sunday Times* 5 August 1990

5 I'm not going to be bloody kebabbed by you. — in *Sunday Times* 14 October 1990
when being interviewed by James Naughtie (the comment was not broadcast, but became widely known through unofficial circulation)

Rudyard Kipling 1865–1936

English writer and poet, cousin of Stanley **Baldwin**

6 Oh, East is East, and West is West, and never the twain
shall meet.
— 'The Ballad of East and West' (1892)

7 Winds of the World, give answer! They are whimpering
to and fro—
And what should they know of England who only
England know?—
The poor little street-bred people that vapour and fume
and brag.
— 'The English Flag' (1892)

8 Ship me somewheres east of Suez, where the best is like
the worst,
Where there aren't no Ten Commandments an' a man
can raise a thirst.
— 'Mandalay' (1892)

9 Now this is the Law of the Jungle—as old and as true as
the sky;
And the Wolf that shall keep it may prosper, but the
Wolf that shall break it must die.
— 'The Law of the Jungle' (1895)

10 We have fed our sea for a thousand years
And she calls us, still unfed,
Though there's never a wave of all her waves
But marks our English dead:
We have strawed our best to the weed's unrest
To the shark and sheering gull.
If blood be the price of admiralty,
Lord God, we ha' paid in full!
— 'The Song of the Dead' (1896)

11 God of our fathers, known of old,
Lord of our far-flung battle-line,
Beneath whose awful Hand we hold
Dominion over palm and pine—
Lord God of Hosts, be with us yet,
— 'Recessional' (1897)

Lest we forget—lest we forget!

The tumult and the shouting dies—
The captains and the kings depart—
Still stands Thine ancient Sacrifice,
An humble and a contrite heart.
Lord God of Hosts, be with us yet,
Lest we forget—lest we forget!

1 A Nation spoke to a Nation,
A Throne sent word to a Throne:
'Daughter am I in my mother's house,
But mistress in my own.
The gates are mine to open,
As the gates are mine to close,
And I abide by my Mother's House.'
Said our Lady of the Snows.

'Our Lady of the Snows' (1898)

2 Take up the White Man's burden—
Send forth the best ye breed—
Go, bind your sons to exile
To serve your captives' need.

'The White Man's Burden' (1899)

3 If you can keep your head when all about you
Are losing theirs and blaming it on you;
If you can trust yourself when all men doubt you,
But make allowance for their doubting too;
If you can wait and not be tired by waiting,
Or being lied about, don't deal in lies,
Or being hated, don't give way to hating,
And yet don't look too good, nor talk too wise;
If you can dream—and not make dreams your master;
If you can think—and not make thoughts your aim,
If you can meet with triumph and disaster
And treat those two imposters just the same...

'If—' (1910)

4 It is always a temptation to a rich and lazy nation,
To puff and look important and to say:-
'Though we know we should defeat you, we have not
the time to meet you,
We will therefore pay you cash to go away.'

And that is called paying the Dane-geld;
But we've proved it again and again,
That if once you have paid him the Dane-geld
You never get rid of the Dane.

'What Dane-geld means' (1911)

5 All Power, each Tyrant, every Mob
Whose head has grown too large,
Ends by destroying its own job
And works its own discharge.

'The Benefactors' (1919)

6 I could not dig: I dared not rob:
Therefore I lied to please the mob.
Now all my lies are proved untrue
And I must face the men I slew.
What tale shall serve me here among
Mine angry and defrauded young?

'Epitaphs of the War: A Dead Statesman' (1919)

1 Power without responsibility: the prerogative of the harlot throughout the ages. — in *Kipling Journal* December 1971

summing up Lord **Beaverbrook**'*s political standpoint* vis-à-vis *the* Daily Express, *after he had said to Kipling, 'What I want is power. Kiss 'em one day and kick 'em the next'; Stanley* **Baldwin**, *Kipling's cousin, subsequently obtained permission to use the phrase in a speech in London on 18 March 1931*

Henry Kissinger 1923–

American politician

2 There cannot be a crisis next week. My schedule is already full. — in *New York Times Magazine* 1 June 1969

3 Power is the great aphrodisiac. — in *New York Times* 19 January 1971

4 We are the President's men and we must behave accordingly. — M. and B. Kalb *Kissinger* (1974)

5 The illegal we do immediately. The unconstitutional takes a little longer. — in *Washington Post* 20 January 1977; attributed

6 Ninety percent of the politicians give the other ten percent a bad name. — in 1978, attributed

7 History knows no resting places and no plateaus. — *White House Years* (1979)

8 The management of a balance of power is a permanent undertaking, not an exertion that has a foreseeable end. — *White House Years* (1979)

9 An Iranian moderate is one who has run out of ammunition. — in *Today* 23 July 1987

10 History has so far shown us only two roads to international stability: domination and equilibrium. — in *The Times* 12 March 1991

11 For other nations, Utopia is a blessed past never to be recovered; for Americans it is just beyond the horizon. — attributed

12 For [Woodrow] Wilson, the justification of America's international role was messianic: America had an obligation not to the balance of power, but to spread its principles throughout the world. — *Diplomacy* (1994)

13 It combined legitimacy and equilibrium, shared values, and balance-of-power diplomacy. Common values restrained the scope of nations' demands while equilibrium limited the capacity to insist upon them. — *Diplomacy* (1994)

of the Congress of Vienna

14 The main advantage of being famous is that when you bore people at dinner parties they think it is their fault. — James Naughtie in *Spectator* 1 April 1995; attributed

Lord Kitchener 1850–1916

British soldier and politician

on Kitchener: see **Asquith** 18:10, **Lloyd George** 231:1

15 You are ordered abroad as a soldier of the King to help our French comrades against the invasion of a common enemy... In this new experience you may find — in *The Times* 19 August 1914

temptations both in wine and women. You must entirely resist both temptations, and, while treating all women with perfect courtesy, you should avoid any intimacy. Do your duty bravely. Fear God. Honour the King.
message to soldiers of the British Expeditionary Force (1914)

1 I don't mind your being killed, but I object to your being taken prisoner.
to the Prince of Wales (later **Edward VIII***) on his asking to be allowed to the Front during the First World War*
in *Journals and Letters of Reginald Viscount Esher* vol. 3 (1938) 18 December 1914

Philander C. Knox 1853–1921

US Attorney-General

Theodore **Roosevelt** *had requested a legal justification for his acquisition of the Panama Canal:*

2 Oh, Mr. President, do not let so great an achievement suffer from any taint of legality.
Tyler Dennett *John Hay: From Poetry to Politics* (1933)

Helmut Kohl 1930–

Chancellor of West Germany (1982–90) and first postwar Chancellor of united Germany (1990–)

3 I have been underestimated for decades. I have done very well that way.
in *New York Times* 25 January 1987

4 My goal, when the historical hour allows it, is the unity of the nation.
to crowds in Dresden on the occasion of his first official visit to East Germany, 19 December 1989
in *The Times* 20 December 1989

5 We Germans now have the historic chance to realize the unity of our fatherland.
in *Guardian* 15 February 1990

Paul Kruger 1825–1904

South African soldier and statesman

6 A bill of indemnity...for raid by Dr Jameson and the British South Africa Company's troops. The amount falls under two heads—first, material damage, total of claim, £677,938 3*s.* 3*d.*—second, moral or intellectual damage, total of claim, £1,000,000.
telegram from the South African Republic, communicated to the House of Commons by Joseph **Chamberlain**
in the House of Commons 18 February 1897

Stanley Kubrick 1928–

American film director and screenwriter

7 The great nations have always acted like gangsters, and the small nations like prostitutes.
in *Guardian* 5 June 1963

Henry Labouchere 1831–1912

British politician

1 I do not object to the old man always having a card up his sleeve, but I do object to his insinuating that the Almighty has placed it there.
on **Gladstone***'s 'frequent appeals to a higher power'*

Earl Curzon *Modern Parliamentary Eloquence* (1913)

Jean de la Bruyère 1645–96

French satiric moralist

2 When the populace is excited, one cannot conceive how calm can be restored; and when it is peaceful, one cannot see how calm can be disturbed.

Characters (1688) 'Of the Sovereign and the State'

Fiorello La Guardia 1882–1947

American politician, mayor of New York City

3 When I make a mistake, it's a beaut!
on the appointment of Herbert O'Brien as a judge in 1936

William Manners *Patience and Fortitude* (1976)

4 Ticker tape ain't spaghetti.

speech to the United Nations Relief and Rehabilitation Administration, 29 March 1946

5 There is no Democratic or Republican way of cleaning the streets.

Charles Garrett *The La Guardia Years, Machine and Reform Politics in New York City* (1961)

John Lambert 1619–83

English soldier and Parliamentary supporter

6 The quarrel is now between light and darkness, not who shall rule, but whether we shall live or be preserved or no. Good words will not do with the cavaliers.
speech in the Parliament of 1656 supporting the rule of the major-generals

in *Dictionary of National Biography*

John George Lambton, Lord Durham 1792–1840

English Whig politician

7 £40,000 a year a moderate income—such a one as a man *might jog on with.*

Thomas Creevey letter to Elizabeth Ord, 13 September 1821

Norman Lamont 1942–

British Conservative politician

8 A price worth paying.
as Chancellor, responding to criticism on the rise in unemployment

in the House of Commons, 16 May 1991

1 The turn of the tide is sometimes difficult to discern. What we are seeing is the return of that vital ingredient—confidence. The green shoots of economic spring are appearing once again.
often quoted as 'the green shoots of recovery'
speech at the Conservative Party Conference, 9 October 1991

2 We give the impression of being in office but not in power.
'in office, but not in power' had earlier been used by A. J. P. **Taylor** *of Ramsay* **Macdonald***'s minority government of 1924*
speech in House of Commons, 9 June 1993

Bert Lance 1931–

American government official

3 If it ain't broke, don't fix it.
in *Nation's Business* May 1977

Walter Savage Landor 1775–1864

English poet

4 The wise become as the unwise in the enchanted chambers of Power, whose lamps make every face the same colour.
Imaginary Conversations (1824–9)

5 George the First was always reckoned
Vile, but viler George the Second;
And what mortal ever heard
Any good of George the Third?
When from earth the Fourth descended
God be praised the Georges ended!
epigram in *The Atlas*, 28 April 1855

Andrew Lang 1844–1912

Scottish man of letters

6 He uses statistics as a drunken man uses lampposts—for support rather than illumination.
Alan L. Mackay *Harvest of a Quiet Eye* (1977); attributed

William Langland *c.*1330–*c.*1400

English poet

7 Brewesters and baksters, bochiers and cokes—
For thise are men on this molde that moost harm
wercheth
To the povere peple.
in an alternative text, 'As bakeres and breweres, bocheres and cokes; / For thyse men don most harm to the mene peple'
The Vision of Piers Plowman

Lao-tzu *c.*604–*c.*531 BC

Chinese philosopher; founder of Taoism

8 Of the best rulers,
The people only know that they exist;
The next best they love and praise;
The next they fear;
The Wisdom of Laotse (1948)

And the next they revile...
But of the best when their task is accomplished, their
work done,
The people all remark, 'We have done it ourselves.'

Duc de la Rochefoucauld-Liancourt

1747–1827

French social reformer

1 LOUIS XVI: It is a big revolt.
LA ROCHEFOUCAULD-LIANCOURT: No, Sire, a big revolution.
on a report reaching Versailles of the Fall of the Bastille, 1789

F. Dreyfus *La Rochefoucauld-Liancourt* (1903)

Harold Laski 1893–1950

British Labour politician and academic

2 Shaw, with incredibly brilliant insolence, began to prove that Foreign Secretaries are by definition cynical and corrupt. Poor Austen, of course, tried to riposte; but he was like an elephant trying to catch an exceedingly agile wasp.
of an encounter between Bernard **Shaw** *and Austen Chamberlain*

letter to Oliver Wendell **Holmes** *Jr., 3 July 1926*

3 I respect fidelity to colleagues even though they are fit for the hangman.

letter to Oliver Wendell **Holmes** Jr., 4 December 1926

4 He searched always to end a sentence with a climax. He looked for antithesis like a monkey looking for fleas.
of Winston **Churchill** *at a dinner at the London School of Economics*

letter to Oliver Wendell **Holmes,** 7 May 1927

Hugh Latimer *c.*1485–1555

English Protestant martyr

5 Be of good comfort Master Ridley, and play the man. We shall this day light such a candle by God's grace in England, as (I trust) shall never be put out.
prior to being burned for heresy, 16 October 1555

John Foxe *Actes and Monuments* (1570 ed.)

Andrew Bonar Law 1858–1923

Canadian-born British Conservative statesman; Prime Minister 1922–3
on Bonar Law: see **Asquith** 18:7, **Beaverbrook** 34:7

6 In war it is necessary not only to be active but to seem active.

letter to **Asquith**, 1916; Robert Blake *The Unknown Prime Minister* (1955)

Richard Law 1901–80

British Conservative politician, son of Andrew Bonar **Law**

1 We do not ask of Mr Chamberlain that he should be Pitt or Chatham—only that he should seem a little less like an alderman exposing a sewage scandal.
of Neville **Chamberlain**
in *Time and Tide* 30 September 1939

Mark Lawson 1962–

British writer and journalist

2 Office tends to confer a dreadful plausibility on even the most negligible of those who hold it.
Joe Queenan *Imperial Caddy* (1992); introduction

Nigel Lawson 1932–

British Conservative politician; Chancellor of the Exchequer 1983–9

3 The Conservative Party has never believed that the business of government is the government of business.
in the House of Commons, 10 November 1981

4 Teenage scribblers.
of the financial press
in *Financial Times* 28 September 1985; coinage attributed to one of Nigel Lawson's Treasury aides

5 It represented the tip of a singularly ill-concealed iceberg, with all the destructive potential that icebergs possess.
of an article by Alan Walters, the Prime Minister's economic adviser, criticizing the Exchange Rate Mechanism
in the House of Commons following his resignation as Chancellor, 31 October 1989

6 When I was a minister I always looked forward to the Cabinet meeting immensely because it was, apart from the summer holidays, the only period of real rest I got in what was a very heavy job.
'Cabinet Government in the Thatcher Years' (1994)

Emma Lazarus 1849–87

American poet

7 Give me your tired, your poor,
Your huddled masses yearning to breathe free,
The wretched refuse of your teeming shore,
Send these, the homeless, tempest-tossed, to me:
I lift my lamp beside the golden door.
inscription on the Statue of Liberty, New York
'The New Colossus' (1883)

Alexandre Auguste Ledru-Rollin 1807–74

French politician

8 Ah well! I am their leader, I really had to follow them!
E. de Mirecourt *Les Contemporains* vol. 14 (1857) 'Ledru-Rollin'

Charles Lee 1731–82

American soldier

1 Beware that your Northern laurels do not change to Southern willows. — on 17 October 1777
to General Horatio Gates after the surrender of Burgoyne at Saratoga

Henry ('Light-Horse Harry') Lee 1756–1818

American soldier and politician

2 A citizen, first in war, first in peace, and first in the hearts of his countrymen. — *Funeral Oration on the death of General Washington* (1800)
of George **Washington**

Richard Henry Lee 1732–94

American politician

3 That these united colonies are, and of right ought to be, free and independent states; that they are absolved from all allegiance to the British crown; and that all political connection between them and the State of Great Britain is, and ought to be, totally dissolved. — resolution moved at the Continental Congress on 7 June 1776; adopted 2 July 1776

Robert E. Lee 1807–70

American Confederate general

4 It is well that war is so terrible. We should grow too fond of it. — attributed
after the battle of Fredericksburg, December 1862

5 There is nothing left for me to do but to go and see General Grant and I would rather die a thousand deaths. — Geoffrey C. Ward *The Civil War* (1991)
just before the Confederate surrender at Appomattox in 1865

6 I have fought against the people of the North because I believed they were seeking to wrest from the South its dearest rights. But I have never cherished toward them bitter or vindictive feelings, and I have never seen the day when I did not pray for them. — Geoffrey C. Ward *The Civil War* (1991)

7 Strike the tent. — on 12 October 1870
last words

Curtis E. LeMay 1906–90

US air-force officer

8 They've got to draw in their horns and stop their aggression, or we're going to bomb them back into the Stone Age. — *Mission with LeMay* (1965)
on the North Vietnamese

Lenin 1870–1924

Russian revolutionary, first Premier (Chairman of the Council of People's Commissars) of the Soviet Union 1918–24

1 What is to be done?
title of pamphlet (1902); originally the title of a novel (1863) by N. G. Chernyshevsky

2 One step forward two steps back
title of book 1904

3 Imperialism is the monopoly stage of capitalism.
Imperialism as the Last Stage of Capitalism (1916) 'Briefest possible definition of imperialism'

4 We must now set about building a proletarian socialist state in Russia.
speech in Petrograd, 7 November 1917

5 A good man fallen among Fabians.
of George Bernard **Shaw**
Arthur Ransome *Six Weeks in Russia in 1919* (1919) 'Notes of Conversations with Lenin'

6 No, Democracy is *not* identical with majority rule. Democracy is a *State* which recognizes the subjection of the minority to the majority, that is, an organization for the systematic use of *force* by one class against the other, by one part of the population against another.
State and Revolution (1919)

7 While the State exists, there can be no freedom. When there is freedom there will be no State.
State and Revolution (1919)

8 Communism equals Soviet power plus the electrification of the whole country.
report to 8th Congress, 1920

9 Who? Whom?
definition of political science, meaning 'Who will outstrip whom?'
in *Polnoe Sobranie Sochinenii* (1970) 17 October 1921

10 An end to bossing.
Neil Harding *Lenin's Political Thought* (1981) vol.2

11 Liberty is precious—so precious that it must be rationed.
Sidney and Beatrice Webb *Soviet Communism* (1935) vol. 2

William Lenthall 1591–1662

Speaker of the House of Commons

12 I have neither eye to see, nor tongue to speak here, but as the House is pleased to direct me.
to **Charles I**, *4 January 1642, on being asked if he had seen any of the five MPs whom the King had ordered to be arrested*
John Rushworth *Historical Collections. The Third Part* vol. 2 (1692)

Doris Lessing 1919–

British novelist and short-story writer, brought up in Rhodesia

13 When old settlers say 'One has to understand the country,' what they mean is, 'You have to get used to our ideas about the native.'
The Grass is Singing (1950)

1 When a white man in Africa by accident looks into the eyes of a native and sees the human being (which it is his chief preoccupation to avoid), his sense of guilt, which he denies, fumes up in resentment and he brings down the whip. — *The Grass is Singing* (1950)

Leslie Lever 1905–77

British Labour politician

2 Generosity is part of my character, and I therefore hasten to assure this Government that I will never make an allegation of dishonesty against it wherever a simple explanation of stupidity will suffice. — Leon Harris *The Fine Art of Political Wit* (1964)

Bernard Levin 1928–

British journalist

3 Whom the mad would destroy, they first make gods.
of **Mao** *Zedong in 1967* — in *The Times* 21 September 1987

4 [Tony] Benn flung himself into the Sixties technology with the enthusiasm (not to say language) of a newly enrolled Boy Scout demonstrating knot-tying to his indulgent parents. — *The Pendulum Years* (1970)

of Harold **Macmillan** *and Harold* **Wilson**:

5 Between them, then, Walrus and Carpenter, they divided up the Sixties. — *The Pendulum Years* (1970)

6 The Stag at Bay with the mentality of a fox at large.
of Harold **Macmillan** — *The Pendulum Years* (1970)

7 Inflation in the Sixties was a nuisance to be endured, like varicose veins or French foreign policy. — *The Pendulum Years* (1970); epilogue

8 Once, when a British Minister sneezed, men half a world away would blow their noses. Now when a British Prime Minister sneezes nobody else will even say, 'Bless You.' — in *The Times* 1976

9 What has happened to architecture since the second world war that the only passers-by who can contemplate it without pain are those equipped with a white stick and a dog? — in *The Times* 1983

10 Since when was fastidiousness a quality useful for political advancement? — *If You Want My Opinion* (1992)

11 Harold Macmillan, whose elevation was achieved by a brutality, cunning and greed for power normally met only in the conclaves of Mafia *capi*, said, after he had climbed the greasy pole and pushed all his rivals off (*takes out handkerchief containing concealed onion*) that the whole thing was Dead Sea Fruit. — *If You Want My Opinion* (1992); cf. **Macmillan** 245:7

12 The less the power, the greater the desire to exercise it. — in *The Times* 21 September 1993

13 I have more than once pointed out that no organization with 'Liberation' in its title has ever, or ever will, liberate anyone or anything. — in *Times* 14 April 1995

Duc de Lévis 1764–1830

French soldier and writer

1 To govern is to choose.

Maximes et Réflexions (1812 ed.) 'Politique: Maximes de Politique'

Willmott Lewis 1877–1950

British journalist and *Times* correspondent in Washington

2 One should perhaps avoid being hypercritical of acts of high policy. Take the charitable view, bearing in mind that every government will do as much harm as it can and as much good as it must.

to Claud **Cockburn**

Claud Cockburn *In Time of Trouble* (1957)

the leader of the French delegation to the Disarmament Conference in Washington after the First World War had described the city as un Versailles nègre:

3 Thus (for you figure to yourself the reactions of Southern senators to whom his ill-timed if apt remark was, I need hardly tell you, instantly communicated) stabbing himself in the back, a performance singularly otiose in a city where so many stand only too eagerly ready to do it for you.

to Claud **Cockburn**

Claud Cockburn *In Time of Trouble* (1957)

Robert Ley 1890–1945

German Nazi; head of the Labour Front from 1933

4 Strength through joy.

German Labour Front slogan from 1933

Basil Henry Liddell Hart 1895–1970

British military historian and strategist

5 Keep strong, if possible. In any case, keep cool. Have unlimited patience. Never corner an opponent, and always assist him to save his face. Put yourself in his shoes—so as to see things through his eyes. Avoid self-righteousness like the devil—nothing so self-blinding.

'Advice to Statesmen'

Deterrent or Defence (1960)

Abbott Joseph Liebling 1904–63

6 Freedom of the press is guaranteed only to those who own one.

in *New Yorker* 14 May 1960

Charles-Joseph, Prince de Ligne

1735–1814

Belgian soldier

1 The Congress makes no progress; it dances.
of the Congress of Vienna

Auguste de la Garde-Chambonas *Souvenirs du Congrès de Vienne* (1820)

Abraham Lincoln 1809–65

American Republican statesman, 16th President of the US 1861–5
on Lincoln: see **Stanton** 348:9, **Whitman** 387:9

2 Politicians [are] a set of men who have interests aside from the interests of the people, and who, to say the most of them, are, taken as a mass, at least one long step removed from honest men. I say this with the greater freedom because, being a politician myself, none can regard it as personal.

speech in the Illinois Legislature, 11 January 1837

3 There is no grievance that is a fit object of redress by mob law.

address at the Young Men's Lyceum, Springfield, Illinois, 27 January 1838

4 Prohibition . . . goes beyond the bounds of reason in that it attempts to control a man's appetite by legislation, and makes a crime out of things that are not crimes. A Prohibition law strikes a blow at the very principles upon which our government was founded.

speech in the Illinois House of Representatives, 18 December 1840

5 Any people anywhere, being inclined and having the power, have the *right* to rise up, and shake off the existing government, and form a new one that suits them better.

in the House of Representatives, 12 January 1848

6 No man is good enough to govern another man without that other's consent.

speech at Peoria, Illinois, 16 October 1854

7 To give victory to the right, not bloody bullets, but peaceful ballots only, are necessary.
usually quoted as, 'The ballot is stronger than the bullet'

speech, 18 May 1858

8 As I would not be a *slave*, so I would not be a *master*. This expresses my idea of democracy. Whatever differs from this, to the extent of the difference, is no democracy.

fragment, 1 August 1858?

9 When . . . you have succeeded in dehumanizing the Negro, when you have put him down and made it forever impossible for him to be but as the beasts of the field; when you have extinguished his soul and placed him where the ray of hope is blown out in darkness like that which broods over the spirits of the damned, are you quite sure that the demon you have roused will not turn and rend you?

speech at Edwardsville, Illinois, 11 September 1858

1 'A house divided against itself cannot stand.' I believe this government cannot endure permanently, half slave and half free.

speech, 16 June 1858

2 I have no purpose to introduce political and social equality between the white and black races. There is a physical difference between the two which, in my judgement, will probably for ever forbid their living together upon the footing of perfect equality; and inasmuch as it becomes a necessity that there must be a difference, I...am in favour of the race to which I belong having the superior position.

speech, 21 August 1858

3 What is conservatism? Is it not adherence to the old and tried, against the new and untried?

speech, 27 February 1860

4 If we do not make common cause to save the good old ship of the Union on this voyage, nobody will have a chance to pilot her on another voyage.

address at Cleveland, Ohio, 15 February 1861

5 It is safe to assert that no government proper ever had a provision in its organic law for its own termination.

first inaugural address, 4 March 1861

6 I take the official oath to-day with no mental reservations, and with no purpose to construe the Constitution or laws by any hypercritical rules.

first inaugural address, 4 March 1861

7 This country, with its institutions, belongs to the people who inhabit it. Whenever they shall grow weary of the existing government, they can exercise their constitutional right of amending it, or their revolutionary right to dismember or overthrow it.

first inaugural address, 4 March 1861

8 The mystic chords of memory, stretching from every battlefield and patriot grave to every living heart and heartstone all over this broad land, will yet swell the chorus of the Union when again touched, as surely they will be, by the better angels of our nature.

first inaugural address, 4 March 1861

9 I think the necessity of being *ready* increases. Look to it.

the whole of a letter to Governor Andrew Curtin of Pennsylvania, 8 April 1861

when asked how he felt about the New York elections:

10 Somewhat like the boy in Kentucky who stubbed his toe while running to see his sweetheart. The boy said he was too big to cry, and far too badly hurt to laugh.

in *Frank Leslie's Illustrated Weekly* 22 November 1862

11 On the first day of January in the year of our Lord, one thousand eight hundred and sixty-three, all persons held as slaves within any state, or designated part of a state, the people whereof shall then be in rebellion against the United States shall be then, thenceforward, and forever free.

Preliminary Emancipation Proclamation, 22 September 1862

12 Fellow citizens, we cannot escape history...No personal significance or insignificance can spare one or another of us. The fiery trial through which we pass will light us down in honour or dishonour to the last generation.

annual message to Congress, 1 December 1862

1 In giving freedom to the slave, we assure freedom to the free—honourable alike in what we give and what we preserve. We shall nobly save, or meanly lose, the last, best hope of earth.

annual message to Congress, 1 December 1862

2 My paramount object in this struggle is to save the Union…If I could save the Union without freeing any slave, I would do it; and if I could save it by freeing all the slaves, I would do it; and if I could save it by freeing some and leaving others alone, I would also do that…I have here stated my purpose according to my views of official duty and I intend no modification of my oft-expressed personal wish that all men everywhere could be free.

letter to Horace **Greeley**, 22 August 1862

3 Fourscore and seven years ago our fathers brought forth upon this continent a new nation, conceived in liberty, and dedicated to the proposition that all men are created equal…In a larger sense we cannot dedicate, we cannot consecrate, we cannot hallow this ground. The brave men, living and these dead, who struggled here, have consecrated it far above our power to add or detract. The world will little note, nor long remember, what we say here, but it can never forget what they did here. It is for us, the living, rather to be dedicated here to the unfinished work which they who fought here have thus far so nobly advanced…we here highly resolve that the dead shall not have died in vain, that this nation, under God, shall have a new birth of freedom; and that government of the people, by the people, and for the people, shall not perish from the earth.

address at the Dedication of the National Cemetery at Gettysburg, 19 November 1863, as reported the following day; the Lincoln Memorial inscription reads 'by the people, for the people'; cf. **Anonymous** 13:6, **Everett** 134:4; cf. also **Parker** 285:6

4 Only those generals who gain success can set up dictators. What I ask of you is military success, and I will risk the dictatorship.

letter appointing Joseph Hooker to command of the Army of the Potomac in 1863

Shelby Foote *The Civil War: Fredericksburg to Meridian* (1991)

5 I claim not to have controlled events, but confess plainly that events have controlled me.

letter to A. G. Hodges, 4 April 1864

6 It is not best to swap horses when crossing streams.

reply to National Union League, 9 June 1864

7 It has long been a grave question whether any government, not too strong for the liberties of its people, can be strong enough to maintain its existence in great emergencies.

response to a serenade, 10 November 1864

8 I desire so to conduct the affairs of this administration that if at the end, when I come to lay down the reins of power, I have lost every other friend on earth, I shall at least have one friend left, and that friend shall be down inside me.

reply to the Missouri Committee of Seventy, 1864

9 Fondly do we hope, fervently do we pray, that this mighty scourge of war may speedily pass away. Yet, if God wills that it continue until all the wealth piled by the bond-man's two hundred and fifty years of unrequited

second inaugural address, 4 March 1865

toil shall be sunk, and until every drop of blood drawn with the lash shall be paid by another drawn with the sword, as was said three thousand years ago, so still it must be said, 'The judgements of the Lord are true and righteous altogether.'

1 With malice toward none; with charity for all; with firmness in the right, as God gives us to see the right, let us strive on to finish the work we are in: to bind up the nation's wounds; to care for him who shall have borne the battle, and for his widow and his orphan, to do all which may achieve and cherish a just and lasting peace among ourselves, and with all nations.

second inaugural address, 4 March 1865

2 As President, I have no eyes but constitutional eyes; I cannot see you.

reply to the South Carolina Commissioners

attributed

3 People who like this sort of thing will find this the sort of thing they like.

judgement of a book

G. W. E. Russell *Collections and Recollections* (1898)

4 So you're the little woman who wrote the book that made this great war!

on meeting Harriet Beecher Stowe, author of Uncle Tom's Cabin *(1852)*

Carl Sandburg *Abraham Lincoln: The War Years* (1936) vol. 2

5 The Lord prefers common-looking people. That is why he makes so many of them.

attributed; James Morgan *Our Presidents* (1928)

6 Whenever I hear anyone arguing for slavery, I feel a strong impulse to see it tried on him personally.

address to an Indiana Regiment, 17 March 1865

7 You cannot help the poor by destroying the rich. You cannot lift the wage earner by pulling down the wage payer.

attributed, but probably apocryphal

8 You may fool all the people some of the time; you can even fool some of the people all the time; but you can't fool all of the people all the time.

Alexander K. McClure *Lincoln's Yarns and Stories* (1904); also attributed to Phineas Barnum

Eric Linklater 1899–1974

Scottish novelist

9 'There won't be any revolution in America,' said Isadore. Nikitin agreed. 'The people are all too clean. They spend all their time changing their shirts and washing themselves. You can't feel fierce and revolutionary in a bathroom.'

Juan in America (1931)

George Linley 1798–1865

English songwriter

10 Among our ancient mountains,
And from our lovely vales,
Oh, let the prayer re-echo:
'God bless the Prince of Wales!'

'God Bless the Prince of Wales' (1862 song)

Walter Lippmann 1889–1974

American journalist

1 Mr Coolidge's genius for inactivity is developed to a very high point. It is far from being an indolent activity. It is a grim, determined, alert inactivity which keeps Mr Coolidge occupied constantly. Nobody has ever worked harder at inactivity, with such force of character, with such unremitting attention to detail, with such conscientious devotion to the task.
Men of Destiny (1927)

2 Private property was the original source of freedom. It still is its main bulwark.
The Good Society (1937)

3 The final test of a leader is that he leaves behind him in other men the conviction and the will to carry on.
in *New York Herald Tribune* 14 April 1945

4 A free press is not a privilege but an organic necessity in a great society.
address at the International Press Institute Assembly in London, 27 May 1965

5 The will to be free is perpetually renewed in every individual who uses his faculties and affirms his manhood.
Arthur Seldon *The State is Rolling Back* (1994)

Maxim Litvinov 1876–1951

Soviet diplomat

6 Peace is indivisible.
note to the Allies, 25 February 1920
A. U. Pope *Maxim Litvinoff* (1943)

Ken Livingstone 1945–

British Labour politician

7 The problem is that many MPs never see the London that exists beyond the wine bars and brothels of Westminster.
in *The Times* 19 February 1987

Livy 59 BC–AD 17

Roman historian

8 *Vae victis.*
Down with the defeated!
cry (already proverbial) of the Gallic King, Brennus, on capturing Rome in 390 BC
Ab Urbe Condita

9 We have been defeated in a great battle.
the announcement of disaster for the Romans in Hannibal's ambush at Lake Trasimene in 217 BC
Ab Urbe Condita

Selwyn Lloyd 1904–78

British Conservative politician

10 I do not speak any foreign language. Except in war, I have never visited any foreign country. I do not like foreigners.
Suez 1956 (1978)

David Lloyd George 1863–1945

British Liberal politician; Prime Minister, 1916–22
on Lloyd George: see **Asquith** 19:2, **Baldwin** 30:1, **Bennett** 37:5, **Churchill** 88:6, **Clemenceau** 98:5, **Grigg** 161:8, **Keynes** 207:11, 208:1, **Massingham** 254:3, **Taylor** 357:12

1 The leal and trusty mastiff which is to watch over our interests, but which runs away at the first snarl of the trade unions... A mastiff? It is the right hon. Gentleman's poodle.
on the House of Lords and Arthur **Balfour** *respectively*
in the House of Commons, 26 June 1907

2 I have no nest-eggs. I am looking for someone else's hen-roost to rob next year.
in 1908, as Chancellor
Frank Owen *Tempestuous Journey* (1954)

3 A fully-equipped duke costs as much to keep up as two Dreadnoughts; and dukes are just as great a terror and they last longer.
speech at Newcastle, 9 October 1909

4 The best example of the unearned increment is the hyphen in the Hon. Member's name.
of William Joynson-Hicks, who had married the daughter of a silk manufacturer and added her name to his own.
*c.*1909, attributed

of the House of Lords, c.1911:

5 A body of five hundred men chosen at random from amongst the unemployed.
speech at Newcastle, 9 October 1909

6 The great peaks of honour we had forgotten—Duty, Patriotism, and—clad in glittering white—the great pinnacle of Sacrifice, pointing like a rugged finger to Heaven.
speech at Queen's Hall, London, 19 September 1914

7 I would as soon go for a sunny evening stroll round Walton Heath with a grasshopper, as try to work with Northcliffe.
of Lord **Northcliffe**, *c.1916*
Frank Owen *Tempestuous Journey* (1954)

8 At eleven o'clock this morning came to an end the cruellest and most terrible war that has ever scourged mankind. I hope we may say that thus, this fateful morning, came to an end all wars.
in the House of Commons, 11 November 1918

9 What is our task? To make Britain a fit country for heroes to live in.
speech at Wolverhampton, 23 November 1918

10 M. Clemenceau... is one of the greatest living orators, but he knows that the finest eloquence is that which gets things done and the worst is that which delays them.
speech at Paris Peace Conference, 18 January 1919
in *The Times* 20 January 1919

11 Wild men screaming through the keyholes.
of the Versailles Peace Conference
in the House of Commons, 16 April 1919

12 If you want to succeed in politics, you must keep your conscience well under control.
Lord Riddell diary 23 April 1919

13 Death is the most convenient time to tax rich people.
in *Lord Riddell's Intimate Diary of the Peace Conference and After, 1918–23* (1933)

1 Unless I am mistaken, by the steps we have taken [in Ireland] we have murder by the throat. — speech at the Mansion House, 9 November 1920

of Arthur **Balfour***'s impact on history:*

2 No more than the whiff of scent on a lady's pocket handkerchief. — Thomas Jones diary 9 June 1922

3 Negotiating with de Valera . . . is like trying to pick up mercury with a fork. — M. J. MacManus *Eamon de Valera* (1944)

to which de Valera replied, 'Why doesn't he use a spoon?'

4 Of all the bigotries that savage the human temper there is none so stupid as the anti-Semitic. — *Is It Peace?* 1923

5 The world is becoming like a lunatic asylum run by lunatics. — in *Observer* 8 January 1933

6 A politician was a person with whose politics you did not agree. When you did agree, he was a statesman. — speech at Central Hall, Westminster, 2 July 1935

7 Neville has a retail mind in a wholesale business. — in 1935; David Dilks *Neville Chamberlain* (1984)

of Neville **Chamberlain**

after meeting **Hitler** *in 1936:*

8 Führer is the proper name for him. He is a great and wonderful leader. — Frank Owen *Tempestuous Journey* (1954)

9 Winston would go up to his Creator and say that he would very much like to meet His Son, of Whom he had heard a great deal and, if possible, would like to call on the Holy Ghost. Winston *loves* meeting people. — A. J. Sylvester diary 2 January 1937

of Winston **Churchill**

10 The Government are behaving like a bevy of maiden aunts who have fallen among buccaneers. — on 21 June 1938; Peter Rowland *Lloyd George* (1975)

during the Spanish Civil War, when British merchant seamen off the east coast of Spain had been bombed

11 The Prime Minister should give an example of sacrifice, because there is nothing which can contribute more to victory than that he should sacrifice the seals of office. — in the House of Commons, 7 May 1940

of Neville **Chamberlain**

on being told by Lord **Beaverbrook***'s butler that, 'The Lord is out walking':*

12 Ah, on the water, I presume. — Lord Cudlipp letter in *Daily Telegraph* 13 September 1993

13 There is no friendship at the top. — habitual remark, said to be quoting **Gladstone**; A. J. P. Taylor *Lloyd George, Rise and Fall* (1961)

14 Truth against the world. — Donald McCormick *The Mask of Merlin* (1963)

Welsh proverb; motto taken on becoming Earl Lloyd-George of Dwyfor, January 1945

15 He has sat on the fence so long the iron has entered into his soul. — attributed

of John Simon

16 He would make a drum out of the skin of his mother in order to sound his own praises. — Peter Rowland *Lloyd George* (1975)

of Winston **Churchill**

1 One of those revolving lighthouses which radiate momentary gleams of light far out into the surrounding gloom, and then suddenly relapse into complete darkness. There were no intermediate stages.
of Kitchener as War Minister

attributed

2 Sufficient conscience to bother him, but not sufficient to keep him straight.
of Ramsay **MacDonald**

A. J. Sylvester *Life with Lloyd George* (1975)

Gwilym Lloyd George, Lord Tenby 1894–1967

British Liberal politician, younger son of David **Lloyd George**

3 Politicians are like monkeys. The higher they climb, the more revolting are the parts they expose.

c. 1954, attributed; Peter Hennessy at the Annual Dinner of the Fabian Society, 25 November 1995

John Locke 1632–1704

English philosopher

4 Whatsoever... [man] removes out of the state that nature hath provided and left it in, he hath mixed his labour with, and joined to it something that is his own, and thereby makes it his property.

Second Treatise of Civil Government (1690)

5 Man... hath by nature a power... to preserve his property—that is, his life, liberty, and estate—against the injuries and attempts of other men.

Second Treatise of Civil Government (1690)

6 Man being... by nature all free, equal, and independent, no one can be put out of this estate, and subjected to the political power of another, without his own consent.

Second Treatise of Civil Government (1690)

7 The great and chief end, therefore, of men's uniting into commonwealths, and putting themselves under government, is the preservation of their property.

Second Treatise of Civil Government (1690)

8 The only way by which any one divests himself of his natural liberty and puts on the bonds of civil society is by agreeing with other men to join and unite into a community.

Second Treatise of Civil Government (1690)

9 This power to act according to discretion for the public good, without the prescription of the law, and sometimes even against it, is that which is called prerogative.

Second Treatise of Civil Government (1690)

Henry Cabot Lodge Snr. 1850–1924

American Republican politician

10 Let us have done with British-Americans and Irish-Americans and German-Americans, and so on, and all be Americans... If a man is going to be an American at all let him be so without any qualifying adjectives; and if he is going to be something else, let him drop the word American from his person description.

The Day We Celebrate (Forefathers' Day) Address, New England Society of Brooklyn, 21 December 1888; cf. **Roosevelt** 311:14

1 It is the flag just as much of the man who was naturalized yesterday as of the man whose people have been here many generations.
address, 1915

Henry Cabot Lodge Jr. 1902–85

American Republican politician

2 It was those damned tea parties that beat me!
attributing the loss of his 1952 senatorial campaign, against the national Republican trend, to the tea parties given by Rose **Kennedy** *on behalf of her son, the Democratic candidate John F.* **Kennedy**
in obituary of Rose **Kennedy** *in Guardian* 24 January 1995

Huey Long 1893–1935

American Democratic politician; Governor of Louisiana

3 For the present you can just call me the Kingfish.
Every Man a King (1933)

answering his opponent's supporters, who said their candidate had gone barefoot as a boy:
4 I can go Mr Wilson one better; I was born barefoot.
T. Harry Williams *Huey Long* (1969)

5 Oh hell, say that I am *sui generis* and let it go at that.
to journalists attempting to analyse his political personality
T. Harry Williams *Huey Long* (1969)

6 Bible's the greatest book ever written. But I sure don't need anybody I can buy for six bits and a chew of tobacco to explain it to me. When I need preachers I buy 'em cheap.
T. Harry Williams *Huey Long* (1969)

7 The time has come for all good men to rise above principle.
attributed

Alice Roosevelt Longworth 1884–1980

daughter of Theodore **Roosevelt**

8 Harding was not a bad man. He was just a slob.
of US President Warren G. **Harding**
Crowded Hours (1933)

Louis XIV (the 'Sun King') 1638–1715

King of France from 1643

9 *L'État c'est moi.*
I am the State.
before the Parlement de Paris, 13 April 1655 (probably apocryphal)
J. A. Dulaure *Histoire de Paris* (1834) vol. 6

10 I was nearly kept waiting.
attribution queried, among others, by E. Fournier in *L'Esprit dans l'Histoire* (1857)

11 Every time I create an appointment, I create a hundred malcontents and one ingrate.
Voltaire *Siècle de Louis XIV* (1768 ed.) vol. 2

1 The Pyrenees are no more.
on the accession of his grandson to the throne of Spain, 1700

attributed to Louis by Voltaire in *Siècle de Louis XIV* (1753), but to the Spanish Ambassador to France in the *Mercure Galant* (Paris) November 1700

Louis XVI 1754–93

King of France from 1774; deposed in 1789 on the outbreak of the French Revolution and executed in 1793

diary entry for 14 July 1789, the day of the storming of the Bastille:

2 *Rien.*
Nothing.

Simon Schama *Citizens* (1989)

Louis XVIII 1755–1824

King of France from 1814; titular king from 1795

3 Remember that there is not one of you who does not carry in his cartridge-pouch the marshal's baton of the duke of Reggio; it is up to you to bring it forth.
speech to Saint-Cyr cadets, 9 August 1819

in *Moniteur Universel* 10 August 1819

4 Punctuality is the politeness of kings.

in *Souvenirs de J. Lafitte* (1844), attributed

David Low 1891–1963

British political cartoonist and creator of 'Colonel Blimp', proponent of reactionary establishment opinions

5 I have never met anyone who wasn't against war. Even Hitler and Mussolini were, according to themselves.

in *New York Times Magazine* 10 February 1946

Robert Lowe, Viscount Sherbrooke 1811–92

British Liberal politician

6 I believe it will be absolutely necessary that you should prevail on our future masters to learn their letters.
on the passing of the Reform Bill, popularized as 'We must educate our masters'

in the House of Commons, 15 July 1867

7 The Chancellor of the Exchequer is a man whose duties make him more or less of a taxing machine. He is intrusted with a certain amount of misery which it is his duty to distribute as fairly as he can.

in the House of Commons, 11 April 1870

James Russell Lowell 1819–91

American poet

8 We've a war, an' a debt, an' a flag; an' ef this
Ain't to be inderpendunt, why, wut on airth is?

The Biglow Papers (Second Series, 1867) no. 4 'A Message of Jeff. Davis in Secret Session'

1 Once to every man and nation comes the moment to decide,
In the strife of Truth with Falsehood, for the good or evil side.

'The Present Crisis' (1845)

2 Truth forever on the scaffold, Wrong forever on the throne,—
Yet that scaffold sways the future, and, behind the dim unknown,
Standeth God within the shadow, keeping watch above his own.

'The Present Crisis' (1845)

Lucan AD 39–65

Roman poet

3 It is not granted to know which man took up arms with more right on his side. Each pleads his cause before a great judge: the winning cause pleased the gods, but the losing one pleased Cato.

Pharsalia

4 There stands the ghost of a great name.
of Pompey

Pharsalia

5 Thinking nothing done while anything remained to be done.

Pharsalia

Martin Luther 1483–1546

German Protestant theologian

6 Here stand I. I can do no other. God help me. Amen.

speech at the Diet of Worms, 18 April 1521; attributed

7 If I had heard that as many devils would set on me in Worms as there are tiles on the roofs, I should none the less have ridden there.

to the Princes of Saxony, 21 August 1524

Rosa Luxemburg 1871–1919

German revolutionary

8 Freedom is always and exclusively freedom for the one who thinks differently.

Die Russische Revolution (1918)

Robert Lynd 1879–1949

Anglo-Irish essayist and journalist

9 The belief in the possibility of a short decisive war appears to be one of the most ancient and dangerous of human illusions.

attributed

Jonathan Lynn 1943– and Antony Jay 1930–

10 Years of political training and experience had taught him to use twenty words where one would do, to write

editors' note, *Yes Minister* vol. 1 (1981)

millions of words where thousands would suffice, to use language to blur and fudge the issues and events so that they become incomprehensible to others. When incomprehensibility has been achieved by a politician, so has safety.
of 'Jim Hacker'

1 'Opposition's about asking awkward questions.' 'Yes... and government's about not answering them.' — *Yes Minister* vol. 1 (1981)

2 'Under consideration' means we've lost the file. 'Under active consideration' means we're trying to find it. — *Yes Minister* vol. 1 (1981)

3 Ministers need activity. It's their substitute for achievement. — *Yes Minister* vol. 1 (1981)

4 The PM—whose motto is... 'In Defeat, Malice—in Victory, Revenge!' — *Yes Minister* vol. 1 (1981)

5 If you wish to describe a proposal in a way that guarantees that a Minister will reject it, describe it as *courageous*. — *Yes Minister* vol. 1 (1981)

6 The Official Secrets Act is not to protect secrets but to protect officials. — *Yes Minister* vol. 1 (1981)

7 *Restricted* means it was in the papers yesterday. *Confidential* means it won't be in the papers till today. — *Yes Minister* vol. 2 (1982)

8 Diplomacy is about surviving till the next century—politics is about surviving till Friday afternoon. — *Yes Prime Minister* vol. 1 (1986)

9 Collective responsibility means that when we do something popular they all leak the fact that it was their idea, and when we do something unpopular they leak the fact that they were against it. — *Yes Prime Minister* vol. 2 (1987)

10 That's another of those irregular verbs, isn't it? I give confidential briefings; you leak; he has been charged under Section 2a of the Official Secrets Act. — *Yes Prime Minister* vol. 2 (1987)

what is known to the Civil Service as the Politicians' Syllogism*:*

11 Step One: We must do something.
Step Two: This is something.
Step Three: Therefore we must do it. — *Yes Prime Minister* vol. 2 (1987)

Douglas MacArthur 1880–1964

American general

12 I came through and I shall return. — in *New York Times* 21 March 1942
on reaching Australia, 20 March 1942, having broken through Japanese lines en route from Corregidor

13 In war, indeed, there can be no substitute for victory. — in *Congressional Record* 19 April 1951, vol. 97

14 I still remember the refrain of one of the most popular barracks ballads of that day, which proclaimed most proudly that old soldiers never die; they just fade away. I now close my military career and just fade away. — address to a Joint Meeting of Congress, 19 April 1951

Lord Macaulay 1800–59

English Whig politician, historian, and poet
on Macaulay: see **Melbourne** 255:10, **Smith** 344:9

1 Thank you, madam, the agony is abated.
aged four, having had hot coffee spilt over his legs

G. O. Trevelyan *Life and Letters of Lord Macaulay* (1876)

2 Obadiah Bind-their-kings-in-chains-and-their-nobles-with-links-of-iron.

'The Battle of Naseby' (1824) fictitious author's name

3 Oh, wherefore come ye forth in triumph from the north,
With your hands, and your feet, and your raiment all red?
And wherefore doth your rout send forth a joyous shout?
And whence be the grapes of the wine-press which ye tread?

'The Battle of Naseby' (1824)

4 And the Man of Blood was there, with his long essenced hair,
And Astley, and Sir Marmaduke, and Rupert of the Rhine.

'The Battle of Naseby' (1824)

5 The object of oratory alone is not truth, but persuasion.

'Essay on Athenian Orators' in *Knight's Quarterly Magazine* August 1824

6 This province of literature [history] is a debatable line. It lies on the confines of two distinct territories. It is under the jurisdiction of two hostile powers; and like other districts similarly situated it is ill-defined, ill-cultivated, and ill-regulated. Instead of being equally shared between its two rulers, the Reason and the Imagination, it falls alternately under the sole and absolute dominion of each. It is sometimes fiction. It is sometimes theory.

'History' (1828)

7 Nothing is so galling to a people not broken in from the birth as a paternal, or in other words a meddling government, a government which tells them what to read and say and eat and drink and wear.

in *Edinburgh Review* January 1830

8 He has one eminent merit—that of being an enthusiastic admirer of mine—so that I may be the Hero of a novel yet, under the name of Delamere or Mortimer. Only think what an honour.
of the novelist and politician **Bulwer Lytton**

letter 5 August 1831

9 He took the praise as a greedy boy takes apple pie, and the criticism as a good dutiful boy takes senna-tea.
of **Bulwer Lytton**, *whose novels he had criticized*

letter 5 August 1831

10 I detest him more than cold boiled veal.
of the Tory essayist and politician John Wilson Croker

letter 5 August 1831

11 We must at present do our best to form a class who may be interpreters between us and the millions whom we govern; a class of persons, Indian in blood and colour, but English in taste, in opinions, in morals, and in intellect.

minute, as Member of Supreme Council of India, 2 February 1835

1 Then none was for a party;
Then all were for the state;
Then the great man helped the poor,
And the poor man loved the great:
Then lands were fairly portioned;
Then spoils were fairly sold:
The Romans were like brothers
In the brave days of old.

Lays of Ancient Rome (1842) 'Horatius'

2 The business of everybody is the business of nobody.

Essays Contributed to the Edinburgh Review (1843) vol. 1 'Hallam'

3 The gallery in which the reporters sit has become a fourth estate of the realm.

Essays Contributed to the Edinburgh Review (1843) vol. 1 'Hallam'

4 He knew that the essence of war is violence, and that moderation in war is imbecility.

Essays Contributed to the Edinburgh Review (1843) vol. 1 'John Hampden'

of Niccolò **Machiavelli**:

5 Out of his surname they have coined an epithet for a knave, and out of his Christian name a synonym for the Devil.

Essays Contributed to the Edinburgh Review (1843) vol. 1 'Machiavelli'

6 Many politicians of our time are in the habit of laying it down as a self-evident proposition, that no people ought to be free till they are fit to use their freedom. The maxim is worthy of the fool in the old story, who resolved not to go into the water till he had learnt to swim. If men are to wait for liberty till they become wise and good in slavery, they may indeed wait for ever.

Essays Contributed to the Edinburgh Review (1843) vol. 1 'Milton'

7 On the rich and the eloquent, on nobles and priests, they [the Puritans] looked down with contempt: for they esteemed themselves rich in a more precious treasure, and eloquent in a more sublime language, nobles by the right of an earlier creation, and priests by the imposition of a mightier hand.

Essays Contributed to the Edinburgh Review (1843) vol. 1 'Milton'

8 We know no spectacle so ridiculous as the British public in one of its periodical fits of morality.

Essays Contributed to the Edinburgh Review (1843) vol. 1 'Moore's *Life of Lord Byron*'

9 We have heard it said that five per cent is the natural interest of money.

Essays Contributed to the Edinburgh Review (1843) vol. 1 'Southey's Colloquies'

10 With the dead there is no rivalry. In the dead there is no change. Plato is never sullen. Cervantes is never petulant. Demosthenes never comes unseasonably. Dante never stays too long. No difference of political opinion can alienate Cicero. No heresy can excite the horror of Bossuet.

Essays Contributed to the Edinburgh Review (1843) vol. 2 'Lord Bacon'

11 An acre in Middlesex is better than a principality in Utopia.

Essays Contributed to the Edinburgh Review (1843) vol. 2 'Lord Bacon'

1 The rising hope of those stern and unbending Tories.
of **Gladstone**

Essays Contributed to the Edinburgh Review (1843) vol. 2 'Gladstone on Church and State'

2 The highest intellects, like the tops of mountains, are the first to catch and to reflect the dawn.

Essays Contributed to the Edinburgh Review (1843) vol. 2 'Sir James Mackintosh'

3 The history of England is emphatically the history of progress.

Essays Contributed to the Edinburgh Review (1843) vol. 2 'Sir James Mackintosh'

4 On the day of the accession of George the Third, the ascendancy of the Whig party terminated; and on that day the purification of the Whig party began.

Essays Contributed to the Edinburgh Review (1843) vol. 2 'William Pitt, Earl of Chatham'

5 The reluctant obedience of distant provinces generally costs more than it [the territory] is worth.

Essays Contributed to the Edinburgh Review (1843) vol. 2 'The War of Succession in Spain'

6 Every schoolboy knows who imprisoned Montezuma, and who strangled Atahualpa.

Essays Contributed to the Edinburgh Review (1843) vol. 3 'Lord Clive'

7 The Chief Justice was rich, quiet, and infamous.

Essays Contributed to the Edinburgh Review (1843) vol. 3 'Warren Hastings'

of Westminster Abbey:

8 That temple of silence and reconciliation where the enmities of twenty generations lie buried.

Essays Contributed to the Edinburgh Review (1843) vol. 3 'Warren Hastings'

9 To my true king I offered free from stain
Courage and faith; vain faith, and courage vain.

'A Jacobite's Epitaph' (1845)

10 By those white cliffs I never more must see,
By that dear language which I spake like thee,
Forget all feuds, and shed one English tear
O'er English dust. A broken heart lies here.

'A Jacobite's Epitaph' (1845)

11 I shall cheerfully bear the reproach of having descended below the dignity of history.

History of England vol. 1 (1849)

12 Thus our democracy was, from an early period, the most aristocratic, and our aristocracy the most democratic in the world.

History of England vol. 1 (1849)

13 Persecution produced its natural effect on them [Puritans and Calvinists]. It found them a sect; it made them a faction.

History of England vol. 1 (1849)

14 [Louis XIV] had shown, in an eminent degree, two talents invaluable to a prince, the talent of choosing his servants well, and the talent of appropriating to himself the chief part of the credit of their acts.

History of England vol. 1 (1849)

15 No man is fit to govern great societies who hesitates about disobliging the few who have access to him for the sake of the many he will never see.

History of England vol. 1 (1849)

1 It was a crime in a child to read by the bedside of a sick parent one of those beautiful collects which had soothed the griefs of forty generations of Christians.

History of England vol. 1 (1849)

2 The Puritan hated bear-baiting, not because it gave pain to the bear, but because it gave pleasure to the spectators.

History of England vol. 1 (1849)

3 It has often been found that profuse expenditure, heavy taxation, absurd commercial restrictions, corrupt tribunals, disastrous wars, seditions, persecutions, conflagrations, inundations, have not been able to destroy capital so fast as the exertions of private citizens have been able to create it.

History of England vol. 1 (1849)

4 In order that he might rob a neighbour whom he had promised to defend, black men fought on the coast of Coromandel, and red men scalped each other by the Great Lakes of North America.

Biographical Essays (1857) 'Frederic the Great'

Eugene McCarthy 1916–

American Democratic politician

5 Being in politics is like being a football coach. You have to be smart enough to understand the game, and dumb enough to think it's important.
while campaigning for the presidency

in an interview, 1968

Joseph McCarthy 1908–57

American politician and anti-Communist agitator

6 I have here in my hand a list of two hundred and five [people] that were known to the Secretary of State as being members of the Communist Party and who nevertheless are still working and shaping the policy of the State Department.

speech at Wheeling, West Virginia, 9 February 1950

7 McCarthyism is Americanism with its sleeves rolled.

speech in Wisconsin, 1952; Richard Rovere *Senator Joe McCarthy* (1973)

Mary McCarthy 1912–89

American writer

8 Bureaucracy, the rule of no one, has become the modern form of despotism.

in *New Yorker* 18 October 1958

George B. McClellan 1826–85

American soldier and politician

9 All quiet along the Potomac.
said at the time of the American Civil War

attributed

Colonel McCormick

of the *Chicago Tribune*

1 The British are no longer important enough for me to dislike.
explaining his willingness to give an interview to the British journalist Woodrow Wyatt
J. K. Galbraith *A Life in Our Times* (1981)

John McCrae 1872–1918

Canadian poet and military physician

2 To you from failing hands we throw
The torch; be yours to hold it high.
If ye break faith with us who die
We shall not sleep, though poppies grow
In Flanders fields.
'In Flanders Fields' (1915)

Ramsay MacDonald 1866–1937

British Labour statesman, Prime Minister 1924, 1929–31, and 1931–5

on MacDonald: see **George V** 149:7, **Lloyd George** 231:2, **Nicolson** 272:4; see also **Lamont** 217:2

3 Wars are popular. Contractors make profits; the aristocracy glean honour.
in *Labour Leader* 11 March 1915

4 A terror decreed by a Secret Committee is child's play compared with a terror instituted by 'lawful authority'.
in *Socialist Review* January-March 1921

5 We hear war called murder. It is not: it is suicide.
in *Observer* 4 May 1930

6 Tomorrow every Duchess in London will be wanting to kiss me!
after forming the National Government, 25 August 1931
Viscount Snowden *An Autobiography* (1934) vol. 2

7 A body representing the citizenship of the whole nation is charged with so much that it can do nothing swiftly and well.
Carl Cohen *Parliament and Democracy* (1962)

Mick McGahey

British miner and trade unionist

8 He mistakes a mass meeting for a mass movement.
of the President of the NUM, Arthur Scargill
in *Independent* 10 March 1990

George McGovern 1922–

American Democratic politician, presidential candidate in 1972

9 Sometimes, when they say you're ahead of your time, it's just a polite way of saying you have a real bad sense of timing.
in *Observer* 18 March 1990 'Sayings of the Week'

Lord McGregor 1921–

British sociologist

1 An odious exhibition of journalists dabbling their fingers in the stuff of other people's souls.
on press coverage of the marriage of the Prince and Princess of Wales, speaking as Chairman of the Press Complaints Commission
in *The Times* 9 June 1992

Niccolò Machiavelli 1469–1527

Florentine statesman and political philosopher

2 Men should be either treated generously or destroyed, because they take revenge for slight injuries—for heavy ones they cannot.
The Prince (1513)

3 This leads to a debate: is it better to be loved than feared, or the reverse? The answer is that it is desirable to be both, but because it is difficult to join them together, it is much safer for a prince to be feared than loved, if he is to fail in one of the two.
The Prince (1513)

4 Let no one oppose this belief of mine with that well-worn proverb: 'He who builds on the people builds on mud.'
The Prince (written 1513)

5 Since, then, a prince is necessitated to play the animal well, he chooses among the beasts the fox and the lion, because the lion does not protect himself from traps; the fox does not protect himself from wolves. The prince must be a fox, therefore, to recognize the traps and a lion to frighten the wolves.
The Prince (1513)

6 So long as the great majority of men are not deprived of either property or honour, they are satisfied.
The Prince (1513)

7 There is no other way for securing yourself against flatteries except that men understand that they do not offend you by telling you the truth; but when everybody can tell you the truth, you fail to get respect.
The Prince (1513)

8 In seizing a state, the usurper ought to examine closely into all those injuries which it is necessary for him to inflict, and to do them all at one stroke, so as not to have to repeat them daily; and thus by not unsettling men he will be able to reassure them, and win them to himself by benefits. He who does otherwise, either from timidity or evil advice, is always compelled to keep the knife in his hand.
The Prince (1513)

9 Princes ought to leave affairs of reproach to the management of others, and keep those of grace in their own hands.
The Prince (1513)

10 It is necessary for him who lays out a state and arranges laws for it to presuppose that all men are evil and that they are always going to act according to the wickedness of their spirits whenever they have free scope.
Discorsi Supra la Prima Deca di Tito Livio (1513–17)

11 Success or failure lies in conforming to the times.
Discourse on Livy (1518)

1 And if, to be sure, sometimes you need to conceal a fact with words, do it in such a way that it does not become known, or, if it does become known, that you have a ready and quick defence.

'Advice to Raffaello Girolami when he went as Ambassador to the Emperor' (October 1522)

2 Wars begin when you will, but they do not end when you please.

History of Florence (1521–4)

James Mackintosh 1765–1832

Scottish philosopher and historian

3 Men are never so good or so bad as their opinions.

Dissertation on the Progress of Ethical Philosophy (1830) 'Jeremy Bentham'

4 The Commons, faithful to their system, remained in a wise and masterly inactivity.

of the French Commons

Vindiciae Gallicae (1791)

Donald McLachlan

first Editor of the *Sunday Telegraph*

on the government of Anthony Eden:

5 Most Conservatives, and almost certainly some of the wiser Trade Union leaders, are waiting to feel the *smack of firm government*.

editorial comment in *Sunday Telegraph* 3 January 1956

Iain Macleod 1913–70

British Conservative politician

on Macleod: see **Butler** 70:6, **Foot** 138:3, **Salisbury** 319:3

6 I want to deal closely and with relish with the vulgar, crude and intemperate speech to which the House of Commons has just listened.

of Aneurin **Bevan***'s speech during the second reading debate on the National Health Service Bill*

in the House of Commons, 27 March 1952

7 To have a debate on the National Health Service without the right hon. Gentleman [Aneurin Bevan] would be like putting on Hamlet with no one in the part of the First Gravedigger.

in the House of Commons, 27 March 1952

8 It is some measure of the tightness of the magic circle on this occasion that neither the Chancellor of the Exchequer nor the Leader of the House of Commons had any inkling of what was happening.

of the 'evolvement' of Alec **Douglas-Home** *as Conservative leader after the resignation of Harold* **Macmillan**

in *The Spectator* 17 January 1964

9 One does not expect to have many people with one in the last ditch.

on remaining firm in his refusal to serve in Lord **Home***'s government of 1963 after his support of Rab* **Butler***, despite seeing others retract or waver*

in *Dictionary of National Biography*

1 The Conservative Party always in time forgives those who were wrong. Indeed often, in time, they forgive those who were right.

in *The Spectator* 21 February 1964

2 Revolutions in this country, and especially within the Tory party, are rarely plotted. They just happen.

of the Conservative leadership election of 1965

in *Spectator* 30 July 1965

comparing his political approach with that of Enoch **Powell**:

3 I am a fellow-traveller but sometimes I leave Powell's train a few stations down the line before it reaches, and sometimes crashes into, the terminal buffers.

in 1965; Nigel Fisher *Iain Macleod* (1973)

4 John Fitzgerald Kennedy described himself, in a brilliant phrase, as an idealist without illusions. I would describe the Prime Minister as an illusionist without ideals.

in the House of Commons, 1 March 1966; cf. **Kennedy** 205:10

5 In Parliament it should not only be the duty but the pleasure of the Opposition to oppose whenever they reasonably can.

in *The Spectator* 26 August 1966

6 I like seeing my political opponents standing shoulder to shoulder on a burning deck.

attributed, 1967

7 I cannot help it if every time the Opposition are asked to name their weapons they pick boomerangs.

in *Dictionary of National Biography*

8 I don't run in a race to run second.

Nigel Fisher *Iain Macleod* (1973)

Marshall McLuhan 1911–80

Canadian communications scholar

9 Television brought the brutality of war into the comfort of the living room. Vietnam was lost in the living rooms of America—not the battlefields of Vietnam.

in *Montreal Gazette* 16 May 1975

Comte de Macmahon 1808–93

French military commander; President of the Third Republic, 1873–9

10 *J'y suis, j'y reste.*

Here I am, and here I stay.

at the taking of the Malakoff fortress during the Crimean War, 8 September 1855

G. Hanotaux *Histoire de la France Contemporaine* (1903–8) vol. 2

William McMahon 1908–88

Australian statesman, Prime Minister 1971–2

11 Politics is trying to get into office.

L. Oakes and D. Solomon *The Making of an Australian Prime Minister* (1973)

Harold Macmillan 1894–1986

British Conservative statesman, Prime Minister 1957–63
on Macmillan: see **Bevan** 41:7, **Birch** 45:8, 45:10, **Headlam** 172:2, **Hennessy** 175:2, **Levin** 222:5, 222:6, 222:11, **Macleod** 242:8, **Thorpe** 364:7

1 Toryism has always been a form of paternal socialism.
in 1936
Anthony Sampson *Macmillan* (1967)

2 We...are Greeks in this American empire...We must run the Allied Forces HQ as the Greeks ran the operations of the Emperor Claudius.
to Richard **Crossman** *in 1944, after French North Africa had become an American sphere of influence, with* **Eisenhower** *as Supreme Allied Commander*
in *Sunday Telegraph* 9 February 1964

3 Germany, now cast down, despised, shunned like an unclean thing, will once more be courted by each of the two groups, and from a starving outcast she will become the pampered courtesan of Europe, selling her favours to the highest bidder.
in the House of Commons, 20 February 1946

4 We have not overthrown the divine right of Kings to fall down before the divine right of experts.
in 1950; Peter Hennessy *Whitehall* (1990)

5 There ain't gonna be no war.
at a London press conference, 24 July 1955, following the Geneva summit
in *News Chronicle* 25 July 1955

6 Forever poised between a cliché and an indiscretion.
on the life of a Foreign Secretary
in *Newsweek* 30 April 1956

7 Let us be frank about it: most of our people have never had it so good. Go around the country, go to the industrial towns, go to the farms, and you'll see a state of prosperity such as we have never had in my lifetime—nor indeed ever in the history of this country. What is beginning to worry some of us is 'Is it too good to be true?' or perhaps I should say 'Is it too good to last?'
'You Never Had It So Good' was the Democratic Party slogan during the 1952 US election campaign
speech at Bedford, 20 July 1957

8 I thought the best thing to do was to settle up these little local difficulties, and then turn to the wider vision of the Commonwealth.
statement at London airport on leaving for a Commonwealth tour, 7 January 1958, following the resignation of the Chancellor of the Exchequer and others
in *The Times* 8 January 1958

9 Do not be impatient with the majors in the party; all regiments have need of majors.
advice to newly elected MPs, at an East India Club dinner in 1959
Julian Critchley *A Bag of Boiled Sweets* (1994)

10 Revolt by all means; but only on one issue at a time; to do more would be to confuse the whips.
advice to newly elected MPs
Julian Critchley *A Bag of Boiled Sweets* (1994)

11 He [Aneurin Bevan] enjoys prophesying the imminent fall of the capitalist system and is prepared to play a part, any part, in its burial, except that of mute.
Michael Foot *Aneurin Bevan* (1962)

1 The wind of change is blowing through this continent, and, whether we like it or not, this growth of [African] national consciousness is a political fact.
speech at Cape Town, 3 February 1960

2 Can we say that with fifteen representatives, Ambassadors or Ministers, in Nato acting in unanimity, the deterrent would continue to be credible? There might be one finger on the trigger. There would be fifteen fingers on the safety catch.
attributed, 1960

3 As usual the Liberals offer a mixture of sound and original ideas. Unfortunately none of the sound ideas is original and none of the original ideas is sound.
speech to London Conservatives, 7 March 1961

4 A successful [political] television show seems to be more and more a cross between a music-hall turn and a scene in a torture-chamber.
speech to the Parliamentary Press Gallery, 14 March 1962

5 [They are a] strange people, tortured by material success and affluence.
of the British, in a confidential memorandum on his possible successors, 1963
in *Independent* 1 January 1995

6 I was determined that no British government should be brought down by the action of two tarts.
comment on the Profumo affair, July 1963
Anthony Sampson *Macmillan* (1967)

7 Power? It's like a Dead Sea fruit. When you achieve it, there is nothing there.
Anthony Sampson *The New Anatomy of Britain* (1971); cf. **Levin** 222:11

8 Churchill was fundamentally what the English call unstable—by which they mean anybody who has that touch of genius which is inconvenient in normal times.
attributed, 1975

9 There are three bodies no sensible man directly challenges: the Roman Catholic Church, the Brigade of Guards and the National Union of Mineworkers.
in *Observer* 22 February 1981; cf. **Baldwin** 29:12

of the office of Prime Minister:

10 Sometimes the strain is awful, you have to resort to Jane Austen.
in the Butler Papers; Peter Hennessy *The Hidden Wiring* (1995)

11 First of all the Georgian silver goes, and then all that nice furniture that used to be in the saloon. Then the Canalettos go.
speech on privatization to the Tory Reform Group, 8 November 1985; often quoted as 'selling the family silver'
in *The Times* 9 November 1985

12 He would have been marvellous in medieval politics, creeping about the Vatican; a tremendous intriguer, he always had some marvellous plan... and he loved the press.
of Rab **Butler**
Alistair Horne *Macmillan* (1988) vol. 1

13 The only quality needed for an MP is the ability to write a good letter.
Julian Critchley *A Bag of Boiled Sweets* (1994)

14 It has always seemed to me more artistic, when the curtain falls on the last performance, to accept the inevitable *E finita la commedia*. It is tempting, perhaps,
At the End of the Day (1973)

but unrewarding to hang about the greenroom after final retirement from the stage.

James Madison 1751–1836

American Democratic Republican statesman, 4th President of the US 1809–17

1 Liberty is to faction what air is to fire, an ailment without which it instantly expires. But it could not be less folly to abolish liberty, which is essential to political life, because it nourishes faction than it would be to wish the annihilation of air, which is essential to animal life, because it imparts to fire its destructive agency.

The Federalist (1787)

2 The diversity in the faculties of men, from which the rights of property originate, is not less an insuperable obstacle to a uniformity of interests. The protection of these faculties is the first object of government. From the protection of different and unequal faculties of acquiring property, the possession of different degrees and kinds of property immediately results.

The Federalist (1787)

3 By a faction, understand a number of citizens, whether amounting to a majority or minority of the whole, who are united and actuated by some common impulse of passion, or of interest, adverse to the rights of other citizens, or to the permanent and aggregate interests of the community.

The Federalist (1787)

4 The most common and durable source of factions has been the various and unequal distribution of property.

The Federalist (1787)

5 The accumulation of all powers, legislative, executive, and judiciary, in the same hands, whether of one, a few, or many, and whether hereditary, self-appointed, or elective, may justly be pronounced the very definition of tyranny.

The Federalist (1787)

6 I believe there are more instances of the abridgement of the freedom of the people by gradual and silent encroachment of those in power than by violent and sudden usurpations.

speech in the Virginia Convention, 16 June 1788

7 In framing a government, which is to be administered by men over men, the great difficulty lies in this: you must first enable the government to control the governed, and in the next place oblige it to control itself.

attributed

John Maffey 1877–1969

British diplomat

as British Ambassador to Dublin:

8 Phrases make history here.

letter 21 May 1945

William Connor Magee 1821–91

English prelate

1 It would be better that England should be free than that England should be compulsorily sober.
on the Intoxicating Liquor Bill
in the House of Lords, 2 May 1872

Magna Carta

Political charter signed by King John at Runnymede, 1215

2 That the English Church shall be free.
Clause 1

3 No free man shall be taken or imprisoned or dispossessed, or outlawed or exiled, or in any way destroyed, nor will we go upon him, nor will we send against him except by the lawful judgement of his peers or by the law of the land.
Clause 39

4 To no man will we sell, or deny, or delay, right or justice.
Clause 40

Alex Magowan

Councillor for Newtonabbey, Northern Ireland

5 A councillor is like a mushroom. You're kept in the dark and now and again manure is thrown over you.
attributed, 1974

Alfred T. Mahan 1840–1914

American naval officer and historian

6 Those far distant, storm-beaten ships, upon which the Grand Army never looked, stood between it and the dominion of the world.
The Influence of Sea Power upon the French Revolution and Empire 1793–1812 (1892) vol. 2

Norman Mailer 1923–

American novelist and essayist

7 All the security around the American President is just to make sure the man who shoots him gets caught.
in *Sunday Telegraph* 4 March 1990

John Major 1943–

British Conservative statesman, Prime Minister since 1990
on Major: see **Blair** 49:1, **Thatcher** 362:11

8 The first requirement of politics is not intellect or stamina but patience. Politics is a very long-run game and the tortoise will usually beat the hare.
in *Daily Express* 25 July 1989

9 If the policy isn't hurting, it isn't working.
speech in Northampton, 27 October 1989

10 If I sounded lukewarm about our commitment to enter the European exchange rate mechanism it was because of a frog in my throat.
in *Independent* 24 March 1990

1 Society needs to condemn a little more and understand a little less.
interview with *Mail on Sunday* 21 February 1993

2 Fifty years on from now, Britain will still be the country of long shadows on county [cricket] grounds, warm beer, invincible green suburbs, dog lovers, and—as George Orwell said—old maids bicycling to Holy Communion through the morning mist.
speech to the Conservative Group for Europe, 22 April 1993; cf. **Orwell** 278:7

3 It is time to get back to basics: to self-discipline and respect for the law, to consideration for others, to accepting responsibility for yourself and your family, and not shuffling it off on the state.
speech to the Conservative Party Conference, 8 October 1993

4 I could name eight people—half of those eight are barmy. How many apples short of a picnic?
of Conservative critics
on 19 September 1993

Josephe de Maistre 1753–1821

French writer and diplomat

5 Every country has the government it deserves.
letter 15 August 1811

Bernard Malamud 1914–86

American novelist and short-story writer

6 There's no such thing as an unpolitical man, especially a Jew.
The Fixer (1966)

Malcolm X 1925–65

American civil rights campaigner

7 If you're born in America with a black skin, you're born in prison.
in an interview, June 1963

8 We are not fighting for integration, nor are we fighting for separation. We are fighting for recognition as human beings. We are fighting for…human rights.
Black Revolution, speech in New York, 1964

Thomas Robert Malthus 1766–1834

English political economist

9 Population, when unchecked, increases in a geometrical ratio. Subsistence only increases in an arithmetical ratio.
Essay on the Principle of Population (1798)

10 The perpetual struggle for room and food.
Essay on the Principle of Population (1798)

11 A man who is born into a world already possessed, if he cannot get subsistence from his parents on whom he has a just demand, and if the society do not want his labour, has no claim of *right* to the smallest portion of food, and, in fact, has no business to be where he is. At Nature's mighty feast there is no vacant cover for him.
Essay on the Principle of Population (1803 ed.)

Earl of Manchester 1602–71

politician and Parliamentary commander in the Civil War

1 If we beat the King ninety-nine times, yet he is king still and so will his posterity be after him; but if the king beat us once we shall all be hanged, and our posterity made slaves.
at a Parliamentary Council-of-War, 10 November 1644
in *Calendar of State Papers, Domestic* 1644–5

Lord Mancroft 1914–87

British Conservative politician

2 Cricket—a game which the English, not being a spiritual people, have invented in order to give themselves some conception of eternity.
Bees in Some Bonnets (1979)

Nelson Mandela 1918–

South African politician and African National Congress activist; President since 1994

3 Through its imperialist system Britain brought about untold suffering of millions of people. And this is an historical fact. To be able to admit this would increase the respect, you know, which we have for British institutions.
in *Guardian* 2 April 1990

Winnie Mandela 1934–

South African political activist

4 With that stick of matches, with our necklace, we shall liberate this country.
speech in black townships, 14 April 1986; a 'necklace' was a tyre soaked or filled with petrol, placed around a victim's neck, and set alight
in *Guardian* 15 April 1986

John Manners, Duke of Rutland 1818–1906

English Tory politician and writer

5 Let wealth and commerce, laws and learning die,
But leave us still our old nobility!
England's Trust (1841)

Lord Mansfield 1705–93

Scottish lawyer and politician

6 The constitution does not allow reasons of state to influence our judgements: God forbid it should! We must not regard political consequences; however formidable soever they might be: if rebellion was the certain consequence, we are bound to say '*fiat justitia, ruat caelum*'.
Rex v. Wilkes, 8 June 1768, in *The English Reports* (1909) vol. 98; cf. **Adams** 4:6

1 Consider what you think justice requires, and decide accordingly. But never give your reasons; for your judgement will probably be right, but your reasons will certainly be wrong.
advice to a newly appointed colonial governor ignorant in the law

Lord Campbell *The Lives of the Chief Justices of England* (1849) vol. 2

Mao Zedong 1893–1976

Chinese statesman, chairman of the Communist Party of the Chinese People's Republic 1949–76 and head of state 1949–59

2 A revolution is not the same as inviting people to dinner, or writing an essay, or painting a picture.

report, March 1927

3 Politics is war without bloodshed while war is politics with bloodshed.

lecture, 1938

4 Every Communist must grasp the truth, 'Political power grows out of the barrel of a gun'.

speech, 6 November 1938

5 The atom bomb is a paper tiger which the United States reactionaries use to scare people. It looks terrible, but in fact it isn't... All reactionaries are paper tigers.

interview, 1946

6 Letting a hundred flowers blossom and a hundred schools of thought contend is the policy for promoting progress in the arts and the sciences and a flourishing socialist culture in our land.

speech in Peking, 27 February 1957

7 People of the world, unite and defeat the US aggressors and all their running dogs!

'Statement Supporting the People of the Congo against US Aggression' 28 November 1964

William Learned Marcy 1786–1857

American politician

8 The politicians of New York... see nothing wrong in the rule, that to the victor belong the spoils of the enemy.

speech to the Senate, 25 January 1832

Marie-Antoinette 1755–93

Queen consort of Louis XVI

9 Let them eat cake.
on being told that her people had no bread

attributed; in *Confessions* (1740) Rousseau refers to a similar remark being a well-known saying; in *Relation d'un Voyage à Bruxelles et à Coblentz en 1791* (1823), Louis XVIII attributes 'Why don't they eat pastry?' to Marie-Thérèse (1638–83), wife of Louis XIV

George C. Marshall 1880–1959

American general and statesman, who as US Secretary of State (1947–9) initiated the programme of economic aid to European countries known as the Marshall Plan

1 If man does find the solution for world peace it will be the most revolutionary reversal of his record we have ever known.
biennal report of the Chief of Staff, United States Army, 1 September 1945

2 Our policy is directed not against any country or doctrine but against hunger, poverty, desperation and chaos. Its purpose should be the revival of a working economy in the world so as to permit the emergence of political and social conditions in which free institutions can exist.
announcing the Marshall Plan
address at Harvard, 5 June 1947

John Marshall 1755–1835

American jurist

3 The power to tax involves the power to destroy.
in *McCulloch v. Maryland* (1819)

4 The people made the Constitution, and the people can unmake it. It is the creature of their own will, and lives only by their will.
in *Cohens v. Virginia* (1821)

Thomas R. Marshall 1854–1925

American politician

5 What this country needs is a really good 5-cent cigar.
in *New York Tribune* 4 January 1920

José Martí 1853–95

6 The spirit of a government must be that of the country. The form of a government must come from the make-up of the country. Government is nothing but the balance of the natural elements of a country.
Our America (1891)

Andrew Marvell 1621–78

English poet

7 *He* nothing common did or mean
Upon that memorable scene:
But with his keener eye
The axe's edge did try:
Nor called the gods with vulgar spite
To vindicate his helpless right,
But bowed his comely head,
Down as upon a bed.
on the execution of **Charles I**
'An Horatian Ode upon Cromwell's Return from Ireland' (written 1650)

8 And now the Irish are ashamed
To see themselves in one year tamed:
'An Horatian Ode upon Cromwell's Return from Ireland' (written 1650)

So much one man can do,
That does both act and know.

1 Choosing each stone, and poising every weight,
Trying the measures of the breadth and height;
Here pulling down, and there erecting new,
Founding a firm state by proportions true.

'The First Anniversary of the Government under His Highness the Lord Protector, 1655'

Karl Marx 1818–83

German political philosopher; founder of modern Communism

2 Religion...is the opium of the people.

A Contribution to the Critique of Hegel's Philosophy of Right (1843–4) introduction

3 The philosophers have only interpreted the world in various ways; the point is to change it.

Theses on Feuerbach (written 1845)

4 Hegel says somewhere that all great events and personalities in world history reappear in one fashion or another. He forgot to add: the first time as tragedy, the second as farce.

The Eighteenth Brumaire of Louis Bonaparte (1852)

5 What I did that was new was to prove...that the class struggle necessarily leads to the dictatorship of the proletariat.

the phrase 'dictatorship of the proletariat' had been used earlier in the Constitution of the World Society of Revolutionary Communists (1850), signed by Marx and others

letter to Georg Weydemeyer 5 March 1852; Marx claimed that the phrase had been coined by Auguste Blanqui (1805–81), but it has not been found in this form in Blanqui's work

6 Mankind always sets itself only such problems as it can solve; since, looking at the matter more closely, it will always be found that the task itself arises only when the material conditions for its solution already exist or are at least in the process of formation.

A Contribution to the Critique of Political Economy (1859) preface

7 It is not the consciousness of men that determines their being, but, on the contrary, their social being that determines their consciousness.

A Contribution to the Critique of Political Economy (1859) preface

8 It is the ultimate aim of this work, to lay bare the economic law of motion of modern society.

Das Kapital (1st German ed., 1867) preface (25 July 1865)

9 From each according to his abilities, to each according to his needs.

Critique of the Gotha Programme (written 1875, but of earlier origin); see Morelly *Code de la nature* (1755), and J. J. L. Blanc *Organisation du travail* (1839) (who, in quoting Saint-Simon, rejects the notion) for possible sources

10 All I know is that I am not a Marxist.

attributed in a letter from Friedrich Engels to Conrad Schmidt, 5 August 1890

Karl Marx 1818–83 and **Friedrich Engels** 1820–95

Co-founders of modern Communism

1 A spectre is haunting Europe—the spectre of Communism.
The Communist Manifesto (1848) opening words

2 The history of all hitherto existing society is the history of class struggles.
The Communist Manifesto (1848)

3 In place of the old bourgeois society, with its classes and class antagonists, we shall have an association, in which the free development of each is the free development of all.
The Communist Manifesto (1848)

4 The proletarians have nothing to lose but their chains. They have a world to win. WORKING MEN OF ALL COUNTRIES UNITE
often quoted as 'Workers of the world, unite!'
The Communist Manifesto (1848) *ad fin.*

Queen Mary 1867–1953

Queen Consort of George V

5 *This* is a pretty kettle of fish!
to the Prime Minister, Stanley **Baldwin,** *after* **Edward VIII** *had told her that he was prepared to give up the throne to marry Mrs Simpson*
James Pope-Hennessy *Life of Queen Mary* (1959)

6 All *this* thrown away for *that.*
on returning home to Marlborough House, London after the abdication of her son, King **Edward VIII,** *December 1936*
David Duff *George and Elizabeth* (1983)

7 I do not think you have ever realised the shock, which the attitude you took up caused your family and the whole nation. It seemed inconceivable to those who had made such sacrifices during the war that you, as their King, refused a lesser sacrifice.
letter to the Duke of Windsor, the former **Edward VIII,** July 1938

Mary, Queen of Scots 1542–87

Queen of Scotland, 1542–67

8 *En ma fin git mon commencement.*
In my end is my beginning.
motto embroidered with an emblem of her mother, Mary of Guise
quoted in a letter from William Drummond of Hawthornden to Ben Jonson in 1619

Mary Tudor 1516–58

Queen of England from 1553

9 When I am dead and opened, you shall find 'Calais' lying in my heart.
in *Holinshed's Chronicles* vol. 4 (1808)

Philip Massinger 1583–1640

English playwright

1 Ambition, in a private man a vice,
Is in a prince the virtue.

The Bashful Lover (licensed 1636, published 1655)

2 Greatness, with private men
Esteemed a blessing, is to me a curse;
And we, whom, for our high births, they conclude
The only freemen, are the only slaves.
Happy the golden mean!

The Great Duke of Florence (licensed 1627, printed 1635)

Henry William Massingham 1860–1924

British journalist; Editor of the *Nation*

3 To me there are few spectacles more melancholy than that of dear old C. P. Scott wearily dredging in a foul pool for the soul of Lloyd George.

of the attempts by C. P. **Scott**, *editor of the* Manchester Guardian, *to find a saving word for* **Lloyd George** *during the last days of the Coalition in 1922*

Vivian Phillipps *My Days and Ways* (1943)

W. Somerset Maugham 1874–1965

British novelist, short-story writer, and dramatist

4 The geniality of the politician who for years has gone out of his way to be cordial with everyone he meets.

A Writer's Notebook (1949) written in 1938

James Maxton 1885–1946

British Labour politician

5 All I say is, if you cannot ride two horses you have no right in the circus.

opposing disaffiliation of the Scottish Independent Labour Party from the Labour Party, often quoted as 'no right in the bloody circus'

in *Daily Herald* 12 January 1931

Horace Maybray-King 1901–86

British Labour politician; Speaker of the House of Commons

6 One of the myths of the British Parliament is that there are three parties there. I can assure you from bitter personal experience there are 629.

in *Observer* 9 October 1966 'Sayings of the Week'

Jonathan Mayhew 1720–66

American divine

7 Rulers have no authority from God to do mischief.

A Discourse Concerning Unlimited Submission and Non-Resistance to the Higher Powers (1750)

1 As soon as the prince sets himself up above the law, he loses the king in the tyrant; he does to all intents and purpose unking himself...And in such cases, has no more right to be obeyed, than any inferior officer who acts beyond his commission.

A Discourse Concerning Unlimited Submission and Non-Resistance to the Higher Powers (1750)

Catherine de' Medici 1518–89

Queen Consort of France, wife of Henri II

2 A false report, if believed during three days, may be of great service to a government.

Isaac D'Israeli *Curiosities of Literature* 2nd series (1849) vol. 2; perhaps apocryphal

Robert Megarry 1910–

3 Whereas in England all is permitted that is not expressly prohibited, it has been said that in Germany all is prohibited unless expressly permitted and in France all is permitted that is expressly prohibited. In the European Common Market (as it then was) no-one knows what is permitted and it all costs more.

'Law and Lawyers in a Permissive Society' (5th Riddell Lecture delivered in Lincoln's Inn Hall 22 March 1972)

Lord Melbourne 1779–1848

British Whig politician; Prime Minister 1834, 1835–41

4 What all the wise men promised has not happened, and what all the d—d fools said would happen has come to pass.
of the Catholic Emancipation Act (1829)

H. Dunckley *Lord Melbourne* (1890)

5 I have always thought complaints of ill-usage contemptible, whether from a seduced disappointed girl or a turned-out Prime Minister.
on being dismissed by William IV

Emily Eden letter to Mrs Lister, 23 November 1834

6 If left out he would be dangerous, but if taken in, he would be simply destructive.
when forming his second administration, Melbourne omitted the former Lord Chancellor, **Brougham**

Lord David Cecil *Lord M* (1954)

7 You domineered too much, you interfered too much with other departments, you encroached upon the provinces of the Prime Minister, you worked, as I believe, with the Press in a manner unbecoming to the dignity of your station.
letter to the former Lord Chancellor, **Brougham**, *explaining why he had been omitted from Melbourne's second administration*

Lord David Cecil *Lord M* (1954)

8 Damn it! Another Bishop dead! I believe they die to vex me.

Lord David Cecil *Lord M* (1954)

9 God help the Minister that meddles with art!

Lord David Cecil *Lord M* (1954)

10 I wish I was as cocksure of anything as Tom Macaulay is of everything.

Earl Cowper *Preface to Lord Melbourne's Papers* (1889)

1 Nobody ever did anything very foolish except from some strong principle.
Lord David Cecil *The Young Melbourne* (1939)

2 Now, is it to lower the price of corn, or isn't it? It is not much matter which we say, but mind, we must all say *the same.*
at the end of a Cabinet meeting to agree a fixed tariff for corn; Melbourne is said to have put his back to the door and only opened it when they agreed
Walter Bagehot *The English Constitution* (1867)

3 Things have come to a pretty pass when religion is allowed to invade the sphere of private life.
on hearing an evangelical sermon
G. W. E. Russell *Collections and Recollections* (1898)

4 What I want is men who will support me when I am in the wrong.
replying to a politician who said 'I will support you as long as you are in the right'
Lord David Cecil *Lord M* (1954)

5 When in doubt what should be done, do nothing.
Lord David Cecil *Lord M* (1954)

6 The whole duty of government is to prevent crime and to preserve contracts.
Lord David Cecil *Lord M* (1954)

David Mellor 1949–

British Conservative politician

7 I do believe the popular press is drinking in the last chance saloon.
interview on *Hard News* (Channel 4), 21 December 1989

H. L. Mencken 1880–1956

American journalist and literary critic

8 Democracy is the theory that the common people know what they want, and deserve to get it good and hard.
A Little Book in C major (1916)

9 The whole aim of practical politics is to keep the populace alarmed (and hence clamorous to be led to safety) by menacing it with an endless series of hobgoblins, all of them imaginary.
In Defence of Women (1923)

10 A good politician is quite as unthinkable as an honest burglar.
Prejudices 4th series (1925)

11 No one in this world, so far as I know—and I have searched the records for years, and employed agents to help me—has ever lost money by underestimating the intelligence of the great masses of the plain people.
in *Chicago Tribune* 19 September 1926

12 The saddest life is that of a political aspirant under democracy. His failure is ignominious and his success is disgraceful.
in *Baltimore Evening Sun* 9 December 1929

13 He [Calvin Coolidge] slept more than any other President, whether by day or by night. Nero fiddled, but Coolidge only snored.
in *American Mercury* April 1933

14 If there had been any formidable body of cannibals in the country he would have promised to provide them with
in *Baltimore Sun* 7 November 1948

free missionaries fattened at the taxpayer's expense.
of Harry **Truman***'s success in the 1948 presidential campaign*

1 Nothing is so abject and pathetic as a politician who has lost his job, save only a retired stud-horse. — *Chrestomathy* (1949)

2 Puritanism. The haunting fear that someone, somewhere, may be happy. — *Chrestomathy* (1949)

3 A government can never be the impersonal thing described in text-books. It is simply a group of men like any other. In every 100 of the men composing it there are two who are honest and intelligent, ten obvious scoundrels, and 88 poor fish. — *Minority Report* (1956)

4 Under democracy one party always devotes its chief energies to trying to prove that the other party is unfit to rule—and both commonly succeed, and are right. — *Minority Report* (1956)

5 The worst government is often the most moral. One composed of cynics is often very tolerant and humane. But when fanatics are on top there is no limit to oppression. — *Minority Report* (1956)

Jean Meslier *c.*1664–1733

French priest

6 I remember, on this matter, the wish made once by an ignorant, uneducated man... He said he wished... that all the great men in the world and all the nobility could be hanged, and strangled with the guts of priests. For myself... I wish I could have the strength of Hercules to purge the world of all vice and sin, and to have the pleasure of destroying all those monsters of error and sin [priests] who make all the peoples of the world groan so pitiably. — *Testament* (1864); cf. **Diderot** 116:1
often quoted as, 'I should like... the last king to be strangled with the guts of the last priest'

Prince Metternich 1773–1859

Austrian statesman

7 Italy is a geographical expression. — *Mémoires, Documents, etc. de Metternich publiés par son fils* (1883) vol. 7; cf. **Bismarck** 46:9
discussing the Italian question with **Palmerston** *in 1847*

of his own downfall:
8 I feel obliged to call to the supporters of the social uprising: Citizens of a dream-world, nothing is altered. On 14 March 1848, there was merely one man fewer. — *Aus Metternich's Nachgelassenen Papieren* (ed. A. von Klinkowström, 1880) vol. 8

9 Error has never approached my spirit. — François Pierre G. Guizot *Mémoires* (1858–67) vol. 4
addressed to Guizot in 1848

10 The Emperor is everything, Vienna is nothing. — letter to Count Bombelles, 5 June 1848

1 The greatest gift of any statesman rests not in knowing what concessions to make, but recognising when to make them.
Concessionen und Nichtconcessionen (1852)

2 The word 'freedom' means for me not a point of departure but a genuine point of arrival. The point of departure is defined by the word 'order'. Freedom cannot exist without the concept of order.
Mein Politisches Testament

Anthony Meyer 1920–

British Conservative politician

3 I question the right of that great Moloch, national sovereignty, to burn its children to save its pride.
speaking against the Falklands War, 1982
in *Listener* 27 September 1990

Jules Michelet 1798–1874

French historian

4 What is the first part of politics? Education. The second? Education. And the third? Education.
Le Peuple (1846)

5 England is an empire, Germany is a nation, a race, France is a person.
Histoire de France (1833–1867)

William Porcher Miles 1822–96

6 'Vote early and vote often,' the advice openly displayed on the election banners in one of our northern cities.
in the House of Representatives, 31 March 1858

John Stuart Mill 1806–73

English philosopher and economist

7 The great majority of those who speak of perfectibility as a dream, do so because they feel that it is one which would afford them no pleasure if it were realized.
Speech on Perfectibility (1828)

8 The sole end for which mankind are warranted, individually or collectively, in interfering with the liberty of action of any of their number, is self-protection.
On Liberty (1859)

9 The only freedom worth the name, is that of pursuing our own good in our own way.
On Liberty (1859)

10 The only purpose for which power can be rightfully exercised over any member of a civilized community, against his will, is to prevent harm to others. His own good, either physical or moral, is not a sufficient warrant.
On Liberty (1859)

11 If all mankind minus one were of one opinion, and only one person were of the contrary opinion, mankind would be no more justified in silencing that one person, than he, if he had the power, would be justified in silencing mankind.
On Liberty (1859)

1 A party of order or stability, and a party of progress or reform, are both necessary elements of a healthy state of political life. — *On Liberty* (1859)

2 The liberty of the individual must be thus far limited; he must not make himself a nuisance to other people. — *On Liberty* (1859)

3 I am not aware that any community has a right to force another to be civilized. — *On Liberty* (1859)

4 Liberty consists in doing what one desires. — *On Liberty* (1859)

5 A State which dwarfs its men, in order that they may be more docile instruments in its hands even for beneficial purposes, will find that with small men no great thing can really be accomplished. — *On Liberty* (1859)

6 When society requires to be rebuilt, there is no use in attempting to rebuild it on the old plan. — *Dissertations and Discussions* vol. 1 (1859) 'Essay on Coleridge'

7 The Conservatives...being by the law of their existence the stupidest party. — *Considerations on Representative Government* (1861)

8 The principle which regulates the existing social relations between the two sexes—the legal subordination of one sex to the other—is wrong in itself, and now one of the chief hindrances to human improvement. — *The Subjection of Women* (1869)

9 Laws and systems of polity always begin by recognising the relations they find already existing between individuals. They convert what was a mere physical fact into a legal right, give it the sanction of society, and principally aim at the substitution of public and organised means of asserting and protecting these rights, instead of the irregular and lawless conflict of physical strength. — *The Subjection of Women* (1869)

10 Everyone who desires power, desires it most over those who are nearest to him, with whom his life is passed, with whom he has most concerns in common, and in whom any independence of his authority is oftenest likely to interfere with his individual preferences. — *The Subjection of Women* (1869)

11 The laws of most countries are far worse than the people who execute them, and many of them are only able to remain laws by being seldom or never carried into effect. If married life were all that it might be expected to be, looking to the laws alone, society would be a hell upon earth. — *The Subjection of Women* (1869)

12 No great improvements in the lot of mankind are possible, until a great change takes place in the fundamental constitution of their modes of thought. — *Autobiography* (1873)

13 Detention by the State of the unearned increment of rent. — *Dissertations and Discussions*

14 In the case of most men the only inducement which has been found sufficiently constant and unflagging to overcome the ever-present influence of indolence and love of ease, and induce men to apply themselves unrelaxingly to work for the most part in itself dull and unexciting, is — in *Fortnightly Review* April 1879

the prospect of bettering their own economic condition and that of their family.

Alice Duer Miller 1874–1942

American writer

1 I am American bred,
I have seen much to hate here—much to forgive,
But in a world where England is finished and dead,
I do not wish to live.

The White Cliffs (1940)

Charles Wright Mills 1916–62

American sociologist

2 By the power elite, we refer to those political, economic, and military circles which as an intricate set of overlapping cliques share decisions having at least national conseqences. In so far as national events are decided, the power elite are those who decide them.

The Power Elite (1956)

Lord Milner 1854–1925

British colonial administrator

3 If we believe a thing to be bad, and if we have a right to prevent it, it is our duty to try to prevent it and to damn the consequences.

speech in Glasgow, 26 November 1909

John Milton 1608–74

English poet, who became a politically active Parliamentarian during the Civil War, publishing the *Areopagitica* (1644) which demanded a free press, and writing a defence of republicanism on the eve of the Restoration (1660)

4 The land had once enfranchised herself from this impertinent yoke of prelaty, under whose inquisitorious and tyrannical duncery no free and splendid wit can flourish.

The Reason of Church Government (1642) bk. 2, introduction

5 Let not England forget her precedence of teaching nations how to live.

The Doctrine and Discipline of Divorce (1643) 'To the Parliament of England'

6 I cannot praise a fugitive and cloistered virtue, unexercised and unbreathed, that never sallies out and sees her adversary, but slinks out of the race, where that immortal garland is to be run for, not without dust and heat.

Areopagitica (1644)

7 Here the great art lies, to discern in what the law is to be to restraint and punishment, and in what things persuasion only is to work.

Areopagitica (1644)

8 None can love freedom heartily, but good men; the rest love not freedom, but licence.

The Tenure of Kings and Magistrates (1649)

1 No man who knows aught, can be so stupid to deny that all men naturally were born free.
The Tenure of Kings and Magistrates (1649)

2 Cromwell, our chief of men.
'To the Lord General Cromwell' (written 1652)

3 ...Peace hath her victories
No less renowned than war.
'To the Lord General Cromwell' (written 1652)

4 What I have spoken, is the language of that which is not called amiss *The good old Cause.*
The Ready and Easy Way to Establish a Free Commonwealth (2nd ed., 1660)

5 They also serve who only stand and wait.
'When I consider how my light is spent' (1673)

Comte de Mirabeau 1749–91

French revolutionary

6 War is the national industry of Prussia.
attributed to Mirabeau by Albert Sorel (1842–1906), based on Mirabeau's introduction to *De la monarchie prussienne sous Frédéric le Grand* (1788)

Joni Mitchell 1943–

Canadian singer and songwriter

7 Lord, there's danger in this land.
You get witch-hunts and wars when church and state hold hands.
Peter McWilliams *Ain't Nobody's Business If You Do* (1993)

François Mitterrand 1916–96

French socialist statesman; President of France 1981–95

8 She has the eyes of Caligula, but the mouth of Marilyn Monroe.
of Margaret **Thatcher**, *briefing his new European Minister Roland Dumas*
in *Observer* 25 November 1990

Walter Monckton 1891–1965

British lawyer and Conservative politician

when offered the post of Minister of Labour, Monckton hesitated on the grounds of inexperience:

9 CHURCHILL: Your qualification is that you have no political past.
MONCKTON: I take it you do not expect me to have any political future.
in *Dictionary of National Biography*

asking his wife to curtsey to the Duchess of Windsor:

10 It does no harm, and makes the little man so happy.
Andrew Roberts *Eminent Churchillians* (1994)

11 Too conventional a thinker to make a great leader.
of Anthony **Eden**
Andrew Roberts *Eminent Churchillians* (1994)

Walter Mondale 1928–

American Democratic politician and Vice-President

1 When I hear your new ideas I'm reminded of that ad, 'Where's the beef?'
alluding to an advertising slogan which made an unfavourable comparison between the relative sizes of a small hamburger and a large bun
in a televised debate with Gary Hart, 11 March 1984

2 Political image is like mixing cement. When it's wet, you can move it around and shape it, but at some point it hardens and there's almost nothing you can do to reshape it.
in *Independent on Sunday* 12 May 1991

Duke of Monmouth 1649–85

illegitimate son of Charles II; focus of the supporters of the Protestant succession in the Exclusion crisis of 1681 (cf. **Dryden**) and leader of the failed Monmouth rebellion against James II

3 Do not hack me as you did my Lord Russell.
words addressed to his executioner; according to a contemporary account five blows were needed
T. B. Macaulay *History of England* vol. 1 (1849)

Jean Monnet 1888–1979

French economist and diplomat; founder of the European Community

of American foreign policy in relation to European integration:

4 It is the first time in history that a great power, instead of basing its policy on ruling by dividing, has consistently and resolutely backed the creation of a large Community uniting peoples previously apart.
in 1953; François Duchêne *Jean Monnet* (1994)

5 Europe has never existed. It is not the addition of national sovereignties in a conclave which creates an entity. One must genuinely *create* Europe.
Anthony Sampson *The New Europeans* (1968)

6 The common market is a process, not a product.
Anthony Sampson *The New Europeans* (1968)

7 I did not understand the politics of Versailles, only the economics.
of the Treaty of Versailles
in an interview in 1971; François Duchêne *Jean Monnet* (1994)

8 It is astonishing how little the word 'alliance', which people find so reassuring, really means in practice if all it implies is the traditional machinery of cooperation... where national sovereignty is ultimately vested in points of prestige and solutions are compromises between them.
in an interview in 1971; François Duchêne *Jean Monnet* (1994)

9 A great statesman is one who can work for long-term goals which eventually suit situations as yet unforeseen.
Memoirs (1978)

10 Each man begins the world afresh. Only institutions grow wiser; they store up the collective experience; and, from this experience and wisdom, men subject to the same
François Duchêne *Jean Monnet* (1994)

laws will gradually find, not that their natures change but that their experience does.
a favourite sentiment ascribed by Monnet to the nineteenth-century Genevese diarist Henri Frédéric Amiel

1 Institutions govern relationships between people. They are the real pillars of civilization. — François Duchêne *Jean Monnet* (1994)

2 We should not create a nation Europe instead of a nation France. — François Duchêne *Jean Monnet* (1994)

James Monroe 1758–1831

American Democratic Republican statesman, 5th President of the US 1817–25, who in 1803 negotiated the Lousiana Purchase, and who formulated the Monroe Doctrine

3 National honour is national property of the highest value. — first inaugural address, 4 March 1817

4 The American continents... are henceforth not to be considered as subjects for future colonization by any European powers. — annual message to Congress, 2 December 1823
first expression of what became the Monroe Doctrine

5 In the wars of the European powers in matters relating to themselves we have never taken any part, nor does it comport with our policy to do so. — annual message to Congress, 2 December 1823

6 With the existing colonies or dependencies of any European power we... shall not interfere. But with the governments... whose independence we have... acknowledged, we could not view any interposition for the purpose of oppressing them, or controlling, in any other manner, their destiny, by any European power, in any other light than as a manifestation of an unfriendly disposition toward the United States. — annual message to Congress, 2 December 1823

Montaigne 1533–92

French moralist and essayist

7 There is scarcely any less bother in the running of a family than in that of an entire state. And domestic business is no less importunate for being less important. — *Essais* (1580)

8 Fame and tranquillity can never be bedfellows. — *Essais* (1580)

9 On the highest throne in the world, we still sit only on our own bottom. — *Essais* (1580)

Montesquieu 1689–1755

French political philosopher

10 Ever since the invention of gunpowder... I continually tremble lest men should, in the end, uncover some secret which would provide a short way of abolishing mankind, of annihilating peoples and nations in their entirety. — *Lettres Persanes* (1721)

1 Just as the sea, which seems to want to cover the whole earth, is checked by the grasses and the smallest bits of gravel on the shore, so monarchs, whose power seems boundless, are checked by the slightest obstacles and submit their natural pride to supplication and prayer. *The Spirit of the Laws* (1748)

2 When the savages of Louisiana want fruit, they cut down the tree and gather the fruit. There you have despotic government. *The Spirit of the Laws* (1748)

3 Republics end in luxury; monarchies, in poverty. *The Spirit of the Laws* (1748)

4 The corruption of each government almost always begins with that of its principles. *The Spirit of the Laws* (1748)

5 The principle of democracy is corrupted not only when the spirit of equality is lost but also when the spirit of extreme equality is taken up and each one wants to be the equal of those chosen to command. *The Spirit of the Laws* (1748)

6 If a republic is small, it is destroyed by a foreign force; if it is large, it is destroyed by an internal vice. *The Spirit of the Laws* (1748)

7 When a neighbouring state is in decline, one should take care not to hasten its ruin, because this is the most fortunate situation possible; there is nothing more suitable for a prince than to be close to another who receives in his stead all the blows and outrages of fortune. *The Spirit of the Laws* (1748)

8 Liberty is the right to do everything the laws permit. *The Spirit of the Laws* (1748)

9 It has eternally been observed that any man who has power is led to abuse it. *The Spirit of the Laws* (1748)

10 Political liberty in a citizen is that tranquillity of spirit which comes from the opinion each one has of his security, and in order for him to have this liberty the government must be such that one citizen cannot fear another citizen. *The Spirit of the Laws* (1748)

11 The English have taken their idea of political government from the Germans. This fine system was found in the forests. *The Spirit of the Laws* (1748)

12 This state [England] will perish when legislative power is more corrupt than executive power. *The Spirit of the Laws* (1748)

13 States are often more flourishing during the imperceptible shift from one constitution to another than they are under either constitution. At that time all the springs of the government are stretched...and there is a noble rivalry between those who defend the declining constitution and those who put forward the one that prevails. *The Spirit of the Laws* (1748)

14 Royal authority is a great spring that should move easily and noiselessly. *The Spirit of the Laws* (1748)

15 In moderate states, there is a compensation for heavy taxes; it is liberty. In despotic states, there is an equivalent for liberty; it is the modest taxes. *The Spirit of the Laws* (1748)

1 Lands produce less by reason of their fertility than by reason of the liberty of their inhabitants.

Alexis de Tocqueville *The Ancien Régime* (1856); attributed

Lord Montgomery 1887–1976

British field marshal

2 War is a very rough game, but I think that politics is worse.

attributed, 1956

3 Rule 1, on page 1 of the book of war, is: 'Do not march on Moscow'...[Rule 2] is: 'Do not go fighting with your land armies in China.'

in the House of Lords, 30 May 1962

4 I have spent much of my life fighting the Germans and fighting the politicians. It is much easier to fight the Germans.

lecture given in Cairo as part of the 25th anniversary commemoration of Alamein, 13 May 1967

in *The Times* 15 May 1967

Thomas More 1478–1535

English scholar and saint; Lord Chancellor of England, 1529–32

on More: see **Whittington** 388:6; see also **Bolt** 51:3

5 Your sheep, that were wont to be so meek and tame, and so small eaters, now, as I hear say, be become so great devourers, and so wild, that they eat up and swallow down the very men themselves.

Utopia (1516); following the marginal précis 'The Disaster Produced by Standing Military Garrisons'

6 If the parties will at my hands call for justice, then, all were it my father stood on the one side, and the Devil on the other, his cause being good, the Devil should have right.

William Roper *Life of Sir Thomas More*

7 'By god's body, master More, *Indignatio principis mors est* [The anger of the sovereign is death].' 'Is that all, my Lord?' quoth he [to the Duke of Norfolk]. 'Then in good faith is there no more difference between your grace and me, but that I shall die to-day, and you to-morrow.'

William Roper *Life of Sir Thomas More*

8 Is not this house [the Tower of London] as nigh heaven as my own?

William Roper *Life of Sir Thomas More*

9 I pray you, master Lieutenant, see me safe up, and my coming down let me shift for my self.

on mounting the scaffold

William Roper *Life of Sir Thomas More*

John Morley 1838–1923

British Liberal politician and writer

10 You have not converted a man, because you have silenced him.

On Compromise (1874)

11 The golden Gospel of Silence is effectively compressed in thirty fine volumes.

on **Carlyle***'s* History of Frederick the Great *(1858–65), Carlyle having written of his subject as 'that strong, silent man'*

Critical Miscellanies (1886) 'Carlyle'

1 Although in Cabinet all its members stand on an equal footing, speak with equal voices and, on the rare occasions when a division is taken, are counted on the fraternal principle of one man, one vote, yet the head of the Cabinet is *primus inter pares*, and occupies a position which, so long as it lasts, is one of exceptional and peculiar authority.
Walpole (1889)

2 Simplicity of character is no hindrance to subtlety of intellect.
Life of Gladstone (1903)

3 The proper memory for a politician is one that knows what to remember and what to forget.
Recollections (1917)

George Pope Morris 1802–64

4 The iron-armed soldier, the true-hearted soldier,
The gallant old soldier of Tippecanoe.
campaign song for William Henry **Harrison**, *1840*
attributed; cf. **Ross** 313:3

William Morris 1834–96

English writer, artist, and designer

5 What is this, the sound and rumour? What is this that all men hear,
Like the wind in hollow valleys when the storm is drawing near,
Like the rolling on of ocean in the eventide of fear?
'Tis the people marching on.
Chants for Socialists (1885) 'The March of the Workers'

Herbert Morrison 1888–1965

British Labour politician

6 Work is the call. Work at war speed. Good-night—and go to it.
broadcast as Minister of Supply, 22 May 1940

Wayne Lyman Morse 1900–74

7 The liberal, emphasizing the civil and property rights of the individual, insists that the individual must remain so supreme as to make the state his servant.
in *New Republic* 22 July 1946

Desmond Morton 1891–1971

British soldier, intelligence officer, and public servant

of **Churchill***'s love for Combined Operations:*
8 He addressed his mind to them as the Managing Director of a vast railway might have, as a hobby, a miniature railway in his garden.
Andrew Roberts *Eminent Churchillians* (1994)

Rogers Morton 1914–79

American public relations officer

1 I'm not going to rearrange the furniture on the deck of the Titanic.
having lost five of the last six primaries as President **Ford**'s *campaign manager*

in *Washington Post* 16 May 1976

Oswald Mosley 1896–1980

English politician and Fascist leader
on Mosley: see **Attlee** 19:7

2 I am not, and never have been, a man of the right. My position was on the left and is now in the centre of politics.

letter to *The Times* 26 April 1968

John Lothrop Motley 1814–77

American historian

3 As long as he lived, he was the guiding-star of a whole brave nation, and when he died the little children cried in the streets.
of William of Orange

The Rise of the Dutch Republic (1856)

Lord Mountbatten 1900–79

British sailor, soldier, and statesman
on Mountbatten: see **Churchill** 91:1, **Whinney** 386:5, **Ziegler** 397:2

4 The nuclear arms race has no military purpose. Wars cannot be fought with nuclear weapons. Their existence only adds to our perils.

speech at Strasbourg, 11 May 1979

Daniel P. Moynihan 1927–

American Democratic politician

5 Welfare became a term of opprobrium—a contentious, often vindictive area of political conflict in which liberals and conservatives clashed and children were lost sight of.

in *The Washington Post* 25 November 1994

Robert Mugabe 1924–

African politician; Prime Minister of Zimbabwe, 1980–7

6 Cricket civilizes people and creates good gentlemen. I want everyone to play cricket in Zimbabwe; I want ours to be a nation of gentlemen.

in *Sunday Times* 26 February 1984

Malcolm Muggeridge 1903–90

British journalist

1 He was not only a bore; he bored for England.
of Anthony **Eden**
Tread Softly (1966)

2 To succeed pre-eminently in English public life it is necessary to conform either to the popular image of a bookie or of a clergyman; Churchill being a perfect example of the former, Halifax of the latter.
The Infernal Grove (1973)

Ed Murrow 1908–65

American broadcaster and journalist

3 I admired your history, doubted your future.
of Britain in the 1930s
radio broadcast; in *Listener* 28 February 1946

4 Future generations who bother to read the official record of proceedings in the House of Commons will discover that British armies retreated from many places, but that there was no retreat from the principles for which your ancestors fought.
radio broadcast; in *Listener* 28 February 1946

of **Winston Churchill**:

5 He mobilized the English language and sent it into battle to steady his fellow countrymen and hearten those Europeans upon whom the long dark night of tyranny had descended.
broadcast, 30 November 1954; *In Search of Light* (1967)

6 When the politicians complain that TV turns their proceedings into a circus, it should be made plain that the circus was already there, and that TV has merely demonstrated that not all the performers are well trained.
attributed, 1959

7 Anyone who isn't confused doesn't really understand the situation.
on the Vietnam War
Walter Bryan *The Improbable Irish* (1969)

Benito Mussolini 1883–1945

Italian Fascist statesman, Prime Minister 1922–43

8 We must leave exactly on time…From now on everything must function to perfection.
to a stationmaster
Giorgio Pini *Mussolini* (1939) vol. 2

Sarojini Naidu 1879–1949

Indian politician

9 If only Bapu [Gandhi] knew the cost of setting him up in poverty!
A. Campbell-Johnson *Mission with Mountbatten* (1951)

Lewis Namier 1888–1960

Polish-born British historian

1 No number of atrocities however horrible can deprive a nation of its right to independence, nor justify its being put under the heel of its worst enemies and persecutors.

in 1919; Julia Namier *Lewis Namier* (1971)

2 What matters most about political ideas is the underlying emotions, the music, to which ideas are a mere libretto, often of very inferior quality.

Personalities and Powers (1955)

Napoleon I 1769–1821

Emperor of France, 1804–15

3 Think of it, soldiers; from the summit of these pyramids, forty centuries look down upon you.

speech to the Army of Egypt on 21 July 1798, before the Battle of the Pyramids

Gaspard Gourgaud *Mémoires* (1823) vol. 2 'Égypte — Bataille des Pyramides'

4 It [the Channel] is a mere ditch, and will be crossed as soon as someone has the courage to attempt it.

letter to Consul Cambacérès, 16 November 1803

5 It is easier to put up with unpleasantness from a man of one's own way of thinking than from one who takes an entirely different point of view.

letter to J. Finckenstein, 14 April 1807

6 A prince who gets a reputation for good nature in the first year of his reign, is laughed at in the second.

letter to the King of Holland, 4 April 1807

7 In war, three-quarters turns on personal character and relations; the balance of manpower and materials counts only for the remaining quarter.

'Observations sur les affaires d'Espagne, Saint-Cloud, 27 août 1808'

8 It is a matter of great interest what sovereigns are doing; but as to what Grand Duchesses are doing—Who cares?

letter 17 December 1811

9 There is only one step from the sublime to the ridiculous.

to De Pradt, Polish ambassador, after the retreat from Moscow in 1812

D. G. De Pradt *Histoire de l'Ambassade dans le grand-duché de Varsovie en 1812* (1815)

10 As to moral courage, I have very rarely met with two o'clock in the morning courage: I mean instantaneous courage.

E. A. de Las Cases *Mémorial de Ste-Hélène* (1823) vol. 1, 4–5 December 1815

11 An army marches on its stomach.

attributed, but probably condensed from a long passage in E. A. de Las Cases *Mémorial de Ste-Hélène* (1823) vol. 4, 14 November 1816; also attributed to **Frederick** the Great

when asked how to deal with the Pope:

12 As though he had 200,000 men.

J. M. Robinson *Cardinal Consalvi* (1987)

13 The career open to the talents.

Barry E. O'Meara *Napoleon in Exile* (1822) vol. 1

1 England is a nation of shopkeepers.

Barry E. O'Meara *Napoleon in Exile* (1822) vol. 2; cf. **Adams** 5:4, **Smith** 341:6

2 Nothing is more contrary to the organization of the mind, of the memory, and of the imagination...The new system of weights and measures will be a stumbling block and the source of difficulties for several generations...It's just tormenting the people with trivia!!!

on the introduction of the metric system

Mémoires...écrits à Ste-Hélène (1823–5)

3 Not tonight, Josephine.

attributed, but probably apocryphal; R. H. Horne *The History of Napoleon* (1841) vol. 2 describes the circumstances in which the affront may have occurred

of **Talleyrand**:

4 A pile of shit in a silk stocking.

attributed

Jawaharlal Nehru 1889–1964

Indian statesman, Prime Minister 1947–64

on Nehru: see **Patil** 287:2

5 There is no easy walk-over to freedom anywhere, and many of us will have to pass through the valley of the shadow again and again before we reach the mountain-tops of our desire.

'From Lucknow to Tripuri' (1939)

6 History is almost always written by the victors and conquerors and gives their viewpoint.

The Discovery of India (1946)

7 At the stroke of the midnight hour, while the world sleeps, India will awake to life and freedom.

immediately prior to Independence

speech to the Indian Constituent Assembly, 14 August 1947

8 The light has gone out of our lives and there is darkness everywhere.

broadcast, 30 January 1948, following **Gandhi**'s *assassination*

Richard J. Walsh *Nehru on Gandhi* (1948)

9 I may lose many things including my temper, but I do not lose my nerve.

at a press conference in Delhi, 4 June 1958

10 Democracy and socialism are means to an end, not the end itself.

'Basic Approach'; written for private circulation and reprinted in Vincent Shean *Nehru: the Years of Power* (1960)

11 Normally speaking, it may be said that the forces of a capitalist society, if left unchecked, tend to make the rich richer and the poor poorer and thus increase the gap between them.

'Basic Approach' in Vincent Shean *Nehru...* (1960)

12 After every other Viceroy has been forgotten, Curzon will be remembered because he restored all that was beautiful in India.

in conversation with Lord Swinton

Kenneth Rose *Superior Person* (1969)

1 I shall be the last Englishman to rule in India. — J. K. Galbraith *A Life in Our Times* (1981)

Allan Nevins 1890–1971

American historian

2 The former Allies had blundered in the past by offering Germany too little, and offering even that too late, until finally Nazi Germany had become a menace to all mankind. — in *Current History* (New York) May 1935

Huey Newton 1942–

American political activist

3 I suggested [in 1966] that we use the panther as our symbol and call our political vehicle the Black Panther Party. The panther is a fierce animal, but he will not attack until he is backed into a corner; then he will strike out. — *Revolutionary Suicide* (1973)

Nicholas I 1796–1855

Russian emperor from 1825

4 Turkey is a dying man. We may endeavour to keep him alive, but we shall not succeed. He will, he must die. — F. Max Müller (ed.) *Memoirs of Baron Stockmar* (1873)

origin of the expression 'the sick man of Europe' referring to Ottoman Turkey

5 Russia has two generals in whom she can confide—Generals Janvier [January] and Février [February]. — attributed; in *Punch* 10 March 1855

Nicias *c.*470–413 BC

Athenian politician and general

6 For a city consists in men, and not in walls nor in ships empty of men. — Thucydides *History of the Peloponnesian Wars*

speech to the defeated Athenian army at Syracuse, 413 BC

Harold Nicolson 1886–1968

English diplomat, politician, and writer; father of Nigel **Nicolson**

7 Ponderous and uncertain is that relation between pressure and resistance which constitutes the balance of power. The arch of peace is morticed by no iron tendons…One night a handful of dust will patter from the vaulting: the bats will squeak and wheel in sudden panic: nor can the fragile fingers of man then stay the rush and rumble of destruction. — *Public Faces* (1932)

of the Duke of York (the future **George VI***), c.1936:*

8 Just a snipe from the great Windsor marshes. — Andrew Roberts *Eminent Churchillians* (1994)

1 Chamberlain (who has the mind and manner of a clothes-brush) aims only at assuring temporary peace at the price of ultimate defeat.
of Neville **Chamberlain**

diary 6 June 1938

on being asked by C. E. Joad if he did not think that Neville **Chamberlain***'s mind had broadened recently:*

2 Yes, in the same way that a darning needle is broader than a sewing-needle.

Nigel Nicolson (ed.) *Diaries and Letters of Harold Nicolson* vol 1 (1966); introduction

3 We shall have to walk and live a Woolworth life hereafter.
anticipating the aftermath of the Second World War

diary 4 June 1941

4 I am haunted by mental decay such as I saw creeping over Ramsay MacDonald. A gradual dimming of the lights.

diary 28 April 1947

comparing **Attlee** *as a public speaker with Winston* **Churchill**:

5 Like a village fiddler after Paganini.

diary 10 November 1947

6 I do not think it is quite fair to say that the British businessman has trampled on the faces of the poor. But he has sometimes not been very careful where he put his feet.
replying to a heckler in the North Croydon by-election, 1948

Nigel Nicolson (ed.) *Diaries and Letters of Harold Nicolson 1945–1962* vol. 3 (1968)

7 For seventeen years he did nothing at all but kill animals and stick in stamps.
of **George V** *as a subject for biography*

letter to Vita Sackville-West, 17 August 1949

8 Suez—a smash and grab raid that was all smash and no grab.

in conversation with Antony Jay, November 1956; see also letter to Vita Sackville-West, 8 November 1956, 'Our smash-and-grab raid got stuck at the smash'

Nigel Nicolson 1917–

British Conservative politician and writer; son of Harold **Nicolson**

9 One final tip to rebels: always have a second profession in reserve.
reflecting on the vote on the Maastricht Treaty in the House of Commons, in the light of having abstained from voting with the Government on the Suez Crisis in 1956 and subsequently lost his seat

in *The Spectator* 7 November 1992

Reinhold Niebuhr 1892–1971

American theologian

10 Man's capacity for justice makes democracy possible, but man's inclination to injustice makes democracy necessary.

Children of Light and Children of Darkness (1944) foreword

Martin Niemöller 1892–1984

German theologian

1 When Hitler attacked the Jews I was not a Jew, therefore, I was not concerned. And when Hitler attacked the Catholics, I was not a Catholic, and therefore, I was not concerned. And when Hitler attacked the unions and the industrialists, I was not a member of the unions and I was not concerned. Then, Hitler attacked me and the Protestant church—and there was nobody left to be concerned.
often quoted in the form 'In Germany they came first for the Communists, and I didn't speak up because I wasn't a Communist…' and so on

in *Congressional Record* 14 October 1968

Friedrich Nietzsche 1844–1900

German philosopher and writer

2 Morality is the herd-instinct in the individual.

Die fröhliche Wissenschaft (1882)

3 I teach you the superman. Man is something to be surpassed.

Also Sprach Zarathustra (1883) prologue

4 Master-morality and slave-morality.

Jenseits von Gut und Böse (1886)

5 At the base of all these aristocratic races the predator is not to be mistaken, the splendorous *blond beast*, avidly rampant for plunder and victory.

Zur Genealogie der Moral (1887)

Richard Milhous Nixon 1913–94

American Republican statesman, 37th President of the US 1969–74; re-elected for a second term in November 1972, it soon became clear that he was implicated in the Watergate scandal, and in 1974 he became the first President to resign from office

on Nixon: see **Abzug** 1:2, **Anonymous** 9:14, 11:4, 14:12, **Conable** 101:6, **Johnson** 195:4, **Stevenson** 350:8, **Ziegler** 397:3

6 Pat and I have the satisfaction that every dime that we've got is honestly ours…Pat doesn't have a mink coat. But she does have a respectable Republican cloth coat. And I always tell her that she'd look good in anything.
having been elected as Vice-President in 1952, in response to criticisms of his electoral campaign

speech on television, 23 September 1952

of the post-election gift of a cocker spaniel, named Checkers by his small daughter:

7 One other thing I probably should tell you, because if I don't they'll probably be saying this about me too, we did get something—a gift—after the election…It was a little cocker-spaniel dog…The kids love that dog and I just want to say this right now, that regardless of what they say about it, we're going to keep it.

speech on television, 23 September 1952

1 There is no such thing as a nonpolitical speech by a politician.
address to Radio-Television Executives Society, New York City, 14 September 1955

2 You won't have Nixon to kick around any more.
at a press conference after losing the election for Governor of California, 5 November 1962
in *New York Times* 8 November 1962

3 Let us begin by committing ourselves to the truth, to see it like it is and tell it like it is, to find the truth, to speak the truth and to live the truth. That's what we will do.
nomination acceptance speech in Miami, 1968
in *New York Times* 9 August 1968

4 There is nothing wrong with this country which a good election can't fix.
at a campaign meeting during the Presidential election
in Syracuse, New York, 29 October 1968

5 This is the greatest week in the history of the world since the Creation.
welcoming the return of the first men to land on the moon
speech, 24 July 1969

6 The great silent majority.
broadcast, 3 November 1969

7 The Chinese are a great and vital people who should not remain isolated from the international community...It is certainly in our interest, and in the interest of peace and stability in Asia and the world, that we take what steps we can toward improved practical relations with Peking.
first foreign policy report to Congress, February 1970

8 In our own lives, let each of us ask—not just what government will do for me, but what can I do for myself?
second inaugural address, 20 January 1973

9 There can be no whitewash at the White House.
television speech on Watergate, 30 April 1973

10 I made my mistakes, but in all my years of public life, I have never profited, never profited from public service. I've earned every cent. And in all of my years in public life I have never obstructed justice...I welcome this kind of examination because people have got to know whether or not their President is a crook. Well, I'm not a crook.
speech at press conference, 17 November 1973

11 This country needs good farmers, good businessmen, good plumbers, good carpenters.
farewell address at White House, 9 August 1974
in *New York Times* 10 August 1974

12 My own view is that taping of conversations for historical purposes was a bad decision.
attributed, 1974

13 When the President does it, that means that it is not illegal.
in conversation; David Frost *I Gave Them a Sword* (1978)

14 I brought myself down. I gave them a sword. And they stuck it in.
television interview, 19 May 1977; David Frost *I Gave Them a Sword* (1978)

15 Foreign aid is the most unpopular damn thing in the world. It is a loser politically.
in *Observer* 21 April 1985 'Sayings of the Week'

16 Finishing second in the Olympics gets you silver. Finishing second in politics gets you oblivion.
in *Sunday Times* 13 November 1988

of the defeat of Michael Dukakis by George **Bush** *in the 1988 presidential election*

1 I played by the rules of politics as I found them. Not taking a higher road than my predecessors and my adversaries was my central mistake. — *In the Arena* (1990)

Charles Howard, Duke of Norfolk

1746–1815

English nobleman

2 I cannot be a good Catholic; I cannot go to heaven; and if a man is to go to the devil, he may as well go thither from the House of Lords as from any other place on earth. — Henry Best *Personal and Literary Memorials* (1829)

Christopher North 1785–1854

Scottish literary critic

3 His Majesty's dominions, on which the sun never sets. — in *Blackwood's Magazine* (April 1829) 'Noctes Ambrosianae'

4 Laws were made to be broken. — in *Blackwood's Magazine* (May 1830) 'Noctes Ambrosianae'

5 I cannot sit still, James, and hear you abuse the shopocracy. — in *Blackwood's Magazine* (February 1835) 'Noctes Ambrosianae'

Lord Northcliffe 1865–1922

British newspaper proprietor

on Northcliffe: see **Taylor** 357:9

6 When I want a peerage, I shall buy it like an honest man. — Tom Driberg *Swaff* (1974)

7 The power of the press is very great, but not so great as the power of suppress.
office message, Daily Mail *1918* — Reginald Rose and Geoffrey Harmsworth *Northcliffe* (1959)

Earl of Northumberland 1564–1632

English nobleman

in a letter to the Council, 11 November 1605, adducing his habits of life as proof that his interests lay elsewhere than in political conspiracy:

8 Examine but my humours in buildings, gardenings, and private expenses these two years past. — in *Dictionary of National Biography*

Julius Nyerere 1922–

Tanzanian statesman, President of Tanganyika 1962–4 and of Tanzania 1964–85

1 Should we really let our people starve so we can pay our debts? — in *Guardian* 21 March 1985

2 We are a poor country and we opted for socialist policies, but to build a socialist society you have to have a developed society. — in *Observer* 28 July 1985 'Sayings of the Week'

Michael Oakeshott 1901–91

British academic

3 A plan to resist all planning may be better than its opposite, but it belongs to the same style of politics. — *Rationalism in Politics* (1962)

of **Hayek**'s The Road to Serfdom

Conor Cruise O'Brien 1917–

Irish politician, writer, and journalist

4 If I saw Mr Haughey buried at midnight at a crossroads, with a stake driven through his heart—politically speaking—I should continue to wear a clove of garlic round my neck, just in case. — in *Observer* 10 October 1982

5 The first great act of intellectual resistance to the first great experiment in totalitarian innovation. — *The Great Melody* (1992)

of **Burke**'s *writings on the French Revolution*

Daniel O'Connell 1775–1847

Irish nationalist leader and social reformer, elected to Parliament in 1828

6 I have given my advice to my countrymen, and whenever I feel it necessary I shall continue to do so, careless whether it pleases or displeases this house or any mad person out of it. — in *Dictionary of National Biography*

James Ogilvy, Lord Seafield 1664–1730

Lord Chancellor of Scotland

7 Now there's ane end of ane old song. — in *The Lockhart Papers* (1817)

as he signed the engrossed exemplification of the Act of Union, 1706

Thomas ('Tip') O'Neill 1912–94

American Democratic politician; Speaker of the House of Representatives 1977–87

8 All politics is local. — in *New York Review of Books* 13 March 1989

P. J. O'Rourke 1947–

American humorous writer and journalist

1 Giving money and power to government is like giving whisky and car keys to teenage boys. *Parliament of Whores* (1991)

2 Politics are, like God's infinite mercy, a last resort. *Parliament of Whores* (1991)

3 I have only one firm belief about the American political system, and that is this: God is a Republican and Santa Claus is a Democrat. *Parliament of Whores* (1991)

4 The Constitution is an equally forthright piece of work and quite succinct... giving the complete operating instructions for a nation of 250 million people. The manual for a Toyota Camry, which only seats five, is four times as long. *Parliament of Whores* (1991)

5 Washington has lots of those Greek- and Roman-style buildings that practically make you feel like a senator just walking up the steps of them. Senators, in particular, are fond of this feeling, and this is one reason official Washington escaped the worst effects of modern architecture. *Parliament of Whores* (1991)

6 The actual work of government is too unglamorous for the people who govern us to do. Important elected office-holders and high appointed officials create bureaucratic departments to perform the humdrum tasks of national supervision. *Parliament of Whores* (1991)

7 Whatever it is that the government does, sensible Americans would prefer that the government does it to somebody else. This is the idea behind foreign policy. *Parliament of Whores* (1991)

8 Every government is a parliament of whores. The trouble is, in a democracy the whores are us. *Parliament of Whores* (1991)

George Orwell 1903–50

English novelist

9 A person of bourgeois origin goes through life with some expectation of getting what he wants, within reasonable limits. Hence the fact that in times of stress 'educated' people tend to come to the front. *The Road to Wigan Pier* (1937)

10 In a Lancashire cotton-town you could probably go for months on end without once hearing an 'educated' accent, whereas there can hardly be a town in the South of England where you could throw a brick without hitting the niece of a bishop. *The Road to Wigan Pier* (1937)

11 The typical Socialist is... a prim little man with a white-collar job, usually a secret teetotaller and often with vegetarian leanings, with a history of Nonconformity behind him, and, above all, with a social position which he has no intention of forfeiting. *The Road to Wigan Pier* (1937)

1 To the ordinary working man, the sort you would meet in any pub on Saturday night, Socialism does not mean much more than better wages and shorter hours and nobody bossing you about.

The Road to Wigan Pier (1937)

2 We of the sinking middle class... may sink without further struggles into the working class where we belong, and probably when we get there it will not be so dreadful as we feared, for, after all, we have nothing to lose but our aitches.

The Road to Wigan Pier (1937)

3 Down here it was still the England I had known in my childhood: the railway cuttings smothered in wild flowers... the red buses, the blue policemen—all sleeping the deep, deep sleep of England, from which I sometimes fear that we shall never wake till we are jerked out of it by the roar of bombs.

Homage to Catalonia (1938)

4 Most revolutionaries are potential Tories, because they imagine that everything can be put right by altering the *shape* of society; once that change is effected, as it sometimes is, they see no need for any other.

Inside the Whale (1940) 'Charles Dickens'

5 England... resembles a family, a rather stuffy Victorian family, with not many black sheep in it but with all its cupboards bursting with skeletons. It has rich relations who have to be kowtowed to and poor relations who are horribly sat upon, and there is a deep conspiracy of silence about the source of the family income. It is a family in which the young are generally thwarted and most of the power is in the hands of irresponsible uncles and bed-ridden aunts. Still, it is a family. It has its private language and its common memories, and at the approach of an enemy it closes its ranks. A family with the wrong members in control.

The Lion and the Unicorn (1941) pt. 1 'England Your England'

6 Probably the battle of Waterloo *was* won on the playing-fields of Eton, but the opening battles of all subsequent wars have been lost there.

The Lion and the Unicorn (1941) pt. 1 'England Your England'; cf. **Wellington** 384:11

7 Old maids biking to Holy Communion through the mists of the autumn mornings... these are not only fragments, but *characteristic* fragments, of the English scene.

The Lion and the Unicorn (1941) pt. 1 'England Your England'; cf. **Major** 248:2

8 Attlee reminds me of nothing so much as a recently dead fish, before it has had time to stiffen.

diary 19 May 1942

9 Man is the only creature that consumes without producing.

Animal Farm (1945)

10 Four legs good, two legs bad.

Animal Farm (1945)

11 All animals are equal but some animals are more equal than others.

Animal Farm (1945)

12 The Catholic and the Communist are alike in assuming that an opponent cannot be both honest and intelligent.

in *Polemic* January 1946 'The Prevention of Literature'

13 The quickest way of ending a war is to lose it.

in *Polemic* May 1946 'Second Thoughts on James Burnham'

14 BIG BROTHER IS WATCHING YOU.

Nineteen Eighty-Four (1949)

1 War is peace. Freedom is slavery. Ignorance is strength. — *Nineteen Eighty-Four* (1949)

2 Who controls the past controls the future: who controls the present controls the past. — *Nineteen Eighty-Four* (1949)

3 Don't you see that the whole aim of Newspeak is to narrow the range of thought? In the end we shall make thoughtcrime literally impossible, because there will be no words in which to express it. — *Nineteen Eighty-Four* (1949)

4 Freedom is the freedom to say that two plus two make four. If that is granted, all else follows. — *Nineteen Eighty-Four* (1949)

5 Syme was not only dead, he was abolished, an unperson. — *Nineteen Eighty-Four* (1949)

6 *Doublethink* means the power of holding two contradictory beliefs in one's mind simultaneously, and accepting both of them. — *Nineteen Eighty-Four* (1949)

7 Power is not a means, it is an end. One does not establish a dictatorship in order to safeguard a revolution; one makes the revolution in order to establish the dictatorship. — *Nineteen Eighty-Four* (1949)

8 If you want a picture of the future, imagine a boot stamping on a human face—for ever. — *Nineteen Eighty-Four* (1949)

9 In our time, political speech and writing are largely the defence of the indefensible. — *Shooting an Elephant* (1950) 'Politics and the English Language'

10 The great enemy of clear language is insincerity. When there is a gap between one's real and one's declared aims, one turns as it were instinctively to long words and exhausted idioms, like a cuttlefish squirting out ink. — *Shooting an Elephant* (1950) 'Politics and the English Language'

11 Political language...is designed to make lies sound truthful and murder respectable, and to give an appearance of solidity to pure wind. — *Shooting an Elephant* (1950) 'Politics and the English Language'

John L. O'Sullivan 1813–95

American journalist and diplomat

12 Understood as a central consolidated power, managing and directing the various general interests of the society, all government is evil, and the parent of evil...The best government is that which governs least. — in *United States Magazine and Democratic Review* (1837) introduction

13 A spirit of hostile interference against us...checking the fulfilment of our manifest destiny to overspread the continent allotted by Providence for the free development of our yearly multiplying millions. — in *United States Magazine and Democratic Review* (1845)

on opposition to the annexation of Texas

James Otis 1725–83

American politician

14 Taxation without representation is tyranny. — in *Dictionary of American Biography*

watchword (c.1761) of the American Revolution

1 An act against the Constitution is void; an act against natural equity is void. — *Argument Against the Writs of Assistance* (1763)

2 Where liberty is, there is my country. — motto used by James Otis; also attributed to Benjamin **Franklin**; cf. **Paine** 283:11

Ovid 43 BC–AD *c.*17

Roman poet

3 I see the better things, and approve; I follow the worse. — *Metamorphoses*

4 How you, rebellious Germany, laid your wretched head beneath the feet of the great general. — *Tristia*

Robert Owen 1771–1858

Welsh-born socialist and philanthropist

5 All the world is queer save thee and me, and even thou art a little queer.
to his partner W. Allen, on severing business relations at New Lanark, 1828 — attributed

Count Oxenstierna 1583–1654

Swedish statesman

6 Dost thou not know, my son, with how little wisdom the world is governed? — letter to his son, 1648; John Selden, in *Table Talk* (1689) 'Pope', quotes 'a certain Pope' (possibly Julius III) saying 'Thou little thinkest what *a little foolery governs the whole world!*'

William Tyler Page 1868–1942

7 I believe in the United States of America as a government of the people, by the people, for the people, whose just powers are derived from the consent of the governed; a democracy in a republic; a sovereign Nation of many sovereign States; a perfect Union, one and inseparable, established upon those principles of freedom, equality, justice, and humanity for which American patriots sacrificed their lives and fortunes. I therefore believe it is my duty to my country to love it, to support its Constitution, to obey its laws, to respect its flag, and to defend it against all enemies. — *American's Creed* (prize-winning competition entry, 1918) in *Congressional Record* vol. 56

Thomas Paine 1737–1809

English political theorist

8 Though we have been wise enough to shut and lock a door against absolute Monarchy, we at the same time — *Common Sense* (1776)

have been foolish enough to put the crown in possession of the key.

1 Government, even in its best state, is but a necessary evil; in its worst state, an intolerable one. Government, like dress, is the badge of lost innocence; the palaces of kings are built upon the ruins of the bowers of paradise. — *Common Sense* (1776)

2 One of the strongest natural proofs of the folly of hereditary right in kings, is that nature disapproves it, otherwise she would not so frequently turn it into ridicule, by giving mankind an *ass for a lion*. — *Common Sense* (1776)

3 Monarchy and succession have laid... the world in blood and ashes. — *Common Sense* (1776)

4 Of more worth is one honest man to society, and in the sight of God, than all the crowned ruffians that ever lived. — *Common Sense* (1776)

5 'Tis not the affair of a city, a county, a province, or a kingdom; but of a continent—of at least one eighth part of the habitable globe. 'Tis not the concern of a day, a year, or an age; posterity are virtually involved in the contest. Now is the seed-time of continental union. — *Common Sense* (1776)

6 Any submission to, or dependence on, Great Britain, tends directly to involve this continent in European wars and quarrels, and set us at variance with nations who would otherwise seek our friendship, and against whom we have neither anger nor complaint. — *Common Sense* (1776)

to America:

7 Freedom hath been hunted round the globe. Asia and Africa have long expelled her. Europe regards her like a stranger, and England hath given her warning to depart. O! receive the fugitive, and prepare in time an asylum for mankind. — *Common Sense* (1776)

8 We have it in our power to begin the world over again. — *Common Sense* (1776)

9 As to religion, I hold it to be the indispensable duty of government to protect all conscientious professors thereof, and I know of no other business which government hath to do therewith. — *Common Sense* (1776)

10 These are the times that try men's souls. The summer soldier and the sunshine patriot will, in this crisis, shrink from the service of their country; but he that stands it *now*, deserves the love and thanks of men and women. — *The Crisis* (December 1776) introduction

11 What we obtain too cheap, we esteem too lightly. — *The Crisis* (December 1776) introduction

of Great Britain:

12 Blessed with all the commerce she could wish for, and furnished, by a vast extension of dominion, with the means of civilizing both the eastern and the western world, she has made no use of both than proudly to idolize her own 'thunder', and rip up the bowels of whole countries for what she could get. — *The American Crisis* pt 2 (1777)

1 I am a farmer of thoughts, and all the crops I raise I give away. — letter to Henry Laurens, *c.* spring 1778

2 A rich man makes a bonny traitor. — letter to Joseph Reed, 4 June 1780

3 A total reformation is wanted in England. She wants an expanded mind—a heart which embraces the universe. Instead of shutting herself up in an island, and quarrelling with the world, she would derive more lasting happiness, and acquire more real riches, by generously mixing with it, and bravely saying, I am the enemy of none. — *Letter to the Abbé Raynal* (1782)

4 [Edmund Burke] is not affected by the reality of distress touching his heart, but by the showy resemblance of it striking his imagination. He pities the plumage, but forgets the dying bird.
on **Burke**'s Reflections on the Revolution in France, *1790* — *The Rights of Man* (1791)

5 Lay then the axe to the root, and teach governments humanity. It is their sanguinary punishments which corrupt mankind. — *The Rights of Man* (1791)

6 [In France] all that class of equivocal generation, which in some countries is called *aristocracy*, and in others *nobility*, is done away, and the peer is exalted into MAN. — *The Rights of Man* (1791)

7 Titles are but nick-names, and every nick-name is a title. — *The Rights of Man* (1791)

8 The idea of hereditary legislators is as inconsistent as that of hereditary judges, or hereditary juries; and as absurd as an hereditary mathematician, or an hereditary wise man; and as ridiculous as an hereditary poet laureate. — *The Rights of Man* (1791)

9 Persecution is not an original feature of *any* religion; but it is always the strongly marked feature of all law-religions, or religions established by law. — *The Rights of Man* (1791)

10 The candidates were not men but principles. — *The Rights of Man* (1791)

11 What were formerly called revolutions were little more than a change of persons...what we now see in the world, from the revolutions of America and France, is a renovation of the natural order of things. — *The Rights of Man* (1791)

12 With respect to the two Houses, of which the English Parliament is composed, they appear to be effectually influenced into one, and as a legislature, to have no temper of its own. The Minister, whoever he at any time may be, touches it as with an opium wand, and it sleeps obedience. — *The Rights of Man* pt. 2 (1792)

13 All hereditary government is in its nature tyranny...To inherit a government, is to inherit the people, as if they were flocks and herds. — *The Rights of Man* pt. 2 (1792)

14 The instant formal government is abolished, society begins to act. A general association takes place, and common interest produces common security. — *The Rights of Man* pt. 2 (1792)

of monarchy:

15 I compare it to something kept behind a curtain, about — *The Rights of Man* pt. 2 (1792) which there is a great deal of bustle and fuss, and a wonderful air of seeming solemnity; but when, by any accident, the curtain happens to be open, and the company see what it is, they burst into laughter.

1 When, in countries that are called civilized, we see age going to the workhouse and youth to the gallows, something must be wrong in the system of government.
The Rights of Man pt. 2 (1792)

2 My country is the world, and my religion is to do good.
The Rights of Man pt. 2 (1792)

3 I do not believe that any two men, on what are called doctrinal points, think alike who think at all. It is only those who have not thought that appear to agree.
The Rights of Man pt. 2 (1792)

4 As he rose like a rocket, he fell like the stick.
on Edmund **Burke***'s losing the parliamentary debate on the French Revolution to Charles James* **Fox**
Letter to the Addressers on the late Proclamation (1792)

5 It is necessary to the happiness of man that he be mentally faithful to himself. Infidelity does not consist in believing, or in disbelieving, it consists in professing to believe what one does not believe.
The Age of Reason pt. 1 (1794)

6 Revelation is necessarily limited to the first communication—after that it is only an account of something which that person says was a revelation made to him; and though he may find himself obliged to believe it, it cannot be incumbent on me to believe it in the same manner; for it was not a revelation made to *me*, and I have only his word for it that it was made to him.
The Age of Reason pt. 1 (1794)

7 To elect, and to reject, is the prerogative of a free people.
in *National Intelligencer* 29 November 1802

8 When moral principles, rather than persons, are candidates for power, to vote is to perform a moral duty, and not to vote is to neglect a duty.
in *Trenton True-American* April 1803

9 The religion of humanity.
Letter… on the Invasion of England (1804)

10 A share in two revolutions is living to some purpose.
Eric Foner *Tom Paine and Revolutionary America* (1976)

11 Where Liberty is not, there is my country.
John Keane *Tom Paine* (1995); cf. **Otis** 280:2

12 When it shall be said in any country in the world, 'My poor are happy; neither ignorance nor distress is to be found among them; my jails are empty of prisoners, my streets of beggars; the aged are not in want, the taxes are not oppressive; the rational world is my friend, because I am the friend of its happiness': when these things can be said, then may that country boast of its constitution and its government.
John Keane *Tom Paine* (1995)

Lord Palmerston 1784–1865

British Whig statesman, Prime Minister 1855–8 and 1859–65

1 We have no eternal allies and we have no perpetual enemies. Our interests are eternal and perpetual, and those interests it is our duty to follow. — in the House of Commons, 1 March 1848

2 I therefore fearlessly challenge the verdict which this House...is to give...whether, as the Roman, in days of old, held himself free from indignity, when he could say *Civis Romanus sum*; so also a British subject, in whatever land he may be, shall feel confident that the watchful eye and the strong arm of England will protect him against injustice and wrong. — in the House of Commons, 25 June 1850

speech in the debate on the protection afforded to the Greek trader David Pacifico (1784–1854), who had been born a British subject at Gibraltar

3 You may call it combination, you may call it the accidental and fortuitous concurrence of atoms. — in the House of Commons, 5 March 1857

on a projected coalition with **Disraeli**

4 We do not want Egypt any more than any rational man with an estate in the north of England and a residence in the south, would have wished to possess the inns on the north road. All he could want would have been that the inns should be well kept, always accessible, and furnishing him, when he came, with mutton chops and post horses. — letter to Earl Cowley, 25 November 1859

5 The function of a government is to calm, rather than to excite agitation. — P. Guedalla *Gladstone and Palmerston* (1928)

6 What is merit? The opinion one man entertains of another. — T. Carlyle *Shooting Niagara: and After?* (1867)

7 Lord Palmerston, with characteristic levity had once said that only three men in Europe had ever understood [the Schleswig-Holstein question], and of these the Prince Consort was dead, a Danish statesman (unnamed) was in an asylum, and he himself had forgotten it. — R. W. Seton-Watson *Britain in Europe 1789–1914* (1937)

on being told that English has no word equivalent to sensibilité*:*

8 Yes we have. Humbug. — attributed

9 Die, my dear Doctor, that's the last thing I shall do! — E. Latham *Famous Sayings and their Authors* (1904)

last words

Christabel Pankhurst 1880–1958

English suffragette; daughter of Emmeline **Pankhurst**

10 We are here to claim our right as women, not only to be free, but to fight for freedom. That it is our right as well as our duty. — in *Votes for Women* 31 March 1911

11 Never lose your temper with the Press or the public is a major rule of political life. — *Unshackled* (1959)

Emmeline Pankhurst 1858–1928

English suffragette leader; founder of the Women's Social and Political Union, 1903

1 There is something that Governments care far more for than human life, and that is the security of property, and so it is through property that we shall strike the enemy...I say to the Government: You have not dared to take the leaders of Ulster for their incitement to rebellion. Take me if you dare.

speech at Albert Hall, 17 October 1912

2 The argument of the broken window pane is the most valuable argument in modern politics.

George Dangerfield *The Strange Death of Liberal England* (1936)

Dorothy Parker 1893–1967

American critic and humorist

on being told that Calvin **Coolidge** *was dead:*

3 How do they know?

Malcolm Cowley *Writers at Work* 1st Series (1958)

Martin Parker d. *c.*1656

English balladmonger

4 But all's to no end, for the times will not mend
Till the King enjoys his own again.

'Upon Defacing of Whitehall' (1671)

Theodore Parker 1810–60

5 Truth never yet fell dead in the streets; it has such affinity with the soul of man, the seed however broadcast will catch somewhere and produce its hundredfold.

A Discourse of Matters Pertaining to Religion (1842)

6 A democracy—that is a government of all the people, by all the people, for all the people; of course, a government of the principles of eternal justice, the unchanging law of God; for shortness' sake I will call it the idea of Freedom.

The American Idea 29 May 1850

C. Northcote Parkinson 1909–

English writer

7 Expenditure rises to meet income.

Parkinson's Law (1958)

8 Work expands so as to fill the time available for its completion.

Parkinson's Law (1958)

9 A committee is organic rather than mechanical in its nature: it is not a structure but a plant. It takes root and grows, it flowers, wilts, and dies, scattering the seed from which other committees will bloom in their turn.

Parkinson's Law (1958)

10 Time spent on any item of the agenda will be in inverse proportion to the sum involved.

Parkinson's Law (1958)

1 The man who is denied the opportunity of taking decisions of importance begins to regard as important the decisions he is allowed to take. — *Parkinson's Law* (1958)

2 Men enter local politics solely as a result of being unhappily married. — *Parkinson's Law* (1958)

Francis Parkman 1823–93

3 The growth of New England was a result of the aggregate efforts of a busy multitude, each in his narrow circle toiling for himself, to gather competence or wealth. The expansion of New France was the achievement of a gigantic ambition striving to grasp a continent. It was a vain attempt. — *Pioneers of France in the New World* (1865); introduction

4 The most momentous and far-reaching question ever brought to issue on this continent [North America] was: Shall France remain here or shall she not? — *Montcalm and Wolfe* (1884); introduction

Charles Stewart Parnell 1846–91

Irish nationalist leader
on Parnell: see **Yeats** 396:1

5 Why should Ireland be treated as a geographical fragment of England... Ireland is not a geographical fragment, but a nation. — in the House of Commons, 26 April 1875

6 My policy is not a policy of conciliation, but a policy of retaliation.
in 1877, on his parliamentary tactics in the House of Commmons as leader of the Irish party — in *Dictionary of National Biography*

7 None of us, whether we are in America or Ireland, or wherever we may be, will be satisfied until we have destroyed the last link which keeps Ireland bound to England. — speech at Cincinnati, 20 February 1880

8 No man has a right to fix the boundary of the march of a nation; no man has a right to say to his country—thus far shalt thou go and no further. — speech at Cork, 21 January 1885

9 Get the advice of everybody whose advice is worth having—they are very few—and then do what you think best yourself. — Conor Cruise O'Brien *Parnell*

Matthew Parris 1949–

British journalist and former Conservative politician

of Lady **Thatcher** *in the House of Lords:*
10 A big cat detained briefly in a poodle parlour, sharpening her claws on the velvet. — *Look Behind You!* (1993)

11 Being an MP feeds your vanity and starves your self-respect. — in *The Times* 9 February 1994

Blaise Pascal 1623–62

French mathematician, physicist, and moralist

1 Had Cleopatra's nose been shorter, the whole face of the world would have changed. — *Pensées* (1909)

Sadashiv Kanoji Patil

Indian politician; Minister for Food and Agriculture in **Nehru**'s government

2 The Prime Minister is like the great banyan tree. Thousands shelter beneath it, but nothing grows.
when asked in an interview who would be **Nehru**'s *successor* — J. K. Galbraith *A Life in Our Times* (1981)

Patrick Pearse 1879–1916

Irish nationalist leader; executed after the Easter Rising
on Pearse: see **Yeats** 395:8

3 The fools, the fools, the fools, they have left us our Fenian dead, and while Ireland holds these graves Ireland unfree shall never be at peace. — oration over the grave of the Fenian Jeremiah O'Donovan Rossa, 1 August 1915

Lester Pearson 1897–1972

Canadian diplomat and Liberal statesman, Prime Minister 1963–8

4 The grim fact is that we prepare for war like precocious giants and for peace like retarded pygmies. — speech in Toronto, 14 March 1955

5 Not only did he not suffer fools gladly, he did not suffer them at all.
of Dean **Acheson** — in *Time* 25 October 1971

6 The chief distinction of a diplomat is that he can say no in such a way that it sounds like yes. — Geoffrey Pearson *Seize the Day* (1993)

7 Canada was supposed to get British government, French culture, and American know-how. Instead it got French government, American culture, and British know-how. — in *The Economist* 27 July 1991

Robert Peel 1788–1850

British Conservative statesman, Prime Minister 1834–5 and 1841–6
on Peel: see **Curran** 107:5, **Disraeli** 117:15, 118:1, 118:13, **Hennessy** 175:2, **Wellington** 384:13

8 What is right must unavoidably be politic. — to Goulburn, 23 September 1822

9 I may be a Tory. I may be an illiberal—but... Tory as I am, I have the further satisfaction of knowing that there is not a single law connected with my name which has not had as its object some mitigation of the severity of the criminal law; some prevention of abuse in the — in the House of Commons, 1 May 1827

exercise of it; or some security for its impartial administration.

1 There is no appetite for truth in Ireland. — to Leveson Gower in 1828

2 As minister of the Crown...I reserve to myself, distinctly and unequivocally, the right of adapting my conduct to the exigency of the moment, and to the wants of the country. — in the House of Commons, 30 March 1829

3 All my experience in public life is in favour of the employment of what the world would call young men instead of old ones. — to Wellington in 1829

4 The longer I live, the more clearly do I see the folly of yielding a rash and precipitate assent to any political measure. — in the House of Commons, 1830

5 Men, if in office, seemed really to be like the Indians—they inherited all the qualities of those enemies they killed. — in the House of Commons,1831

6 We are here to consult the interests and not to obey the will of the people, if we honestly believe that that will conflicts with those interests. — in the House of Commons, 1831

7 No man attached to his country could always acquiesce in the opinions of the majority. — in the House of Commons, 1831

8 No government can exist which does not control and restrain the popular sentiments. — in the House of Commons, 1832

9 There will always be found a permanent fund of discontent and dissatisfaction in every country. — in the House of Commons, 1832

10 The hasty inordinate demand for peace might be just as dangerous as the clamour for war. — in the House of Commons, 1832

11 I see no dignity in persevering in error. — in the House of Commons, 1833

of Robert **Walpole**:

12 So far as the great majority of his audience was concerned, he had blocks to cut, and he chose a fitter instrument than a razor to cut them with. — to Mahon in 1833

13 I am not sure that those who clamour most, suffer most. — in the House of Commons, 1834

14 Of all vulgar arts of government, that of solving every difficulty which might arise by thrusting the hand into the public purse is the most delusory and contemptible. — in the House of Commons, 1834

15 English grouse are to Scotch what Scotchmen are to Englishmen. They are much more wary and provident birds more given to locomotion. — to Aberdeen in 1836

16 The true policy in public life is to act with decision and as far as possible to adhere to what is decided, but not to decide before the time for decision shall have arrived, and carefully to consider in the interval every mode of solving a difficulty. — to Graham in 1841

17 The distinction of being without an honour is becoming a rare and valuable one and should not become extinct. — to Graham in 1841

1 A cordial and good understanding between France and England is essential to the peace and welfare of Europe. — in the House of Commons, 1841

2 Speaking with that caution with which I am sometimes taunted but which I find a great convenience. — in the House of Commons, 1842

3 There are those who seem to have nothing else to do but to suggest modes of taxation to men in office. — in the House of Commons, 1842

4 The great art of government is to work by such instruments as the world supplies. — in Cabinet, 1844

5 There are many parties in Ireland who desire to have a grievance and prefer the grievance to the remedy. — to the Queen, 1844

6 Philosophers are very regardless of expense when the public has to bear it. — to Haddington in 1844

7 Priests are not above sublunary considerations. Priests have nephews. — to Graham, 13 August 1845

8 An Irishman has no sense of the ridiculous when office is in question. — to Graham, 28 December 1845

9 There seem to me very few facts, at least ascertainable facts, in politics. — to Lord **Brougham** in 1846

10 Great public measures cannot be carried by the influence of mere reason. — to Lord Radnor in 1846

Charles Péguy 1873–1914

French poet and essayist

11 Tyranny is always better organized than freedom. — *Basic Verities* (1943) 'War and Peace'

Henry Herbert, Lord Pembroke

*c.*1534–1601

12 A parliament can do any thing but make a man a woman, and a woman a man. — quoted by his son, the 4th Earl, in a speech on 11 April 1648, proving himself Chancellor of Oxford

William Penn 1644–1718

English Quaker; founder of Pennsylvania

13 It is a reproach to religion and government to suffer so much poverty and excess. — *Some Fruits of Solitude* (1693)

14 The taking of a bribe or gratuity, should be punished with as severe penalties as the defrauding of the State. — *Some Fruits of Solitude* (1693)

Samuel Pepys 1633–1703

English diarist

15 I went out to Charing Cross, to see Major-general Harrison hanged, drawn, and quartered; which was done — diary 13 October 1660

there, he looking as cheerful as any man could do in that condition.

1 But methought it lessened my esteem of a king, that he should not be able to command the rain.
diary 19 July 1662

2 I see it is impossible for the King to have things done as cheap as other men.
diary 21 July 1662

3 While we were talking came by several poor creatures carried by, by constables, for being at a conventicle... I would to God they would either conform, or be more wise, and not be catched!
diary 7 August 1664

4 Pretty witty Nell.
of Nell Gwyn
diary 3 April 1665

Pericles *c.*495–429 BC

Athenian statesman

5 For famous men have the whole earth as their memorial.
Thucydides *History of the Peloponnesian War*

Juan Perón 1895–1974

Argentinian soldier and statesman, President 1946–55 and 1973–4

6 If I had not been born Perón, I would have liked to be Perón.
in *Observer* 21 February 1960

H. Ross Perot 1930–

American businessman; independent presidential candidate in the 1992 election

7 After the election people like us to go back to work. We have to go back to work because we've got to work five months just to pay our taxes.
speech to the Symposium for Better Government, 2 November 1991

8 An activist is the guy who cleans the river, not the guy who concludes it's dirty.
a favourite saying; Ken Gross *Ross Perot* (1992)

after George **Bush** *had laid stress on the value of experience in the 1992 presidential debates:*

9 I don't have any experience in running up a $4 trillion debt.
in *Newsweek* 19 October 1992

on his political future:

10 Look, I would like to go away, but if I go away, the odds we'll get reforms are zero, so I kind of have to stay around.
in *Observer* 20 August 1995 'Sayings of the Week'

Henri Philippe Pétain 1856–1951

French general and statesman, head of state 1940–2

11 To write one's memoirs is to speak ill of everybody except oneself.
in *Observer* 26 May 1946

Mike Peters

American cartoonist

1 When I go into the voting booth, do I vote for the person who is the best President? Or the slime bucket who will make my life as a cartoonist wonderful?

in *Wall Street Journal* 20 January 1993

Roger Peyrefitte 1907–

French writer

2 The ideal civil servant should always be colourless, odourless and tasteless.

Diplomatic Diversions (1953)

Edward John Phelps 1822–1900

American lawyer and diplomat

3 The man who makes no mistakes does not usually make anything.

speech at the Mansion House, London, 24 January 1889

Kim Philby 1912–88

British intelligence officer and Soviet spy

4 To betray, you must first belong.

in *Sunday Times* 17 December 1967

Prince Philip 1921–

husband of **Elizabeth II**

5 Just at this moment we are suffering a national defeat comparable to any lost military campaign, and what is more it is self-inflicted...I think it is about time we pulled our finger out.

speech to businessmen, 17 October 1961

6 If at any stage people feel that the Monarchy has no further part to play, then for goodness sake let's end the thing on amicable grounds without having a row.
to the Canadians

attributed, 1969

Morgan Phillips 1902–63

British Labour politician

7 The Labour Party owes more to Methodism than to Marxism.

James Callaghan *Time and Chance* (1987)

Wendell Phillips 1811–84

American abolitionist and orator

8 Revolutions are not made; they come. A revolution is as natural a growth as an oak. It comes out of the past. Its foundations are laid far back.

speech 8 January 1852

9 The best use of laws is to teach men to trample bad laws under their feet.

speech 12 April 1852

1 One on God's side is a majority. — speech 1 November 1859

2 Every man meets his Waterloo at last. — speech 1 November 1859

3 Whether in chains or in laurels, Liberty knows nothing but victories. — speech 1 November 1859

4 Truth is one forever absolute, but opinion is truth filtered through the moods, the blood, the disposition of the spectator. — in *Idols* 4 October 1859

Phocion *c.*402–317 BC

Athenian soldier

5 DEMOSTHENES: The Athenians will kill thee, Phocion, should they go crazy.
PHOCION: But they will kill thee, should they come to their senses. — Plutarch *Parallel Lives* 'Phocion'

Kenneth Pickthorn 1892–1975

British Conservative politician and historian

6 Procedure is all the poor Briton has, now that any Government which commands 51 per cent of the House can at any moment do anything they like with retrospective or prospective intention. — in the House of Commons, 8 February 1960

William Pitt, Earl of Chatham 1708–78

British Whig statesman; he became Secretary of State (effectively Prime Minister) in 1756 and headed coalition governments 1756–61 and 1766–8; father of William **Pitt** (1759–1806)
on Pitt: see **Walpole** 378:4

7 The atrocious crime of being a young man...I shall neither attempt to palliate nor deny. — in the House of Commons, 2 March 1741

8 I must now address a few words to the Solicitor; they shall be few, but they shall be daggers.
to William Murray, the Attorney-General, in the House of Commons — Basil Williams *William Pitt, Earl of Chatham* (1913)

9 The poorest man may in his cottage bid defiance to all the forces of the Crown. It may be frail—its roof may shake—the wind may blow through it—the storm may enter—the rain may enter—but the King of England cannot enter! — speech, *c.* March 1763

10 Confidence is a plant of slow growth in an aged bosom: youth is the season of credulity. — in the House of Commons, 14 January 1766

11 Unlimited power is apt to corrupt the minds of those who possess it. — in the House of Lords, 9 January 1770

12 There is something behind the throne greater than the King himself. — in the House of Lords, 2 March 1770

1 We have a Calvinistic creed, a Popish liturgy, and an Arminian clergy.
in the House of Lords, 19 May 1772

2 You cannot conquer America.
in the House of Lords, 18 November 1777

3 I invoke the genius of the Constitution!
in the House of Lords, 18 November 1777

4 Shall a people that fifteen years ago was the terror of the world now stoop so low as to tell its ancient inveterate enemy, 'Take all we have, only give us peace?'
in his last speech in the Lords, shortly before his death, opposing a surrender to the American colonists and their ally France
Basil Williams *William Pitt, Earl of Chatham* (1913)

5 Our watchword is security.
attributed

6 The parks are the lungs of London.
quoted in the House of Commons by William Windham, 30 June 1808

William Pitt 1759–1806

British statesman, Prime Minister 1783–1801 and 1804–6; second son of William **Pitt**, Earl of Chatham

on Pitt: see **Burke** 65:6, **Fox** 140:4, **Fox** 140:5

7 Necessity is the plea for every infringement of human freedom: it is the argument of tyrants; it is the creed of slaves.
in the House of Commons, 18 November 1783

8 We must anew commence the salvation of Europe.
in 1795; in *Dictionary of National Biography*

9 We must recollect... what it is we have at stake, what it is we have to contend for. It is for our property, it is for our liberty, it is for our independence, nay, for our existence as a nation; it is for our character, it is for our very name as Englishmen, it is for everything dear and valuable to man on this side of the grave.
on the rupture of the Peace of Amiens and the resumption of war with Napoleon, 22 July 1803
Speeches of the Rt. Hon. William Pitt (1806)

10 England has saved herself by her exertions, and will, as I trust, save Europe by her example.
replying to a toast in which he had been described as the saviour of his country in the wars with France
R. Coupland *War Speeches of William Pitt* (1915)

11 Roll up that map; it will not be wanted these ten years.
of a map of Europe, on hearing of **Napoleon***'s victory at Austerlitz, December 1805*
Earl Stanhope *Life of the Rt. Hon. William Pitt* (1862)

12 Oh, my country! how I leave my country!
last words; oral tradition reports 'I think I could eat one of Bellamy's veal pies'
Earl Stanhope *Life of the Rt. Hon. William Pitt* vol. 3 (1879) ('How I love my country' in the 1st ed., vol. 4 (1862) ch. 43); G. Rose *Diaries and Correspondence* (1860) vol. 2, 23 January 1806, cites 'My country! oh, my country!'

Pius VII 1742–1823

Pope from 1800

1 We are prepared to go to the gates of Hell—but no further.
attempting to reach an agreement with **Napoleon,** *c.1800–1*
J. M. Robinson *Cardinal Consalvi* (1987)

Plato 429–347 BC

Greek philosopher

2 What I say is that 'just' or 'right' means nothing but what is in the interest of the stronger party.
spoken by Thrasymachus in *The Republic*

3 One of the penalties for refusing to participate in politics is that you end up being governed by your inferiors.
The Republic

4 When the tyrant has disposed of foreign enemies by conquest or treaty, and there is nothing to fear from them, then he is always stirring up some war or other, in order that the people may require a leader.
'foreign enemies' here means 'exiled opponents'
The Republic

Pliny the Elder AD 23–79

Roman statesman and scholar

5 *Ex Africa semper aliquid novi.*
Always something new out of Africa.
traditional form of *Semper aliquid novi Africam adferre*; *Historia Naturalis*

George Washington Plunkitt 1842–1924

American politician

6 I seen my opportunities and I took 'em.
William L. Riordan *Plunkitt of Tammany Hall* (1905)

7 The politician who steals is worse than a thief. He is a fool. With all the grand opportunities around for the man with a political pull, there's no excuse for stealin' a cent.
William L. Riordan *Plunkitt of Tammany Hall* (1905)

Plutarch AD *c.*46–*c.*120

Greek philosopher and biographer

8 For we are told that when a certain man was accusing both of them to him, he [Caesar] said that he had no fear of those fat and long-haired fellows, but rather of those pale and thin ones.
Parallel Lives 'Anthony'

9 The man who is thought to have been the first to see beneath the surface of Caesar's public policy and to fear it, as one might fear the smiling surface of the sea.
of **Cicero**
Parallel Lives 'Julius Caesar'

Georges Pompidou 1911–74

French statesman, Prime Minister 1962–8 and President 1969–74

1 A statesman is a politician who places himself at the service of the nation. A politician is a statesman who places the nation at his service.

in 1973, attributed

Alexander Pope 1688–1744

English poet

2 Here thou, great Anna! whom three realms obey,
Dost sometimes counsel take—and sometimes tea.

The Rape of the Lock (1714)

3 Statesman, yet friend to Truth! of soul sincere,
In action faithful, and in honour clear;
Who broke no promise, served no private end,
Who gained no title, and who lost no friend.

Epistles to Several Persons 'To Mr Addison' (1720)

4 For forms of government let fools contest;
Whate'er is best administered is best.

An Essay on Man Epistle 3 (1733)

5 If parts allure thee, think how Bacon shined,
The wisest, brightest, meanest of mankind:
Or ravished with the whistling of a name,
See Cromwell, damned to everlasting fame!

An Essay on Man Epistle 4 (1734)

6 Old politicians chew on wisdom past,
And totter on in business to the last.

Epistles to Several Persons 'To Lord Cobham' (1734)

7 Get place and wealth, if possible, with grace;
If not, by any means get wealth and place.

Imitations of Horace Horace bk. 1, Epistle 1 (1738); cf. **Horace** 183:3

8 Lo! thy dread empire, Chaos! is restored;
Light dies before thy uncreating word:
Thy hand, great Anarch! lets the curtain fall;
And universal darkness buries all.

The Dunciad (1742)

John Popham 1531?–1607

Speaker of the House of Commons and Chief Justice

on being asked by the Queen what had passed in the Lower House in the Parliament of 1581:

9 If it please your Majesty, seven weeks.

Bacon *Apopthegms*

Karl Popper 1902–95

Austrian-born philosopher

10 We may become the makers of our fate when we have ceased to pose as its prophets.

The Open Society and its Enemies (1945) introduction

11 We must plan for freedom, and not only for security, if for no other reason than that only freedom can make security secure.

The Open Society and its Enemies (1945)

12 There is no history of mankind, there are only many histories of all kinds of aspects of human life. And one of

The Open Society and its Enemies (1945)

these is the history of political power. This is elevated into the history of the world.

1 Marxism is only an episode—one of the many mistakes we have made in the perennial and dangerous struggle for building a better and a freer world.
The Open Society and its Enemies (rev. ed., 1952)

2 Piecemeal social engineering resembles physical engineering in regarding the *ends* as beyond the province of technology.
The Poverty of Historicism (1957)

David Morris Potter 1901–71

3 Democracy is clearly most appropriate for countries which enjoy an economic surplus and least appropriate for countries where there is an economic insufficiency.
People of Plenty (1954)

Henry Codman Potter 1835–1908

Bishop of New York from 1887

4 We have exchanged the Washingtonian dignity for the Jeffersonian simplicity, which was, in truth, only another name for the Jacksonian vulgarity.
Bishop Potter's Address (1890)

Colin Powell 1937–

American general

5 My philosophy in all this is rather simple: match political expectations to military means in a wholly realistic way. Don't slide in, don't mislead yourself.
in *The National Interest* Spring 1994
speech at the National Press Club luncheon, 28 September 1993

Enoch Powell 1912–

British Conservative politician
on Powell: see **Macleod** 243:3

6 In politics it is more blessed not to take than to give.
in *Daily Telegraph* 31 January 1964

7 A little nonsense now and then is not a bad thing. Where would we politicians be if we were not allowed to talk it sometimes.?
attributed, 1964

8 The professional politician can sympathize with the professional advertiser...both must resign themselves to a low public estimation of their veracity and sincerity.
attributed, 1965

9 History is littered with the wars which everybody knew would never happen.
speech to the Conservative Party Conference, 19 October 1967

10 Those whom the gods wish to destroy, they first make mad. We must be mad, literally mad, as a nation to be permitting the annual inflow of some 50,000 dependents, who are for the most part the material of the future growth of the immigrant descended population. It is like watching a nation busily engaged in heaping up its own funeral pyre.
speech at Birmingham, 20 April 1968

1 As I look ahead, I am filled with foreboding. Like the Roman, I seem to see 'the River Tiber foaming with much blood'.
speech at Birmingham, 20 April 1968; cf. **Virgil** 375:6

2 'Helping industry' is the elephant pit of socialism, a deep hole with sharp spikes at the bottom, covered over with twigs and fresh grass.
speech in Eastbourne, 24 September 1969

3 No one is forced to be a politician. It can only compare with fox-hunting and writing poetry. These are two things that men do for sheer enjoyment too.
attributed, 1973

4 There is a mania in legislation in detecting discrimination. But all life is about discrimination.
attributed, 1975

5 A party...is not a faction or club of individuals who associate for mutual assistance in acquiring and retaining office. It is a body of persons who hold, advocate and desire to bring into effect certain political principles and policies.
speech 30 September 1976

6 Office before honour was the password of Conservative government.
of the 1970–4 Conservative administration
in *Spectator* 15 October 1977

7 All political lives, unless they are cut off in midstream at a happy juncture, end in failure, because that is the nature of politics and of human affairs.
Joseph Chamberlain (1977); epilogue

8 Take Parliament out of the history of England and that history itself becomes meaningless.
in 'The Parliamentarians' (BBC TV), a discussion between Enoch Powell and Robin Day, 4 February 1979

9 For a politician to complain about the press is like a ship's captain complaining about the sea.
in *Guardian* 3 December 1984

10 A Tory is someone who thinks institutions are wiser than those who operate them.
in *Daily Telegraph* 31 March 1986

11 ANNE BROWN: How would you like to be remembered?
ENOCH POWELL: I should like to have been killed in the war.
in a radio interview, 13 April 1986

12 The politician has to simplify in order to do his business with his public: but the historian can be so obsessed with the falsity of simplification as to qualify his subject out of recognizability.
in *Spectator* 26 November 1988

13 To pretend that you cannot exchange goods and services freely with a Frenchman or an Italian, unless there is an identical standard of bathing beaches or tap water in the different countries is not logic. It is naked aggression.
in *Guardian* 22 May 1990

14 To be and to remain a member of the House of Commons was the overriding and undiscussable motivation of my life as a politician.
'Theory and Practice' 1990

15 What is history except a nation's collective memory?
on BBC Radio 4 10 February 1991

16 Lift the curtain and 'the State' reveals itself as a little group of fallible men in Whitehall, making guesses about the future, influenced by political prejudices and partisan
attributed

prejudices, and working on projections drawn from the past by a staff of economists.

John O'Connor Power b. 1846

Irish lawyer and politician

of the Liberal Unionists:

1 The mules of politics: without pride of ancestry, or hope of posterity. — H. H. Asquith *Memories and Reflections* (1928); cf. **Disraeli** 117:9, **Donnelly** 122:7

John Prescott 1938–

British Labour politician; Deputy Leader of the Labour Party from 1994

on the contest for the Labour leadership, during a debate between himself, Tony **Blair**, *and Margaret Beckett:*

2 We're in danger of loving ourselves to death. — in *Observer* 19 June 1994 'Sayings of the Week'

Richard Price 1723–91

English nonconformist minister

3 Now, methinks, I see the ardour for liberty catching and spreading; a general amendment beginning in human affairs; the dominion of kings changed for the dominion of laws, and the dominion of priests giving way to the dominion of reason and conscience. — *A Discourse on the Love of our Country* (1790)

Matthew Prior 1664–1721

English poet

4 What is a King?—a man condemned to bear
The public burden of the nation's care. — *Solomon* (1718)

Pierre-Joseph Proudhon 1809–65

French social reformer

5 Property is theft. — *Qu'est-ce que la propriété?* (1840)

John Pym 1584–1643

English Parliamentary leader

6 To have granted liberties, and not to have liberties in truth and realities, is but to mock the kingdom. — in *Dictionary of National Biography*

after the battle of Edgehill, in a speech at Guildhall to the citizens of London pointing out the illusory nature of **Charles I**'s *promises*

Pyrrhus 319–272 BC

King of Epirus from 306 BC

1 One more such victory and we are lost. — Plutarch *Parallel Lives* 'Pyrrhus'
on defeating the Romans at Asculum, 279 BC; origin of the phrase 'Pyrrhic victory'

François Quesnay 1694–1774

French political economist

2 *Vous ne connaissez qu'une seule règle du commerce; c'est (pour me servir de vos propres termes) de laisser passer et de laisser faire tous les acheteurs et tous les vendeurs quelconques.*
You recognize but one rule of commerce; that is (to avail myself of your own terms) to allow free passage and freedom of action to all buyers and sellers whoever they may be. — letter from M. Alpha to de Quesnay, 1767, in L. Salleron *François Quesnay et la Physiocratie* (1958) vol. 2, but not found in de Quesnay's writings; cf. **Argenson** 16:1

Josiah Quincy 1772–1864

American Federalist politician

3 As it will be the right of all, so it will be the duty of some, definitely to prepare for a separation, amicably if they can, violently if they must. — in *Abridgement of Debates of Congress* 14 January 1811

Yitzhak Rabin 1922–95

Israeli statesman and military leader, Prime Minister 1974–7 and 1992–5

4 We say to you today in a loud and a clear voice: enough of blood and tears. Enough. — in Washington, 13 September 1993
to the Palestinians, at the signing of the Israel–Palestine Declaration

Lord Radcliffe 1899–1977

British lawyer and public servant

5 Society has become used to the standing armies of power—the permanent Civil Service, the police force, the tax-gatherer—organized on a scale which was unknown to earlier centuries. — *Power and the State* (BBC Reith Lectures, 1951)

6 Governments always tend to want not really a free press but a managed or well-conducted one. — in 1967; Peter Hennessy *What the Papers Never Said* (1985)

Thomas Rainborowe d. 1648

English soldier and parliamentarian

1 The poorest he that is in England hath a life to live as the greatest he.
during the Army debates at Putney, 29 October 1647
C. H. Firth (ed.) *The Clarke Papers* vol. 1 (1891)

Milton Rakove 1918–83

2 The second law, Rakove's law of principle and politics, states that the citizen is influenced by principle in direct proportion to his distance from the political situation.
in *Virginia Quarterly Review* (1965)

Walter Ralegh *c.*1552–1618

English explorer and courtier

3 Fain would I climb, yet fear I to fall.
line written on a window-pane; cf. **Elizabeth I** 131:8
Thomas Fuller *History of the Worthies of England* (1662) 'Devonshire'

4 Say to the court, it glows
And shines like rotten wood;
Say to the church, it shows
What's good, and doth no good:
If church and court reply,
Then give them both the lie.
'The Lie' (1608)

5 'Tis a sharp remedy, but a sure one for all ills.
on feeling the edge of the axe prior to his execution
D. Hume *History of Great Britain* (1754)

6 So the heart be right, it is no matter which way the head lies.
at his execution, on being asked which way he preferred to lay his head
W. Stebbing *Sir Walter Raleigh* (1891)

7 I have a long journey to take, and must bid the company farewell.
parting words
E. Thompson *Sir Walter Raleigh* (1935)

John Randolph 1773–1833

American politician

8 The surest way to prevent war is not to fear it.
in the House of Representatives, 5 March 1806

9 God has given us Missouri, and the devil shall not take it from us.
in the debate in the US Senate in 1820 on the admission of Missouri to the Union as a slave state
Robert V. Remini *Henry Clay* (1991)

10 Never were abilities so much below mediocrity so well rewarded; no, not when Caligula's horse was made Consul.
on John Quincy **Adams***'s appointment of Richard Rush as Secretary of the Treasury*
speech 1 February 1828

1 He is a man of splendid abilities but utterly corrupt. He shines and stinks like rotten mackerel by moonlight.
of Edward Livingston
W. Cabell Bruce *John Randolph of Roanoke* (1923) vol. 2

2 He rowed to his object with muffled oars.
of Martin Van Buren
W. Cabell Bruce *John Randolph of Roanoke* (1923) vol. 2

3 That most delicious of all privileges—spending other people's money.
William Cabell Bruce *John Randolph of Roanoke* (1923) vol. 2

Sam Rayburn 1882–1961

American politician

4 If you want to get along, go along.
Neil MacNeil *Forge of Democracy* (1963)

Ronald Reagan 1911–

American Republican statesman, 40th President of the US 1981–9; former Hollywood actor
on Reagan: see **Keillor** 203:3, **Schroeder** 321:8, **Vidal** 375:2; see also **Dempsey** 113:3, **Gipp** 153:5

5 Government is like a big baby—an alimentary canal with a big appetite at one end and no responsibility at the other.
campaigning for the governorship of California, 1965
attributed

6 Politics is just like show business, you have a hell of an opening, coast for a while and then have a hell of a close.
in 1966; Mark Green and Gail MacColl (eds.) *There He Goes Again* (1983)

7 Government does not solve problems; it subsidizes them.
speech 11 December 1972

8 Politics is supposed to be the second oldest profession. I have come to realize that it bears a very close resemblance to the first.
at a conference in Los Angeles, 2 March 1977

9 I've noticed that everybody who is for abortion has already been born.
presidential campaign debate, 21 September 1980

10 You can tell a lot about a fellow's character by his way of eating jellybeans.
in *New York Times* 15 January 1981

11 We're the party that wants to see an America in which people can still get rich.
at a Republican congressional dinner, 4 May 1982

12 So in your discussions of the nuclear freeze proposals, I urge you to beware the temptation of pride—the temptation blithely to declare yourselves above it all and label both sides equally at fault, to ignore the facts of history and the aggressive impulses of an evil empire.
speech to the National Association of Evangelicals, 8 March 1983

13 My fellow Americans, I am pleased to tell you I just signed legislation which outlaws Russia forever. The bombing begins in five minutes.
said during radio microphone test, 11 August 1984
in *New York Times* 13 August 1984

14 The taxpayer—that's someone who works for the federal government but doesn't have to take a Civil Service examination.
attributed, 1985

1 We are especially not going to tolerate these attacks from outlaw states run by the strangest collection of misfits, Looney Tunes, and squalid criminals since the advent of the Third Reich.
speech following the hijack of a US plane, 8 July 1985
in *New York Times* 9 July 1985

2 This mad dog of the Middle East.
of Colonel Gadaffi of Libya, 9 April 1986
in *New York Times* 10 April 1986

3 It's difficult to believe that people are starving in this country because food isn't available.
at a press conference, 11 June 1986

4 The nine most terrifying words in the English language are, 'I'm from the government and I'm here to help.'
on assistance to farmers
at a press conference in Chicago, 2 August 1986

5 Mr Gorbachev, tear down this wall.
in Berlin, 12 June 1987

6 I don't resent his popularity or anything else. Good Lord, I co-starred with Errol Flynn once.
of Mikhail **Gorbachev**
address to schoolchildren in Jacksonville, Florida, 1 December 1987

7 To grasp and hold a vision, that is the very essence of successful leadership—not only on the movie set where I learned it, but everywhere.
in *The Wilson Quarterly* Winter 1994; attributed

8 I now begin the journey that will lead me into the sunset of my life.
statement to the American people revealing that he had Alzheimer's disease, 1994
in *Daily Telegraph* 5 January 1995

John Redmond 1856–1918

Irish politician and nationalist leader

in the Spring of 1914 Redmond was asked by a friend, a priest from Tipperary, if anything could now rob them of Home Rule:

9 A European war might do it.
in *Dictionary of National Biography*

Joseph Reed 1741–85

American Revolutionary politician

10 I am not worth purchasing, but such as I am, the King of Great Britain is not rich enough to do it.
replying to an offer from Governor George Johnstone of £10,000, and any office in the Colonies in the King's gift, if he were able successfully to promote a Union between the United Kingdom and the American Colonies
W. B. Read *Life and Correspondence of Joseph Reed* (1847)

Thomas Brackett Reed 1839–1902

American politician and member of Congress

of two fellow congressmen:

11 They never open their mouths without subtracting from the sum of human knowledge.
Samuel W. McCall *The Life of Thomas Brackett Reed* (1914)

Montague John Rendall 1862–1950

member of the first BBC Board of Governors

1 Nation shall speak peace unto nation. — motto of the BBC; cf. **Bible** 43:18

James Reston 1909–95

American journalist

2 This is the devilish thing about foreign affairs: they are foreign and will not always conform to our whim. — in *New York Times* 16 December 1964

3 All politics, however, are based on the indifference of the majority. — in *New York Times* 12 June 1968

Walter Reuther 1907–70

American labour leader

4 If it looks like a duck, walks like a duck and quacks like a duck, then it just may be a duck. — attributed
as a test, during the McCarthy era, of Communist affiliations

5 Injustice was as common as streetcars. When men walked into their jobs, they left their dignity, their citizenship and their humanity outside. — attributed
on working life in America before the Wagner Act

Paul Revere 1735–1818

American patriot

6 To the memory of the glorious Ninety-two: members of the Honorable House of Representatives of the Massachusetts Bay who, undaunted by the insolent menaces of villains in power, from a strict regard to conscience and the liberties of their constituents on the 30th June 1768 voted NOT TO RESCIND. — attributed
inscription on Revere's silver 'Liberty' bowl, 1768

7 If the British went out by water, to show two lanterns in the North Church steeple; and if by land, one as a signal, for we were apprehensive it would be difficult to cross the Charles River or get over Boston Neck. — letter to Jeremy Belknap
signal code arranged with Colonel Conant of the Charlestown Committee of Safety, 16 April 1775

Joshua Reynolds 1723–92

English painter

8 The House of Commons resembles a private company. How seldom is any man convinced by another's argument; passion and pride rise against it. — James Boswell *Life of Samuel Johnson* (1791) 3 April 1778

Cecil Rhodes 1853–1902

British-born South African diamond prospector and statesman, Prime Minister of Cape Colony 1890–6

1 Ask any man what nationality he would prefer to be, and ninety-nine out of a hundred will tell you that they would prefer to be Englishmen. — Gordon Le Sueur *Cecil Rhodes* (1913)

2 Being an Englishman is the greatest prize in the lottery of life. — A. W. Jarvis *Jottings from an Active Life* (1928)

3 So little done, so much to do.
said on the day of his death — Lewis Michell *Life of Rhodes* (1910)

David Ricardo 1772–1823

British economist

4 Rent is that portion of the earth, which is paid to the landlord for the use of the original and indestructible powers of the soil. — *On the Principles of Political Economy and Taxation* (1817)

Grantland Rice 1880–1954

American sportswriter

5 All wars are planned by old men
In council rooms apart. — 'The Two Sides of War' (1955)

Stephen Rice 1637–1715

Irish lawyer

6 I will drive a coach and six horses through the Act of Settlement. — W. King *State of the Protestants of Ireland* (1672)

Tim Rice 1944–

English lyricist

7 Don't cry for me, Argentina.
from the musical Evita, *based on the life of Eva Perón* — title of song (1976)

Mandy Rice-Davies 1944–

English courtesan

at the trial of Stephen Ward, 29 June 1963, on being told that Lord Astor claimed that her allegations, concerning himself and his house parties at Cliveden, were untrue:

8 He would, wouldn't he? — in *Guardian* 1 July 1963

Ann Richards 1933–

American Democratic politician; State Treasurer, and later Governor, of Texas

1 That dog won't hunt.
of Republican policies
keynote speech at the Democratic convention, 1988; Wallace O. Chariton *This Dog'll Hunt* (1989)

2 Poor George, he can't help it—he was born with a silver foot in his mouth.
of George **Bush**
keynote speech at the Democratic convention, 1988; in *Independent* 20 July 1988

Johann Paul Friedrich Richter ('Jean Paul') 1763–1825

German novelist

3 Providence has given to the French the empire of the land, to the English that of the sea, and to the Germans that of—the air!
Thomas Carlyle 'Jean Paul Friedrich Richter' in *Edinburgh Review* no. 91 (1827)

Adam Ridley 1942–

British economist, former Director of the Conservative Research Department

4 Parties come to power with silly, inconsistent and impossible policies because they have spent their whole period in opposition forgetting about the real world, destroying the lessons they learnt in government and clambering slowly back on to the ideological plain where they feel happiest.
in *RIPA Report* Winter 1985

Nicholas Ridley 1929–93

British Conservative politician

5 The last thing I want is to spend more time with my family.
as Trade and Industry Secretary, replying to taunts that he had more past than future as a minister
in *Independent* 10 March 1990

of the European monetary union:

6 This is all a German racket designed to take over the whole of Europe.
in an interview with Dominic Lawson, in the aftermath of which Ridley resigned from the Government
in *Spectator* 14 July 1990

7 Seventeen unelected reject politicians with no accountability to anybody, who are not responsible for raising taxes, just spending money, who are pandered to by a supine parliament which also is not responsible for raising taxes.
of the European Community
in *Spectator* 14 July 1990

8 I'm not against giving up sovereignty in principle, but not to this lot. You might just as well give it to Adolf
in *Spectator* 14 July 1990

Hitler, frankly.
of the European Community

Hal Riney 1932–

American advertising executive

1 It's morning again in America. — in *Newsweek* 6 August 1984
slogan for Ronald **Reagan***'s 1984 election campaign*

Geoffrey Rippon 1924–

British Conservative politician

2 The world is divided into three classes. The Haves, the Have-nots, and the Haves but Have not Paid. — attributed, May 1987

3 An opposition politician must at all times avoid being contaminated by the truth. — attributed, May 1987

Maximilien Robespierre 1758–94

French revolutionary
on Robespierre: see **Carlyle** 75:9

4 I am no courtesan, nor moderator, nor Tribune, nor defender of the people: I am myself the people. — speech at the Jacobin Club, 27 April 1792

5 The general will rules in society as the private will governs each separate individual. — *Lettres à ses commettans* (2nd series) 5 January 1793

6 Any law which violates the inalienable rights of man is essentially unjust and tyrannical; it is not a law at all. — *Déclaration des droits de l'homme* 24 April 1793, article 6; this article, in slightly different form, is recorded as having figured in Robespierre's *Projet* of 21 April 1793

7 Any institution which does not suppose the people good, and the magistrate corruptible, is evil. — *Déclaration des droits de l'homme* 24 April 1793, article 25

8 The revolutionary government is the despotism of liberty against tyranny. — speech 5 February 1794

9 Wickedness is the root of despotism as virtue is the essence of the Republic. — in the Convention, 7 May 1794

10 One single will is necessary. — private note; S. A. Berville and J. F. Barrière *Papiers inédits trouvés chez Robespierre* vol. 2 (1828)

11 If the basis of popular government in time of peace is virtue, its basis in a time of revolution is both virtue and intimidation. Intimidation without virtue is disastrous; virtue without intimidation is powerless. — J. M. Thompson *The French Revolution*; attributed

James Harvey Robinson 1863–1936

12 Political campaigns are designedly made into emotional orgies which endeavour to distract attention from the — *The Human Comedy* (1937)

real issues involved, and they actually paralyze what slight powers of cerebration man can normally muster.

1 With supreme irony, the war to 'make the world safe for democracy' ended by leaving democracy more unsafe in the world than at any time since the collapse of the revolutions of 1848. — *The Human Comedy* (1937)

Joan Robinson 1903–

British economist

2 Current experience suggests that socialism is not a stage beyond capitalism but a substitute for it—a means by which the nations which did not share in the Industrial Revolution can imitate its technical achievements; a means to achieve rapid accumulation under a different set of rules of the game. — 'Marx, Marshall and Keynes' (1955)

Mary Robinson 1944–

Irish Labour stateswoman; President from 1990

3 Instead of rocking the cradle, they rocked the system.
in her victory speech, paying tribute to the women of Ireland — in *The Times* 10 November 1990

Boyle Roche 1743–1807

Irish politician

4 Mr Speaker, I smell a rat; I see him forming in the air and darkening the sky; but I'll nip him in the bud. — attributed

Lord Rochester 1647–80

English poet

5 Here lies a great and mighty king
Whose promise none relies on;
He never said a foolish thing,
Nor ever did a wise one.
of **Charles II**; *an alternative first line reads: 'Here lies our sovereign lord the King'* — 'The King's Epitaph'; C. E. Doble et al. *Thomas Hearne: Remarks and Collections* (1885–1921) 17 November 1706; cf. **Charles II** 83:1

6 A merry monarch, scandalous and poor. — 'A Satire on King Charles II' (1697)

Will Rogers 1879–1935

American humorist

7 The more you read and observe about this Politics thing, you got to admit that each party is worse than the other. The one that's out always looks the best. — *Illiterate Digest* (1924)

8 Communism is like prohibition, it's a good idea but it won't work. — in 1927; *Weekly Articles* (1981) vol. 3

9 I don't know jokes—I just watch the government and report the facts. — 'A Rogers Thesaurus' in *Saturday Review* 25 August 1962

Mme Roland 1754–93

French revolutionary

1 O liberty! O liberty! what crimes are committed in thy name! — A. de Lamartine *Histoire des Girondins* (1847)

Oscar Romero 1917–80

Salvadorean Roman Catholic priest, Archbishop of San Salvador

2 When a dictatorship seriously violates human rights and attacks the common good of the nation, when it becomes unbearable and closes all channels of dialogue, of understanding, of rationality, when this happens, the Church speaks of the legitimate right of insurrectional violence. — Alan Riding 'The Cross and the Sword in Latin America' (1981)

Eleanor Roosevelt 1884–1962

American humanitarian and diplomat, wife of Franklin **Roosevelt**
on Roosevelt: see **Stevenson** 350:14

3 No one can make you feel inferior without your consent. — in *Catholic Digest* August 1960

Franklin D. Roosevelt 1882–1945

American Democratic statesman, 32nd President of the US 1933–45
on Roosevelt: see **Churchill** 92:5, **Holmes** 181:8, **Truman** 371:1

4 These unhappy times call for the building of plans that... build from the bottom up and not from the top down, that put their faith once more in the forgotten man at the bottom of the economic pyramid. — radio address, 7 April 1932

5 The country needs and, unless I mistake its temper, the country demands bold, persistent experimentation. It is common sense to take a method and try it. If it fails, admit it frankly and try another. But above all, try something. — address at Oglethorpe University, Atlanta, Georgia, 22 May 1932

6 I pledge you, I pledge myself, to a new deal for the American people.
accepting the presidential nomination — speech to the Democratic Convention in Chicago, 2 July 1932

7 There is no indispensable man. — campaign speech, New York, 3 November 1932

8 The only thing we have to fear is fear itself. — inaugural address, 4 March 1933

9 In the field of world policy I would dedicate this Nation to the policy of the good neighbour. — inaugural address, 4 March 1933

10 This generation of Americans has a rendezvous with destiny. — speech accepting renomination as President, 27 June 1936

1 I have seen war. I have seen war on land and sea. I have seen blood running from the wounded. I have seen men coughing out their gassed lungs. I have seen the dead in the mud. I have seen cities destroyed. I have seen 200 limping, exhausted men come out of line—the survivors of a regiment of 1,000 that went forward 48 hours before. I have seen children starving. I have seen the agony of mothers and wives. I hate war.

speech at Chautauqua, NY, 14 August 1936

2 I should like to have it said of my first Administration that in it the forces of selfishness and of lust for power met their match. I should like to have it said of my second Administration that in it these forces met their master.

speech at Madison Square Garden, 31 October 1936

3 I see one-third of a nation ill-housed, ill-clad, ill-nourished.

second inaugural address, 20 January 1937

4 War is a contagion.

speech at Chicago, 5 October 1937

5 The only sure bulwark of continuing liberty is a government strong enough to protect the interests of the people, and a people strong enough and well enough informed to maintain its sovereign control over its government.

'Fireside Chat' radio broadcast, 14 April 1938

6 When peace has been broken anywhere, the peace of all countries everywhere is in danger.

'Fireside Chat' radio broadcast, 3 September 1939

7 I am reminded of four definitions: A Radical is a man with both feet firmly planted—in the air. A Conservative is a man with two perfectly good legs who, however, has never learned to walk forward. A Reactionary is a somnambulist walking backwards. A Liberal is a man who uses his legs and his hands at the behest—at the command—of his head.

radio address to *New York Herald Tribune* Forum, 26 October 1939

8 On this tenth day of June 1940 the hand that held the dagger has struck it into the back of its neighbour.

on hearing that Italy had declared war on France

address at the University of Virginia, Charlottesville, 10 June 1940

9 I have said this before, but I shall say it again and again and again: Your boys are not going to be sent into any foreign wars.

speech in Boston, 30 October 1940

10 We have the men—the skill—the wealth—and above all, the will... We must be the great arsenal of democracy.

'Fireside Chat' radio broadcast, 29 December 1940

11 We look forward to a world founded upon four essential human freedoms. The first is freedom of speech and expression—everywhere in the world. The second is freedom of every person to worship God in his own way—everywhere in the world. The third is freedom from want... everywhere in the world. The fourth is freedom from fear... anywhere in the world.

message to Congress, 6 January 1941

12 We, too, born to freedom, and believing in freedom, are willing to fight to maintain freedom. We, and all others who believe as deeply as we do, would rather die on our feet than live on our knees.

on receiving the degree of Doctor of Civil Law from Oxford

on 19 June 1941; cf. **Ibarruri** 186:6

1 Yesterday, December 7, 1941—a date which will live in infamy—the United States of America was suddenly and deliberately attacked by naval and air forces of the Empire of Japan.
address to Congress, 8 December 1941

2 Books can not be killed by fire. People die, but books never die. No man and no force can abolish memory... In this war, we know, books are weapons. And it is a part of your dedication always to make them weapons for man's freedom.
'Message to the Booksellers of America' 6 May 1942

3 It is fun to be in the same decade with you.
cabled reply to Winston Churchill, acknowledging congratulations on his 60th birthday
W. S. Churchill *The Hinge of Fate* (1950)

4 All of our people all over the country—except the pure-blooded Indians—are immigrants or descendants of immigrants, including even those who came over here on the Mayflower.
campaign speech in Boston, 4 November 1944

5 The American people are quite competent to judge a political party that works both sides of the street.
campaign speech in Boston, 4 November 1944

6 We have learned that we cannot live alone, at peace; that our own well-being is dependent on the well-being of other nations, far away. We have learned that we must live as men, and not as ostriches, no as dogs in the manger. We have learned to be citizens of the world, members of the human community.
fourth inaugural address, 20 January 1945

7 You've convinced me. Now go out and put pressure on me.
attributed; Peter Hennessy *Whitehall* (1990)

8 The work, my friend, is peace. More than an end of this war—an end to the beginnings of all wars.
undelivered address for Jefferson Day, 13 April 1945, the day after Roosevelt died
Public Papers (1950) vol. 13

9 The only limit to our realization of tomorrow will be our doubts of today. Let us move forward with strong and active faith.
undelivered address for Jefferson Day, 13 April 1945, final lines
Public Papers (1950) vol. 13

Theodore Roosevelt 1858–1919

American Republican statesman, 26th President of the US 1901–9

on Roosevelt: see **Hanna** 168:1, **Knox** 215:2

10 I wish to preach, not the doctrine of ignoble ease, but the doctrine of the strenuous life.
speech to the Hamilton Club, Chicago, 10 April 1899

11 Far better it is to dare mighty things, to win glorious triumphs, even though checkered by failure, than to take rank with those poor spirits who neither enjoy much nor suffer much, because they live in the grey twilight that knows not victory nor defeat.
speech to the Hamilton Club, Chicago, 10 April 1899

12 I am as strong as a bull moose and you can use me to the limit.
letter to Mark **Hanna**, 27 June 1900

'Bull Moose' subsequently became the popular name of the Progressive Party

1 In life, as in a football game, the principle to follow is: Hit the line hard.
The Strenuous Life (1900)

2 McKinley has no more backbone than a chocolate éclair!
of William McKinley (1843–1901), Republican statesman and 25th President of the US, whose assassination brought about the accession of Roosevelt
H. T. Peck *Twenty Years of the Republic* (1906)

3 The first requisite of a good citizen in this Republic of ours is that he shall be able and willing to pull his weight.
speech in New York, 11 November 1902

4 There is a homely old adage which runs: 'Speak softly and carry a big stick; you will go far.' If the American nation will speak softly, and yet build and keep at a pitch of the highest training a thoroughly efficient navy, the Monroe Doctrine will go far.
speech in Chicago, 3 April 1903

5 A man who is good enough to shed his blood for the country is good enough to be given a square deal afterwards. More than that no man is entitled to, and less than that no man shall have.
speech at the Lincoln Monument, Springfield, Illinois, 4 June 1903

6 Far and away the best prize that life offers is the chance to work hard at work worth doing.
address at the State Fair, Syracuse, New York Labour Day, 7 September 1903

7 No man is above the law and no man is below it; nor do we ask any man's permission when we require him to obey it. Obedience to the law is demanded as a right; not asked as a favour.
third annual message to Congress, 7 December 1903

8 The men with the muckrakes are often indispensable to the well-being of society; but only if they know when to stop raking the muck.
speech in Washington, 14 April 1906

9 Malefactors of great wealth.
speech at Provincetown, Massachusetts, 20 August 1907

10 It is not the critic who counts; not the man who points out how the strong man stumbles, or where the doer of deeds could have done better. The credit belongs to the man who is actually in the arena.
'Citizenship in a Republic', speech at the Sorbonne, Paris, 23 April 1910

11 Every man holds his property subject to the general right of the community to regulate its use to whatever degree the public welfare may require it.
speech at Osawatomie, 31 August 1910

12 We stand at Armageddon and we battle for the Lord.
speech at Progressive Party Convention, Chicago, 17 June 1912

13 Foolish fanatics...the men who form the lunatic fringe in all reform movements.
Autobiography (1913)

14 There is no room in this country for hyphenated Americanism...The one absolutely certain way of bringing this nation to ruin, of preventing all possibility of its continuing to be a nation at all, would be to permit it to become a tangle of squabbling nationalities.
speech in New York, 12 October 1915

1 One of our defects as a nation is a tendency to use what have been called 'weasel words'. When a weasel sucks eggs the meat is sucked out of the egg. If you use a 'weasel word' after another, there is nothing left of the other.
speech in St Louis, 31 May 1916

2 There can be no fifty-fifty Americanism in this country. There is room here for only 100 per cent Americanism, only for those who are Americans and nothing else.
speech in Saratoga, 19 July 1918

3 No man is justified in doing evil on the ground of expediency.
Works (1925) vol. 15 'Latitude and Longitude among Reformers'

4 Put out the light.
last words
on 6 January 1919

Lord Rosebery 1847–1929

British Liberal statesman, Prime Minister 1894–5

5 There is no need for any nation, however great, leaving the Empire, because the Empire is a commonwealth of nations.
speech in Adelaide, Australia, 18 January 1884

6 There was no retirement, no concealment. He died by inches in public, sole mourner at his own protracted funeral.
of Lord Randolph **Churchill**
attributed

7 I have never known the sweets of place with power, but of place without power, of place with the minimum of power—that is a purgatory, and if not a purgatory it is a hell.
in *The Spectator* 6 July 1895

8 Imperialism, sane Imperialism, as distinguished from what I may call wild-cat Imperialism, is nothing but this—a larger patriotism.
speech, City of London Liberal Club, 5 May 1899

9 There are two supreme pleasures in life. One is ideal, the other real. The ideal is when a man receives the seals of office from his Sovereign. The real pleasure comes when he hands them back.
Sir Robert Peel (1899)

10 It is beginning to be hinted that we are a nation of amateurs.
Rectorial address at Glasgow University, 16 November 1900

11 No one outside an asylum wishes to be rid of it.
of the British Empire
Rectorial address at Glasgow University, 16 November 1900

12 I must plough my furrow alone.
speech on remaining outside the Liberal Party leadership, 19 July 1901
in *The Times* 20 July 1901

13 Men who sit still with the fly-blown phylacteries bound round their obsolete policy.
on certain members of the Liberal Party
speech at Chesterfield, 16 December 1901

Ethel Rosenberg 1916–53 and Julius Rosenberg 1918–53

American husband and wife; convicted of spying for the Russians and executed

1 We are innocent...To forsake this truth is to pay too high a price even for the priceless gift of life.
petition for executive clemency, filed 9 January 1953
Ethel Rosenberg *Death House Letters* (1953)

2 We are the first victims of American Fascism.
letter from Julius to Emanuel Bloch before the Rosenbergs' execution, 19 June 1953
Testament of Ethel and Julius Rosenberg (1954)

A. C. Ross fl. 1840

3 Tippecanoe and Tyler, too.
presidential campaign song for William Henry **Harrison**, *1840*
attributed; cf. **Morris** 266:4

Dick Ross

British economist, former Deputy Director of the Central Policy Review Staff

4 You must think the unthinkable, but always wear a dark suit when presenting the results.
in the early 1970s; Peter Hennessy *Whitehall* (1990)

Christina Rossetti 1830–94

English poet; sister of D. G. Rossetti

5 Our Indian Crown is in great measure the trapping of a splendid misery.
on the siege of Kandahar
letter to Amelia Heimann, 29 July 1880

Jean Rostand 1894–1977

French biologist

6 Stupidity, outrage, vanity, cruelty, iniquity, bad faith, falsehood—we fail to see the whole array when it is facing in the same direction as we.
Pensées d'un biologiste (1939)

Lord Rothschild 1910–90

British administrator and scientist, first Director of the Central Policy Review Staff
on Rothschild: see **Hurd** 185:8

on being appointed to the Government think-tank in 1970 where he met Burke **Trend**, *the Cabinet Secretary, and William* **Armstrong**, *Secretary to the Treasury:*

7 Until this week I never realized that the country was run by two men I'd never heard of.
Peter Hennessy *Whitehall* (1990)

1 Politicians often believe that their world is the real one. Officials sometimes take a different view.
on resigning as Director of the Central Policy Review Staff
in *The Times* 13 October 1974

2 The promises and panaceas that gleam like false teeth in the party manifestoes.
Meditations of a Broomstick (1977)

Claude-Joseph Rouget de Lisle

1760–1836

French soldier

3 *Allons, enfants de la patrie,*
Le jour de gloire est arrivé...
Aux armes, citoyens!
Formez vos battaillons!
Come, children of our country, the day of glory has arrived... To arms, citizens! Form your battalions!
'La Marseillaise' (25 April 1792)

Jean-Jacques Rousseau 1712–78

French philosopher and novelist

4 The social contract
title of book, 1762

5 Man was born free, and everywhere he is in chains.
The Social Contract (1762)

6 Slaves become so debased by their chains as to lose even the desire of breaking from them.
The Social Contract 1762

Maude Royden 1876–1956

English religious writer, social reformer, and preacher

7 The Church should go forward along the path of progress and be no longer satisfied only to represent the Conservative Party at prayer.
address at Queen's Hall, London, 16 July 1917

Paul Alfred Rubens 1875–1917

English songwriter

8 Oh! we don't want to lose you but we think you ought
to go
For your King and your Country both need you so;
We shall want you and miss you but with all our might
and main
We shall cheer you, thank you, kiss you
When you come back again.
'Your King and Country Want You' (1914 song)

Richard Rumbold c.1622–85

English republican conspirator

9 I never could believe that Providence had sent a few men into the world, ready booted and spurred to ride, and millions ready saddled and bridled to be ridden.
on the scaffold
T. B. Macaulay *History of England* vol. 1 (1849)

Dean Rusk 1909–94

US politician; Secretary of State, 1961–9

1 We're eyeball to eyeball, and I think the other fellow just blinked.
on the Cuban missile crisis, 24 October 1962
in *Saturday Evening Post* 8 December 1962

2 Only one-third of human beings are asleep at one time, and the other two-thirds are awake and up to some mischief somewhere.
attributed, 1966

3 Scratch any American and underneath you'll find an isolationist.
to the British Foreign Secretary, George Brown; Tony Benn diary 12 January 1968

4 It has been said that power tends to corrupt, but that loss of power tends to corrupt absolutely.
attributed, 1968

John Ruskin 1819–1900

English art and social critic

5 It ought to be quite as natural and straightforward a matter for a labourer to take his pension from his parish, because he has deserved well of his parish, as for a man in higher rank to take his pension from his country, because he has deserved well of his country.
Unto this Last (1862) preface

6 The force of the guinea you have in your pocket depends wholly on the default of a guinea in your neighbour's pocket. If he did not want it, it would be of no use to you.
Unto this Last (1862)

7 Government and co-operation are in all things the laws of life; anarchy and competition the laws of death.
Unto this Last (1862)

8 Whereas it has long been known and declared that the poor have no right to the property of the rich, I wish it also to be known and declared that the rich have no right to the property of the poor.
Unto this Last (1862)

9 The first duty of a State is to see that every child born therein shall be well housed, clothed, fed and educated, till it attain years of discretion.
Time and Tide (1867)

10 All mastership is not alike in principle; there are just and unjust masterships.
Time and Tide (1867)

11 You want to have voices in Parliament! Your voices are not worth a rat's squeak, either in Parliament or out of it, till you have some ideas to utter with them.
Time and Tide (1867)

12 Consider, for instance, the ridiculousness of the division of parties into 'Liberal' and 'Conservative'. There is no opposition whatever between those two kinds of men. There is opposition between Liberals and Illiberals; that is to say, between people who desire liberty, and who dislike it. I am a violent Illiberal; but it does not follow that I must be a Conservative. A Conservative is a person who wishes to keep things as they are; and he is opposed
Fors Clavigera (1871)

to a Destructive, who wishes to destroy them, or to an Innovator, who wishes to alter them. Now, though I am an Illiberal, there are many things I should like to destroy.

1 We Communists of the old school think that our property belongs to everybody, and everybody's property to us; so of course I thought the Louvre belonged to me as much as to the Parisians, and expected they would have sent word over to me, being an Art Professor, to ask whether I wanted it burnt down. But no message or intimation to that effect ever reached me. *Fors Clavigera* (1871)

2 You have founded an entire Science of Political Economy, on what you have stated to be the constant instinct of man—the desire to defraud his neighbour. *Fors Clavigera* (1871)

3 Visible governments are the toys of some nations, the diseases of others, the harness of some, the burdens of more, the necessity of all. *Fors Clavigera* (1871)

4 I am, and my father was before me, a violent Tory of the old school; Walter Scott's school, that is to say, and Homer's. *Praeterita* (1885)

Bertrand Russell 1872–1970

British philosopher and mathematician

5 Next to enjoying ourselves, the next greatest pleasure consists in preventing others from enjoying themselves, or, more generally, in the acquisition of power. *Sceptical Essays* (1928)

6 The opinions that are held with passion are always those for which no good ground exists; indeed the passion is the measure of the holder's lack of rational conviction. *Sceptical Essays* (1928)

7 Envy is the basis of democracy. *The Conquest of Happiness* (1930)

8 One should as a rule respect public opinion in so far as is necessary to avoid starvation and to keep out of prison, but anything that goes beyond this is voluntary submission to an unnecessary tyranny. *The Conquest of Happiness* (1930)

9 If the Communists conquered the world it would be very unpleasant for a while, but not for ever. attributed, 1958

10 Few people can be happy unless they hate some other person, nation, or creed. attributed

11 Religion may in most of its forms be defined as the belief that the gods are on the side of the Government. attributed

12 The trouble with the world is that the stupid are cocksure and the intelligent are full of doubt. attributed

Lord John Russell 1792–1878

British Whig statesman, Prime Minister 1846–52 and 1865–6
on Russell: see **Derby** 114:2

1 It is impossible that the whisper of a faction should prevail against the voice of a nation.
reply to an Address from a meeting of 150,000 persons at Birmingham on the defeat of the second Reform Bill, October 1831
S. Walpole *Life of Lord John Russell* (1889)

2 If peace cannot be maintained with honour, it is no longer peace.
speech at Greenock, 19 September 1853

3 Among the defects of the Bill, which were numerous, one provision was conspicuous by its presence and another by its absence.
speech to the electors of the City of London, April 1859

Anwar al-Sadat 1918–81

Egyptian statesman, President 1970–81

4 Peace is much more precious than a piece of land.
speech in Cairo, 8 March 1978

Lord St John of Fawsley 1929–

British Conservative politician and author

5 The monarchy has become our only truly popular institution at a time when the House of Commons has declined in public esteem and the Lords is a matter of controversy. The monarchy is, in a real sense, underpinning the other two estates of the realm.
in *The Times* 1 February 1982

Saki 1870–1916

Scottish writer

6 We all know that Prime Ministers are wedded to the truth, but like other married couples they sometimes live apart.
The Unbearable Bassington (1912)

Lord Salisbury 1830–1903

British Conservative statesman, Prime Minister 1885–6, 1886–92, and 1895–1902
on Salisbury: see **Bismarck** 47:2, **Disraeli** 120:5, **Goschen** 158:4, **Hennessy** 175:2

7 English policy is to float lazily downstream, occasionally putting out a diplomatic boathook to avoid collisions.
letter to Lord Lytton, 9 March 1877

8 A great deal of misapprehension arises from the popular use of maps on a small scale. As with such maps you are able to put a thumb on India and a finger on Russia, some persons at once think that the political situation is alarming and that India must be looked to. If the noble
in the House of Lords, 11 June 1877

Lord would use a larger map—say one on the scale of the Ordnance Map of England—he would find that the distance between Russia and British India is not to be measured by the finger and thumb, but by a rule.

1 No lesson seems to be so deeply inculcated by the experience of life as that you never should trust experts. If you believe the doctors, nothing is wholesome: if you believe the theologians, nothing is innocent: if you believe the soldiers, nothing is safe. They all require to have their strong wine diluted by a very large admixture of insipid common sense.
letter to Lord Lytton, 15 June 1877

2 The agonies of a man who has to finish a difficult negotiation, and at the same time to entertain four royalties at a country house can be better imagined than described.
letter to Lord Lyons, 5 June 1878

3 What with deafness, ignorance of French, and Bismarck's extraordinary mode of speech, Beaconsfield has the dimmest idea of what is going on—understands everything crossways—and imagines a perpetual conspiracy.
letter to Lady Salisbury from the Congress of Berlin, 23 June 1878
Lady Gwendolen Cecil *Life of Robert, Marquis of Salisbury* (1921–32)

4 A party whose mission it is to live entirely upon the discovery of grievances are apt to manufacture the element upon which they subsist.
speech at Edinburgh, 24 November 1882

5 They who have the absolute power of preventing lamentable events, and knowing what is taking place, refuse to exercise that power, are responsible for what happens.
in the House of Lords, 12 February 1884

6 We are part of the community of Europe and we must do our duty as such.
speech at Caernarvon, 10 April 1888

7 Where property is in question I am guilty…of erecting individual liberty as an idol, and of resenting all attempts to destroy or fetter it; but when you pass from liberty to life, in no well-governed State, in no State governed according to the principles of common humanity, are the claims of mere liberty allowed to endanger the lives of the citizens.
in the House of Lords, 29 July 1897

8 Horny-handed sons of toil.
in *Quarterly Review* October 1873; later popularized in the US by Denis Kearney, 1847–1907

9 I rank myself no higher in the scheme of things than a policeman—whose utility would disappear if there were no criminals.
comparing his role in the Conservative Party with that of **Gladstone**
Lady Gwendolen Cecil *Biographical Studies… of Robert, Third Marquess of Salisbury* (1962)

10 By office boys for office boys.
of the Daily Mail
H. Hamilton Fyfe *Northcliffe, an Intimate Biography* (1930)

11 To defend a bad policy as an 'error of judgement' does not excuse it—the right functioning of a man's judgement is his most fundamental responsibility.
Gwendolen Cecil *Life of Robert, Marquis of Salisbury* (1921–32) vol. 3

1 If these gentlemen had their way, they would soon be asking me to defend the moon against a possible attack from Mars.
of his senior military advisers, and their tendency to see threats which did not exist

Robert Taylor *Lord Salisbury* (1975)

2 Too much poring over maps drives men mad.

Peter Hennessy *Never Again* (1992)

Lord Salisbury 1893–1972

British Conservative politician

3 Too clever by half.
of Iain **Macleod***, Colonial Secretary, 'in his relationship to the white communities of Africa'*

in the House of Lords, 7 March 1961

Sallust 86–35 BC

Roman historian

4 Greedy for the property of others, extravagant with his own.

Catiline

5 To stir up undisputed matters seemed a great reward in itself.

Catiline

6 He preferred to be rather than to seem good.
of Cato

Catiline

7 A venal city ripe to perish, if a buyer can be found.
of Rome

Jugurtha

8 *Punica fide.*
With Carthaginian trustworthiness.
meaning treachery

Jugurtha

Anthony Sampson 1926–

British author and journalist

9 Members [of the Order of St Michael and St George] rise from CMG (known sometimes in Whitehall as 'Call Me God') to the KCMG ('Kindly Call Me God') to—for a select few governors and super-ambassadors—the GCMG ('God Calls Me God').

Anatomy of Britain (1962)

10 A secret tome of *The Great and the Good* is kept, listing everyone who has the right, safe qualifications of worthiness, soundness and discretion; and from this tome came the stage army of committee people.

Anatomy of Britain Today (1965)

11 Of all the legacies of empire, the most dangerous is surely an immobile bureaucracy which can perpetuate its own interests and values, like those ancient hierarchies which presided over declining civilizations... As the British mandarins reinforce their defences, awarding each other old imperial honours, do they hear any echoes from Castile or Byzantium?

The Changing Anatomy of Britain (1982)

Paul A. Samuelson 1915–

American economist

1 The consumer, so it is said, is the king...each is a voter who uses his money as votes to get the things done that he wants done. — *Economics* (8th ed., 1970)

Lord Sandwich 1718–92

British politician and diplomat; First Lord of the Admiralty

2 If any man will draw up his case, and put his name at the foot of the first page, I will give him an immediate reply. Where he compels me to turn over the sheet, he must wait my leisure. — N. W. Wraxall *Memoirs* (1884) vol. 1

on appeals made by officers to the Navy Board

George Santayana 1863–1962

Spanish-born philosopher and critic

3 Fanaticism consists in redoubling your effort when you have forgotten your aim. — *The Life of Reason* (1905); introduction

4 Those who cannot remember the past are condemned to repeat it. — *The Life of Reason* (1905)

Jean-Paul Sartre 1905–80

French philosopher, novelist, playwright, and critic

5 When the rich wage war it's the poor who die. — *Le Diable et le bon Dieu* (1951)

Hugh Scanlon 1913–

British trade union leader

6 Of course liberty is not licence. Liberty in my view is conforming to majority opinion. — television interview, 9 August 1977

Arthur Scargill 1938–

British trade union leader

7 Parliament itself would not exist in its present form had people not defied the law. — evidence to House of Commons Select Committee on Employment, 2 April 1980

Lord Scarman 1911–

British judge

on the need for a written constitution:

8 No bevy of men, not even parliament, could always be trusted to safeguard human rights. — in conversation, 1982; Anthony Sampson *The Essential Anatomy of Britain* (1992)

1 The people as a source of sovereign power are in truth only occasional partners in the constitutional minuet danced for most of the time by Parliament and the political party in power.

The Shape of Things to Come (1989)

2 Time and the development of our society have rendered the checks and balances, such as they now are, of the constitution of no avail...to restrain an oppressively minded executive if it should win control of a majority of the House of Commons...The path to an 'elected dictatorship' is open and must be blocked now before the bad boys realize their opportunity and organize a takeover of the British Constitution.

The Shape of Things to Come (1989)

3 A government above the law is a menace to be defeated.

Why Britain Needs a Written Constitution 1992

4 Men still feel the need to keep the government in order. The feeling is deep, and as old as man.

Why Britain Needs a Written Constitution 1992

5 When times are abnormally alive with fear and prejudice, the common law is at a disadvantage: it cannot resist the will, however frightened and prejudiced it may be, of parliament.

after delivering a lecture advocating the establishment of a Bill of Rights

in conversation, 20 July 1992; Anthony Sampson *The Essential Anatomy of Britain* (1992)

Arthur M. Schlesinger Jr. 1917–

American historian

6 The answer to the runaway Presidency is not the messenger-boy Presidency. The American democracy must discover a middle way between making the President a czar and making him a puppet.

The Imperial Presidency (1973); preface

7 Suppose...that Lenin had died of typhus in Siberia in 1895 and Hitler had been killed on the western front in 1916. What would the twentieth century have looked like now?

The Cycles of American History (1986)

Patricia Schroeder 1940–

American Democratic politician; Congresswoman

8 Ronald Reagan...is attempting a great breakthrough in political technology—he has been perfecting the Teflon-coated Presidency. He sees to it that nothing sticks to him.

speech in the US House of Representatives, 2 August 1983

9 We've got the kind of President who thinks arms control means some kind of deodorant.

in *Observer* 9 August 1987 'Sayings of the Week'

E. F. Schumacher 1911–77

German-born economist

10 Small is beautiful. A study of economics as if people mattered.

title of book, 1973

1 Call a thing immoral or ugly, soul-destroying or a degradation of man, a peril to the peace of the world or to the well-being of future generations: as long as you have not shown it to be 'uneconomic' you have not really questioned its right to exist, grow, and prosper.

Small is Beautiful (1973)

Carl Schurz 1829–1906

American soldier and politician

2 My country, right or wrong; if right, to be kept right; and if wrong, to be set right!

speech, US Senate, 29 February 1872

Claud Schuster 1869–1956

British civil servant

of the relationship between the Prime Minister and the Cabinet:

3 Like the procreation of eels, [it] is slippery and mysterious.

G. H. L. Le May *The Victorian Constitution* (1979)

C. P. Scott 1846–1932

British journalist; editor of the Manchester Guardian, 1872–1929

4 A newspaper is of necessity something of a monopoly, and its first duty is to shun the temptations of monopoly. Its primary office is the gathering of news. At the peril of its soul it must see that the supply is not tainted. Neither in what it gives, nor in what it does not give, nor in the mode of presentation must the unclouded face of truth suffer wrong. Comment is free, but facts are sacred.

in *Manchester Guardian* 5 May 1921

Sir Walter Scott 1771–1832

Scottish novelist and poet

5 Breathes there the man, with soul so dead,
Who never to himself hath said,
This is my own, my native land!
Whose heart hath ne'er within him burned,
As home his footsteps he hath turned
From wandering on a foreign strand!

The Lay of the Last Minstrel (1805)

John Seeley 1834–95

English historian

6 We [the English] seem, as it were, to have conquered and peopled half the world in a fit of absence of mind.

The Expansion of England (1883); cf. **Hailsham** 163:12

John Selden 1584–1654

English historian and antiquary

1 Ignorance of the law excuses no man; not that all men know the law, but because 'tis an excuse every man will plead, and no man can tell how to confute him. — *Table Talk* (1689) 'Law'

2 A king is a thing men have made for their own sakes, for quietness' sake. Just as in a family one man is appointed to buy the meat. — *Table Talk* (1689) 'Of a King'

3 There is not anything in the world so much abused as this sentence, *Salus populi suprema lex esto.* — *Table Talk* (1689) 'People'; cf. **Cicero** 95:6

Arthur Seldon 1916–

British economist

4 Government of the busy by the bossy for the bully. — *Capitalism* (1990)
subheading on over-government

W. C. Sellar 1898–1951 and R. J. Yeatman 1898–1968

British writers

5 The Cavaliers (Wrong but Wromantic) and the Roundheads (Right but Repulsive). — *1066 and All That* (1930)

6 The Rump Parliament—so called because it had been sitting for such a long time. — *1066 and All That* (1930)

7 Charles II was always very merry and was therefore not so much a king as a Monarch. — *1066 and All That* (1930)

8 The National Debt is a very Good Thing and it would be dangerous to pay it off, for fear of Political Economy. — *1066 and All That* (1930)

9 Most memorable...was the discovery (made by all the rich men in England at once) that women and children could work twenty-five hours a day in factories without many of them dying or becoming excessively deformed. This was known as the Industrial Revelation. — *1066 and All That* (1930)

10 Gladstone...spent his declining years trying to guess the answer to the Irish Question; unfortunately whenever he was getting warm, the Irish secretly changed the Question. — *1066 and All That* (1930)

11 AMERICA was thus clearly top nation, and History came to a . — *1066 and All That* (1930)

Nassau William Senior 1790–1864

British economist

12 Though it is in the power of human institutions to make everybody poor, they cannot make everybody rich. — diary 1849

William Seward 1801–72

American politician

1 I know, and all the world knows, that revolutions never go backward. — speech at Rochester, 25 October 1858

Edward Sexby d. 1658

English conspirator

2 Killing no murder briefly discourst in three questions. — title of pamphlet (an apology for tyrannicide, 1657)

Anthony Ashley Cooper, Lord Shaftesbury 1621–83

in the English Civil War, adherent first of the royalist and then (from 1644) of the Parliamentary cause; in the reign of **Charles II**, supporter of **Monmouth**'s claim to the succession
on Shaftesbury: see **Cromwell** 106:2, **Dryden** 125:4

refusing the claims of Cromwell's House of Lords:

3 Admit lords, and you admit all. — in *Dictionary of National Biography*

William Shakespeare 1564–1616

English playwright

4 What's the matter, you dissentious rogues,
That, rubbing the poor itch of your opinion,
Make yourselves scabs? — *Coriolanus* (1608)

5 He that depends
Upon your favours swims with fins of lead,
And hews down oaks with rushes. — *Coriolanus* (1608)

6 Hear you this Triton of the minnows? mark you
His absolute 'shall'? — *Coriolanus* (1608)

7 What is the city but the people? — *Coriolanus* (1608)

8 You common cry of curs! whose breath I hate
As reek o' the rotten fens, whose loves I prize
As the dead carcases of unburied men
That do corrupt my air,—I banish you. — *Coriolanus* (1608)

9 Despising,
For you, the city, thus I turn my back:
There is a world elsewhere. — *Coriolanus* (1608)

10 The beast
With many heads butts me away. — *Coriolanus* (1608)

11 Let me have war, say I; it exceeds peace as far as day does night; it's spritely, waking, audible, and full of vent. Peace is a very apoplexy, lethargy: mulled, deaf, sleepy, insensible; a getter of more bastard children than war's a destroyer of men. — *Coriolanus* (1608)

1 I think he'll be to Rome
As is the osprey to the fish, who takes it
By sovereignty of nature.

Coriolanus (1608)

2 Why should we pay tribute? If Caesar can hide the sun from us with a blanket, or put the moon in his pocket, we will pay him tribute for light; else, sir, no more tribute.

Cymbeline (1609–10)

3 The art o'th' court,
As hard to leave as keep, whose top to climb
Is certain falling, or so slipp'ry that
The fear's as bad as falling.

Cymbeline (1609–10)

4 But in the gross and scope of my opinion,
This bodes some strange eruption to our state.

Hamlet (1601)

5 His greatness weighed, his will is not his own,
For he himself is subject to his birth.
He may not, as unvalued persons do,
Carve for himself, for on his choice depends
The sanity and health of the whole state;
And therefore must his choice be circumscribed
Unto the voice and yielding of that body
Whereof he is the head.

Hamlet (1601)

6 Something is rotten in the state of Denmark.

Hamlet (1601)

7 The time is out of joint; O cursèd spite,
That ever I was born to set it right!

Hamlet (1601)

8 For who would bear the whips and scorns of time,
The oppressor's wrong, the proud man's contumely,
The pangs of disprized love, the law's delay,
The insolence of office, and the spurns
That patient merit of the unworthy takes,
When he himself might his quietus make
With a bare bodkin?...
Thus conscience doth make cowards of us all.

Hamlet (1601)

9 Madness in great ones must not unwatched go.

Hamlet (1601)

10 Indeed this counsellor
Is now most still, most secret, and most grave,
Who was in life a foolish prating knave.

Hamlet (1601)

11 And where the offence is let the great axe fall.

Hamlet (1601)

12 The great man down, you mark his favourite flies;
The poor advanced makes friends of enemies.

Hamlet (1601)

13 The cease of majesty
Dies not alone, but like a gulf doth draw
What's near with it. It is a massy wheel,
Fixed on the summit of the highest mount,
To whose huge spokes ten thousand lesser things
Are mortised and adjoined; which when it falls,
Each small annexment, petty consequence,
Attends the boist'rous ruin. Never alone
Did the King sigh, but with a general groan.

Hamlet (1601)

1 Diseases desperate grown,
By desperate appliances are relieved,
Or not at all.
Hamlet (1601)

2 We go to gain a little patch of ground,
That hath in it no profit but the name.
Hamlet (1601)

3 Rightly to be great
Is not to stir without great argument,
But greatly to find quarrel in a straw
When honour's at the stake.
Hamlet (1601)

4 There's such divinity doth hedge a king,
That treason can but peep to what it would.
Hamlet (1601)

5 Rebellion lay in his way, and he found it.
Henry IV, Part 1 (1597)

6 It was always yet the trick of our English nation, if they have a good thing, to make it too common.
Henry IV, Part 2 (1597)

7 Uneasy lies the head that wears a crown.
Henry IV, Part 2 (1597)

8 This is the English, not the Turkish court;
Not Amurath an Amurath succeeds,
But Harry, Harry.
Henry IV, Part 2 (1597)

9 O England! model to thy inward greatness,
Like little body with a mighty heart,
What might'st thou do, that honour would thee do,
Were all thy children kind and natural!
But see thy fault!
Henry V (1599)

10 A little touch of Harry in the night.
Henry V (1599)

11 Discuss unto me; art thou officer?
Or art thou base, common and popular?
Henry V (1599)

12 I think the king is but a man, as I am: the violet smells to him as it doth to me.
Henry V (1599)

13 I am afeard there are few die well that die in a battle; for how can they charitably dispose of any thing when blood is their argument?
Henry V (1599)

14 Every subject's duty is the king's; but every subject's soul is his own.
Henry V (1599)

15 Upon the king! let us our lives, our souls,
Our debts, our careful wives,
Our children, and our sins lay on the king!
We must bear all. O hard condition!
Henry V (1599)

16 What infinite heart's ease
Must kings neglect, that private men enjoy!
And what have kings that privates have not too,
Save ceremony, save general ceremony?
Henry V (1599)

17 Put forth thy hand, reach at the glorious gold.
Henry VI, Part 2 (1592)

18 Is this the fashion of the court of England?
Is this the government of Britain's isle,
And this the royalty of Albion's king?
Henry VI, Part 2 (1592)

19 I say it was never merry world in England since gentlemen came up.
Henry VI, Part 2 (1592)

1 CADE: There shall be in England seven halfpenny loaves sold for a penny; the three-hooped pot shall have ten hoops; and I will make it felony to drink small beer. All the realm shall be in common, and in Cheapside shall my palfrey go to grass. And when I am king,—as king I will be,—...there shall be no money; all shall eat and drink on my score; and I will apparel them all in one livery, that they may agree like brothers, and worship me their lord.
DICK: The first thing we do, let's kill all the lawyers.

Henry VI, Part 2 (1592)

2 Is not this a lamentable thing, that of the skin of an innocent lamb should be made parchment? that parchment, being scribbled o'er, should undo a man?

Henry VI, Part 2 (1592)

3 Thou hast most traitorously corrupted the youth of the realm in erecting a grammar school: and whereas, before, our forefathers had no other books but the score and the tally, thou hast caused printing to be used; and, contrary to the king, his crown and dignity, thou hast built a paper-mill.

Henry VI, Part 2 (1592)

4 Peace! impudent and shameless Warwick, peace;
Proud setter up and puller down of kings.

Henry VI, Part 3 (1592)

5 Farewell! a long farewell, to all my greatness!

Henry VIII (1613)

6 I have ventured,
Like little wanton boys that swim on bladders,
This many summers in a sea of glory,
But far beyond my depth...
Vain pomp and glory of this world, I hate ye:
I feel my heart new opened. O how wretched
Is that poor man that hangs on princes' favours!
There is, betwixt that smile we would aspire to,
That sweet aspect of princes, and their ruin,
More pangs and fears than wars or women have;
And when he falls, he falls like Lucifer,
Never to hope again.

Henry VIII (1613)

7 Cromwell, I charge thee, fling away ambition:
By that sin fell the angels; how can man then,
The image of his Maker, hope to win by't?
Love thyself last: cherish those hearts that hate thee;
Corruption wins not more than honesty.
Still in thy right hand carry gentle peace,
To silence envious tongues: be just, and fear not.
Let all the ends thou aim'st at be thy country's,
Thy God's, and truth's: then if thou fall'st, O Cromwell!
Thou fall'st a blessed martyr.

Henry VIII (1613)

8 Had I but served my God with half the zeal
I served my king, he would not in mine age
Have left me naked to mine enemies.

Henry VIII (1613)

9 In her days every man shall eat in safety
Under his own vine what he plants; and sing
The merry songs of peace to all his neighbours.

Henry VIII (1613)

1 You blocks, you stones, you worse than senseless things! *Julius Caesar* (1599)
O you hard hearts, you cruel men of Rome,
Knew you not Pompey?

2 CAESAR: Who is it in the press that calls on me? *Julius Caesar* (1599)
I hear a tongue, shriller than all the music,
Cry 'Caesar'. Speak; Caesar is turned to hear.
SOOTHSAYER: Beware the ides of March.

3 Ye gods, it doth amaze me, *Julius Caesar* (1599)
A man of such a feeble temper should
So get the start of the majestic world,
And bear the palm alone.

4 Why, man, he doth bestride the narrow world *Julius Caesar* (1599)
Like a Colossus; and we petty men
Walk under his huge legs, and peep about
To find ourselves dishonourable graves.
Men at some time are masters of their fates:
The fault, dear Brutus, is not in our stars,
But in ourselves, that we are underlings.

5 'Brutus' will start a spirit as soon as 'Caesar'. *Julius Caesar* (1599)
Now in the names of all the gods at once,
Upon what meat doth this our Caesar feed,
That he is grown so great?

6 When could they say, till now, that talked of Rome, *Julius Caesar* (1599)
That her wide walls encompassed but one man?
Now is it Rome indeed and room enough,
When there is in it but one only man.

7 Let me have men about me that are fat; *Julius Caesar* (1599)
Sleek-headed men and such as sleep o' nights;
Yond' Cassius has a lean and hungry look;
He thinks too much: such men are dangerous.

8 Such men as he be never at heart's ease, *Julius Caesar* (1599)
Whiles they behold a greater than themselves,
And therefore are they very dangerous.

9 Th' abuse of greatness is, when it disjoins *Julius Caesar* (1599)
Remorse from power.

10 'Tis a common proof, *Julius Caesar* (1599)
That lowliness is young ambition's ladder,
Whereto the climber-upward turns his face;
But when he once attains the upmost round,
He then unto the ladder turns his back,
Looks in the clouds, scorning the base degrees
By which he did ascend.

11 O conspiracy! *Julius Caesar* (1599)
Sham'st thou to show thy dangerous brow by night,
When evils are most free?

12 Let us be sacrificers, but not butchers, Caius. *Julius Caesar* (1599)

13 Let's carve him as a dish fit for the gods, *Julius Caesar* (1599)
Not hew him as a carcass fit for hounds.

1 But when I tell him he hates flatterers,
He says he does, being then most flattered.
Julius Caesar (1599)

2 CAESAR: The ides of March are come.
SOOTHSAYER: Ay, Caesar; but not gone.
Julius Caesar (1599)

3 If I could pray to move, prayers would move me;
But I am constant as the northern star,
Of whose true-fixed and resting
There is no fellow in the firmament.
The skies are painted with unnumbered sparks,
They are all fire and every one doth shine,
But there's but one in all doth hold his place:
So, in the world; 'tis furnished well with men,
And men are flesh and blood, and apprehensive;
Yet in the number I do know but one
That unassailable holds on his rank,
Unshaked of motion: and that I am he.
Julius Caesar (1599)

4 *Et tu, Brute?* Then fall, Caesar!
Julius Caesar (1599)

5 Ambition's debt is paid.
Julius Caesar (1599)

6 CASSIUS: How many ages hence
Shall this our lofty scene be acted o'er,
In states unborn, and accents yet unknown!
BRUTUS: How many times shall Caesar bleed in sport.
Julius Caesar (1599)

7 Waving our red weapons o'er our heads
Let's all cry 'Peace, freedom, and liberty!'
Julius Caesar (1599)

8 O mighty Caesar! dost thou lie so low?
Are all thy conquests, glories, triumphs, spoils,
Shrunk to this little measure?
Julius Caesar (1599)

9 Caesar's spirit, ranging for revenge,
With Ate by his side, come hot from hell,
Shall in these confines, with a monarch's voice
Cry, 'Havoc!' and let slip the dogs of war;
That this foul deed shall smell above the earth
With carrion men, groaning for burial.
Julius Caesar (1599)

10 Not that I loved Caesar less, but that I loved Rome more.
Julius Caesar (1599)

11 As he was valiant, I honour him: but, as he was ambitious, I slew him.
Julius Caesar (1599)

12 Who is here so base that would be a bondman? If any, speak; for him have I offended. Who is here so rude that would not be a Roman? If any, speak; for him have I offended. Who is here so vile that will not love his country? If any, speak; for him have I offended. I pause for a reply.
Julius Caesar (1599)

13 Friends, Romans, countrymen, lend me your ears;
I come to bury Caesar, not to praise him.
The evil that men do lives after them,
The good is oft interrèd with their bones;
So let it be with Caesar. The noble Brutus
Hath told you Caesar was ambitious;
Julius Caesar (1599)

If it were so, it was a grievous fault;
And grievously hath Caesar answered it.

1 He was my friend, faithful and just to me:
But Brutus says he was ambitious;
And Brutus is an honourable man.
Julius Caesar (1599)

2 When that the poor have cried, Caesar hath wept;
Ambition should be made of sterner stuff.
Julius Caesar (1599)

3 On the Lupercal
I thrice presented him a kingly crown
Which he did thrice refuse: was this ambition?
Julius Caesar (1599)

4 You all did love him once, not without cause.
Julius Caesar (1599)

5 But yesterday the word of Caesar might
Have stood against the world; now lies he there,
And none so poor to do him reverence.
Julius Caesar (1599)

6 This was the most unkindest cut of all.
Julius Caesar (1599)

7 O! what a fall was there, my countrymen;
Then I, and you, and all of us fell down,
Whilst bloody treason flourished over us.
Julius Caesar (1599)

8 I come not, friends, to steal away your hearts:
I am no orator, as Brutus is;
But, as you know me all, a plain, blunt man,
That love my friend.
Julius Caesar (1599)

9 For I have neither wit, nor words, nor worth,
Action, nor utterance, nor power of speech,
To stir men's blood; I only speak right on;
I tell you that which you yourselves do know.
Julius Caesar (1599)

10 But were I Brutus,
And Brutus Antony, there were an Antony
Would ruffle up your spirits, and put a tongue
In every wound of Caesar, that should move
The stones of Rome to rise and mutiny.
Julius Caesar (1599)

11 Now let it work; mischief, thou art afoot,
Take thou what course thou wilt!
Julius Caesar (1599)

12 He shall not live; look, with a spot I damn him.
Julius Caesar (1599)

13 This is a slight unmeritable man,
Meet to be sent on errands.
Julius Caesar (1599)

14 There is a tide in the affairs of men,
Which, taken at the flood, leads on to fortune;
Omitted, all the voyage of their life
Is bound in shallows and in miseries.
On such a full sea are we now afloat,
And we must take the current when it serves,
Or lose our ventures.
Julius Caesar (1599)

15 O Julius Caesar! thou art mighty yet!
Thy spirit walks abroad, and turns our swords
In our own proper entrails.
Julius Caesar (1599)

16 This was the noblest Roman of them all;
All the conspirators save only he
Julius Caesar (1599)

Did that they did in envy of great Caesar;
He only in a general honest thought
And common good to all, made one of them.
His life was gentle, and the elements
So mixed in him that Nature might stand up
And say to all the world, 'This was a man!'

1 This England never did, nor never shall, *King John* (1591–8)
Lie at the proud foot of a conqueror,
But when it first did help to wound itself.
Now these her princes are come home again,
Come the three corners of the world in arms,
And we shall shock them: nought shall make us rue,
If England to itself do rest but true.

2 Think'st thou that duty shall have dread to speak *King Lear* (1605–6)
When power to flattery bows? To plainness honour's
bound
When majesty falls to folly.

3 Let go thy hold when a great wheel runs down a hill, *King Lear* (1605–6)
lest it break thy neck with following; but the great one
that goes upward, let him draw thee after.

4 A dog's obeyed in office. *King Lear* (1605–6)

5 Get thee glass eyes; *King Lear* (1605–6)
And, like a scurvy politician, seem
To see the things thou dost not.

6 MALCOLM: Nothing in his life *Macbeth* (1606)
Became him like the leaving it: he died
As one that had been studied in his death
To throw away the dearest thing he owed
As 'twere a careless trifle.
DUNCAN: There's no art
To find the mind's construction in the face;
He was a gentleman on whom I built
An absolute trust.

7 Besides, this Duncan *Macbeth* (1606)
Hath borne his faculties so meek, hath been
So clear in his great office, that his virtues
Will plead like angels trumpet-tongued, against
The deep damnation of his taking-off.

8 I have no spur *Macbeth* (1606)
To prick the sides of my intent, but only
Vaulting ambition, which o'erleaps itself,
And falls on the other.

9 Confusion now hath made his masterpiece! *Macbeth* (1606)
Most sacrilegious murder hath broke ope
The Lord's anointed temple, and stole thence
The life o' the building!

10 Thou hast it now: King, Cawdor, Glamis, all, *Macbeth* (1606)
As the weird women promised; and, I fear,
Thou play'dst most foully for't.

1 LADY MACBETH: Things without all remedy
Should be without regard: what's done is done.
MACBETH: We have scotched the snake, not killed it:
She'll close and be herself.

Macbeth (1606)

2 Duncan is in his grave;
After life's fitful fever he sleeps well;
Treason has done his worst: nor steel, nor poison,
Malice domestic, foreign levy, nothing,
Can touch him further.

Macbeth (1606)

3 Stands Scotland where it did?

Macbeth (1606)

4 Now, as fond fathers,
Having bound up the threat'ning twigs of birch,
Only to stick it in their children's sight
For terror, not to use, in time the rod
Becomes more mocked than feared; so our decrees,
Dead to infliction, to themselves are dead,
And liberty plucks justice by the nose;
The baby beats the nurse, and quite athwart
Goes all decorum.

Measure for Measure (1604)

5 We must not make a scarecrow of the law,
Setting it up to fear the birds of prey,
And let it keep one shape, till custom make it
Their perch and not their terror.

Measure for Measure (1604)

6 'Tis one thing to be tempted, Escalus,
Another thing to fall. I not deny,
The jury, passing on the prisoner's life,
May in the sworn twelve have a thief or two
Guiltier than him they try.

Measure for Measure (1604)

7 No ceremony that to great ones 'longs,
Not the king's crown, nor the deputed sword,
The marshal's truncheon, nor the judge's robe,
Become them with one half so good a grace
As mercy does.

Measure for Measure (1604)

8 O! it is excellent
To have a giant's strength, but it is tyrannous
To use it like a giant.

Measure for Measure (1604)

9 Man, proud man,
Drest in a little brief authority,
Most ignorant of what he's most assured,
His glassy essence, like an angry ape,
Plays such fantastic tricks before high heaven,
As make the angels weep.

Measure for Measure (1604)

10 The quality of mercy is not strained,
It droppeth as the gentle rain from heaven
Upon the place beneath.

The Merchant of Venice (1596–8)

11 A substitute shines brightly as a king
Until a king be by, and then his state
Empties itself, as doth an inland brook
Into the main of waters.

The Merchant of Venice (1596–8)

1 The purest treasure mortal times afford *Richard II* (1595)
Is spotless reputation; that away,
Men are but gilded loam or painted clay.
A jewel in a ten-times-barred-up chest
Is a bold spirit in a loyal breast.
Mine honour is my life; both grow in one;
Take honour from me, and my life is done.

2 We were not born to sue, but to command. *Richard II* (1595)

3 How long a time lies in one little word! *Richard II* (1595)
Four lagging winters and four wanton springs
End in a word; such is the breath of kings.

4 This royal throne of kings, this sceptered isle, *Richard II* (1595)
This earth of majesty, this seat of Mars,
This other Eden, demi-paradise,
This fortress built by Nature for herself
Against infection and the hand of war,
This happy breed of men, this little world,
This precious stone set in the silver sea,
Which serves it in the office of a wall,
Or as a moat defensive to a house,
Against the envy of less happier lands,
This blessèd plot, this earth, this realm, this England,
This nurse, this teeming womb of royal kings,
Feared by their breed and famous by their birth,
Renownèd for their deeds as far from home,—
For Christian service and true chivalry,—
As is the sepulchre in stubborn Jewry
Of the world's ransom, blessèd Mary's Son:
This land of such dear souls, this dear, dear land,
Dear for her reputation through the world,
Is now leased out,—I die pronouncing it,—
Like to a tenement or pelting farm:
England, bound in with the triumphant sea,
Whose rocky shore beats back the envious siege
Of watery Neptune, is now bound in with shame,
With inky blots, and rotten parchment bonds:
That England, that was wont to conquer others,
Hath made a shameful conquest of itself.

5 The caterpillars of the commonwealth. *Richard II* (1595)

6 Not all the water in the rough rude sea *Richard II* (1595)
Can wash the balm from an anointed king;
The breath of worldly men cannot depose
The deputy elected by the Lord.

7 Is not the king's name twenty thousand names? *Richard II* (1595)
Arm, arm, my name! A puny subject strikes
At thy great glory.

8 For God's sake, let us sit upon the ground *Richard II* (1595)
And tell sad stories of the death of kings:
How some have been deposed, some slain in war,
Some haunted by the ghosts they have deposed,
Some poisoned by their wives, some sleeping killed;

All murdered: for within the hollow crown
That rounds the mortal temples of a king
Keeps Death his court, and there the antick sits,
Scoffing his state and grinning at his pomp;
Allowing him a breath, a little scene,
To monarchize, be feared, and kill with looks,
Infusing him with self and vain conceit
As if this flesh which walls about our life
Were brass impregnable; and humoured thus
Comes at the last, and with a little pin
Bores through his castle wall, and farewell king!

1 See, see, King Richard doth himself appear,
As doth the blushing discontented sun
From out the fiery portal of the east.
Richard II (1595)

2 What must the king do now? Must he submit?
The king shall do it: must he be deposed?
The king shall be contented: must he lose
The name of king? o' God's name, let it go.
Richard II (1595)

3 Give me the crown. Here, cousin, seize the crown;
Here cousin,
On this side my hand and on that side thine.
Now is this golden crown like a deep well
That owes two buckets filling one another;
The emptier ever dancing in the air,
The other down, unseen, and full of water:
That bucket down and full of tears am I,
Drinking my griefs, whilst you mount up on high.
Richard II (1595)

4 You may my glories and my state depose,
But not my griefs; still am I king of those.
Richard II (1595)

5 Now mark me how I will undo myself.
Richard II (1595)

6 With mine own tears I wash away my balm,
With mine own hands I give away my crown.
Richard II (1595)

7 Mine eyes are full of tears, I cannot see:
And yet salt water blinds them not so much
But they can see a sort of traitors here.
Nay, if I turn my eyes upon myself,
I find myself a traitor with the rest.
Richard II (1595)

8 Now is the winter of our discontent
Made glorious summer by this sun of York.
Richard III (1591)

9 Grim-visaged war hath smoothed his wrinkled front;
And now, instead of mounting barbèd steeds,
To fright the souls of fearful adversaries,—
He capers nimbly in a lady's chamber
To the lascivious pleasing of a lute.
Richard III (1591)

10 Since every Jack became a gentleman
There's many a gentle person made a Jack.
Richard III (1591)

11 And thus I clothe my naked villainy
With odd old ends stol'n forth of holy writ,
And seem a saint when most I play the devil.
Richard III (1591)

1 Woe to the land that's governed by a child! *Richard III* (1591)

2 Talk'st thou to me of 'ifs'? Thou art a traitor:
Off with his head! *Richard III* (1591)

3 I am not in the giving vein to-day. *Richard III* (1591)

4 Men shut their doors against a setting sun. *Timon of Athens* (c.1607)

5 A stone is soft as wax, tribunes more hard than stones.
A stone is silent and offendeth not,
And tribunes with their tongues doom men to death. *Titus Andronicus* (1590)

6 Rome is but a wilderness of tigers. *Titus Andronicus* (1590)

7 The heavens themselves, the planets, and this centre
Observe degree, priority, and place,
Insisture, course, proportion, season, form,
Office, and custom, in all line of order. *Troilus and Cressida* (1602)

8 O! when degree is shaked,
Which is the ladder to all high designs,
The enterprise is sick. *Troilus and Cressida* (1602)

9 Take but degree away, untune that string,
And, hark! what discord follows; each thing meets
In mere oppugnancy. The bounded waters
Should lift their bosoms higher than the shores
And make a sop of all this sordid globe;
Strength should be lord of imbecility
And the rude son should strike his father dead. *Troilus and Cressida* (1602)

10 A plague of opinion! a man may wear it on both sides, like a leather jerkin. *Troilus and Cressida* (1602)

11 How my achievements mock me! *Troilus and Cressida* (1602)

Robert Shapiro 1942–

American lawyer; originally leader of the defence team at the trial of O. J. Simpson

of the change of strategy embraced after Johnnie Cochran took over from him the leadership of the defence team:

12 Not only did we play the race card, we played it from the bottom of the deck. in *The Times* 5 October 1995; cf. **Churchill** 86:8

to which Cochran responded, 'We didn't play the race card, we played the credibility card'

George Bernard Shaw 1856–1950

Irish playwright

13 There is nothing so bad or so good that you will not find Englishmen doing it; but you will never find an Englishman in the wrong. He does everything on principle. He fights you on patriotic principles; he robs you on business principles; he enslaves you on imperial principles; he bullies you on manly principles; he supports his king on loyal principles and cuts off his king's head on republican principles. *The Man of Destiny* (1898)

1 SWINDON: What will history say? BURGOYNE: History, sir, will tell lies as usual. — *The Devil's Disciple* (1901)

2 He [the Briton] is a barbarian, and thinks that the customs of his tribe and island are the laws of nature. — *Caesar and Cleopatra* (1901)

3 Your friend the British soldier can stand up to anything except the British War Office. — *The Devil's Disciple* (1901)

4 Englishmen never will be slaves: they are free to do whatever the Government and public opinion allow them to do. — *Man and Superman* (1903)

5 In the arts of peace Man is a bungler. — *Man and Superman* (1903)

6 Revolutions have never lightened the burden of tyranny: they have only shifted it to another shoulder. — *Man and Superman* (1903) 'The Revolutionist's Handbook' foreword

7 Democracy substitutes election by the incompetent many for appointment by the corrupt few. — *Man and Superman* (1903) 'Maxims: Democracy'

8 Liberty means responsibility. That is why most men dread it. — *Man and Superman* (1903) 'Maxims: Liberty and Equality'

9 The art of government is the organization of idolatry. — *Man and Superman* (1903) 'Maxims: Idolatry'

10 Titles distinguish the mediocre, embarrass the superior, and are disgraced by the inferior. — *Man and Superman* (1903) 'Maxims for Revolutionists: Titles'

11 Money is indeed the most important thing in the world; and all sound and successful personal and national morality should have this fact for its basis. — *The Irrational Knot* (1905) preface

12 An Irishman's heart is nothing but his imagination. — *John Bull's Other Island* (1907)

13 He knows nothing; and he thinks he knows everything. That points clearly to a political career. — *Major Barbara* (1907)

14 Nothing is ever done in this world until men are prepared to kill one another if it is not done. — *Major Barbara* (1907)

15 Assassination is the extreme form of censorship. — *The Showing-Up of Blanco Posnet* (1911) 'Limits to Toleration'

16 Anarchism is a game at which the police can beat you. — *Misalliance* (1914)

17 Go anywhere in England where there are natural, wholesome, contented, and really nice English people; and what do you always find? That the stables are the real centre of the household. — *Heartbreak House* (1919)

18 The captain is in his bunk, drinking bottled ditch-water; and the crew is gambling in the forecastle. She will strike and sink and split. Do you think the laws of God will be suspended in favour of England because you were born in it? — *Heartbreak House* (1919)

19 You'll never have a quiet world till you knock the patriotism out of the human race. — *O'Flaherty V.C.* (1919)

20 All great truths begin as blasphemies. — *Annajanska* (1919)

21 It is evident that if the incomes of the rich were taken from them and divided among the poor as we stand at — *The Intelligent Woman's Guide to Socialism and Capitalism* (1928)

present, the poor would be very little less poor; the supply of capital would cease because nobody could afford to save; the country houses would fall into ruins; and learning and science and art and literature and all the rest of what we call culture would perish.

1 What Englishman will give his mind to politics as long as he can afford to keep a motor car?
The Apple Cart (1930)

2 A government which robs Peter to pay Paul can always depend on the support of Paul.
Everybody's Political What's What? (1944)

3 England and America are two countries divided by a common language.
attributed in this and other forms, but not found in Shaw's published writings; cf. **Wilde** 388:7

Hartley Shawcross 1902–

British Labour politician and barrister

4 'But,' said Alice, 'the question is whether you can make a word mean different things.' 'Not so,' said Humpty-Dumpty, 'the question is which is to be the master. That's all.' We are the masters at the moment, and not only at the moment, but for a very long time to come.
often quoted as 'We are the masters now'
in the House of Commons, 2 April 1946; cf. **Carroll** 77:1

Charles Shaw-Lefevre 1794–1888

5 What is that fat gentleman in such a passion about?
as a child, on hearing Charles James **Fox** *speak in Parliament*
G. W. E. Russell *Collections and Recollections* (1898)

Lord Shelburne 1737–1805

British Whig politician; Prime Minister

6 The country will neither be united at home nor respected abroad, till the reins of government are lodged with men who have some little pretensions to common sense and common honesty.
in the House of Lords, 22 November 1770

of the defence of the king's speech at the opening of the parliamentary session:

7 Nothing more than a string of sophisms, no less wretched in their texture than insolent in their tenor.
in the House of Lords, 31 October 1776

8 The sun of Great Britain will set whenever she acknowledges the independence of America... the independence of America would end in the ruin of England.
in the House of Lords, October 1782

Percy Bysshe Shelley 1792–1822

English poet

9 'My name is Ozymandias, king of kings:
Look on my works, ye Mighty, and despair!'
'Ozymandias' (1819)

1 An old, mad, blind, despised, and dying king.
'Sonnet: England in 1819' (written 1819)

2 I met Murder on the way—
He had a mask like Castlereagh.
'The Mask of Anarchy' (1819)

3 Men of England, wherefore plough
For the lords who lay ye low?
'Song to the Men of England' (written 1819)

4 The seed ye sow, another reaps;
The wealth ye find, another keeps;
The robes ye weave, another wears;
The arms ye forge, another bears.
'Song to the Men of England' (written 1819)

5 Kingly conclaves stern and cold
Where blood with guilt is bought and sold.
Prometheus Unbound (1820)

6 Tyranny entrenches itself within the existing interests of the most refined citizens of a nation and says 'If you dare trample upon these, be free.'
A Philosophical View of Reform (written 1819–20)

7 Monarchy is only the string that ties the robber's bundle.
A Philosophical View of Reform (written 1819–20)

8 Let there be light! said Liberty,
And like sunrise from the sea,
Athens arose!
Hellas (1822)

William Shenstone 1714–63

English poet and essayist

9 Laws are generally found to be nets of such a texture, as the little creep through, the great break through, and the middle-sized are alone entangled in.
Works in Verse and Prose (1764) vol. 2 'On Politics'; cf. **Anarcharsis** 8:3, **Swift** 353:4

Philip Henry Sheridan 1831–88

American Union cavalry commander in the Civil War

10 The only good Indian is a dead Indian.
at Fort Cobb, January 1869
attributed; perhaps already proverbial

Richard Brinsley Sheridan 1751–1816

Anglo-Irish playwright and Whig politician

11 The newspapers! Sir, they are the most villainous—licentious—abominable—infernal—Not that I ever read them—No—I make it a rule never to look into a newspaper.
The Critic (1779)

12 The throne *we* honour is the *people's choice.*
Pizarro (1799)

13 The Right Honourable gentleman is indebted to his memory for his jests, and to his imagination for his facts.
in reply to Mr Dundas
in the House of Commons; T. Moore *Life of Sheridan* (1825) vol. 2

William Tecumseh Sherman 1820–91

American general; from 1864 chief Union commander in the west in succession to Ulysses S. **Grant**

1 War is the remedy our *enemies* have chosen, and I say let us give them all they want.

in 1864; Geoffrey C. Ward *The Civil War* (1991)

2 [Grant] stood by me when I was crazy, and I stood by him when he was drunk; and now we stand by each other always.

of his relationship with his fellow Union commander, Ulysses S. ***Grant***

in 1864; Geoffrey C. Ward *The Civil War* (1991)

3 I think we understand what military fame is. To be killed on the field of battle and have our name spelled wrong in the newspapers.

Ken Burns *The Civil War* (documentary, 1989) episode 9

4 I will not accept if nominated, and will not serve if elected.

on being urged to stand as Republican candidate in the 1884 presidential election

telegram to General Henderson; *Memoirs* (4th ed., 1891)

Emanuel Shinwell 1884–1986

British Labour politician

5 We know that the organised workers of the country are our friends. As for the rest, they don't matter a tinker's cuss.

speech to the Electrical Trades Union conference at Margate, 7 May 1947

Jonathan Shipley 1714–88

English clergyman, Bishop of St Asaph

6 I look upon North America as the only great nursery of freemen left on the face of the earth.

in 1774, after voting against the alteration of the constitution of Massachusetts, proposed as a punishment for the tea-ship riots at Boston

in *Dictionary of National Biography*

William Shippen 1673–1743

English Jacobite politician

7 Robin and I are two honest men: he is for King George and I for King James, but those men in long cravats [Sandys, Rushout, Pulteney, and their following] only desire places under one or the other.

view of his relationship with his political opponent Robert ***Walpole***

in *Dictionary of National Biography*

Algernon Sidney 1622–83

English conspirator, executed for his alleged part in the Rye House Plot, 1683

1 Liars ought to have good memories.
Discourses concerning Government (1698)

2 Men lived like fishes; the great ones devoured the small.
Discourses concerning Government (1698)

3 'Tis not necessary to light a candle to the sun.
Discourses concerning Government (1698)

Emmanuel Joseph Sieyès 1748–1836

French abbot and statesman

4 Death, without rhetoric.
on voting in the French Convention for the death of **Louis XVI**, *16 January 1793*
attributed to Sieyès, but afterwards repudiated by him (*Le Moniteur* 20 January 1793 records his vote as 'La mort')

when asked what he had done during the French Revolution:
5 I survived.
F. A. M. Mignet *Notice historique sur la vie et les travaux de M. le Comte de Sieyès* (1836)

Simonides *c.*556–468 BC

Greek poet

6 Go, tell the Spartans, thou who passest by,
That here obedient to their laws we lie.
epitaph on the Spartans who died heroically defending the pass of Thermopylae against the Persians
Herodotus *Histories*; attributed

Kirke Simpson

American journalist

7 [Warren] Harding of Ohio was chosen by a group of men in a smoke-filled room early today as Republican candidate for President.
news report, 12 June 1920; cf. **Daugherty** 109:9

C. H. Sisson 1914–

English poet

8 Here lies a civil servant. He was civil
To everyone, and servant to the devil.
The London Zoo (1961)

Noel Skelton 1880–1935

British Conservative politician

9 To state as clearly as may be what means lie ready to develop a property-owning democracy, to bring the industrial and economic status of the wage-earner
in *The Spectator* 19 May 1923

abreast of his political and educational, to make democracy stable and four-square.

Adam Smith 1723–90

Scottish philosopher and economist

1 Little else is requisite to carry a state to the highest degree of opulence from the lowest barbarism, but peace, easy taxes, and a tolerable administration of justice; all the rest being brought about by the natural course of things.

in 1755; *Essays on Philosophical Subjects* (1795)

2 And thus, *Place*, that great object which divides the wives of aldermen, is the end of half the labours of human life; and is the cause of all the tumult and bustle, all the rapine and injustice, which avarice and ambition have introduced into this world.

Theory of Moral Sentiments (1759)

3 [The man of system] seems to imagine that he can arrange the different members of a great society with as much ease as the hand arranges the different pieces upon a chessboard; he does not consider that the pieces upon the chessboard have no other principle of motion besides that which the hand impresses upon them; but that, in the great chessboard of human society, every single piece has a principle of motion of its own, altogether different from that which the legislator might choose to impress upon it.

Theory of Moral Sentiments (1759)

4 It is not from the benevolence of the butcher, the brewer, or the baker, that we expect our dinner, but from their regard to their own interest. We address ourselves not to their humanity but their self love, and never talk to them of our necessities but of their advantages.

Wealth of Nations (1776)

5 People of the same trade seldom meet together, even for merriment and diversion, but the conversation ends in a conspiracy against the public, or in some contrivance to raise prices.

Wealth of Nations (1776)

6 To found a great empire for the sole purpose of raising up a people of customers, may at first sight appear a project fit only for a nation of shopkeepers. It is, however, a project altogether unfit for a nation of shopkeepers; but extremely fit for a nation whose government is influenced by shopkeepers.

Wealth of Nations (1776); cf. **Adams** 5:4, **Napoleon** 270:1

7 It is the highest impertinence and presumption, therefore, in kings and ministers, to pretend to watch over the economy of private people, and to restrain their expense... They are themselves always, and without any exception, the greatest spendthrifts in society. Let them look well after their own expense, and they may safely trust private people with theirs. If their own extravagance does not ruin the state, that of their subjects never will.

Wealth of Nations (1776)

1 Consumption is the sole end and purpose of production; and the interest of the producer ought to be attended to only so far as it may be necessary for promoting that of the consumer. *Wealth of Nations* (1776)

2 There is no art which one government sooner learns of another than that of draining money from the pockets of the people. *Wealth of Nations* (1776)

3 If any of the provinces of the British empire cannot be made to contribute towards the support of the whole empire, it is surely time that Great Britain should free herself from the expense of defending those provinces in time of war, and of supporting any part of their civil or military establishments in time of peace, and endeavour to accommodate her future views and designs to the real mediocrity of her circumstances. *Wealth of Nations* (1776)

4 Every individual necessarily labours to render the annual revenue of society as great as he can. He generally neither intends to promote the public interest, nor knows how much he is promoting it. He intends only his own gain, and he is, in this, as in many other cases, led by an invisible hand to promote an end which was no part of his intention. *Wealth of Nations* (1776)

5 Great nations are never impoverished by private, though they sometimes are by public prodigality and misconduct. The whole, or almost the whole public revenue, is in most countries employed in maintaining unproductive hands. *Wealth of Nations* (1776)

6 What is prudence in the conduct of every private family, can scarce be folly in that of a great kingdom. If a foreign country can supply us with a commodity cheaper than we ourselves can make it, better buy it of them with some part of the produce of our own industry, employed in a way in which we have some advantage. *Wealth of Nations* (1776)

7 The natural advantages which one country has over another in producing particular commodities are sometimes so great, that it is acknowledged by all the world to be in vain to struggle with them. By means of glasses, hotbeds, and hotwalls, very good grapes can be raised in Scotland, and very good wine too can be made of them at about thirty times the expense for which at least equally good can be bought from foreign countries. Would it be a reasonable law to prohibit the importation of all foreign wines, merely to encourage the making of claret and burgundy in Scotland? But if there would be manifest absurdity in turning towards any employment, thirty times more of the capital and industry of the country, than would be necessary to purchase from foreign countries an equal quantity of the commodities wanted, there must be an absurdity, though not altogether so glaring, yet exactly of the same kind, in turning towards any such employment a thirtieth, or even a three hundredth part more of either. *Wealth of Nations* (1776)

1 Those parts of education, it is to be observed, for the teaching of which there are no public institutions, are generally the best taught. — *Wealth of Nations* (1776)

2 Princes . . . have frequently engaged in many . . . mercantile projects, and have been willing, like private persons, to mend their fortunes by becoming adventurers in the common branches of trade. They have scarcely ever succeeded. The profusion with which the affairs of princes are always managed, renders it almost impossible that they should. The agents of a prince regard the wealth of their master as inexhaustible; are careless at which price they buy; are careless at which price they sell; are careless at what expense they transport his goods from one place to another. — *Wealth of Nations* (1776)

3 The natural effort of every individual to better his own condition . . . is so powerful, that it is alone, and without any assistance, not only capable of carrying on the society to wealth and prosperity, but of surmounting a hundred impertinent obstructions with which the folly of human laws too often encumbers its operations. — *Wealth of Nations* (1776)

Alfred Emanuel Smith 1873–1944

American politician; presidential candidate in 1928

4 The crowning climax to the whole situation is the undisputed fact that William Randolph Hearst gave him the kiss of death. — in *New York Times* 25 October 1926

on **Hearst***'s support for Ogden Mills, Smith's unsuccessful opponent for the governorship of New York State*

5 All the ills of democracy can be cured by more democracy. — speech in Albany, 27 June 1933

6 No sane local official who has hung up an empty stocking over the municipal fireplace, is going to shoot Santa Claus just before a hard Christmas. — in *New Outlook* December 1933

comment on the New Deal

Cyril Smith 1928–

British Liberal politician

of the House of Commons:

7 The longest running farce in the West End. — *Big Cyril* (1977)

F. E. Smith, Lord Birkenhead 1872–1930

British Conservative politician and lawyer

on Smith: see **Asquith** 19:1

8 The world continues to offer glittering prizes to those who have stout hearts and sharp swords. — Rectorial address, Glasgow University, 7 November 1923

9 We have the highest authority for believing that the meek shall inherit the earth; though I have never found — *Contemporary Personalities* (1924) 'Marquess Curzon'

any particular corroboration of this aphorism in the records of Somerset House.

1 Nature has no cure for this sort of madness [Bolshevism], though I have known a legacy from a rich relative work wonders.
Law, Life and Letters (1927)

2 Austen [Chamberlain] always played the game, and he always lost it.
Lord Beaverbrook *Men and Power* (1956)

Howard Smith 1919–

British diplomat; former Ambassador to Moscow

3 I have not had major experience of talking with people once pronounced brain-dead, but I think we could be safe in saying he did not have great zip.
of Leonid Brezhnev
in *Times* 8 September 1988

Ian Smith 1919–

Rhodesian politician; Prime Minister, 1964–79

4 I don't believe in black majority rule in Rhodesia—not in a thousand years.
broadcast speech, 20 March 1976

Samuel Francis Smith 1808–95

American poet and divine

5 My country, 'tis of thee,
Sweet land of liberty,
Of thee I sing:
Land where my fathers died,
Land of the pilgrims' pride,
From every mountain-side
Let freedom ring.
'America' (1831)

Sydney Smith 1771–1845

English clergyman and essayist

6 The moment the very name of Ireland is mentioned, the English seem to bid adieu to common feeling, common prudence, and common sense, and to act with the barbarity of tyrants, and the fatuity of idiots.
Letters of Peter Plymley (1807)

7 Tory and Whig in turns shall be my host,
I taste no politics in boiled and roast.
letter to John Murray, November 1834

8 Daniel Webster struck me much like a steam-engine in trousers.
Lady Holland *Memoir* (1855)

9 He [Macaulay] has occasional flashes of silence, that make his conversation perfectly delightful.
Lady Holland *Memoir* (1855)

10 Minorities...are almost always in the right.
H. Pearson *The Smith of Smiths* (1934)

1 My brother [Bobus] and I have inverted the laws of nature. He rose by his gravity; I sank by my levity.
Alan Bell (ed.) *The Sayings of Sydney Smith* (1993); attributed

Tobias Smollett 1721–71

Scottish novelist

2 I think for my part one half of the nation is mad—and the other not very sound.
The Adventures of Sir Launcelot Greaves (1762)

3 Mourn, hapless Caledonia, mourn
Thy banished peace, thy laurels torn.
'The Tears of Scotland' (1746)

C. P. Snow 1905–80

English novelist and scientist

4 The official world, the corridors of power.
Homecomings (1956)

Philip Snowden 1864–1937

British Labour politician

5 It would be desirable if every Government, when it comes to power, should have its old speeches burnt.
C. E. Bechofer Roberts ('Ephesian') *Philip Snowden* (1929)

6 This is not Socialism. It is Bolshevism run mad.
on the Labour Party's 1931 election programme
radio broadcast, 17 October 1931

Socrates 469–399 BC

Greek philosopher

7 Most excellent man, are you who are a citizen of Athens, the greatest of cities and the most famous for wisdom and power, not ashamed to care for the acquisition of wealth and for reputation and honour, when you neither care nor take thought for wisdom and truth and the perfection of your soul?
Plato *Apology*

8 And I tell you that virtue does not come from money, but from virtue comes money and all other good things to man, both to the individual and to the state.
Plato *Apology*

Alexander Solzhenitsyn 1918–

Russian novelist

9 The thoughts of a prisoner—they're not free either. They keep returning to the same things.
One Day in the Life of Ivan Denisovich (1962)

10 You only have power over people as long as you don't take *everything* away from them. But when you've robbed a man of *everything* he's no longer in your power—he's free again.
The First Circle (1968)

11 Mankind's salvation lies exclusively in everyone's making everything his business, in the people of the East being anything but indifferent to what is thought in the West,
Nobel Prize Lecture, 1970

and in the people of the West being anything but indifferent to what happens in the East.

1 In our country the lie has become not just a moral category but a pillar of the State. — interview in 1974; in appendix to *The Oak and the Calf* (1975)

2 The Gulag Archipelago. — title of book (1973–5)
referring to the political prison camps dotted around the Soviet Union

3 Yes, we are still the prisoners of communism, and yet, for us in Russia, Communism is a dead dog, while for many people in the West it is still a living lion. — broadcast on BBC Russian Service, in *Listener* 15 February 1979

4 In the United States the difficulties are not a Minotaur or a dragon—not imprisonment, hard labour, death, government harassment, and censorship—but cupidity, boredom, sloppiness, and indifference. Not the acts of a mighty all-pervading repressive government but the failure of a listless public to make use of the freedom that is its birthright. — in *Policy Review* Winter 1994

Anastasio Somoza 1925–80

elected President of Nicaragua in 1967, he was overthrown by the Sandinistas in 1979, and assassinated while in exile in Paraguay

replying to an accusation of ballot-rigging:
5 You won the elections, but I won the count. — in *Guardian* 17 June 1977

Susan Sontag 1933–

American writer

6 The white race *is* the cancer of human history, it is the white race, and it alone—its ideologies and inventions—which eradicates autonomous civilizations wherever it spreads, which has upset the ecological balance of the planet, which now threatens the very existence of life itself. — in *Partisan Review* Winter 1967

Lord Soper 1903–

British Methodist minister

of the quality of debate in the House of Lords:
7 It is, I think, good evidence of life after death. — in *Listener* 17 August 1978

John L. B. Soule 1815–91

American journalist

8 Go West, young man, go West! — in *Terre Haute* [Indiana] *Express* (1851) editorial

Robert Southey 1774–1843

English poet and writer

1 Now tell us all about the war,
And what they fought each other for.

'The Battle of Blenheim' (1800)

2 'And everybody praised the Duke,
Who this great fight did win.'
'But what good came of it at last?'
Quoth little Peterkin.
'Why that I cannot tell,' said he,
'But 'twas a famous victory.'

'The Battle of Blenheim' (1800)

3 The death of Nelson was felt in England as something more than a public calamity; men started at the intelligence, and turned pale, as if they had heard of the loss of a dear friend.

The Life of Nelson (1813)

Henry D. Spalding d. 1990

4 I like Ike.

US button badge first used in 1947 when General **Eisenhower** *was seen as a potential presidential nominee*

in *New Republic* 27 October 1947

Herbert Spencer 1820–1903

Engish philosopher

5 The Republican form of Government is the highest form of government; but because of this it requires the highest type of human nature—a type nowhere at present existing.

Essays (1891) vol. 3 'The Americans'

6 The ultimate result of shielding men from the effects of folly, is to fill the world with fools.

Essays (1891) vol. 3 'State Tamperings with Money and Banks'

Oswald Spengler 1880–1936

German historian

7 Socialism is nothing but the capitalism of the working class.

The Hour of Decision (1933)

Edmund Spenser *c.*1552–99

English poet

8 Ill can he rule the great that cannot reach the small.

The Faerie Queen (1596)

Benjamin Spock 1903–

American paediatrician

9 To win in Vietnam, we will have to exterminate a nation.

Dr Spock on Vietnam (1968)

Cecil Spring-Rice 1859–1918

British diplomat; Ambassador to Washington from 1912

1 I vow to thee, my country—all earthly things above—
Entire and whole and perfect, the service of my love,
The love that asks no question: the love that stands the test,
That lays upon the altar the dearest and the best:
The love that never falters, the love that pays the price,
The love that makes undaunted the final sacrifice.

'I Vow to Thee, My Country' (written on the eve of his departure from Washington, 12 January 1918)

2 Wilson is the nation's shepherd and McAdoo his crook.
of President Woodrow **Wilson** *and his secretary of the treasury, a remark considered unfortunate in the light of British attempts to draw the US into the First World War*

Robert Skidelsky *John Maynard Keynes* vol. 1 (1983)

Joseph Stalin 1879–1953

Soviet dictator

3 The State is an instrument in the hands of the ruling class, used to break the resistance of the adversaries of that class.

Foundations of Leninism (1924)

4 There is the question: Can Socialism *possibly* be established in one country alone by that country's unaided strength? The question must be answered in the affirmative.

Problems of Leninism (1926)

5 The Pope! How many divisions has *he* got?
on being asked to encourage Catholicism in Russia by way of conciliating the Pope

on 13 May 1935; W. S. Churchill *The Gathering Storm* (1948)

6 There is one eternally true legend—that of Judas.
at the trial of Radek in 1937

Robert Payne *The Rise and Fall of Stalin* (1966)

7 One death is a tragedy, one million is a statistic.

attributed

Charles E. Stanton 1859–1933

American soldier

8 Lafayette, we are here.
at the tomb of Lafayette in Paris, 4 July 1917

in *New York Tribune* 6 September 1917

Edwin McMasters Stanton 1814–69

American lawyer

9 Now he belongs to the ages.
of Abraham **Lincoln**, *following his assassination, 15 April 1865*

I. M. Tarbell *Life of Abraham Lincoln* (1900)

David Steel 1938–

British Liberal politician; Leader of the Liberal Party 1976–88
on Steel: see **Foot** 138:8

10 I have the good fortune to be the first Liberal leader for over half a century who is able to say to you at the end

speech to the Liberal Party Assembly, 18 September 1981

of our annual assembly: go back to your constituencies and prepare for government.

Lincoln Steffens 1866–1936

American journalist

1 I have seen the future; and it works.
following a visit to the Soviet Union in 1919

Letters (1938) vol. 1; see J. M. Thompson *Russia, Bolshevism and the Versailles Treaty* (1954), where it is recalled that Steffens had composed the expression before he had even arrived in Russia

Gertrude Stein 1874–1946

American writer

2 In the United States there is more space where nobody is than where anybody is. That is what makes America what it is.

The Geographical History of America (1936)

James Fitzjames Stephen 1829–94

English lawyer

3 The way in which the man of genius rules is by persuading an efficient minority to coerce an indifferent and self-indulgent majority.

Liberty, Equality and Fraternity (1873)

Thaddeus Stevens 1792–1868

American politician

4 Though the President is Commander-in-Chief, Congress is his commander; and, God willing, he shall obey. He and his minions shall learn that this is not a Government of kings and satraps, but a Government of the people, and that Congress is the people.

speech in House of Representatives, 3 January 1867

Adlai Stevenson 1900–65

American Democratic politician

5 I am not a politician, I am a citizen.
speech during the 1948 election campaign

Bert Cochran *Adlai Stevenson* (1969)

6 We must be patient—making peace is harder than making war.

speech to Chicago Council on Foreign Relations, 21 March 1946

7 I suppose flattery hurts no one, that is, if he doesn't inhale.

television broadcast, 30 March 1952

8 Better we lose the election than mislead the people.
on accepting the Democratic nomination in 1952

Herbert Muller *Adlai Stevenson* (1968)

9 Let's talk sense to the American people. Let's tell them the truth, that there are no gains without pains.
accepting the Democratic nomination

speech at the Democratic National Convention, Chicago, Illinois, 26 July 1952

1 If they [the Republicans] will stop telling lies about the Democrats, we will stop telling the truth about them. — speech during 1952 Presidential campaign; J. B. Martin *Adlai Stevenson and Illinois* (1976)

2 When an American says that he loves his country, he… means that he loves an inner air, an inner light in which freedom lives and in which a man can draw the breath of self-respect. — speech in New York City, 27 August 1952

3 A hungry man is not a free man. — speech at Kasson, Minnesota, 6 September 1952

4 The time to stop a revolution is at the beginning, not the end. — speech in San Francisco, 9 September 1952

5 There is no evil in the atom; only in men's souls. — speech at Hartford, Connecticut, 18 September 1952

6 In America any boy may become President and I suppose it's just one of the risks he takes! — speech in Indianapolis, 26 September 1952

7 A free society is a society where it is safe to be unpopular. — speech in Detroit, 7 October 1952

8 The Republican party did not have to… encourage the excesses of its Vice-Presidential nominee [Richard Nixon]—the young man who asks you to set him one heart-beat from the Presidency of the United States. — speech at Cleveland, Ohio, 23 October 1952

commonly quoted as 'just a heart-beat away…'

9 A funny thing happened to me on the way to the White House. — Alden Whitman *Portrait: Adlai E. Stevenson* (1965)

speech in Washington, 13 December 1952, following his defeat in the Presidential election

10 We hear the Secretary of State [John Foster Dulles] boasting of his brinkmanship—the art of bringing us to the edge of the abyss. — speech in Hartford, Connecticut, 25 February 1956; cf. **Dulles** 126:9

11 The idea that you can merchandize candidates for high office like breakfast cereal—that you can gather votes like box tops—is, I think, the ultimate indignity to the democratic process. — speech at the Democratic National Convention, 18 August 1956

12 You have taught me a lesson I should have learned long ago—to take counsel always of your courage and never of your fears. — Herbert J. Muller *Adlai Stevenson* (1968)

on losing the Presidential nomination in 1960

13 Do you remember that in classical times when Cicero had finished speaking, the people said, 'How well he spoke', but when Demosthenes had finished speaking, they said, 'Let us march.' — Bert Cochran *Adlai Stevenson* (1969)

introducing John Fitzgerald ***Kennedy*** *in 1960*

14 She would rather light a candle than curse the darkness, and her glow has warmed the world. — in *New York Times* 8 November 1962

on learning of Eleanor ***Roosevelt****'s death*

15 Eggheads of the world unite; you have nothing to lose but your yolks. — attributed

perhaps a reworking of 'Eggheads of the world, arise — I was even going to add that you have nothing to lose but your yolks', speech at Oakland, 1 February 1956

1 If I had any epitaph that I would rather have more than another, it would be to say that I had disturbed the sleep of my generation. — epigraph to Jack W. Germand and Jules Witcover *Wake Us When It's Over* (1985)

2 A politician is a person who approaches every subject with an open mouth. — attributed

3 The sound of tireless voices is the price we pay for the right to hear the music of our own opinions. — in *The Guide to American Law* (1984)

Robert Louis Stevenson 1850–94

Scottish writer

4 Politics is perhaps the only profession for which no preparation is thought necessary. — *Familiar Studies of Men and Books* (1882)

Caskie Stinnett 1911–

5 A diplomat...is a person who can tell you to go to hell in such a way that you actually look forward to the trip. — *Out of the Red* (1960)

Baroness Stocks 1891–1975

British educationist

6 The House of Lords is a perfect eventide home. — *My Commonplace Book* (1970)

Tom Stoppard 1937–

British playwright

7 The House of Lords, an illusion to which I have never been able to subscribe—responsibility without power, the prerogative of the eunuch throughout the ages. — *Lord Malquist and Mr Moon* (1966)

8 It's not the voting that's democracy, it's the counting. — *Jumpers* (1972)

9 War is capitalism with the gloves off and many who go to war know it but they go to war because they don't want to be a hero. — *Travesties* (1975)

10 Comment is free but facts are on expenses. — *Night and Day* (1978); cf. **Scott** 322:4

11 I'm with you on the free press. It's the newspapers I can't stand. — *Night and Day* (1978)

William Stoughton 1631–1701

12 God hath sifted a nation that he might send choice grain into this wilderness. — election sermon in Boston, 29 April 1669

Lord Stowell 1745–1836

English jurist

1 A precedent embalms a principle.
an opinion, while Advocate-General, 1788

quoted by Disraeli in the House of Commons, 22 February 1848

2 The elegant simplicity of the three per cents.

Lord Campbell *Lives of the Lord Chancellors* (1857); cf. **Disraeli** 120:19

Thomas Wentworth, Lord Strafford 1593–1641

English statesman

3 The authority of a King is the keystone which closeth up the arch of order and government which, once shaken, all the frame falls together in a confused heap of foundation and battlement.

Hugh Trevor-Roper *Historical Essays* (1952)

Simeon Strunsky 1879–1948

4 People who want to understand democracy should spend less time in the library with Aristotle and more time on buses and in the subway.

No Mean City (1944)

Louis Sullivan 1933–

American Secretary of Health and Human Services

on the probable nature of a nationalized health service:

5 What we would have is a combination of the compassion of the Internal Revenue Service and the efficiency of the post office.

in *Newsweek* February 1992

Maximilien de Béthune, Duc de Sully 1559–1641

French statesman

6 Tilling and grazing are the two breasts by which France is fed.

Mémoires (1638)

7 The English take their pleasures sadly after the fashion of their country.

attributed

Arthur Hays Sulzberger 1891–1968

American newspaper proprietor

8 We tell the public which way the cat is jumping. The public will take care of the cat.
on journalism

in *Time* 8 May 1950

Charles Sumner 1811–74

American politician and orator
on Sumner: see **Adams** 2:9

1 Where Slavery is, there Liberty cannot be; and where Liberty is, there Slavery cannot be.
'Slavery and the Rebellion'; speech at Cooper Institute 5 November 1864

2 There is the National flag. He must be cold, indeed, who can look upon its folds rippling in the breeze without pride of country. If in a foreign land, the flag is companionship, and country itself, with all its endearments.
Are We a Nation? 19 November 1867

Hannen Swaffer 1879–1962

British journalist

3 Freedom of the press in Britain means freedom to print such of the proprietor's prejudices as the advertisers don't object to.
said to Tom Driberg *c.*1928; Tom Driberg *Swaff* (1974)

Jonathan Swift 1667–1745

Anglo-Irish poet and satirist

4 Laws are like cobwebs, which may catch small flies, but let wasps and hornets break through.
A Critical Essay upon the Faculties of the Mind (1709); cf. **Anarcharsis** 8:3, **Shenstone** 338:9

5 It is the folly of too many, to mistake the echo of a London coffee-house for the voice of the kingdom.
The Conduct of the Allies (1711)

6 I cannot but conclude the bulk of your natives to be the most pernicious race of little odious vermin that nature ever suffered to crawl upon the surface of the earth.
Gulliver's Travels (1726) 'A Voyage to Brobdingnag'

7 And he gave it for his opinion, that whoever could make two ears of corn or two blades of grass to grow upon a spot of ground where only one grew before, would deserve better of mankind, and do more essential service to his country than the whole race of politicians put together.
Gulliver's Travels (1726) 'A Voyage to Brobdingnag'

8 These unhappy people were proposing schemes for persuading monarchs to choose favourites upon the score of their wisdom, capacity and virtue; of teaching ministers to consult the public good; of rewarding merit, great abilities and eminent services; of instructing princes to know their true interest by placing it on the same foundation with that of their people: of choosing for employment persons qualified to exercise them; with many other wild impossible chimeras, that never entered before into the heart of man to conceive, and confirmed in me the old observation, that there is nothing so extravagant and irrational which some philosophers have not maintained for truth.
Gulliver's Travels (1726) 'A Voyage to Laputa, etc.'

1 I have been assured by a very knowing American of my acquaintance in London, that a young healthy child well nursed is at a year old a most delicious, nourishing, and wholesome food, whether stewed, roasted, baked, or boiled, and I make no doubt that it will equally serve in a fricassee, or a ragout.

A Modest Proposal for Preventing the Children of Ireland from being a Burden to their Parents or Country (1729)

Tacitus AD *c.*56–AFTER 117

Roman senator and historian

2 Now the boundary of Britain is revealed, and everything unknown is held to be glorious.
reporting the speech of a British leader, Calgacus

Agricola

3 They make a wilderness and call it peace.

Agricola

4 You were indeed fortunate, Agricola, not only in the distinction of your life, but also in the lucky timing of your death.

Agricola

5 With neither anger nor partiality.

Annals

6 The more corrupt the republic, the more numerous the laws.

Annals

7 These times having the rare good fortune that you may think what you like and say what you think.

Histories

8 He seemed much greater than a private citizen while he still was a private citizen, and by everyone's consent capable of reigning if only he had not reigned.
of the Emperor Galba

Histories

9 The gods are on the side of the stronger.

Histories; cf. **Voltaire** 375:8

William Howard Taft 1857–1930

American Republican statesman, 27th President of the US 1909–13

10 Next to the right of liberty, the right of property is the most important individual right guaranteed by the Constitution and the one which, united with that of personal liberty, has contributed more to the growth of civilization than any other institution established by the human race.

Popular Government (1913)

Charles-Maurice de Talleyrand 1754–1838

French statesman
on Talleyrand: see **Napoleon** 270:4

of the Bourbons in exile:

11 They have learnt nothing, and forgotten nothing.
a similar comment on the courtiers of **Louis XVIII**, *attributed to the French general Dumouriez, was quoted by* **Napoleon** *in his Declaration to the French on his return from Elba*

oral tradition, attributed to Talleyrand by the Chevalier de Panat, January 1796

on hearing of **Napoleon***'s costly victory at Borodino, 1812:*

1 This is the beginning of the end.
Sainte-Beuve *M. de Talleyrand* (1870); attributed

2 It is not an event, it is an item of news.
on hearing of the death of **Napoleon** *in 1821*
Philip Henry Stanhope *Notes of Conversations with the Duke of Wellington* (1888) 1 November 1831

3 Above all, gentlemen, not the slightest zeal.
P. Chasles *Voyages d'un critique à travers la vie et les livres* (1868) vol. 2

4 He who has not lived during the years around 1789 can not know what is meant by the pleasure of life.
M. Guizot *Mémoires pour servir à l'histoire de mon temps* (1858) vol. 1

5 [Treason] is a question of dates.
Duff Cooper *Talleyrand* (1932)

R. H. Tawney 1880–1962

British economic historian

6 By making the most fundamental of all industries a public service carried on in partnership between the state and the workers, it will call into operation motives of public spirit and professional zeal which are at present stifled by subordination of the industry to the pursuit of private gain, and will raise the whole tone and quality of our industrial civilization.
on the nationalization of the coal industry in 1919
Anthony Sampson *The Changing Anatomy of Britain* (1982)

7 The characteristic virtue of Englishmen is power of sustained practical activity and their characteristic vice a reluctance to test the quality of that activity by reference to principles.
The Acquisitive Society (1921)

8 Militarism . . . is fetish worship. It is the prostration of men's souls and the laceration of their bodies to appease an idol.
The Acquisitive Society (1921)

9 Those who dread a dead-level of income or wealth . . . do not dread, it seems, a dead-level of law and order, and of security for life and property.
Equality (1931 ed.)

10 Private property is a necessary institution, at least in a fallen world; men work more and dispute less when goods are private than when they are common. But it is to be tolerated as a concession to human frailty, not applauded as desirable in itself.
Religion and the Rise of Capitalism (1926)

11 To take usury is contrary to Scripture; it is contrary to Aristotle; it is contrary to nature, for it is to live without labour; it is to sell time, which belongs to God, for the advantage of wicked men; it is to rob those who use the money lent, and to whom, since they make it profitable, the profits should belong.
Religion and the Rise of Capitalism (1926)

12 Both the existing economic order, and too many of the projects advanced for reconstructing it, break down
Religion and the Rise of Capitalism (1926) conclusion

through their neglect of the truism that, since even quite common men have souls, no increase in material wealth will compensate them for arrangements which insult their self-respect and impair their freedom. A reasonable estimate of economic organisation must allow for the fact that, unless industry is to be paralysed by recurrent revolts on the part of outraged human nature, it must satisfy criteria which are not purely economic.

1 Freedom for the pike is death for the minnows.
Equality (1938 ed.)

2 Democracy a society where ordinary men exercise initiative. Dreadful respect for superiors. Mental enlargement...Real foe to be overcome...fact that large section of the public *like* plutocratic government, and are easily gullible. How shake them!
unpublished fragment of Chicago lecture (1939), read at Tawney's funeral

3 That seductive border region where politics grease the wheels of business and polite society smiles hopefully on both.
Business and Politics under James I (1958)

declining the offer of a peerage:

4 What harm have I ever done to the Labour Party?
in *Evening Standard* 18 January 1962

A. J. P. Taylor 1906–90

British historian

5 Without democracy socialism would be worth nothing, but democracy is worth a great deal even when it is not socialist.
in *Manchester Guardian* 7 March 1941

6 What is wrong with Germany is there is too much of it. There are too many Germans, and Germany is too strong, too well organized, too well equipped with industrial resources.
in *Manchester Guardian* 29 March 1944

7 The British political system has no room for the rogue elephant.
in *History Today* July 1951 'Lord Palmerston'

8 Crimea: The War That Would Not Boil.
Rumours of Wars (1952); originally the title of an essay in *History Today* 2 February 1951

9 Bismarck was a political genius of the highest rank, but he lacked one essential quality of the constructive statesman: he had no faith in the future.
in *Encyclopedia Britannica* (1954)

10 The politician performs upon the stage; the historian looks behind the scenery.
Englishmen and Others (1956)

11 We may remind ourselves over and over again, that the foreign policy of a country is made by a few experts and a few rather less expert politicians...We write 'the British' when we mean 'the few members of the Foreign Office who happened to concern themselves with this question'.
The Troublemakers (1957)

12 Conformity may give you a quiet life; it may even bring you a University Chair. But all change in history, all
The Troublemakers (1957)

advance, comes from the nonconformist. If there had been no trouble makers, no Dissenters, we should still be living in caves.

1 Appeasement was a sensible course, even though it was tried with the wrong man; and it remains the noblest word in the diplomatist's vocabulary.
in *Manchester Guardian* 30 September 1958

2 A racing tipster who only reached Hitler's level of accuracy would not do well for his clients.
The Origins of the Second World War (1961)

3 Communism continued to haunt Europe as a spectre—a name men gave to their own fears and blunders. But the crusade against Communism was even more imaginary than the spectre of Communism.
The Origins of the Second World War (1961)

4 Human blunders, however, usually do more to shape history than human wickedness.
The Origins of the Second World War (1961)

5 With Hitler guilty, every other German could claim innocence.
The Origins of the Second World War (1961)

6 'Democratic, federal Yugoslavia' translated into practice the great might-have-been of Habsburg history.
The Habsburg Monarchy, 1809–1918 (2nd ed. 1961)

7 Like most of those who study history, he [Napoleon III] learned from the mistakes of the past how to make new ones.
in *Listener* 6 June 1963 'Mistaken Lessons from the Past'

8 The First World War had begun—imposed on the statesmen of Europe by railway timetables. It was an unexpected climax to the railway age.
The First World War (1963)

9 He aspired to power instead of influence, and as a result forfeited both.
of Lord **Northcliffe**
English History 1914–45 (1965)

10 History gets thicker as it approaches recent times.
English History 1914–45 (1965) Bibliography

11 In the Second World War the British people came of age. This was a people's war...Few now sang *Land of Hope and Glory*. Few even sang *England Arise*. England had risen all the same.
English History, 1914–1945 (1965)

12 He aroused every feeling except trust.
of **Lloyd George**
English History 1914–1945 (1965)

of the period after the First World War:

13 Civilization was held together by the civilized behaviour of ordinary people...In reality the masses were calmer and more sensible than those who ruled over them.
From Sarajevo to Potsdam (1966)

14 Like Johnson's friend Edwards, I, too have tried to be a Marxist but common sense kept breaking in.
'Accident Prone' in *Journal of Modern History* 1977

15 If men are to respect each other for what they are, they must cease to respect each other for what they own.
Politicians, Socialism and Historians (1980)

Henry Taylor 1800–86

British writer and civil servant

1 It is of far greater importance to a statesman to make one friend who will hold out with him for twenty years, than to find twenty followers in each year, losing as many. *The Statesman* (1836)

2 No statesman, be he as discreet as he may, will escape having ascribed to him, as the result of interviews, promises and understandings which it was not his purpose to convey; and yet in a short time he will be unable to recollect what was said with sufficient distinctness to enable him to give a confident contradiction. *The Statesman* (1836)

3 The conscience of a statesman should be rather a strong conscience than a tender conscience. *The Statesman* (1836)

4 It is very certain that there may be met with, in public life, a species of conscience which is all bridle and no spurs. *The Statesman* (1836)

5 The hand which executes a measure should belong to the head which propounds it. *The Statesman* (1836)

6 One who would thrive by seeking favours from the great, should never trouble them for small ones. *The Statesman* (1836)

7 [A statesman] should steer by the compass, but he must lie with the wind. *The Statesman* (1836)

8 A secret may be sometimes best kept by keeping the secret of its being a secret. *The Statesman* (1836)

9 Indecisiveness will be *caeteris paribus* most pernicious in affairs which require secrecy;—1st. Because the greatest aid to secrecy is celerity; 2nd. Because the undecided man, seeking after various counsels, necessarily multiplies confidences. *The Statesman* (1836)

10 To choose that which will bring him the most credit with the least trouble, has hitherto been the sole care of the statesman in office. *The Statesman* (1836)

11 Good nature and kindness towards those with whom they come in personal contact, at the expense of public interests, that is of those whom they never see, is the besetting sin of public men. *The Statesman* (1836)

12 He who has once advanced by a stride will not be content to advance afterwards by steps. Public servants, therefore, like racehorses, should be well fed with reward, but not to fatness. *The Statesman* (1836)

13 Men in high places, from having less personal interest in the characters of others—being safe from them—are commonly less acute observers, and with their progressive elevation in life become, as more and more indifferent to what other men are, so more and more ignorant of them. *The Statesman* (1836)

Norman Tebbit 1931–

British Conservative politician
on Tebbit: see **Foot** 138:7

1 I grew up in the Thirties with our unemployed father. He did not riot, he got on his bike and looked for work.
speech at Conservative Party Conference, 15 October 1981

2 The trigger of today's outburst of crime and violence... lies in the era and attitudes of postwar funk which gave birth to the 'permissive society'.
in *Guardian* 4 November 1985

3 The word 'conservative' is used by the BBC as a portmanteau word of abuse for anyone whose views differ from the insufferable, smug, sanctimonious, naive, guilt-ridden, wet, pink orthodoxy of that sunset home of the third-rate minds of that third-rate decade, the nineteen-sixties.
in *Independent* 24 February 1990

4 The cricket test—which side do they cheer for?... Are you still looking back to where you came from or where you are?
on the loyalties of Britain's immigrant population
interview in *Los Angeles Times*, reported in *Daily Telegraph* 20 April 1990

William Temple 1881–1944

English theologian; Archbishop of Canterbury from 1942

5 In place of the conception of the power-state we are led to that of the welfare-state.
Citizen and Churchman (1941)

John Tenniel 1820–1914

English draughtsman

6 Dropping the pilot.
cartoon caption, and title of poem, on **Bismarck**'s *dismissal from office by Kaiser* **Wilhelm II**
in *Punch* 29 March 1890

Lord Tennyson 1809–92

English poet

7 Forward, forward let us range,
Let the great world spin for ever down the ringing
grooves of change.
'Locksley Hall' (1842)

8 A land of settled government,
A land of just and old renown,
Where Freedom slowly broadens down
From precedent to precedent.
'You ask me, why, though ill at ease' (1842)

9 The last great Englishman is low.
'Ode on the Death of the Duke of Wellington' (1852)

10 O good grey head which all men knew!
'Ode on the Death of the Duke of Wellington' (1852)

11 O fall'n at length that tower of strength
Which stood four-square to all the winds that blew!
'Ode on the Death of the Duke of Wellington' (1852)

1 That world-earthquake, Waterloo! — 'Ode on the Death of the Duke of Wellington' (1852)

2 Who never sold the truth to serve the hour,
Nor paltered with Eternal God for power. — 'Ode on the Death of the Duke of Wellington' (1852)

3 Not once or twice in our rough island-story,
The path of duty was the way to glory. — 'Ode on the Death of the Duke of Wellington' (1852)

4 Authority forgets a dying king. — 'The Passing of Arthur' (1869)

5 The old order changeth, yielding place to new,
And God fulfils himself in many ways,
Lest one good custom should corrupt the world. — 'The Passing of Arthur' 1869

Terence 190–159 BC

Roman comic playwright

6 *Quot homines tot sententiae: suus cuique mos.*
There are as many opinions as there are people: each has his own correct way. — *Phormio*

Margaret Thatcher 1925–

British Conservative stateswoman, Prime Minister 1979–90
on Thatcher: see **Anonymous** 11:2, **Biffen** 45:1, **Callaghan** 73:2, **Critchley** 104:5, 104:8, **Healey** 173:1, 173:2, 173:4, **Hennessy** 175:2, **Kinnock** 211:9, **Mitterrand** 261:8, **Parris** 286:10, **West** 385:8

7 No woman in my time will be Prime Minister or Chancellor or Foreign Secretary—not the top jobs. Anyway I wouldn't want to be Prime Minister. You have to give yourself 100%.
on her appointment as Shadow Education Spokesman — in *Sunday Telegraph* 26 October 1969

8 In politics if you want anything said, ask a man. If you want anything done, ask a woman. — in *People* (New York) 15 September 1975

9 I'll always be fond of dear Ted, but there's no sympathy in politics.
of her predecessor, Edward **Heath** — attributed, 1975

10 I stand before you tonight in my red chiffon evening gown, my face softly made up, my fair hair gently waved…the Iron Lady of the Western World! Me? A cold war warrior? Well, yes—if that is how they wish to interpret my defence of values and freedoms fundamental to our way of life. — speech at Finchley, 31 January 1976

11 I've got no hang-ups about my background, like you intellectual commentators in the south-east. When you're actually *doing* things you don't have time for hang-ups. — in conversation with Anthony Sampson in 1977; Anthony Sampson *The Changing Anatomy of Britain* (1982)

12 Pennies don't fall from heaven. They have to be earned on earth. — in *Observer* 18 November 1979 'Sayings of the Week'

13 I don't mind how much my Ministers talk, as long as they do what I say. — in *Observer* 27 January 1980

1 We have to get our production and our earnings in balance. There's no easy popularity in what we are proposing, but it is fundamentally sound. Yet I believe people accept there is no real alternative.
popularly encapsulated in the acronym TINA

speech at Conservative Women's Conference, 21 May 1980

2 To those waiting with bated breath for that favourite media catch-phrase, the U-turn, I have only this to say. 'You turn if you want; the lady's not for turning.'

speech at Conservative Party Conference in Brighton, 10 October 1980

3 Economics are the method; the object is to change the soul.

in *Sunday Times* 3 May 1981

4 My politics are based... on things I and millions like me were brought up with. An honest day's work for an honest day's pay; live within your means; put by a nest egg for a rainy day; pay your bills on time; support the police.

in *News of the World* 20 September 1981

5 Let me make one thing absolutely clear. The National Health Service is safe with us.

speech at Conservative Party Conference, 8 October 1982

6 Just rejoice at that news and congratulate our armed forces and the Marines. Rejoice!
on the recapture of South Georgia, usually quoted as, 'Rejoice, rejoice!'

to newsmen outside 10 Downing Street, 25 April 1982

7 It is exciting to have a real crisis on your hands, when you have spent half your political life dealing with humdrum issues like the environment.
on the Falklands campaign, 1982

speech to Scottish Conservative Party conference, 14 May 1982

8 I was asked whether I was trying to restore Victorian values. I said straight out I was. And I am.

speech to the British Jewish Community, 21 July 1983, referring to an interview with Brian Walden on 17 January 1983

9 Now it must be business as usual.
on the steps of Brighton police station a few hours after the bombing of the Grand Hotel, Brighton; often quoted as 'We shall carry on as usual'

in *The Times* 13 October 1984

10 In church on Sunday morning—it was a lovely morning and we haven't had many lovely days—the sun was coming through a stained glass window and falling on some flowers, falling right across the church. It just occurred to me that this was the day I was meant not to see. Then all of a sudden I thought, 'there are some of my dearest friends who are not seeing this day.'
after the Brighton bombing

television interview, 15 October 1984

of Mikhail **Gorbachev**:

11 We can do business together.

in *The Times* 18 December 1984

12 We got a really good consensus during the last election. Consensus behind my convictions.

attributed, 1984

13 We must try to find ways to starve the terrorist and the hijacker of the oxygen of publicity on which they depend.

speech to American Bar Association in London, 15 July 1985

14 I don't spend a lifetime watching which way the cat jumps. I know really which way I want the cats to go.

interview with Michael Charlton on BBC radio, 17 December 1985

1 No one would remember the Good Samaritan if he'd only had good intentions. He had money as well.
television interview, 6 January 1986

2 There is no such thing as Society. There are individual men and women, and there are families.
in *Woman's Own* 31 October 1987

3 We have become a grandmother.
in *The Times* 4 March 1989

4 I am extraordinarily patient, provided I get my own way in the end.
in *Observer* 4 April 1989

5 Advisers advise and ministers decide.
on the respective roles of the her personal economic adviser, Alan Walters, and her Chancellor, Nigel **Lawson** *(who resigned the following day)*
in the House of Commons, 26 October 1989

of Nigel **Lawson**, *who had resigned two days before:*
6 To me, the Chancellor's position was unassailable.
in an interview with Brian Walden, 29 October 1989

7 You don't reach Downing Street by pretending you've travelled the road to Damascus when you haven't even left home.
of Neil **Kinnock**
in *Independent* 14 October 1989

8 I am naturally very sorry to see you go, but understand...your wish to be able to spend more time with your family.
reply to Norman **Fowler**'*s resignation letter*
in *Guardian* 4 January 1990; cf. **Fowler** 140:3

9 Others bring me problems, David brings me solutions.
of Lord Young
in *Observer* 1 July 1990

10 No! No! No!
making clear her opposition to a single European currency, and more centralized controls from Brussels
in the House of Commons, 30 October 1990

11 I shan't be pulling the levers there but I shall be a very good back-seat driver.
on the appointment of John **Major** *as the next Prime Minister*
in *Independent* 27 November 1990

12 Every Prime Minister needs a Willie.
at the farewell dinner to Lord **Whitelaw**
in *Guardian* 7 August 1991

of being told by a majority of her Cabinet that she could not continue as Prime Minister:
13 Treachery with a smile on its face.
on 'The Thatcher Years' (BBC 1), 20 October 1993

14 I think sometimes the Prime Minister should be intimidating. There's not much point being a weak, floppy thing in the chair, is there?
on 'The Thatcher Years' (BBC 1), 21 October 1993

of the poll tax:
15 Given time, it would have been seen as one of the most far-reaching and beneficial reforms ever made in the working of local government.
The Downing Street Years (1993)

William Roscoe Thayer 1859–1923

American biographer and historian

1 From log-cabin to White House.

title of biography (1910) of James **Garfield**

Louis Adolphe Thiers 1797–1877

French statesman and historian

2 The king reigns, and the people govern themselves.

unsigned article in *Le National*, 20 January 1830; a signed article, 4 February 1830, reads: 'The king neither administers nor governs, he reigns'

Dylan Thomas 1914–53

Welsh poet

3 The hand that signed the paper felled a city;
Five sovereign fingers taxed the breath,
Doubled the globe of death and halved a country;
These five kings did a king to death.

'The Hand That Signed the Paper Felled a City'

4 The hand that signed the treaty bred a fever,
And famine grew, and locusts came;
Great is the hand that holds dominion over
Man by a scribbled name.

'The Hand That Signed the Paper Felled a City'

J. H. Thomas 1874–1949

British Socialist politician

5 And now 'ere we 'ave this obstinate little man with 'is Mrs Simpson. Hit won't do, 'arold, I tell you that straight.

to Harold **Nicolson** *on* **Edward VIII** *and the Abdication crisis*

Harold Nicolson letter 26 February 1936

6 They 'ate 'aving no family life at Court.

of the British people and the Abdication crisis

Harold Nicolson letter 26 February 1936

Norman Thomas 1884–1968

American Presbyterian minister and writer

7 I'd rather see America save her soul than her face.

protesting against the Vietnam War

speech in Washington, DC, 27 November 1965

Lord Thomson of Fleet 1894–1976

Canadian-born British newspaper and television proprietor

on owning a commercial television station:

8 Like having your own licence to print money.

R. Braddon *Roy Thomson* (1965)

Henry David Thoreau 1817–62

American writer

1 I heartily accept the motto, 'That government is best which governs least'…Carried out, it finally amounts to this, which I also believe,—'That government is best which governs not at all.' — *Civil Disobedience* (1849)

2 Under a government which imprisons any unjustly, the true place for a just man is also a prison. — *Civil Disobedience* (1849)

3 It takes two to speak the truth,—one to speak, and another to hear. — *A Week on the Concord and Merrimack Rivers* (1849) 'Wednesday'

4 The oldest, wisest politician grows not more human so, but is merely a grey wharf-rat at last. — *Journal* 1853

5 The government of the world I live in was not framed, like that of Britain, in after-dinner conversations over the wine. — *Walden* (1854) 'Conclusion'

Julian Thompson 1934–

British soldier, second-in-command of the land forces during the Falklands campaign.

6 You don't mind dying for Queen and country, but you certainly don't want to die for politicians. — 'The Falklands War – the Untold Story' (Yorkshire Television) 1 April 1987

Jeremy Thorpe 1929–

British Liberal politician; Liberal Party leader 1967–76

of Harold **Macmillan***'s sacking seven of his Cabinet on 13 July 1962*

7 Greater love hath no man than this, that he lay down his friends for his life. — D. E. Butler and Anthony King *The General Election of 1964* (1965)

James Thurber 1894–1961

American humorist

8 You can fool too many of the people too much of the time. — *Fables for our Time* (1940); cf. **Lincoln** 227:8

Lord Thurlow 1731–1806

English jurist; Lord Chancellor, 1778–83, 1783–92

9 Corporations have neither bodies to be punished, nor souls to be condemned, they therefore do as they like. — John Poynder *Literary Extracts* (1844) vol. 1

usually quoted as 'Did you ever expect a corporation to have a conscience, when it has no soul to be damned, and no body to be kicked?'

Alexis de Tocqueville 1805–59

French historian and politician

1 The French want no-one to be their *superior.* The English want *inferiors.* The Frenchman constantly raises his eyes above him with anxiety. The Englishman lowers his beneath him with satisfaction. On either side it is pride, but understood in a different way.

Voyage en Angleterre et en Irlande de 1835 (1958) 8 May 1835

2 It is from the midst of this putrid sewer that the greatest river of human industry springs up and carries fertility to the whole world. From this foul drain pure gold flows forth. Here it is that humanity achieves for itself both perfection and brutalization, that civilization produces its wonders, and that civilized man becomes again almost a savage.

of Manchester

Voyage en Angleterre et en Irlande de 1835 (1958) 2 July 1835

3 The surface of American society is covered with a layer of democratic paint, but from time to time one can see the old aristocratic colours breaking through.

Democracy in America (1835–40) vol.1

4 Americans rightly think their patriotism is a sort of religion strengthened by practical service.

Democracy in America (1835–40) vol.1

5 The President may slip without the state suffering, for his duties are limited. Congress may slip without the Union perishing, for above Congress there is the electoral body which can change its spirit by changing its membership. But if ever the Supreme Court came to be composed of rash or corrupt men, the confederation would be threatened by anarchy or civil war.

Democracy in America (1835–40) vol.1

6 Providence has not created mankind entirely independent or entirely free. It is true that around every man a fatal circle is traced, beyond which he cannot pass; but within the wide verge of that circle he is powerful and free.

Democracy in America (1835–40) vol. 1

7 Of all nations, those submit to civilization with the most difficulty which habitually live by the chase.

Democracy in America (1835–40) vol. 1

8 What is understood by republican government in the United States is the slow and quiet action of society upon itself.

Democracy in America (1835–40) vol. 1

9 There are, at the present time, two great nations in the world, which seem to tend towards the same end, although they started from different points; I allude to the Russians and the Americans... Their starting point is different, and their courses are not the same; yet each of them seems to be marked out by the will of Heaven to sway the destinies of half the globe.

Democracy in America (1835–40) vol. 1

10 Unable to judge at once of the social position of those he meets, an Englishman prudently avoids all contact with them. Men are afraid less some slight service rendered should draw them into an unsuitable acquaintance; they dread civilities, and they avoid the obtrusive gratitude of a stranger quite as much as his hatred.

Democracy in America (1835–40) vol. 2

1 On my arrival in the United States I was struck by the degree of ability among the governed and the lack of it among the governing.

Democracy in America (1835–40) vol. 2

2 Freedom alone...substitutes from time to time for the love of material comfort more powerful and more lofty passions; it alone supplies ambition with greater objectives than the acquisition of riches, and creates the light that makes it possible to see and to judge the vices and virtues of mankind.

The Ancien Régime (1856)

3 Where is the man of soul so base that he would prefer to depend on the caprices of one of his fellow men rather than obey the laws which he has himself contributed to establish?

The Ancien Régime (1856)

4 Despots themselves do not deny that freedom is excellent; only they desire it for themselves alone, and they maintain that everyone else is altogether unworthy of it.

The Ancien Régime (1856)

5 The French Revolution operated in reference to this world in exactly the same manner as religious revolutions acted in view of the other world. It considered the citizen as an abstract proposition apart from any particular society, in the same way as religions considered man as man, independent of country and time.

The Ancien Régime (1856)

6 History is a gallery of pictures in which there are few originals and many copies.

The Ancien Régime (1856)

7 When a nation abolishes aristocracy, centralization follows as a matter of course.

The Ancien Régime (1856)

8 The only substantial difference between the custom of those days and our own resides in the price paid for office. Then they were sold by government, now they are bestowed; it is no longer necessary to pay money; the object can be attained by selling one's soul.

The Ancien Régime (1856)

9 The student of our revolution soon discovers that it was led and managed by the same spirit which gave birth to so many abstract treatises on government. In both he finds the same love for general theories, sweeping legislative systems, and symmetrical laws; the same confidence in theory; the same desire for new and original institutions; the same wish to reconstruct the whole Constitution according to the rules of logic, and in conformity with a set plan, instead of attempting partial amendments. A terrible sight! for what is merit in an author is often a defect in a statesman, and characteristics which improve a book may be fatal to a revolution.

The Ancien Régime (1856)

10 Centralization and socialism are native of the same soil: one is the wild herb, the other the garden plant.

The Ancien Régime (1856)

11 What do men need in order to remain free? A taste for freedom. Do not ask me to analyze that sublime taste; it can only be felt. It has a place in every great heart which

The Ancien Régime (1856)

God has prepared to receive it; it fills and inflames it. To try to explain it to those inferior minds who have never felt it is to waste time.

1 No example is so dangerous as that of violence employed by well-meaning people for beneficial objects. *The Ancien Régime* (1856)

2 He who desires in liberty anything other than itself is born to be a servant. *The Ancien Régime* (1856)

3 It is not always by going from bad to worse that a society falls into revolution...The social order destroyed by a revolution is almost always better than that which immediately preceded it, and experience shows that the most dangerous moment for a bad government is generally that in which it sets about reform. *The Ancien Régime* (1856)

Robert Torrens 1780–1864

British economist

4 In the first stone which he [the savage] flings at the wild animals he pursues, in the first stick that he seizes to strike down the fruit which hangs above his reach, we see the appropriation of one article for the purpose of aiding in the acquisition of another, and thus discover the origin of capital. *An Essay on the Production of Wealth* (1821) ch. 2

Arnold Toynbee 1889–1975

English historian

5 America is a large, friendly dog in a very small room. Every time it wags its tail it knocks over a chair. attributed

Joseph Trapp 1679–1747

English poet and pamphleteer

6 The King, observing with judicious eyes
The state of both his universities,
To Oxford sent a troop of horse, and why?
That learned body wanted loyalty;
To Cambridge books, as very well discerning
How much that loyal body wanted learning.

lines written on **George I***'s donation of the Bishop of Ely's Library to Cambridge University*

John Nichols *Literary Anecdotes* (1812–16) vol. 3; cf. **Browne** 59:6

Lord Trend 1914–87

British civil servant; Cabinet Secretary 1963–73

on Trend: see **Rothschild** 313:7

7 The acid test of any political decision is, 'What is the alternative?' attributed, 1975

Charles Trevelyan 1807–86

British civil servant

on the organization of a new system of admission into the civil service:

1 It is proposed to invite the flower of our youth to the aid of public service.

to John Thadeus Delane, Editor of *The Times*, in 1853; Asa Briggs *Victorian People* (1965)

G. M. Trevelyan 1876–1962

English historian

2 If the French noblesse had been capable of playing cricket with their peasants, their chateaux would never have been burnt.

English Social History (1942)

3 In a world of voluble hates, he plotted to make men like, or at least tolerate one another.
of Stanley **Baldwin**

in *Dictionary of National Biography 1941–50* (1959)

William Trevor 1928–

Anglo-Irish novelist and short story writer

of the troubles in Northern Ireland:

4 A disease in the family that is never mentioned.

in *Observer* 18 November 1990

Hugh Trevor-Roper 1914–

British historian

5 Aristocracies…may preserve themselves longest, but only democracies, which refresh their ruling class, can expand.

Historical Essays (1952)

6 Any reaction which is to be successful over a long period must have radical origins…A reaction which is to last, which is to be accepted as orthodoxy over several generations, must spring out of the same social circumstances as the progress which it resists.

The Rise of Christian Europe (1965)

7 Historians in general are great toadies of power.

History and Imagination (1981)

8 Those who exercise power and determine policy are generally men whose minds have been formed by events twenty or thirty years before.

From Counter-Reformation to Glorious Revolution (1992); introduction

9 How are we to disentangle religion from politics in a revolution? Religion may form the outlook of an individual. It may serve as an ideological intoxicant for a crowd. But in high politics it is a variable.

From Counter-Reformation to Glorious Revolution (1992)

Tommy Trinder 1909–89

British comedian

of American troops in Britain during the Second World War:

1 Overpaid, overfed, oversexed, and over here. — associated with Trinder, but probably not his invention

Anthony Trollope 1815–82

English novelist

2 No reform, no innovation...stinks so foully in the nostrils of an English Tory politician as to be absolutely irreconcilable to him. When taken in the refreshing waters of office any such pill can be swallowed. — *The Bertrams* (1859)

3 To me it seems that no form of existing government—no form of government that ever did exist, gives or has given so large a measure of individual freedom to all who live under it as a constitutional monarchy. — *North America* (1862)

4 There is nothing more tyrannical than a strong popular feeling among a democratic people. — *North America* (1862)

5 I have sometimes thought that there is no being so venomous, so bloodthirsty as a professed philanthropist. — *North America* (1862)

6 [Equality] is a doctrine to be forgiven when he who preaches it is...striving to raise others to his own level. — *North America* (1862)

7 Mr Palliser was one of those politicians in possessing whom England has perhaps more reason to be proud than of any other of her resources, and who, as a body, give to her that requisite combination of conservatism and progress which is her present strength and best security for the future. — *Can You Forgive Her?* (1864)

8 A fainéant government is not the worst government that England can have. It has been the great fault of our politicians that they have all wanted to do something. — *Phineas Finn* (1869)

of the radical politician:

9 Having nothing to construct, he could always deal with generalities. Being free from responsibility, he was not called upon either to study details or to master even great facts. It was his business to inveigh against existing evils, and perhaps there is no easier business when once the privilege of an audience has been attained. It was his work to cut down forest-trees, and he had nothing to do with the subsequent cultivation of the land. — *Phineas Finn* (1869)

10 The first necessity for good speaking is a large audience. — *Phineas Finn* (1869)

11 It is the necessary nature of a political party in this country to avoid, as long as it can be avoided, the consideration of any question which involves a great change...The best carriage horses are those which can most steadily hold back against the coach as it trundles down the hill. — *Phineas Redux* (1874)

1 A man destined to sit conspicuously on our Treasury Bench, or on the seat opposite to it, should ask the Gods for a thick skin as a first gift. — *Phineas Redux* (1874)

2 Equality would be a heaven, if we could attain it. — *The Prime Minister* (1876)

3 I have hardly as yet met two Englishmen who were agreed as to the political power of the sovereign. — *The American Senator* (1877)

4 What Good Government ever was not stingy? — *South Africa* (1878)

5 How seldom is it that theories stand the wear and tear of practice! — *Thackeray* (1879)

6 Let the Toryism of the Tory be ever so strong, it is his destiny to carry out the purposes of his opponents. — *Why Frau Frohmann Raised Her Prices* (1882)

7 A man who entertains in his mind any political doctrine, except as a means of improving the condition of his fellows, I regard as a political intriguer, a charlatan, and a conjuror. — *Autobiography* (1883)

of political life:

8 The hatreds which sound so real when you read the mere words, which look so true when you see their scornful attitudes, on which for the time you are inclined to pin your faith so implicitly, amount to nothing. — *The Landleaguers* (1883)

9 But in truth the capacity of a man...[to be Prime Minister] does not depend on any power of intellect, or indomitable courage, or far-seeing cunning. The man is competent simply because he is believed to be so. — *Lord Palmerston* (1882)

Leon Trotsky 1879–1940

Russian revolutionary

10 Where force is necessary, there it must be applied boldly, decisively and completely. But one must know the limitations of force; one must know when to blend force with a manoeuvre, a blow with an agreement. — *What Next?* (1932)

11 Civilization has made the peasantry its pack animal. The bourgeoisie in the long run only changed the form of the pack. — *History of the Russian Revolution* (1933) vol. 3

12 You [the Mensheviks] are pitiful isolated individuals; you are bankrupts; your role is played out. Go where you belong from now on—into the dustbin of history! — *History of the Russian Revolution* (1933) vol. 3

13 Old age is the most unexpected of all things that happen to a man. — *Diary in Exile* (1959) 8 May 1935

14 In a country where the sole employer is the State, opposition means death by slow starvation. The old principle: who does not work shall not eat, has been replaced by a new one: who does not obey shall not eat. — attributed

15 Not believing in force is the same thing as not believing in gravitation. — G. Maximov *The Guillotine at Work* (1940)

Harry S Truman 1884–1972

American Democratic statesman, 33rd President of the US 1945–53

on Truman: see **Mencken** 256:14; cf. **Vaughan** 373:4

to reporters the day after his accession to the Presidency on the death of Franklin **Roosevelt***:*

1 When they told me yesterday what had happened, I felt like the moon, the stars and all the planets had fallen on me. — on 13 April 1945

2 Sixteen hours ago an American airplane dropped one bomb on Hiroshima...The force from which the sun draws its power has been loosed against those who brought war to the Far East. — on 6 August 1945

first announcement of the dropping of the atomic bomb

3 The release of atomic energy constitutes a new force too revolutionary to consider in the framework of old ideas. — message to Congress 3 October 1945

4 Effective, reciprocal, and enforceable safeguards acceptable to all nations. — on 15 November 1945

Declaration on Atomic Energy by President Truman, Clement **Attlee***, and W. L. Mackenzie King, Prime Minister of Canada*

5 All the President is, is a glorified public relations man who spends his time flattering, kissing and kicking people to get them to do what they are supposed to do anyway. — letter to his sister, 14 November 1947; *Off the Record* (1980)

6 Those who want the Government to regulate matters of the mind and spirit are like men who are so afraid of being murdered that they commit suicide to avoid assassination. — address at the National Archives, Washington, DC, 15 December 1952

7 Once a decision was made, I did not worry about it afterward. — *Memoirs* (1955) vol. 2

8 Most of the problems a President has to face have their roots in the past. — *Memoirs* (1955) vol. 2

9 To me, party platforms are contracts with the people. — *Memoirs* (1955) vol. 2

10 A President needs political understanding to *run* the government, but he may be *elected* without it. — *Memoirs* (1955) vol. 2

11 If there is one basic element in our Constitution, it is civilian control of the military. — *Memoirs* (1955) vol. 2

12 I never give them [the public] hell. I just tell the truth, and they think it is hell. — in *Look* 3 April 1956

13 A politician is a man who understands government, and it takes a politician to run a government. A statesman is a politician who's been dead 10 or 15 years. — in *New York World Telegram and Sun* 12 April 1958

14 It's a recession when your neighbour loses his job; it's a depression when you lose yours. — in *Observer* 13 April 1958

15 Wherever you have an efficient government you have a dictatorship. — lecture at Columbia University, 28 April 1959

16 Always be sincere, even if you don't mean it. — Attributed

1 The buck stops here. — unattributed motto
on Truman's desk

2 I didn't fire him [General MacArthur] because he was a dumb son of a bitch, although he was, but that's not against the law for generals. If it was, half to three-quarters of them would be in jail. — Merle Miller *Plain Speaking* (1974)

3 Secrecy and a free, democratic government don't mix. — Merle Miller *Plain Speaking* (1974)

Barbara W. Tuchman 1912–89

American historian and writer

4 Dead battles, like dead generals, hold the military mind in their dead grip and Germans, no less than other peoples, prepare for the last war. — *August 1914* (1962)

5 No more distressing moment can ever face a British government than that which requires it to come to a hard, fast and specific decision. — *August 1914* (1962)

6 For one August in its history Paris was French—and silent. — *August 1914* (1962)

A. R. J. Turgot 1727–81

French economist and statesman

7 He snatched the lightning shaft from heaven, and the sceptre from tyrants. — inscription
for a bust of Benjamin **Franklin**, *inventor of the lightning conductor and one of those who drafted the Declaration of Independence*

Mark Twain 1835–1910

American writer

8 It could probably be shown by facts and figures that there is no distinctly native American criminal class except Congress. — *Following the Equator* (1897)

9 It is by the goodness of God in our country that we have those three unspeakably precious things: freedom of speech, freedom of conscience, and the prudence never to practise either of them. — *Following the Equator* (1897)

10 Get your facts first, and then you can distort them as much as you please. — Rudyard Kipling *From Sea to Sea* (1899)

11 Suppose you were an idiot. And suppose you were a member of Congress. But I repeat myself. — A. B. Paine *Mark Twain* (1912)

Paul Valéry 1871–1945

French poet, critic, and man of letters

12 An attitude of permanent indignation signifies great mental poverty. Politics compels its votaries to take that — *Tel Quel* (1941–3)

line and you can see their minds growing more and more impoverished every day, from one burst of righteous anger to the next.

1 Politics is the art of preventing people from taking part in affairs which properly concern them. — *Tel Quel* (1941–3)

William Henry Vanderbilt 1821–85

American railway magnate

2 The public be damned!
on whether the public should be consulted about luxury trains — A. W. Cole letter to *New York Times* 25 August 1918

Laurens van der Post 1906–

South African explorer and writer

3 Human beings are perhaps never more frightening than when they are convinced beyond doubt that they are right. — *The Lost World of the Kalahari* (1958)

Harry Vaughan

4 If you can't stand the heat, get out of the kitchen. — in *Time* 28 April 1952; associated with Harry S **Truman**, but attributed by him to Vaughan, his 'military jester'

Thorstein Veblen 1857–1929

American economist and social scientist

5 Conspicuous consumption of valuable goods is a means of reputability to the gentleman of leisure. — *Theory of the Leisure Class* (1899)

6 From the foregoing survey of conspicuous leisure and consumption, it appears that the utility of both alike for the purposes of reputability lies in the element of waste that is common to both. In the one case it is a waste of time and effort, in the other it is a waste of goods. — *Theory of the Leisure Class* (1899)

Vegetius AD 379–95

Roman military writer

7 Let him who desires peace, prepare for war.
usually quoted as 'If you want peace, prepare for war' — *Epitoma Rei Militaris*

Pierre Vergniaud 1753–93

French revolutionary; executed with other Girondists

8 There was reason to fear that the Revolution, like Saturn, might devour in turn each one of her children. — Alphonse de Lamartine *Histoire des Girondins* (1847)

Hendrik Frensch Verwoerd 1901–66

South African statesman, Prime Minister 1958–66

1 Up till now he [the Bantu] has been subjected to a school system which drew him away from his own community and practically misled him by showing him the green pastures of the European but still did not allow him to graze there…It is abundantly clear that unplanned education creates many problems, disrupts the communal life of the Bantu and endangers the communal life of the European.

speech in South African Senate, 7 June 1954

Vespasian AD 9–79

Roman emperor from AD 69

2 *Pecunia non olet.*
Money has no smell.
replying to Titus's objection to his tax on public lavatories; holding a coin to Titus's nose and being told it didn't smell, he replied, 'Atque e lotio est [*Yes, that's made from urine*]'

traditional summary of Suetonius *Lives of the Caesars* 'Vespasian'

3 Woe is me, I think I am becoming a god.
when fatally ill

Suetonius *Lives of the Caesars* 'Vespasian'

Queen Victoria 1819–1901

Queen of the United Kingdom from 1837
on Victoria: see **Gladstone** 155:10

4 I will be good.
on being shown a chart of the line of succession, 11 March 1830

Theodore Martin *The Prince Consort* (1875)

5 The Queen is most anxious to enlist every one who can speak or write to join in checking this mad, wicked folly of 'Woman's Rights', with all its attendant horrors, on which her poor feeble sex is bent, forgetting every sense of womanly feeling and propriety.

letter to Theodore Martin, 29 May 1870

on **Gladstone**'*s last appointment as Prime Minister:*

6 The danger to the country, to Europe, to her vast Empire, which is involved in having all these great interests entrusted to the shaking hand of an old, wild, and incomprehensible man of 82, is very great!

letter to Lord Lansdowne, 12 August 1892

7 The future Viceroy must…not be guided by the *snobbish* and vulgar, over-bearing and offensive behaviour of our Civil and Political Agents, if we are to go on peaceably and happily in India…not trying to trample on the people and continuously reminding them and making them feel they are a conquered people.

letter to Lord **Salisbury**, 27 May 1898

8 He speaks to Me as if I was a public meeting.
of **Gladstone**

G. W. E. Russell *Collections and Recollections* (1898)

9 We are not interested in the possibilities of defeat; they do not exist.
on the Boer War during 'Black Week', December 1899

Lady Gwendolen Cecil *Life of Robert, Marquis of Salisbury* (1931)

1 We are not amused. — attributed; Caroline Holland *Notebooks of a Spinster Lady* (1919), 2 January 1900

Gore Vidal 1925–

American novelist and critic

of Ronald **Reagan**:

2 A triumph of the embalmer's art. — in *Observer* 26 April 1981

José Antonio Viera Gallo 1943–

Chilean politician

3 Socialism can only arrive by bicycle. — Ivan Illich *Energy and Equity* (1974) epigraph

Virgil 70–19 BC

Roman poet

4 So massive was the effort to found the Roman nation. — *Aeneid*

5 Do not trust the horse, Trojans. Whatever it is, I fear the Greeks even when they bring gifts. — *Aeneid*

6 I see wars, horrible wars, and the Tiber foaming with much blood. — *Aeneid*; cf. **Powell** 297:1

Voltaire 1694–1778

French writer and philosopher

7 Governments need both shepherds and butchers. — 'The Piccini Notebooks' (*c.*1735–50)

8 God is on the side not of the heavy battalions, but of the best shots. — 'The Piccini Notebooks' (*c.*1735–50)

9 This agglomeration which was called and which still calls itself the Holy Roman Empire was neither holy, nor Roman, nor an empire. — *Essai sur l'histoire générale et sur les moeurs et l'esprit des nations* (1756)

10 *Dans ce pays-ci il est bon de tuer de temps en temps un amiral pour encourager les autres.*
In this country [England] it is thought well to kill an admiral from time to time to encourage the others. — *Candide* (1759)

11 I disapprove of what you say, but I will defend to the death your right to say it. — in *The Friends of Voltaire* (1907)

attributed; the words are in fact S. G. Tallentyre's summary of Voltaire's attitude towards Helvétius following the burning of the latter's De l'esprit *in 1759*

what Voltaire apparently *said on the burning of* De l'esprit:

12 What a fuss about an omelette! — James Parton *Life of Voltaire* (1881) vol. 2

13 Whatever you do, stamp out abuses, and love those who love you. — letter to M. d'Alembert, 28 November 1762

1 The art of government consists in taking as much money as possible from one class of citizens to give to the other.
Dictionnaire philosophique (1764) 'Money'

2 Superstition sets the whole world in flames; philosophy quenches them.
Dictionnaire philosophique (1764) 'Superstition'

3 Indeed, history is nothing more than a tableau of crimes and misfortunes.
L'Ingénu (1767)

4 If one must serve, I hold it better to serve a well-bred lion, who is naturally stronger than I am, than two hundred rats of my own breed.
letter to a friend; Alexis de Tocqueville *The Ancien Régime* (1856)

5 To succeed in chaining the crowd you just seem to wear the same fetters.
attributed

William Waldegrave 1946–

British Conservative politician

6 In exceptional circumstances it is necessary to say something that is untrue in the House of Commons.
to a House of Commons select committee, in *Guardian* 9 March 1994

George Walden 1939–

British Conservative politician and columnist

7 Our politics seem to be increasingly about the management of illusions.
announcing that he would not seek re-election to Parliament
on 23 July 1995

Felix Walker fl. 1820

American politician

excusing a long, dull, irrelevant speech in the House of Representatives, c.1820 (Buncombe being his constituency):

8 I'm talking to Buncombe ['bunkum'].
W. Safire *New Language of Politics* (2nd ed., 1972); cf. **Carlyle** 76:7

George Wallace 1919–

American Democratic politician; Governor of Alabama

9 Segregation now, segregation tomorrow and segregation forever!
inaugural speech as Governor of Alabama, January 1963

Henry Wallace 1888–1965

American Democratic politician

10 The century on which we are entering—the century which will come out of this war—can be and must be the century of the common man.
speech, 8 May 1942

Edmund Waller 1606–87

English poet

1 Rome, though her eagle through the world had flown,
Could never make this island all her own.
'Panegyric to My Lord Protector' (1655)

2 Others may use the ocean as their road,
Only the English make it their abode.
'Of a War with Spain' (1658)

3 Under the tropic is our language spoke,
And part of Flanders hath received our yoke.
'Upon the Late Storm, and of the Death of His Highness Ensuing the Same' (1659)

Horace Walpole 1717–97

English writer and connoisseur, son of Robert **Walpole**

4 Our supreme governors, the mob.
letter to Horace Mann, 7 September 1743

5 Everybody talks of the constitution, but all sides forget that the constitution is extremely well, and would do very well, if they would but let it alone.
letter to Horace Mann, 18–19 January 1770

6 His speeches were fine, but as much laboured as his extempore sayings.
of Lord **Chesterfield,** *1751*
Memoirs of the Reign of King George II (1846) vol. 1

7 Whoever knows the interior of affairs, must be sensible to how many more events the faults of statesmen give birth, than are produced by their good intentions.
in 1754; *Memoirs of the Reign of King George II* (1846) vol. 1

8 The keenness of his sabre was blunted by the difficulty with which he drew it from the scabbard; I mean, the hesitation and ungracefulness of his delivery took off from the force of his arguments.
of Henry Fox, Lord **Holland,** *1755*
Memoirs of the Reign of King George II (1846) vol. 2

9 While he felt like a victim, he acted like a hero.
of Admiral Byng, on the day of his execution, 1757
Memoirs of the Reign of King George II (1846) vol. 2

10 Perhaps those, who, trembling most, maintain a dignity in their fate, are the bravest: resolution on reflection is real courage.
in 1757; *Memoirs of the Reign of King George II* (1846) vol. 2

11 They seem to know no medium between a mitre and a crown of martyrdom. If the clergy are not called to the latter, they never deviate from the pursuit of the former. One would think their motto was, *Canterbury or Smithfield*.
in 1758; *Memoirs of the Reign of King George II* (1846) vol. 3

12 All his passions were expressed by one livid smile.
of George **Grenville,** *1763*
Memoirs of the Reign of King George III (1845) vol. 1

13 He lost his dominions in America, his authority over Ireland, and all influence in Europe, by aiming at despotism in England; and exposed himself to more mortifications and humiliations than can happen to a quiet Doge of Venice.
of **George III,** *1770*
Memoirs of the Reign of King George III (1845) vol. 4

1 It was easier to conquer it [the East] than to know what to do with it. — letter to Horace Mann, 27 March 1772

2 By the waters of Babylon we sit down and weep, when we think of thee, O America! — letter to Revd William Mason, 12 June 1775

Robert Walpole 1676–1745

English Whig statesman; first British Prime Minister, 1721–42; father of Horace **Walpole**

on Walpole: see **Peel** 288:12, **Shippen** 339:7

3 Madam, there are fifty thousand men slain this year in Europe, and not one Englishman.
to Queen Caroline, 1734, on the war of the Polish succession, in which the English had refused to participate — John Hervey *Memoirs* (written 1734–43, published 1848) vol. 1

4 We must muzzle this terrible young cornet of horse.
of the elder William **Pitt***, who had held a cornetcy before his election to Parliament, but whose speech in support of the congratulatory address on the Prince of Wales's marriage in 1736 was regarded as so offensive through its covert satire that he was shortly afterwards dismissed from the army* — in *Dictionary of National Biography*

5 They now *ring* the bells, but they will soon *wring* their hands.
on the declaration of war with Spain, 1739 — W. Coxe *Memoirs of Sir Robert Walpole* (1798) vol. 1

6 All those men have their price.
of fellow parliamentarians — W. Coxe *Memoirs of Sir Robert Walpole* (1798) vol. 1

7 [Gratitude of place-expectants] is a lively sense of future favours. — W. Hazlitt *Lectures on the English Comic Writers* (1819) 'On Wit and Humour'

the normally imperturbable Walpole, having lost his temper at a Council, broke up the meeting:

8 No man is fit for business with a ruffled temper. — Edmund Fitzmaurice *Life of Shelburne* (1875)

9 There is enough pasture for all the sheep.
on his ability to spread round patronage satisfactorily — attributed

on seeing Henry Fox (Lord **Holland***) reading in the library at Houghton:*

10 You can read. It is a great happiness. I totally neglected it while I was in business, which has been the whole of my life, and to such a degree that I cannot now read a page—a warning to all Ministers. — Edmund Fitzmaurice *Life of Shelburne* (1875) vol. 1

Charles Dudley Warner 1829–1900

US author and editor

11 Politics makes strange bedfellows. — *My Summer in a Garden* (1871)

Earl Warren 1891–1974

American Chief Justice

1 In civilized life, law floats in a sea of ethics. — in *New York Times* 12 November 1962

Booker T. Washington 1856–1915

American educationist and emancipated slave

2 In all things that are purely social we can be as separate as the fingers, yet one as the hand in all things essential to mutual progress. — speech at the Cotton States and International Exposition, Atlanta, 18 September 1895

3 No race can prosper till it learns that there is as much dignity in tilling a field as in writing a poem. — *Up from Slavery* (1901)

4 You can't hold a man down without staying down with him. — attributed

George Washington 1732–99

American soldier and statesman, 1st President of the US 1789–97

on Washington: see **Byron** 71:2, **Franklin** 142:3, 142:5, **Lee** 220:2

5 I can't tell a lie, Pa; you know I can't tell a lie. I did cut it with my hatchet. — M. L. Weems *Life of George Washington* (10th ed., 1810)

6 The time is now near at hand which must probably determine whether Americans are to be freemen or slaves; whether they are to have any property they can call their own…The fate of unborn millions will now depend, under God, on the courage and conduct of this army. Our cruel and unrelenting enemy leaves us only the choice of brave resistance, or the most abject submission. We have, therefore, to resolve to conquer or die. — general orders, 2 July 1776

7 Few men have virtue to withstand the highest bidder. — letter 17 August 1779

8 Without a decisive naval force we can do nothing definitive. And with it, everything honorable and glorious. — to Lafayette, 15 November 1781

9 There can be no greater error than to expect or calculate upon real favours from nation to nation. — *President's Address…retiring from Public Life* (17 September 1796)

10 'Tis our true policy to steer clear of permanent alliances, with any portion of the foreign world. — *President's Address…* (17 September 1796)

11 Let me…warn you in the most solemn manner against the baneful effects of the spirit of party. — *President's Address…* (17 September 1796)

12 The nation which indulges toward another an habitual hatred or an habitual fondness is in some degree a slave. It is a slave to its animosity or to its affection, either of — *President's Address…* (17 September 1796) which is sufficient to lead it astray from its duty and its interest.

1 Liberty, when it begins to take root, is a plant of rapid growth. — attributed

2 It is well, I die hard, but I am not afraid to go. — on 14 December 1799
last words

William Watson *c.*1559–1603

English Roman Catholic conspirator

3 *Fiat justitia et ruant coeli.*
Let justice be done even though the heavens fall. — *A Decacordon of Ten Quodlibeticall Questions Concerning Religion and State* (1602), being the first citation in an English work of a famous maxim; cf. **Adams** 4:6

Evelyn Waugh 1903–66

English novelist

4 *The Beast* stands for strong mutually antagonistic governments everywhere... Self-sufficiency at home, self-assertion abroad. — *Scoop* (1938)

5 Remember that the Patriots are in the right and are going to win... But they must win quickly. The British public has no interest in a war that drags on indecisively. A few sharp victories, some conspicuous acts of personal bravery on the Patriot side and a colourful entry into the capital. That is *The Beast* Policy for the war. — *Scoop* (1938)

6 Other nations use 'force'; we Britons alone use 'Might'. — *Scoop* (1938)

7 'In a democracy,' said Mr Pinfold, with more weight than originality, 'Men do not seek authority so that they may impose a policy. They seek a policy so that they may achieve authority.' — *The Ordeal of Gilbert Pinfold* (1957)

8 Is there any place that is free from evil? It is too simple to say that only the Nazis wanted war... Even good men thought that their private honour would be satisfied by war. They could assert their manhood by killing and being killed. They would accept hardship in recompense for having been selfish and lazy. Danger justified privilege. — *Unconditional Surrender* (1961)

9 Randolph Churchill went into hospital... to have a lung removed. It was announced that the trouble was not 'malignant'... it was a typical triumph of modern science to find the only part of Randolph that was not malignant and remove it. — Michael Davie (ed.) *Diaries of Evelyn Waugh* (1976) 'Irregular Notes 1960–65', March 1964

10 George VI's reign will go down in history as the most disastrous my country has known since Matilda and Stephen. — Andrew Roberts *Eminent Churchillians* (1994)

1 The trouble with the Conservative Party is that it has not turned the clock back a single second.

attributed

Beatrice Webb 1858–1943

English socialist, wife of Sidney **Webb**

2 Restless, almost intolerably so, without capacity for sustained and unexcited labour, egotistical, bumptious, shallow-minded and reactionary, but with a certain personal magnetism, great pluck and some originality, not of intellect but of character.

in 1903, of Winston **Churchill**

Martin Gilbert *In Search of Churchill* (1994)

3 I never visualised labour as separate men and women of different sorts and kinds...labour was an abstraction, which seemed to denote an arithmetically calculable mass of human beings, each individual a repetition of the other.

My Apprenticeship (1926)

Sidney Webb 1859–1947

English socialist, husband of Beatrice **Webb**

4 Once we face the necessity of putting our principles first into Bills, to be fought through committee clause by clause; and then into the appropriate machinery for carrying them into execution from one end of the kingdom to the other...the inevitability of gradualness cannot fail to be appreciated.

presidential address to the annual conference of the Labour Party, 26 June 1923

5 Nobody told us we could do this.

when the new National Government came off the Gold Standard in 1931, the outgoing Labour Government not having resorted to this tactic

Nigel Rees *Brewer's Quotations* (1994)

6 Marriage is the waste-paper basket of the emotions.

Bertrand Russell *Autobiography* (1967) vol. 1

Max Weber 1864–1920

German economist

7 The Protestant ethic and the spirit of capitalism.

Archiv für Sozialwissenschaft Sozialpolitik vol. 20 (1904–5) (title of article)

8 The State is a relation of men dominating men, a relation supported by means of legitimate (i.e. considered to be legitimate) violence.

'*Politik als Beruf*' (1919)

9 The authority of the 'eternal yesterday'.

'*Politik als Beruf*' (1919)

10 The experience of the irrationality of the world has been the driving force of all religious revolution.

'*Politik als Beruf*' (1919)

11 The concept of the 'official secret' is its [bureaucracy's] specific invention.

'*Politik als Beruf*' (1919)

1 In Baxter's view the care for external goods should only lie on the shoulders of the saint like 'a light cloak, which can be thrown aside at any moment.' But fate decreed that the cloak should become an iron cage.

Gesammelte Aufsätze zur Religionssoziologie (1920) vol. 1

Daniel Webster 1782–1852

American politician
on Webster: see **Smith** 344:8

2 The people's government, made for the people, made by the people, and answerable to the people.

second speech in the Senate on Foote's Resolution, 26 January 1830; cf. **Lincoln** 226:3

3 Liberty *and* Union, now and forever, one and inseparable!

second speech in the Senate on Foote's Resolution, 26 January 1830

4 When my eyes shall be turned to behold for the last time the sun in heaven, may I not see him shining on the broken and dishonored fragments of a once glorious Union; on States dissevered, discordant, belligerent; on a land rent with civil feuds, or drenched, it may be, in fraternal blood.

second speech in the Senate on Foote's Resolution, 26 January 1830

5 Fearful concatenation of circumstances.
argument on the murder of Captain Joseph White

speech on 6 April 1830

6 He smote the rock of the national resources, and abundant streams of revenue gushed forth. He touched the dead corpse of the Public Credit, and it sprung upon its feet.
of Alexander **Hamilton**

speech 10 March 1831

7 On this question of principle, while actual suffering was yet afar off, they [the Colonies] raised their flag against a power, to which, for purposes of foreign conquest and subjugation, Rome, in the height of her glory, is not to be compared; a power which has dotted over the surface of the whole globe with her possessions and military posts, whose morning drum-beat, following the sun, and keeping company with the hours, circles the earth with one continuous and unbroken strain of the martial airs of England.

speech in the Senate on the President's Protest, 7 May 1834

8 Whatever government is not a government of laws, is a despotism, let it be called what it may.

at a reception in Bangor, Maine, 25 August 1835

9 One country, one constitution, one destiny.

speech 15 March 1837

10 Thank God, I—I also—am an American!
speech on the completion of Bunker Hill Monument, 17 June 1843

Writings and Speeches vol. 1 (1903)

11 The Law: It has honoured us, may we honour it.

speech at the Charleston Bar Dinner, 10 May 1847

12 I was born an American; I will live an American; I shall die an American.

speech in the Senate on 'The Compromise Bill', 17 July 1850

1 There is always room at the top.
on being advised against joining the overcrowded legal profession
attributed

Josiah Wedgwood 1730–95

English potter

2 Am I not a man and a brother.
legend on Wedgwood cameo, depicting a kneeling Negro slave in chains
reproduced in facsimile in E. Darwin *The Botanic Garden* pt. 1 (1791)

Simone Weil 1909–43

French essayist and philosopher

3 I would suggest that barbarism be considered as a permanent and universal human characteristic which becomes more or less pronounced according to the play of circumstances.
Écrits Historiques et politiques (1960) 'Réflexions sur la barbarie' (written *c.*1939)

4 A right is not effectual by itself, but only in relation to the obligation to which it corresponds... An obligation which goes unrecognized by anybody loses none of the full force of its existence. A right which goes unrecognized by anybody is not worth very much.
L'Enracinement (1949) 'Les Besoins de l'âme'

5 What a country calls its vital economic interests are not the things which enable its citizens to live, but the things which enable it to make war.
W. H. Auden *A Certain World* (1971)

Stanley Weiser and Oliver Stone 1946–

6 Greed—for lack of a better word—is good. Greed is right. Greed works.
Wall Street (1987 film); cf. **Boesky** 50:4

Orson Welles 1915–85

American actor and film director

7 In Italy for thirty years under the Borgias they had warfare, terror, murder, bloodshed—they produced Michelangelo, Leonardo da Vinci and the Renaissance. In Switzerland they had brotherly love, five hundred years of democracy and peace and what did that produce...? The cuckoo clock.
The Third Man (1949 film); words added by Welles to Graham Greene's script

Duke of Wellington 1769–1852

British general and statesman; Prime Minister 1828–30
on Wellington: see **Tennyson** 359:9, 359:10, 360:2

8 As Lord Chesterfield said of the generals of his day, 'I only hope that when the enemy reads the list of their names, he trembles as I do.'
usually quoted as 'I don't know what effect these men will have upon the enemy, but, by God, they frighten me'
letter, 29 August 1810

1 Trust nothing to the enthusiasm of the people. Give them a strong and a just, and, if possible, a good, government; but, above all, a strong one.
letter to Lord William Bentinck, 24 December 1811

2 Up Guards and at them!
letter from an officer in the Guards, 22 June 1815, in *The Battle of Waterloo* by a Near Observer [J. Booth] (1815); later denied by Wellington

3 Hard pounding this, gentlemen; let's see who will pound longest.
at the Battle of Waterloo
Sir Walter Scott *Paul's Letters* (1816)

4 Publish and be damned.
replying to Harriette Wilson's blackmail threat, c.1825
attributed; Elizabeth Longford *Wellington: The Years of the Sword* (1969)

of his first Cabinet meeting as Prime Minister:
5 An extraordinary affair. I gave them their orders and they wanted to stay and discuss them.
Peter Hennessy *Whitehall* (1990)

6 I used to say of him [Napoleon] that his presence on the field made the difference of forty thousand men.
Philip Henry Stanhope *Notes of Conversations with the Duke of Wellington* (1888) 2 November 1831

7 Ours [our army] is composed of the scum of the earth—the mere scum of the earth.
Philip Henry Stanhope *Notes of Conversations with the Duke of Wellington* (1888) 4 November 1831

8 I never saw so many shocking bad hats in my life.
on seeing the first Reformed Parliament
William Fraser *Words on Wellington* (1889)

9 Nothing the people of this country like so much as to see their great men take part in their amusements. The aristocracy will commit a great error if they ever fail to mix freely with their neighbours.
on foxhunting
in 1836; Philip Henry Stanhope *Notes of Conversations with the Duke of Wellington* (1888)

10 All the business of war, and indeed all the business of life, is to endeavour to find out what you don't know by what you do; that's what I called 'guessing what was at the other side of the hill'.
in *The Croker Papers* (1885) vol. 3

11 The battle of Waterloo was won on the playing fields of Eton.
oral tradition, but not found in this form of words; C. F. R. Montalembert *De l'avenir politique de l'Angleterre* (1856); cf. **Orwell** 278:6

to a gentleman who had accosted him in the street saying, 'Mr Jones, I believe?
12 If you believe that, you'll believe anything.
George Jones RA (1786–1869), painter of military subjects, bore a striking resemblance to Wellington
Elizabeth Longford *Pillar of State* (1972)

13 I have no small talk and Peel has no manners.
G. W. E. Russell *Collections and Recollections* (1898)

1 Next to a battle lost, the greatest misery is a battle gained.

in *Diary of Frances, Lady Shelley 1787–1817* (ed. R. Edgcumbe); see S. Rogers *Recollections* (1859) for variations on the theme

2 You must build your House of Parliament upon the river... the populace cannot exact their demands by sitting down round you.

William Fraser *Words on Wellington* (1889)

H. G. Wells 1866–1946

English novelist

3 The Social Contract is nothing more or less than a vast conspiracy of human beings to lie to and humbug themselves and one another for the general Good. Lies are the mortar that bind the savage individual man into the social masonry.

Love and Mr Lewisham (1900)

4 The war that will end war.

title of book (1914)

5 In England we have come to rely upon a comfortable time-lag of fifty years or a century intervening between the perception that something ought to be done and a serious attempt to do it.

The Work, Wealth and Happiness of Mankind (1931)

of Lord **Beaverbrook**:

6 If Max gets to Heaven he won't last long. He will be chucked out for trying to pull off a merger between Heaven and Hell... after having secured a controlling interest in key subsidiary companies in both places, of course.

A. J. P. Taylor *Beaverbrook* (1972)

Rebecca West 1892–1983

writer, journalist, and literary critic

7 It was in dealing with the early feminist that the Government acquired the tact and skilfulness with which it is now handling Ireland.

in 1916; *The Young Rebecca* (1982)

8 Whatever happens, never forget that people would rather be led to *perdition* by a man, than to *victory* by a woman.

in conversation in 1979, just before Margaret **Thatcher***'s first election victory*

in *Sunday Telegraph* 17 January 1988

9 Having watched the form of our traitors for a number of years, I cannot think that espionage can be recommended as a technique for building an impressive civilization. It's a lout's game.

The Meaning of Treason (1982 ed.)

John Fane, Lord Westmorland 1759–1841

English nobleman

10 *Merit*, indeed!... We are come to a pretty pass if they talk of *merit* for a bishopric.

noted in Lady Salisbury's diary, 9 December 1835

Charles Wetherell 1770–1846

English lawyer and politician

1 Then there is my noble and biographical friend who has added a new terror to death.
of Lord Campbell

Lord St Leonards *Misrepresentations in Campbell's Lives of Lyndhurst and Brougham* (1869); also attributed to Lord Lyndhurst

Grover A. Whalen 1886–1962

2 There's a lot of law at the end of a nightstick.

Quentin Reynolds *Courtroom* (1950)

Thomas, Lord Wharton 1648–1715

English Whig politician

3 Ara! but why does King James stay behind?
Lilli burlero bullen a la
Ho! by my shoul 'tis a Protestant wind
Lilli burlero bullen a la.
a Williamite song in mockery of Richard Talbot, newly created Earl of Tyrconnell by the Catholic James II in Dublin in 1688; the refrain parodies the Irish language

'A New Song' (written 1687); Thomas Kinsella *The New Oxford Book of Irish Verse* (1986); attribution to Wharton has been disputed

4 I sang a king out of three kingdoms.
said to have been Wharton's boast after 'A New Song' became a propaganda weapon against James II

in *Dictionary of National Biography*

Robert Whinney

Captain in the British Navy

5 As a captain in command he was consistently unfortunate, with one glorious defeat after another.
on **Mountbatten***'s wartime naval career*

Andrew Roberts *Eminent Churchillians* (1994)

E. B. White 1899–1985

American humorist

6 Democracy is the recurrent suspicion that more than half of the people are right more than half of the time.

in *New Yorker* 3 July 1944

7 The so-called science of poll-taking is not a science at all but a mere necromancy. People are unpredictable by nature, and although you can take a nation's pulse, you can't be sure that the nation hasn't just run up a flight of stairs.

in *New Yorker* 13 November 1948

Theodore H. White

American author and journalist

1 Johnson's instinct for power is as primordial as a salmon's going upstream to spawn.
of Lyndon **Johnson**
The Making of the President (1964)

2 The flood of money that gushes into politics today is a pollution of democracy.
in *Time* 19 November 1984

William Allen White 1868–1944

American journalist and editor

3 Tinhorn politicians.
in *Emporia Gazette* 25 October 1901

4 Liberty is the only thing you cannot have unless you are willing to give it to others.
attributed

William Whitelaw 1918–

British Conservative politician
on Whitelaw: see **Thatcher** 362:12

5 It is never wise to appear to be more clever than you are. It is sometimes wise to appear slightly less so.
attributed, 1975

6 The Labour Party is going around stirring up apathy.
recalled by Alan Watkins as a characteristic 'Willieism'
in *Observer* 1 May 1983

Gough Whitlam 1916–

Australian Labor politician, Prime Minister 1972–5

the Governor-General, Sir John Kerr, had dismissed the Labor government headed by Gough Whitlam in November 1975:

7 Well may he say 'God Save the Queen'. But after this nothing will save the Governor-General... Maintain your rage and your enthusiasm through the campaign for the election now to be held and until polling day.
speech in Canberra, 11 November 1975

Walt Whitman 1819–92

American poet

8 The United States themselves are essentially the greatest poem.
Leaves of Grass (1855) preface

9 O Captain! my Captain! our fearful trip is done,
The ship has weathered every rack, the prize we sought is won,
The port is near, the bells I hear, the people all exulting.
allegorical poem on the death of Abraham **Lincoln**
'O Captain! My Captain!' (1871)

10 The ship is anchored safe and sound, its voyage closed and done.
From fearful trip the victor ship comes in with object won;
'O Captain! My Captain!' (1871)

Exult O shores, and ring O bells! But I with mournful tread
Walk the deck my Captain lies, Fallen cold and dead.

1 This dust was once the man,
Gentle, plain, just and resolute, under whose cautious hand,
Against the foulest crime in history known in any land or age,
Was saved the Union of these States.

'This dust was once the man' (1881)

2 Where the populace rise at once against the never-ending audacity of elected persons.

'Song of the Broad Axe' (1881)

3 Where the city of the healthiest fathers stands,
Where the city of the best-bodied mothers stands,
There the great city stands.

'Song of the Broad Axe' (1881)

4 Strange, (is it not?) that battles, martyrs, blood, even assassination, should so condense—perhaps only really, lastingly condense—a Nationality.

of the American Civil War

Geoffrey C. Ward *The Civil War* (1991)

John Greenleaf Whittier 1807–92

American poet

5 'Shoot, if you must, this old grey head,
But spare your country's flag,' she said.
A shade of sadness, a blush of shame,
Over the face of the leader came.

'Barbara Frietchie' (1863)

Robert Whittington

6 As time requireth, a man of marvellous mirth and pastimes, and sometime of as sad gravity, as who say: a man for all seasons.

of Thomas **More**

in *Vulgaria* (1521) pt. 2; Erasmus famously applied the idea to More, writing in his prefatory letter to *In Praise of Folly* (1509) that he played *'omnium horarum hominem* [a man of all hours]'

Oscar Wilde 1854–1900

Anglo-Irish playwright and poet

7 We have really everything in common with America nowadays except, of course, language.

The Canterville Ghost (1887); cf. **Shaw** 337:3

8 If the country doesn't go to the dogs or the Radicals, we shall have you Prime Minister, some day.

An Ideal Husband (1895)

Wilhelm II 1859–1941

German Emperor and King of Prussia, 1888–1918

9 We have…fought for our place in the sun and have won it. It will be my business to see that we retain this place in the sun unchallenged, so that the rays of that sun

speech in Hamburg, 18 June 1901; cf. **Bülow** 61:7

may exert a fructifying influence upon our foreign trade and traffic.

John Wilkes 1727–97

English parliamentary reformer

1 EARL OF SANDWICH: 'Pon my soul, Wilkes, I don't know whether you'll die upon the gallows or of the pox.
WILKES: That depends, my Lord, whether I first embrace your Lordship's principles, or your Lordship's mistresses.

Charles Petrie *The Four Georges* (1935); probably apocryphal

2 Give me a grain of truth and I will mix it up with a great mass of falsehood so that no chemist will ever be able to separate them.

Adrian Hamilton *The Infamous Essay on Women, or John Wilkes seated between Vice and Virtue* (1972)

William III 1650–1702

Stadtholder of the Netherlands from 1672; King of Great Britain and Ireland from 1688

3 'Do you not see your country is lost?' asked the Duke of Buckingham. 'There is one way never to see it lost' replied William, 'and that is to die in the last ditch.'

Bishop Gilbert Burnet *History of My Own Time* (1838 ed.)

4 Every bullet has its billet.

John Wesley *Journal* (1827) 6 June 1765

Wendell Willkie 1892–1944

American lawyer and politician

5 Freedom is an indivisible word. If we want to enjoy it, and fight for it, we must be prepared to extend it to everyone, whether they are rich or poor, whether they agree with us or not, no matter what their race or the colour of their skin.

One World (1943)

6 The constitution does not provide for first and second class citizens.

An American Programme (1944)

Charles E. Wilson 1890–1961

American industrialist
see also **Anonymous** 9:2

7 For years I thought what was good for our country was good for General Motors and vice versa. The difference did not exist. Our company is too big. It goes with the welfare of the country.

testimony to the Senate Armed Services Committee on his proposed nomination to be Secretary of Defence, 15 January 1953

Harold Wilson 1916–95

British Labour statesman, Prime Minister 1964–70 and 1974–6

on Wilson: see **Benn** 36:6, **Birch** 46:1, **Bulmer-Thomas** 61:6, **Home** 182:3, **Junor** 201:4

1 All these financiers, all the little gnomes in Zurich and the other financial centres about whom we keep on hearing.

in the House of Commons, 12 November 1956

2 I myself have always deprecated . . . in crisis after crisis, appeals to the Dunkirk spirit as an answer to our problems.

in the House of Commons, 26 July 1961; cf. **Wilson** 390:9

3 This party is a moral crusade or it is nothing.

speech at the Labour Party Conference, 1 October 1962

4 If I had the choice between smoked salmon and tinned salmon I'd have it tinned. With vinegar.

in *Observer* 11 November 1962

5 We are restating our socialism in terms of the scientific revolution . . . the Britain that is going to be forged in the white heat of this revolution will be no place for restrictive practices or outdated methods on either side of industry.

usually quoted as, 'the white heat of the technological revolution'

speech at the Labour Party Conference, 1 October 1963

6 What I think we are going to need is something like what President Kennedy had when he came in after years of stagnation in the United States. He had a programme of a hundred days—a hundred days of dynamic action.

in a party political broadcast, 15 July 1964

7 The Smethwick Conservatives can have the satisfaction of having topped the poll, and of having sent here as their Member one who, until a further General Election restores him to oblivion, will serve his term here as a Parliamentary leper.

on the outcome of a by-election with racist overtones

in the House of Commons, 3 November 1964

8 A week is a long time in politics.

probably first said at a lobby briefing at the time of the 1964 sterling crisis

Nigel Rees *Sayings of the Century* (1984); cf. **Chamberlain** 80:1

9 I believe that the spirit of Dunkirk will carry us through . . . to success.

speech to the Labour Party Conference, 12 December 1964; cf. **Wilson** 390:2

10 [Labour is] the natural party of government.

in 1965; Anthony Sampson *The Changing Anatomy of Britain*

11 On the expert advice available to me the cumulative effects of the economic and financial sanctions might well bring the rebellion to an end within a matter of weeks rather than months.

on Rhodesia's Unilateral Declaration of Independence

at the Lagos Conference, final communiqué, 12 January 1966

12 From now the pound abroad is worth 14 per cent or so less in terms of other currencies. It does not mean, of

ministerial broadcast, 19 November 1967

course, that the pound here in Britain, in your pocket or purse or in your bank, has been devalued.

1 Get your tanks off my lawn, Hughie.
to the trade union leader Hugh Scanlon, at Chequers in June 1969
Peter Jenkins *The Battle of Downing Street* (1970)

2 I know what is going on. I am going on.
at the Labour Party Conference, commenting on rumours of conspiracies against his leadership
attributed, 1969

3 One man's wage increase is another man's price increase.
speech at Blackburn, 8 January 1970

4 If one buys land on which there is a slag heap 120 ft. high and it costs £100,000 to remove that slag, that is not land speculation in the sense that we condemn it. It is land reclamation.
in the House of Commons, 4 April 1974

5 This party is a bit like an old stagecoach. If you drive along at a rapid rate, everyone aboard is either so exhilarated or so seasick that you don't have a lot of difficulty.
of the Labour Party
Anthony Sampson *The Changing Anatomy of Britain* (1982)

6 Whichever party is in office, the Treasury is in power.
while in opposition
Anthony Sampson *The Changing Anatomy of Britain* (1982)

7 The Monarchy is a labour-intensive industry.
in *Observer* 13 February 1977

of Tony **Benn**:

8 He immatures with age.
in 1981; Anthony Sampson *The Changing Anatomy of Britain* (1982)

9 The one thing we need to nationalize in this country is the Treasury, but no one has ever succeeded.
in 1984; Peter Hennessy *Whitehall* (1990)

Henry Wilson 1864–1922

British soldier, Churchill's principal military adviser 1919–21

10 He has many good qualities, some of which lie hidden, and he has many bad ones, all of which are in the shop window.
of Winston **Churchill**, *in a letter to a senior military colleague*
Martin Gilbert *In Search of Churchill* (1994)

Woodrow Wilson 1856–1924

American Democratic statesman, 28th President of the US 1913–21
on Wilson: see **Clemenceau** 98:5, **Keynes** 207:4, **Kissinger** 214:12

11 Liberty has never come from the government. Liberty has always come from the subjects of government. The history of liberty is the history of resistance. The history of liberty is a history of the limitation of governmental power, not the increase of it.
speech to the New York Press Club, 9 September 1912

1 The United States must be neutral in fact as well as in name. — message to the Senate, 19 August 1914
at the outbreak of the First World War

2 It is like writing history with lightning. And my only regret is that it is all so terribly true. — at the White House, 18 February 1915
on seeing D. W. Griffith's film The Birth of a Nation

3 No nation is fit to sit in judgement upon any other nation. — speech in New York, 20 April 1915

4 There is such a thing as a man being too proud to fight; there is such a thing as a nation being so right that it does not need to convince others by force that it is right. — speech in Philadelphia, 10 May 1915

5 We have stood apart, studiously neutral. — speech to Congress, 7 December 1915

6 [It] created in this country what had never existed before—a national consciousness. It was not the salvation of the Union; it was the rebirth of the Union. — Memorial Day address 1915
of the Civil War

7 America can not be an ostrich with its head in the sand. — speech at Des Moines, 1 February 1916

8 It must be a peace without victory... Only a peace between equals can last. — speech to US Senate, 22 January 1917

9 A little group of wilful men representing no opinion but their own, have rendered the Great Government of the United States helpless and contemptible. — in *New York Times* 5 March 1917
statement, 4 March 1917, after a successful filibuster against his bill to arm American merchant ships

10 Armed neutrality is ineffectual enough at best. — speech to Congress, 2 April 1917

11 The day has come when America is privileged to spend her blood and her might for the principles that gave her birth and happiness and the peace which she has treasured. — speech to Congress, 2 April 1917

12 The world must be made safe for democracy. — speech to Congress, 2 April 1917

13 The right is more precious than peace. — speech to Congress, 2 April 1917

14 Once lead this people into war and they will forget there ever was such a thing as tolerance. — John Dos Passos *Mr Wilson's War* (1917)

15 The programme of the world's peace... is this:
1. Open covenants of peace, openly arrived at. — speech to Congress, 8 January 1918

16 A general association of nations must be formed... for the purpose of affording mutual guarantees of political independence and territorial integrity to great and small states alike. — speech to Congress, 8 January 1918

17 America is the only idealistic nation in the world. — speech at Sioux Falls, South Dakota, 8 September 1919

18 If I am to speak for ten minutes, I need a week for preparation; if fifteen minutes, three days; if half an hour, two days; if an hour, I am ready now. — Josephus Daniels *The Wilson Era* (1946)

William Windham 1750–1810

English politician

1 Those entrusted with arms...should be persons of some substance and stake in the country.

in the House of Commons, 22 July 1807

John Winthrop 1588–1649

American settler

2 We must consider that we shall be a city upon a hill, the eyes of all people are on us; so that if we shall deal falsely with our God in this work we have undertaken, and so cause Him to withdraw His present help from us, we shall be made a story and a byword through the world.

Christian Charity, A Model Hereof (sermon, 1630)

Robert Charles Winthrop 1809–94

3 A Star for every State, and a State for every Star.

speech on Boston Common, 27 August 1862

Humbert Wolfe 1886–1940

British poet

4 You cannot hope
to bribe or twist,
thank God! the
British journalist.
But, seeing what
the man will do
unbribed, there's
no occasion to.

'Over the Fire' (1930)

James Wolfe 1727–59

British general; captor of Quebec

5 The General...repeated nearly the whole of Gray's Elegy...adding, as he concluded, that he would prefer being the author of that poem to the glory of beating the French to-morrow.

J. Playfair *Biographical Account of J. Robinson* in *Transactions of the Royal Society of Edinburgh* vol. 7 (1815)

Thomas Wolfe 1900–38

American novelist

6 'Where they got you stationed now, Luke?' said Harry Tugman peering up snoutily from a mug of coffee. 'At the p-p-p-present time in Norfolk at the Navy base,' Luke answered, 'm-m-making the world safe for hypocrisy.'

Look Homeward, Angel (1929); cf. **Wilson** 392:12

Tom Wolfe 1931–

American writer

1 A cult is a religion with no political power. — *In Our Time* (1980)

Thomas Wolsey c.1475–1530

English cardinal; Lord Chancellor, 1515–29

2 Father Abbot, I am come to lay my bones amongst you. — George Cavendish *Negotiations of Thomas Wolsey* (1641)

3 Had I but served God as diligently as I have served the King, he would not have given me over in my grey hairs. — George Cavendish *Negotiations of Thomas Wolsey* (1641)

Alexander Woollcott 1887–1943

American writer

4 I think your slogan 'Liberty or Death' is splendid, and whichever one you decide on will be all right with me. — attributed

William Wordsworth 1770–1850

English poet

5 In our halls is hung
Armoury of the invincible Knights of old:
We must be free or die, who speak the tongue
That Shakespeare spake; the faith and morals hold
Which Milton held. In every thing we are sprung
Of Earth's first blood, have titles manifold.

'It is not to be thought of that the Flood' (1807)

6 Once did she hold the gorgeous East in fee,
And was the safeguard of the West.

'On the Extinction of the Venetian Republic' (1807)

7 Bliss was it in that dawn to be alive,
But to be young was very heaven!

'The French Revolution, as it Appeared to Enthusiasts' (1809); also *The Prelude* (1850)

Henry Wotton 1568–1639

English poet and diplomat

8 Dazzled thus with height of place,
Whilst our hopes our wits beguile,
No man marks the narrow space
'Twixt a prison and a smile.

'Upon the sudden restraint of the Earl of Somerset' (1651)

9 An ambassador is an honest man sent to lie abroad for the good of his country. — written in the album of Christopher Fleckmore in 1604

Neville Wran 1926–

Australian politician

10 The average footslogger in the New South Wales Right... generally speaking carries a dagger in one hand and — in 1973; Michael Gordon *A Question of Leadership* (1993)

a Bible in the other and doesn't put either to really elegant use.

John Wycliff *c.*1330–82

English religious reformer

1 The Bible is for the government of the people, by the people, and for the people.

general prologue to the Wycliff translation of the Bible, 1384

Augustin, Marquis de Ximénèz
1726–1817

French poet

2 Let us attack in her own waters perfidious Albion!

'L'Ère des Français' (October 1793)

William Yancey 1814–63

American Confederate politician

of Jefferson **Davis**, *President-elect of the Confederacy, in 1861:*

3 The man and the hour have met.

Shelby Foote *The Civil War: Fort Sumter to Perryville* (1991)

W. B. Yeats 1865–1939

Irish poet; senator of the Irish Free State 1922–8

4 Romantic Ireland's dead and gone,
It's with O'Leary in the grave.

'September, 1913' (1914)

5 I think it better that at times like these
We poets keep our mouths shut, for in truth
We have no gift to set a statesman right.

'A Reason for Keeping Silent' (1916)

6 Turning and turning in the widening gyre
The falcon cannot hear the falconer;
Things fall apart; the centre cannot hold;
Mere anarchy is loosed upon the world,
The blood-dimmed tide is loosed, and everywhere
The ceremony of innocence is drowned;
The best lack all conviction, while the worst
Are full of passionate intensity.

'The Second Coming' (1920)

7 Too long a sacrifice
Can make a stone of the heart.
O when may it suffice?

'Easter, 1916' (1921)

8 I write it out in a verse—
MacDonagh and MacBride
And Connolly and Pearse
Now and in time to be,
Wherever green is worn,
Are changed, changed utterly:
A terrible beauty is born.

'Easter, 1916' (1921)

of the Anglo-Irish:

1 We... are no petty people. We are one of the great stocks of Europe. We are the people of Burke; we are the people of Swift, the people of Emmet, the people of Parnell. We have created most of the modern literature of this country. We have created the best of its political intelligence.
speech in the Irish Senate, 11 June 1925, in the debate on divorce

2 Out of Ireland have we come.
Great hatred, little room,
Maimed us at the start.
I carry from my mother's womb
A fanatic heart.
'Remorse for Intemperate Speech' (1933)

3 Cast your mind on other days
That we in coming days may be
Still the indomitable Irishry.
'Under Ben Bulben' (1939)

Boris Yeltsin 1931–

Russian statesman, President of the Russian Federation from 1990

4 Today is the last day of an era past.
at a Berlin ceremony to end the Soviet military presence in Germany
in *Guardian* 1 September 1994

5 Europe is in danger of plunging into a cold peace.
at the summit meeting of the Conference on Security and Co-operation in Europe, December 1994
in *Newsweek* 19 December 1994

Andrew Young 1932–

American Democratic politician and minister

6 Nothing is illegal if one hundred well-placed business men decide to do it.
Morris K. Udall *Too Funny to be President* (1988)

Michael Young 1915–

British writer

7 Today we frankly recognize that democracy can be no more than aspiration, and have rule not so much by the people as by the cleverest people; not an aristocracy of birth, not a plutocracy of wealth, but a true meritocracy of talent.
The Rise of the Meritocracy (1958)

Israel Zangwill 1864–1926

British author and philanthropist, son of a Russian refugee

8 America is God's Crucible, the great Melting-Pot where all the races of Europe are melting and re-forming!
The Melting Pot (1908)

Emiliano Zapata 1879–1919

Mexican revolutionary

1 Many of them, so as to curry favour with tyrants, for a fistful of coins, or through bribery or corruption, are shedding the blood of their brothers.

on the maderistas *who, in Zapata's view, had betrayed the revolutionary cause*

Plan de Ayala 28 November 1911

Philip Ziegler 1929–

British historian

2 Remember. In Spite of Everything, He Was A Great Man.

notice kept on his desk while working on his biography of **Mountbatten** *(published 1985)*

Andrew Roberts *Eminent Churchillians* (1994)

Ronald L. Ziegler 1939–

American government spokesman

reminded of the President's previous statements that the White House was not involved in the Watergate affair:

3 [Mr Nixon's latest statement] is the Operative White House Position . . . and all previous statements are inoperative.

in *Boston Globe* 18 April 1973

Grigori Zinoviev 1883–1936

Soviet politician

4 Armed warfare must be preceded by a struggle against the inclinations to compromise which are embedded among the majority of British workmen, against the ideas of evolution and peaceful extermination of capitalism. Only then will it be possible to count upon complete success of an armed insurrection.

letter to the British Communist Party, 15 September 1924, in *The Times* 25 October 1924 (the 'Zinoviev Letter', said by some to be a forgery)

Émile Zola 1840–1902

French novelist

5 *J'accuse.*

I accuse.

title of an open letter to the President of the French Republic, in connection with the Dreyfus affair

in *L'Aurore* 13 January 1898

Keyword Index

abilities according to his a. MARX 252:9
uncommon a. BAG 23:14
ability a. among the governed TOCQ 366:1
abode English make it their a. WALL 377:2
abolish a. the cult of the individual KHR 209:2
abolished state is not 'a.' ENG 133:6
aborigines then upon the a. EVAR 134:3
abortion everybody who is for a. REAG 301:9
abroad angel of death has been a. BRIG 56:4
honest man sent to lie a. WOTT 394:9
resolved to go a. no more CHAR 83:4
Thy spirit walks a. SHAK 330:15
When I am a. I always CHUR 93:2
absence could shoot me in my a. BEHAN 34:10
in a fit of a. of mind SEEL 322:6
presence and another by its a. RUSS 317:3
absentee a. aristocracy DISR 117:13
absolute a. power corrupts ACTON 1:9
house of Commons is a. DISR 117:2
absolutes a. in our Bill of Rights BLACK 48:3
absolutism a. moderated by assassination ANON 9:12
abstract A. liberty BURKE 63:9
abuse has power is led to a. it MONT 264:9
more dangerous the a. BURKE 63:7
portmanteau word of a. TEBB 359:3
prevention of a. in the exercise PEEL 287:9
abused so much a. as this sentence SELD 323:3
uncomfortable when being a. BALF 31:4
abuses attended with considerable a. BURKE 64:14
conceal its own a. CLAY 97:7
Whatever you do, stamp out a. VOLT 375:13
abyss to the edge of the a. STEV 350:10
accent hearing an 'educated' a. ORW 277:10
accents a. yet unknown SHAK 329:6
accept I will not a. if nominated SHER 339:4
acceptable a. to all nations TRUM 371:4
accepted comfortable and the a. GALB 145:8
access few who have a. MAC 238:15
accident by the a. of death CHES 84:3
according a. to his abilities MARX 252:9
account to call to a. GLAD 154:4
accountable a. shambles HUNT 185:7
To whom are you a. BENN 36:11
accumulated a. wrong CAS 78:2
accumulation a. of all powers MAD 246:5
accuracy some degree of a. JOHN 197:5
accuse a. himself of courage BIRCH 46:1
J'a. ZOLA 397:5
accused or apology before you be a. CHAR 82:2
ace turn out the a. of trumps CHUR 86:8
achieve Together we shall a. victory EIS 129:3
achievements How my a. mock me SHAK 335:11
Achitophel false A. was first DRYD 125:4
acknowledgement a. of inferiority CALH 72:4
acquiesce a. with silence JOHN 197:2
If we accept and a. BETH 39:9
acquired way in which she a. it HARL 169:3
acquiring a. their institutions HAIL 163:12
acquisition aiding in the a. TORR 367:4
acre a. in Middlesex is better MAC 237:11
acres Three a. and a cow ANON 14:1
act a. against the Constitution OTIS 280:1
a. only according to that maxim KANT 202:2
easier to a. than to think AREN 15:11
fun in any A. of Parliament HERB 176:11
six horses through the a. RICE 304:6
That does both a. and know MARV 251:8
to a. with decision PEEL 288:16
acted our lofty scene be a. o'er SHAK 329:6
action hundred days of dynamic a. WILS 390:6
In a. faithful POPE 295:3
interfering with the liberty of a. MILL 258:8
responsibility for a. GALB 145:5
single moral a. of a single man GLAD 156:3
thought, as preliminary to a. HALD 164:2
thought is the child of a. DISR 116:4
actions my a. are my ministers' CHAR 83:1
active be a. but to seem active LAW 218:6
activist a. is the guy who cleans PEROT 290:8
activity ministers need a. LYNN 235:3
acts manly examination of the a. HARR 170:1
ad I'm reminded of that a. MOND 262:1
adamant a. for drift CHUR 89:7
added a. to his dignity CHUR 94:13
addiction prisoners of a. ILL 187:4
adjectives qualifying a. LODGE 231:10
administered best a. is best POPE 295:4
administration affairs of this a. LINC 226:8
criticism of a. as much a part BAG 24:14
In public a. good sense GALB 146:6
said of my first A. ROOS 309:2
admiral kill an a. from time to time VOLT 375:10
admiralty If blood be the price of a. KIPL 212:10
admired more a. CALL 73:2
admirer enthusiastic a. of mine MAC 236:8
admiring a. the House of Lords BAG 26:4
admit A. lords, and you admit all SHAF 324:3
adolescence petrified a. BEVAN 40:12

adultery committed a. in my heart CART 77:7
advance retrograde if it does not a. GIBB 151:13
advancement a. in this man's party HILL 178:7
quality useful for political a. LEVIN 222:10
advantage undertaking of Great a. ANON 9:8
adventurer a. pure and simple FOOT 138:6
greatest a. of modern political BUTL 70:2
adversary No, sir! I am his a. GLAS 156:4
adverse a. to the rights MAD 246:3
advertise a. food to hungry GALB 145:4
advertisement no a. for a prosperous HES 178:2
advertiser professional a. POW 296:8
advertisers a. don't object to SWAF 353:3
advice Get the a. of everybody PARN 286:9
given my a. to my countrymen O'CON 276:6
advise Advisers a. THAT 362:5
advisers A. advise THAT 362:5
advocate with the intellect of an a. BAG 24:5
advocates potent a. of peace GEOR 149:6
affairs beginning in human a. PRICE 298:3
phrase 'foreign a.' DISR 120:1
tide in the a. of men SHAK 330:14
Whoever knows the interior of a. WALP 377:7
affections a. must be confined GALB 146:3
affluent a. society GALB 145:6
afraid I am not a. to go WASH 380:2
afresh begins the world a. MONN 262:10
Africa something new out of A. PLINY 294:5
white man in A. LESS 222:1
African A. is conditioned KENY 206:6
[A.] national consciousness MACM 245:1
again to begin the world over a. PAINE 281:8
against a. everything all the time KENN 206:3
He was a. it COOL 103:5
met anyone who wasn't a. war LOW 233:5
most people vote a. ADAMS 2:6
not with me is a. me BIBLE 44:6
age a. fatal to Revolutionists DESM 114:4
a. going to the workhouse PAINE 283:1
a. of chivalry is gone BURKE 66:16
complain of the a. we live in BURKE 62:10
every a. had consisted of crises ATK 19:5
He immatures with a. WILS 391:8
not the a. of pamphleteers HOGB 181:1
old a. is the most unexpected TROT 370:13
agenda on any item of the a. PARK 285:10
agents a. of a prince regard SMITH 343:2
our Civil and Political a. VICT 374:7
ages nations, and the next a. BACON 23:10
Now he belongs to the a. STAN 348:9
aggression a. abroad CHUR 87:3
It is naked a. POW 297:13
aggressions Whensoever hostile a. JEFF 192:11
aggressors defeat the US a. MAO 250:7
agitation rather than to excite a. PALM 284:5
agonizing a. reappraisal DULL 126:8
agony a. is abated MAC 236:1
That a. is over CHES 83:9
agree a., he was a statesman LLOY 230:6
a. in the dark BACON 23:6
appear to a. PAINE 283:3
agreeable a. to their temper BURKE 62:6
agreement a. between two men CECIL 79:5
a. with hell GARR 148:4
blow with an a. TROT 370:10
ahead a. of your time MCG 240:9
aid foreign a. NIXON 274:15
Aids stop them catching A. CURR 107:7
aim forgotten your a. SANT 320:3
air out in healthy fresh a. GALB 146:8
to the Germans that of—the a. RICH 305:3
Alamein Before A. we never had CHUR 93:10
Albert to take a message to A. DISR 122:2
alcohol A. didn't cause BOAZ 50:1
a. has taken out of me CHUR 94:12
alderman little less like an a. LAW 219:1
aldermen divides the wives of a. SMITH 341:2
alien quick to blame the a. AESC 6:3
aliens a. to this kingdom GEOR 149:4
alimentary a. canal REAG 301:5
alive if I am a. I shall be HOLL 181:5
in that dawn to be a. WORD 394:7
Not while I'm a. 'e ain't BEVIN 43:3
all A. the way with LBJ ANON 8:6
fair shares for a., is Labour's call JAY 190:5
man for a. seasons WHIT 388:6
presuppose that a. men are evil MACH 241:10
allegiance I pledge a. to the flag BELL 34:11
mystic reverence, the religious a. BAG 24:9
pledged a. to you BALD 28:6
alliance how little the word 'a.' MONN 262:8
rumours of a morganatic a. HARD 168:4
alliances entangling a. with none JEFF 192:7
steer clear of permanent a. WASH 379:10
allies no a. to be polite to GEOR 150:4
no eternal a. PALM 284:1
allons *a., enfants de la patrie* ROUG 314:3
almighty A. has placed it there LAB 216:1
Even the a. took seven CHUR 92:4
alone And bear the palm a. SHAK 328:3
plough my furrow a. ROS 312:12
right to be let a. BRAN 55:2
they would but let it a. WALP 377:5
we cannot live a. ROOS 310:6
When he is a. in the room KEYN 208:8
along If you want to get a. RAYB 301:4
altar lays upon the a. SPR 348:1
altars threw our a. to the ground JORD 199:5
alteration A. though it be from HOOK 182:6
alterations a. on the map of Europe CHUR 87:6
alternative there is no real a. THAT 361:1
What is the a. TREND 367:7

armed A. neutrality WILS 392:10
A. warfare must be preceded by ZIN 397:4
armes *Aux a., citoyens* ROUG 314:3
armies commander of the American a. FRAN 142:5
greatly interested in a. AUDEN 21:5
standing a. of power RADC 299:5
stronger than all the a. ANON 13:8
Arminian A. clergy PITT 293:1
armistice a. for twenty years FOCH 138:2
armour a. of a righteous cause BRYAN 60:4
armoury a. of the invincible WORD 394:5
arms a. control means some kind SCHR 321:9
a. ye forge, another bears SHEL 338:4
but it hath very long a. HAL 166:2
corners of the world in a. SHAK 331:1
Those entrusted with a. WIND 393:1
to keep and bear a. ANON 14:11
took up a. with more right LUCAN 234:3
youth of a state a. do flourish BACON 23:7
army a. marches on its stomach NAP 269:11
a. would be a base rabble BURKE 64:6
contemptible little a. ANON 10:1
Grand a. never looked MAHAN 247:6
made against invasion by an a. HUGO 184:5
[our a.] is composed of the scum WELL 384:7
Your poor a. CROM 105:12
arrest police are those who a. you HARR 169:6
arse politician is an a. upon CUMM 107:2
arsenal great a. of democracy ROOS 309:10
art a. establishes the basic KENN 205:8
a. of government consists VOLT 376:1
a. of leadership is saying no BLAIR 48:12
a. o'th' court SHAK 325:3
great a. of government is to work PEEL 289:4
Here the great a. lies MILT 260:7
In free society a. is not a weapon KENN 205:9
minister that meddles with a. MELB 255:9
no a. which one government SMITH 342:2
politics is the a. of acquiring GAND 147:2
politics is the a. of preventing VAL 373:1
politics is the a. of the possible BISM 46:6
politics not the a. of the possible GALB 145:12
triumph of the embalmer's a. VIDAL 375:2
article non-violence is the first a. GAND 147:3
artificial a. man HOBB 179:9
artists a. are not engineers KENN 205:9
arts France, mother of a. DU B 126:4
No a.; no letters HOBB 180:2
Of all vulgar a. of government PEEL 288:14
ascendancy a. of the Whig party MAC 238:4
ascent a. to greatness GIBB 151:5
ascertainable a. facts PEEL 289:9
ashes Scatter my a. GRAH 159:2
Asian A. boys ought to be doing JOHN 196:4
ask a. not what your country KENN 204:7
but what I intend to a. of them KENN 203:9
could he see you now, a. why AUDEN 21:6
They will a., what is the road BURKE 65:8
askance looking a. GOGOL 156:8
asleep human beings are a. RUSK 315:2
aspirant political a. MENC 256:12
aspiration no more than a. YOUNG 396:7
ass kiss my a. JOHN 196:8
assassination absolutism moderated by a. ANON 9:12
A. has never changed DISR 119:11
A. is the extreme form SHAW 336:15
battles, martyrs, blood, even a. WHIT 388:4
commit suicide to avoid a. TRUM 371:6
assent rash and precipitate a. PEEL 288:4
asserted whatever is boldly a. BURR 69:1
associate good must a. BURKE 63:4
association general a. of nations WILS 392:17
assurance a. of a sleepwalker HITL 179:5
astonished a. at my own moderation CLIVE 99:9
asylum lunatic a. run by lunatics LLOY 230:5
No one outside an a. wishes ROS 312:11
statesman was in an a. PALM 284:7
ate Jefferson a. alone KENN 205:1
With A. by his side SHAK 329:9
atheist town drunkard, a town a. BROG 57:6
Athenians A. will kill thee PHOC 292:5
Athens A. arose SHEL 338:8
what Pericles felt of A. KEYN 207:3
who are a citizen of A. SOCR 345:7
Atlanta A. is gone CHES 83:9
atom a. bomb is a paper tiger MAO 250:5
best defence against the a. bomb ANON 8:11
grasped the mystery of the a. BRAD 54:4
no evil in the a. STEV 350:5
atomic black portent of a new a. age BAR 32:4
release of a. energy constitutes TRUM 371:3
way to win an a. war BRAD 54:3
atoms concurrence of a. PALM 284:3
atrocities No number of a. NAM 269:1
atrophied a. Englishmen JOHN 196:13
attainable We look at the a. GLAD 155:3
attempt a. a measure of authority BURKE 62:9
attention a. of the nation BAG 25:9
attentive a. and favourable hearers HOOK 182:5
Attlee A. reminds me of ORW 278:8
door was opened A. got out CHUR 94:9
attribution a. of false motive BALD 29:11
audace *toujours de l'a.* DANT 109:6
audacity a. of elected persons WHIT 388:2
audible spritely, waking, a. SHAK 324:11
audience large a. TROL 369:10
August For one A. in its history TUCH 372:6
Austen have to resort to Jane A. MACM 245:10
Australia take A. right back KEAT 202:7
author a. who speaks about DISR 120:3
authority attempt a measure of a. BURKE 62:9
A. doesn't work without DE G 112:1

authority (*cont.*):
A. forgets a dying king TENN 360:4
a. of a King is STR 352:3
a. of the 'eternal yesterday' WEBER 381:9
drest in a little brief a. SHAK 332:9
English people is to resist a. BAG 27:3
independence of his a. MILL 259:10
no a. from God to do mischief MAYH 254:7
royal a. is a great spring MONT 264:14
so that they may achieve a. WAUGH 380:7
terror instituted by 'lawful a.' MACD 240:4
authors We a., Ma'am DISR 119:15
autocracy Russian a. turned HERZ 177:7
autocrat a.: that's my trade CATH 78:4
autres *pour encourager les a.* VOLT 375:10
autumn mists of the a. mornings ORW 278:7
avalanche mighty a. HOUS 183:8
avarice a. and ambition SMITH 341:2
avoided a. simply by postponing CHUR 94:16
awake other two-thirds are a. RUSK 315:2
awareness positive signs of his a. BLUNT 49:7
axe a.'s edge did try MARV 251:7
Lay then the a. to the root PAINE 282:5
let the great a. fall SHAK 325:11
Axis sword is the a. of the world DE G 112:2
under-belly of the A. CHUR 91:11

babble coffee house b. DISR 120:7
babies putting milk into b. CHUR 92:1
baby b. beats the nurse SHAK 332:4
Burn, b., burn ANON 9:5
government is like a big b. REAG 301:5
Babylon By the waters of B. WALP 378:2
London is a modern B. DISR 118:10
back b. to basics MAJOR 248:3
boys in the b. rooms BEAV 33:8
going into their own b. garden KERR 206:7
stabbing himself in the b. LEWIS 223:3
very good b.-seat driver THAT 362:11
Winston is b. ANON 15:4
backbone no more b. ROOS 311:2
backed never so perfectly b. HAL 165:11
backing b. a quitter KERR 206:8
I'm b. Britain ANON 10:10
backstairs prefers the b. CAMP 74:4
backward look b. to their ancestors BURKE 66:10
revolutions never go b. SEW 324:1
Bacon think how B. shined POPE 295:5
When their lordships asked B. BENT 38:1
bad almost always b. men ACTON 1:10
as b. as we'd been saying KENN 204:9
B. laws are the worst sort BURKE 65:4
B. money drives out good ANON 8:8
brave b. man CLAR 96:5
so many shocking b. hats WELL 384:8
To defend a b. policy SAL 318:11
told how b. things are CHUR 91:4
trample b. laws PHIL 291:9
When b. men combine BURKE 63:4
bag b. and baggage GLAD 154:12
like an old b. lady HEAL 173:4
baggage bag and b. GLAD 154:12
bagman Cobden is an inspired b. CARL 76:13
bakeres *As b. and breweres* LANG 217:7
balance b. of our population JOS 200:3
b. of power NIC 271:7
government is nothing but the b. MART 251:6
management of a b. of power KISS 214:8
redress the b. of the Old CANN 75:4
tongue in the b. BISM 47:13
tyrannize over his bank b. KEYN 208:2
balances checks and b. SCAR 321:2
balancing B. the budget GRAMM 159:3
bald b. eagle FRAN 142:7
fight between two b. men BORG 52:7
Balkans silly thing in the B. BISM 47:8
ballads permitted to make all the b. FLET 137:8
ballot b.-boxing, Nigger-emancipating CARL 76:11
b. is stronger than the bullet LINC 224:7
rap at the b. box CHILD 85:3
right of all to the b. ANTH 15:7
vote by b. is the dyspepsia of CARL 76:15
ballots peaceful b. only LINC 224:7
balm Can wash the b. SHAK 333:6
ban B. the bomb ANON 8:9
baneful b. effects of the spirit WASH 379:11
bang bigger b. for a buck ANON 9:2
Not with a b. but a whimper ELIOT 130:2
banish I b. you SHAK 324:8
bank tyrannize over his b. balance KEYN 208:2
banknotes to fill old bottles with b. KEYN 208:4
bankrupts more b. JOS 200:4
you are b. TROT 370:12
banner Freedom's b. streaming DRAKE 124:8
star-spangled b. KEY 207:1
banners enlisting under other b. ADAMS 4:8
Bantu [B.] has been subjected VERW 374:1
banyan like the great b. tree PATIL 287:2
bar member of the b. BOK 50:5
barbarians b. are to arrive today CAV 79:2
b., Philistines, and Populace ARN 17:2
become of us without the b. CAV 79:3
in my own mind *the b.* ARN 17:4
barbarism b. be considered WEIL 383:3
methods of b. in South Africa CAMP 74:2
barbarity b. of tyrants SMITH 344:6
bard this goat-footed b. KEYN 207:11
barefoot I was born b. LONG 232:4
bark don't b. yourself ATTL 20:13
barrel out of the b. of a gun MAO 250:4
barren I am but a b. stock ELIZ 130:5
It seems to me a b. thing DISR 117:9

bar-room America is like a b. drunk ALLEN 7:2
base b., common and popular SHAK 326:11
man of soul so b. TOCQ 366:3
scorning the b. degrees SHAK 328:10
basest swayed by the b. men CLAY 97:6
basics back to b. MAJOR 248:3
basis b. of popular government ROB 306:11
bastard b. who gets the mail KEAT 203:1
getter of more b. children SHAK 324:11
bathing caught the Whigs b. DISR 117:15
bathroom revolutionary in a b. LINK 227:9
baton marshal's b. LOU 233:3
bats like b. amongst birds BACON 23:2
batsmen sending your opening b. HOWE 184:1
battalions side not of the heavy b. VOLT 375:8
battle B., *n.* A method BIER 44:15
b., sir, is not to the strong HENRY 176:7
b. to the strong BIBLE 43:16
defeated in a great b. LIVY 228:9
die well that die in a b. SHAK 326:13
France has lost a b. DE G 112:3
glad of them in the b. of Britain BEVIN 42:9
lost the b. of Jena ANON 10:3
Next to a b. lost WELL 385:1
who shall have borne the b. LINC 227:1
battles b., martyrs, blood WHIT 388:4
dead b., like dead generals TUCH 372:4
forced marches, b. and death GAR 148:1
mother of b. HUSS 186:1
opening b. of all subsequent ORW 278:6
bauble fool's b., the mace CROM 105:9
baubles *take away these b.* CROM 105:9
bayonet b. is a weapon ANON 8:10
bayonets throne of b. INGE 187:7
beaches We shall fight on the b. CHUR 90:7
bear b. the palm alone SHAK 328:3
not to embrace the Russian b. CHAN 81:8
so b. ourselves CHUR 90:8
to keep and b. arms ANON 14:11
We must b. all SHAK 326:15
bear-baiting Puritan hated b. MAC 239:2
beard King of Spain's b. DRAKE 124:6
beareth b. up things light BACON 22:15
beast *B.* stands for strong WAUGH 380:4
b. With many heads SHAK 324:10
dying b. lying across a railway JENK 194:5
either a b. or a god ARIS 16:6
splendorous *blond b.* NIET 273:5
beat b. their swords into plowshares BIBLE 43:18
b. the King ninety-nine times MANC 249:1
beating glory of b. the French WOLFE 393:5
beaut make a mistake, it's a b. LA G 216:3
beautiful black is b. ANON 9:3
This *is* a b. country BROWN 59:4
beauty b. of the mountain rose BEAV 34:2
terrible b. is born YEATS 395:8
Beaverbrook that of Lord B. ATTL 20:1
become b. President DARR 109:8
bed Down as upon a b. MARV 251:7
bedfellows strange b. WARN 378:11
beef roast b. of old England BURKE 63:3
Where's the b. MOND 262:1
beer to drink small b. SHAK 327:1
torrent of gin and b. GLAD 154:9
beg to b. in the streets FRAN 141:2
begin But let us b. KENN 204:5
to b. the world over again PAINE 281:8
wars b. when you will MACH 242:2
beginning b. of the end TALL 355:1
In my end is my b. MARY 253:8
not even the b. of the end CHUR 91:10
revolution is at the b. STEV 350:4
beginnings All b. are small JOUB 200:6
time the b. and endings BACON 22:7
begun I have not yet b. to fight JONES 199:1
behind something b. the throne PITT 292:12
being their social b. MARX 252:7
Belgium until B. recovers ASQ 18:3
belief attacks my b. JOHN 198:5
believe B. nothing until it has been COCK 100:6
If you b. that, you'll b. anything WELL 384:12
professing to b. PAINE 283:5
willing to b. what they wish CAES 71:8
believed b. during three days MED 255:2
b. to be so TROL 370:9
believing b. their own lies ARB 15:8
Not b. in force TROT 370:15
Bellamy *one of B.'s veal pies* PITT 293:12
bells b. I hear WHIT 387:9
They now *ring* the b. WALP 378:5
belong To betray, you must first b. PHIL 291:4
below b. the dignity of history MAC 238:11
belt see a b. without hitting ASQ 19:2
bench hut, with only a simple b. GARF 147:9
on our Treasury b. TROL 370:1
beneficent purposes are b. BRAN 55:3
beneficial b. objects TOCQ 367:1
benevolence b. of the butcher SMITH 341:4
enticed by b. BAG 28:2
Benn B. flung himself LEVIN 222:4
Berliner *Ich bin ein B.* KENN 205:6
best b. administered is best POPE 295:4
b. is like the worst KIPL 212:8
b. lack all conviction YEATS 395:6
It was the b. of times DICK 115:4
Send forth the b. ye breed KIPL 213:2
we will do our b. CHUR 91:5
bestow b. on every airth a limb GRAH 159:2
bestride b. the narrow world SHAK 328:4
betray guts to b. my country FORS 139:4
To b., you must first belong PHIL 291:4
betrayal b. of Ulster CAIR 72:1

betrayed one of them b. me BEAV 34:7
better b. his own condition SMITH 343:3
b. if he had never lived CHUR 92:13
b. off than they are DISR 118:4
B. red than dead ANON 9:1
B. than a play CHAR 83:2
b. than light and safer than HASK 170:2
b. to be in chains KAFKA 201:9
from worse to b. HOOK 182:6
see the b. things, and approve OVID 280:3
times that were are b. GRE 161:1
bettering prospect of b. MILL 259:14
Bevan [B.] enjoys prophesying MACM 244:11
Bevin speech from Ernest B. FOOT 138:4
beware B. the ides of March SHAK 328:2
bible b. in the other WRAN 394:10
B. is for the government of WYCL 395:1
Written by b. readers BAIN 28:3
bicker safely afford to b. BALF 31:2
bicycle only arrive by b. VIER 375:3
bidder withstand the highest b. WASH 379:7
big B. BROTHER IS WATCHING YOU ORW 278:14
b. enough to take away FORD 138:10
carry a b. stick ROOS 311:4
too b. for them BULM 61:6
bigger b. bang for a buck ANON 9:2
bigot mind of a b. HOLM 182:1
bigotries b. that savage LLOY 230:4
bike got on his b. TEBB 359:1
bill absolutes in our b. of Rights BLACK 48:3
b. of indemnity KRUG 215:6
b. of Rights was not ordained JORD 199:4
called upon to pay the b. HARD 168:4
billet Every bullet has its b. WILL 389:4
billion b. dollar country FOST 139:7
bind Go, b. your sons to exile KIPL 213:2
Obadiah b.-their-kings-in-chains MAC 236:2
biographical noble and b. friend WETH 386:1
biography B. should be written by BALF 31:1
Read no history: nothing but b. DISR 116:7
bird b. of bad moral character FRAN 142:7
catch the b. of paradise KHR 209:4
forgets the dying b. PAINE 282:4
birds b., wild flowers BALD 29:3
I see all the b. are flown CHAR 82:3
like bats amongst b. BACON 23:2
one's eye for the high b. HAL 166:13
Birkenhead Lord B. is very clever ASQ 19:1
birth accident of b. CHES 84:3
b. as a mark of distinction BUR 69:2
bishop Another b. dead MELB 255:8
b. of Rome hath no jurisdiction BOOK 51:6
hitting the niece of a b. ORW 277:10
Make him a b. CLARE 95:14
No b., no King JAM 189:9
now he makes me a b. KING 210:1
bishopric talk of *merit* for a b. WEST 385:10
Bismarck B. was a political genius TAYL 356:9
his theory of politics was B.'s KEYN 207:3
bitches businessmen were sons of b. KENN 205:2
bite b. the hand that fed BURKE 68:6
bites dead woman b. not GRAY 160:7
black B. dog is back again CHUR 94:8
B. is beautiful ANON 9:3
b. majority rule in Rhodesia SMITH 344:4
b. men fought on the coast MAC 239:4
B. Panther Party NEWT 271:3
B. power CARM 76:16
Black's not so b. CANN 75:2
born in America with a b. skin MALC 248:7
equality between the white and b. LINC 225:2
man has a b. face EDW 128:2
blacks running from b. JACK 189:8
bladders boys that swim on b. SHAK 327:6
blame b. the alien AESC 6:3
bland b. lead the bland GALB 145:8
blank political b. cheque GOSC 158:4
blasphemies truths begin as b. SHAW 336:20
blazing *eyes b. with insincerity* ANON 13:10
bleed Caesar b. in sport SHAK 329:6
Blenheim fighting B. BEVAN 40:10
bless God b. the Prince of Wales LINL 227:10
blessed b. mother of us all JEFF 193:12
This b. plot SHAK 333:4
Thou fall'st a b. martyr SHAK 327:7
blessing be to us a national b. HAM 167:1
blind b., despised, and dying king SHEL 338:1
In the country of the b. ERAS 133:10
blinked other fellow just b. RUSK 315:1
bliss b. was it in that dawn WORD 394:7
block old b. itself BURKE 65:6
blocks b. to cut PEEL 288:12
You b., you stones SHAK 328:1
blond splendorous *b. beast* NIET 273:5
blood And men are flesh and b. SHAK 329:3
b. and iron BISM 47:4
b. and the sweat of JACK 189:6
b. drawn with the lash LINC 226:9
b. of patriots and tyrants JEFF 191:7
B. sport is brought to its INGH 187:10
b., toil, tears and sweat CHUR 90:5
drains all the b. from the head BEVAN 40:4
enough of b. and tears RABIN 299:4
guiltless of his country's b. GRAY 160:8
If b. be the price of admiralty KIPL 212:10
In the b. of the socialist CROS 106:7
left this tincture in the b. DEFOE 111:12
Of earth's first b. WORD 394:5
privileged to spend her b. WILS 392:11
rivers of b. JEFF 193:11
shedding the b. of their brothers ZAP 397:1
stream of b. coming from beneath ANON 12:1
Tiber foaming with much b. POW 297:1

Tiber foaming with much b. VIRG 375:6
when b. is their argument SHAK 326:13
Where b. with guilt is bought SHEL 338:5
blood-dimmed b. tide is loosed YEATS 395:6
bloodshed war without b. MAO 250:3
bloodthirsty so b. TROL 369:5
bloody b. curtain ELIS 130:3
no right in the b. circus MAXT 254:5
blossom hundred flowers b. MAO 250:6
blot b. on the escutcheon GRAY 160:6
blow b. with an agreement TROT 370:10
blubbering b. Cabinet GLAD 155:9
Blücher Napoleon forgot B. CHUR 86:9
blunder crime, it is a b. BOUL 53:5
blunders human b., however TAYL 357:4
blunt plain, b. man SHAK 330:8
blushing b. discontented sun SHAK 334:1
board on b. while asleep HUME 184:9
There wasn't any b. HERB 176:9
boast b. of its constitution PAINE 283:12
Such is the patriot's b. GOLD 157:3
boat They sank my b. KENN 205:11
boathook diplomatic b. SAL 317:7
bodes b. some strange eruption SHAK 325:4
bodies B. tied together BURKE 64:16
three b. no sensible man MACM 245:9
bodkin With a bare b. SHAK 325:8
body b. of a weak and feeble woman ELIZ 130:9
liberation of the human b. GOLD 157:2
no b. to be kicked THUR 364:9
yielding of that b. SHAK 325:5
Bognor Bugger B. GEOR 149:11
bogy b. man BEVAN 40:9
boil War That Would Not B. TAYL 356:8
boiled bag of b. sweets CRIT 104:4
no politics in b. and roast SMITH 344:7
bold b. spirit in a loyal breast SHAK 333:1
boldness b., and again boldness DANT 109:6
b. is a child of ignorance BACON 22:4
Bolshevism B. run mad SNOW 345:6
this sort of madness [B.] SMITH 344:1
bomb Ban the b. ANON 8:9
best defence against the atom b. ANON 8:11
b. them back into the Stone LEMAY 220:8
bombed glad we've been b. ELIZ 132:8
protect him from being b. BALD 29:6
bomber b. will always get through BALD 29:6
bombing b. begins in five minutes REAG 301:13
bondman base that would be a b. SHAK 329:12
b.'s two hundred and fifty years LINC 226:9
bonds b. of civil society LOCKE 231:8
boneless b. wonder CHUR 89:1
bones lay my b. amongst you WOLS 394:2
Not worth the healthy b. BISM 47:10
bonkers stark, raving b. HAIL 163:6
bonny rich man makes a b. traitor PAINE 282:2
book improve a b. TOCQ 366:9
little woman who wrote the b. LINC 227:4
when he can read the b. BEVAN 40:8
bookie b. or of a clergyman MUGG 268:2
books b. are weapons ROOS 310:2
to Cambridge b. he sent BROW 59:6
Wherever b. will be burned HEINE 174:1
write it in the b. of law JOHN 195:8
boomerangs they pick b. MACL 243:7
boot b. stamping on a human face ORW 279:8
order of the b. CHUR 92:7
booted b. and spurred to ride RUMB 314:9
boots without any b. BULM 61:6
bore b. people at dinner parties KISS 214:14
not only a b.; he bored MUGG 268:1
bored I am b. BISM 47:5
boredom b. on a large scale INGE 187:9
born all men naturally were b. free MILT 261:1
because you were b. in it SHAW 336:18
b. free and equal in dignity ANON 8:4
for abortion has already been b. REAG 301:9
If I had not been b. Perón PERÓN 290:6
I was b. barefoot LONG 232:4
Man was b. free ROUS 314:5
not b. to sue, but to command SHAK 333:2
That ever I was b. to set it right SHAK 325:7
That's b. into the world alive GILB 152:6
those who are to be b. BURKE 67:5
borough b.-mongering DISR 117:5
bossing end to b. LENIN 221:10
nobody b. you about ORW 278:1
Bossuet excite the horror of B. MAC 237:10
bossy of the busy by the b. SELD 323:4
Boston long way from East B. KENN 205:13
Botany Bay colonies seek for at B. FRE 143:6
both man may wear it on b. sides SHAK 335:10
bottles fill old b. with banknotes KEYN 208:4
new wine into old b. ATTL 20:5
bottom b. of the economic pyramid ROOS 308:4
sit only on our own b. MONT 263:9
bought blood with guilt is b. SHEL 338:5
when he's b. stays bought CAM 73:6
bounded b. on the north by FISKE 137:5
bounds shall thy b. be set BENS 37:6
bourgeois old b. society MARX 253:3
person of b. origin ORW 277:9
Too old, too b. GISC 153:6
bourgeoisie b. in the long run only TROT 370:11
bowels in the b. of Christ CROM 105:6
boy b. may become President STEV 350:6
b. will ruin himself GEOR 149:10
boys b. in the back rooms BEAV 33:8
By office b. for office boys SAL 318:10
little wanton b. that swim SHAK 327:6
not about to send American b. JOHN 196:4
Your b. are not going ROOS 309:9

brag that vapour and fume and b. KIPL 212:7
brain leave that b. outside GILB 152:8
once pronounced b.-dead SMITH 344:3
workers by hand or by b. ANON 14:3
brains b. go to his head ASQ 19:1
brave b. bad man CLAR 96:5
b. man inattentive to his duty JACK 188:7
home of the b. KEY 207:1
bravery acts of personal b. WAUGH 380:5
Bray vicar of B. ANON 10:12
bread He took the b. and brake it ELIZ 131:4
looked to government for b. BURKE 68:6
reap, we should soon want b. JEFF 193:16
break to b. his spirit HOLL 181:4
breast dauntless b. GRAY 160:8
breasts b. by which France is fed SULLY 352:6
breath b. of worldly men SHAK 333:6
breathes b. there the man SCOTT 322:5
breed Feared by their b. SHAK 333:4
this happy b. of men SHAK 333:4
breweres *As bakeres and b.* LANG 217:7
bribe taking of a b. or gratuity PENN 289:14
to b. or twist WOLFE 393:4
bribes How many b. he had taken BENT 38:1
brick inherited it b. AUG 21:8
throw a b. without hitting ORW 277:10
bride b. at a wedding HEAD 172:1
bridge b. scores in his head BUTL 70:6
b. too far BROW 59:7
promise to build a b. KHR 209:6
bridle all b. and no spurs TAYL 358:4
brief drest in a little b. authority SHAK 332:9
briefing b. is what *I* do CALL 72:6
briefings I give confidential b. LYNN 235:10
Brigade B. of Guards MACM 245:9
brink We walked to the b. DULL 126:9
brinkmanship boasting of his b. STEV 350:10
Britain boundary of B. is revealed TAC 354:2
B. will still be MAJOR 248:2
dependence on, Great B. PAINE 281:6
further you got from B. CALL 73:2
Great B. has a series of capitals CURZ 108:1
I'm backing B. ANON 10:10
make B. a fit country for heroes LLOY 229:9
You speak for B. BOOT 52:4
British allegiance to the B. crown LEE 220:3
American culture, and B. know-how PEAR 287:7
better rating in B. mythology GRIGG 161:8
B. are no longer important MCC 240:1
B. Constitution has always been ELIZ 132:7
[B. Constitution] presumes more GLAD 154:13
B. electors will not vote for BEAV 34:6
B. Empire ROS 312:11
B. government forms the best HAM 167:2
B. have the distinction ATTL 20:5
B. institutions MAND 249:3
B. nation is unique in this CHUR 91:4
B. people came of age TAYL 357:11
B. political system has no room TAYL 356:7
B. Prime Minister sneezes LEVIN 222:8
B. subject, in whatever land PALM 284:2
destinies of the B. Empire DISR 119:7
If the B. public falls for this HAIL 163:6
intervene to help B. companies HES 178:4
liquidation of the B. Empire CHUR 91:9
myths of the B. Parliament MAYB 254:6
provinces of the B. empire SMITH 342:3
ridiculous as the B. public MAC 237:8
shadow of the B. oak BURKE 67:3
tugged the forelock to the B. KEAT 202:8
Briton glory in the name of B. GEOR 149:1
procedure is all the poor B. has PICK 292:6
Britons B. alone use 'Might' WAUGH 380:6
broadcasters to be left to the b. BENN 36:2
broadcasting B. is too important BENN 36:2
broadened b. into a brotherhood JOHN 195:9
broke If it ain't b., don't fix it LANCE 217:3
broken bats have been b. HOWE 184:1
Can it be b. JENK 194:4
Don't tell me peace has b. out BREC 55:10
laws were made to be b. NORTH 275:4
taken up the b. blade DE G 112:4
When peace has been b. ROOS 309:6
broker honest b. BISM 47:1
bronze noontide was b. CHUR 89:9
brook as doth an inland b. SHAK 332:11
broomstick who can tether a b. KEYN 208:1
brother BIG B. IS WATCHING YOU ORW 278:14
not a man and a b. WEDG 383:2
to be the white man's b. KING 210:2
brotherhood broadened into a b. JOHN 195:9
together at the table of b. KING 210:10
brother-in-law brother, not his b. KING 210:2
brothers learn to live together as b. KING 211:2
that they may agree like b. SHAK 327:1
brought b. down by the action MACM 245:6
brow upon the b. of labour BRYAN 60:6
Browning safety-catch of my B. JOHST 198:14
bruiser piratical old b. HAIL 163:10
brute *Et tu, B.* CAES 71:13
Et tu, B. SHAK 329:4
finest b. votes in Europe BAG 26:6
should be treated as a b. EDW 128:2
brutish nasty, b., and short HOBB 180:2
Brutus 'B.' will start a spirit as SHAK 328:5
You too, B. CAES 71:13
buccaneers fallen among b. LLOY 230:10
buck bigger bang for a b. ANON 9:2
b. stops here TRUM 372:1
bucket That b. down SHAK 334:3
buckle *b.* which fastens BAG 24:13
bud I'll nip him in the b. ROCHE 307:4

budget balancing the b. GRAMM 159:3
buffers terminal b. MACL 243:3
bugger B. Bognor GEOR 149:11
builds b. up a man only if BENN 36:6
bull strong as a b. moose ROOS 310:12
bullet *ballot is stronger than the b.* LINC 224:7
Every b. has its billet WILL 389:4
bullets not bloody b. LINC 224:7
bully by the bossy for the b. SELD 323:4
bulwark floating b. of the island BLAC 48:7
only sure b. of continuing liberty ROOS 309:5
Buncombe I'm talking to B. WALK 376:8
speaking through reporters to B. CARL 76:7
bungler good nature is a b. in it HAL 166:12
of peace Man is a b. SHAW 336:5
burden heavy b. of responsibility EDW 128:5
pay any price, bear any b. KENN 204:2
public b. of the nation's care PRIOR 298:4
white Man's b. KIPL 213:2
bureaucracy b. is sure to think that BAG 26:10
b. of the corporation state DOUG 123:4
[b.'s] specific invention WEBER 381:11
B., the rule of no one MCC 239:8
immobile b. SAMP 319:11
bureaucrats b. will care more for BAG 26:9
Guidelines for b. BOREN 52:6
burglar b. of others' intellect DISR 118:13
honest b. MENC 256:10
burial groaning for b. SHAK 329:9
part, any part, in its b. MACM 244:11
Burke [Edmund B.] is not affected PAINE 282:4
with B. under a shed JOHN 198:11
burn B., baby, burn ANON 9:5
b. your fingers in public life BEAV 33:4
to b. its children to save its MEYER 258:3
burned also, in the end, are b. HEINE 174:1
burnt b., tortured, fined JEFF 191:2
chateaux would never have been b. TREV 368:2
bury I come to b. Caesar SHAK 329:13
We will b. you KHR 209:3
bus he missed the b. CHAM 81:4
under Sulla was like a b. ADC 5:7
business b. carried on as usual CHUR 87:6
b. of government LAWS 219:3
b. of nobody MAC 237:2
difficulties in princes' b. BACON 22:8
fit for b. with a ruffled temper WALP 378:8
hundred well-placed b. men YOUNG 396:6
liberty is always unfinished b. ANON 11:14
making everything his b. SOLZ 345:11
Men in b. are in as much danger HAL 165:4
Now it must be b. as usual THAT 361:9
of the American people is b. COOL 103:3
politics grease the wheels of b. TAWN 356:3
totter on in b. to the last POPE 295:6
Treasury is the spring of b. BAG 24:12
We can do b. together THAT 361:11
businessman British b. has trampled NIC 272:6
businessmen all b. were sons of bitches KENN 205:2
message to the b. of this country CURR 107:7
busy of the b. by the bossy SELD 323:4
butcher benevolence of the b. SMITH 341:4
on the way to the b. CHUR 89:6
Prime Minister has to be a b. BUTL 70:5
butchers sacrificers, but not b. SHAK 328:12
shepherds and b. VOLT 375:7
butter b. or guns GOER 156:6
manage without b. GOEB 156:5
butts With many heads b. me SHAK 324:10
buy b. it like an honest man NORT 275:6
Don't b. a single vote more KENN 203:8
buyer if a b. can be found SALL 319:7
byword made a story and a b. WINT 393:2

cabinet blubbering c. GLAD 155:9
c. consists of reporting HOGG 181:3
c. does not propose, it decides ATTL 20:6
c. government 'a shambles' HUNT 185:7
c. is a combining committee BAG 24:13
c. ministers are educated BENN 37:4
C. minutes are studied KAUF 202:3
c.'s gone to its dinner ANON 12:12
consequence of c. government BAG 24:14
group of c. Ministers CURZ 108:3
head of the c. is *primus inter* MORL 266:1
looked forward to the c. meeting LAWS 219:6
mislead the c. ASQ 18:6
of his first c. meeting WELL 384:5
Prime Minister and the c. SCH 322:3
sandhills of the Baldwin c. ASQ 18:8
say one of two things in c. ANON 12:6
ways of getting into the c. BEVAN 41:11
Caesar appealed unto C. BIBLE 44:12
Aut C., aut nihil BORG 53:1
But yesterday the word of C. SHAK 330:5
C. bleed in sport SHAK 329:6
C. hath wept SHAK 330:2
C.'s wife must be above suspicion CAES 71:9
Came from C.'s laurel crown BLAKE 49:3
died—that c. might be great CAMP 73:8
envy of great C. SHAK 330:16
Et tu, Brute? Then fall, C. SHAK 329:4
Fox divided the kingdom with C. JOHN 198:12
If C. can hide the sun SHAK 325:2
Not that I loved C. less SHAK 329:10
O mighty C.! dost thou lie so low SHAK 329:8
render therefore unto C. BIBLE 44:7
Speak; C. is turned to hear SHAK 328:2
surface of C.'s public policy PLUT 294:9
what meat doth this our C. feed SHAK 328:5

Caesars C. and Napoleons HUXL 186:3
cage anybody outside the c. DALT 108:9
cloak should become an iron c. WEBER 382:1
cake Let them eat c. MAR 250:9
Calais 'C.' lying in my heart MARY 253:9
calamity more than a public c. SOUT 347:3
calculate c. upon real favours WASH 379:9
calculating desiccated c. machine BEVAN 41:5
Caledonia mourn, hapless C. SMOL 345:3
calico c. millenium CARL 76:13
Caligula C.'s horse RAND 300:10
eyes of C. MITT 261:8
call c. Me God SAMP 319:9
c. to account those who do GLAD 154:4
Fair shares for all, is Labour's c. JAY 190:5
Work is the c. MORR 266:6
calling Germany c. JOYCE 200:8
calls in the press that c. on me SHAK 328:2
calm pilot of the c. BAG 25:3
to c., rather than to excite PALM 284:5
Calvinistic We have a C. creed PITT 293:1
Cambridge To C. books TRAPP 367:6
to C. books BROW 59:6
came I c., I saw, I conquered CAES 71:12
I c. through and I shall return MAC 235:12
campaign You c. in poetry CUOMO 107:3
campaigns political c. ROB 306:12
Campbell-Bannerman C. is a mere BALF 30:5
can label on the c. of worms CRIT 104:8
Canada C. was supposed to get PEAR 287:7
Canalettos Then the C. go MACM 245:11
cancer We have a c. within DEAN 110:6
white race *is* the c. SONT 346:6
candidate Democratic Party's c. KENN 204:1
candidates c. were not men PAINE 282:10
merchandize c. for high office STEV 350:11
when c. appeal to 'Every' ADAMS 2:4
candle c. in that great turnip CHUR 93:3
light a c. to the sun SIDN 340:3
light such a c. by God's grace LAT 218:5
rather light a c. than curse STEV 350:14
candles to carry c. HERV 177:6
cannibals formidable body of c. MENC 256:14
cant c. of 'Measures not men' CANN 74:9
Canterbury *C. or Smithfield* WALP 377:11
Cantuar O Lord, how full of C. BULL 61:5
canvasses good in c. BACON 22:5
capable c. of reigning if only TAC 354:8
capers He c. nimbly SHAK 334:9
capital c. must be propelled by BAG 28:2
colourful entry into the c. WAUGH 380:5
interests of c. and labour ATK 19:6
not been able to destroy c. MAC 239:3
thus discover the origin of c. TORR 367:4
capitalism C., as an institutional BERG 38:5
c. of the working class SPEN 347:7
C., wisely managed KEYN 207:7
kindly c. KINN 211:8
monopoly stage of c. LENIN 221:3
peaceful extermination of c. ZIN 397:4
spirit of c. WEBER 381:7
stage beyond c. but a substitute ROB 307:2
unacceptable face of c. HEATH 173:8
Under c. man exploits man ANON 14:5
war is c. with the gloves off STOP 351:9
capitalist forces of a c. society NEHRU 270:11
worker is the slave of c. society CONN 102:2
capitals Britain has a series of c. CURZ 108:1
Capri letter came from C. JUV 201:7
caprices depend on the c. TOCQ 366:3
captain c. is in his bunk, drinking SHAW 336:18
game by the team c. HOWE 184:1
like a ship's c. complaining POW 297:9
O c.! my Captain WHIT 387:9
Walk the deck my c. lies WHIT 387:10
captains c. and the kings depart KIPL 212:11
car afford to keep a motor c. SHAW 337:1
c. in every garage and HOOV 182:9
carcases dead c. of unburied men SHAK 324:8
carcass c. fit for hounds SHAK 328:13
card c. up his sleeve LAB 216:1
Orange c. CHUR 86:8
play the race c. SHAP 335:12
cards pack the c. BACON 22:5
care c. fifty times more BAG 25:8
c. of human life and happiness JEFF 193:1
career I now close my military c. MAC 235:14
loyal to his own c. DALT 109:2
points clearly to a political c. SHAW 336:13
careless As 'twere a c. trifle SHAK 331:6
C. talk costs lives ANON 9:7
cares c. and pleasures of domestic GIBB 151:7
caring prosperous or c. society HES 178:2
carnivorous sheep are born c. FAG 135:1
carpenter walrus and c. LEVIN 222:5
carrion With c. men SHAK 329:9
carry c. a big stick ROOS 311:4
We shall c. on as usual THAT 361:10
Carthage C. must be destroyed CATO 79:1
Carthaginian C. trustworthiness SALL 319:8
cartoonist life as a c. PET 291:1
carve Let's c. him as a dish fit SHAK 328:13
case civil servant a good c. CLARK 96:7
cash In epochs when c. payment CARL 76:2
pay you c. to go away KIPL 213:4
cast c. your mind on other days YEATS 396:3
die is c. CAES 71:11
castle rich man in his c. ALEX 7:1
Castlereagh He had a mask like C. SHEL 338:2
casualty truth is the first c. JOHN 197:4
cat big c. detained briefly PARR 286:10
colour of the c. doesn't matter DENG 113:4
Like a powerful graceful c. CHUR 88:3
take care of the c. SULZ 352:8

catalogue c. of human crime CHUR 90:6
catched more wise, and not be c. PEPYS 290:3
categorical c. imperative KANT 202:2
caterpillars c. of the commonwealth SHAK 333:5
Catherine Marx and C. the Great ATTL 20:8
Catholic C. and the Communist ORW 278:12
C. candidate for President KENN 204:1
Gentlemen, I am a C. BELL 35:2
I cannot be a good C. NORF 275:2
Roman C. Church MACM 245:9
Catholics Hitler attacked the C. NIEM 273:1
Cato losing one pleased C. LUCAN 234:3
Voice of C. is the voice of Rome JONS 199:3
cats which way I want the c. to go THAT 361:14
cat's-paws really mere c. COCK 100:7
cattle thousands of great c. BURKE 67:3
cause *good old c.* MILT 261:4
his c. being good MORE 265:6
just c. reaches its flood-tide CATT 78:7
Our c. is just DICK 115:9
winning c. pleased the gods LUCAN 234:3
causes declare the c. JEFF 190:7
tough on the c. of crime BLAIR 48:11
caution Speaking with that c. PEEL 289:2
Cavaliers C. (Wrong) SELL 323:5
will not do with the c. LAMB 216:6
Cave of Adullam political C. BRIG 56:8
cease c. of majesty SHAK 325:13
war will c. when men refuse ANON 14:6
celerity aid to secrecy is c. TAYL 358:9
cement like mixing c. MOND 262:2
censors without c. JEFF 191:12
censorship extreme form of c. SHAW 336:15
centralization c. and socialism TOCQ 366:10
c. follows TOCQ 366:7
centre c. cannot hold YEATS 395:6
My c. is giving way FOCH 138:1
now in the c. of politics MOSL 267:2
soft c. has always melted HAIL 163:9
stables are the real c. SHAW 336:17
centuries All c. but this GILB 152:10
forty c. look down upon you NAP 269:3
century c. of the common man WALL 376:10
twentieth c. have looked like SCHL 321:7
ceremonial All c. is ridiculous COBB 100:5
ceremony c. of innocence YEATS 395:6
No c. that to great ones 'longs SHAK 332:7
Save ceremony, save general c. SHAK 326:16
Cervantes C. is never petulant MAC 237:10
chain c. about the ankle DOUG 124:3
chaining c. the crowd VOLT 376:5
chains everywhere he is in c. ROUS 314:5
freedom from c. BERL 39:3
nothing to lose but their c. MARX 253:4
often better to be in c. KAFKA 201:9
so debased by their c. ROUS 314:6
Whether in c. or in laurels PHIL 292:3
chairs carry candles and set c. HERV 177:6
challenge times of c. KING 210:6
chamber naked into the conference c. BEVAN 41:3
second c. selected by the Whips FOOT 138:5
Chamberlain [C.] has been able CHUR 89:11
speech by C. BEVAN 40:3
chambers enchanted c. of Power LAND 217:4
chameleon Who shall paint the c. KEYN 208:1
chance taking a c. on peace BUSH 69:8
Chancellor C. of the Exchequer is LOWE 233:7
C.'s position was unassailable THAT 362:6
rid of a C. of the Exchequer BIRCH 45:8
talk with the German C. CHAM 80:10
chances take c. for peace DULL 126:9
change all c. in history TAYL 356:12
c. is constant DISR 119:13
commends a radical c. FISH 137:2
continent of revolutionary c. BUSH 69:9
down the ringing grooves of c. TENN 359:7
involves a great c. TROL 369:11
little more than a c. of persons PAINE 282:11
make c. our friend CLIN 99:7
necessary not to c. FALK 135:3
occasion for fundamental c. BENN 36:4
point is to c. it MARX 252:3
times c., and we c. with them ANON 13:7
torrent of c. CHES 84:4
why it's time for a c. DEWEY 114:5
wind of c. is blowing MACM 245:1
without the means of some c. BURKE 66:8
changed changed, c. utterly YEATS 395:8
that it be not c. BIBLE 43:20
changes c. we fear JOHN 197:2
channel [c.] is a mere ditch NAP 269:4
c. through which KENN 203:7
chaos desperation and c. MARS 251:2
thy dread empire, c. POPE 295:8
chapter now to write the next c. JOHN 195:8
character by the content of their c. KING 210:10
change the c. of the nation CECIL 79:8
fellow's c. by his way of eating REAG 301:10
men of the highest c. CIC 95:8
not of intellect but of c. WEBB 381:2
simplicity of c. is no hindrance MORL 266:2
turns on personal c. NAP 269:7
charge trumpet for the c. CHAM 80:3
When in c., ponder BOREN 52:6
charitably how can they c. dispose SHAK 326:13
charity with c. for all LINC 227:1
Charles C. II was always SELL 323:7
C. I lost his head for CRO 107:1
In good King C.'s golden days ANON 10:12
cheap have things done as c. PEPYS 290:2
What we obtain too c. PAINE 281:11
Cheapside in C. shall my palfrey SHAK 327:1

cheating period of c. BIER 44:17
check c. upon both ADAMS 3:12
mutual c. upon each other BLAC 48:10
checked c. by the slightest MONT 264:1
checks c. and balances SCAR 321:2
cheerful c. as any man could PEPYS 289:15
cheers Two c. for Democracy FORS 139:5
cheese 246 varieties of c. DE G 112:11
cheque political blank c. GOSC 158:4
cherry American as c. pie BROWN 58:7
chess playing their high c.-game CARL 76:10
chessboard c. of human society SMITH 341:3
chicken *c. in every pot* HOOV 182:9
c. in his pot every Sunday HENR 175:5
overnight c. shit can turn JOHN 195:4
some c.! Some neck CHUR 91:7
chief c. executive of this country ACH 1:8
Cromwell, our c. of men MILT 261:2
Chief Justice C. was rich, quiet MAC 238:7
not a C. CLARE 95:14
child every c. born therein RUSK 315:9
illegitimate c. of Karl Marx ATTL 20:8
land that's governed by a c. SHAK 335:1
Right...is the c. of law BENT 37:7
when thy king is a c. BIBLE 43:17
young healthy c. well nursed SWIFT 354:1
children burn its c. to save its pride MEYER 258:3
c. could work twenty-five hours SELL 323:9
c. of a larger growth CHES 83:10
faults which 'only c.' are said BAG 24:7
In peace, c. inter their parents HER 177:3
in turn each one of her c. VERG 373:8
labouring c. can look out CLEG 98:3
no illegitimate c. JOS 200:5
Were all thy c. kind and natural SHAK 326:9
when he cried the little c. died AUDEN 21:5
when he died the little c. cried MOTL 267:3
who talks about her own c. DISR 120:3
Chimborazo He is a C. or Everest ASQ 18:8
chimeras wild impossible c. SWIFT 353:8
China with your land armies in C. MONT 265:3
Chinese C. are a great and vital NIXON 274:7
chip c. of the old 'block' BURKE 65:6
chips given them nothing but c. CHUR 86:5
chivalry age of c. is gone BURKE 66:16
I adore his c. GIBB 151:14
choice c. of working or starving JOHN 197:6
hunger allows no c. AUDEN 21:2
state of perpetual potential c. BAG 26:7
we honour is the *people's c.* SHER 338:12
choose to be free to c. BERL 39:5
To govern is to c. LÉVIS 223:1
choosing c. between the disastrous GALB 145:12
c. each stone MARV 252:1
chosen not be c. for BERL 39:5
Christ as though C. were coming CART 77:5
C. and His saints slept ANON 12:5
C. crucified Pontius Pilate HOUS 183:7
Christian C. that it is better CECIL 79:7
I die a C. CHAR 82:7
Christianity C. is part of the laws HALE 164:5
C., of course BALF 30:9
Christians forty generations of C. MAC 239:1
like Gibbon on the C. BUTL 70:7
Christmas just before a hard C. SMITH 343:6
vote for an early C. CALL 73:1
chuck C. it, Smith CHES 84:6
church c. and state forever GRANT 160:3
c. speaks of the legitimate right ROM 308:2
English c. shall be free MAGN 247:2
free c. in a free state CAV 79:4
Say to the c., it shows RAL 300:4
wall between c. and state BLACK 48:2
when c. and state hold hands MITC 261:7
Churchill C. being a perfect MUGG 268:2
C. was fundamentally MACM 245:8
heard was that of Mr C. ATTL 20:1
never was a C. from John GLAD 155:2
Randolph C. went into hospital WAUGH 380:9
Church of England profession of the C. CHAR 82:7
Cicero opinion can alienate C. MAC 237:10
when C. had finished speaking STEV 350:13
cigar really good 5-cent c. MARS 251:5
Cincinnatus C. of the West BYRON 71:2
circle c. of our felicities JEFF 192:3
fatal c. is traced TOCQ 365:6
tightness of the magic c. MACL 242:8
circles c. the earth WEBS 382:7
circumstances concatenation of c. WEBS 382:5
play of c. WEIL 383:3
circus no right in the c. MAXT 254:5
turns their proceedings into a c. MURR 268:6
circuses bread and c. JUV 201:8
cities government of c. BRYCE 61:2
streets of a hundred c. HOOV 182:10
citizen c. as an abstract TOCQ 366:5
c., first in war LEE 220:2
c. in this world city AUR 21:9
c. is influenced by RAK 300:2
c. of no mean city BIBLE 44:11
first requisite of a good c. ROOS 311:3
greater than a private c. TAC 354:8
humblest c. of all the land BRYAN 60:4
I am a c. STEV 349:5
I am a Roman c. CIC 95:10
No cold relation is a zealous c. BURKE 67:9
political liberty in a c. MONT 264:10
citizens c. of the world ROOS 310:6
first and second class c. WILL 389:6
most refined c. SHEL 338:6
rights of c. HAM 167:8

coach (*cont.*):
football c. MCC 239:5
coal island is made mainly of c. BEVAN 40:5
miners' c. dust BOOT 52:5
coalition rainbow c. JACK 189:7
coalitions England does not love c. DISR 118:17
coals c. to Newcastle GEOR 149:9
coat republican cloth c. NIXON 273:6
riband to stick in his c. BROW 60:1
cobwebs laws are like c. SWIFT 353:4
cock c. crowing on its own dunghill ALD 6:9
Our c. won't fight BEAV 33:6
There you are, fixed, old c. CHUR 91:8
cocksure I wish I was as c. MELB 255:10
stupid are c. RUSS 316:12
coercion effect of c. JEFF 191:2
co-exist peacefully c. KHR 209:3
coexistence peaceful c. FULB 144:4
coffee c. house babble DISR 120:7
London c.-house SWIFT 353:5
poison in your c. ASTOR 19:3
coffin silver plate on a c. CURR 107:5
coins fistful of c. ZAP 397:1
cold captain lies, fallen c. WHIT 387:10
c. and are not clothed EIS 129:4
c. peace YELT 396:5
c. war BAR 32:5
c. war warrior THAT 360:10
c. war which is getting warmer BAR 32:6
hotbed of c. feet EBAN 127:6
No c. relation is a zealous citizen BURKE 67:9
offspring of c. hearts BURKE 66:17
Our sympathy is c. GIBB 151:11
colleague c.-free day DALT 109:3
execution of a senior c. CLARK 96:9
colleagues fidelity to c. LASKI 218:3
collective C. responsibility LYNN 235:9
sense of c. responsibility ALD 6:9
collects one of those beautiful c. MAC 239:1
collision avoid foreign c. CLAY 97:2
colonies c. do not cease to be DISR 119:6
c. seek for at Botany Bay FRE 143:6
commerce with our c. BURKE 64:13
existing c. or dependencies MONR 263:6
united c. LEE 220:3
wretched c. DISR 119:2
colonization subjects for future c. MONR 263:4
colony fuzzy wuzzy c. CAIR 72:1
Colossus Like a C. SHAK 328:4
colour c. of the cat doesn't matter DENG 113:4
c. of their skin KING 210:10
met by the c. line DOUG 124:2
Our constitution is c.-blind HARL 169:2
problem of the c. line DU B 126:5
coloured c. man DOUG 124:1
'white' or 'c.' signs KENN 205:5
colourless c., odourless PEYR 291:2
colours c. will agree in the dark BACON 23:6
columnists political c. ADAMS 2:4
comb two bald men over a c. BORG 52:7
combination You may call it c. PALM 284:3
combine bad men c. BURKE 63:4
combining cabinet is a c. committee BAG 24:13
come Out of Ireland have we c. YEATS 396:2
We are c. for your good GEOR 148:8
When you c. back again RUB 314:8
comeback c. kid CLIN 99:6
comfort And a' the c. we're to get BURNS 68:13
Be of good c. Master Ridley LAT 218:5
for the love of material c. TOCQ 366:2
My c. hath been in my people's ELIZ 131:2
comfortable c. and the accepted GALB 145:8
comical I often think it's c. GILB 152:6
coming as though Christ were c. CART 77:5
my c. down MORE 265:9
that c. storm GLAD 154:1
they will be c. for us BALD 28:9
command able to c. the rain PEPYS 290:1
not born to sue, but to c. SHAK 333:2
commander c. of the American FRAN 142:5
Congress is his c. STEV 349:4
commanding c. heights BEVAN 41:6
commandments ten c. BIGG 45:3
comment c. is free, but facts SCOTT 322:4
c. is free but facts STOP 351:10
I couldn't possibly c. DOBBS 122:4
commerce c. with our colonies BURKE 64:13
matters of c. CANN 75:3
peace, c., and honest friendship JEFF 192:7
commercial c. world BURKE 68:8
commissions *royal c.* FRAN 142:12
committed [Earl Haig] c. suicide BEAV 34:4
committee cabinet is a combining c. BAG 24:13
c. is organic PARK 285:9
committing c. another evil HAVEL 170:6
c. ourselves to the truth NIXON 274:3
commodities particular c. SMITH 342:7
commodity supply us with a c. SMITH 342:6
common according to the c. weal JAM 190:2
carrying on the c. cause HAL 166:6
century of the c. man WALL 376:10
c. interest PAINE 282:14
c. interests of capital and labour ATK 19:6
c. law JEFF 192:2
c. law is at a disadvantage SCAR 321:5
C. Law of England HERB 177:1
c. man, I think BEVIN 42:10
c. market is a process MONN 262:6
c. opinion and uncommon abilities BAG 23:14
c. sense and c. honesty SHEL 337:6
c. sense kept breaking in TAYL 357:14
He nothing c. did or mean MARV 251:7
Lord prefers c.-looking people LINC 227:5

conflict (*cont.*):
risks of spreading c. JOHN 196:3
tragic c. of loyalties HOWE 184:2
conflicts disputes or c. BRI 56:2
conform either c., or be more wise PEPYS 290:3
conforming c. to the times MACH 241:11
confound c. their politics ANON 9:9
confrontation c. with the politics HAIL 163:9
confused Anyone who isn't c. MURR 268:7
confusion c. now hath made SHAK 331:9
confute man can tell how to c. him SELD 323:1
Congress C. is his commander STEV 349:4
C. makes no progress LIGNE 224:1
C. may slip without the Union TOCQ 365:5
criminal class except C. TWAIN 372:8
you were a member of C. TWAIN 372:11
conjuror superlative Hebrew c. CARL 76:12
conquer it is possible to c. poverty JOHN 196:1
It was easier to c. it WALP 378:1
resolve to c. or die WASH 379:6
wont to c. others SHAK 333:4
conquered feel they are a c. people VICT 374:7
I came, I saw, I c. CAES 71:12
If the Communists c. the world RUSS 316:9
perpetually to be c. BURKE 64:12
to have c. and peopled SEEL 322:6
conqueror Every other c. BURKE 65:9
proud foot of a c. SHAK 331:1
conquest for purposes of foreign c. WEBS 382:7
shameful c. of itself SHAK 333:4
conquests Are all thy c., glories SHAK 329:8
conscience c. is a still small voice ATTL 20:7
c. of a statesman TAYL 358:3
dominion of reason and c. PRICE 298:3
England was the 'courage of c.' CHO 85:6
freedom of speech, freedom of c. TWAIN 372:9
have a c., when it has no soul THUR 364:9
human happiness or a quiet c. BERL 39:1
keep your c. well under control LLOY 229:12
meddle not with any man's c. CROM 105:5
power without c. BRAD 54:5
public life, a species of c. TAYL 358:4
Sufficient c. to bother him LLOY 231:2
taking your c. round BEVIN 42:7
will not cut my c. HELL 174:3
consciences binding on the c. JOHN 195:1
conscientious c. stupidity KING 210:5
consciousness determines their c. MARX 252:7
consecrated c. by the experience GIBB 152:2
c. obstruction BAG 25:10
consensus c. behind my convictions THAT 361:12
c. breaking up CROS 106:11
consent c. of the governed PAGE 280:7
feel inferior without your c. ROOS 308:3
voice of Rome is the c. of heaven JONS 199:3
without his c. CAMD 73:5
consequence c. of cabinet government BAG 24:14
consequences damn the c. MILN 260:3
I renounce war for its c. FOSD 139:6
political c. GALB 146:12
We must not regard political c. MANS 249:6
conservation means of its c. BURKE 66:8
conservatism c. and progress TROL 369:7
C.—an unhappy cross-breed DISR 117:9
C. discards Prescription DISR 117:6
c. is based upon the idea CHES 84:4
harder shores of modern C. HENN 175:1
meanness in the argument of c. EMER 133:3
party of C. and that of Innovation EMER 133:2
What is c. LINC 225:3
conservative belief that it is really c. FISH 137:2
C. Government DISR 117:17
C. is a man ROOS 309:7
c., *n.* A statesman BIER 44:16
c. on the day after the revolution AREN 15:10
C. Party always in time forgives MACL 243:1
C. Party at prayer ROYD 314:7
C. party must rule BAG 27:7
C. party takes office BISM 47:7
fear it would make me c. FROST 144:3
I must be a C. RUSK 315:12
most c. man in this world BEVIN 42:6
Or else a little C. GILB 152:6
password of C. government POW 297:6
sound C. government DISR 117:7
trouble with the C. Party WAUGH 381:1
We [the C. Party] found it hard JOS 199:7
which makes a man more c. KEYN 207:9
word 'c.' is used by the BBC TEBB 359:3
conservatives C. being by the law MILL 259:7
C. do not believe HAIL 163:3
C. were to set the people free HEATH 173:7
liberals and c. clashed MOYN 267:5
more formalistic than c. CALV 73:4
trouble with c. CARV 78:1
consideration Under active c. LYNN 235:2
consistency no c., except BYRON 71:1
conspicuous c. by its presence RUSS 317:3
c. consumption VEBL 373:5
conspiracy c. against the public SMITH 341:5
imagines a perpetual c. SAL 318:3
kind of c. against the rest HAL 166:4
O c. SHAK 328:11
society is in an organized c. DOUG 124:4
conspirators All the c. save only SHAK 330:16
constant c. as the northern star SHAK 329:3
His inconstancy is his great c. DUPIN 127:2
constellation bright c. JEFF 192:8
constituencies go back to your c. STEEL 348:10
constituents mob of their c. BURKE 66:3
constitution act against the C. OTIS 280:1
boast of its c. PAINE 283:12

British C. ELIZ 132:7
[British C.] presumes GLAD 154:13
c. does not provide WILL 389:6
C., in all its provisions CHASE 83:7
C. is an equally forthright piece O'RO 277:4
c. is extremely well WALP 377:5
C. is what happens GRIF 161:6
C. of the United States is DAVIS 110:2
C. of the United States was CLAY 98:1
[C.] was framed upon CARD 75:7
construe the C. or laws LINC 225:6
English c. BLAC 48:8
Every country has its own c. ANON 9:12
invoke the genius of the C. PITT 293:3
need for a written c. SCAR 320:8
oath to support the c. JACK 188:9
one basic element in our C. TRUM 371:11
One country, one c., one destiny WEBS 382:9
Our c. is colour-blind HARL 169:2
Our C. works FORD 138:12
people made the C. MARS 251:4
principles of a free c. GIBB 151:4
reconstruct the whole C. TOCQ 366:9
set down in writing a C. DANG 109:4
support its C., to obey its laws PAGE 280:7
takeover of the British C. SCAR 321:2
very essence of the c. JUN 200:9
What's the C. between friends? CAMP 74:1
When the C. was framed BEARD 33:3
written c. CALL 73:3
constitutional c. right LINC 225:7
I have no eyes but c. eyes LINC 227:2
live under it as a c. monarchy TROL 369:3
most influential of c. statesmen BAG 23:15
only fit material for a c. king BAG 26:2
partners in the c. minuet SCAR 321:1
constitutions c. of later Greece BAG 25:7
constrained by violence c. ELIZ 130:4
construct Having nothing to c. TROL 369:9
construction mind's c. in the face SHAK 331:6
consul horse was made C. RAND 300:10
consult here to c. the interests PEEL 288:6
consulted right to be c. BAG 26:1
consume c. more than HAYEK 171:10
consumer c., is the king SAM 320:1
c. society ILL 187:4
consumes c. without producing ORW 278:9
consumption conspicuous c. VEBL 373:5
c. is the sole end SMITH 342:1
not increase its c. KEYN 208:3
contagion War is a c. ROOS 309:4
contemptible c. little army ANON 10:1
ill-usage c. MELB 255:5
those poor c. men CROM 105:12
contending fierce c. nations ADD 5:9
content I am c. ADAMS 5:1
Nothing less will c. me BURKE 64:8
contented king shall be c. SHAK 334:2
continent c. allotted by Providence O'SUL 279:13
c., frozen in hostility BUSH 69:9
c. will [not] suffer England DISR 117:1
involve this c. PAINE 281:6
striving to grasp a c. PARK 286:3
upon this c. a new nation LINC 226:3
continental c. union PAINE 281:5
continentally Learn to think c. HAM 167:7
continents American c. MONR 263:4
contingent play of the c. FISH 136:8
continuation *war is the c. of politics* CLA 96:11
continue c. for five years too long BIFF 45:2
continuous c. tolerance BAG 27:6
contract labour c. CHUR 87:4
new social c. CALL 72:7
social c. ROUS 314:4
social c. is left-wing DEBR 111:1
social c. is nothing more or less WELLS 385:3
society is indeed a c. BURKE 67:5
contracting high c. powers BRI 56:2
contracts party platforms are c. TRUM 371:9
preserve c. MELB 256:6
contradict I never deny; I never c. DISR 121:7
Never c. FISH 137:4
contrary Every law is c. to liberty BENT 37:10
To take usury is c. to Scripture TAWN 355:11
contrive How nature always does c. GILB 152:6
control c. the governed MAD 246:7
controlling no longer c. events HATT 170:3
controls Who c. the past ORW 279:2
controversy man of c. GALB 145:8
times of challenge and c. KING 210:6
contumely proud man's c. SHAK 325:8
conventional c. wisdom GALB 145:7
Too c. a thinker MONC 261:11
conversation c. perfectly delightful SMITH 344:9
His c. turned on BEAV 34:2
conversations after-dinner c. THOR 364:5
taping of c. NIXON 274:12
converted You have not c. a man MORL 265:10
conviction best lack all c. YEATS 395:6
c. politicians BANC 32:1
convictions behind my c. THAT 361:12
convince we c. ourselves JUN 200:11
convinced c. beyond doubt VAN 373:3
You've c. me ROOS 310:7
cool In any case, keep c. LIDD 223:5
Coolidge admiration for Mr C. ANON 13:12
Mr C.'s genius for inactivity LIPP 228:1
Nero fiddled, but C. only snored MENC 256:13
Cooper Gary C. killing off BALD 28:6
co-operation government and c. RUSK 315:7
copies few originals and many c. TOCQ 366:6
cord triple c. BURKE 68:3
cordial c. with everyone MAUG 254:4

Corinthian C. capital BURKE 67:6
corn lower the price of c. MELB 256:2
raise the price of c. BYRON 71:5
two ears of c. SWIFT 353:7
corner Never c. an opponent LIDD 223:5
corners three c. of the world SHAK 331:1
turn square c. HOLM 181:6
cornet muzzle this terrible young c. WALP 378:4
Cornish twenty thousand C. men HAWK 170:7
coronation king's c. BLUNT 49:7
corporate c. officials FRI 143:7
corporation c. state DOUG 123:4
expect a c. THUR 364:9
corps effete c. of impudent snobs AGNEW 6:6
strike at the whole c. BURKE 66:1
Corps d'Armée Tory C. GLAD 154:14
corpse c. at the funeral HEAD 172:1
politician's c. was laid away BELL 35:5
corridors c. of power SNOW 345:4
corrupt equally wicked and c. BURKE 63:2
good custom should c. the world TENN 360:5
legislative power is more c. MONT 264:12
more c. the republic TAC 354:6
most c. government on the earth JEFF 192:2
people generally c. BURKE 64:18
power tends to c. RUSK 315:4
That do c. my air,—I banish you SHAK 324:8
Unlimited power is apt to c. PITT 292:11
corrupted c. governments HAL 165:12
c. the youth of the realm SHAK 327:3
principle of democracy is c. MONT 264:5
corruption c. at home CHUR 87:3
c. of each government MONT 264:4
c., the most infallible symptom GIBB 151:9
c. wins not more than honesty SHAK 327:7
corrupts absolute power c. ACTON 1:9
cosmopolitan c. critics DISR 120:8
cost c. of liberty DU B 126:7
c. of setting him up NAIDU 268:9
costs duke c. as much to keep up LLOY 229:3
obedience generally c. more MAC 238:5
cottage poorest man may in his c. PITT 292:9
the c. is not happy DISR 121:13
cotton C. is King CHR 86:1
council In c. rooms apart RICE 304:5
labour c. hiring taxis KINN 211:11
councillor c. is like a mushroom MAG 247:5
councillors c. of state CARL 76:10
counsel Dost sometimes c. take POPE 295:2
intention to keep my c. GLAD 155:6
religion, justice, c., and treasure BACON 22:16
take c. always of your courage STEV 350:12
counsellor Indeed this c. SHAK 325:10
counsels crooked c. fit DRYD 125:4
seeking after various c. TAYL 358:9
count I won the c. SOM 346:5
counted the faster we c. EMER 133:4
counting it's the c. STOP 351:8
countries bowels of whole c. PAINE 281:12
country Anyone who loves his c. GAR 148:1
Britain a fit c. for heroes LLOY 229:9
choose between betraying my c. FORS 139:4
c. which has 246 varieties DE G 112:11
c. will be called upon HARD 168:4
dying for Queen and c. THOM 364:6
ends thou aim'st at be thy c.'s SHAK 327:7
established in one c. alone STAL 348:4
ever exist in a free c. BURKE 64:9
every c. but his own GILB 152:10
Every c. has its own constitution ANON 9:12
Every c. has the government MAIS 248:5
fate of this c. depends DISR 120:6
fight for its king and c. GRAH 158:6
for the good of his c. WOTT 394:9
friend of every c. but his own CANN 75:1
friends of every c. DISR 120:8
His first, best c. GOLD 157:3
how I leave my c. PITT 293:12
insular c., subject to fogs DISR 120:15
In the c. of the blind ERAS 133:10
I pray for the c. HALE 164:4
Isn't this a billion dollar c. FOST 139:7
leave his c. as good COBB 100:4
Liberty is not, there is my c. PAINE 283:11
life to lose for my c. HALE 164:6
Love thy c. DOD 122:5
may our c. be always successful ADAMS 4:6
merchants have no c. JEFF 193:5
My c. is the world PAINE 283:2
My c., right or wrong CHES 84:1
My c., right or wrong; if right SCH 322:2
My c., 'tis of thee SMITH 344:5
never let my c. die for me KINN 212:1
No man attached to his c. PEEL 288:7
not see much of the c. GLAD 154:8
old c. must wake up GEOR 149:5
One c., one constitution WEBS 382:9
our c., right or wrong DEC 111:4
party before c. CREWE 104:2
prepare the mind of the c. DISR 119:12
quarrel in a far away c. CHAM 80:9
right to leave any c. ANON 9:13
says that he loves his c. STEV 350:2
serve my c. as a faithful servant GIBR 152:3
serve our c. ADD 5:8
service of their c. PAINE 281:10
take a c. into a war CHAM 81:2
that will not love his c. SHAK 329:12
these c. patriots BYRON 71:5
The union, sir, is my c. CLAY 97:12
They died to save their c. CHES 84:10
This c. needs good farmers NIXON 274:11
This c. was a lot better off DEL 113:1

This *is* a beautiful c. BROWN 59:4
tremble for my c. JEFF 191:3
understand the c. LESS 221:13
wants of the c. PEEL 288:2
what was good for our c. WILS 389:7
Where liberty is, there is my c. OTIS 280:2
with women, to a single c. GALB 146:3
you can do for your c. KENN 204:7
your c. is lost WILL 389:3
Your king and c. need you FIELD 136:5
your king and your c. RUB 314:8
countrymen Friends, Romans, c. SHAK 329:13
given my advice to my c. O'CON 276:6
hearts of his c. LEE 220:2
rebels are our c. again GRANT 159:8
counts not the critic who c. ROOS 311:10
courage accuse himself of c. BIRCH 46:1
c. is the rarest of all DISR 121:19
c. of conscience CHO 85:6
c. to be the secret of liberty BRAN 54:10
One man with c. JACK 189:4
resolution on reflection is real c. WALP 377:10
take counsel always of your c. STEV 350:12
two o'clock in the morning c. NAP 269:10
vain faith, and c. vain MAC 238:9
courageous describe it as *c.* LYNN 235:5
course c. by course CHUR 89:11
c. of human events JEFF 190:7
Take thou what c. thou wilt SHAK 330:11
court art o'th' c. SHAK 325:3
'aving no family life at c. THOM 363:6
bright lustre of a c. CECIL 79:9
mean c. BAG 25:11
Say to the c., it glows RAL 300:4
courtesan pampered c. of Europe MACM 244:3
courtmartialled I was c. BEHAN 34:10
Coutts banks with C. GILB 152:11
covenant c. with death GARR 148:4
covenants open c. of peace WILS 392:15
cow Three acres and a c. ANON 14:1
cowboy that damned c. HANNA 168:1
cracking c. sound CROS 106:11
cradle from the c. to the grave CHUR 91:12
rocking the c. ROB 307:3
crash c. will come BISM 47:6
cravats men in long c. SHIP 339:7
crawl c. up the staircase BEVAN 41:11
crazy should they go c. PHOC 292:5
when I was c. SHER 339:2
create c. the current of events BISM 47:9
One must genuinely *c.* Europe MONN 262:5
qualities which c. publicity ATTL 20:4
created all men are c. equal JEFF 191:1
creates not only in what it c. BAG 26:3
creation since the c. NIXON 274:5
creative destruction is also a c. urge BAK 28:4
creator go up to his c. and say LLOY 230:9
credibility *we played the c. card* SHAP 335:12
credit most c. TAYL 358:10
credulity present age is craving c. DISR 119:8
soften into a c. BURKE 63:2
youth is the season of c. PITT 292:10
creed c. of slaves PITT 293:7
c. of the moment BAG 23:15
last article of my c. GAND 147:3
political c. ADAMS 4:3
creep ambition can c. BURKE 68:5
cricket c.—a game MANC 249:2
c. civilizes people MUG 267:6
c. test TEBB 359:4
playing c. with their peasants TREV 368:2
cried he died the little children c. MOTL 267:3
poor have c., Caesar hath wept SHAK 330:2
when he c. the little children died AUDEN 21:5
Crillon brave C. HENR 175:3
crime catalogue of human c. CHUR 90:6
c. of being a young man PITT 292:7
foulest c. in history WHIT 388:1
high c. rates BOAZ 50:1
parent of revolution and c. ARIS 16:8
prevent c. MELB 256:6
today's outburst of c. TEBB 359:2
tough on c. and tough on BLAIR 48:11
worse than a c. BOUL 53:5
crimes register of the c. GIBB 151:6
criminal c. element DEBS 111:3
ends I think c. KEYN 207:2
native American c. class TWAIN 372:8
severity of the c. law PEEL 287:9
criminals if there were no c. SAL 318:9
squalid c. REAG 302:1
cringe cultural c. KEAT 202:7
crises c. that seemed intolerable ATK 19:5
crisis c. in American leadership BALT 31:9
c. that we inherit BENN 36:4
C.? What Crisis? ANON 9:10
fit for a great c. BAG 25:2
never panics, except in a c. HOSK 183:6
real c. on your hands THAT 361:7
There cannot be a c. KISS 214:2
criterion infallible c. of wisdom BURKE 67:13
critic not the c. who counts ROOS 311:10
criticism c. as a good dutiful boy MAC 236:9
c. of administration BAG 24:14
permits c. FORS 139:5
criticize never to c. or attack CHUR 93:2
critics cosmopolitan c. DISR 120:8
crocodile one who feeds a c. CHUR 90:3
Cromwell C., damned to everlasting fame POPE 295:5
C. guiltless GRAY 160:8
C., I charge thee SHAK 327:7
C., our chief of men MILT 261:2

Cromwell (*cont.*):
They set up C. and his heir JORD 199:5
crony against government by c. ICKES 187:3
crook McAdoo his c. SPR 348:2
their President is a c. NIXON 274:10
crops all the c. I raise PAINE 282:1
cross c. of gold BRYAN 60:6
crosses And tumbled down the c. JORD 199:5
Are they clinging to their c. CHES 84:5
crossroads midnight at a c. O'BR 276:4
crossways understands everything c. SAL 318:3
crowd chaining the c. VOLT 376:5
crown allegiance to the British c. LEE 220:3
As minister of the C. PEEL 288:2
can't have the c. of thorns BEVAN 41:1
C. is, according to the saying BAG 24:12
Give me the c. SHAK 334:3
glory of my c. ELIZ 132:1
head that wears a c. SHAK 326:7
I give away my c. SHAK 334:6
influence of the C. DUNN 127:1
never wears the c. HES 177:9
Not the king's c. SHAK 332:7
Our Indian C. ROSS 313:5
power of the c. BURKE 63:1
put the c. in possession PAINE 280:8
restore the C. JOHN 198:2
this c. of thorns BRYAN 60:6
thrice presented him a kingly c. SHAK 330:3
understand the power of the C. BENN 36:12
within the hollow c. SHAK 333:8
crowned all the c. ruffians PAINE 281:4
Roman Empire, sitting c. HOBB 180:9
crowning c. mercy CROM 105:7
crowns c. are empty things DEFOE 111:11
crucible America is God's c. ZANG 396:8
crucify you shall not c. mankind BRYAN 60:6
cruel c. men of Rome SHAK 328:1
c. necessity CROM 105:4
state business is a c. trade HAL 166:12
crusade party is a moral c. WILS 390:3
crush c. people to the earth CHILD 85:2
cry Don't c. for me, Argentina RICE 304:7
he was too big to c. LINC 225:10
crystal Why read the c. BEVAN 40:8
cuckoo The c. clock WELL 383:7
cult c. is a religion WOLFE 394:1
c. of the individual KHR 209:2
cultural c. cringe KEAT 202:7
culture men of c. ARN 17:3
Whenever I hear the word c. JOHST 198:14
cunning c. men pass for wise BACON 22:6
cure c. for admiring the House BAG 26:4
we palliate what we cannot c. JOHN 197:2
cured ills of democracy can be c. SMITH 343:5
currency debauch the c. KEYN 207:5
current create the c. of events BISM 47:9
we must take the c. SHAK 330:14
curs You common cry of c. SHAK 324:8
curst to all succeeding ages c. DRYD 125:4
curtain bloody c. ELIS 130:3
iron c. has descended CHUR 92:10
lets the c. fall POPE 295:8
Lift the c. POW 297:16
something kept behind a c. PAINE 282:15
Curzon C. will be remembered NEHRU 270:12
cuss don't matter a tinker's c. SHIN 339:5
custodes *ipsos C.* JUV 201:6
custodiet Sed quis c. ipsos JUV 201:6
custom c., that unwritten law D'AV 110:1
Lest one good c. should corrupt TENN 360:5
unwritten c. CATT 78:6
customary action, which is not c. CORN 103:8
customers people of c. SMITH 341:6
customs survives by its ancient c. ENN 133:8
cut he had blocks to c. PEEL 288:12
most unkindest c. of all SHAK 330:6
So he has c. his throat at last BYRON 71:4
they will c. off my head CHAR 82:5
will not c. my conscience HELL 174:3
cuttlefish idioms, like a c. ORW 279:10
cycle c. of deprivation JOS 199:6
cyclops state policy, a c. COL 101:3
czar making the President a c. SCHL 321:6
Czechoslovakia gain for C. CHUR 89:11

dabbling d. their fingers MCGR 241:1
daddy Look, d., no hands ANON 12:6
dagger d. in one hand WRAN 394:10
hand that held the d. ROOS 309:8
daggers few, but they shall be d. PITT 292:8
damage moral or intellectual d. KRUG 215:6
Damascus road to D. THAT 362:7
damn d. the consequences MILN 260:3
look, with a spot I d. him SHAK 330:12
damnation deep d. of his taking-off SHAK 331:7
damned d. to everlasting fame POPE 295:5
lies, d. lies and statistics DISR 121:15
public be d. VAND 373:2
publish and be d. WELL 384:4
dances makes no progress; it d. LIGNE 224:1
dancing d. on a torrent BALF 30:5
Dane never get rid of the D. KIPL 213:4
Dane-geld paying the D. KIPL 213:4
danger d. justified privilege WAUGH 380:8
d. of great nations BAG 27:12
d. to the country, to Europe VICT 374:6
in as much d. HAL 165:4
Pleased with the d. DRYD 125:5
dangerous he would be d. MELB 255:6
most d. moment TOCQ 367:3
such men are d. SHAK 328:7

when they are no longer d. BOUL 53:6
Dante D. never stays too long MAC 237:10
dare none d. call it treason HAR 169:1
Take me if you d. PANK 285:1
dark always wear a d. suit ROSS 313:4
colours will agree in the d. BACON 23:6
things go around in the d. HOOV 182:11
darkness curse the d. STEV 350:14
Go out into the d. HASK 170:2
light cut into the d. KENN 205:7
there is d. everywhere NEHRU 270:8
universal d. buries all POPE 295:8
darning d. needle is broader NIC 272:2
Darwin evidence to upset D. ADAMS 2:10
date d. which will live ROOS 310:1
dates question of d. TALL 355:5
daughter d. am I in my mother's KIPL 213:1
d. of debate, that eke discord ELIZ 130:8
dauntless with d. breast GRAY 160:8
dawn bliss was it in that d. WORD 394:7
catch and to reflect the d. MAC 238:2
day close the drama with the d. BERK 38:4
d. I was meant not to THAT 361:10
d. of small nations CHAM 80:6
not a second on the d. COOK 102:5
daylight not let in d. upon magic BAG 25:13
days cast your mind on other d. YEATS 396:3
finished in the first 1,000 d. KENN 204:5
hundred d. of dynamic action WILS 390:6
In the brave d. of old MAC 237:1
dazzled d. thus with height WOTT 394:8
dead better red than d. ANON 9:1
d. battles, like dead generals TUCH 372:4
d., but in the Elysian fields DISR 121:6
d. or dying beast JENK 194:5
d. shall not have died in vain LINC 226:3
d. woman bites not GRAY 160:7
democracy of the d. CHES 84:2
if I am d. he would like to see HOLL 181:5
protection is not only d. DISR 121:11
those who are d. BURKE 67:5
we are all d. KEYN 207:6
With the d. there is no rivalry MAC 237:10
dead-level d. of income or wealth TAWN 355:9
deadliness d. to fight Germany CHUR 86:2
Dead Sea like a D. fruit MACM 245:7
whole thing was D. Fruit LEVIN 222:11
deal I want to d. closely MACL 242:6
new d. ROOS 308:6
square d. ROOS 311:5
dean no dogma, no D. DISR 121:10
dear fault, d. Brutus SHAK 328:4
this d., dear land SHAK 333:4
dearest throw away the d. thing SHAK 331:6
death added a new terror to d. WETH 386:1
anger of the sovereign is d. MORE 265:7
certain, except d. and taxes FRAN 142:9
covenant with d. GARR 148:4
d. and sorrow CHUR 90:11
d. for the minnows TAWN 356:1
D. is the most convenient time LLOY 229:13
d. of any state HOBB 180:7
d. of democracy is not likely HUTC 186:2
d., without rhetoric SIEY 340:4
disqualified by the accident of d. CHES 84:3
forced marches, battles and d. GAR 148:1
give me d. HENRY 176:5
kiss of d. SMITH 343:4
laws of d. RUSK 315:7
loving ourselves to d. PRES 298:2
lucky timing of your d. TAC 354:4
nearest thing to d. in life ANON 12:8
One d. is a tragedy, one million STAL 348:7
signed my d. warrant COLL 101:4
sign her own d.-warrant BAG 25:12
sorry for the d. BAG 24:4
studied in his d. SHAK 331:6
suicide 25 years after his d. BEAV 34:4
tell sad stories of the d. of kings SHAK 333:8
their tongues doom men to d. SHAK 335:5
Those by d. are few JEFF 192:9
While there is d. there is hope CROS 106:9
your slogan 'liberty or d.' WOOL 394:4
debatable d. line MAC 236:6
debate better to d. a question JOUB 200:7
daughter of d. ELIZ 130:8
d. on public issues BREN 55:11
Rupert of d. BULW 62:1
talk fluently, d. forcefully HOGB 181:1
debating reporting, rather than d. HOGG 181:3
debt ambition's d. is paid SHAK 329:5
national d. HAM 167:1
national d. is a very Good Thing SELL 323:8
running up a $4 trillion d. PEROT 290:9
We've a war, an' a d. LOW 233:8
debts so we can pay our d. NYER 276:1
decade in the same d. with you ROOS 310:3
decades underestimated for d. KOHL 215:3
deceiving nearly d. your friends CORN 103:9
decide ministers d. THAT 362:5
moment to d. LOW 234:1
power elite are those who d. MILLS 260:2
decides does not propose, it d. ATTL 20:6
decision hard, fast and specific d. TUCH 372:5
life is to act with d. PEEL 288:16
monologue is not a d. ATTL 19:10
offhand d. HARDY 168:7
Once a d. was made TRUM 371:7
political d. TREND 367:7
that is a power of d. HEAD 172:5
decisions d. of importance PARK 286:1
important d. ATTL 20:14
decisive short d. war LYND 234:9

deck to shoulder on a burning d. MACL 243:6
Walk the d. WHIT 387:10
declaration D. of Independence CHO 85:8
There has been no d. of war EDEN 127:7
decline neighbouring state is in d. MONT 264:7
orderly management of d. ARMS 17:1
decorated d., and got rid of CIC 95:13
decorum Goes all d. SHAK 332:4
decree establish the d. BIBLE 43:20
decry not one of those who d. Eton BEVIN 42:9
defeat d. is an orphan CIANO 95:4
In d.: defiance CHUR 93:5
In d., Malice LYNN 235:4
In d. unbeatable CHUR 94:5
knows not victory nor d. ROOS 310:11
one glorious d. after another WHIN 386:5
possibilities of d.; they do not exist VICT 374:9
price of ultimate d. NIC 272:1
we know we should d. you KIPL 213:4
we never had a d. CHUR 93:10
defeated d. in a great battle LIVY 228:9
Down with the d. LIVY 228:8
defence best d. against the atom ANON 8:11
d. of the indefensible ORW 279:9
extremism in the d. of liberty GOLD 157:8
millions for d., but not one cent HARP 169:5
Never make a d. or apology CHAR 82:2
only d. is in offence, which means BALD 29:6
think of the d. of England BALD 29:7
defend d. to the death your right VOLT 375:11
refuses to d. his rights JACK 188:6
defiance In defeat: d. CHUR 93:5
definitive we can do nothing d. WASH 379:8
defrauding d. of the State PENN 289:14
degree Observe d. SHAK 335:7
O! when d. is shaked SHAK 335:8
dehumanizing d. the Negro LINC 224:9
Dei *vox D.* ALC 6:8
delay d., right or justice MAGN 247:4
delaying by d. put the state to rights ENN 133:9
delenda *D. est Carthago* CATO 79:1
deleted expletive d. ANON 9:14
delighteth king d. to honour BIBLE 43:13
delivered d. him into mine hand BIBLE 43:11
delivery ungracefulness of his d. WALP 377:8
deluge as the d. subsides CHUR 88:4
demand inordinate d. for peace PEEL 288:10
demands cannot exact their d. WELL 385:2
demi-paradise This other Eden, d. SHAK 333:4
demise its own d. BLAIR 49:1
democracies d. against despots DEM 113:2
d., which refresh their ruling class TREV 368:5
sacred thing; in d. FRAN 141:3
democracy be an empire or a d. BRZ 61:3
before D. go through its due CARL 75:8
cured by more d. SMITH 343:5
death of d. HUTC 186:2
D. and proper drains BETJ 40:1
D. and socialism NEHRU 270:10
D. a society where ordinary men TAWN 356:2
d. can be no more than YOUNG 396:7
d., for the starvation FOSD 139:6
d. in a republic PAGE 280:7
D. is a *State* which recognizes LENIN 221:6
D. is clearly most appropriate POTT 296:3
d. is that it has tolerated BEVAN 40:2
D. is the name we give FLERS 137:7
D. is the recurrent suspicion WHITE 386:6
D. is the theory MENC 256:8
D. means government ATTL 20:11
D. means government CHES 85:1
D. never lasts long ADAMS 4:2
D. no longer works FIELD 136:6
d. of the dead CHES 84:2
D. substitutes election SHAW 336:7
d.—that is a government PARK 285:6
d. the worst form of Government CHUR 93:1
D., which means despair CARL 76:14
D. will not be salvaged HOGB 181:1
envy is the basis of d. RUSS 316:7
extreme d. or absolute oligarchy ARIS 16:9
great arsenal of d. ROOS 309:10
grieved under a *d.* HOBB 180:8
holy name of liberty or d. GAND 147:5
'In a d.,' said Mr Pinfold WAUGH 380:7
in a d. the whores are us O'RO 277:8
justice makes d. possible NIEB 272:10
leaving d. more unsafe ROB 307:1
made safe for d. WILS 392:12
myth of d. CROS 106:12
no d. can afford BEV 42:4
not the voting that's d. STOP 351:8
our d. was, from an early period MAC 238:12
People who want to understand d. STR 352:4
perfect d. BURKE 67:4
political aspirant under d. MENC 256:12
pollution of d. WHITE 387:2
principle of d. MONT 264:5
property-owning d. SKEL 340:9
there is a little less d. to save ATK 19:4
This expresses my idea of d. LINC 224:8
Two cheers for D. FORS 139:5
Under d. one party always MENC 257:4
what Tory D. is CHUR 86:3
Wisconsin was a triumph for d. HOPE 183:2
Without d. socialism would TAYL 356:5
democrat called himself or herself a d. BEARD 33:3
Santa Claus is a D. O'RO 277:3
United States senator, and a D. JOHN 195:5
democratic among a d. people TROL 369:4
d. and accountable HUNT 185:7
D. Party is like a mule DONN 122:7
d. socialism FOOT 138:9

dwelling in a state of d. freedom CHUR 88:14
free, d. government TRUM 372:3
indignity to the d. process STEV 350:11
layer of d. paint TOCQ 365:3
no D. or Republican LA G 216:5
democratically d. governed HAIL 164:1
democratization d. of civil society KEANE 202:5
democrats all D. were saloon keepers GRE 161:2
D. object CHES 84:3
stop telling lies about the D. STEV 350:1
town atheist, and a few D. BROG 57:6
Demosthenes D. had finished STEV 350:13
D. never comes MAC 237:10
denied until it has been officially d. COCK 100:6
Denmark rotten in the state of D. SHAK 325:6
deny d. them this participation BURKE 63:12
I never d.; I never contradict DISR 121:7
will we sell, or d., or delay MAGN 247:4
deodorant some kind of d. SCHR 321:9
depart D., I say AMERY 8:1
departed glory is d. BIBLE 43:10
departments other d. MELB 255:7
departure point of d. METT 258:2
twenty years after my d. BISM 47:6
depose my glories and my state d. SHAK 334:4
depositary d. of power DISR 117:10
depression d. when you lose TRUM 371:14
deprivation cycle of d. JOS 199:6
depths d. of insincerity ANON 13:10
deputy d. elected by the Lord SHAK 333:6
deserve d. to get it MENC 256:8
desiccated d. calculating machine BEVAN 41:5
designs ladder to all high d. SHAK 335:8
desire d. for honour CIC 95:8
d. of power HOBB 179:10
desires doing what one d. MILL 259:4
desk subservience to the d. FRAN 142:10
desolated province they have d. GLAD 154:12
desolation d. of war GEOR 149:6
years of d. pass over JEFF 193:11
despair ye Mighty, and d. SHEL 337:9
desperate Diseases d. grown SHAK 326:1
desperation hunger, poverty, d. MARS 251:2
despised old, mad, blind, d. SHEL 338:1
despot wise d. HERB 177:2
despotic create a d. government HERB 177:2
d. states MONT 264:15
There you have d. government MONT 264:2
despotism D. accomplishes great things BALZ 31:10
d. in England WALP 377:13
D. is essential in most enterprises CARL 76:6
d. of liberty against tyranny ROB 306:8
d., or unlimited sovereignty ADAMS 4:3
d. tempered by epigrams CARL 75:11
d. will come ARIS 16:9
government of laws, is a d. WEBS 382:8
modern form of d. MCC 239:8
translated from d. to liberty JEFF 191:11
wickedness is the root of d. ROB 306:9
despots democracies against d. DEM 113:2
D. themselves do not deny TOCQ 366:4
destinies d. of half the globe TOCQ 365:9
d. of the British Empire DISR 119:7
development of human d. FISH 136:8
destiny one constitution, one d. WEBS 382:9
our manifest d. O'SUL 279:13
rendezvous with d. ROOS 308:10
walking with d. CHUR 90:4
destroy d. all respect CHUR 94:14
d. the juridical safeguards HAYEK 171:9
d. the town to save it ANON 11:3
tax involves the power to d. MARS 251:3
Whom the mad would d. LEVIN 222:3
destroyed Carthage must be d. CATO 79:1
treated generously or d. MACH 241:2
destruction happiness, and not their d. JEFF 193:1
law on the side of d. KEYN 207:5
mad d. GAND 147:5
rush and rumble of d. NIC 271:7
urge for d. is also a creative urge BAK 28:4
world peace or world d. BAR 32:4
destructive he would be simply d. MELB 255:6
detected he was d. only once BENN 37:5
detest I d. him more than cold MAC 236:10
detestation d. of the high DICK 115:6
Deutschland *D. über alles* HOFF 180:11
de Valera negotiating with d. LLOY 230:3
developed have a d. society NYER 276:2
devil first Whig was the d. JOHN 198:8
go to the d., he may as well go NORF 275:2
his cause being good, the d. MORE 265:6
name a synonym for the d. MAC 237:5
when most I play the d. SHAK 334:11
devils many d. would set on me LUTH 234:7
devour always opened to d. ADAMS 3:3
devourers become so great d. MORE 265:5
diaper Dewey threw his d. ICKES 187:2
dictator begin a career as a d. DE G 112:7
German d., instead of snatching CHUR 89:11
dictators d. ride to and fro upon CHUR 89:8
evil weed, which d. may cultivate BEV 42:4
gain success can set up d. LINC 226:4
dictatorship d. of the proletariat MARX 252:5
d. seriously violates human ROM 308:2
elective d. HAIL 163:8
government you have a d. TRUM 371:15
inherent inefficiencies of d. GALB 145:3
One does not establish a d. ORW 279:7
path to an 'elected d.' SCAR 321:2
dictatorships d. it puts in FOSD 139:6
die afeard there are few d. well SHAK 326:13
And shall Trelawny d. HAWK 170:7

die (*cont.*):
better to d. on your feet than to IBAR 186:6
d. in the last ditch WILL 389:3
d. is cast CAES 71:11
D., my dear Doctor, that's PALM 284:9
d. to-day, and you to-morrow MORE 265:7
don't want to d. for politicians THOM 364:6
faith is something you d. for BENN 36:10
He will, he must d. NICH 271:4
I believe they d. to vex me MELB 255:8
I d. a Christian, according to CHAR 82:7
I d. happy FOX 141:1
in the sky when you d. HILL 178:8
It is well, I d. hard WASH 380:2
I will d. like a true-blue rebel HILL 178:9
leased out,—I d. pronouncing it SHAK 333:4
Let us do—or d. BURNS 68:12
never let my country d. for me KINN 212:1
People d., but books never die ROOS 310:2
something he will d. for KING 210:9
That we can d. but once to serve ADD 5:8
to resolve to conquer or d. WASH 379:6
you asked this man to d. AUDEN 21:6
youth who must fight and d. HOOV 183:1
died As He d. to make men holy HOWE 184:4
He d. by inches in public ROS 312:6
on its tombstone: *d. of a Theory* DAVIS 110:3
They d. to save their country CHES 84:10
difference d. of forty thousand men WELL 384:6
no more d. between your grace MORE 265:7
tough-minded…respect d. BEN 35:7
What d. does it make GAND 147:5
differences of course a nation of d. CART 77:6
differently for the one who thinks d. LUX 234:8
difficult d. to speak BURKE 66:4
difficulties d. in princes' business BACON 22:8
source of d. for several NAP 270:2
these little local d. MACM 244:8
dig D. for Victory DORM 123:1
digging you're in a hole, stop d. HEAL 173:3
dignified *d.* parts BAG 24:10
dignities men come to d. BACON 22:11
dignity added to his d. CHUR 94:13
as much d. in tilling a field WASH 379:3
below the d. of history MAC 238:11
d. of a person is acknowledged JOHN 195:3
free and equal in d. and rights ANON 8:4
I see no d. in persevering in error PEEL 288:11
kept up the d. of the office GEOR 149:7
maintain a d. in their fate WALP 377:10
diminished ought to be d. DUNN 127:1
dimming gradual d. of the lights NIC 272:4
dinner inviting people to d. MAO 250:2
to their talking politics after d. DISR 120:4
we expect our d. SMITH 341:4
dinners consists in giving d. ADAMS 4:10
diplomacy d. is about surviving till LYNN 235:8
d. is saying 'Nice doggie' CATL 78:5
d. is to do and say GOLD 156:9
science of d. consists ADAMS 4:10
diplomat chief distinction of a d. PEAR 287:6
d.…is a person who can tell STIN 351:5
diplomatic d. boathook SAL 317:7
diplomatist d.'s vocabulary TAYL 357:1
directed d. from Washington JEFF 193:16
direction facing in the same d. ROST 313:6
dirt D. is only matter out of GRAY 160:6
thicker will be the d. GALB 145:11
disappearance d. from the human CLAY 97:5
disappointing be the least d. BAR 32:7
disapprove I d. of what you say VOLT 375:11
disaster meet with triumph and d. KIPL 213:3
press lives on d. ATTL 20:10
disastrous between the d. GALB 145:12
discipline d., unless operated COCK 100:8
discontent D. arises from BEVAN 40:11
permanent fund of d. PEEL 288:9
winter of our d. SHAK 334:8
discontented blushing d. sun SHAK 334:1
discord And, hark! what d. follows SHAK 335:9
debate, that eke d. doth sow ELIZ 130:8
What dire effects from civil d. flow ADD 5:9
discoveries consequence of d. BACON 22:2
discovery d. of grievances SAL 318:4
discretion inform their d. JEFF 193:8
their happiness in thy d. ELIZ 131:2
discrimination all life is about d. POW 297:4
in the face of d. BETH 39:9
discuss stay and d. them WELL 384:5
discussion administration is by d. GALB 146:11
after reasonable d. CHUR 93:11
capable of enduring continuous d. BAG 27:6
government by d. ATTL 20:11
disease desperate d. requires FAWK 136:1
D., Ignorance, Squalor BEV 42:3
d. in the family that is TREV 368:4
mortal d. by which the Socialist CHUR 88:8
diseases D. desperate grown SHAK 326:1
disgraces Labour d. no man GRANT 160:4
disguised England is a d. republic BAG 27:2
dish d. fit for the gods SHAK 328:13
dishonesty allegation of d. LEVER 222:2
dishonour in honour or d. LINC 225:12
dishonourable find ourselves d. graves SHAK 328:4
dishwatery silly, flat, d. utterances ANON 13:6
disillusion one d.—mankind KEYN 207:3
disintegration through rapine to d. GLAD 154:16
disinter not be too ready to d. JOUB 200:6
disloyalty D. is the secret weapon CRIT 104:9
dismal D. Science CARL 76:9
dismemberment disintegration and d. GLAD 154:16

dismount they dare not d. CHUR 89:8
disobliging d. the few MAC 238:15
disorder to preserve d. DALEY 108:8
disorderly in a d. government HAL 165:13
disposed way she d. of an empire HARL 169:3
dispossessed imprisoned or d. MAGN 247:3
disputes solution of all d. BRI 56:2
dissatisfaction discontent and d. PEEL 288:9
dissent in the West is called 'd.' HAVEL 170:4
dissentious you d. rogues SHAK 324:4
dissimulation by one word—d. DISR 116:8
dissolved union will be d. COBB 100:1
distance d. between Russia and SAL 317:8
prestige without d. DE G 112:1
distant too bourgeois, too d. GISC 153:6
distinction birth as a mark of d. BUR 69:2
d. of being without an honour PEEL 288:17
distinctions artificial d. JACK 189:1
distort then you can d. them TWAIN 372:10
distress when they are in obvious d. BALF 30:8
distresses d. of humanity JOHN 197:2
distribute d. as fairly as he can LOWE 233:7
ditch [Channel] is a mere d. NAP 269:4
die in the last d. WILL 389:3
environed with a great d. CROM 105:13
with one in the last d. MACL 242:9
diversity world safe for d. KENN 205:4
divided d. by a common language SHAW 337:3
Fox d. the kingdom with Caesar JOHN 198:12
Gaul as a whole is d. into three CAES 71:7
world is d. into three classes RIPP 306:2
dividing by d. we fall DICK 115:8
divine no government by d. right HARR 169:7
divinity d. doth hedge a king SHAK 326:4
division d. of Europe into a number GIBB 151:2
do diplomacy is to d. and say GOLD 156:9
government is not to d. KEYN 207:10
I am to d. what I please FRED 143:4
I can d. no other LUTH 234:6
Let us d.—or die BURNS 68:12
little done, so much to d. RHOD 304:3
machinery so that we can d. CHOD 85:9
Nobody told us we could d. this WEBB 381:5
Step One: We must d. something LYNN 235:11
supposed to d. anyway TRUM 371:5
what can I d. for myself? NIXON 274:8
what it can d. for the nation HARD 168:5
docile more d. instruments MILL 259:5
doctors If you believe the d. SAL 318:1
doctrine any political d., except TROL 370:7
d. is something you kill for BENN 36:10
d. to be forgiven TROL 369:6
not the d. of ignoble ease ROOS 310:10
dog America is a large, friendly d. TOYN 367:5
Black d. is back again CHUR 94:8
Communism is a dead d. SOLZ 346:3
d.'s obeyed in office SHAK 331:4
drover's d. could lead HAYD 171:3
I must love the d. GIBB 152:1
kids love that d. NIXON 273:7
That d. won't hunt RICH 305:1
This mad d. of the Middle East REAG 302:2
very good d. in Mr Ernest Bevin ATTL 20:13
woman's preaching is like a d.'s JOHN 197:9
Doge quiet D. of Venice WALP 377:13
doggie diplomacy is saying 'Nice d.' CATL 78:5
dogma no d., no Dean DISR 121:10
dogs country doesn't go to the d. WILDE 388:8
let slip the d. of war SHAK 329:9
their running d. MAO 250:7
dole 1930s d. queue JOS 199:7
dollar billion d. country FOST 139:7
domestic d. business MONT 263:7
pleasures of d. life GIBB 151:7
dominating relation of men d. men WEBER 381:8
domination d. and equilibrium KISS 214:10
Soviet d. FORD 139:2
dominion d. of kings PRICE 298:3
d. of laws, and the dominion PRICE 298:3
d. of religion; the liberation of GOLD 157:2
d. of the master HUME 184:9
d. of the world MAHAN 247:6
d. over palm and pine KIPL 212:11
D., the blessed mother JEFF 193:12
inglorious period of our d. BURKE 65:9
dominions His Majesty's d. NORTH 275:3
domino 'falling d.' principle EIS 129:5
done anything remained to be d. LUCAN 234:5
at present are not d. at all KEYN 207:10
d. very well out of the war BALD 29:1
should be d., do nothing MELB 256:5
something ought to be d. WELLS 385:5
surprised to find it d. at all JOHN 197:9
that which gets things d. LLOY 229:10
want anything d., ask a woman THAT 360:8
We have d. it ourselves LAO-T 217:8
what is to be d. LENIN 221:1
door from beneath a closed d. ANON 12:1
open d. HAY 171:2
prejudices through the d. FRED 143:3
shut and lock a d. PAINE 280:8
doors Men shut their d. SHAK 335:4
doorstep do this on the d. JUNOR 201:4
dots what those damned d. meant CHUR 87:1
doublethink *d.* means the power ORW 279:6
doubt intelligent are full of d. RUSS 316:12
When in d. MELB 256:5
When in d., mumble BOREN 52:6
Dover chalk cliffs of D. BALD 29:7
down many kicked d. stairs HAL 165:1
You can't hold a man d. WASH 379:4
downhearted We are not d. CHAM 80:7
Downing Street from Germany to D. CHAM 81:1
You don't reach D. THAT 362:7

drain From this foul d. pure gold TOCQ 365:2
drains democracy and proper d. BETJ 40:1
drawers d. of water BIBLE 43:8
drawing through my d. room EDEN 128:1
drawing-room same men in the d. HAL 165:8
dread That is why most men d. it SHAW 336:8
Dreadnoughts to keep up as two D. LLOY 229:3
dream I have a d. KING 210:10
perfectibility as a d. MILL 258:7
vision and the old men's d. DRYD 125:7
dreams not make d. your master KIPL 213:3
dredging Scott wearily d. MASS 254:3
dregs among the d. of Romulus CIC 95:5
d. are often filthy-tasting CHUR 87:2
drest d. in a little brief authority SHAK 332:9
drift adamant for d. CHUR 89:7
drinking d. my griefs SHAK 334:3
drive difficult to d. BRO 58:2
driver be a very good back-seat d. THAT 362:11
providing he was in the d.'s seat BEAV 34:5
drizzle d. of Empires CHUR 88:1
drollery That fatal d. DISR 118:7
dropping D. the pilot TENN 359:6
drover d.'s dog could lead HAYD 171:3
drowns d. things weighty and solid BACON 22:15
drum-beat morning d. WEBS 382:7
drunk America is like a bar-room d. ALLEN 7:2
My mother, d. or sober CHES 84:1
stood by him when he was d. SHER 339:2
duchess every d. in London MACD 240:6
duchesses what Grand d. are doing NAP 269:8
duck Honey, I just forgot to d. DEMP 113:3
If it looks like a d. REUT 303:4
ducking see a parapet without d. CRIT 104:7
duke everybody praised the d. SOUT 347:2
Had we beaten the d. CLAY 97:11
dukes d. are just as great LLOY 229:3
dull statesman is that he be d. ACH 1:6
dullness d. in Parliamentary BAG 23:12
duncery tyrannical d. MILT 260:4
dunghill cock crowing on its own d. ALD 6:9
Dunkirk D. spirit WILS 390:2
spirit of D. will carry us through WILS 390:9
duplicity continuous acts of d. COCK 100:9
dust not without d. and heat MILT 260:6
O'er English d. MAC 238:10
This d. was once the man WHIT 388:1
dustbin d. of history TROT 370:12
Dutch commerce the fault of the D. CANN 75:3
duty brave man inattentive to his d. JACK 188:7
Do your d. bravely KITC 214:15
d. of an Opposition DERBY 114:1
every man's d. to do all COBB 100:4
Every subject's d. is the king's SHAK 326:14
first d. of a State RUSK 315:9
indispensable d. of government PAINE 281:9
path of d. was the way to glory TENN 360:3
right as well as our d. PANK 284:10
we must do our d. SAL 318:6
dwarfs state which d. its men MILL 259:5
dwellings our d. shape us CHUR 92:3
dying At last d. in the last dyke BURKE 66:5
forgets a d. king TENN 360:4
Turkey is a d. man NICH 271:4
unconscionable time d. CHAR 83:6
without many of them d. SELL 323:9
dyke last d. of prevarication BURKE 66:5
dyspepsia d. of the society CARL 76:15

eagle bald e. had not been chosen FRAN 142:7
Rome, though her e. WALL 377:1
ear right sow by the e. HENR 176:2
earl As far as the fourteenth e. is HOME 182:3
e. and a knight ATTL 20:9
early vote for an e. Christmas CALL 73:1
earned They have to be e. on earth THAT 360:12
earnest I am in e. GARR 148:3
ears countrymen, lend me your e. SHAK 329:13
earth Everything on e. is flying past GOGOL 156:8
have to be earned on e. THAT 360:12
meek shall inherit the e. SMITH 343:9
Of e.'s first blood WORD 394:5
returning him safely to e. KENN 204:8
return seven years later to e. BEAV 34:1
This e. of majesty SHAK 333:4
this is the end of e. ADAMS 5:1
whole e. as their memorial PER 290:5
ease he be never at heart's e. SHAK 328:8
not the doctrine of ignoble e. ROOS 310:10
easier It is e. to make war CLEM 98:6
It will be e. for you CHIL 85:4
east fiery portal of the e. SHAK 334:1
hold the gorgeous e. in fee WORD 394:6
Oh, E. is E., and West is West KIPL 212:6
politics in the e. may be defined DISR 116:8
ship me somewheres e. of Suez KIPL 212:8
what happens in the e. SOLZ 345:11
East End I can look the E. in the face ELIZ 132:8
Easter E. Island statue with an arse KEAT 202:6
eastern civilizing both the e. PAINE 281:12
spectre is haunting e. Europe HAVEL 170:4
easy no e. walk-over to freedom NEHRU 270:5
eat *e. one of Bellamy's veal pies* PITT 293:12
hoping it will e. him last CHUR 90:3
I have often had to e. my words CHUR 94:15
Let them e. cake MAR 250:9
so wild, that they e. up MORE 265:5
You will e., bye and bye HILL 178:8
ecclesiastic e. tyranny's the worst DEFOE 111:10
éclair than a chocolate é. ROOS 311:2

ecological upset the e. balance SONT 346:6
economic bettering their own e. condition MILL 259:14
countries which enjoy an e. surplus POTT 296:3
criteria which are not purely e. TAWN 355:12
e. ones are incomprehensible HOME 182:4
great social and e. experiment HOOV 182:7
green shoots of e. spring LAM 217:1
hidden forces of e. law KEYN 207:5
lay bare the e. law of motion MARX 252:8
read e. documents HOME 182:2
vital e. interests WEIL 383:5
economical e. with the truth ARMS 16:12
economics e. are the method THAT 361:3
I evidently knew more about e. KEYN 208:5
politics of Versailles, only the e. MONN 262:7
speech on e. like pissing JOHN 196:12
economist death of a political e. BAG 24:4
no e. should be denied it GALB 146:5
no need for the e. to prove KALD 201:10
slaves of some defunct e. KEYN 208:6
economists e. may not know how FRI 143:8
ideas of e. and political KEYN 208:6
sophisters, e., and calculators BURKE 66:16
economy e. of private people SMITH 341:7
e. of truth BURKE 68:2
for fear of political e. SELL 323:8
heights of the e. BEVAN 41:6
in favour of general e. EDEN 127:8
no e. where there is no efficiency DISR 119:14
not know how to run the e. FRI 143:8
science of political e. RUSK 316:2
Eden This other E., demi-paradise SHAK 333:4
edge e. of the abyss STEV 350:10
educate e. our party DISR 119:12
We must e. our masters LOWE 233:6
educated by the badly e. CHES 85:1
times of stress 'e.' people tend ORW 277:9
well housed, clothed, fed and e. RUSK 315:9
education as in the case of e. JAY 190:4
E. makes a people easy to BRO 58:2
first part of politics? e. MICH 258:4
No part of the e. of a politician CHUR 89:10
parts of e., it is to be observed SMITH 343:1
unplanned e. creates problems VERW 374:1
Upon the e. of the people DISR 120:6
Edward VIII this boy [the future E.] HARD 168:4
eels e. get used to skinning CHUR 90:9
procreation of e. SCH 322:3
effects What dire e. ADD 5:9
efficiencies inherent e. of freedom GALB 145:3
efficiency e. of the post office SULL 352:5
where there is no e. DISR 119:14
efficient e. government TRUM 371:15
next, the *e.* parts BAG 24:10
effort redoubling your e. SANT 320:3
egg e. of a North African GLAD 155:4
eggheads e. of the world unite STEV 350:15
Egypt Our first site in E. GLAD 155:4
We do not want E. any more PALM 284:4
eight We want e. ANON 14:10
ein *E. Reich, ein Volk, ein Führer* ANON 9:11
elder rising hope to e. statesman FOOT 138:8
elect To e., and to reject PAINE 283:7
we must e. world peace BAR 32:4
elected audacity of e. persons WHIT 388:2
e. a Labour Government ANON 9:6
will not serve if e. SHER 339:4
election After the e. PEROT 290:7
Better we lose the e. than STEV 349:8
e. by the incompetent many SHAW 336:7
e. is coming ELIOT 130:1
I've won the e. GEOR 150:5
loss of the e. BALD 29:10
right of e. is the very essence JUN 200:9
Tories, every e., must have BEVAN 40:9
which a good e. can't fix NIXON 274:4
elections e. are won ADAMS 2:6
fighting of e. CHUR 89:10
I do not like e. CHUR 89:2
You won the e., but I won SOM 346:5
elective e. dictatorship HAIL 163:8
In e. monarchies GIBB 151:1
electors British e. will not vote BEAV 34:6
electricity *usefulness of e.* FAR 135:4
electrification e. of the whole LENIN 221:8
elegant e. simplicity of the three STOW 352:2
elegy whole of Gray's E. WOLFE 393:5
elements e. of modern civilization CARL 75:12
life was gentle, and the e. SHAK 330:16
natural e. of a country MART 251:6
elephant e. pit of socialism POW 297:2
he was like an e. LASKI 218:2
no room for the rogue e. TAYL 356:7
elite power e. MILLS 260:2
eloquence finest e. is that which LLOY 229:10
I admire his e. GIBB 151:14
parliamentary e. CARL 76:8
eloquent e., impressive and wrong BLYT 49:8
e. in a more sublime MAC 237:7
Elysian dead, but in the E. fields DISR 121:6
embalmer triumph of the e.'s art VIDAL 375:2
embarrassed e. phantom DISR 120:14
emblem e. of mortality DISR 121:12
embrace e. your Lordship's WILK 389:1
emergency one e. following FISH 136:8
emotion never a dependable e. ALSOP 7:5
emotional e. orgies ROB 306:12
e. spasm BEVAN 41:4
emotions e., the music NAM 269:2
waste-paper basket of the e. WEBB 381:6

emperor e. is everything METT 257:10
to which the e. holds the key CUST 108:6
emperors e. can actually do nothing BREC 55:8
empire All e. is no more than DRYD 125:8
British E. ROS 312:11
course of e. takes its way BERK 38:4
destinies of the British E. DISR 119:7
dismemberment of the E. GLAD 154:16
E. is a commonwealth of nations ROS 312:5
England is an e., Germany is MICH 258:5
Great Britain has lost an e. ACH 1:5
great e. and little minds BURKE 64:7
great Mother E. stands FOST 140:1
Greeks in this American e. MACM 244:2
holy, nor Roman, nor an e. VOLT 375:9
How's the E. GEOR 150:1
impulses of an evil e. REAG 301:12
legacies of e. SAMP 319:11
liquidation of the British E. CHUR 91:9
metropolis of the e. COBB 100:3
preserve the unity of the e. BURKE 63:12
provinces of the British e. SMITH 342:3
Russia can be an e. or a democracy BRZ 61:3
strength of the E., India GLAD 155:1
that is the meaning of E. Day CHES 84:11
This e., vast as it is CUST 108:6
this E. will perish DISR 121:17
To found a great e. SMITH 341:6
way she disposed of an e. HARL 169:3
wilderness into a glorious e. BURKE 63:11
empires day of E. has come CHAM 80:6
drizzle of E. CHUR 88:1
e. of the mind CHUR 92:2
employed innocently e. JOHN 198:1
employer sole e. is the State TROT 370:14
employers e. of past generations BALD 29:5
employment e. of what the world PEEL 288:3
known as gainful e. ACH 1:4
empty e. taxi arrived CHUR 94:9
flamboyant labels on e. luggage BEVAN 41:7
patriot on an e. stomach BRANN 55:5
encompassed her wide walls e. SHAK 328:6
encourage right to e. BAG 26:1
to e. the others VOLT 375:10
encourager *pour e. les autres* VOLT 375:10
encourages It only e. them ANON 11:1
encroachment gradual and silent e. MAD 246:6
end beginning of the e. TALL 355:1
but the e. is not yet BIBLE 44:8
came to an e. all wars LLOY 229:8
e. of ane old song OGIL 276:7
e. of a thousand years of GAIT 145:2
e. of the beginning CHUR 91:10
In my e. is my beginning MARY 253:8
Power is not a means, it is an e. ORW 279:7
reserved for some e. or other CLIVE 99:8
This, this is the e. of earth ADAMS 5:1
war that will e. war WELLS 385:4
ended Georges e. LAND 217:5
ending quickest way of e. a war ORW 278:13
endings beginnings and e. BACON 22:7
endogenous e. growth theory BROWN 58:6
ends e. I think criminal KEYN 207:2
in regarding the *e.* as beyond POPP 296:2
Let all the e. thou aim'st at SHAK 327:7
outdistanced the e. KING 211:1
endure of all that human hearts e. JOHN 197:7
enemies e. in war, in peace friends JEFF 190:6
e. of Freedom INGE 187:8
e. of man: tyranny, poverty KENN 204:6
for the e. he has made BRAGG 54:9
just friends and brave e. JEFF 192:11
left me naked to mine e. SHAK 327:8
priests have been e. of liberty HUME 185:1
remedy our *e.* have chosen SHER 339:1
they will be e. to laws BURKE 65:3
we have no perpetual e. PALM 284:1
enemy ancient inveterate e. PITT 293:4
e., but, by God, they frighten me WELL 383:8
more formidable e. than Germany BROG 57:5
our friend and not our e. CLIN 99:7
spoils of the e. MARCY 250:8
written by an acute e. BALF 31:1
energy atomic e. TRUM 371:3
problems of our country—e. CART 77:8
enfants *allons, e. de la patrie* ROUG 314:3
enforce how to e. with temper GREN 161:4
enforced laws which cannot be e. EINS 128:7
Engels Marx, E. and Lenin KHR 209:1
engine not connected to the e. GOOD 158:1
stopped the e. in its tracks JENK 194:3
engineering Piecemeal social e. POPP 296:2
engineers artists are not e. KENN 205:9
engines cannot be amiss for the e. BURKE 66:7
England better that E. should be free MAGEE 247:1
between France and E. PEEL 289:1
bored for E. MUGG 268:1
deep sleep of E. ORW 278:3
defence of E. BALD 29:7
Elizabethan E. INGE 187:6
end in the ruin of E. SHEL 337:8
E. and America are two SHAW 337:3
E. does not love coalitions DISR 118:17
E. had risen all the same TAYL 357:11
E. has saved herself PITT 293:10
E. is a disguised republic BAG 27:2
E. is a nation of shopkeepers NAP 270:1
E. is an empire, Germany is MICH 258:5
E. . . . resembles a family ORW 278:5
E.'s not a bad country DRAB 124:5
E. was too pure an Air ANON 12:13
E. will have her neck wrung CHUR 91:7
fashion of the court of E. SHAK 326:18

God punish E. FUNKE 144:7
Gott strafe E. FUNKE 144:7
history of E. POW 297:8
history of E. is emphatically MAC 238:3
In E.'s green and pleasant land BLAKE 49:6
jurisdiction in this Realm of E. BOOK 51:6
keeps Ireland bound to E. PARN 286:7
last king of E. EDW 128:3
Let not E. forget her precedence MILT 260:5
never have seen E. more CROM 105:1
no man in E. CHAR 83:3
[not] suffer E. to be the workshop DISR 117:1
not yet ordained that E. ELIZ 131:6
O E.! model to thy inward SHAK 326:9
people of E., that never CHES 84:7
roast beef of old E. BURKE 63:3
Speak for E. AMERY 7:7
strong arm of E. will protect PALM 284:2
suspended in favour of E. SHAW 336:18
this earth, this realm, this E. SHAK 333:4
This E. never did SHAK 331:1
This state [E.] will perish MONT 264:12
total reformation is wanted in E. PAINE 282:3
weave old E.'s winding sheet BLAKE 49:4
what is left of E. HUGO 184:6
Whereas in E. all is permitted MEG 255:3
where E. is finished and dead MILL 260:1
who only E. know KIPL 212:7

English But marks our E. dead KIPL 212:10
characteristic of the E. Monarchy BAG 25:7
cricket—a game which the E. MANC 249:2
E. have taken their idea MONT 264:11
E. in taste, in opinions MAC 236:11
E., not the Turkish court SHAK 326:8
E. people never expect any one BAG 23:13
E. policy is to float lazily SAL 317:7
E. subject's sole prerogative DRYD 125:14
E. take their pleasures sadly SULLY 352:7
E. up with which I will not put CHUR 93:4
E. want *inferiors* TOCQ 365:1
excellence of the E. government BLAC 48:10
fragments, of the E. scene ORW 278:7
if the E. people, directing BAG 26:11
impulse of the E. people BAG 27:3
in favour of boys learning E. CHUR 88:12
Only the E. make it their abode WALL 377:2
principle of the E. constitution BLAC 48:8
really nice E. people SHAW 336:17
Roman-Saxon-Danish-Norman E. DEFOE 111:7
seven feet of E. ground HAR 169:4
shed one E. tear MAC 238:10
talent of our E. nation DRYD 125:2
to the E. that of the sea RICH 305:3
yet the trick of our E. nation SHAK 326:6

Englishman Being an E. is the greatest prize RHOD 304:2
can be offered to an E.—a seat DISR 120:18
E. prudently avoids all contact TOCQ 365:10
E.'s heaven-born privilege ARN 17:5
in Europe, and not one E. WALP 378:3
last E. to rule in India NEHRU 271:1
last great E. TENN 359:9
never find an E. in the wrong SHAW 335:13
religious rights of an E. JUN 201:3
vain, ill-natured thing, an E. DEFOE 111:6
What E. will give his mind SHAW 337:1

Englishmen E. never will be slaves SHAW 336:4
our very name as E. PITT 293:9
they would prefer to be E. RHOD 304:1
Tories, in short, are atrophied E. JOHN 196:13
virtue of E. TAWN 355:7
what Scotchmen are to E. PEEL 288:15

enigma in a mystery inside an e. CHUR 90:1

enjoy private men e. SHAK 326:16

enjoying e. themselves RUSS 316:5

enmities e. of twenty MAC 238:8

enough e. of blood and tears RABIN 299:4

enslave impossible to e. BRO 58:2

entangled alone e. SHEN 338:9

enter king of England cannot e. PITT 292:9

enterprise e. is sick SHAK 335:8

enterprises essential in most e. CARL 76:6

entertain e. four royalties SAL 318:2

enthusiasm e. moves the world BALF 30:4
e. of the people WELL 384:1

enthusiasts few e. can be trusted BALF 30:4

entire e. and whole and perfect SPR 348:1

entitled no man is e. to ROOS 311:5

entourage e. before the Party GORB 158:2

entrails In our own proper e. SHAK 330:15

entreat I do e. heaven daily ELIZ 131:2

entrusted Those e. with arms WIND 393:1

envious e. siege SHAK 333:4
To silence e. tongues: be just SHAK 327:7

environed e. with a great ditch CROM 105:13

environment issues like the e. THAT 361:7

envy Against the e. of less SHAK 333:4
e. is the basis of democracy RUSS 316:7
in e. of great Caesar SHAK 330:16
prisoners of e. ILL 187:4

epigrams despotism tempered by e. CARL 75:11

episode Marxism is only an e. POPP 296:1

epitaph If I had any e. STEV 351:1

equal All shall e. be GILB 152:11
born free and e. in dignity ANON 8:4
can be both free and e. BAG 24:6
created e. and independent JEFF 191:1
created e.... In a larger sense LINC 226:3
created e., that they are ANON 14:7
earth the separate and e. station JEFF 190:7
E. Pay for Equal Work ANTH 15:6
e. rights JOHN 195:8
For e. division of unequal earnings ELL 133:1
we are all e. JUN 200:12

equality [e.] is a doctrine TROL 369:6
e. would be a heaven TROL 370:2
general state of e. JOHN 198:6
liberty is liberty, not e. BERL 39:1
majestic e. of the law FRAN 141:2
makes e. such a difficult BECQ 34:8
neither e. nor freedom FRI 143:10
political and social e. LINC 225:2
spirit of extreme e. MONT 264:5
this pretty state of e. JOHN 198:13
true apostles of e. ARN 17:3
We wish, in a word, e. BAK 28:5
equalize attempt to level never e. BURKE 66:11
equals peace between e. WILS 392:8
pigs treat us as e. CHUR 94:11
equanimity face with e. GILB 152:9
equation e. is something for eternity EINS 129:2
equilibrium legitimacy and e. KISS 214:13
stability: domination and e. KISS 214:10
equipped e. to be the chief executive ACH 1:8
equivocate I will not e. GARR 148:3
erecting there e. new MARV 252:1
err e. as grossly as the few DRYD 125:11
errands Meet to be sent on e. SHAK 330:13
error e. has never approached METT 257:9
no dignity in persevering in e. PEEL 288:11
than all the hosts of e. BRYAN 60:4
errors e. of those who think BID 44:14
eruption strange e. to our state SHAK 325:4
escutcheon e. of the Common Law GRAY 160:6
espionage I cannot think that e. WEST 385:9
essenced his long e. hair MAC 236:4
essentials all the e. of life CHUR 87:8
established e. Clergy GLAD 154:14
socialism *possibly* be e. STAL 348:4
establishment British e. KEAT 202:8
estate And ordered their e. ALEX 7:1
dealing with e. workers DOUG 123:5
e.-owners, in come the e. agents HEATH 173:11
fourth e. of the realm MAC 237:3
esteem too cheap, we e. too lightly PAINE 281:11
État *L'É. c'est moi* LOU 232:9
eternal e. yesterday WEBER 381:9
eternity some conception of e. MANC 249:2
ethical nuclear giants and e. infants BRAD 54:5
ethics floats in a sea of e. WARR 379:1
Eton decry E. and Harrow BEVIN 42:9
on the playing fields of E. WELL 384:11
eunuch prerogative of the e. STOP 351:7
eunuchs seraglio of e. FOOT 138:5
Europe alterations on the map of E. CHUR 87:6
commence the salvation of E. PITT 293:8
Communism continued to haunt E. TAYL 357:3
division of E. GIBB 151:2
domination of Eastern E. FORD 139:2
E. des patries DE G 112:10
E. has never existed MONN 262:5
E. is a continent of energetic FISH 137:1
E. is in danger of plunging YELT 396:5
glory of E. is extinguished BURKE 66:16
great stocks of E. YEATS 396:1
kind of United States of E. CHUR 92:11
lamps are going out all over E. GREY 161:5
map of E. has been changed CHUR 88:4
pampered courtesan of E. MACM 244:3
part of the community of E. SAL 318:6
rest of E. is marching HEAL 173:4
save E. by her example PITT 293:10
should not create a nation E. MONN 263:2
smaller nationalities of E. ASQ 18:3
spectre is haunting eastern E. HAVEL 170:4
take over the whole of E. RIDL 305:6
Whoever speaks of E. is wrong BISM 46:9
whole of E., that will decide DE G 112:8
word E. on the lips BISM 46:10
European any E. power MONR 263:6
colonization by any E. powers MONR 263:4
common E. causes and affairs BAG 26:11
communal life of the E. VERW 374:1
descendant of a E. CRÈV 104:1
E. exchange rate mechanism MAJOR 247:10
E. talks of progress DISR 118:9
E. war might do it REDM 302:9
E. wars and quarrels PAINE 281:6
head of E. liberal principles CLAY 97:4
instruments of E. greatness HAM 167:5
not be involved in a E. war BEAV 33:7
of the E. Community RIDL 305:7
opposition to a single E. currency THAT 362:10
wars of the E. powers MONR 263:5
Europeans E. often ask BRYCE 61:1
event greatest e. it is FOX 140:6
It is not an e., it is an item TALL 355:2
eventide perfect e. home STOC 351:6
events current of e. BISM 47:9
e. have controlled me LINC 226:5
We cannot make e. ADAMS 5:6
Everest He is a Chimborazo or E. ASQ 18:8
everything for e. dear and valuable PITT 293:9
Macaulay is of e. MELB 255:10
robbed a man of *e.* SOLZ 345:10
Woolworth's: e. in its place BEVAN 40:3
evidence e. of life after death SOPER 346:7
give e. against their own HAL 165:9
evil all government is e. O'SUL 279:12
but a necessary e. PAINE 281:1
do nothing for e. to triumph BURKE 68:7
e. that men do lives after them SHAK 329:13
He overcame e. with good KING 210:4
impulses of an e. empire REAG 301:12
indistinguishable from the e. DAWS 110:4
justified in doing e. ROOS 312:3

no e. in the atom STEV 350:5
place that is free from e. WAUGH 380:8
presuppose that all men are e. MACH 241:10
respond to e. by committing HAVEL 170:6
evils no necessary e. in government JACK 189:2
not live only by fighting e. BERL 39:4
When e. are most free SHAK 328:11
evolution against the ideas of e. ZIN 397:4
progress of e. ADAMS 2:10
examination e. of the acts of HARR 170:1
examine e. but my humours NORT 275:8
examiners economics than my e. KEYN 208:5
example save Europe by her e. PITT 293:10
excess poverty and e. PENN 289:13
excited When the populace is e. LA BR 216:2
excitement means of intellectual e. BAG 24:3
excuse e. every man will plead SELD 323:1
will not equivocate—I will not e. GARR 148:3
execute people who e. them MILL 259:11
executes hand which e. a measure TAYL 358:5
execution fascination of a public e. FOOT 138:4
imminent e. of a senior colleague CLARK 96:9
so effective as their stringent e. GRANT 160:2
executive both the legislative and e. ADAMS 3:12
more corrupt than e. power MONT 264:12
new powers of the e. DENN 113:8
power is nominated by the e. GIBB 151:4
exercise greater the desire to e. it LEVIN 222:12
exhausted enemies are not yet e. GLAD 154:15
exile therefore I die in e. GREG 161:3
exiled outlawed or e. MAGN 247:3
exiles politicians are e. GRIGG 161:9
exist questioned its right to e. SCH 322:1
existence our e. as a nation PITT 293:9
strong enough to maintain its e. LINC 226:7
Their e. only adds to our perils MOUN 267:4
existing shake off the e. government LINC 224:5
exit Such a graceful e. JUNOR 201:4
expectation public e. be kept GALB 146:6
expectations political e. to military POW 296:5
revolution of rising e. CLEV 99:4
expected what we least e. DISR 116:11
expediency on the ground of e. ROOS 312:3
taint pure laws with mere e. AESC 6:2
expedient not a principle, but an e. DISR 117:16
expenditure annual e. nineteen DICK 115:3
economy and particular e. EDEN 127:8
e. rises to meet income PARK 285:7
expense regardless of e. PEEL 289:6
expenses facts are on e. STOP 351:10
private e. NORT 275:8
experience e. is the child of DISR 116:4
e. of being disastrously wrong GALB 146:5
man of no e. CURZ 108:4
that is the lamp of e. HENRY 176:6
experiment full tide of successful e. JEFF 192:6
great social and economic e. HOOV 182:7
experimentation persistent e. ROOS 308:5
experts divine right of e. MACM 244:4
'e.' make the worst possible ATTL 20:12
few e. and a few rather less TAYL 356:11
you never should trust e. SAL 318:1
explain e. why it didn't happen CHUR 94:6
Never complain and never e. BALD 29:11
Never complain and never e. DISR 121:8
never e. FISH 137:4
explained when being e. BALF 31:4
explanation simple e. of stupidity LEVER 222:2
expletive e. deleted ANON 9:14
exploits capitalism man e. man ANON 14:5
extempore his e. sayings WALP 377:6
exterminate e. a nation SPOCK 347:9
extol How shall we e. thee BENS 37:6
extraordinary this is an e. man JOHN 198:11
extravagant e. with his own SALL 319:4
nothing so e. and irrational SWIFT 353:8
extreme e. party is most irritated BAG 27:11
extremism e. in the defence GOLD 157:8
e. in the pursuit JOHN 196:5
exult e. O shores, and ring WHIT 387:10
exulting people all e. WHIT 387:9
eye cast a longing e. on them JEFF 191:14
e. to the main chance CECIL 79:6
neither e. to see, nor tongue LENT 221:12
spoils one's e. for the high birds HAL 166:13
watchful e. and the strong arm PALM 284:2
eyeball We're e. to eyeball RUSK 315:1
eyes *e. blazing with insincerity* ANON 13:10
e. of Caligula, but the mouth MITT 261:8
Get thee glass e. SHAK 331:5
have no e. but constitutional e. LINC 227:2
Mine e. are full of tears SHAK 334:7
Mine e. have seen the glory HOWE 184:3

Fabians F.... found socialism HEAL 172:6
farmyard civilization of the F. INGE 187:9
good man fallen among F. LENIN 221:5
face changed the whole f. BACON 22:2
mind's construction in the f. SHAK 331:6
not lose its human f. DUBC 126:3
save her soul than her f. THOM 363:7
stamping on a human f. ORW 279:8
unacceptable f. of capitalism HEATH 173:8
whole f. of the world PASC 287:1
faces private f. in public places AUDEN 21:1
facing f. in the same direction ROST 313:6
fact certain superiority in its f. EMER 133:3
physical f. into a legal right MILL 259:9
faction By a f. MAD 246:3
it made them a f. MAC 238:13
liberty is to f. what air is to fire MAD 246:1
men who shine in a f. HAL 166:5
party...is not a f. POW 297:5

faction (*cont.*):
whisper of a f. should prevail RUSS 317:1
factions canvasses and f. BACON 22:5
durable source of f. MAD 246:4
facts f. are on expenses STOP 351:10
f. are sacred SCOTT 322:4
few f., at least ascertainable f. PEEL 289:9
Get your f. first TWAIN 372:10
ignoring f. ADAMS 3:1
report the f. ROG 307:9
to his imagination for his f. SHER 338:13
faculties diversity in the f. of men MAD 246:2
From each according to his f. BAK 28:5
Hath borne his f. so meek SHAK 331:7
fade just f. away MAC 235:14
fail f. from not comprehending BAG 27:12
We shall not flag or f. CHUR 90:7
failing from f. hands we throw MCCR 240:2
failure end in f. POW 297:7
f. of a listless public SOLZ 346:4
His f. is ignominious MENC 256:12
fair f. shares for all JAY 190:5
fairness liberty, not equality or f. BERL 39:1
faith Courage and f.; vain f. MAC 238:9
f. and morals WORD 394:5
f. in a nation of sectaries DISR 117:11
f. is something you die for BENN 36:10
first article of my f. GAND 147:3
good sense and the good f. GLAD 154:13
If ye break f. with us who die MCCR 240:2
Marxism is now a world f. BENN 36:7
My f. in the people governing DICK 115:7
faithful He was my friend, f. SHAK 330:1
mentally f. to himself PAINE 283:5
falcon f. cannot hear the falconer YEATS 395:6
Falklands F. thing was a fight BORG 52:7
fall Another thing to f. SHAK 332:6
by dividing we f. DICK 115:8
Et tu, Brute? Then f., Caesar SHAK 329:4
O! what a f. was there SHAK 330:7
things f. apart YEATS 395:6
fallacies f. leading to inappropriate BAL 31:7
fallen all the planets had f. on me TRUM 371:1
captain lies, f. cold and dead WHIT 387:10
good man f. among Fabians LENIN 221:5
falling 'f. domino' principle EIS 129:5
fear's as bad as f. SHAK 325:3
false attribution of f. motive BALD 29:11
equally f. GIBB 151:3
f. report, if believed MED 255:2
falsehood great mass of f. WILK 389:2
strife of truth with f. LOW 234:1
falsehoods f. which interest dictates JOHN 197:4
falters love that never f. SPR 348:1
fame damned to everlasting f. POPE 295:5
F. and tranquillity MONT 263:8
F. is like a river BACON 22:15
understand what military f. SHER 339:3
We came here for f. DISR 121:16
families Great f. of yesterday DEFOE 111:9
women, and there are f. THAT 362:2
family f. with the wrong members ORW 278:5
I have a young f. FOWL 140:3
in the running of a f. MONT 263:7
no f. life at Court THOM 363:6
selling the f. silver MACM 245:11
spend more time with my f. RIDL 305:5
spend more time with your f. THAT 362:8
famous But 'twas a f. victory SOUT 347:2
f. by their birth SHAK 333:4
For f. men have the whole earth PER 290:5
Let us now praise f. men BIBLE 44:2
main advantage of being f. KISS 214:14
fanatic f. heart YEATS 396:2
f. is a great leader BROUN 58:3
fanaticism F. consists in SANT 320:3
fanatics But when f. are on top MENC 257:5
far bridge too f. BROW 59:7
It is a f., far better thing GALB 145:9
Poor Mexico, so f. from God DIAZ 114:6
quarrel in a f. away country CHAM 80:9
farce as tragedy, the second as f. MARX 252:4
longest running f. SMITH 343:7
farewell F.! a long f. SHAK 327:5
f. king SHAK 333:8
must bid the company f. RAL 300:7
farmer I am a f. of thoughts PAINE 282:1
farmers country needs good f. NIXON 274:11
fart My Lord, I had forgot the f. ELIZ 131:11
So dumb he can't f. JOHN 196:10
fascination f. of a public execution FOOT 138:4
subject myself to his f. GLAS 156:4
Fascism first victims of American F. ROS 313:2
Fascists to include F. ANON 10:2
fashion f. in these things FRAN 142:12
fashionable join the f. madmen DID 116:2
fashions to fit this year's f. HELL 174:3
fastidiousness Since when was f. LEVIN 222:10
fat Butter merely makes us f. GOER 156:6
f. and long-haired fellows PLUT 294:8
men about me that are f. SHAK 328:7
What is that f. gentleman SHAW 337:5
fate arbiter of others' f. BYRON 71:3
become the makers of our f. POPP 295:10
decide the f. of the world DE G 112:8
f. of this country depends DISR 120:6
f. of unborn millions WASH 379:6
German whom f. has raised up BRY 60:7
grief to thy too rigid f. GRAH 159:1
fates masters of their f. SHAK 328:4
father Lloyd George knew my f. ANON 12:2
my f. was before me RUSK 316:4
polite f. of his people JAM 189:10
rude son should strike his f. dead SHAK 335:9

they will cut off thy f.'s head CHAR 82:5
fatherland unity of our f. KOHL 215:5
fathers city of the healthiest f. WHIT 388:3
our f. brought forth LINC 226:3
victory has a hundred f. CIANO 95:4
fatuity f. of idiots SMITH 344:6
fault But see thy f. SHAK 326:9
f., dear Brutus, is not SHAK 328:4
it was a grievous f. SHAK 329:13
faults f. of statesmen WALP 377:7
f. which 'only children' BAG 24:7
Faust this shabby F. HEAL 173:1
favour f. of the people BURKE 62:11
Fools out of f. DEFOE 111:5
favourable most f. opportunity BISM 47:14
favourite mark his f. flies SHAK 325:12
favourites choose f. SWIFT 353:8
favours calculate upon real f. WASH 379:9
lively sense of future f. WALP 378:7
man that hangs on princes' f. SHAK 327:6
seeking f. from the great TAYL 358:6
Upon your f. swims SHAK 324:5
fear acting and reasoning as f. BURKE 62:3
be just, and f. not SHAK 327:7
But let us never f. to negotiate KENN 204:4
concessions of f. BURKE 64:11
do not wholly banish f. AESC 6:2
F. God KITC 214:15
F. is the foundation ADAMS 3:11
f. of the political consequences GALB 146:12
f.'s as bad as falling SHAK 325:3
freedom from f. ROOS 309:11
hate, so long as they f. ACC 1:3
In politics, what begins in f. COL 101:2
No tyrant need f. till men ARIS 16:11
ocean in the eventide of f. MORR 266:5
prevent war is not to f. it RAND 300:8
thing we have to f. is f. itself ROOS 308:8
will try to have no f. CHES 83:9
feared prince to be f. than loved MACH 241:3
fearful our f. trip is done WHIT 387:9
fears bondage of irrational f. BRAN 55:1
never of your f. STEV 350:12
feast At nature's mighty f. MALT 248:11
LIBERTY's a glorious f. BURNS 68:11
featherbed liberty in a f. JEFF 191:11
fed We have f. our sea KIPL 212:10
federal Our f. Union JACK 188:8
Federalists we are all F. JEFF 192:4
fee hold the gorgeous east in f. WORD 394:6
feeble f. can seldom persuade GIBB 151:12
man of such a f. temper SHAK 328:3
unjust as a f. government BURKE 67:12
feed meat doth this our Caesar f. SHAK 328:5
feeling appeals to diffused f. BAG 25:9
He aroused every f. except trust TAYL 357:12
feelings governed more by their f. ADAMS 5:6
feet better to die on your f. IBAR 186:6
careful where he put his f. NIC 272:6
f. are always in the water AMES 8:2
hotbed of cold f. EBAN 127:6
seven f. of English ground HAR 169:4
would rather die on our f. ROOS 309:12
felicities close the circle of our f. JEFF 192:3
fellow ankle of his f. man DOUG 124:3
I am a f.-traveller MACL 243:3
felony f. to drink small beer SHAK 327:1
female f. worker is the slave CONN 102:2
patriotism in the f. sex ADAMS 2:3
feminist dealing with the early f. WEST 385:7
fence sat on the f. so long LLOY 230:15
Fenian left us our F. dead PEAR 287:3
fens rotten f., whose loves SHAK 324:8
Fermanagh dreary steeples of F. CHUR 88:4
fertility less by reason of their f. MONT 265:1
fetish militarism...is f. worship TAWN 355:8
fetters his f. fall GAND 147:7
seem to wear the same f. VOLT 376:5
feuds forget all f. MAC 238:10
fever After life's fitful f. SHAK 332:2
bred a f. THOM 363:4
février f. [February] NICH 271:5
few by so many to so f. CHUR 90:10
f. thought he was even ATTL 20:9
fewer there was merely one man f. METT 257:8
fiat *f. justitia et pereat mundus* FERD 136:4
f. justitia et ruant coeli WATS 380:3
say '*f. justitia, ruat caelum*' MANS 249:6
fiction f. lags after truth BURKE 64:13
It is sometimes f. MAC 236:6
my one form of continuous f. BEVAN 41:9
fiddler Like a village f. NIC 272:5
fide *Punica f.* SALL 319:8
fidelity I respect f. to colleagues LASKI 218:3
malignant f. BALF 31:3
field f. of human conflict CHUR 90:10
fiery out the f. portal of the east SHAK 334:1
fifth F. Amendment is an old friend DOUG 123:3
f. of November ANON 13:2
fifty f.-four forty, or fight ALLEN 7:3
no f.-fifty Americanism ROOS 312:2
fight cease when men refuse to f. ANON 14:6
deadliness to f. Germany CHUR 86:2
fifty-four forty, or f. ALLEN 7:3
f. and f. and f. again GAIT 145:1
f. for freedom and truth IBSEN 186:9
f. for its King and Country GRAH 158:6
f. it out on this line GRANT 159:7
f. on to the end HAIG 163:2
For those who bade me f. EWER 134:5
have not yet begun to f. JONES 199:1
it is youth who must f. and die HOOV 183:1
man being too proud to f. WILS 392:4

fight (*cont.*):
Ulster will f. CHUR 86:6
We shall f. on the beaches CHUR 90:7
You cannot f. against the future GLAD 154:6
fighting between two periods of f. BIER 44:17
f. the politicians MONT 265:4
He is still f. Blenheim BEVAN 40:10
war consisteth not in actual f. HOBB 180:1
fights knows what he f. for CROM 105:3
figure extraordinary f. of our time KEYN 207:11
figures prove anything by f. CARL 76:1
file we've lost the f. LYNN 235:2
filtered opinion is truth f. PHIL 292:4
finality f. is not the language DISR 119:3
finance f. is, as it were GLAD 154:3
financial unsordid f. act CHUR 92:5
financiers All these f. WILS 390:1
finest This was their f. hour CHUR 90:8
finger measured by the f. SAL 317:8
pointing like a rugged f. LLOY 229:6
time we pulled our f. out PHIL 291:5
whose f. do you want ANON 15:1
fingers as separate as the f. WASH 379:2
burn your f. in public life BEAV 33:4
fifteen f. on the safety catch MACM 245:2
journalists dabbling their f. MCGR 241:1
finish tools and we will f. the job CHUR 91:6
finished All this will not be f. KENN 204:5
England is f. and dead MILL 260:1
fins swims with f. of lead SHAK 324:5
fire f. brigade and the fire CHUR 88:7
I didn't f. him TRUM 372:2
our neighbour's house is on f. BURKE 66:7
take a walk into the f. ENG 133:7
firebell f. in the night JEFF 193:7
firm *smack of f. government* MCL 242:5
first ever be done for the f. time CORN 103:8
F. Amendment has erected a wall BLACK 48:2
f. and second class citizens WILL 389:6
f. article of my faith GAND 147:3
f. in peace, and f. in the hearts LEE 220:2
f. to catch and to reflect MAC 238:2
guarantee of the F. Amendment BLACK 48:4
rather be f. in a village CAES 71:10
fish 88 poor f. MENC 257:3
pretty kettle of f. MARY 253:5
recently dead f. ORW 278:8
surrounded by f. BEVAN 40:5
fishes like f. in a saucepan KHR 209:5
men lived like f. SIDN 340:2
fistful for a f. of coins ZAP 397:1
fit I am f. for nothing but to carry HERV 177:6
fitful After life's f. fever he sleeps SHAK 332:2
fitting It is f. ASQ 18:7
five f. per cent is the natural MAC 237:9
Want is one only of f. giants BEV 42:3
fix If it ain't broke, don't f. it LANCE 217:3
which a good election can't f. NIXON 274:4
fixed There you are, f., old cock CHUR 91:8
fixers We need fixed rules, not f. HAYEK 171:8
flag debt, an' a f. LOW 233:8
discover that the f. BALD 28:6
f. is companionship SUMN 353:2
I pledge allegiance to the f. BELL 34:11
It is the f. just as much of LODGE 232:1
raised their f. against WEBS 382:7
respect its f. PAGE 280:7
spare your country's f. WHIT 388:5
that does not carry the f. CHO 85:7
We'll keep the red f. flying here CONN 101:7
We shall not f. or fail CHUR 90:7
flagpole run it up the f. and see ANON 11:12
Flanders In F. fields MCCR 240:2
part of F. hath received WALL 377:3
they had brought him a F. mare HENR 176:1
flashes occasional f. of silence SMITH 344:9
flattered being then most f. SHAK 329:1
flatterers I tell him he hates f. SHAK 329:1
sycophants and f. HARD 168:4
within a week the same f. HAL 165:8
flatteries against f. MACH 241:7
flattering f., kissing and kicking TRUM 371:5
flattery Everyone likes f. DISR 121:4
f. corrupts both the receiver BURKE 66:13
I suppose f. hurts no one STEV 349:7
When power to f. bows SHAK 331:2
fleas like a monkey looking for f. LASKI 218:4
flesh f. which walls about our life SHAK 333:8
men are f. and blood SHAK 329:3
flies catch small f. SWIFT 353:4
for you to keep the f. off the meat CHUR 90:14
you mark his favourite f. SHAK 325:12
float f. lazily downstream SAL 317:7
floating f. bulwark of the island BLAC 48:7
flog f. the rank and file ARN 17:6
flood just cause reaches its f.-tide CATT 78:7
return it as a f. GLAD 155:11
taken at the f., leads on SHAK 330:14
floor I could f. them all DISR 116:9
floppy weak, f. thing in the chair THAT 362:14
flourish princes and lords may f. GOLD 157:6
flow rivers of blood must yet f. JEFF 193:11
flower f. of our youth TREV 368:1
little f., this delicate little beauty KEAT 202:9
flowers wild f., and Prime Ministers BALD 29:3
flowing Suez Canal was f. through EDEN 128:1
flown all the birds are f. CHAR 82:3
fluidity solid for f. CHUR 89:7
fly they ever f. by twilight BACON 23:2
fly-blown f. phylacteries ROS 312:13
foaming Tiber f. with much blood POW 297:1
focus f. of politics on real people HAVEL 170:5

foe friend than as a f. GLAD 156:1
Where breathes the f. DRAKE 124:8
willing f. and sea room ANON 15:3
foliage f. which we call the myth CROS 106:12
follies crimes, f., and misfortunes GIBB 151:6
follow I f. the worse OVID 280:3
I really had to f. them LEDR 219:8
following to find nobody f. CHAM 80:3
folly effects of f., is to fill the world SPEN 347:6
He knew human f. AUDEN 21:5
usually ends in f. COL 101:2
wicked f. of 'Woman's Rights' VICT 374:5
fond We should grow too f. of it LEE 220:4
fondly f. do we hope LINC 226:9
fondness habitual f. WASH 379:12
food advertise f. to hungry GALB 145:4
because f. isn't available REAG 302:3
struggle for room and f. MALT 248:10
wholesome f., whether stewed SWIFT 354:1
fool f. all of the people all ADAMS 2:5
f. too many of the people THUR 364:8
Take away that f.'s bauble CROM 105:9
wisest f. in Christendom HENR 175:4
You may f. all the people some of LINC 227:8
foolish He never said a f. thing ROCH 307:5
Nobody ever did anything very f. MELB 256:1
fools did he not suffer f. gladly PEAR 287:5
fill the world with f. SPEN 347:6
f. are in a terrible IBSEN 186:8
f. out of favour DEFOE 111:5
f. said would happen has MELB 255:4
f., they have left us our PEAR 287:3
make one half the world f. JEFF 191:2
perish together as f. KING 211:2
foot at the f. of the first page SAND 320:2
born with a silver f. in his mouth RICH 305:2
football In life, as in a f. game ROOS 311:1
politics is like being a f. coach MCC 239:5
footlights couldn't get in the f. COOK 102:7
footslogger average f. WRAN 394:10
forbearance f. ceases to be a virtue BURKE 62:8
force blend f. with a manoeuvre TROT 370:10
driving f. of all religious WEBER 381:10
f., and fraud, are in war HOBB 180:3
f. from which the sun TRUM 371:2
f. is not a remedy BRIG 57:1
Not believing in f. TROT 370:15
Other nations use 'f.' WAUGH 380:6
use of f. alone is but *temporary* BURKE 64:12
use of *f.* by one class against LENIN 221:6
forcibly f. if we must CLAY 97:3
Ford I am a F., not a Lincoln FORD 138:11
forefathers contemplate our f. ADAMS 5:2
think of your f. ADAMS 4:5
foreign destroyed by a f. force MONT 264:6
devilish thing about f. affairs REST 303:2
f. aid is the most unpopular NIXON 274:15
f. policy of a country TAYL 356:11
From wandering on a f. strand SCOTT 322:5
I do not speak any f. language LLOYD 228:10
If a f. country can supply us SMITH 342:6
If in a f. land, the flag SUMN 353:2
If you wish to avoid f. collision CLAY 97:2
influences on our f. policy GALB 146:12
my f. policy: I wage war CLEM 98:4
phrase 'f. affairs' DISR 120:1
purchase from f. countries SMITH 342:7
This is the idea behind f. policy O'RO 277:7
to be sent into any f. wars ROOS 309:9
foreigners I do not like f. LLOYD 228:10
To admit f. indiscriminately HAM 167:8
Foreign Secretary attacking the F. BEVAN 41:2
send Britain's F. naked BEVAN 41:3
forelock tugged the f. KEAT 202:8
forest f. laments CHUR 86:4
like an American f. BAG 27:5
foretell f. what is going to happen CHUR 94:6
forged f. in controversies FRAN 141:8
forget do not quite f. CHES 84:7
f. all feuds, and shed one MAC 238:10
I never contradict; I sometimes f. DISR 121:7
lest we f. KIPL 212:11
never forgive but I always f. BALF 31:5
not to f. we are gentlemen BURKE 63:6
they will f. there ever was WILS 392:14
forgets authority f. a dying king TENN 360:4
forgive f. those who were right MACL 243:1
good Lord will f. me CATH 78:4
I never f. but I always forget BALF 31:5
Reason to rule, but mercy to f. DRYD 125:15
forgot Honey, I just f. to duck DEMP 113:3
My Lord, I had f. the fart ELIZ 131:11
forgotten f. man at the bottom ROOS 308:4
learnt nothing, and f. nothing TALL 354:11
fork pick up mercury with a f. LLOY 230:3
formalistic revolutionaries more f. CALV 73:4
forms For f. of government POPE 295:4
fortnight beyond the next f. CHAM 80:1
fortress This f. built by Nature SHAK 333:4
fortune leads on to f. SHAK 330:14
fortunes greater part of our f. CHUR 93:8
forward F., forward let us range TENN 359:7
not look f. to posterity BURKE 66:10
fought we f. at Arques HENR 175:3
what they f. each other for SOUT 347:1
foully Thou play'dst most f. for't SHAK 331:10
found as good as he had f. it COBB 100:4
effort to f. the Roman nation VIRG 375:4
has not yet f. a role ACH 1:5
foundation f. of morals BENT 37:9
Good order is the f. BURKE 67:10
founding f. a firm state MARV 252:1
fountain He is the f. of honour BACON 23:8
saying, the 'f. of honour' BAG 24:12

four f. essential human ROOS 309:12
f. lagging winters SHAK 333:3
F. legs good, two legs bad ORW 278:10
two plus two make f. ORW 279:4
fourteenth f. Mr Wilson HOME 182:3
fourth f. estate of the realm MAC 237:3
This is the f. JEFF 194:1
your f. of July DOUG 123:6
fox F. divided the kingdom JOHN 198:12
mentality of a f. at large LEVIN 222:6
My God! They've shot our f. BIRCH 45:6
prince must be a f. MACH 241:5
foxes f. have a sincere interest ELIOT 130:1
foxholes 'coloured' signs on the f. KENN 205:5
fox-hunting f. and writing poetry POW 297:3
simplest of them prefer f. HAIL 163:3
fracture f. the Labour party KINN 212:3
fragment geographical f. PARN 286:5
France between F. and England PEEL 289:1
F.... a nation of forty millions CRILE 104:3
F. has lost a battle DE G 112:3
F., mother of arts, of warfare DU B 126:4
F. was long a despotism tempered CARL 75:11
He felt about F. what Pericles KEYN 207:3
in F. all is permitted MEG 255:3
nation, a race, F. is a person MICH 258:5
nation F. MONN 263:2
political thought, in F. ARON 17:7
Shall F. remain here PARK 286:4
two breasts by which F. is fed SULLY 352:6
until F. is adequately secured ASQ 18:3
wield the sword of F. DE G 112:4
frank f. and explicit DISR 118:5
fraud force, and f., are in war HOBB 180:3
frauds all great men are f. BON 51:5
Frederick death of F. the Great BISM 47:6
free all men everywhere could be f. LINC 226:2
all men naturally were born f. MILT 261:1
assure freedom to the f. LINC 226:1
better that England should be f. MAGEE 247:1
born f. and equal in dignity ANON 8:4
comment is f. but facts are STOP 351:10
dare trample upon these, be f. SHEL 338:6
die to make men f. HOWE 184:4
English church shall be f. MAGN 247:2
essence of a f. government CALH 72:2
expects to be ignorant and f. JEFF 193:6
forever f. LINC 225:11
f. as they want to be BALD 28:7
f. at last! Thank God Almighty KING 210:11
f. development of each MARX 253:3
f. press is not a privilege LIPP 228:4
f. society is a society where STEV 350:7
F. speech, free passes BETJ 40:1
function of speech to f. men BRAN 55:1
half slave and half f. LINC 225:1
he is powerful and f. TOCQ 365:6
he's f. again SOLZ 345:10
hungry man is not a f. man STEV 350:3
I am a f. man, an American JOHN 195:5
I'm with you on the f. press STOP 351:11
in chains than to be f. KAFKA 201:9
in prison, I am not f. DEBS 111:3
land of the f. KEY 207:1
leave their citizens f. JEFF 193:15
Long Live F. Quebec DE G 112:14
man is either f. or he is not BAR 32:2
Man was born f. ROUS 314:5
men can be both f. and equal BAG 24:6
mother of the f. BENS 37:6
must ever exist in a f. country BURKE 64:9
need in order to remain f. TOCQ 366:11
No f. man shall be taken MAGN 247:3
no such thing as a f. lunch ANON 13:9
only maxim of a f. government ADAMS 3:5
prerogative of a f. people PAINE 283:7
set the people f. HEATH 173:7
should themselves be f. BRO 57:7
so far kept us f. and firm JEFF 192:6
they are f. to do whatever SHAW 336:4
through f. trade CHOD 85:10
truth which makes men f. AGAR 6:4
want not really a f. press RADC 299:6
Was he f.? Was he happy AUDEN 21:4
We must be f. or die WORD 394:5
wholly slaves or wholly f. DRYD 125:16
will to be f. is perpetually LIPP 228:5
women, not only to be f. PANK 284:10
work makes f. ANON 8:7
yearning to breathe f. LAZ 219:7
freed not be many f. men HAL 166:9
freedom better organized than f. PÉGUY 289:11
born to f., and believing in f. ROOS 309:12
call it the idea of f. PARK 285:6
cannot be any apprenticeship for f. BAR 32:2
deny them this participation of f. BURKE 63:12
do not deny that f. is excellent TOCQ 366:4
enemies of f. do not argue INGE 187:8
fit to use their f. MAC 237:6
F. alone ... substitutes TOCQ 366:2
F. and not servitude BURKE 64:1
F. and slavery are mental states GAND 147:7
f. cannot exist without METT 258:2
F. for the pike is death TAWN 356:1
F. hath been hunted round PAINE 281:7
F. is always and exclusively LUX 234:8
F. is an indivisible word WILL 389:5
F. is slavery ORW 279:1
f. is something people take BALD 28:7
F. is the freedom to say ORW 279:4
f. of the press CHUR 94:7
f. of the press, and f. of person JEFF 192:8
F. of the press in Britain SWAF 353:3
F. of the press is guaranteed LIEB 223:6

f. of thought ADAMS 5:5
f. of thought HAYEK 171:7
f. of which Europe has little KENY 206:6
f. that is its birthright SOLZ 346:4
f. which in no other land DRYD 125:14
go out to fight for f. and truth IBSEN 186:9
I desire their liberty and f. CHAR 82:6
I gave my life for f. EWER 134:5
impair their f. TAWN 355:12
In giving f. to the slave LINC 226:1
inherent efficiencies of f. GALB 145:3
Let f. ring SMITH 344:5
love not f., but licence MILT 260:8
love of f. itself GLAD 154:11
measure of individual f. TROL 369:3
most important guarantee of f. HAYEK 171:4
neither equality nor f. FRI 143:10
no easy walk-over to f. NEHRU 270:5
not f. from, but f. to BERL 39:2
O f., what liberties are taken GEOR 150:9
of the f. of the people MAD 246:6
only f. worth the name MILL 258:9
original source of f. LIPP 228:2
peace, f., and liberty SHAK 329:7
precious things: f. of speech TWAIN 372:9
principles of f., equality, justice PAGE 280:7
rights of f. we are all equal JUN 200:12
right to f. of movement ANON 9:13
safeguards of individual f. HAYEK 171:9
sense of f. is f. from chains BERL 39:3
taste for f. TOCQ 366:11
we can do for the f. of man KENN 204:7
We must plan for f. POPP 295:11
When there is f. LENIN 221:7
When we let f. ring KING 210:11
Where f. slowly broadens down TENN 359:8
With f.'s soil beneath our feet DRAKE 124:8
freedoms four essential human f. ROOS 309:11
freeing f. some and leaving others LINC 226:2
freemen f. or slaves WASH 379:6
only f. MASS 254:2
only great nursery of f. SHIP 339:6
To rule o'er f. BRO 57:7
frei *Arbeit macht f.* ANON 8:7
French beating the F. WOLFE 393:5
F. are with equal advantage CANN 75:3
F. government, American culture PEAR 287:7
F. noblesse TREV 368:2
F. Revolution operated TOCQ 366:5
F. want no-one to be TOCQ 365:1
in its history Paris was F. TUCH 372:6
Providence has given to the F. RICH 305:3
fresh healthy f. air GALB 146:8
fricassee equally serve in a f. SWIFT 354:1
friend betraying my f. FORS 139:4
Fifth Amendment is an old f. DOUG 123:3
f. in power is a f. lost ADAMS 2:8
f. of every country but his own CANN 75:1
lose her as a f. than as a foe GLAD 156:1
loss of a dear f. SOUT 347:3
make change our f. CLIN 99:7
make one f. TAYL 358:1
my f., faithful and just to me SHAK 330:1
one f. left LINC 226:8
That love my f. SHAK 330:8
who lost no f. POPE 295:3
friends between f. CAMP 74:1
enemies in war, in peace f. JEFF 190:6
f. of every country DISR 120:8
F., Romans, countrymen SHAK 329:13
just f. and brave enemies JEFF 192:11
lay down his f. for his life THOR 364:7
There are no true f. in politics CLARK 96:10
very nearly deceiving your f. CORN 103:9
workers of the country are our f. SHIN 339:5
friendship honest f. with all nations JEFF 192:7
In f. false DRYD 125:6
There is no f. at the top LLOY 230:13
fright f. the souls SHAK 334:9
frighten *by God, they f. me* WELL 383:8
frightening never more f. than VAN 373:3
fringe lunatic f. ROOS 311:13
frivolity irresponsible f. DISR 120:12
frog f. in my throat MAJOR 247:10
from not freedom f. BERL 39:2
front I've been stabbed in the f. INGH 188:2
frontier edge of a new f. KENN 203:9
frontiers old f. are gone BALD 29:7
frozen f. in an out-of-date mould JENK 194:4
fructify f. in the pockets GLAD 156:2
frustrate f. their knavish tricks ANON 9:9
frying-pan frizzled in my f. ENG 133:7
fugitive f. and cloistered virtue MILT 260:6
Führer *Ein Reich, ein Volk, ein F.* ANON 9:11
F. is the proper name LLOY 230:8
full God, we ha' paid in f. KIPL 212:10
fun It is f. ROOS 310:3
Mr Gladstone read Homer for f. CHUR 88:13
no reference to f. HERB 176:11
function must f. to perfection MUSS 268:8
fundamental f. sense of freedom BERL 39:3
funeral corpse at the f. HEAD 172:1
heaping up its own f. pyre POW 296:10
funk attitudes of postwar f. TEBB 359:2
funny f. thing happened to me STEV 350:9
furnish f. the pictures and I'll f. HEAR 173:5
furniture all that nice f. MACM 245:11
not going to rearrange the f. MORT 267:1
furrow I must plough my f. alone ROS 312:12
further f. you got from Britain CALL 73:2
gates of hell—but no f. PIUS 294:1
fuss What a f. about an omelette VOLT 375:12
future controls the f. ORW 279:2
doubted your f. MURR 268:3

future (*cont.*):
empires of the f. CHUR 92:2
extravagant hopes of the f. BURKE 62:10
have any political f. MONC 261:9
if you want a f. in politics HES 178:1
I have seen the f.; and it works STEF 349:1
lively sense of f. favours WALP 378:7
never plan the f. by the past BURKE 67:16
no preparation for the f. DISR 117:6
no way of judging the f. HENRY 176:6
picture of the f., imagine a boot ORW 279:8
promise us everything for the f. KHR 209:8
that scaffold sways the f. LOW 234:2
You cannot fight against the f. GLAD 154:6
Fyfe Is David Patrick Maxwell F. ANON 12:8

gained misery is a battle g. WELL 385:1
gainful g. employment ACH 1:4
gains no g. without pains STEV 349:9
gallery history is a g. of pictures TOCQ 366:6
Gallia *G. est omnis divisa in partes* CAES 71:7
gallows die upon the g. WILK 389:1
you see nothing but the g. BURKE 67:1
gambler whore and g. BLAKE 49:4
game always played the g. SMITH 344:2
anarchism is a g. SHAW 336:16
war is a very rough g. MONT 265:2
win this g., and to thrash DRAKE 124:7
Gandhi If only Bapu [G.] knew NAIDU 268:9
gangsters acted like g. KUBR 215:7
garage to the full g. HOOV 182:9
garden their own back g. KERR 206:7
wild herb, the other the g. plant TOCQ 366:10
gardening g. with a staff of three BIRCH 45:7
garland immortal g. MILT 260:6
garlic wear a clove of g. O'BR 276:4
garments reasons are not like g. ESSEX 134:2
garter Order of the G. CHUR 92:7
gate poor man at his g. ALEX 7:1
stood at the g. of the year HASK 170:2
gates And shut the g. of mercy GRAY 160:8
g. are mine to open KIPL 213:1
open the g. of opportunity JOHN 196:7
prepared to go to the g. of Hell PIUS 294:1
Gaul G. as a whole is divided CAES 71:7
general feet of the great g. OVID 280:4
hands of the g. government JEFF 192:1
generalities g. of natural right CHO 85:8
General Motors good for G. WILS 389:7
generals dead battles, like dead g. TUCH 372:4
not against the law for g. TRUM 372:2
Only those g. who gain success LINC 226:4
Russia has two g. NICH 271:5
generation sleep of my g. STEV 351:1
generations thousand g. KINN 212:2
generously treated g. or destroyed MACH 241:2
geniality g. of the politician MAUG 254:4
genius Bismarck was a political g. TAYL 356:9
g. of its scientists EIS 129:4
g. of the Constitution PITT 293:3
talent and g. in this house KENN 205:1
times in which a g. ADAMS 2:2
gent gentleman is to a g. BALD 30:2
gentle droppeth as the g. rain SHAK 332:10
His life was g. SHAK 330:16
gentleman cannot make a g. BURKE 67:17
g. in Whitehall JAY 190:4
No real English g. BAG 24:4
scribbling—never a g. DISR 121:9
Since every Jack became a g. SHAK 334:10
that which you call 'a g.' CROM 105:3
to the intelligentsia what a g. is BALD 30:2
gentlemen creates good g. MUG 267:6
g. do not take soup CURZ 108:5
not to forget we are g. BURKE 63:6
since g. came up SHAK 326:19
When g. cease to be returned DISR 121:17
geographical g. concept BISM 46:9
Ireland is not a g. fragment PARN 286:5
Italy is a g. expression METT 257:7
geometrical increases in a g. ratio MALT 248:9
George Any good of G. the Third LAND 217:5
G. III was a kind of BAG 25:10
G. the First knew nothing JOHN 198:2
G. the First was always reckoned LAND 217:5
G. the Third BENT 38:2
G. VI's reign will go down WAUGH 380:10
Georges G. ended LAND 217:5
Georgia on the red hills of G. KING 210:10
Georgian G. silver goes MACM 245:11
German G. Chancellor, Herr Hitler CHAM 80:10
G. dictator CHUR 89:11
great G. whom fate has raised up BRY 60:7
This is all a G. racket RIDL 305:6
With Hitler guilty, every other G. TAYL 357:5
Germans G. down ISMAY 188:4
G., if this Government GEDD 148:7
government from the G. MONT 264:11
much easier to fight the G. MONT 265:4
There are too many G. TAYL 356:6
to the G. that of—the air RICH 305:3
We G. now have the historic KOHL 215:5
Germany country is at war with G. CHAM 81:3
deadliness to fight G. CHUR 86:2
from G. to Downing Street CHAM 81:1
G. above all HOFF 180:11
G. calling! Germany calling JOYCE 200:8
G. is a nation, a race MICH 258:5
G., now cast down, despised MACM 244:3
G. was rearming BALD 29:10
How you, rebellious G. OVID 280:4
in G. all is prohibited MEG 255:3

Let us...put G. in the saddle BISM 46:8
offering G. too little NEV 271:2
What is wrong with G. TAYL 356:6
get governments had better g. out EIS 129:7
If you want to g. along RAYB 301:4
ghost conjure a great g. DANG 109:4
g. of a great name LUCAN 234:4
g. of the deceased Roman HOBB 180:9
giant To have a g.'s strength SHAK 332:8
giants one only of five g. BEV 42:3
prepare for war like precocious g. PEAR 287:4
world of nuclear g. BRAD 54:5
Gibbon like G. on the Christians BUTL 70:7
gibes master of g. and flouts DISR 120:5
gifts even when they bring g. VIRG 375:5
gilded Men are but g. loam SHAK 333:1
gin torrent of g. and beer GLAD 154:9
Gipper win just one for the G. GIPP 153:5
girls treaties, you see, are like g. DE G 112:13
give g. me back my legions AUG 21:7
g. us the tools CHUR 91:6
never g. up their liberties BURKE 65:10
not to take than to g. POW 296:6
willing to g. it to others WHITE 387:4
given I would have g. gladly JOHN 195:7
not have g. me over WOLS 394:3
giver both the receiver and the g. BURKE 66:13
giving not in the g. vein to-day SHAK 335:3
glad I'm g. we've been bombed ELIZ 132:8
never g. confident morning BROW 60:2
gladly I would have given g. JOHN 195:7
Gladstone G.... spent his declining SELL 323:10
in order that Mr G. may perspire CHUR 86:4
Mr G. read Homer for fun CHUR 88:13
voting against G. all my life KING 210:1
glass Get thee g. eyes SHAK 331:5
glittering g. and sounding generalities CHO 85:8
merely the g. scum CHUR 88:9
world continues to offer g. prizes SMITH 343:8
glitters medal g., but it also CHUR 91:2
globe hunted round the g. PAINE 281:7
sop of all this sordid g. SHAK 335:9
glories my g. and my state depose SHAK 334:4
glorious reach at the g. gold SHAK 326:17
To the memory of the g. REV 303:6
What a g. morning is this ADAMS 5:3
glory day of g. has arrived ROUG 314:3
duty was the way to g. TENN 360:3
g. is departed from Israel BIBLE 43:10
I g. in the name of Briton GEOR 149:1
I name thee Old G. DRIV 124:9
land of hope and g. BENS 37:6
lost the hope of g. BALF 30:10
Mine eyes have seen the g. HOWE 184:3
not the g. of rulers or of races BEV 42:2
this I count the g. of my crown ELIZ 132:1
Vain pomp and g. of this world SHAK 327:6
gloves capitalism with the g. off STOP 351:9
glow her g. has warmed STEV 350:14
glue truth is the g. FORD 139:1
gnomes little g. in Zurich WILS 390:1
go g. anywhere I damn well please BEVIN 43:4
Good-night—and g. to it MORR 266:6
In the name of God, g. AMERY 8:1
In the name of God, g. CROM 105:8
let my people g. BIBLE 43:7
thus far shalt thou g. PARN 286:8
unto Caesar shalt thou g. BIBLE 44:12
we think you ought to g. RUB 314:8
you want to get along, g. along RAYB 301:4
goals They live by positive g. BERL 39:4
work for long-term g. MONN 262:9
God but for the grace of G. CHUR 93:12
Caesar's; and unto G. the things BIBLE 44:7
either a beast or a g. ARIS 16:6
Fellow-citizens: G. reigns GARF 147:8
GCMG ('G. Calls Me God') SAMP 319:9
G. also is a Trinity man BIRR 46:2
G. bless America BERL 38:6
G. bless the Prince of Wales LINL 227:10
G. fulfils himself TENN 360:5
G. has given us Missouri RAND 300:9
G. has more right JOHN 195:1
G. help the Minister that meddles MELB 255:9
G. is any respecter of persons BROWN 59:2
G. is a Republican O'RO 277:3
G. is on the side VOLT 375:8
G. punish England FUNKE 144:7
G. save the king HOGG 181:2
G. who made thee mighty BENS 37:6
Had I but served G. as diligently WOLS 394:3
Had I but served my G. SHAK 327:8
hand into the Hand of G. HASK 170:2
he hears the steps of G. BISM 47:11
In the name of G., go AMERY 8:1
like G.'s infinite mercy O'RO 277:2
Nor paltered with Eternal G. TENN 360:2
of the people is the voice of G. ALC 6:8
One on G.'s side is a majority PHIL 292:1
Standeth G. within the shadow LOW 234:2
thick skin is a gift from G. ADEN 6:1
think I am becoming a g. VESP 374:3
This is the negation of G. GLAD 154:2
when I reflect that G. is just JEFF 191:3
gods dish fit for the g. SHAK 328:13
g. are on the side of RUSS 316:11
g. are on the side of the stronger TAC 354:9
they are called g. JAM 189:11
would destroy, they first make g. LEVIN 222:3
goes As Maine g., so g. Vermont FARL 135:5
for the grace of God, g. God CHUR 93:12
going Everything is g. nowadays GEOR 150:8
g. gets tough, the tough get g. KENN 206:2
I am g. on WILS 391:2

going (*cont.*):
knows not whither he is g. CROM 106:1
gold *came off the G. Standard* WEBB 381:5
I stuffed their mouths with g. BEVAN 41:10
mankind upon a cross of g. BRYAN 60:6
pure g. flows forth TOCQ 365:2
reach at the glorious g. SHAK 326:17
golden g. moments of our history GLAD 155:7
Happy the g. mean MASS 254:2
In good King Charles's g. days ANON 10:12
lift my lamp beside the g. door LAZ 219:7
morning had been g. CHUR 89:9
golf g.-links lie so near the mill CLEG 98:3
gone what haste I can to be g. CROM 106:3
good And common g. to all SHAK 330:16
Any g. of George the Third LAND 217:5
as much g. as it must LEWIS 223:2
Asquith is g. and immoral CHUR 88:2
discretion for the public g. LOCKE 231:9
g. government could never be CAMP 74:3
g. is oft interrèd SHAK 329:13
g. must associate BURKE 63:4
g. nature is a bungler HAL 166:12
g. of subjects DEFOE 111:11
g. of the people CIC 95:6
'g. old days' were a myth ATK 19:5
g. words will not do LAMB 216:6
Great and the G. SAMP 319:10
He overcame evil with g. KING 210:4
His own g. MILL 258:10
If he is no g. he must CHUR 93:6
if they have a g. thing SHAK 326:6
I will be g. VICT 374:4
know better what is g. for people JAY 190:4
leave his country as g. COBB 100:4
maintain g. government HAM 167:3
Men are never so g. or so bad MACK 242:3
necessary only for the g. man BURKE 68:7
never had it so g. MACM 244:7
not called amiss *The g. old Cause* MILT 261:4
object of g. government JEFF 193:1
only g. Indian is a dead Indian SHER 338:10
policy of the g. neighbour ROOS 308:9
pursuing our own g. MILL 258:9
rather than to seem g. SALL 319:6
That would be a g. idea GAND 147:4
their g. becomes indistinguishable DAWS 110:4
Therefore, the g. of man must be ARIS 16:2
This is the sum of g. government JEFF 192:3
We are come for your g. GEOR 148:8
We threw g. housekeeping KEYN 208:7
What g. Government ever TROL 370:4
What's g., and doth no g. RAL 300:4
what was g. for our country was WILS 389:7
goods care for external g. WEBER 382:1
dispute less when g. are TAWN 355:10
your good, for all your g. GEOR 148:8
goodwill In peace: g. CHUR 93:5
goose common from the g. ANON 14:2
Goose Green on the ground at G. KINN 211:9
Gorbachev Mr G., tear down REAG 302:5
Goschen I forgot G. CHUR 86:9
gossip in the g. columns INGH 187:10
govern easy to g., but impossible BRO 58:2
good enough to g. another man LINC 224:6
Go out and g. New South Wales BELL 35:3
g. according to the common weal JAM 190:2
heroes to g. you CARL 76:14
How can you g. a country DE G 112:11
No man is fit to g. great societies MAC 238:15
not to g. the country but GLAD 154:4
people g. themselves THI 363:2
To g. is to choose LÉVIS 223:1
You g. in prose CUOMO 107:3
governed ability among the g. TOCQ 366:1
democratically g. republic HAIL 164:1
g. by your inferiors PLATO 294:3
government to control the g. MAD 246:7
my faith in The People g. is DICK 115:7
nation is not g. BURKE 64:12
not so well g. as they ought HOOK 182:5
People must be g. in a manner BURKE 62:6
they are g. by the weakness BAG 25:6
To understand how we're g. BENN 36:12
governing lack of it among the g. TOCQ 366:1
right of g. was not property FOX 140:5
totally incapable of g. CHES 83:12
government abandon a g. JEFF 192:6
actual work of g. O'RO 277:6
America as a g. of the people PAGE 280:7
any established institution of g. BURKE 65:7
any G. which commands PICK 292:6
art of g. consists in taking VOLT 376:1
art of g. is the organization SHAW 336:9
asks you to form a G. you say ATTL 19:9
attack the G. of my country CHUR 93:2
basis of popular g. ROB 306:11
be outlawed in a well-ordered g. HAL 165:6
best definition of the best g. is HAL 165:14
best g. is that which O'SUL 279:12
Bible is for the g. of the people WYCL 395:1
British g. forms the best model HAM 167:2
cheerfully support their g. CLEV 99:3
consequence of cabinet g. BAG 24:14
corruption of each g. MONT 264:4
dangerous moment for a bad g. TOCQ 367:3
democracy means g. by discussion ATTL 20:11
determined that no British g. MACM 245:6
dullness in parliamentary g. BAG 23:12
duty of g. is to prevent crime MELB 256:6
efficient g. you have a dictatorship TRUM 371:15
erected into a system of G. GLAD 154:2
essence of a free g. CALH 72:2

every g. will do as much harm LEWIS 223:2
every politician not in G. must JENK 194:10
examination of the acts of g. HARR 170:1
excellence of the English g. BLAC 48:10
face a British g. TUCH 372:5
feel the *smack of firm g.* MCL 242:5
first enable the g. to control MAD 246:7
For forms of g. let fools contest POPE 295:4
formal g. is abolished, society PAINE 282:14
four pillars of g. BACON 22:16
Giving money and power to g. O'RO 277:1
glue that holds G. together FORD 139:1
Good g. depends BAG 27:10
good G. ever was not stingy TROL 370:4
g. above the law SCAR 321:3
G. acquired the tact WEST 385:7
G. and co-operation RUSK 315:7
G. and public opinion SHAW 336:4
G. are behaving LLOY 230:10
G. at Washington lives GARF 147:8
g. by the uneducated CHES 85:1
g. can never be the impersonal MENC 257:3
g. could never be a substitute CAMP 74:3
G. does not solve problems REAG 301:7
G., even in its best state PAINE 281:1
g. intervention DICEY 114:7
G. is a contrivance BURKE 66:12
g. is influenced by shopkeepers SMITH 341:6
G. is like a big baby REAG 301:5
G. is nothing but the balance MART 251:6
G.... is simply not the channel KENN 203:7
g. it deserves MAIS 248:5
g. of business LAWS 219:3
g. of cities BRYCE 61:2
g. of laws, and not of men ADAMS 3:7
g. of statesmen or of clerks DISR 117:4
G. of the busy by the bossy SELD 323:4
g. of the world I live in THOR 364:5
g. of the world is carried DISR 120:12
g.'s about not answering LYNN 235:1
g.'s purposes are beneficent BRAN 55:3
g. strong enough to protect ROOS 309:5
g. that runs that machine DOUG 123:4
g. was a practical thing BURKE 64:17
g. which robs Peter to pay SHAW 337:2
g. without a king BANC 31:11
g. without newspapers JEFF 191:4
grave question whether any g. LINC 226:7
great art of g. is to work PEEL 289:4
grow weary of the existing g. LINC 225:7
hands of the general g. JEFF 192:1
has never come from the g. WILS 391:11
having looked to g. for bread BURKE 68:6
highest form of g. SPEN 347:5
how the G. feels in its inside BENN 37:3
I am against g. by crony ICKES 187:3
idea of political g. from the Germans MONT 264:11
if every G., when it comes SNOW 345:5
if possible, a good, g. WELL 384:1
If the G. is big enough FORD 138:10
I just watch the g. and report ROG 307:9
I'm from the g. and I'm here REAG 302:4
important thing for G. is not to KEYN 207:10
in a disorderly g. as in a river HAL 165:13
indispensable duty of g. PAINE 281:9
in moderate g. HAM 167:4
in other words a meddling g. MAC 236:7
In revealing the workings of g. BLACK 48:5
In the life of any g. BOOK 51:7
in the working of local g. THAT 362:15
Is this the g. of Britain's isle SHAK 326:18
its constitution and its g. PAINE 283:12
I work for a G. I despise KEYN 207:2
know the intentions of a g. GALB 145:13
land of settled g. TENN 359:8
least g. was the best FEIN 136:3
legitimate powers of g. JEFF 193:13
might as well be in g. HELL 174:2
most corrupt g. on the earth JEFF 192:2
natural party of g. WILS 390:10
need to keep the g. in order SCAR 321:4
no form of g. that ever did exist TROL 369:3
no g. by divine right HARR 169:7
No G. can be long secure without DISR 117:12
No g. can exist which does not PEEL 288:8
No g. ought to be without JEFF 191:12
no g. proper ever had a provision LINC 225:5
no necessary evils in g. JACK 189:2
not for having share in g. CHAR 82:6
not get all of the g. FRI 144:2
not interested too much in g. BAR 32:8
not just what g. will do for me NIXON 274:8
not the worst g. that England TROL 369:8
object of g. in peace and in war BEV 42:2
Of all vulgar arts of g. PEEL 288:14
of great service to a g. MED 255:2
Of the increase of his g. and peace BIBLE 43:19
one g. sooner learns of another SMITH 342:2
only legitimate object of good g. JEFF 193:1
on the side of the G. RUSS 316:11
our great republic is a G. of laws FORD 138:12
overdoes the quantity of g. BAG 26:10
parliamentary G. as the noblest DISR 119:17
parliamentary g. is impossible DISR 119:18
people's g., made for the people WEBS 382:2
politician to run a g. TRUM 371:13
prepare for g. STEEL 348:10
public *like* plutocratic g. TAWN 356:2
regarded popular g. rather as a means BAG 24:3
representative g. DISR 118:7
republican g. in the United States TOCQ 365:8

government (*cont.*):
revolutionary g. is the despotism ROB 306:8
rights when called by his G. JACK 188:6
risen up in the g. greater than CALH 72:3
second office of g. is honourable JEFF 191:13
secrecy and a free, democratic g. TRUM 372:3
shackles and restraints of g. GOLD 157:2
shake off the existing g. LINC 224:5
signifies the want of g. HOBB 180:8
society is the end of g. ADAMS 3:10
springs of the g. are stretched MONT 264:13
sum of good g. JEFF 192:3
That g. is best which governs not THOR 364:1
that g. of the people LINC 226:3
Then they were sold by g. TOCQ 366:8
There you have despotic g. MONT 264:2
To inherit a g., is to inherit PAINE 282:13
Under a g. which imprisons THOR 364:2
under one form of g. rather than JOHN 197:13
Unfortunately, it's the g. ALLEN 7:4
unjust as a feeble g. BURKE 67:12
virtue of paper g. BURKE 64:3
want the G. to regulate TRUM 371:6
Whatever g. is not a g. of laws WEBS 382:8
Whatever it is that the g. does O'RO 277:7
what the g. can do for it HARD 168:5
when a g. can only secure BLAIR 49:1
when they deal with the G. HOLM 181:6
Why has g. been instituted HAM 167:6
why monarchy is a strong g. BAG 25:5
will ever maintain good g. HAM 167:3
will never use arbitrary g. CHAR 83:5
wise g. knows how to enforce GREN 161:4
works for the federal g. REAG 301:14
worst form of G. except CHUR 93:1
worst g. is often the most moral MENC 257:5
you will create a despotic g. HERB 177:2
governmental unwarranted g. intrusion BREN 56:1
governments foundation of most g. ADAMS 3:11
G. always tend to want RADC 299:6
G. are far more stupid EIS 129:6
g. had better get out EIS 129:7
G. need both shepherds VOLT 375:7
g. to gain ground JEFF 191:8
In all tyrannical g. BLAC 48:9
In corrupted g. the place is given HAL 165:12
Visible g. are the toys RUSK 316:3
governor once knew a g. BOK 50:5
save the G.-General WHIT 387:7
governors Our supreme g. WALP 377:4
governs best which g. not at all THOR 364:1
that which g. least O'SUL 279:12
grab all smash and no g. NIC 272:8
grace keep those of g. MACH 241:9
retains the means of g. BALF 30:10
graces ought to sacrifice to the g. BURKE 67:11
gradualness inevitability of g. WEBB 381:4
grain send choice g. STO 351:12
grammar erecting a g. school SHAK 327:3
every fucking g. school CROS 106:5
talking bad g. DISR 122:1
grandmother We have become a g. THAT 362:3
Grant go and see General G. LEE 220:5
grapes g. can be raised SMITH 342:7
g. of the wine-press MAC 236:3
g. of wrath are stored HOWE 184:3
grass g. will grow in the streets BRYAN 60:5
g. will grow in the streets HOOV 182:10
they nibble g. FAG 135:1
This party comes from the g. roots BEV 42:1
two blades of g. SWIFT 353:7
grasshopper with a g. LLOY 229:7
grasshoppers half a dozen g. BURKE 67:3
gratitude g. is not a normal feature KILM 209:10
G., like love ALSOP 7:5
obtrusive g. of a stranger TOCQ 365:10
gratuity taking of a bribe or g. PENN 289:14
grave crowned upon the g. HOBB 180:9
from the cradle to the g. CHUR 91:12
Is that ayont the g., man BURNS 68:13
It's with O'Leary in the g. YEATS 395:4
life beyond the g. KHR 209:8
ought to be g., and not taunting BACON 22:12
Gravedigger part of the First G. MACL 242:7
graves dishonourable g. SHAK 328:4
graveyards fills political g. KINN 211:7
foxholes or g. of battle KENN 205:5
gravitation not believing in g. TROT 370:15
gravity He rose by his g. SMITH 345:1
Gray whole of G.'s Elegy WOLFE 393:5
graze not allow him to g. there VERW 374:1
greasy to the top of the g. pole DISR 121:5
great All g. men make mistakes CHUR 86:9
g. break through SHEN 338:9
G., Good and Just GRAH 159:1
G. hatred, little room YEATS 396:2
g. man down, you mark SHAK 325:12
G. men are almost always bad ACTON 1:10
G. men are not always wise BIBLE 43:14
g. ones devoured the small SIDN 340:2
g. that cannot reach the small SPEN 347:8
He Was A G. Man ZIEG 397:2
If I am a g. man, then all g. men BON 51:5
madness in g. ones SHAK 325:9
Rightly to be g. SHAK 326:3
seeking favours from the g. TAYL 358:6
That he is grown so g. SHAK 328:5
Then the g. man helped the poor MAC 237:1
tome of *The G. and the Good* SAMP 319:10
upward to the G. Society JOHN 196:2
with small men no g. thing MILL 259:5

Great Britain G. has lost an empire ACH 1:5
G. is going to make war BETH 39:8
G. should free herself SMITH 342:3
G. will not be involved BEAV 33:7
sun of G. will set SHEL 337:8
greater behold a g. than themselves SHAK 328:8
g. than a private citizen TAC 354:8
g. the power, the more dangerous BURKE 63:7
greatest g. happiness of the g. number BENT 37:9
How much the g. event FOX 140:6
greatness ascent to g. GIBB 151:5
G., with private men Esteemed MASS 254:2
His g. weighed SHAK 325:5
long farewell, to all my g. SHAK 327:5
nature of all g. not to be exact BURKE 64:14
Th' abuse of g. SHAK 328:9
Those who have g. within them CAMUS 74:5
Grecian admit the G. horse HAM 167:8
Greece constitutions of later G. BAG 25:7
greed g. is all right...G. is healthy BOES 50:4
g. is right WEIS 383:6
greedy G. for the property SALL 319:4
Greek G. as a treat CHUR 88:12
Greeks G. in this American empire MACM 244:2
I fear the G. even when VIRG 375:5
green for the wearin' o' the g. ANON 10:11
g. shoots of economic spring LAM 217:1
In England's g. and pleasant land BLAKE 49:6
Wherever g. is worn YEATS 395:8
greenroom hang about the g. MACM 245:14
grenadier single Pomeranian g. BISM 47:10
grey given me over in my g. hairs WOLS 394:3
this old g. head WHIT 388:5
gridlock g. might be good DOLE 122:6
grief My g. to thy too rigid fate GRAH 159:1
griefs drinking my g. SHAK 334:3
ere England's g. began GOLD 157:6
g. of forty generations MAC 239:1
not my g.; still am I king of SHAK 334:4
grievance prefer the g. PEEL 289:5
There is no g. that is a fit object LINC 224:3
grievances discovery of g. SAL 318:4
grieve one suffer, than a nation g. DRYD 125:9
grind laws g. the poor GOLD 157:4
grooves ringing g. of change TENN 359:7
grotesque g. chaos of a Labour KINN 211:11
ground every rood of g. GOLD 157:6
gain a little patch of g. SHAK 326:2
g. which a coloured man DOUG 124:1
let us sit upon the g. SHAK 333:8
seven feet of English g. HAR 169:4
grounds g. to make war FAIR 135:2
grouse English g. are to Scotch PEEL 288:15
grovelling g. tyranny DISR 118:12
groves In the g. of *their* academy BURKE 67:1
growth endogenous g. theory BROWN 58:6
plant of rapid g. WASH 380:1
guards up g. and at them WELL 384:2
who is to guard the g. themselves JUV 201:6
guessing what I called 'g.' WELL 384:10
guided g. missiles and misguided KING 211:1
guiding g. star of my political life CARS 77:4
guiding-star g. of a whole brave nation MOTL 267:3
guilt blood with g. is bought SHEL 338:5
g. of Stalin GORB 158:2
not allow middle-class g. HEAL 172:9
guiltier g. than him SHAK 332:6
guilty With Hitler g. TAYL 357:5
guinea g. you have in your pocket RUSK 315:6
rank is but the g.'s stamp BURNS 68:10
Gulag G. Archipelago SOLZ 346:2
gum can't fart and chew g. JOHN 196:10
gun barrel of a g. MAO 250:4
Every g. that is made EIS 129:4
We have got the Maxim G. BELL 35:1
gun-boat send a g. BEVAN 40:10
gunfire towards the sound of g. GRIM 162:1
gunpowder civilization, g., Printing CARL 75:12
inglorious; namely, printing, g. BACON 22:2
invention of g. MONT 263:10
no reason why g. treason ANON 13:2
guns not, for example, without g. GOEB 156:5
rather have butter or g. GOER 156:6
guts g. of the last priest DID 116:1
strangled with the g. of the last MESL 257:6
gyre turning in the widening g. YEATS 395:6

habeas corpus protection of *h.* JEFF 192:8
habits respect the prejudices and h. GIBB 152:2
habitual h. hatred WASH 379:12
Habsburg H. history TAYL 357:6
hack Do not h. me MONM 262:3
Haig [Earl H.] committed suicide BEAV 34:4
hair his long essenced h. MAC 236:4
Haldane H. always prefers CAMP 74:4
half h. slave and half free LINC 225:1
Too clever by h. SAL 319:3
Halifax H. of the latter MUGG 268:2
halitosis h. of the intellect ICKES 187:1
hallow cannot h. this ground LINC 226:3
halls In our h. is hung WORD 394:5
Hamlet like putting on H. with no MACL 242:7
hamsters tigress surrounded by h. BIFF 45:1
hand bite the h. that fed them BURKE 68:6
delivered him into mine h. BIBLE 43:11
h. into the H. of God HASK 170:2
h. that held the dagger ROOS 309:8
h. that signed the paper THOM 363:3
h. to execute GIBB 151:10
h. to execute any mischief CLAR 96:2

hand (*cont.*):
h. which executes a measure TAYL 358:5
invisible h. in politics FRI 144:1
led by an invisible h. SMITH 342:4
never stretch out the h. HES 177:10
one as the h. WASH 379:2
On this side my h. SHAK 334:3
workers by h. or by brain ANON 14:3
handbag hitting it with her h. CRIT 104:5
handkerchief lady's pocket h. LLOY 230:2
hands *chained up the h. of the loyal* ANON 13:3
h. of the oppressor BIKO 45:4
Look, daddy, no h. ANON 12:6
With mine own h. SHAK 334:6
hang h. yourself, brave Crillon HENR 175:3
We must indeed all h. together FRAN 142:2
we ought to let him h. there EHRL 128:6
hanged had longed to see him h. BELL 35:5
h., drawn, and quartered PEPYS 289:15
Men are not h. for stealing horses HAL 166:10
hanging h.' men an' women ANON 10:11
hangman fit for the h. LASKI 218:3
only the arm of the h. ANON 13:3
hangs h. on princes' favours SHAK 327:6
hang-ups don't have time for h. THAT 360:11
happen d—d fools said would h. MELB 255:4
what is going to h. tomorrow CHUR 94:6
happens constitution is what h. GRIF 161:6
happiness greatest h. of the greatest number BENT 37:9
h. of an individual JOHN 197:13
h. of society is the end ADAMS 3:10
h. of the common man BEV 42:2
hath been in my people's h. ELIZ 131:2
in America, the politics of h. HUMP 185:5
justice or human h. BERL 39:1
liberty and the pursuit of h. ANON 14:7
liberty, and the pursuit of h. JEFF 191:1
secret of h. and courage BRAN 54:10
happy accounted yourselves h. CROM 105:13
Few people can be h. unless RUSS 316:10
h. is that city ANON 10:4
I'm h. tonight KING 211:4
My poor are h. PAINE 283:12
someone, somewhere, may be h. MENC 257:2
splendid and a h. land GOLD 157:7
than that none should be h. JOHN 198:6
this h. breed of men SHAK 333:4
Was he free? Was he h. AUDEN 21:4
hard I die h., but I am not afraid WASH 380:2
hard-faced lot of h. men BALD 29:1
hare-brained h. chatter DISR 120:12
hark h. the herald angels sing ANON 10:5
harlot prerogative of the h. KIPL 214:1
harm government will do as much h. LEWIS 223:2
his will, is to prevent h. to others MILL 258:10
It does no h. MONC 261:10
thyse men don most h. LANG 217:7
Harrow who decry Eton and H. BEVIN 42:9
worthy to pass into H. CHUR 88:10
Harry But H., H. SHAK 326:8
little touch of H. in the night SHAK 326:10
haste make what h. I can CROM 106:3
hat who does not wear a h. BEAV 34:6
hatchet did cut it with my h. WASH 379:5
hate h. some other person RUSS 316:10
I h. war ROOS 309:1
I have seen much to h. here MILL 260:1
implacable in h. DRYD 125:6
Let them h., so long as they fear ACC 1:3
hated He rather h. the ruling few BENT 37:11
hates In a world of voluble h. TREV 368:3
hating By h. vices too much BURKE 67:8
don't give way to h. KIPL 213:3
hatred burning h. for the Tory Party BEVAN 40:6
great h., little room YEATS 396:2
toward another an habitual h. WASH 379:12
undying h. it arouses FOSD 139:6
hatreds h. which sound so real TROL 370:8
systematic organization of h. ADAMS 2:7
hats so many shocking bad h. WELL 384:8
Haughey Mr H. buried at midnight O'BR 276:4
have between the House of H. GEOR 150:10
only thing you cannot h. WHITE 387:4
havoc Cry, 'h.!' and let slip SHAK 329:9
hawk Browne was like a h. ANON 9:4
hawking *h. his conscience* BEVIN 42:7
hay work and pray, live on h. HILL 178:8
he h. would, wouldn't he? RICE 304:8
live as the greatest h. RAIN 300:1
head all the blood from the h. BEVAN 40:4
bad legs, but for your good h. ELIZ 131:3
bridge scores in his h. BUTL 70:6
But bowed his comely h. MARV 251:7
Charles I lost his h. for no less CRO 107:1
h. of the Cabinet MORL 266:1
h. that wears a crown SHAK 326:7
h. to contrive, and a hand GIBB 151:10
h. to contrive, a tongue CLAR 96:2
his brains go to his h. ASQ 19:1
If you can keep your h. KIPL 213:3
if you strike at the h. BURKE 66:1
laid your wretched h. OVID 280:4
make you shorter by the h. ELIZ 130:7
no matter which way the h. lies RAL 300:6
not tell which was the h. BRIG 56:9
O good grey h. TENN 359:10
"On my h.," was the reply DISR 116:10
parboiled h. upon a stake GRAH 159:2
should belong to the h. TAYL 358:5
show my h. to the people DANT 109:7
Whereof he is the h. SHAK 325:5

wholly admirable h. of state HAIL 164:1
headline I don't want the last h. HES 178:1
headmasters h. have powers CHUR 88:11
healing not heroics, but h. HARD 168:6
health case of nutrition and h. JAY 190:4
National H. Service is safe THAT 361:5
war is the h. of the state BOUR 53:7
healthy Greed is h. BOES 50:4
h. state of political life MILL 259:1
hear I h. a smile CROSS 106:8
men prefer not to h. AGAR 6:4
one to speak, and another to h. THOR 364:3
will come when you will h. me DISR 116:12
heard by two men I'd never h. of ROTH 313:7
I will be h. GARR 148:3
right to be h. HUMP 185:4
we should certainly have h. AUDEN 21:4
hearers favourable h. HOOK 182:5
Hearst William Randolph H. SMITH 343:4
heart broken h. lies here MAC 238:10
committed adultery in my h. CART 77:7
fanatic h. YEATS 396:2
find 'Calais' lying in my h. MARY 253:9
h. and stomach of a king ELIZ 130:9
he had a h. to resolve GIBB 151:10
I feel my h. new opened SHAK 327:6
If thy h. fails thee, climb not ELIZ 131:8
Irishman's h. SHAW 336:12
key to my h. CLAY 97:9
largely a matter of h. BUTL 70:8
little body with a mighty h. SHAK 326:9
make a stone of the h. YEATS 395:7
So the h. be right RAL 300:6
heart-beat *just a h. away* STEV 350:8
hearts all that human h. endure GOLD 157:5
h. of his countrymen LEE 220:2
offspring of cold h. BURKE 66:17
O you hard h. SHAK 328:1
to steal away your h. SHAK 330:8
heat can't stand the h., get out of VAUG 373:4
not without dust and h. MILT 260:6
white h. of the technological revolution WILS 390:5
heaven consent of h. JONS 199:3
equality would be a h. TROL 370:2
I cannot go to h. NORF 275:2
If Max gets to H. WELLS 385:6
like going to h. GRAMM 159:3
not go to H. but with a party JEFF 191:9
pennies don't fall from h. THAT 360:12
Son of Saint Louis, ascend to h. FIRM 136:7
sudden journey to h. BEAV 34:1
to be young was very h. WORD 394:7
[Tower of London] as nigh h. MORE 265:8
heavens h. themselves, the planets SHAK 335:7
Hebrew superlative H. conjuror CARL 76:12
hedge such divinity doth h. a king SHAK 326:4
hedgehogs start throwing h. KHR 209:7
heights h. of the economy BEVAN 41:6
helicopters stay up in h. BEVIN 43:2
hell agreement with h. GARR 148:4
come hot from h. SHAK 329:9
go to the gates of H. PIUS 294:1
H. of not making money CARL 76:4
h. upon earth MILL 259:11
tell you to go to h. STIN 351:5
they think it is h. TRUM 371:12
help do without the h. EDW 128:5
God h. me LUTH 234:6
I'm here to h. REAG 302:4
helped We shall have h. it DICK 115:5
helping h. industry POW 297:2
hen better take a wet h. KHR 209:4
h.-roost to rob LLOY 229:2
herd-instinct Morality is the h. NIET 273:2
here H. I am MACM 243:10
hereditary folly of h. right in kings PAINE 281:2
h. government PAINE 282:13
idea of h. legislators PAINE 282:8
in 1802 every h. monarch BAG 27:1
heresy h. signifies no more than HOBB 179:11
No h. can excite the horror MAC 237:10
heretic oppressor or a h. CAMUS 74:8
hero he acted like a h. WALP 377:9
I may be the h. of a novel MAC 236:8
heroes Britain a fit country for h. LLOY 229:9
despair of finding any h. CARL 76:14
unhappy the land that needs h. BREC 55:6
heroics not h., but healing HARD 168:6
Herr H.... H. and there COOK 102:6
hew Not h. him as a carcass SHAK 328:13
hewers let them be h. of wood BIBLE 43:8
hide nothing to h. CHUR 92:9
hiding bloody good h. GRANT 159:5
high Be ye never so h., the law DENN 113:6
Be you never so h., the law FULL 144:6
detestation of the h. DICK 115:6
Men in h. places TAYL 358:13
None climbs so h. CROM 106:1
spoils one's eye for the h. birds HAL 166:13
higher h. they climb LLOY 231:3
hijacker terrorist and the h. THAT 361:13
hill be a city upon a h. WINT 393:2
other side of the h. WELL 384:10
hills on the red h. of Georgia KING 210:10
hip He smote them h. and thigh BIBLE 43:9
hippopotamus tact than a h. CAMP 74:4
hired They h. the money COOL 103:4
hireling pay given to a state h. JOHN 197:3
Hiroshima one bomb on H. TRUM 371:2
historian h. can be so obsessed POW 297:12
h. looks behind the scenery TAYL 356:10
one safe rule for the h. FISH 136:8

historians h. in general TREV 368:7
historical for h. purposes NIXON 274:12
history But all change in h. TAYL 356:12
cancer of human h. SONT 346:6
descended below the dignity of h. MAC 238:11
do more to shape h. TAYL 357:4
dustbin of h. TROT 370:12
H. came to a SELL 323:11
H. consists, for the greater part BURKE 67:7
H. gets thicker TAYL 357:10
H. is a gallery of pictures TOCQ 366:6
H. is almost always written NEHRU 270:6
H....is, indeed, little more GIBB 151:6
H. is littered with the wars POW 296:9
h. is on our side KHR 209:3
H. is past politics FRE 143:5
H. knows no resting places KISS 214:7
h. of all hitherto existing society MARX 253:2
h. of England POW 297:8
h. of progress MAC 238:3
h. to his patriotism ADAMS 4:11
I admired your h. MURR 268:3
I have discerned in h. a plot FISH 136:8
Indeed, h. is nothing more VOLT 376:3
in the h. of the world NIXON 274:5
like writing h. with lightning WILS 392:2
marked through h. BAG 24:2
never changed the h. DISR 119:11
never learned anything from h. HEGEL 173:12
not learning from our h. BLAIR 49:2
One of the uses of h. is to free us BORK 53:2
Phrases make h. here MAFF 246:8
political h. of the West HAIL 163:7
Read no h. DISR 116:7
Thames is liquid h. BURNS 68:9
There is no h. of mankind POPP 295:12
This province of literature [h.] MAC 236:6
thousand years of h. GAIT 145:2
we cannot escape h. LINC 225:12
What is h. except a nation's POW 297:15
What will h. say SHAW 336:1
Hitler for a man like Adolf H. BUCH 61:4
H. and Mussolini LOW 233:5
H.'s level of accuracy TAYL 357:2
H. swept out of his Berlin ANON 11:5
H. thought he might get away CHAM 81:4
that villain H. GEOR 150:3
well give it to Adolf H., frankly RIDL 305:8
When H. attacked the Jews NIEM 273:1
With H. guilty, every other TAYL 357:5
Hoares no more H. to Paris GEOR 149:9
hobby as a h., a miniature MORT 266:8
hobgoblins endless series of h. MENC 256:9
hoi polloi multitude, the *h.* DRYD 125:1
hold Once did she h. the gorgeous WORD 394:6
we can neither h. him JEFF 193:9
You can't h. a man down WASH 379:4
holder what its h. chooses ASQ 18:5
hole when you're in a h. HEAL 173:3
hollow within the h. crown SHAK 333:8
holy He died to make men h. HOWE 184:4
neither h., nor Roman VOLT 375:9
old ends stol'n forth of h. writ SHAK 334:11
homage h. of the low DICK 115:6
home her princes are come h. again SHAK 331:1
h. his footsteps he hath SCOTT 322:5
h. of the brave KEY 207:1
homeless send these, the h. LAZ 219:7
Homer Mr Gladstone read H. for fun CHUR 88:13
Home Ruler Be H. if you must CHAM 80:2
homines *Quot h. tot sententiae* TER 360:6
honest buy it like an h. man NORT 275:6
few h. men are better CROM 105:2
He only in a general h. thought SHAK 330:16
h. man is laughed at HAL 166:11
h. politician CAM 73:6
more that of an h. broker BISM 47:1
Of more worth is one h. man PAINE 281:4
Robin and I are two h. men SHIP 339:7
unthinkable as an h. burglar MENC 256:10
honesty common h. SHEL 337:6
honour *All is lost, save h.* FRAN 141:4
As he was valiant, I h. him SHAK 329:11
but a peace I hope with h. DISR 120:9
deprived of either property or h. MACH 241:6
for reputation and h. SOCR 345:7
fountain of h. BAG 24:12
gained immortal h. CLAY 97:11
great peaks of h. LLOY 229:6
He is the fountain of h. BACON 23:8
h. the King KITC 214:15
In action faithful, and in h. clear POPE 295:3
in politics there is no h. DISR 116:5
light us down in h. LINC 225:12
louder he talked of his h. EMER 133:4
maintained with h. RUSS 317:2
may we h. it WEBS 382:11
Mine h. is my life SHAK 333:1
national h. MONR 263:3
office before h. POW 297:6
peace with h. CHAM 81:1
roll of h. CLEV 99:2
safety, h., and welfare CHAR 82:8
their private h. WAUGH 380:8
throne *we* h. SHER 338:12
When h.'s at the stake SHAK 326:3
whom the king delighteth to h. BIBLE 43:13
without an h. PEEL 288:17
honourable Brutus is an h. man SHAK 330:1
h. alike in what we give LINC 226:1
honours Examine the H. List BENN 37:3
Excluded from h. and from offices ADAMS 2:3
flagrant sale of h. DISR 117:5
good card to play for H. BENN 37:4

hunger against h., poverty MARS 251:2
h. allows no choice AUDEN 21:2
I offer you h., thirst GAR 148:1
those who h. and are not fed EIS 129:4
hungry advertise food to h. people GALB 145:4
And the tigers are getting h. CHUR 89:8
Cassius has a lean and h. look SHAK 328:7
h. man is not a free man STEV 350:3
hunt That dog won't h. RICH 305:1
hunting Very humorous, all h. ATTL 20:15
hurry old man in a h. CHUR 86:7
hurt Nothing doth more h. BACON 22:6
hurting If the policy isn't h. MAJOR 247:9
husband words 'My h. and I' ELIZ 132:5
hypercritical any h. rules LINC 225:6
hyphen *h.* which joins BAG 24:13
hyphenated h. Americanism ROOS 311:14
hypocrisy organized h. DISR 117:17
world safe for h. WOLFE 393:6
hypocrites other half h. JEFF 191:2
hysteria h. is heard in the land DID 116:2

I I am a free man JOHN 195:5
words 'My husband and I' ELIZ 132:5
iceberg ill-concealed i. LAWS 219:5
idea i. whose time has come ANON 13:8
invasion by an i. HUGO 184:5
That would be a good i. GAND 147:4
idealism i. is the noble toga HUXL 186:4
some spark of i. BRAN 55:4
idealist I'm an i. without illusions KENN 205:10
idealistic only i. nation WILS 392:16
ideals illusionist without i. MACL 243:4
ideas I still have the i., Walter CHUR 94:4
it would be to have i. FRANK 141:5
none of the sound i. MACM 245:3
political i. NAM 269:2
resistance of established i. BERL 39:6
ideological i. difference KENN 203:5
ides Beware the i. of March SHAK 328:2
i. of March are come SHAK 329:2
idiot i. who praises GILB 152:10
Suppose you were an i. TWAIN 372:11
idiots fatuity of i. SMITH 344:6
idle vivacity of an i. man BAG 27:8
idleness i. and pride FRAN 142:1
idol obvious and natural i. BAG 26:3
to appease an i. TAWN 355:8
idolatry organization of i. SHAW 336:9
if i. I had to choose between FORS 139:4
ifs Talk'st thou to me of 'i.' SHAK 335:2
ignoble not the doctrine of i. ease ROOS 310:10
ignorance boldness is a child of i. BACON 22:4
I. is an evil weed BEV 42:4
I. is strength ORW 279:1
I. of the law excuses no man SELD 323:1
just i. CURR 107:6
more dangerous than sincere i. KING 210:5
ignorant expects to be i. and free JEFF 193:6
right of the i. man CARL 76:3
Ike I like I. SPAL 347:4
ill i.-concealed iceberg LAWS 219:5
I. fares the land GOLD 157:6
warn you not to fall i. KINN 211:10
illegal i. we do immediately KISS 214:5
it is not i. NIXON 274:13
Nothing is i. if YOUNG 396:6
illegally accomplishes great things i. BALZ 31:10
illegitimate i. child of Karl Marx ATTL 20:8
no i. children, only i. parents JOS 200:5
ill-housed one-third of a nation i. ROOS 309:3
illiberal I am a violent i. RUSK 315:12
illimitable unlimited and i. BARK 32:3
ill-nourished ill-housed, ill-clad, i. ROOS 309:3
ills All the i. of democracy SMITH 343:5
illumination support rather than i. LANG 217:6
ill-usage complaints of i. MELB 255:5
illusion He had one i.—France KEYN 207:3
i. that times that were GRE 161:1
illusionist Prime Minister as an i. MACL 243:4
illusions I'm an idealist without i. KENN 205:10
management of i. WALD 376:7
image political i. is like mixing MOND 262:2
images reflects i. ADAMS 2:9
imagination initiative and i. GALB 145:5
nothing but his i. SHAW 336:12
reason and the i. MAC 236:6
to his i. for his facts SHER 338:13
Wanting i. he lacked prescience DISR 119:1
imaginations weakness of their i. BAG 25:6
imagined free us of a falsely i. past BORK 53:2
immatures He i. with age WILS 391:8
immaturity human i. BRIT 57:3
immigrants i. or descendants of i. ROOS 310:4
immobility i. of British institutions ASQ 18:4
immoral Asquith is good and i. CHUR 88:2
Call a thing i. or ugly SCH 322:1
impartial for its i. administration PEEL 287:9
I decline utterly to be i. CHUR 88:7
impeached Richard Nixon i. himself ABZUG 1:2
imperative one categorical i. KANT 202:2
imperfect on i. knowledge ATTL 20:14
imperial our great i. family ELIZ 132:4
imperialism i. is the monopoly LENIN 221:3
what I may call wild-cat i. ROS 312:8
imperialisms prey of rival i. KENY 206:6
imperialist Through its i. system MAND 249:3
imperialists make the i. dance KHR 209:5
imperially Learn to think i. CHAM 80:5
imperium *i. et Libertas* DISR 120:13
implacable i. in hate DRYD 125:6
important British are no longer i. MCC 240:1
less importunate for being less i. MONT 263:7

influence i. of the Crown DUNN 127:1
odium, under the name of i. BURKE 63:1
power instead of i. TAYL 357:9
public opinion is a permeating i. BAG 24:1
inform not to i. the reader ACH 1:7
information war-time Minister of i. COCK 100:9
ingeminate i. the word *Peace* CLAR 96:3
inhale I didn't i. CLIN 99:5
if he doesn't i. STEV 349:7
inherent i. efficiencies of freedom GALB 145:3
inherited Indians—they i. PEEL 288:5
iniquity loved justice and hated i. GREG 161:3
initiative i. and imagination GALB 145:5
injuries against the i. LOCKE 231:5
take revenge for slight i. MACH 241:2
injustice I. anywhere is a threat KING 210:7
i. done to an individual JUN 201:1
I., poverty, slavery BERL 39:4
I. was as common as streetcars REUT 303:5
man's inclination to i. NIEB 272:10
protect him against i. PALM 284:2
rapine and i. SMITH 341:2
innocence ceremony of i. YEATS 395:6
other German could claim i. TAYL 357:5
innocent Millions of i. men JEFF 191:2
sweat of the i. JACK 189:6
We are i. ROS 313:1
innovate To i. is not to reform BURKE 68:4
innovation In well-framed politics, i. BAG 27:7
totalitarian i. O'BR 276:5
inns i. should be well kept PALM 284:4
inoperative statements are i. ZIEG 397:3
inquisition little less than an i. HAL 166:6
insane hereditary monarch was i. BAG 27:1
inseparable one and i. WEBS 382:3
inside i. the tent pissing out JOHN 196:9
insignificance And of the utmost i. CURZ 108:4
insignificant most i. office ADAMS 4:1
insincerity depths of i. ANON 13:10
enemy of clear language is i. ORW 279:10
insistence i. of some liberals HAYEK 171:5
insolence i. is not invective DISR 118:16
insoluble political ones are i. HOME 182:4
instability mark of i. GALB 145:8
instantaneous i. courage NAP 269:10
institution Any i. which does not ROB 306:7
cannot see an i. without hitting CRIT 104:5
destroy any established i. BURKE 65:7
institutions acquiring their i. HAIL 163:12
British i. MAND 249:3
great i. which they have created BAG 27:12
immobility of British i. ASQ 18:4
I. govern relationships MONN 263:1
in the power of human i. SEN 323:12
It is the same with i. JOUB 200:6
nations begin by forming their i. HAIL 163:11
Only i. grow wiser MONN 262:10
public i. SMITH 343:1
Tory is someone who thinks i. POW 297:10
instructions operating i. O'RO 277:4
instrument state is an i. STAL 348:3
instruments work by such i. PEEL 289:4
insular i. both in situation BAG 26:11
i. country, subject to fogs DISR 120:15
insurance National compulsory i. CHUR 91:12
insurrection success of an armed i. ZIN 397:4
insurrectional right of i. violence ROM 308:2
integration not fighting for i. MALC 248:8
intellect burglar of others' i. DISR 118:13
i. of an advocate BAG 24:5
no hindrance to subtlety of i. MORL 266:2
originality, not of i. WEBB 381:2
second-class i. HOLM 181:8
suffering from halitosis of the i. ICKES 187:1
intellects highest i. MAC 238:2
intellectual act of i. resistance O'BR 276:5
i. commentators THAT 360:11
means of i. excitement BAG 24:3
moral or i. damage KRUG 215:6
intellectuals themselves as i. AGNEW 6:6
treachery of the i. BENDA 35:6
intelligence i. of the great masses MENC 256:11
personality with so little i. JENK 194:2
intelligent Every i. voter ADAMS 2:4
i. are full of doubt RUSS 316:12
i. are to the intelligentsia BALD 30:2
intelligentsia intelligent are to the i. BALD 30:2
intelligible it is an i. government BAG 25:5
intensity full of passionate i. YEATS 395:6
intent prick the sides of my i. SHAK 331:8
intention i. to keep my counsel GLAD 155:6
intentions if he'd only had good i. THAT 362:1
i. of a government GALB 145:13
their good i. WALP 377:7
interest common i. always will DRYD 125:10
common i. produces PAINE 282:14
from its duty and its i. WASH 379:12
I., not sentiment, directs them CHES 83:11
it's i. that keeps peace CROM 105:10
natural i. of money MAC 237:9
their regard to their own i. SMITH 341:4
interested not i. too much BAR 32:8
interests common i. of capital and labour ATK 19:6
consult the i. PEEL 288:6
men who have i. aside from LINC 224:2
Our i. are eternal and perpetual PALM 284:1
interfered i. in behalf of the rich BROWN 59:1
i. too much with other MELB 255:7
interfering i. with the liberty MILL 258:8
internal destroyed by an i. vice MONT 264:6
international dependable i. emotion ALSOP 7:5
interpreted only i. the world MARX 252:3

interpreters class who may be i. MAC 236:11
interrèd oft i. with their bones SHAK 329:13
intervene i. to help British HES 178:4
intervention effect of state i. DICEY 114:7
interviews result of i., promises TAYL 358:2
intimacy you should avoid any i. KITC 214:15
intimidating Minister should be i. THAT 362:14
intoxicated once i. with power BURKE 67:14
intrusion governmental i. BREN 56:1
invasion i. by an idea HUGO 184:5
invective insolence is not i. DISR 118:16
invention [bureaucracy's] specific i. WEBER 381:11
since the i. of gunpowder MONT 263:10
inverse in i. proportion HAIL 163:4
inverted i. the laws of nature SMITH 345:1
There they sit, like i. Micawbers GUED 162:5
investigation duty of i. HALD 164:2
invisible i. hand in politics FRI 144:1
led by an i. hand SMITH 342:4
invitations don't accept our i. KHR 209:3
involuntary It was i. KENN 205:11
Iranian I. moderate is one who KISS 214:9
Ireland How's poor ould I. ANON 10:11
I. is not a geographical PARN 286:5
I.! that cloud in the west GLAD 154:1
I. unfree shall never be PEAR 287:3
keeps I. bound to England PARN 286:7
many parties in I. who desire PEEL 289:5
My mission is to pacify I. GLAD 154:7
name of I. is mentioned SMITH 344:6
no appetite for truth in I. PEEL 288:1
One prayer absorbs all others: I. GLAD 155:8
Out of I. have we come YEATS 396:2
romantic I.'s dead and gone YEATS 395:4
We are bound to lose I. GLAD 156:1
with which it is now handling I. WEST 385:7
Irish answer to the I. Question SELL 323:10
now the I. are ashamed MARV 251:8
That is the I. Question DISR 117:13
Irishman I. has no sense of PEEL 289:8
I.'s heart is nothing but SHAW 336:12
Irishry Still the indomitable I. YEATS 396:3
iron become an i. cage WEBER 382:1
i. curtain at its frontier CRILE 104:3
i. curtain has descended CHUR 92:10
i. has entered into his soul LLOY 230:15
i. lady ANON 11:2
I. Lady of the Western World THAT 360:10
nice smile, but he's got i. teeth GROM 162:4
through blood and i. BISM 47:4
wood painted to look like i. BISM 47:2
irrational bondage of i. fears BRAN 55:1
extravagant and i. SWIFT 353:8
irrationality [House of] Lords is its i. CAMP 73:7
i. of the world WEBER 381:10
irregular another of those i. verbs LYNN 235:10
irritated most i. against the party BAG 27:11
Islam If laws are needed, I. KHOM 208:9
island floating bulwark of the i. BLAC 48:7
honour the people of this i. CHUR 89:2
never make this i. WALL 377:1
This i. is made mainly of coal BEVAN 40:5
twice in our rough i.-story TENN 360:3
isle this sceptered i. SHAK 333:4
isms All the 'i. are wasms ANON 8:5
isolationist find an i. RUSK 315:3
Israel glory is departed from I. BIBLE 43:10
there is a prophet in I. BIBLE 43:12
issue It *is* a moral i. HALEY 164:7
one i. at a time MACM 244:10
Italy I. is a geographical expression METT 257:7

Jack J. became a gentleman SHAK 334:10
Jacksonian J. vulgarity POTT 296:4
jail would be in j. TRUM 372:2
jam j. we thought was BENN 36:3
never j. today CARR 77:2
James why does King J. stay WHAR 386:3
Jameson raid by Dr J. KRUG 215:6
janvier Generals J. [January] NICH 271:5
Japan forces of the Empire of J. ROOS 310:1
not necessarily to J.'s advantage HIR 179:1
Japanese reconcile J. action CHUR 91:3
jaw-jaw To j. is always better CHUR 94:2
jaws j. of power are always opened ADAMS 3:3
jeers gibes and flouts and j. DISR 120:5
Jefferson Thomas—J. ADAMS 4:4
when Thomas J. ate alone KENN 205:1
Jeffersonian J. simplicity POTT 296:4
jellybeans his way of eating j. REAG 301:10
Jena battle of J. ANON 10:3
J. came twenty years after BISM 47:6
Jerusalem And was J. builded here BLAKE 49:5
Till we have built J. BLAKE 49:6
jests to his memory for his j. SHER 338:13
Jesus *bon Sansculotte J.* DESM 114:4
thinks he is J. Christ CLEM 98:5
Jew am a J. of Tarsus BIBLE 44:11
especially a J. MAL 248:6
old J.! That is the man BISM 47:3
jewel Common Law may be a j. GRAY 160:6
Jewish home for the J. people BALF 30:6
total solution of the J. question GOER 156:7
Jews When Hitler attacked the J. NIEM 273:1
jingo But be a little j. if you can CHAM 80:2
job MI5 is a j. creation scheme HENN 174:8
MP is the sort of j. ABB 1:1
politician who has lost his j. MENC 257:1
really get on with the j. DALT 109:3
we will finish the j. CHUR 91:6

jog as a man *might j. on with* LAMB 216:7
joint time is out of j. SHAK 325:7
joints know the j. BUTL 70:5
jokes civil servant doesn't make j. ION 188:3
I don't know j. ROG 307:9
Josephine Not tonight, J. NAP 270:3
journalism why j. BALF 30:9
journalist British j. WOLFE 393:4
journalists j. dabbling their fingers MCGR 241:1
journey companions of our j. CHUR 90:11
I have a long j. to take RAL 300:7
I now begin the j. REAG 302:8
joy politics of j. HUMP 185:5
strength through j. LEY 223:4
Judas true legend—that of J. STAL 348:6
judge j. is a member BOK 50:5
J. not, that ye be not judged BIBLE 44:4
Justly to j. BRO 57:7
nor the j.'s robe SHAK 332:7
judged not be j. by the colour KING 210:10
judgement j. is a mere lottery DRYD 125:1
j. which is needed ATTL 20:14
lawful j. of his peers MAGN 247:3
Nor is the people's j. DRYD 125:11
not his industry only, but his j. BURKE 63:8
right functioning of a man's j. SAL 318:11
sit in j. upon any other nation WILS 392:3
your j. MANS 250:1
judges independence of j. DENN 113:7
judicial j. power ADAMS 3:12
jump what Trojan 'orses will j. out BEVIN 43:5
jumps which way the cat j. THAT 361:14
jungle air-conditioned j. KINN 211:8
law of the j. KIPL 212:9
juridical destroy the j. safeguards HAYEK 171:9
jurisdiction Rome hath no j. BOOK 51:6
jury j., passing on the prisoner's SHAK 332:6
just be j., and fear not SHAK 327:7
I reflect that God is j. JEFF 191:3
j. and unjust masterships RUSK 315:10
j. cause reaches its flood-tide CATT 78:7
'j.' or 'right' means nothing PLATO 294:2
land of j. and old renown TENN 359:8
my friend, faithful and j. to me SHAK 330:1
this may not be a j. peace IZET 188:5
true place for a j. man THOR 364:2
justice administration of j. SMITH 341:1
And liberty plucks j. by the nose SHAK 332:4
call for j. MORE 265:6
deny, or delay, right or j. MAGN 247:4
furtherance of the ends of j. BROWN 59:3
humanity, reason, and j. BURKE 64:5
human j. is ever lagging GLAD 154:10
I have never obstructed j. NIXON 274:10
J. is in one scale JEFF 193:9
J. is truth in action DISR 118:14
j. should not only be done HEW 178:5
kings the sword of j. DEFOE 111:11
let j. be done, though the world FERD 136:4
loved j. and hated iniquity GREG 161:3
Man's capacity for j. NIEB 272:10
more devoted to order than to j. KING 210:8
not equality or fairness or j. BERL 39:1
of moral good and of j. JOHN 195:3
threat to j. everywhere KING 210:7
what you think j. requires MANS 250:1
justifiable perfectly j. BURKE 65:12
justification j. of America's KISS 214:12
justified No man is j. in doing evil ROOS 312:3
justitia *fiat j. et pereat mundus* FERD 136:4

Kaiser put the kibosh on the K. ELL 132:10
kebabbed not going to be bloody k. KINN 212:5
keener But with his k. eye MARV 251:7
keep If you can k. your head KIPL 213:3
intention to k. my counsel GLAD 155:6
keeping k. the secret TAYL 358:8
Kennedy senator, you're no Jack K. BENT 38:3
kettle back to the tea-k. DISR 118:1
This is a pretty k. of fish MARY 253:5
key emperor holds the k. CUST 108:6
in possession of the k. PAINE 280:8
k. of India is London DISR 121:2
take the k. of the Union CLAY 97:9
keyholes screaming through the k. LLOY 229:11
keystone king is the k. STR 352:3
kibosh put the k. on the Kaiser ELL 132:10
kick *k. 'em the next* KIPL 214:1
k. them in the teeth BEVAN 41:11
won't have Nixon to k. around NIXON 274:2
kicked k. up stairs HAL 165:1
no body to be k. THUR 364:9
kicking kissing and k. people TRUM 371:5
kid comeback k. CLIN 99:6
kids k. love that dog NIXON 273:7
LBJ, LBJ, how many k. ANON 11:11
kill But they will k. thee PHOC 292:5
did nothing at all but k. animals NIC 272:7
doctrine is something you k. for BENN 36:10
let's k. all the lawyers SHAK 327:1
until men are prepared to k. SHAW 336:14
you must k. him EMER 133:5
killed don't mind your being k. KITC 215:1
kids have you k. today ANON 11:11
like to have been k. in the war POW 297:11
killing assert their manhood by k. WAUGH 380:8
k. no murder briefly discourst SEXBY 324:2
kindly KCMG ('K. Call Me God') SAMP 319:9
king And when I am k. SHAK 327:1
as I have served the K. WOLS 394:3
As to the K., the laws of the land CHAR 82:6
authority forgets a dying k. TENN 360:4
authority of a K. is the keystone STR 352:3

away my life to make you K. CHAR 83:3
beat the K. ninety-nine times MANC 249:1
benefit of the K.'s Coronation BLUNT 49:7
blind, despised, and dying k. SHEL 338:1
blind the one-eyed man is k. ERAS 133:10
Cotton is K. CHR 86:1
cuts off his k.'s head SHAW 335:13
Did the K. sigh SHAK 325:13
Every subject's duty is the k.'s SHAK 326:14
For your K. and your Country RUB 314:8
God bless the K. BYROM 70:10
God save the k. HOGG 181:2
government without a k. BANC 31:11
great and mighty k. ROCH 307:5
heart and stomach of a k. ELIZ 130:9
If the K. asks you ATTL 19:9
I served my k. SHAK 327:8
I think the k. is but a man SHAK 326:12
it is impossible for the K. PEPYS 290:2
k. can do no wrong BLAC 48:8
k. delighteth to honour BIBLE 43:13
k. is a thing men have made SELD 323:2
k. is truly *parens patriae* JAM 189:10
k. may make a nobleman BURKE 67:17
k. never dies BLAC 48:6
K., observing with judicious eyes TRAPP 367:6
K. of England cannot enter PITT 292:9
K. of Great Britain is not REED 302:10
K. over the Water ANON 11:6
K., refused a lesser sacrifice MARY 253:7
k. reigns, and the people govern THI 363:2
K.'s life is moving peacefully DAWS 110:5
K.'s Moll ANON 11:7
k.'s name twenty thousand names SHAK 333:7
K. to Oxford sent a troop BROW 59:6
K. will get away with it CHAN 81:5
K. will never leave ELIZ 132:9
last K. of England EDW 128:3
last k. to be strangled MESL 257:6
lessened my esteem of a k. PEPYS 290:1
loses the k. in the tyrant MAYH 255:1
material for a constitutional k. BAG 26:2
More of a royalist than the k. ANON 13:3
Mrs Simpson's pinched our k. ANON 10:5
my griefs; still am I k. of those SHAK 334:4
neck of the last k. DID 116:1
No bishop, no K. JAM 189:9
no circumstances fight for its K. GRAH 158:6
Northcliffe has sent for the K. ANON 10:6
not so much a k. as a Monarch SELL 323:7
our sins lay on the k. SHAK 326:15
sang a k. out of three kingdoms WHAR 386:4
substitute shines brightly as a k. SHAK 332:11
such divinity doth hedge a k. SHAK 326:4
These five kings did a k. to death THOM 363:3
Till the K. enjoys his own again PARK 285:4
To my true k. I offered MAC 238:9
What is a K.?—a man PRIOR 298:4
What must the k. do now SHAK 334:2
whatsoever K. shall reign ANON 10:12
when thy k. is a child BIBLE 43:17
When you strike at a k. EMER 133:5
you must not be a k., so long as CHAR 82:5
Your K. and Country need you FIELD 136:5

kingdom but to mock the k. PYM 298:6
k. against k. BIBLE 44:9
that of a great k. SMITH 342:6
they become aliens to this k. GEOR 149:4
voice of the k. SWIFT 353:5

kingdoms king out of three k. WHAR 386:4

kingfish can just call me the K. LONG 232:3

kingly K. conclaves stern and cold SHEL 338:5

kings captains and the k. depart KIPL 212:11
commonwealths and ruin k. DRYD 125:3
divine right of K. to fall MACM 244:4
folly of hereditary right in k. PAINE 281:2
good of subjects is the end of k. DEFOE 111:11
heart's ease Must k. neglect SHAK 326:16
heroic k. governed BAG 25:7
k. and ministers SMITH 341:7
k. are not only God's lieutenants JAM 189:11
K. will be tyrants from policy BURKE 67:2
laws or k. can cause GOLD 157:5
laws or k. can cause JOHN 197:7
people keep even k. in awe D'AV 110:1
punctuality is the politeness of k. LOU 233:4
setter up and puller down of k. SHAK 327:4
stories of the death of k. SHAK 333:8
there will be only five K. left FAR 135:6
Through talk, we tamed k. BENN 36:8
with a heavier hand than k. FRAN 142:1

kiss cheer you, thank you, k. you RUB 314:8
gave him the k. of death SMITH 343:4
k. 'em one day and kick 'em KIPL 214:1
k. my ass in Macy's JOHN 196:8
London will be wanting to k. MACD 240:6

kitchen get out of the k. VAUG 373:4

Kitchener K. is a great poster ASQ 18:10

Klondike beer of a man in K. CHES 84:11

knave coined an epithet for a k. MAC 237:5
in life a foolish prating k. SHAK 325:10
man must be supposed a k. HUME 185:2
To feed the titled k. BURNS 68:13
Wherever a k. is not punished HAL 166:11

knavery k. seems to be so much GEOR 149:4

knaves grudge at k. in place DEFOE 111:5

knees first fell upon their own k. EVAR 134:3
live on our k. ROOS 309:12
live on your k. IBAR 186:6

knell k. of the Union JEFF 193:7

knife He who wields the k. HES 177:9
keep the k. in his hand MACH 241:8

knight earl and a k. of the garter ATTL 20:9

knights invincible k. of old WORD 394:5
knives night of the long k. HITL 179:4
knot political k. BIER 44:15
know do not k. what they have said CHUR 87:5
find out what you don't k. WELL 384:10
How do they k. PARK 285:3
It is better to k. nothing BILL 45:5
learnt to k. and honour CHUR 89:2
no one to k. what it is ANON 9:8
that which you yourselves do k. SHAK 330:9
what did the President k. ANON 14:12
knowledge envied kind of k. ADAMS 3:4
k. itself is power BACON 22:1
k. of everything but power HER 177:4
k. of the possible BEVAN 40:11
such a k., in its ultimate GLAD 156:3
sum of human k. REED 302:11
known safer than a k. way HASK 170:2
knows He k. nothing SHAW 336:13

label l. on the can of worms CRIT 104:8
labels l. on empty luggage BEVAN 41:7
laborious assiduity of a very l. one BAG 27:8
labour common interests of capital and l. ATK 19:6
ever done to the L. Party TAWN 356:4
Fair shares for all, is L.'s call JAY 190:5
I did not enter the L. Party BENN 36:9
it is to live without l. TAWN 355:11
kind of leader for the L. Party BEVAN 41:5
L. council hiring taxis KINN 211:11
L. disgraces no man GRANT 160:4
L. isn't working ANON 11:8
[L. is] the natural party of WILS 390:10
L. is the party of law BLAIR 48:11
L. Party is going around stirring WHIT 387:6
L. Party owes more to Methodism PHIL 291:7
l. spread her wholesome store GOLD 157:6
leader of the L. party KINN 212:4
never visualised L. as separate WEBB 381:3
of the L. Party JENK 194:5
parliamentary L. Party DALT 108:9
they've elected a L. Government ANON 9:6
trouble with the L. Party GRIM 162:3
trying to fracture the L. party KINN 212:3
upon the brow of l. BRYAN 60:6
We l. soon, we l. late BURNS 68:13
laboured l. as his extempore WALP 377:6
labourer l. to take his pension RUSK 315:5
labouring l. children can look out CLEG 98:3
labour-intensive monarchy is a l. WILS 391:7
labours wasting the l. of the people JEFF 192:10
laceration l. of their bodies TAWN 355:8
ladder l. called 'the status quo' BENN 37:2
l. to all high designs SHAK 335:8
lowliness is young ambition's l. SHAK 328:10
ladies remember the l. ADAMS 2:1
lady in a l.'s chamber SHAK 334:9
iron l. ANON 11:2
l.'s not for turning THAT 361:2
l.'s pocket handkerchief LLOY 230:2
Said our L. of the Snows KIPL 213:1
Lafayette L., we are here STAN 348:8
lagging justice is ever l. after GLAD 154:10
laisser faire *l.* ARG 16:1
l. tous les acheteurs QUES 299:2
laissez-faire l. and noblesse oblige HES 178:3
principle of *l.* HAYEK 171:5
lamb skin of an innocent l. SHAK 327:2
lamentable dark, l. catalogue CHUR 90:6
laments forest l. in order that CHUR 86:4
lamp carrying her l. GRIF 161:7
I lift my l. beside the golden door LAZ 219:7
l. of experience HENRY 176:6
lampposts drunken man uses l. LANG 217:6
lamps l. are going out GREY 161:5
Lancashire L. merchants CHES 84:11
land abroad throughout the l. BRIG 56:4
empire of the l. RICH 305:3
ill fares the l. GOLD 157:6
It is l. reclamation WILS 391:4
l. for the people ANON 11:10
L. of Hope and Glory BENS 37:6
l. that I love BERL 38:6
l. where my fathers died SMITH 344:5
more precious than a piece of l. SADAT 317:4
new people takes the l. CHES 84:8
O'er the l. of the free KEY 207:1
splendid and a happy l. GOLD 157:7
This l. of such dear souls SHAK 333:4
woe to the l. that's governed SHAK 335:1
landing l. was made EIS 129:3
we shall fight on the l. grounds CHUR 90:7
landlord paid to the l. for the use RIC 304:4
though he were a feudal l. ATTL 19:7
lands envy of less happier l. SHAK 333:4
l. produce less by reason of MONT 265:1
Then l. were fairly portioned MAC 237:1
landslide going to pay for a l. KENN 203:8
Lang How L., O Lord BULL 61:5
language By that dear l. MAC 238:10
divided by a common l. SHAW 337:3
enemy of clear l. is insincerity ORW 279:10
He mobilized the English l. MURR 268:5
l. of priorities is the religion BEVAN 40:7
of course, l. WILDE 388:7
political l.... is designed ORW 279:11
riot is the l. of the unheard KING 211:3
Under the tropic is our l. spoke WALL 377:3
Lansbury conscience like L. BEVIN 42:7
lanterns show two l. REV 303:7
larger children of a l. growth CHES 83:10

lascivious l. pleasing of a lute SHAK 334:9
lash blood drawn with the l. LINC 226:9
rum, sodomy, prayers, and the l. CHUR 93:7
lass It came with a l. JAM 190:3
last God's infinite mercy, a l. resort O'RO 277:2
I don't want the l. headline HES 178:1
l. article of my creed GAND 147:3
l. chance saloon MELL 256:7
l. great Englishman is low TENN 359:9
l. King of England EDW 128:3
l. thing I shall do PALM 284:9
like girls and roses: they l. DE G 112:13
marks of the l. person HAIG 163:1
people with one in the l. ditch MACL 242:9
today is the l. day of an era past YELT 396:4
lasts democracy never l. long ADAMS 4:2
late offering even that too l. NEV 271:2
lath l. of wood painted to look BISM 47:2
lathe could not tell a l. from JOS 200:1
Latin learn L. as an honour CHUR 88:12
laugh far too badly hurt to l. LINC 225:10
laughable very l. things JOHN 197:10
laughed honest man is l. at HAL 166:11
l. at in the second NAP 269:6
When he l., respectable senators AUDEN 21:5
laurels l. to paeans CIC 95:7
Northern l. do not change LEE 220:1
Thy banished peace, thy l. torn SMOL 345:3
Whether in chains or in l. PHIL 292:3
law books of l. JOHN 195:8
common l. is at a disadvantage SCAR 321:5
custom, that unwritten l. D'AV 110:1
dead-level of l. and order TAWN 355:9
destroy all respect for the l. CHUR 94:14
doctrine of liberty under the l. HAIL 163:7
enforce a l. not supported HUMP 185:3
entitled to protection by l. JACK 189:1
Every l. is contrary to liberty BENT 37:10
fig for those by l. protected BURNS 68:11
first is l., the last prerogative DRYD 125:15
For where no l. is BIBLE 44:13
good of the people is the chief l. CIC 95:6
government above the l. SCAR 321:3
had people not defied the l. SCAR 320:7
ignorance of the l. excuses no SELD 323:1
In civilized life, l. floats in a sea WARR 379:1
it is not a l. at all ROB 306:6
Labour is the party of l. and order BLAIR 48:11
l. is above you DENN 113:6
l. is above you FULL 144:6
l. is to be to restraint MILT 260:7
L. is whatever is boldly asserted BURR 69:1
L.: It has honoured us WEBS 382:11
l. of motion of modern society MARX 252:8
l. of the Medes and Persians BIBLE 43:20
l.'s delay SHAK 325:8
majestic equality of the l. FRAN 141:2
make a scarecrow of the l. SHAK 332:5
necessity hath no l. CROM 105:11
No man is above the l. ROOS 311:7
Now this is the L. of the Jungle KIPL 212:9
on the silence of the l. HOBB 180:5
People crushed by l. BURKE 65:3
prevail, of a common l. JEFF 192:2
provision in its organic l. LINC 225:5
right...is the child of l. BENT 37:7
rule of l. in England DENN 113:7
severity of the criminal l. PEEL 287:9
strict observance of the written l. JEFF 193:2
There's a lot of l. WHAL 386:2
this is the royal L. COR 103:10
lawful instituted by 'l. authority' MACD 240:4
lawn Get your tanks off my l. WILS 391:1
tell a lathe from a l. mower JOS 200:1
laws arranges l. MACH 241:10
arts, of warfare, and of l. DU B 126:4
bad l. are the worst sort BURKE 65:4
best use of l. is to teach men PHIL 291:9
can be made so by l. BOL 50:6
Christianity is part of the l. HALE 164:5
construe the constitution or l. LINC 225:6
country's planted thick with l. BOLT 51:3
do everything the l. permit MONT 264:8
Do not taint pure l. with mere AESC 6:2
folly of human l. SMITH 343:3
government of l., and not of men ADAMS 3:7
If l. are needed, Islam KHOM 208:9
If l. are their enemies BURKE 65:3
If the l. could speak for themselves HAL 166:1
l. and learning die MANN 249:5
L. and systems of polity MILL 259:9
L. are generally found to be SHEN 338:9
L. are like cobwebs SWIFT 353:4
L. are silent in time of war CIC 95:12
L. grind the poor GOLD 157:4
L., like houses, lean on BURKE 62:5
l. of God will be suspended SHAW 336:18
l. of morality BURKE 65:11
l. of most countries MILL 259:11
l. of necessity, of self-preservation JEFF 193:2
l. of the land CHAR 82:6
L. were made to be broken NORTH 275:4
makers, and their l. approve DRYD 126:1
make the l. of a nation FLET 137:8
more numerous the l. TAC 354:6
neither the l. made JOHN 195:1
not a government of l. WEBS 382:8
nothing to do with the l. HORS 183:4
passing l. which cannot EINS 128:7
rather than obey the l. TOCQ 366:3
repeal of bad or obnoxious l. GRANT 160:2
That part which l. or kings GOLD 157:5
That part which l. or kings JOHN 197:7
Written l. are like spider's webs ANAC 8:3

lawyer l. tells me I *may* do BURKE 64:5
lawyers complain of the l. HAL 166:1
let's kill all the l. SHAK 327:1
one hundred and fifty l. JEFF 193:10
lay that he l. down his friends THOR 364:7
lazy His l., long, lascivious reign DEFOE 111:8
lead easy to l., but difficult to drive BRO 58:2
evening l. CHUR 89:9
leader Ah well! I am their l. LEDR 219:8
fanatic is a great l. BROUN 58:3
final test of a l. LIPP 228:3
great and wonderful l. LLOY 230:8
importance of a plebeian l. DISR 118:18
l. of the Labour party KINN 212:4
make a great l. MONC 261:11
one realm, one people, one l. ANON 9:11
Over the face of the l. WHIT 388:5
people may require a l. PLATO 294:4
political l. must keep looking BAR 32:9
right kind of l. for the Labour Party BEVAN 41:5
leaders not the l. of a revolution CONR 102:4
up more to the political l. HEAD 172:4
leadership crisis in American l. BALT 31:9
l. is not about being nice KEAT 203:2
l. is saying no, not yes BLAIR 48:12
very essence of successful l. REAG 302:7
leak confidential briefings; you l. LYNN 235:10
they all l. the fact LYNN 235:9
leaking l. is what you do CALL 72:6
lean laws, like houses, l. on BURKE 62:5
l. and hungry look SHAK 328:7
l. and tight-lipped JOS 199:7
leap must l. into the ocean HUME 184:9
learned governments have never l. HEGEL 173:12
learning in the middle age of a state, l. BACON 23:7
liberty without l. KENN 205:3
not l. from our history BLAIR 49:2
of light, of liberty, and of l. DISR 120:2
that loyal body wanted l. TRAPP 367:6
learnt They have l. nothing TALL 354:11
least l. government was the best FEIN 136:3
line of l. resistance AMERY 7:6
man who promises l. BAR 32:7
leave couldn't l. without the King ELIZ 132:9
right to l. any country ANON 9:13
wiser to l. five minutes too soon BIFF 45:2
leaving Became him like the l. it SHAK 331:6
left l. out he would be dangerous MELB 255:6
l. to the politicians DE G 112:9
My position was on the l. MOSL 267:2
leg like pissing down your l. JOHN 196:12
legacies l. of empire SAMP 319:11
legacy l. from a rich relative SMITH 344:1
legal fact into a l. right MILL 259:9
legality suffer from any taint of l. KNOX 215:2
legalize l. it and it splits BAG 24:8
legally accomplishing small things l. BALZ 31:10
legend true l.—that of Judas STAL 348:6
legions Varus, give me back my l. AUG 21:7
legislation morals and l. BENT 37:9
There is a mania in l. POW 297:4
legislative distinct from both the l. ADAMS 3:12
l. power is nominated GIBB 151:4
when l. power is more corrupt MONT 264:12
legislator people is the true l. BURKE 62:4
legislators idea of hereditary l. PAINE 282:8
legislature l. is in session ANON 12:10
legitimacy l. and equilibrium KISS 214:13
legitimate l. powers of government JEFF 193:13
legs dog's walking on his hinder l. JOHN 197:9
four legs good, two l. bad ORW 278:10
not for your bad l. ELIZ 131:3
walk under his huge l., and peep SHAK 328:4
leisure increased l. DISR 119:20
politicians also have no l. ARIS 16:4
survey of conspicuous l. VEBL 373:6
lemon as a l. is squeezed GEDD 148:7
lend l. me your ears SHAK 329:13
Lend-Lease assistance called L. CHUR 92:5
Lenin L. was right KEYN 207:5
teaching of Marx, Engels and L. KHR 209:1
leper here as a parliamentary l. WILS 390:7
lesser refused a l. sacrifice MARY 253:7
lest l. we forget KIPL 212:11
let L. justice be done FERD 136:4
L. my people go BIBLE 43:7
L. the word go forth KENN 204:2
letter ability to write a good l. MACM 245:13
huge wordy l. came from Capri JUV 201:7
letters No arts; no l. HOBB 180:2
level Those who attempt to l. BURKE 66:11
levellers l. wish to level *down* JOHN 197:8
levelling cannot bear l. *up* JOHN 197:8
levers I shan't be pulling the l. THAT 362:11
Leviathan that great L. HOBB 179:9
levity I sank by my l. SMITH 345:1
lex *salus populi suprema est l.* CIC 95:6
salus populi suprema l. esto SELD 323:3
liar easy virtue and a proved l. HAIL 163:5
known l. should be outlawed HAL 165:6
liars l. ought to have good SIDN 340:1
liberal between l. concessions BOOK 52:1
first L. leader for over half STEEL 348:10
head of European l. principles CLAY 97:4
ineffectual l.'s problem FRAYN 143:1
Is either a little L. GILB 152:6
'L.' and 'Conservative' RUSK 315:12
l., emphasizing the civil MORSE 266:7
L. is a man who uses ROOS 309:7
L. party takes the rudder BISM 47:7

lied Therefore I l. to please the mob KIPL 213:6
lies believing their own l. ARB 15:8
History, sir, will tell l. as usual SHAW 336:1
It produces l. like sand ANON 14:13
l. about the Democrats STEV 350:1
l., damned l. and statistics DISR 121:15
l. it lives on and propagates FOSD 139:6
make l. sound truthful ORW 279:11
swallowing their own l. ARB 15:9
lieutenants God's l. upon earth JAM 189:11
life After l.'s fitful fever he sleeps SHAK 332:2
all the voyage of their l. SHAK 330:14
best prize that l. offers ROOS 311:6
But all l. is about discrimination POW 297:4
doctrine of the strenuous l. ROOS 310:10
England will take away my l. CHAR 83:3
evidence of l. after death SOPER 346:7
heaven daily for your longer l. ELIZ 131:2
His l. was gentle SHAK 330:16
I gave my l. for freedom EWER 134:5
in the distinction of your l. TAC 354:4
It is not a L. at all GLAD 155:12
Just gave what l. required GOLD 157:6
lay down his friends for his l. THOR 364:7
l., and liberty, and the pursuit JEFF 191:1
l. beyond the grave KHR 209:8
l., liberty and the pursuit of ANON 14:7
l. of man, solitary, poor HOBB 180:2
my whole l., whether it be long ELIZ 132:4
nearest thing to death in l. ANON 12:8
Nothing in his l. SHAK 331:6
one l. to lose for my country HALE 164:6
only honour and l. FRAN 141:4
priceless gift of l. ROS 313:1
right to a dignified l. JOHN 195:3
should forfeit my l. BROWN 59:3
walk and live a Woolworth l. NIC 272:3
light creates the l. that makes TOCQ 366:2
Give me a l. that I may tread HASK 170:2
Let there be l.! said Liberty SHEL 338:8
l. has gone NEHRU 270:8
l., of liberty, and of learning DISR 120:2
pay him tribute for l. SHAK 325:2
Put out the l. ROOS 312:4
radiate momentary gleams of l. LLOY 231:1
shaft of l. cut into the darkness KENN 205:7
thousand points of l. BUSH 69:6
lighthouse great l. which stands JENK 194:8
lighthouses those revolving l. LLOY 231:1
lightning He snatched the l. shaft TURG 372:7
like writing history with l. WILS 392:2
loosed the fateful l. HOWE 184:3
lights gradual dimming of the l. NIC 272:4
like I l. Ike SPAL 347:4
now she is l. everyone else DE G 112:6
People who l. this sort of thing LINC 227:3
plotted to make men l. TREV 368:3
likes privilege of doing as he l. ARN 17:5
Lilli burlero L. bullen a la WHAR 386:3
limit l. to our realization ROOS 310:9
limitation history of the l. WILS 391:11
limited revelation is necessarily l. PAINE 283:6
limpet-like l. Prime Ministers JENK 194:7
Lincoln am a Ford, not a L. FORD 138:11
shared the fate of Abraham L. GRIGG 161:8
line Hit the l. hard ROOS 311:1
l. of least resistance AMERY 7:6
no party l. DJIL 122:3
link last l. which keeps Ireland PARN 286:7
lion better to serve a well-bred l. VOLT 376:4
globe that had the l.'s heart CHUR 94:1
l. to frighten the wolves MACH 241:5
still a living l. SOLZ 346:3
lips my l. are not yet unsealed BALD 29:9
Read my l.: no new taxes BUSH 69:7
liquid But the Thames is l. history BURNS 68:9
liquidation l. of the British Empire CHUR 91:9
list Examine the honours l. BENN 37:3
l. of two hundred and five MCC 239:6
listen l. to their critics GALB 146:13
literature l.'s always a good card BENN 37:4
little It has been a splendid l. war HAY 171:1
l. local difficulties MACM 244:8
Little man, l. man ELIZ 132:2
l. woman who wrote the book LINC 227:4
makes the l. man so happy MONC 261:10
offering Germany too l. NEV 271:2
So l. done, so much to do RHOD 304:3
texture, as the l. creep through SHEN 338:9
littleness ruined by the l. BREC 55:8
live date which will l. in infamy ROOS 310:1
he isn't fit to l. KING 210:9
He shall not l. SHAK 330:12
l. on your knees IBAR 186:6
l. together as brothers KING 211:2
l. within your means THAT 361:4
l. without labour TAWN 355:11
make war that we may l. in peace ARIS 16:3
rascals, would you l. for ever FRED 143:2
sometimes l. apart SAKI 317:6
teaching nations how to l. MILT 260:5
unable to l. in society ARIS 16:6
which enable its citizens to l. WEIL 383:5
work and pray, l. on hay HILL 178:8
lived better if he had never l. CHUR 92:13
who has not l. during the years TALL 355:4
lively l. Oracles of God COR 103:10
livery apparel them all in one l. SHAK 327:1
lives All political l. POW 297:7
careless talk costs l. ANON 9:7
evil that men do l. after them SHAK 329:13
live our l. as though Christ CART 77:5
living between those who are l. BURKE 67:5
learning from our history but l. it BLAIR 49:2

l. to some purpose PAINE 283:10
Vietnam was lost in the l. rooms MCL 243:9
Lloyd George [L.] did not seem BEAV 34:5
L. knew my father ANON 12:2
[L.] thinks he is Napoleon CLEM 98:5
L. would have a better rating GRIGG 161:8
pool for the soul of L. MASS 254:3
loaves seven halfpenny l. sold SHAK 327:1
lobby into the l. against us BALD 29:9
local All politics is l. O'NE 276:8
little l. difficulties MACM 244:8
Men enter l. politics solely PARK 286:2
working of l. government THAT 362:15
log Give me a l. hut GARF 147:9
log-cabin From l. to White House THAY 363:1
London L. is a modern Babylon DISR 118:10
parks are the lungs of L. PITT 293:6
people of L. with one voice CHUR 91:5
long How l. a time SHAK 333:3
In the l. run we are all dead KEYN 207:6
it hath very l. arms HAL 166:2
night of the l. knives HITL 179:4
Too l. a sacrifice YEATS 395:7
week is a l. time in politics WILS 390:8
longer heaven daily for your l. life ELIZ 131:2
longest l. running farce SMITH 343:7
l. suicide note in history KAUF 202:4
longing cast a l. eye on them JEFF 191:14
look I l. at the senators HALE 164:4
l. the East End in the face ELIZ 132:8
L. to it LINC 225:9
l. to your Moat HAL 165:3
someone to l. down on JOHN 195:6
looking L. for houses, Nye ATTL 20:2
no use l. beyond CHAM 80:1
politics is the art of l. for trouble BENN 35:8
looks If it l. like a duck REUT 303:4
Looney misfits, L. Tunes REAG 302:1
lord *L. is out walking* LLOY 230:12
L.'s anointed temple SHAK 331:9
of the coming of the L. HOWE 184:3
we battle for the L. ROOS 311:12
lords admiring the House of L. BAG 26:4
Admit l., and you admit all SHAF 324:3
And l. whose parents DEFOE 111:9
For the l. who lay ye low SHEL 338:3
hand of new unhappy l. CHES 84:9
House of L., an illusion STOP 351:7
House of L. is a perfect eventide STOC 351:6
[House of] L. is its irrationality CAMP 73:7
L. do not encourage wit DISR 116:6
L. is a matter of controversy ST J 317:5
only a wit among L. JOHN 197:1
reform the House of L. DANG 109:4
thither from the House of L. NORF 275:2
lordships good enough for their l. ANON 13:11
lose be on the right side and l. GALB 146:1
Better we l. the election STEV 349:8
I would rather l. her as a friend GLAD 156:1
meanly l., the last, best hope LINC 226:1
much to hope and nothing to l. BURKE 65:3
nothing to l. but our aitches ORW 278:2
nothing to l. but their chains MARX 253:4
Oh! we don't want to l. you RUB 314:8
Or l. our ventures SHAK 330:14
seek power and to l. liberty BACON 22:10
take care not to l. wars CHUR 92:12
We should never l. an occasion DISR 118:11
loser It is a l. politically NIXON 274:15
losers no winners, but all are l. CHAM 80:8
losing conduct of a l. party BURKE 67:13
l. one pleased Cato LUCAN 234:3
loss l. of a dear friend SOUT 347:3
l. of power tends to corrupt RUSK 315:4
losses l. to a nation CECIL 79:8
lost France has not l. the war DE G 112:3
Frederick the Great l. the battle ANON 10:3
Great Britain has l. an empire ACH 1:5
he always l. it SMITH 344:2
L. is our old simplicity ANON 12:3
Next to a battle l. WELL 385:1
not see your country is l. WILL 389:3
Vietnam was l. MCL 243:9
we are l. PYRR 299:1
lot Their l. forbad GRAY 160:8
lottery prize in the l. of life RHOD 304:2
their judgement is a mere l. DRYD 125:1
louder l. he talked of his honour EMER 133:4
loud-mouthed l. fellow ATTL 20:3
loudspeaker small voice and not a l. ATTL 20:7
lout It's a l.'s game WEST 385:9
love come to l. men too little BURKE 67:8
Greater l. hath no man THOR 364:7
I must l. the dog GIBB 152:1
It is the l. of the people BURKE 64:6
land that I l. BERL 38:6
l. of freedom itself GLAD 154:11
l. that asks no question SPR 348:1
l. those who l. you VOLT 375:13
Only L. the Beloved Republic FORS 139:5
That l. my friend SHAK 330:8
They l. him most for the enemies BRAGG 54:9
to save the party we l. GAIT 145:1
will not l. his country SHAK 329:12
You all did l. him once SHAK 330:4
loved Not that I l. Caesar less SHAK 329:10
prince to be feared than l. MACH 241:3
to Washington to be l. GRAMM 159:4
loves I have reigned with your l. ELIZ 132:1
l. what he knows CROM 105:3
loving l. ourselves to death PRES 298:2
low Caesar! dost thou lie so l. SHAK 329:8
involuntary homage of the l. DICK 115:6

low (*cont.*):
malice is of a l. stature HAL 166:2
lower l. than vermin BEVAN 40:6
never knew that the l. classes CURZ 108:2
they call the L. House DISR 117:3
while there is a l. class DEBS 111:3
lowliness l. is young ambition's SHAK 328:10
loyal He is l. to his own career DALT 109:2
loyalties l. which centre CHUR 93:6
tragic conflict of l. HOWE 184:2
loyalty I want *l.* JOHN 196:8
l., a principle BOSW 53:4
L. is a fine quality KINN 211:7
L. is the Tory's secret weapon KILM 209:9
That learned body wanted l. TRAPP 367:6
Lucifer he falls like L. SHAK 327:6
luck l. to be called upon CHUR 94:1
luggage labels on empty l. BEVAN 41:7
lunatic l. fringe ROOS 311:13
lunatics lunatic asylum run by l. LLOY 230:5
lunch no such thing as a free l. ANON 13:9
luncheon do not take soup at l. CURZ 108:5
lungs parks are the l. of London PITT 293:6
Lupercal On the L. SHAK 330:3
lustre bright l. of a court CECIL 79:9
lute lascivious pleasing of a l. SHAK 334:9
luxury republics end in l. MONT 264:3
lying branch of the art of l. CORN 103:9

MacArthur General M. TRUM 372:2
Macaulay [M.] has occasional flashes SMITH 344:9
Tom M. MELB 255:10
machinery [Our] whole political m. BALF 31:2
political m. CHOD 85:9
whole m. of the State BRO 58:1
macht *Arbeit m. frei* ANON 8:7
mackerel stinks like rotten m. RAND 301:1
mad half of the nation is m. SMOL 345:2
old, m., blind, despised SHEL 338:1
This m. dog of the Middle East REAG 302:2
Whom the m. would destroy LEVIN 222:3
madam m. I may not call you ELIZ 131:10
made revolutions are not m. PHIL 291:8
madmen m. in authority KEYN 208:6
when we join the fashionable m. DID 116:2
madness m. in great ones SHAK 325:9
sort of m. [Bolshevism] SMITH 344:1
magic not let in daylight upon m. BAG 25:13
tightness of the m. circle MACL 242:8
magistrate m. corruptible ROB 306:7
Magna Charta M. is such a fellow COKE 101:1
magnanimity In victory: m. CHUR 93:5
m. in politics BURKE 64:7
magnet m. [Mariner's Needle] BACON 22:2
magpie would have a m. society CHUR 94:3
maiden bevy of m. aunts LLOY 230:10
maids Old m. biking to Holy ORW 278:7
mail bastard who gets the m. KEAT 203:1
maimed m. us at the start YEATS 396:2
main Into the m. of waters SHAK 332:11
with an eye to the m. chance CECIL 79:6
Maine As M. goes, so goes Vermont FARL 135:5
maintain m. good government HAM 167:3
maintained plausibly m. BURR 69:1
majestic m. equality of the law FRAN 141:2
majesty cease of m. Dies not alone SHAK 325:13
This earth of m. SHAK 333:4
When m. falls to folly SHAK 331:2
majority as a rule the m. are wrong DEBS 111:2
As for our m.... one is enough DISR 120:17
great silent m. NIXON 274:6
however safe its m. BOOK 51:7
indifference of the m. REST 303:3
indifferent and self-indulgent m. STEP 349:3
in the opinions of the m. PEEL 288:7
m. is always the best repartee DISR 118:8
m. never has right on its side IBSEN 186:8
man with courage makes a m. JACK 189:4
minority to the m. LENIN 221:6
on God's side is a m. PHIL 292:1
vast untutored m. HEAD 172:3
will of the m. is in all cases JEFF 192:5
majors m. in the party MACM 244:9
make does not usually m. PHEL 291:3
king may m. a nobleman BURKE 67:17
to m. as much money FRI 143:7
maker am prepared to meet my m. CHUR 93:14
making m. the world safe for WOLFE 393:6
malaise energy and m. CART 77:8
malefactors m. of great wealth ROOS 311:9
malice m. is of a low stature HAL 166:2
With m. toward none LINC 227:1
malignant not m. and remove it WAUGH 380:9
with m. fidelity BALF 31:3
malignity m. truly diabolical BURKE 63:2
man affinity with the soul of m. PARK 285:5
Am I not a m. and a brother WEDG 383:2
And the M. of Blood was there MAC 236:4
but make a m. a woman PEMB 289:12
century of the common m. WALL 376:10
encompassed but one m. SHAK 328:6
every m. against every man HOBB 179:12
everyone has sat except a m. CUMM 107:2
figure of 'The Reasonable M.' HERB 177:1
It's that m. again ANON 11:5
landing a m. on the Moon KENN 204:8
led to *perdition* by a m. WEST 385:8
m. and the hour have met YANC 395:3
M. being... by nature all free LOCKE 231:6
m. for all seasons WHIT 388:6
M. is something to be surpassed NIET 273:3

m. is the only animal JEFF 191:5
M. is the only creature ORW 278:9
M., proud man SHAK 332:9
m. who stood at the gate HASK 170:2
once to every m. and nation LOW 234:1
plain, blunt m. SHAK 330:8
right m. in the right place JEFF 193:14
right to be obeyed than m. JOHN 195:1
theories about the rights of m. BURKE 66:14
this is an extraordinary m. JOHN 198:11
this was a m. SHAK 330:16
unpleasantness from a m. NAP 269:5
want anything said, ask a m. THAT 360:8
Would this m., could he see AUDEN 21:6
managed m. or well-conducted RADC 299:6
management m. of a balance KISS 214:8
m. of illusions WALD 376:7
telling British m. off JOS 200:1
Manchester school of M. DISR 121:14
manhood customs and its m. ENN 133:8
They could assert their m. WAUGH 380:8
Youth is a blunder; M. a struggle DISR 117:8
manifesto have our m. written BENN 36:9
manifestoes party m. ROTH 314:2
mankind gates of mercy on m. GRAY 160:8
M. always sets itself MARX 252:6
m. and posterity INGE 187:6
M. are happier JOHN 198:13
M. must put an end KENN 204:10
M.'s salvation lies exclusively SOLZ 345:11
not created m. entirely TOCQ 365:6
short way of abolishing m. MONT 263:10
There is no history of m. POPP 295:12
war with the rights of m. JEFF 191:10
you shall not crucify m. BRYAN 60:6
manners Oh, the times! Oh, the m. CIC 95:9
Peel has no m. WELL 384:13
manoeuvre blend force with a m. TROT 370:10
manufacturing m. the plausible BALD 30:1
manure It is its natural m. JEFF 191:7
many makes so m. of them LINC 227:5
so much owed by so m. to so few CHUR 90:10
map Lord would use a larger m. SAL 317:8
roll up that m. PITT 293:11
maps m. on a small scale SAL 317:8
Too much poring over m. SAL 319:2
marble left it m. AUG 21:8
March beware the ides of M. SHAK 328:2
Do not m. on Moscow MONT 265:3
ides of M. are come SHAK 329:2
I intend to m. my troops GRIM 162:1
m. as an alternative to jogging FITT 137:6
m. of a nation PARN 286:8
these gentlemen wish to m. GLAD 154:16
they said, 'Let us m.' STEV 350:13
You can m. towards it CALL 72:9
marches forced m., battles GAR 148:1
marching His truth is m. on HOWE 184:3
'Tis the people m. on MORR 266:5
mare brought him a Flanders m. HENR 176:1
marijuana I experimented with m. CLIN 99:5
mark Now m. me how I will undo SHAK 334:5
market gentle m. economy KINN 211:8
m. has no morality HES 177:11
market-place gathered in the m. CAV 79:2
marks bears the m. of the last HAIG 163:1
marriage fifty times more for a m. BAG 25:8
m. is the waste-paper basket WEBB 381:6
married If m. life were all MILL 259:11
like other m. couples SAKI 317:6
marrow largest vegetable m. ASQ 18:9
Mars possible attack from M. SAL 319:1
marshal m.'s baton of the duke LOU 233:3
martial become valiant and m. BACON 23:4
m. airs of England WEBS 382:7
martyr has the soul of a m. BAG 24:5
I am the m. of the people CHAR 82:6
Thou fall'st a blessed m. SHAK 327:7
martyrdom crown of m. WALP 377:11
torches of m. JEFF 193:3
Marx illegitimate child of Karl M. ATTL 20:8
M is for M. CONN 102:1
teaching of M. KHR 209:1
Marxism M. is now a world faith BENN 36:7
M. is only an episode POPP 296:1
monetarism, like M. GILM 153:1
more to Methodism than to M. PHIL 291:7
Marxist I am not a M. MARX 252:10
tried to be a M. TAYL 357:14
mask He had a m. like Castlereagh SHEL 338:2
mass arithmetically calculable m. WEBB 381:3
broad m. of a nation HITL 179:3
m. meeting for a m. movement MCG 240:8
Paris is well worth a m. HENR 175:6
masses And Movement of M. CONN 102:1
back the m. against the classes GLAD 155:5
m. were calmer TAYL 357:13
Your huddled m. yearning LAZ 219:7
master between M. and Servant CHUR 88:6
but one mistress, and no m. ELIZ 131:1
dominion of the m. HUME 184:9
I would not be a *m.* LINC 224:8
m. of very little else BEV 42:5
these forces met their m. ROOS 309:2
master-morality m. and slave NIET 273:4
masters *educate our m.* LOWE 233:6
I have had two m. BEAV 34:7
m. of their fates SHAK 328:4
new m. HAL 166:7
people are the m. BURKE 65:5
We are the m. now SHAW 337:4
masterships just and unjust m. RUSK 315:10

mastiff leal and trusty m. LLOY 229:1
mat put them under the m. GURN 162:6
matches have a box of m. HOME 182:2
With that stick of m. MAND 249:4
material tortured by m. success MACM 245:5
Matilda since M. and Stephen WAUGH 380:10
matter dirt is only m. out of place GRAY 160:6
take away the m. of them BACON 23:1
Max If M. gets to Heaven WELLS 385:6
maxim It is a just political m. HUME 185:2
only m. of a free government ADAMS 3:5
We have got The M. Gun BELL 35:1
may lawyer tells me I *m.* do BURKE 64:5
Mayflower here on the M. ROOS 310:4
maypole organ and the m. JORD 199:5
McCarthyism M. is Americanism MCC 239:7
McKinley M. has no more ROOS 311:2
me thee and m. OWEN 280:5
mean citizen of no m. city BIBLE 44:11
even if you don't m. it TRUM 371:16
Happy the golden m. MASS 254:2
having a m. Court BAG 25:11
He nothing common did or m. MARV 251:7
meanest brightest, m. of mankind POPE 295:5
meanly nobly save, or m. lose LINC 226:1
means cease to be a mere m. HAYEK 171:6
continuation of politics by other m. CLA 96:11
he still retains the m. of Grace BALF 30:10
Increased m. DISR 119:20
it m. just what I choose CARR 77:1
live within your m. THAT 361:4
m. by which we live KING 211:1
m. of rising in the world JOHN 198:4
political expectations to military m. POW 296:5
measles m. of the human race EINS 129:1
measure assent to any political m. PEEL 288:4
shrunk to this little m. SHAK 329:8
ultimate m. of a man KING 210:6
measures cant of 'm. not men' CANN 74:9
cant of *Not men, but m.* BURKE 63:5
Great public m. PEEL 289:10
meat appointed to buy the m. SELD 323:2
keep the flies off the m. CHUR 90:14
teeth are in the real m. GRIM 162:2
Upon what m. SHAK 328:5
mechanical m. arts BACON 23:7
organic rather than m. PARK 285:9
medal m. glitters, but it also casts CHUR 91:2
meddle m. and muddle DERBY 114:2
m. not with any man's conscience CROM 105:5
meddling m. government MAC 236:7
media m., I tell pedants INGH 188:1
medieval marvellous in m. politics MACM 245:12
mediocre titles distinguish the m. SHAW 336:10
mediocrity real m. SMITH 342:3
meek borne his faculties so m. SHAK 331:7
m. shall inherit the earth SMITH 343:9
meet prepared to m. my Maker CHUR 93:14
meeting He mistakes a mass m. MCG 240:8
Winston *loves* m. people LLOY 230:9
Melting-Pot crucible, the great M. ZANG 396:8
members m. of the Communist MCC 239:6
memoirs To write one's m. PÉT 290:11
memorable Upon that m. scene MARV 251:7
memorandum m. is written ACH 1:7
memorial whole earth as their m. PER 290:5
memories ought to have good m. SIDN 340:1
memory For my name and m. BACON 23:10
indebted to his m. for his jests SHER 338:13
nation's collective m. POW 297:15
no force can abolish m. ROOS 310:2
proper m. for a politician MORL 266:3
men all m. are created JEFF 191:1
all m. would be tyrants ADAMS 2:1
As though he had 200,000 m. NAP 269:12
cant of 'measures not m.' CANN 74:9
cant of *Not m., but measures* BURKE 63:5
For thyse m. don most harm LANG 217:7
individual m. and women THAT 362:2
m. and nations behave EBAN 127:5
m. dominating men WEBER 381:8
m. in great place BACON 22:9
m. know so little of m. DU B 126:6
m. lived like fishes SIDN 340:2
Millions of innocent m., women JEFF 191:2
not m. but principles PAINE 282:10
political question from the m. BURKE 66:2
state which dwarfs its m. MILL 259:5
stupid to deny that all m. MILT 261:1
wealth accumulates, and m. GOLD 157:6
What I want is m. who will MELB 256:4
menace m. to be defeated SCAR 321:3
mental and slavery are m. states GAND 147:7
I am haunted by m. decay NIC 272:4
mentioned family that is never m. TREV 368:4
Mephistopheles who is the M. HEAL 173:1
mercantile m. projects SMITH 343:2
merchandise arts and m. BACON 23:7
merchandize m. candidates STEV 350:11
merchantman monarchy is a m. AMES 8:2
merchants m. have no country JEFF 193:5
mercury pick up m. with a fork LLOY 230:3
mercy As m. does SHAK 332:7
crowning m. CROM 105:7
quality of m. is not strained SHAK 332:10
reason to rule, but m. to forgive DRYD 125:15
shut the gates of m. GRAY 160:8
merit *m.* for a bishopric WEST 385:10
What is m. PALM 284:6
meritocracy true m. of talent YOUNG 396:7

merits m. of any political question BURKE 66:2
merry Charles II was very m. SELL 323:7
m. monarch, scandalous ROCH 307:6
never m. world in England SHAK 326:19
message take a m. to Albert DISR 122:2
messenger very well paid m. boy ASH 17:8
messianic role was m.: America KISS 214:12
met man and the hour have m. YANC 395:3
m. by the colour line DOUG 124:2
method economics are the m. THAT 361:3
Methodism owes more to M. PHIL 291:7
metropolis m. of the empire COBB 100:3
Mexico Poor M., so far from God DIAZ 114:6
MI5 M. is a job creation scheme HENN 174:8
Micawbers like inverted M. GUED 162:5
mice as long as it catches the m. DENG 113:4
middle in politics the m. way ADAMS 3:8
in the m. of the road BEVAN 40:13
middle class m. is in control ARIS 16:10
m. was quite prepared BELL 35:3
philistines proper, or m. ARN 17:4
powerful m. DISR 120:15
We of the sinking m. ORW 278:2
We should not allow m. guilt HEAL 172:9
Middle East mad dog of the M. REAG 302:2
Middlesex An acre in M. MAC 237:11
middle-sized m. are alone SHEN 338:9
midnight stroke of the m. hour NEHRU 270:7
might Britons alone use 'M.' WAUGH 380:6
might-have-been great m. TAYL 357:6
mightier make thee m. yet BENS 37:6
spark-gap is m. than the pen HOGB 181:1
mighty thou art m. yet SHAK 330:15
militarism M.... is fetish worship TAWN 355:8
military arms race has no m. purpose MOUN 267:4
civilian control of the m. TRUM 371:11
I now close my m. career MAC 235:14
matter to entrust to m. men CLEM 98:7
m. action GALB 146:11
m. mind in their dead grip TUCH 372:4
political expectations to m. means POW 296:5
understand what m. fame is SHER 339:3
milk putting m. into babies CHUR 92:1
millenium believes in a calico m. CARL 76:13
millionaire m. has just as good HOPE 183:2
millionaires need more m. JOS 200:4
millionairess semi-royal m. CHAN 81:10
millions m. for defence HARP 169:5
tear-wrung m. BYRON 71:6
What m. died—that Caesar CAMP 73:8
yearly multiplying m. O'SUL 279:13
mills dark Satanic m. BLAKE 49:5
millstone m. round our necks DISR 119:2
Milton Some mute inglorious M. GRAY 160:8
Which M. held WORD 394:5
mind cast your m. on other days YEATS 396:3
[Charles] Sumner's m. ADAMS 2:9
conceal your own m. DISR 118:5
empires of the m. CHUR 92:2
fit of absence of m. SEEL 322:6
hundred-horse-power m. BALD 30:3
liberation of the human m. GOLD 157:2
m. of a bigot HOLM 182:1
m. of the oppressed BIKO 45:4
m.'s construction in the face SHAK 331:6
m. was that of Lord Beaverbrook ATTL 20:1
Neville has a retail m. LLOY 230:7
passion so effectually robs the m. BURKE 62:3
prepare the m. of the country DISR 119:12
minds great empire and little m. BURKE 64:7
miners like m.' coal dust BOOT 52:5
Mineworkers Union of M. MACM 245:9
minister As m. of the Crown PEEL 288:2
decide whether a M. HEND 174:6
First M. whose self-righteous JENK 194:6
God help the M. that meddles MELB 255:9
House, and cheer the m. CANN 75:5
M., whoever he at any time PAINE 282:12
M. will reject it LYNN 235:5
When I was a m. I always LAWS 219:6
wisdom of a great m. JUN 200:10
yes, M.! No, Minister CROS 106:10
ministers cabinet m. are educated BENN 37:4
group of Cabinet M. begins CURZ 108:3
how much my M. talk THAT 360:13
in kings and m. SMITH 341:7
m. decide THAT 362:5
M. have to make good BAG 26:8
M. need activity LYNN 235:3
M. say one of two things ANON 12:6
my actions are my m. CHAR 83:1
page—a warning to all M. WALP 378:10
teaching m. to consult SWIFT 353:8
worst possible M. ATTL 20:12
ministries made many m. BAG 25:1
ministry for a marriage than a m. BAG 25:8
m. of all the talents ANON 12:7
mink doesn't have a m. coat NIXON 273:6
minnows pike is death for the m. TAWN 356:1
this Triton of the m. SHAK 324:6
minorities M.... are almost SMITH 344:10
minority majority with a helpless m. HEAD 172:3
m. are right DEBS 111:2
m. possess their equal rights JEFF 192:5
most vilified and persecuted m. FRAN 141:7
persuading an efficient m. STEP 349:3
subjection of the m. LENIN 221:6
minuet constitutional m. SCAR 321:1
minutes as you did in two m. EVER 134:4
Cabinet m. are studied KAUF 202:3
writes the m. rules the roost ANON 10:8
you can have the seven m. COLL 101:5

mischief execute any m. CLAR 96:2
In every deed of m. GIBB 151:10
m., thou art afoot SHAK 330:11
miserable arise and make them m. HUXL 186:3
miseries m. brought upon the world BURKE 67:7
misery certain amount of m. LOWE 233:7
greatest m. is a battle gained WELL 385:1
relation of distant m. GIBB 151:11
trapping of a splendid m. ROSS 313:5
misfits strangest collection of m. REAG 302:1
misfortunes crimes, follies, and m. GIBB 151:6
tableau of crimes and m. VOLT 376:3
misguided guided missiles and m. KING 211:1
mislead m. the people STEV 349:8
one to m. the public ASQ 18:6
misplaced rise of m. power EIS 129:8
missed he m. the bus CHAM 81:4
mission My m. is to pacify Ireland GLAD 154:7
missionaries free m. MENC 256:14
Missouri God has given us M. RAND 300:9
mistake Biggest damfool m. EIS 129:9
When I make a m., it's a beaut LA G 216:3
mistaken you may be m. CROM 105:6
mistakes All great men make m. CHUR 86:9
If he makes m. CHUR 93:6
learned from the m. of the past TAYL 357:7
man who makes no m. PHEL 291:3
mistress But m. in my own KIPL 213:1
but one m., and no Master ELIZ 131:1
m. I am ashamed to call you ELIZ 131:10
mistresses your Lordship's m. WILK 389:1
mitre between a m. and a crown WALP 377:11
moat look to your m. HAL 165:3
mob amphibious ill-born m. DEFOE 111:6
do what the m. do DICK 115:1
each tyrant, every m. KIPL 213:5
fit object of redress by m. law LINC 224:3
I lied to please the m. KIPL 213:6
m. of their constituents BURKE 66:3
m., Parliament COBB 100:2
Our supreme governors, the m. WALP 377:4
mock but to m. the kingdom PYM 298:6
How my achievements m. me SHAK 335:11
model best m. the world ever HAM 167:2
m. of a modern Prime HENN 175:2
moderate in m. government HAM 167:4
Iranian m. is one who KISS 214:9
m. income LAMB 216:7
white m. KING 210:8
moderation astonished at my own m. CLIVE 99:9
deviate into m. BURKE 66:3
M. in the affairs of the nation JOHN 196:5
m. in war is imbecility MAC 237:4
modern m. Prime Minister HENN 175:2
thought of m. civilization GAND 147:4
modest much to be m. about CHUR 93:13
moll King's M. Reno'd ANON 11:7
Moloch right of that great M. MEYER 258:3
moment creed of the m. BAG 23:15
exigency of the m. PEEL 288:2
monarch hereditary m. was insane BAG 27:1
merry m., scandalous ROCH 307:6
not so much a king as a M. SELL 323:7
monarchical m. or popular HOBB 180:4
monarchies In elective m. GIBB 151:1
m., in poverty MONT 264:3
monarchize To m., be feared SHAK 333:8
monarchs For righteous m. BRO 57:7
m., whose power seems MONT 264:1
schemes for persuading m. SWIFT 353:8
monarchy characteristic of the English M. BAG 25:7
constitutional m. TROL 369:3
constitutional m. such as ours BAG 26:1
discontented under *m.* HOBB 180:8
essential to a true m. BAG 24:9
lock a door against absolute M. PAINE 280:8
M. and succession PAINE 281:3
m. has become ST J 317:5
M. has no further part PHIL 291:6
M. is a labour-intensive industry WILS 391:7
m. is a merchantman AMES 8:2
M. is a strong government BAG 25:5
M. is only the string SHEL 338:7
of m. PAINE 282:15
state of m. is the supremest JAM 189:11
monetarism m., like Marxism GILM 153:1
money as much m. as possible VOLT 376:1
bad m. drives out good ANON 8:8
can be master of m. BEV 42:5
draining m. from the pockets SMITH 342:2
flood of m. that gushes WHITE 387:2
getting m. JOHN 198:1
Giving m. and power O'RO 277:1
He had m. as well THAT 362:1
hell of not making m. CARL 76:4
If you have m. you spend it KENN 206:4
mark of distinction with m. BUR 69:2
m. for their stockholders FRI 143:7
M. has no smell VESP 374:2
M. is indeed the most important SHAW 336:11
M. . . . is none of the wheels HUME 184:7
Neither is m. the sinews of war BACON 23:3
not spending m. alone EIS 129:4
sinews of war, unlimited m. CIC 95:11
spending other people's m. RAND 301:3
spending the public m. COOL 103:6
there shall be no m. SHAK 327:1
They hired the m., didn't they COOL 103:4
virtue does not come from m. SOCR 345:8
voter who uses his m. SAM 320:1
your own licence to print m. THOM 363:8

moneybag Aristocracy of the M. CARL 75:10
mongrels continent of energetic m. FISH 137:1
monk cloistered m. BIRCH 45:9
monkey m. looking for fleas LASKI 218:4
no reason to attack the m. BEVAN 41:2
monkeys politicians are like m. LLOY 231:3
monologue m. is not a decision ATTL 19:10
monopoly best of all m. profits HICKS 178:6
m. stage of capitalism LENIN 221:3
shun the temptations of m. SCOTT 322:4
Monroe M. Doctrine ROOS 311:4
mouth of Marilyn M. MITT 261:8
monstrous against a m. tyranny CHUR 90:6
Montezuma who imprisoned M. MAC 238:6
monument left some m. BURKE 65:9
m. was erected by the state AUDEN 21:4
Pentagon, that immense m. FRAN 142:10
moon defend the m. SAL 319:1
I felt like the m., the stars TRUM 371:1
landing a man on the m. KENN 204:8
moonlight rotten mackerel by m. RAND 301:1
moose strong as a bull m. ROOS 310:12
moral Arthur is wicked and m. CHUR 88:2
attainment of m. good JOHN 195:3
government is often the most m. MENC 257:5
It *is* a m. issue HALEY 164:7
m. imperative that we have it DID 116:2
m. or intellectual damage KRUG 215:6
m. principles PAINE 283:8
scarcely a single m. action GLAD 156:3
This party is a m. crusade WILS 390:3
morality laws of m. are the same BURKE 65:11
market has no m. HES 177:11
M. is the herd-instinct NIET 273:2
periodical fits of m. MAC 237:8
personal and national m. SHAW 336:11
morally not m. sure BURKE 62:9
morals either m. or principles GLAD 155:2
faith and m. hold WORD 394:5
foundation of m. BENT 37:9
more some animals are m. equal ORW 278:11
mores *O tempora, O m.* CIC 95:9
morganatic m. alliance HARD 168:4
morning It's m. again in America RINEY 306:1
m. had been golden CHUR 89:9
never glad confident m. again BROW 60:2
they take you in the m. BALD 28:9
What a glorious m. is this ADAMS 5:3
mors *principis m. est* MORE 265:7
mortality emblem of m. DISR 121:12
mortifications m. and humiliations WALP 377:13
Moscow Do not march on M. MONT 265:3
Mosley Why does M. always ATTL 19:7
mother France, m. of arts, of warfare DU B 126:4
m. of battles HUSS 186:1
m. of Parliaments BRIG 56:7
M. of the Free BENS 37:6
m. who talks about DISR 120:3
My m., drunk or sober CHES 84:1
skin of his m. LLOY 230:16
mothers city of the best-bodied m. WHIT 388:3
mothers-in-law m. and Wigan Pier BRID 56:3
motion economic law of m. MARX 252:8
renders the m. of the wheels HUME 184:7
motivation undiscussable m. POW 297:14
motive noble in m. HOOV 182:7
motives two m., neither of them BURKE 65:12
mould out-of-date m. JENK 194:4
Mount Sermon on the M. BRAD 54:4
mountain beauty of the m. rose BEAV 34:2
go up to the m. KING 211:4
mourn M., hapless Caledonia, m. SMOL 345:3
mourner sole m. at his own ROS 312:6
mourning waste any time in m. HILL 178:9
mouth m. of Marilyn Monroe MITT 261:8
silver foot in his m. RICH 305:2
subject with an open m. STEV 351:2
mouths I stuffed their m. with gold BEVAN 41:10
move If I could pray to m. SHAK 329:3
moved We shall not be m. ANON 14:8
movement mass m. MCG 240:8
right of free m. JOHN 195:3
moving king's life is m. peacefully DAWS 110:5
MP Being an M. feeds your vanity PARR 286:11
Being an M. is the sort of job ABB 1:1
only quality needed for an M. MACM 245:13
MPs dull M. in close proximity GILB 152:9
healthy cynicism of M. CREWE 104:2
I've seen M. on both sides BROWN 58:5
many M. never see LIV 228:7
When in that House M. divide GILB 152:8
much So little done, so m. to do RHOD 304:3
so m. owed by so many CHUR 90:10
muck when to stop raking the m. ROOS 311:8
mud builds on m. MACH 241:4
muddle meddle and m. DERBY 114:2
m. through BRIG 56:6
muddy m. understandings BURKE 66:17
muffled with m. oars RAND 301:2
mufflered m. men in the 1930s dole JOS 199:7
mule like a m. DONN 122:7
m. of politics DISR 117:9
What that Sicilian m. was to me GLAD 155:10
mules m. of politics POWER 298:1
multitude m., such as Mob COBB 100:2
mundus *fiat justitia et pereat m.* FERD 136:4
murder I met m. on the way SHEL 338:2
Killing no m. briefly discourst SEXBY 324:2
Most sacrilegious m. SHAK 331:9
m. respectable ORW 279:11
we have m. by the throat LLOY 230:1
We hear war called m. MACD 240:5
muse talked shop like a tenth m. ANON 10:7

mushroom councillor is like a m. MAG 247:5
music m. of our own opinions STEV 351:3
shriller than all the m. SHAK 328:2
music-hall cross between a m. turn MACM 245:4
Mussolini Hitler and M. LOW 233:5
must Is *m.* a word to be addressed ELIZ 132:2
mutability large republics is m. BOL 51:1
mutamur *et nos m. in illis* ANON 13:7
mute that of m. MACM 244:11
mutiny rise and m. SHAK 330:10
muzzle m. this terrible young WALP 378:4
myself I find m. a traitor SHAK 334:7
never thought of thinking for m. GILB 152:4
mystery grasped the m. of the atom BRAD 54:4
Its m. is its life BAG 25:13
m. of the king's power JAM 190:1
riddle wrapped in a m. CHUR 90:1
myth 'good old days' were a m. ATK 19:5
m. of democracy CROS 106:12
mythology British m. GRIGG 161:8
myths devoid of plausible m. BERG 38:5
m. of the British Parliament MAYB 254:6

nabobs n. of negativism AGNEW 6:7
naked It is n. aggression POW 297:13
left me n. to mine enemies SHAK 327:8
n. into the conference chamber BEVAN 41:3
thus I clothe my n. villainy SHAK 334:11
name For my n. and memory BACON 23:10
ghost of a great n. LUCAN 234:4
have our n. spelled wrong SHER 339:3
I glory in the n. of Briton GEOR 149:1
In the n. of God, go AMERY 8:1
In the n. of God, go CROM 105:8
Is not the king's n. SHAK 333:7
liberties are taken in thy n. GEOR 150:9
n. is Ainsley Gotto ERWIN 134:1
n. is neither one thing CHUR 95:3
n. to all succeeding ages curst DRYD 125:4
n. we give the people FLERS 137:7
whistling of a n. POPE 295:5
names little man with three n. CROM 106:2
Napoleon N. forgot Blücher CHUR 86:9
thinks he is N. CLEM 98:5
used to say of him [N.] WELL 384:6
Napoleons Caesars and N. HUXL 186:3
nastiest n. thing in the nicest way GOLD 156:9
nasty n., brutish, and short HOBB 180:2
nation against the rest of the n. HAL 166:4
against the voice of a n. RUSS 317:1
American n. BAG 24:7
AMERICA was thus clearly top n. SELL 323:11
bind up the n.'s wounds LINC 227:1
broad mass of a n. HITL 179:3
citizenship of the whole n. MACD 240:7
deprive a n. of its right to NAM 269:1
England is a n. of shopkeepers NAP 270:1
existence as a n. ADAMS 4:7
find faith in a n. of sectaries DISR 117:11
fit only for a n. of shopkeepers SMITH 341:6
For n. shall rise against n. BIBLE 44:9
France...a n. of forty millions CRILE 104:3
geographical fragment, but a n. PARN 286:5
God hath sifted a n. STO 351:12
If a n. expects to be ignorant JEFF 193:6
Licensed build that n.'s fate BLAKE 49:4
losses to a n. may be so great CECIL 79:8
Maine goes, so goes the n. FARL 135:5
march of a n. PARN 286:8
n. is not governed BURKE 64:12
n. is only at peace KING 211:6
n. of differences CART 77:6
n. of shopkeepers are very seldom ADAMS 5:4
n.'s collective memory POW 297:15
n. shall not lift up sword BIBLE 43:18
N. shall speak peace unto n. REND 303:1
N. spoke to a Nation KIPL 213:1
n. which indulges toward WASH 379:12
new n., conceived in liberty LINC 226:3
No n. is fit to sit in judgement WILS 392:3
No n. was ever ruined by trade FRAN 142:6
once to every man and n. LOW 234:1
one-third of a n. ill-housed ROOS 309:3
operating instructions for a n. O'RO 277:4
our existence as a n. PITT 293:9
places the n. at his service POMP 295:1
public burden of the n.'s care PRIOR 298:4
real favours from n. to n. WASH 379:9
rich and lazy n. KIPL 213:4
should not create a n. Europe MONN 263:2
things which make a n. great BACON 23:9
Think of what our N. stands for BETJ 40:1
unity of the n. KOHL 215:4
watching a n. busily engaged POW 296:10
we are a n. of amateurs ROS 312:10
We are a n. of communities BUSH 69:6
what it can do for the n. HARD 168:5
will have to exterminate a n. SPOCK 347:9
national n. debt HAM 167:1
N. Debt is a very Good Thing SELL 323:8
n. events are decided MILLS 260:2
n. home for the Jewish BALF 30:6
N. honour is n. property MONR 263:3
There is the N. flag SUMN 353:2
nationalism N. is an infantile sickness EINS 129:1
N. is a silly cock crowing ALD 6:9
nationalities smaller n. of Europe ASQ 18:3
squabbling n. ROOS 311:14
nationality condense—a N. WHIT 388:4
what n. he would prefer RHOD 304:1
nationalization *n. of the coal* TAWN 355:6

nationalize n. in this country WILS 391:9
nations acceptable to all n. TRUM 371:4
and the people formed Two N. DISR 118:3
characteristic danger of great n. BAG 27:12
day of small n. has long passed CHAM 80:6
empire is a commonwealth of n. ROS 312:5
Europe of n. DE G 112:10
friendship with all n. JEFF 192:7
general association of n. WILS 392:17
Great n. are never impoverished SMITH 342:5
great n. have always acted KUBR 215:7
let fierce contending n. know ADD 5:9
n. and states draw aside GOGOL 156:8
N. begin by forming HAIL 163:11
N., like men, have their infancy BOL 50:8
N. touch at their summits BAG 26:5
n. which have put mankind INGE 187:6
Other n. use 'force' WAUGH 380:6
teaching n. how to live MILT 260:5
two great n. in the world TOCQ 365:9
two n.; between whom DISR 118:2
native eyes of a n. LESS 222:1
ideas about the n. LESS 221:13
This is my own, my n. land SCOTT 322:5
NATO N. exists for three reasons ISMAY 188:4
nattering n. nabobs of negativism AGNEW 6:7
natural irresistible n. laws BON 51:4
n. effort of every individual SMITH 343:3
n. order of things PAINE 282:11
n. party of government WILS 390:10
n. rights is simple nonsense BENT 37:8
naturalized man who was n. LODGE 232:1
nature better angels of our n. LINC 225:8
How n. always does contrive GILB 152:6
n. has no cure for this SMITH 344:1
n. of all greatness BURKE 64:14
n. of war consisteth not HOBB 180:1
n.'s mighty feast MALT 248:11
state that n. hath provided LOCKE 231:4
naval decisive n. force WASH 379:8
n. tradition CHUR 93:7
navy head of the N. CARS 77:3
It is upon the n. CHAR 82:8
n. nothing but rotten timber BURKE 64:6
royal n. of England BLAC 48:7
thoroughly efficient n. ROOS 311:4
Nazi N. Germany NEV 271:2
Nazis N. wanted war WAUGH 380:8
nearest those who are n. to him MILL 259:10
nearly I was n. kept waiting LOU 232:10
necessary but a n. evil PAINE 281:1
It became n. to destroy the town ANON 11:3
no n. evils in government JACK 189:2
not n. to change FALK 135:3
necessities Great n. call out ADAMS 2:2
people's hard n. BEV 42:1
necessity cruel n. CROM 105:4
laws of n., of self-preservation JEFF 193:2
n. hath no law CROM 105:11
n. is the plea PITT 293:7
pragmatic n. DID 116:2
neck lest it break thy n. SHAK 331:3
Roman people had but one n. CAL 72:5
some chicken! Some n. CHUR 91:7
necklace with our n. MAND 249:4
necks throw the reins over their n. CLAY 97:10
necromancy mere n. WHITE 386:7
need whenever we n. them FLERS 137:7
needle darning n. is broader NIC 272:2
needs to each according to his n. BAK 28:5
to each according to his n. MARX 252:9
negation This is the n. of God GLAD 154:2
negative prefers a n. peace KING 210:8
negativism nattering nabobs of n. AGNEW 6:7
negotiate never n. out of fear KENN 204:4
negotiating n. with de Valera LLOY 230:3
negotiation finish a difficult n. SAL 318:2
Negro dehumanizing the N. LINC 224:9
living with the N. BALD 28:8
N.'s great stumbling block KING 210:8
negroes drivers of n. JOHN 198:9
neighbour n.'s house is on fire BURKE 66:7
policy of the good n. ROOS 308:9
neighbourhood narrow into a n. JOHN 195:9
neighbouring n. state is in decline MONT 264:7
neighbours peace to all his n. SHAK 327:9
what is happening to our n. CHAM 80:7
neither n. one thing nor CHUR 95:3
Nell Pretty witty N. PEPYS 290:4
Nelson death of N. was felt SOUT 347:3
neo-classical post n. BROWN 58:6
nephews Priests have n. PEEL 289:7
Nero N. fiddled MENC 256:13
nerve I do not lose my n. NEHRU 270:9
nest I have no n.-eggs LLOY 229:2
nets n. of such a texture SHEN 338:9
neutral studiously n. WILS 392:5
United States must be n. WILS 392:1
neutrality armed n. is ineffectual WILS 392:10
Just for a word 'n.' BETH 39:8
never n. explain FISH 137:4
n. glad confident morning again BROW 60:2
n. had it so good MACM 244:7
n. in the field of human CHUR 90:10
n. was and n. will be JEFF 193:6
new against the n. and untried LINC 225:3
n. deal for the American people ROOS 308:6
n. wine into old bottles ATTL 20:5
Newcastle no more coals to N. GEOR 149:9
New England growth of N. PARK 286:3
New France expansion of N. PARK 286:3
news item of n. TALL 355:2
President who never told bad n. KEIL 203:3

New South Wales govern N. BELL 35:3
newspaper never to look into a n. SHER 338:11
n. is of necessity something SCOTT 322:4
newspapers government without n. JEFF 191:4
I read the n. avidly BEVAN 41:9
It's the n. I can't stand STOP 351:11
Vietnam War, the n. nobly BLACK 48:5
Newspeak aim of N. is to narrow ORW 279:3
New World N. into existence CANN 75:4
nexus n. of man to man CARL 76:2
nice not about being n. KEAT 203:2
nicest nastiest thing in the n. way GOLD 156:9
nick-name every n. is a title PAINE 282:7
niece hitting the n. of a bishop ORW 277:10
night long dark n. of tyranny MURR 268:5
n. of the long knives HITL 179:4
show thy dangerous brow by n. SHAK 328:11
touch of Harry in the n. SHAK 326:10
Nightingale Florence N. GRIF 161:7
nightmare national n. is over FORD 138:12
nightstick at the end of a n. WHAL 386:2
nihil *Aut Caesar, aut n.* BORG 53:1
ninety n. percent of the politicians KISS 214:6
Ninety-two glorious N. REV 303:6
nip n. him in the bud ROCHE 307:4
Nixon You won't have N. NIXON 274:2
no he can say n. in such a way PEAR 287:6
leadership is saying n., not yes BLAIR 48:12
N.! No! No THAT 362:10
rebel? A man who says n. CAMUS 74:6
nobility and in others *n.* PAINE 282:6
leave us still our old n. MANN 249:5
n. is a graceful ornament BURKE 67:6
n. is the act of time BACON 22:14
order of n. is of great use BAG 26:3
nobleman king may make a n. BURKE 67:17
nobles n. by the right MAC 237:7
noblesse laissez-faire and n. oblige HES 178:3
noblest n. Roman of them all SHAK 330:16
remains the n. word TAYL 357:1
nobly We shall n. save LINC 226:1
nobody n. left to be concerned NIEM 273:1
there is n. there KEYN 208:8
To n. GURN 162:6
nominated I will not accept if n. SHER 339:4
nomination decide the n. DAUG 109:9
nonconformist comes from the n. TAYL 356:12
nonconformity history of N. ORW 277:11
none With malice toward n. LINC 227:1
nonexistence nonviolence or n. KING 210:3
nonpolitical n. speech NIXON 274:1
nonsense little n. now and then POW 296:7
n. upon stilts BENT 37:8
non-violence n. is the first article GAND 147:3
n. or nonexistence KING 210:3
organization of n. BAEZ 23:11
north against the people of the N. LEE 220:6
forth in triumph from the n. MAC 236:3
men and women of the N. ANTH 15:5
N. is determined to preserve HOUS 183:8
North African egg of a N. Empire GLAD 155:4
Northcliffe N. has sent for the King ANON 10:6
northern constant as the n. star SHAK 329:3
N. laurels LEE 220:1
N. States will manage somehow BRIG 56:6
southern efficiency and n. charm KENN 205:12
nose Do not run up your n. BALD 29:12
Had Cleopatra's n. been shorter PASC 287:1
liberty plucks justice by the n. SHAK 332:4
nothing better to know n. BILL 45:5
desired to know n. JOHN 198:2
do n. MELB 256:5
good man to do n. BURKE 68:7
Having n. to construct TROL 369:9
n. LOU 233:2
n. is ever done SHAW 336:14
n. should ever be done for CORN 103:8
Thinking n. done LUCAN 234:5
nought n. shall make us rue SHAK 331:1
nouns n. of number, or multitude COBB 100:2
novel be the hero of a n. yet MAC 236:8
November remember the fifth of N. ANON 13:2
now n. she is like everyone else DE G 112:6
nuclear forces of n. destruction KENN 205:7
n. arms race has no military MOUN 267:4
n. freeze proposals REAG 301:12
n. giants and ethical infants BRAD 54:5
nuisance not make himself a n. MILL 259:2
n. in time of war CHUR 92:8
NUM against the Pope or the N. BALD 29:12
number centre upon n. one CHUR 93:6
greatest n. BENT 37:9
nouns of n., or multitude COBB 100:2
numbers better than n. CROM 105:2
nurse baby beats the n. SHAK 332:4
nursery great n. of freemen SHIP 339:6
not a n. of future revolutions BURKE 66:9
nut sledgehammer to miss a n. BOOK 52:2
nutrition n. and health JAY 190:4

oaks hews down o. with rushes SHAK 324:5
oars to his object with muffled o. RAND 301:2
Obadiah O. Bind-their-kings MAC 236:2
obedience o. to the law ROOS 311:7
rebellion to tyrants is o. to God BRAD 54:8
reluctant o. of distant provinces MAC 238:5
obedient o. to their laws we lie SIM 340:6
obey laws but to o. them HORS 183:4
not to o. the will of the people PEEL 288:6
obeyed more right to be o. JOHN 195:1
objections o. may be made JOHN 197:11

obligation o. of subjects HOBB 180:6
o. which goes unrecognized WEIL 383:4
oblivion gets you o. NIXON 274:16
observance o. of procedural FRAN 141:6
strict o. of the written law JEFF 193:2
obstinate o. little man THOM 363:5
obstruction kind of 'consecrated o.' BAG 25:10
obtain What we o. too cheap PAINE 281:11
obvious in o. distress BALF 30:8
occasion never lose an o. DISR 118:11
occupations O let us love our o. DICK 115:2
occurred Ought never to have o. BENT 38:2
ocean leap into the o., and perish HUME 184:9
Like the rolling on of o. MORR 266:5
use the o. as their road WALL 377:2
you had better abandon the o. CLAY 97:2
oceans To the o. white with foam BERL 38:6
odds o. we'll get reforms PEROT 290:10
Odysseus Like O., the President KEYN 207:4
off o. with his head SHAK 335:2
offence only defence is in o. BALD 29:6
where the o. is SHAK 325:11
offended speak; for him have I o. SHAK 329:12
offer not what I intend to o. KENN 203:9
office By o. boys for o. boys SAL 318:10
candidates for high o. STEV 350:11
chances of getting o. HAIL 163:4
commonplace mind high in o. HARDY 168:7
dignity of the o. GEOR 149:7
dog's obeyed in o. SHAK 331:4
going to run his o. HEND 174:6
I found myself without an o. CHUR 89:3
in o. but not in power LAM 217:2
insolence of o. SHAK 325:8
lifetime in public o. GALB 146:7
Men, if in o., seemed PEEL 288:5
men in o. PEEL 289:3
most insignificant o. ADAMS 4:1
o. before honour POW 297:6
o.-building and o.-hunting JEFF 192:1
o. is something that builds up BENN 36:6
o. of the Prime Minister ASQ 18:5
o. tends to confer LAWS 219:2
party or statesman got into o. CHUR 93:9
price paid for o. TOCQ 366:8
receives the seals of o. ROS 312:9
refreshing waters of o. TROL 369:2
second o. of government JEFF 191:13
statesman in o. TAYL 358:10
trusted with the o. BROD 57:4
trying to get into o. MCM 243:11
unfit to hold an o. FAB 134:6
when o. is in question PEEL 289:8
When we got into o. KENN 204:9
Whichever party is in o. WILS 391:6
officer art thou o. SHAK 326:11
offices Excluded from o. ADAMS 2:3
o. are acceptable here JEFF 191:14
o. as public trusts CALH 72:2
official concept of the 'o. secret' WEBER 381:11
its duty is to augment o. power BAG 26:10
No sane local o. SMITH 343:6
This high o., all allow HERB 176:9
officially o. denied COCK 100:6
officials high appointed o. O'RO 277:6
o. are the servants GOW 158:5
o. sometimes take a different ROTH 314:1
protect o. LYNN 235:6
tell the permanent o. HARC 168:3
offspring time's noblest o. BERK 38:4
oil like an o. painting INGH 188:1
o. which renders the motion HUME 184:7
old All wars are planned by o. men RICE 304:5
call young men instead of o. ones PEEL 288:3
conservative when o. FROST 144:3
'good o. days' were a myth ATK 19:5
I name thee O. Glory DRIV 124:9
new wine into o. bottles ATTL 20:5
not adherence to the o. and tried LINC 225:3
O. Age a regret DISR 117:8
o. age is the most unexpected TROT 370:13
O. Country must wake up GEOR 149:5
o., mad, blind, despised SHEL 338:1
o. man in a hurry CHUR 86:7
o. order changeth TENN 360:5
o., white-headed and large BUSH 69:4
redress the balance of the o. CANN 75:4
shaking hand of an o., wild VICT 374:6
Too o., too bourgeois GISC 153:6
violent Tory of the o. school RUSK 316:4
warn you not to grow o. KINN 211:10
older o. men declare war HOOV 183:1
oligarchy *aristocracy*, call it *o.* HOBB 180:8
extreme democracy or absolute o. ARIS 16:9
Olympian O. bolts DISR 118:15
omelette What a fuss about an o. VOLT 375:12
omitted o., all the voyage SHAK 330:14
omnibus man on the Clapham o. BOWEN 54:1
once o. is more than enough BIRCH 45:8
o. lead this people into war WILS 392:14
o. to every man and nation LOW 234:1
one encompassed but o. man SHAK 328:6
merely o. man fewer METT 257:8
o. as the hand WASH 379:2
O. man shall have one vote CART 77:9
O. realm, one people, one leader ANON 9:11
our majority…o. is enough DISR 120:17
win just o. for the Gipper GIPP 153:5
one-eyed o. man is king ERAS 133:10
only o. thing we have to fear ROOS 308:8
open enter the o. society CARM 76:17
If you o. that Pandora's Box BEVIN 43:5
o. covenants of peace WILS 392:15

open (*cont.*):
o. door HAY 171:2
with an o. mouth STEV 351:2
opening sending your o. batsmen HOWE 184:1
operating o. instructions O'RO 277:4
operative o. White House Position ZIEG 397:3
opinion being without an o. BAG 27:9
conforming to majority o. SCAN 320:6
gross and scope of my o. SHAK 325:4
man of common o. BAG 23:14
of one o. MILL 258:11
o. is truth filtered PHIL 292:4
o. one man entertains PALM 284:6
Our researchers into public o. AUDEN 21:3
Party is organized o. DISR 119:9
plague of o. SHAK 335:10
poor itch of your o. SHAK 324:4
public o. is a permeating influence BAG 24:1
representing no o. but their own WILS 392:9
respect public o. RUSS 316:8
sacrifices it to your o. BURKE 63:8
supported by popular o. CATT 78:6
They that approve a private o. HOBB 179:11
opinions by men's o., by blame FAB 134:6
delivers his o. CIC 95:5
music of our own o. STEV 351:3
o. of the majority PEEL 288:7
o. that are held with passion RUSS 316:6
so bad as their o. MACK 242:3
That he held the proper o. AUDEN 21:3
There are as many o. TER 360:6
opium o. of the people MARX 252:2
touches it as with an o. wand PAINE 282:12
opponent Never corner an o. LIDD 223:5
o. cannot be both honest ORW 278:12
opponents political o. MACL 243:6
purposes of his o. TROL 370:6
opportunism principally o. CHUR 86:3
opportunist What is an o. BISM 47:14
opportunities I seen my o. PLUN 294:6
our history, one of those o. GLAD 155:7
opportunity greatest o. DISR 120:18
I am a product of o. HEATH 173:10
open the gates of o. JOHN 196:7
o. is more powerful DISR 118:11
o. of taking decisions PARK 286:1
uses the most favourable o. BISM 47:14
oppose o. everything DERBY 114:1
pleasure of the opposition to o. MACL 243:5
opposing more in the wrong in o. BISM 46:5
opposition duty of an O. DERBY 114:1
every time the o. are asked MACL 243:7
government must needs be in O. JENK 194:10
make a figure by o. HAL 166:5
Minister or Leader of the O. DISR 121:9
O. is four or five years' HATT 170:3
o. means death TROT 370:14
O., on coming into power BAG 26:8
o. politician must at all times RIPP 306:3
O.'s about asking LYNN 235:1
phrase, 'Her Majesty's O.' BAG 24:14
phrase 'His Majesty's O.' HOBH 180:10
pleasure of the O. to oppose MACL 243:5
whole period in o. forgetting RIDL 305:4
without a formidable O. DISR 117:12
oppressed mind of the o. BIKO 45:4
oppression there is no limit to o. MENC 257:5
to violate would be o. JEFF 192:5
oppressive so o. and unjust BURKE 67:12
oppressor in the hands of the o. BIKO 45:4
o.'s wrong SHAK 325:8
revolutionary ends as an o. CAMUS 74:8
opprobrium term of o. MOYN 267:5
oppugnancy In mere o. SHAK 335:9
opulence private o. GALB 145:10
oracles lively o. of God COR 103:10
orange *quoted as 'Play the o. card'* CHUR 86:8
orang-outang o. or the tiger BURKE 65:9
orator I am no o., as Brutus is SHAK 330:8
No o. ever made an impression BAG 24:11
orators one of those o. CHUR 87:5
oratory appetite for o. GALB 146:9
contemporary parliamentary o. CRIT 104:6
object of o. alone is not truth MAC 236:5
order and a Democrat, in that o. JOHN 195:5
custom, in all line of o. SHAK 335:7
given me the o. of the boot CHUR 92:7
Good o. is the foundation BURKE 67:10
is defined by the word 'o.' METT 258:2
keep the government in o. SCAR 321:4
more devoted to o. than to justice KING 210:8
old o. changeth TENN 360:5
only war creates o. BREC 55:7
o. destroyed by a revolution TOCQ 367:3
o. reigns in Warsaw ANON 13:1
party of o. or stability MILL 259:1
renovation of the natural o. PAINE 282:11
social progress, o., security JOHN 195:2
ordered o. their estate ALEX 7:1
orders I gave them their o. WELL 384:5
ordinary behaviour of o. people TAYL 357:13
warn you not to be o. KINN 211:10
organ great o. of public opinion DISR 118:15
o. grinder BEVAN 41:2
organic committee is o. PARK 285:9
organization o. of idolatry SHAW 336:9
o. of non-violence BAEZ 23:11
o. with 'Liberation' LEVIN 222:13
systematic o. of hatreds ADAMS 2:7
organize mourning—o. HILL 178:9
organized party is o. opinion DISR 119:9
organs all the other o. GLAD 154:3
orgies emotional o. ROB 306:12

original expect any one to be o. BAG 23:13
none of the sound ideas is o. MACM 245:3
originality o. is taken to be a mark GALB 145:8
pluck and some o. WEBB 381:2
originals few o. and many copies TOCQ 366:6
origins disinter the o. of those JOUB 200:6
must have radical o. TREV 368:6
ornament o. to the civil order BURKE 67:6
orphan defeat is an o. CIANO 95:4
osprey As is the o. to the fish SHAK 325:1
ostrich America can not be an o. WILS 392:7
other guessing what was at the o. side WELL 384:10
spending o. people's money RAND 301:3
This o. Eden, demi-paradise SHAK 333:4
without that o.'s consent LINC 224:6
ought didn't o. never BEVIN 43:6
something o. to be done WELLS 385:5
tells me I o. to do BURKE 64:5
ourselves We have done it o. LAO-T 217:8
out one that's o. ROG 307:7
went o., like all good things DISR 121:1
out-argue we will o. them JOHN 198:7
outdoor gigantic system of o. relief BRIG 57:2
outlaw attacks from o. states REAG 302:1
outlawed known liar should be o. HAL 165:6
o. or exiled MAGN 247:3
out of touch say he is o. DOUG 123:5
outside than o. pissing in JOHN 196:9
out-vote we cannot o. them JOHN 198:7
over oversexed, and o. here TRIN 369:1
over-bearing o. and offensive VICT 374:7
overcame He o. evil with good KING 210:4
overcome we shall o. ANON 14:9
overpaid grossly o. HERB 176:9
o., overfed, oversexed TRIN 369:1
oversexed overpaid, overfed, o. TRIN 369:1
overstated being o. BERL 39:6
own every country but his o. CANN 75:1
for my words are my o. CHAR 83:1
for what they o. TAYL 357:15
Oxford king To O. sent a troop BROW 59:6
secret in the O. sense FRAN 142:11
To O. sent a troop of horse TRAPP 367:6
oxygen o. of publicity THAT 361:13
Ozymandias O., king of kings SHEL 337:9

pacific by p. means BRI 56:2
pacify My mission is to p. Ireland GLAD 154:7
pack can p. the cards BACON 22:5
made the peasantry its p. animal TROT 370:11
running with the p. BUTL 70:9
pack-horse posterity is a p. DISR 119:4
Paddington As London is to P. CANN 74:10
paeans yield to peace, laurels to p. CIC 95:7
Paganini village fiddler after P. NIC 272:5
page foot of the first p. SAND 320:2
paid Lord God, we ha' p. in full KIPL 212:10
pain gave p. to the bear MAC 239:2
pains by p. men come to greater BACON 22:11
no gains without p. STEV 349:9
paint layer of democratic p. TOCQ 365:3
painted gilded loam or p. clay SHAK 333:1
lath of wood p. to look like iron BISM 47:2
painting writing and p. CHUR 87:7
palace p. is not safe DISR 121:13
Palestine establishment in P. BALF 30:6
Palladium *P.* of all the civil JUN 201:3
palliate p. what we cannot cure JOHN 197:2
palm And bear the p. alone SHAK 328:3
dominion over p. and pine KIPL 212:11
paltered Nor p. with Eternal God TENN 360:2
pamphleteers not the age of p. HOGB 181:1
Pandora If you open that P.'s Box BEVIN 43:5
panics Tory party never p. HOSK 183:6
Panther Black P. Party NEWT 271:3
papacy p. is not other HOBB 180:9
paper hand that signed the p. THOM 363:3
I ran the p. [the *Daily Express*] BEAV 33:9
just for a scrap of p. BETH 39:8
reactionaries are p. tigers MAO 250:5
virtue of p. government BURKE 64:3
paper-mill thou hast built a p. SHAK 327:3
papers in the p. yesterday LYNN 235:7
paradise cannot catch the bird of p. KHR 209:4
paragraphs p. and plausibilities CARL 76:5
parapet could not see a p. without CRIT 104:7
parboiled place my p. head GRAH 159:2
parchment p., being scribbled o'er SHAK 327:2
rotten p. bonds SHAK 333:4
pardon God may p. you ELIZ 131:5
parens king is truly *p. patriae* JAM 189:10
parent poverty is the p. of revolution ARIS 16:8
Revolution a p. of settlement BURKE 66:9
parents illegitimate p. JOS 200:5
In peace, children inter their p. HER 177:3
lords whose p. were DEFOE 111:9
Paris no more Hoares to P. GEOR 149:9
P. was French TUCH 372:6
parish take his pension from his p. RUSK 315:5
parks p. are the lungs of London PITT 293:6
parliament build your house of P. WELL 385:2
cease to be returned to P. DISR 121:17
duty as a Member of P. BIGG 45:3
English P. is composed PAINE 282:12
government is a p. of whores O'RO 277:8
In P. it should not only MACL 243:5
most of the time by P. SCAR 321:1
multitude, such as mob, P. COBB 100:2
My desire to get here [P.] BOOT 52:5
myths of the British P. MAYB 254:6
not even p. SCAR 320:8

parliament (*cont.*):
pandered to by a supine p. RIDL 305:7
p. can do any thing but PEMB 289:12
P. itself would not exist SCAR 320:7
P. speaking through reporters CARL 76:7
prejudiced it may be, of p. SCAR 321:5
Take P. out of the history POW 297:8
They [p.] are a lot of hard-faced BALD 29:1
This P. is enough to discourage HEAD 172:3
want to have voices in P. RUSK 315:11
parliamentarian pleasure for a p. CRIT 104:4
parliamentary cage of the P. Labour Party DALT 108:9
contemporary P. oratory CRIT 104:6
next p. opportunity FOOT 138:9
P. government BAG 23:12
P. Government as the noblest DISR 119:17
P. leper WILS 390:7
unhappy bag of p. eloquence CARL 76:8
without party P. government DISR 119:18
parliaments heavier hand than kings and p. FRAN 142:1
In p., men wrangle HAL 166:3
mother of P. BRIG 56:7
parson become the world's p. HEAL 172:8
see a Whig in a p.'s gown JOHN 197:14
part p. of the solution CLE 98:2
play a p., any p., in its burial MACM 244:11
partiality With neither anger nor p. TAC 354:5
participate p. in politics PLATO 294:3
parties All political p. die at last ARB 15:9
both our political p. will bid BAG 27:4
P. come to power RIDL 305:4
P. must ever exist BURKE 64:9
ridiculousness of the division of p. RUSK 315:12
three p. there MAYB 254:6
two p. which divide the state EMER 133:2
warns the heads of p. ARB 15:8
parts *dignified* p. BAG 24:10
party best p. is but a kind HAL 166:4
competent to judge a political p. ROOS 310:5
conduct of a losing p. BURKE 67:13
each p. is worse than the other ROG 307:7
educate our p. DISR 119:12
effects of the spirit of p. WASH 379:11
extreme p. is most irritated BAG 27:11
false teeth in the p. manifestoes ROTH 314:2
fight again to save the P. we love GAIT 145:1
great p. is not to be brought HAIL 163:5
I always voted at my p.'s call GILB 152:4
meanness of which a political p. DISR 116:5
natural p. of government WILS 390:10
necessary nature of a political p. TROL 369:11
P. is little less HAL 166:6
P.... is not a faction or club POW 297:5
P. is organized opinion DISR 119:9
p. of order or stability MILL 259:1
p. platforms are contracts TRUM 371:9
p.'s over CROS 106:6
p. whose mission it is SAL 318:4
political p. in power SCAR 321:1
prove that the other p. is unfit MENC 257:4
put p. before country CREWE 104:2
responsibility of a political p. HAIL 163:4
Stick to your p. DISR 121:3
stupidest p. MILL 259:7
Then none was for a p. MAC 237:1
there is no P. line DJIL 122:3
This p. comes from the grass roots BEV 42:1
This p. is a bit like WILS 391:5
This p. of two BRIG 56:9
to heaven but with a p. JEFF 191:9
when any particular p. CHUR 93:9
Whichever p. is in office WILS 391:6
without a seat, without a p. CHUR 89:3
without p. DISR 119:18
with the majors in the p. MACM 244:9
pass cunning men p. for wise BACON 22:6
p. the ammunition FORGY 139:3
They shall not p. ANON 10:9
They shall not p. IBAR 186:7
passer *laisser p.* QUES 299:2
passeront *Ils ne p. pas* ANON 10:9
passes free speech, free p. BETJ 40:1
passion No p. so effectually robs BURKE 62:3
opinions that are held with p. RUSS 316:6
political p. ANON 11:9
such a p. SHAW 337:5
Passionaria La P. of middle-class HEAL 173:2
passionate full of p. intensity YEATS 395:6
passions All his p. were expressed WALP 377:12
more powerful and more lofty p. TOCQ 366:2
p. of men will not conform HAM 167:6
past cannot remember the p. SANT 320:4
controls the p. ORW 279:2
falsely imagined p. BORK 53:2
future but by the p. HENRY 176:6
have their roots in the p. TRUM 371:8
lament the p. BURKE 62:10
last day of an era p. YELT 396:4
no political p. MONC 261:9
nothing but the p. KEYN 207:9
plan the future by the p. BURKE 67:16
remember what is p. HAL 165:5
Utopia is a blessed p. KISS 214:11
pasture enough p. for all the sheep WALP 378:9
pastures green p. of the European VERW 374:1
paternal form of p. socialism MACM 244:1
p., or in other words MAC 236:7
paternalism lessons of p. CLEV 99:3
path p. of great principles BAG 24:2
patience my p. is now at an end HITL 179:7
not stamina but p. MAJOR 247:8

patient I am extraordinarily p. THAT 362:4
patrie Allons, enfants de la p. ROUG 314:3
patries *europe des p.* DE G 112:10
patriot Never was p. yet DRYD 125:12
p. on an empty stomach BRANN 55:5
steady p. of the world CANN 75:1
Such is the p.'s boast GOLD 157:3
Would the honest p. JEFF 192:6
patriotism history to his p. ADAMS 4:11
nothing but this—a larger p. ROS 312:8
p. in the female sex ADAMS 2:3
p. is a lively sense ALD 6:9
p. is a sort of religion TOCQ 365:4
p. is the last refuge JOHN 198:3
till you knock the p. out SHAW 336:19
patriots all these country p. BYRON 71:5
blood of p. and tyrants JEFF 191:7
p. are in the right WAUGH 380:5
so to be p. BURKE 63:6
this last effort of the p. ADAMS 3:6
pattern predetermined p. FISH 136:8
pause I p. for a reply SHAK 329:12
pawns p. are men CARL 76:10
pay *Equal P. for Equal Work* ANTH 15:6
Not a penny off the p. COOK 102:5
p. given to a state hireling JOHN 197:3
that we are made to p. for FRI 144:2
ulcer Man on 4 Ulcer p. EARLY 127:4
we shall p. any price KENN 204:2
paying p. the Dane-geld KIPL 213:4
price worth p. LAM 216:8
peace advocates of p. upon earth GEOR 149:6
arch of p. is morticed by no iron NIC 271:7
call it p. TAC 354:3
carry gentle p. SHAK 327:7
cherish a just and lasting p. LINC 227:1
Don't tell me p. has broken out BREC 55:10
enemies in war, in p. friends JEFF 190:6
find the solution for world p. MARS 251:1
for p. like retarded pygmies PEAR 287:4
fortunes in p. and in war CHUR 93:8
good war, or a bad p. FRAN 142:4
hasty inordinate demand for p. PEEL 288:10
have to take chances for p. DULL 126:9
I believe it is p. for our time CHAM 81:1
If p. cannot be maintained RUSS 317:2
If you want p., prepare for war VEG 373:7
ingeminate the word *P.* CLAR 96:3
In p., children inter their parents HER 177:3
In p.: goodwill CHUR 93:5
In the arts of p. Man is SHAW 336:5
in time of p. thinks of war ANON 10:4
Let us have p. GRANT 160:1
Let war yield to p. CIC 95:7
make war than to make p. CLEM 98:6
making p. is harder STEV 349:6
may not be a just p. IZET 188:5
merry songs of p. SHAK 327:9
nation is only at p. KING 211:6
nation shall speak p. unto nation REND 303:1
not to send p., but a sword BIBLE 44:5
only give us p. PITT 293:4
open covenants of p. WILS 392:15
p. at the price of NIC 272:1
p. between equals WILS 392:8
P., commerce JEFF 192:7
p., easy taxes SMITH 341:1
P., freedom, and liberty SHAK 329:7
P. hath her victories MILT 261:3
p. I hope with honour DISR 120:9
P. is a very apoplexy SHAK 324:11
P. is indivisible LITV 228:6
P. is much more precious SADAT 317:4
P. is nothing but slovenliness BREC 55:7
P., *n.* BIER 44:17
P., retrenchment, and reform BRIG 56:5
p. with honour CHAM 81:1
people want p. so much EIS 129:7
plunging into a cold p. YELT 396:5
prefers a negative p. KING 210:8
right is more precious than p. WILS 392:13
security and p. of each country JOHN 195:2
shameless Warwick, p. SHAK 327:4
taking a chance on p. BUSH 69:8
that we may live in p. ARIS 16:3
This is not a p. treaty FOCH 138:2
Thy banished p. SMOL 345:3
war is p. ORW 279:1
we cannot live alone, at p. ROOS 310:6
When p. has been broken ROOS 309:6
When there was p. AUDEN 21:3
work, my friend, is p. ROOS 310:8
world p. or world destruction BAR 32:4
yet it's interest that keeps p. CROM 105:10
peaceably p. if we can CLAY 97:3
peaceful p. coexistence FULB 144:4
peacefully moving p. towards DAWS 110:5
peach When a man wants a p. ASQ 18:9
peasantry But a bold p. GOLD 157:6
made the p. its pack animal TROT 370:11
peasants cricket with their p. TREV 368:2
pecker I want his p. in my pocket JOHN 196:8
Pecunia *p. non olet* VESP 374:2
Peel P. has no manners WELL 384:13
peer Not a reluctant p. BENN 36:1
p. is exalted into MAN PAINE 282:6
peerage We owe the English p. DISR 117:5
When I want a p., I shall buy it NORT 275:6
Peers House of P. GILB 152:7
My Lord in the P. will take BRO 57:8
we love our House of P. GILB 152:5
Peking relations with P. NIXON 274:7
pen mightier than the p. HOGB 181:1

pendulum vibration of a p. JUN 200:10
pennies P. don't fall from heaven THAT 360:12
penny Not a p. off the pay COOK 102:5
pension p. list of the republic CLEV 99:2
P. Pay given to JOHN 197:3
take his p. from his parish RUSK 315:5
Pentagon P., that immense FRAN 142:10
people About one-fifth of the p. KENN 206:3
And a new p. takes the land CHES 84:8
belongs to the p. LINC 225:7
city but the p. SHAK 324:7
common p. know MENC 256:8
contracts with the p. TRUM 371:9
does not suppose the p. good ROB 306:7
enthusiasm of the p. WELL 384:1
far more stupid than their p. EIS 129:6
fool all the p. some of the time LINC 227:8
fool too many of the p. THUR 364:8
For we are the p. of England CHES 84:7
from the interests of the p. LINC 224:2
good of the p. is the chief law CIC 95:6
government by the p. CAMP 74:3
government of the p., by the p. WYCL 395:1
great masses of the plain p. MENC 256:11
He who builds on the p. MACH 241:4
I am myself the p. ROB 306:4
include the support of the p. CLEV 99:3
indictment against an whole p. BURKE 64:2
in favour of the p. BURKE 62:11
land for the p. ANON 11:10
law for rulers and p. DAVIS 110:2
Let my p. go BIBLE 43:7
love of the p. BURKE 64:6
made for the p., made by the p. WEBS 382:2
many opinions as there are p. TER 360:6
more than half of the p. WHITE 386:6
My faith in the p. governing DICK 115:7
my p.'s happiness ELIZ 131:2
of the p., by the p. PAGE 280:7
one realm, one p., one leader ANON 9:11
p. are never so perfectly backed HAL 165:11
p. are the masters BURKE 65:5
p. as a source of sovereign SCAR 321:1
p. formed Two Nations DISR 118:3
p. govern themselves THI 363:2
p. is the true legislator BURKE 62:4
p. made the Constitution MARS 251:4
p. only know that they exist LAO-T 217:8
p. overlaid with taxes BACON 23:4
p.'s choice SHER 338:12
p. strong enough ROOS 309:5
p. that has licked BROG 57:5
pockets of the p. GLAD 156:2
power to the p. ANON 13:4
'Tis the p. marching on MORR 266:5
voice of the p. is the voice of God ALC 6:8
wasting the labours of the p. JEFF 192:10
We...are no petty p. YEATS 396:1
we were to set the p. free HEATH 173:7
What kind of a p. do they think CHUR 91:3
worship the p. BACON 22:3
peopled p. half the world SEEL 322:6
Peoria It'll play in P. ANON 11:4
perch Their p. and not their terror SHAK 332:5
perdition led to *p.* by a man WEST 385:8
pereat *fiat justitia et p. mundus* FERD 136:4
perestroika restructuring [*p.*] GORB 158:3
perfect entire and whole and p. SPR 348:1
p. democracy BURKE 67:4
perfectibility p. as a dream MILL 258:7
perfection Ideal p. GLAD 155:3
must function to p. MUSS 268:8
perfidious p. Albion XIM 395:2
Pericles what P. felt of Athens KEYN 207:3
perils adds to our p. MOUN 267:4
period p. of our dominion BURKE 65:9
p. of silence on your part ATTL 19:8
perish no vision, the people p. BIBLE 43:15
ordained that England shall p. ELIZ 131:6
p. together as fools KING 211:2
though the world p. FERD 136:4
venal city ripe to p. SALL 319:7
permanent p. indignation VAL 372:12
tell the p. officials HARC 168:3
permitted if a man were p. FLET 137:8
Whereas in England all is p. MEG 255:3
pernicious most p. race SWIFT 353:6
Perón had not been born P. PERÓN 290:6
perpetual p. quarrel BURKE 64:4
persecute p. a sect BAG 24:8
persecuted p. minority FRAN 141:7
persecution p. is not an original PAINE 282:9
p. produced MAC 238:13
persevering p. in error PEEL 288:11
person only one p. at a time FRAN 142:11
personal come in p. contact TAYL 358:11
personality political p. JENK 194:2
persons principles, rather than p. PAINE 283:8
perspiration p. of firm confidence FOOT 138:3
perspire Mr Gladstone may p. CHUR 86:4
persuade p. a multitude HOOK 182:5
persuading By p. others JUN 200:11
persuasion in what things p. only MILT 260:7
not truth, but p. MAC 236:5
P. is the resource of the feeble GIBB 151:12
pertness obliged to put up with p. DISR 116:6
petrified p. adolescence BEVAN 40:12
petticoat in my p. ELIZ 130:4
petty We...are no p. people YEATS 396:1
we p. men SHAK 328:4
petty larceny political p. DISR 118:13
petulance p. is not sarcasm DISR 118:16
pews Talk about the p. and steeples CHES 84:6

phantom p. of Lord Goderich DISR 120:14
philanthropist professed p. TROL 369:5
Philistines barbarians, P. ARN 17:2
from the P. proper ARN 17:4
philosopher p. may preach GIBB 152:2
philosophers p. are very regardless of expense PEEL 289:6
political p. KEYN 208:6
some p. have not maintained SWIFT 353:8
philosophy p. quenches them VOLT 376:2
This barbarous p. BURKE 66:17
Phrases P. make history here MAFF 246:8
phylacteries fly-blown p. ROS 312:13
picked hastily p. himself up CHUR 94:10
picking won't notice you're p. JOHN 195:6
pickle weaned on a p. ANON 13:12
picnic many apples short of a p. MAJOR 248:4
pictures You furnish the p. HEAR 173:5
pie You'll get p. in the sky HILL 178:8
piebald p. complexion CHUR 90:13
pies *eat one of Bellamy's veal p.* PITT 293:12
pigmies built by p. CHUR 89:5
pigs p. treat us as equals CHUR 94:11
pike freedom for the p. is death TAWN 356:1
pilgrims Land of the p.' pride SMITH 344:5
pillar p. of the State SOLZ 346:1
pillars four p. of government BACON 22:16
real p. of civilization MONN 263:1
pillow like the feather p. HAIG 163:1
pilot daring p. in extremity DRYD 125:5
dropping the p. TENN 359:6
replace the p. BAG 25:3
pin with a little p. SHAK 333:8
pinched Mrs Simpson's p. our king ANON 10:5
pine dominion over palm and p. KIPL 212:11
pinstripe have to come in a p. suit FEIN 136:2
pips until the p. squeak GEDD 148:7
piratical p. old bruiser HAIL 163:10
piss worth a pitcher of warm p. GARN 148:2
pissing inside the tent p. out JOHN 196:9
p. down your leg JOHN 196:12
pistol found the smoking p. CON 101:6
I reach for my p. JOHST 198:14
pitcher p. of warm piss GARN 148:2
Pitt P. is to Addington CANN 74:10
pity p. never ceases to be shown DRYD 125:10
place All rising to great p. BACON 22:13
fought for our p. in the sun WILH 388:9
Get p. and wealth, if possible POPE 295:7
In p. of strife CAST 78:3
men in great p. BACON 22:9
Observe degree, priority, and p. SHAK 335:7
our own p. in the sun BÜLOW 61:7
p. is given for the sake HAL 165:12
p., that great object SMITH 341:2
p. with power ROS 312:7
right man in the right p. JEFF 193:14
rising unto p. is laborious BACON 22:11
place-expectants Gratitude of p. WALP 378:7
places desire p. under one SHIP 339:7
Men in high p. TAYL 358:13
private faces in public p. AUDEN 21:1
plagues of all p. DEFOE 111:10
plain p., blunt man SHAK 330:8
plaintive p. treble DISR 118:15
plan p. the future by the past BURKE 67:16
p. to resist all planning OAK 276:3
rebuild it on the old p. MILL 259:6
rest on its original p. BURKE 65:2
planets heavens themselves, the p. SHAK 335:7
planning plan to resist all p. OAK 276:3
professed aims of p. HAYEK 171:6
plans finest p. are always ruined BREC 55:8
plant confidence is a p. of slow PITT 292:10
p. of rapid growth WASH 380:1
planted p. thick with laws BOLT 51:3
plateaus no p. KISS 214:7
platforms party p. are contracts TRUM 371:9
platitude p. is simply a truth BALD 29:2
Plato living in P.'s Republic CIC 95:5
P. is never sullen MAC 237:10
plausibilities p. bring votes CARL 76:5
plausibility confer a dreadful p. LAWS 219:2
plausible manufacturing the p. BALD 30:1
play better than a p. CHAR 83:2
It'll p. in Peoria ANON 11:4
Not only did we p. the race card SHAP 335:12
watch the men at p. CLEG 98:3
yet cannot p. well BACON 22:5
play'dst Thou p. most foully for't SHAK 331:10
played always p. the game SMITH 344:2
I p. by the rules of politics NIXON 275:1
your role is p. out TROT 370:12
playing p. fields of Eton WELL 384:11
please am to do what I p. FRED 143:4
p. myself or you HEND 174:5
To tax and to p. BURKE 64:15
pleasure gave p. to the spectators MAC 239:2
what is meant by the p. of life TALL 355:4
would afford them no p. MILL 258:7
pleasures English take their p. SULLY 352:7
two supreme p. in life ROS 312:9
plebeian importance of a p. leader DISR 118:18
plot Gunpowder Treason and p. ANON 13:2
This blessèd p., this earth SHAK 333:4
plots p., true or false DRYD 125:3
plotted rarely p. MACL 243:2
plough I must p. my furrow alone ROS 312:12
Men of England, wherefore p. SHEL 338:3
ploughed have p. the sea BOL 51:2
ploughman even the poorest p. CHAR 82:4
plowshares swords into p. BIBLE 43:18
plumage pities the p., but forgets PAINE 282:4

plumbers good p. NIXON 274:11
plutocracy not a p. of wealth YOUNG 396:7
plutocratic *like* p. government TAWN 356:2
Plymouth pious ones of P. EVAR 134:3
PM But he ended P. ATTL 20:9
only P. in England DALT 109:1
P.—whose motto LYNN 235:4
pocket in your neighbour's p. RUSK 315:6
in your p. or purse WILS 390:12
put the house in his p. GARV 148:6
want his pecker in my p. JOHN 196:8
won't notice you're picking his p. JOHN 195:6
pockets p. of the people GLAD 156:2
poem p. to the glory of beating WOLFE 393:5
poetry power corrupts, p. cleanses KENN 205:8
writing p. POW 297:3
You campaign in p. CUOMO 107:3
poets p. keep our mouths shut YEATS 395:5
point different p. of view NAP 269:5
points thousand p. of light BUSH 69:6
poised p. between a cliché MACM 244:6
poising p. every weight MARV 252:1
poison put p. in your coffee ASTOR 19:3
strongest p. ever known BLAKE 49:3
pole top of the greasy p. DISR 121:5
polecat semi-house-trained p. FOOT 138:7
police For the urban poor the p. HARR 169:6
p. can beat you SHAW 336:16
p. were to blame GRANT 159:5
policeman p. is there to preserve disorder DALEY 108:8
p.—whose utility SAL 318:9
terrorist and the p. CONR 102:3
world's p. HEAL 172:8
policies but rarely p. HURD 185:8
catastrophic, p. BAL 31:7
impossible p. RIDL 305:4
principles and p. POW 297:5
policy directing their own p. BAG 26:11
English p. is to float lazily SAL 317:7
exercise power and determine p. TREV 368:8
[foreign] p. is to be able BEVIN 43:4
from your p. do not wholly AESC 6:2
idea behind foreign p. O'RO 277:7
If the p. isn't hurting MAJOR 247:9
incomes p. alone JOS 200:2
kings will be tyrants from p. BURKE 67:2
My home p.: I wage war CLEM 98:4
not a p. of conciliation PARN 286:6
p. of the American government JEFF 193:15
p. of the good neighbour ROOS 308:9
state p., a cyclops with one eye COL 101:3
That p. is violent HUME 184:8
They seek a p. WAUGH 380:7
To defend a bad p. SAL 318:11
polite have no allies to be p. to GEOR 150:4
p. father of his people JAM 189:10
p. society smiles hopefully TAWN 356:3
politeness p. of kings LOU 233:4
politic must unavoidably be p. PEEL 287:8
political adventurer of modern p. history BUTL 70:2
All p. lives, unless they are cut POW 297:7
anyone's p. prospects HEAD 172:2
any p. doctrine TROL 370:7
beyond p. life itself ARIS 16:4
capacity for p. passion ANON 11:9
death of a p. economist BAG 24:4
distance from the p. situation RAK 300:2
entering p. life HEAD 172:3
expect me to have any p. future MONC 261:9
exudes from every p. pore FOOT 138:3
for fear of P. Economy SELL 323:8
get hold of the p. machinery CHOD 85:9
healthy state of p. life MILL 259:1
in excess it fills p. graveyards KINN 211:7
In our time, p. speech ORW 279:9
Man is by nature a p. animal ARIS 16:5
match p. expectations POW 296:5
no p. or ideological difference KENN 203:5
not a normal feature of p. life KILM 209:10
of p. life TROL 370:8
[Our] whole p. machinery BALF 31:2
points clearly to a p. career SHAW 336:13
p. campaigns ROB 306:12
p. country is like an American BAG 27:5
p. heads of departments HARC 168:3
p. image is like mixing cement MOND 262:2
p. language ORW 279:11
p. liberty in a citizen MONT 264:10
p. life dealing with humdrum THAT 361:7
p. ones are insoluble HOME 182:4
p. power grows MAO 250:4
p. power of another LOCKE 231:6
p. power of the sovereign TROL 370:3
p. thought, in France ARON 17:7
powerful p. personality JENK 194:2
religion with no p. power WOLFE 394:1
schemes of p. improvement JOHN 197:10
Science of P. Economy RUSK 316:2
social and p. problems BAL 31:8
test of any p. decision TREND 367:7
politically It is a loser p. NIXON 274:15
politician achieved by a p. LYNN 234:10
education of a p. CHUR 89:10
Every p. ought to sacrifice BURKE 67:11
forced to be a p. POW 297:3
geniality of the p. who for years MAUG 254:4
good p. is quite as unthinkable MENC 256:10
greatest art of a p. BOL 50:7
honest p. is one who CAM 73:6
I am not a p., I am a citizen STEV 349:5
like a scurvy p. SHAK 331:5
my life as a p. POW 297:14

nonpolitical speech by a p. NIXON 274:1
nostrils of an English Tory p. TROL 369:2
oldest, wisest p. THOR 364:4
opposition p. must at all times RIPP 306:3
pathetic as a p. who has MENC 257:1
p. has not to revenge BISM 46:7
p. has to simplify POW 297:12
p. is a man who understands TRUM 371:13
p. is an arse CUMM 107:2
p. is a person who approaches STEV 351:2
p. is a statesman POMP 295:1
p. never believes what he says DE G 112:12
p. performs upon the stage TAYL 356:10
p.'s corpse was laid away BELL 35:5
p. to complain about the press POW 297:9
p. was a person with whose LLOY 230:6
p. who steals PLUN 294:7
professional p. can sympathize POW 296:8
proper memory for a p. MORL 266:3
radical p. TROL 369:9

politicians conviction p., certainly BANC 32:1
done to death by p. CHES 83:8
don't want to die for p. THOM 364:6
fighting the p. MONT 265:4
great fault of our p. TROL 369:8
If p. lived on praise and thanks HEATH 173:9
left to the p. DE G 112:9
ninety percent of the p. KISS 214:6
Old p. chew on wisdom past POPE 295:6
P. also have no leisure ARIS 16:4
P. [are] a set of men LINC 224:2
P. are exiles GRIGG 161:9
P. are like monkeys LLOY 231:3
P. are the same all over KHR 209:6
p. in possessing whom TROL 369:7
P. in pursuit of votes GALB 146:10
P. neither love nor hate CHES 83:11
P. often believe that their world ROTH 314:1
P.' Syllogism LYNN 235:11
p. who wanted something BISM 46:10
poor if p. treat them FIELD 136:6
schemes of visionary p. BURKE 64:17
Seventeen unelected reject p. RIDL 305:7
tinhorn p. WHITE 387:3
to do with politics or p. CHUR 87:7
too many p. who believe ADAMS 2:5
When the p. complain that TV MURR 268:6
Where would we p. be POW 296:7
whole race of p. put together SWIFT 353:7

politics aim of practical p. MENC 256:9
All p., however, are based on REST 303:3
All p. is local O'NE 276:8
ascertainable facts, in p. PEEL 289:9
Being in p. is like being a football MCC 239:5
confound their p. ANON 9:9
definition of the art of p. ATTL 20:14
disentangle religion from p. TREV 368:9
do not go in for p. CAMUS 74:5
first part of p.? Education MICH 258:4
first requirement of p. is not MAJOR 247:8
focus of p. on real people HAVEL 170:5
From p., it was an easy step AUST 21:10
give his mind to p. SHAW 337:1
great reform in p. if wisdom CHUR 92:14
holy mistaken zeal in p. JUN 200:11
I approve his p. GIBB 151:14
I must study p. and war ADAMS 3:13
in America, the p. of happiness HUMP 185:5
In p. if you want anything said THAT 360:8
In p. I think it is wiser BIFF 45:2
In p. it is more blessed POW 296:6
in p. that you are much exposed BALD 29:11
in p. the middle way ADAMS 3:8
in p. there is no honour DISR 116:5
In p., there is no use looking CHAM 80:1
In p. you must keep running BUTL 70:9
invariably of the p. of the people BORR 53:3
invisible hand in p. FRI 144:1
In well-framed p., innovation BAG 27:7
I taste no p. in boiled and roast SMITH 344:7
I think that p. is worse MONT 265:2
I will not close my p. FOX 140:7
long time in p. WILS 390:8
Magnanimity in p. BURKE 64:7
marvellous in medieval p. MACM 245:12
Men enter local p. solely PARK 286:2
money that gushes into p. WHITE 387:2
mule of p. DISR 117:9
My p. are based...on things THAT 361:4
no consistency, except in p. BYRON 71:1
no sympathy in p. THAT 360:9
Nothing in p. is ever as good BOYLE 54:2
no true friends in p. CLARK 96:10
not the language of p. DISR 119:3
now in the centre of p. MOSL 267:2
objective of the science of p. ARIS 16:2
Our p. seem to be increasingly WALD 376:7
people who went into p. COOK 102:7
played by the rules of p. NIXON 275:1
P. are, like God's infinite mercy O'RO 277:2
P. are now nothing more JOHN 198:4
P. are too serious a matter DE G 112:9
P. are usually the executive BRIT 57:3
P., as a practice ADAMS 2:7
P. compels its votaries VAL 372:12
p. consists in ignoring facts ADAMS 3:1
p. grease the wheels TAWN 356:3
p. is about surviving LYNN 235:8
P. is for the present EINS 129:2
P. is just like show business REAG 301:6
P. is largely a matter BUTL 70:8
P. is not an exact science BISM 46:4
P. is not the art of GALB 145:12
P. is perhaps the only profession STEV 351:4

politics (*cont.*):
p. is present history FRE 143:5
P. is supposed to be REAG 301:8
P. is the art of acquiring GAND 147:2
P. is the art of looking BENN 35:8
P. is the art of preventing VAL 373:1
P. is the art of the possible BISM 46:6
P. is trying to get into office MCM 243:11
P. is war without bloodshed MAO 250:3
P., like religion, hold up JEFF 193:3
P. makes strange bedfellows WARN 378:11
p. of the left and centre JENK 194:4
p. of Versailles MONN 262:7
p. only one thing really counts HEAD 172:5
p. to a spectator sport GALB 146:4
practice of p. in the East DISR 116:8
refusing to participate in p. PLATO 294:3
same style of p. OAK 276:3
second in p. gets you oblivion NIXON 274:16
secret of p.? Make a good treaty BISM 46:3
talking p. after dinner DISR 120:4
theory of p. was Bismarck's KEYN 207:3
this P. thing ROG 307:7
times in p. when GALB 146:1
to do with p. or politicians CHUR 87:7
want to succeed in p. LLOY 229:12
war is the continuation of p. CLA 96:11
poll-taking so-called science of p. WHITE 386:7
poll tax *of the p.* THAT 362:15
pollution p. of democracy WHITE 387:2
Pomeranian P. grenadier BISM 47:10
pomp grinning at his p. SHAK 333:8
Vain p. and glory of this world SHAK 327:6
Pompey Knew you not P. SHAK 328:1
Pontius Pilate Christ crucified P. HOUS 183:7
pony piebald complexion of my p. CHUR 90:13
poodle Gentleman's p. LLOY 229:1
in a p. parlour PARR 286:10
poor better to be rich than p. CECIL 79:7
decent provision for the p. JOHN 197:12
For the urban p. the police HARR 169:6
Give me your tired, your p. LAZ 219:7
help the many who are p. KENN 204:3
laws grind the p. GOLD 157:4
make everybody p. SEN 323:12
My p. are happy PAINE 283:12
no longer works for the p. FIELD 136:6
none so p. to do him reverence SHAK 330:5
not that men are p. DU B 126:6
of the rich on the p. JEFF 191:5
peasant in my kingdom so p. HENR 175:5
p. fish MENC 257:3
p. have cried, Caesar hath wept SHAK 330:2
p. have no right RUSK 315:8
p. man at his gate ALEX 7:1
p. man loved the great MAC 237:1
p. people in rich countries BAUER 33:1
p. relations who are horribly ORW 278:5
p. to sleep under bridges FRAN 141:2
p. would be very little less SHAW 336:21
RICH AND THE P. DISR 118:2
rich richer and the p. poorer NEHRU 270:11
rich wage war it's the p. who die SART 320:5
You cannot help the p. LINC 227:7
poorest p. he that is in England RAIN 300:1
p. man may in his cottage PITT 292:9
Pope against the P. or the NUM BALD 29:12
P.! How many divisions STAL 348:5
Popish P. liturgy PITT 293:1
To tie a p. successor with laws HAMP 167:9
populace keep the p. alarmed MENC 256:9
philistines, and p. ARN 17:2
propriety give the name of p. ARN 17:5
When the p. is excited LA BR 216:2
popular base, common and p. SHAK 326:11
basis of p. government ROB 306:11
custom supported by p. opinion CATT 78:6
monarchical or p. HOBB 180:4
p. feeling TROL 369:4
regarded p. government BAG 24:3
restrain the p. sentiments PEEL 288:8
wars are p. MACD 240:3
popularity I don't resent his p. REAG 302:6
population balance of our p. JOS 200:3
one part of the p. LENIN 221:6
p., when unchecked MALT 248:9
populi *salus p. suprema est lex* CIC 95:6
salus p. suprema lex esto SELD 323:3
voice of God [*vox p., vox Dei*] ALC 6:8
porcupines throw a couple of p. KHR 209:7
pore from every political p. FOOT 138:3
poring Too much p. over maps SAL 319:2
pornography statistics as p. JENK 194:9
port p. is near WHIT 387:9
portal From out the fiery p. SHAK 334:1
portmanteau p. word of abuse TEBB 359:3
position Every p. must be held HAIG 163:2
positive p. peace KING 210:8
wish that he gave more p. signs BLUNT 49:7
possessed limited in order to be p. BURKE 65:1
possessions All my p. ELIZ 132:3
possibilities land of unlimited p. GOLD 157:1
possible art of the p. BISM 46:6
knowledge of the p. BEVAN 40:11
not the art of the p. GALB 145:12
p. you may be mistaken CROM 105:6
poster Kitchener is a great p. ASQ 18:10
posterity ancestry or hope of p. DONN 122:7
ancestry, or hope of p. POWER 298:1
enjoy what p. will say FRAN 142:3
looked upon by p. CLAR 96:5
Nation are the trustees of p. DISR 118:6
not go down to p. DISR 122:1
not look forward to p. BURKE 66:10

our forefathers, and p. ADAMS 5:2
p. is a pack-horse DISR 119:4
p. most in their debt INGE 187:6
p. will do justice DISR 121:9
Think of your p. ADAMS 4:5
post office efficiency of the p. SULL 352:5
postponing avoided simply by p. CHUR 94:16
postwar attitudes of p. funk TEBB 359:2
pot *chicken in every p.* HOOV 182:9
chicken in his p. every Sunday HENR 175:5
potent p. advocates of peace GEOR 149:6
Potomac All quiet along the P. MCCL 239:9
poultry lives of the p. ELIOT 130:1
pound p. here in Britain WILS 390:12
pounding Hard p. this, gentlemen WELL 384:3
poverty against hunger, p. MARS 251:2
it is possible to conquer p. JOHN 196:1
monarchies, in p. MONT 264:3
p. is the parent of revolution ARIS 16:8
setting him up in p. NAIDU 268:9
suffer so much p. and excess PENN 289:13
war on p. in America JOHN 195:10
power absolute p. ADAMS 4:3
absolute p. of preventing SAL 318:5
All p., each Tyrant, every Mob KIPL 213:5
all p. is a trust DISR 116:3
any man who has p. is led MONT 264:9
arts of p. and its minions CLAY 97:7
aspired to p. instead of influence TAYL 357:9
black p.... is a call CARM 76:16
but the act of p. BACON 22:14
candidates for p. PAINE 283:8
civil to persons in p. under her DERBY 114:3
command, p., and glory CIC 95:8
conception of the p.-state TEMP 359:5
constitutes the balance of p. NIC 271:7
corridors of p. SNOW 345:4
depositary of p. DISR 117:10
disastrous rise of misplaced p. EIS 129:8
drape over their will to p. HUXL 186:4
duty is to augment official p. BAG 26:10
enchanted chambers of p. LAND 217:4
encroachment of those in p. MAD 246:6
Everyone who desires p. MILL 259:10
For also knowledge itself is p. BACON 22:1
friend in p. is a friend lost ADAMS 2:8
from which the sun draws its p. TRUM 371:2
general are great toadies of p. TREV 368:7
generally, in the acquisition of p. RUSS 316:5
Giving money and p. O'RO 277:1
government, when it comes to p. SNOW 345:5
greater the p. BURKE 63:7
greed for p. normally met LEVIN 222:11
history of political p. POPP 295:12
holding, and wielding p. GAND 147:2
individual liberty is individual p. ADAMS 4:9
inherit when we come to p. BENN 36:4
in office but not in p. LAM 217:2
jaws of p. are always opened ADAMS 3:3
Johnson's instinct for p. WHITE 387:1
less the p., the greater the desire LEVIN 222:12
limitation of governmental p. WILS 391:11
lost, when the legislative p. GIBB 151:4
lust for p. ROOS 309:2
management of a balance of p. KISS 214:8
men live without a common p. HOBB 179:12
monarchs, whose p. seems MONT 264:1
most of the p. is in the hands ORW 278:5
mystery of the king's p. JAM 190:1
no hopes but from p. BURKE 65:3
once intoxicated with p. BURKE 67:14
only have p. over people as long SOLZ 345:10
opposition, on coming into p. BAG 26:8
outrun our spiritual p. KING 211:1
paltered with Eternal God for p. TENN 360:2
parties come to p. with silly RIDL 305:4
place without p. ROS 312:7
political p. grows out of the barrel MAO 250:4
political p. of another LOCKE 231:6
political p. of the sovereign TROL 370:3
politics of p. HAIL 163:9
p. can be rightfully exercised MILL 258:10
p. corrupts, poetry cleanses KENN 205:8
p. elite are those who decide MILLS 260:2
p. has risen up CALH 72:3
p. in trust DRYD 125:8
p. is an indispensable condition KEANE 202:5
P. is not a means ORW 279:7
P. is so apt to be insolent HAL 166:8
P. is the great aphrodisiac KISS 214:3
P.? It's like a Dead Sea MACM 245:7
p. of decision HEAD 172:5
p. of the crown BURKE 63:1
p. of the press NORT 275:7
p. over nothing HER 177:4
p. should always be distrusted JONES 199:2
p. tends to corrupt RUSK 315:4
P. tends to corrupt ACTON 1:9
p. to act according to discretion LOCKE 231:9
p. to endanger the public liberty ADAMS 3:5
p. to tax MARS 251:3
P. to the people ANON 13:4
p. which has dotted over WEBS 382:7
p. without conscience BRAD 54:5
P. without responsibility KIPL 214:1
religion with no political p. WOLFE 394:1
remorse from p. SHAK 328:9
responsibility without p. STOP 351:7
restless desire of p. after p. HOBB 179:10
road to p., credit BURKE 65:8
standing armies of p. RADC 299:5
strange desire to seek p. BACON 22:10
supreme p. must be arbitrary HAL 165:10
Those who exercise p. TREV 368:8

power (*cont.*):
Treasury is in p. WILS 391:6
Unlimited p. is apt to corrupt PITT 292:11
utility of monarchical p. BOSW 53:4
What p. have you got BENN 36:11
When p. to flattery bows SHAK 331:2
powerful p. and free TOCQ 365:6
rich society and the p. society JOHN 196:2
powers accumulation of all p. MAD 246:5
headmasters have p. CHUR 88:11
high contracting p. BRI 56:2
jurisdiction of two hostile p. MAC 236:6
legitimate p. of government JEFF 193:13
little-celebrated p. of Presidents GALB 146:13
new p. of the executive DENN 113:8
real separation of p. DENN 113:7
ultimate p. of the society JEFF 193:8
wars of the European p. MONR 263:5
pox gallows or of the p. WILK 389:1
practical government was a p. thing BURKE 64:17
power of sustained p. activity TAWN 355:7
p. men, who believe KEYN 208:6
we look at the p. GLAD 155:3
practice intention of putting it into p. BISM 48:1
put into p. GILM 153:1
wear and tear of p. TROL 370:5
praise If politicians lived on p. HEATH 173:9
Let us now p. famous men BIBLE 44:2
P. the Lord and pass FORGY 139:3
took the p. as a greedy boy MAC 236:9
praised less happy when being p. BALF 31:4
p., decorated, and got rid of CIC 95:13
pray day when I did not p. for them LEE 220:6
If I could p. to move SHAK 329:3
I p. for the country HALE 164:4
p., that this mighty scourge LINC 226:9
work and p., live on hay HILL 178:8
prayer Conservative Party at p. ROYD 314:7
One p. absorbs all others GLAD 155:8
people's p. DRYD 125:7
preachers I need p. I buy 'em LONG 232:6
preaching woman's p. is like JOHN 197:9
precedent From precedent to p. TENN 359:8
p. embalms a principle STOW 352:1
precious liberty is p. LENIN 221:11
right is more p. than peace WILS 392:13
This p. stone set in the silver SHAK 333:4
predictable seldom p. BERL 39:4
pre-eminence p. in her Colonial GEOR 149:5
preferences individual p. MILL 259:10
pregnant like being a little p. HEND 174:7
prejudices p. through the door FRED 143:3
respect the p. and habits GIBB 152:2
such of the proprietor's p. SWAF 353:3
prelate religion without a p. BANC 31:11
prelaty impertinent yoke of p. MILT 260:4
Premier great P. must add BAG 27:8
will probably be p. for years CHAN 81:7
preparation I need a week for p. WILS 392:18
no p. is thought necessary STEV 351:4
prerogative English subject's sole p. DRYD 125:14
first is law, the last p. DRYD 125:15
p. of the harlot KIPL 214:1
rotten as p. BURKE 63:1
that which is called p. LOCKE 231:9
prescience he lacked p. DISR 119:1
prescription discards P. DISR 117:6
presence conspicuous by its p. RUSS 317:3
p. on the field WELL 384:6
present know nothing but the p. KEYN 207:9
offers no redress for the p. DISR 117:6
politics is for the p. EINS 129:2
preservation p. of their property LOCKE 231:7
preserve p. contracts MELB 256:6
p. disorder DALEY 108:8
preserved it must be p. JACK 188:8
Presidency close to the P. DEAN 110:6
in the pursuit of the P. JOHN 196:5
one heart-beat from the P. STEV 350:8
runaway P. SCHL 321:6
Teflon-coated P. SCHR 321:8
wants the p. so much BROD 57:4
President All the P. is TRUM 371:5
America any boy may become P. STEV 350:6
anybody could become P. DARR 109:8
As P., I have no eyes but LINC 227:2
candidate for P. KENN 204:1
damned cowboy is P. HANNA 168:1
making the P. a czar SCHL 321:6
P. is Commander-in-Chief STEV 349:4
P. may slip without the state TOCQ 365:5
P. needs political understanding TRUM 371:10
P.'s hardest task is not to JOHN 196:6
P.'s spouse BUSH 69:3
P. who never told bad news KEIL 203:3
P. who thinks arms control SCHR 321:9
problems a P. has to face TRUM 371:8
rather be right than be P. CLAY 97:8
republican candidate for P. SIMP 340:7
security around the American P. MAIL 247:7
slept more than any other P. MENC 256:13
their P. is a crook NIXON 274:10
We are the P.'s men KISS 214:4
what did the P. know ANON 14:12
When the P. does it NIXON 274:13
who is the best P. PET 291:1
Presidents powers of P. GALB 146:13
press complain about the p. POW 297:9
freedom of the p. CHUR 94:7
freedom of the p. JEFF 192:8
freedom of the p. in Britain SWAF 353:3

freedom of the p. is guaranteed LIEB 223:6
free p. is not a privilege LIPP 228:4
liberty of the p. JUN 201:3
lose your temper with the P. PANK 284:11
popular p. is drinking in MELL 256:7
power of the p. is very great NORT 275:7
P. lives on disaster ATTL 20:10
To the p. alone JEFF 191:15
want not really a free p. RADC 299:6
where the p. is free JEFF 191:12
with the P. in a manner MELB 255:7
with you on the free p. STOP 351:11

pressure go out and put p. on me ROOS 310:7
relation between p. and resistance NIC 271:7

prestige doesn't work without p. DE G 112:1
points of p. MONN 262:8

pretender But who p. is BYROM 70:10

pretending p. that people DISR 118:4

pretexts tyrants seldom want p. BURKE 67:15

prevarication last dyke of p. BURKE 66:5

prevent our duty to try to p. it MILN 260:3
way to p. war is not to fear RAND 300:8

preventing art of p. people VAL 373:1
p. lamentable events SAL 318:5

prevents but in what it p. BAG 26:3

prey to hast'ning ills a p. GOLD 157:6

price All those men have their p. WALP 378:6
another man's p. increase WILS 391:3
If blood be the p. of admiralty KIPL 212:10
love that pays the p. SPR 348:1
p. of repression DU B 126:7
p. worth paying LAM 216:8
resides in the p. paid for office TOCQ 366:8

prices contrivance to raise p. SMITH 341:5

prick To p. the sides of my intent SHAK 331:8

pride idleness and p. tax FRAN 142:1
On either side it is p. TOCQ 365:1
to save its p. MEYER 258:3

priest guts of the last p. DID 116:1
guts of the last p. MESL 257:6
rid me of this turbulent p. HENR 175:7

priests dominion of p. PRICE 298:3
p. by the imposition MAC 237:7
p. have been enemies HUME 185:1
P. have nephews PEEL 289:7

prig not too much of the p. CROS 106:7

Prime Minister best P. we have BUTL 70:3
buried the unknown P. ASQ 18:7
capacity of a man ... [to be P.] TROL 370:9
Every P. needs a Willie THAT 362:12
fresh to be our war P. BALD 29:8
Great of Finchley, the P. herself HEAL 173:1
I think a P. has to be a butcher BUTL 70:5
It's no part of a P.'s duty CHAM 81:2
model of a modern P. HENN 175:2
more often than the P. BIRCH 46:1
next P. but three BELL 35:3
office of P. MACM 245:10
office of the P. is what its holder ASQ 18:5
power of the P. BENN 36:12
P. and the Cabinet SCH 322:3
P. has an absolute genius BEVAN 41:7
P. has had a very difficult GEOR 150:6
P. has nothing to hide CHUR 92:9
P. has resigned and Northcliffe ANON 10:6
P. is like the great banyan PATIL 287:2
P. is shuffling along HEAL 173:4
P. or Chancellor THAT 360:7
P. or Leader DISR 121:9
P. should be intimidating THAT 362:14
P. should give an example LLOY 230:11
radicals, we shall have you P. WILDE 388:8
second time the P. has got rid BIRCH 45:8
see a woman becoming a P. ASQ 18:11
turned-out P. MELB 255:5
upon the provinces of the P. MELB 255:7
when a British P. sneezes LEVIN 222:8

Prime Ministers Even P. CLARK 96:6
P. are wedded to the truth SAKI 317:6
P. can be easily disposed of JENK 194:7
P. have never CHUR 88:11
wild flowers, and P. BALD 29:3

primordial p. condition of liberty BAK 28:5

primus *p. inter pares* MORL 266:1

prince constitutional king is a p. BAG 26:2
Is in a p. the virtue MASS 254:1
p. sets himself up above MAYH 255:1
p. who gets a reputation NAP 269:6
two talents invaluable to a p. MAC 238:14
under the dominion of a p. HUME 184:9

Prince of Wales God bless the P. LINL 227:10

princes difficulties in p.' business BACON 22:8
p. and lords may flourish GOLD 157:6
p. ... have frequently engaged SMITH 343:2
p. in this case DAN 109:5
p. ought to leave MACH 241:9
That sweet aspect of p. SHAK 327:6
these her p. are come home SHAK 331:1
wade into the weakness of p. JAM 190:1

principis *indignatio p.* MORE 265:7

principle approves of something in p. BISM 48:1
call the 'falling domino' p. EIS 129:5
citizen is influenced by p. RAK 300:2
except from some strong p. MELB 256:1
good men to rise above p. LONG 232:7
He does everything on p. SHAW 335:13
precedent embalms a p. STOW 352:1
p. of the English constitution BLAC 48:8
protection is not a p. DISR 117:16
shrinks from p. DISR 117:6
when subjects are rebels from p. BURKE 67:2
women's rights is the basic p. FOUR 140:2

principles begins with that of its p. MONT 264:4
by reference to p. TAWN 355:7

principles (*cont.*):
certain political p. POW 297:5
Damn your p. DISR 121:3
embrace your Lordship's p. WILK 389:1
had either morals or p. GLAD 155:2
moral p., rather than persons PAINE 283:8
no retreat from the p. MURR 268:4
not men but p. PAINE 282:10
path of great p. is marked BAG 24:2
p. of a free constitution GIBB 151:4
p. that gave her birth WILS 392:11
Their p. are the same JOHN 198:10
We need good p. HAYEK 171:8
print in Britain means freedom to p. SWAF 353:3
licence to p. money THOM 363:8
printing gunpowder, p. CARL 75:12
namely, p., gunpowder BACON 22:2
thou hast caused p. to be used SHAK 327:3
priorities language of p. BEVAN 40:7
priority Observe degree, p. SHAK 335:7
prison black, you're born in p. MALC 248:7
just man is also a p. THOR 364:2
p. to which the emperor holds CUST 108:6
soul in p., I am not free DEBS 111:3
'Twixt a p. and a smile WOTT 394:8
prisoner object to your being taken p. KITC 215:1
passing on the p.'s life SHAK 332:6
thoughts of a p. SOLZ 345:9
prisoners p. of addiction ILL 187:4
privacy right of p. means anything BREN 56:1
private conduct of every p. family SMITH 342:6
economy of p. people SMITH 341:7
exertions of p. citizens MAC 239:3
invade the sphere of p. life MELB 256:3
kings neglect, that p. men enjoy SHAK 326:16
lovely in p. life BURKE 63:6
no liberty of p. opinion HAL 166:6
p. faces in public places AUDEN 21:1
p. opinion HOBB 179:11
p. opulence and public squalor GALB 145:10
p. property LIPP 228:2
p. property is a necessary TAWN 355:10
p. will governs ROB 306:5
right of p. judgement ADAMS 5:5
system of p. property HAYEK 171:4
privilege danger justified p. WAUGH 380:8
Englishman's heaven-born p. ARN 17:5
free press is not a p. LIPP 228:4
not a product of p. HEATH 173:10
Privileged P. and the People DISR 118:3
prize Far and away the best p. ROOS 311:6
p. in the lottery of life RHOD 304:2
prizes offer glittering p. SMITH 343:8
probabilities human p. FAIR 135:2
problem or you're part of the p. CLE 98:2
p. of the colour line DU B 126:5
p. very often for people CURR 107:6
problems government does not solve p. REAG 301:7
Others bring me p. THAT 362:9
p. a President has to face TRUM 371:8
social and political p. BAL 31:8
such p. as it can solve MARX 252:6
Two p. of our country CART 77:8
procedural p. standards FRAN 141:6
procedure p. is all the poor Briton PICK 292:6
process common market is a p. MONN 262:6
procreation Like the p. of eels SCH 322:3
prodigality public p. and misconduct SMITH 342:5
produce more than they p. HAYEK 171:10
product I am not a p. of privilege HEATH 173:10
process, not a p. MONN 262:6
production purpose of p. SMITH 342:1
upon the deep river of p. CHUR 88:9
productivity increase p. HEATH 173:6
profaned desolated and p. GLAD 154:12
professed p. philanthropist TROL 369:5
profession be the second oldest p. REAG 301:8
have a second p. NIC 272:9
professional p. politician POW 296:8
professors all conscientious p. PAINE 281:9
profit no p. but the name SHAK 326:2
profited p. from public service NIXON 274:10
profits best of all monopoly p. HICKS 178:6
civilization and p. go hand COOL 103:2
p. should belong TAWN 355:11
progress basic principle of all social p. FOUR 140:2
Congress makes no p. LIGNE 224:1
conservatism and p. TROL 369:7
disavows P. DISR 117:6
emphatically the history of p. MAC 238:3
European talks of p. DISR 118:9
party of p. or reform MILL 259:1
policy for promoting p. MAO 250:6
p. is not real GEOR 150:10
p. of evolution ADAMS 2:10
social p., order, security JOHN 195:2
progression Nothing in p. can rest BURKE 65:2
progressive p. country DISR 119:13
prohibited in Germany all is p. MEG 255:3
prohibition by the P. laws EINS 128:7
Communism is like p. ROG 307:8
more successful than P. BOAZ 50:2
of the '20s and '30s, P. BOAZ 50:1
P.... goes beyond the bounds LINC 224:4
proletarian p. socialist state LENIN 221:4
proletariat dictatorship of the p. MARX 252:5
promise Who broke no p. POPE 295:3
Whose p. none relies on ROCH 307:5
promised As the weird women p. SHAK 331:10
I've seen the p. land KING 211:4

You never reach the p. land CALL 72:9
promises make good their p. BAG 26:8
p. and panaceas ROTH 314:2
result of interviews, p. TAYL 358:2
vote for the man who p. least BAR 32:7
young man of p. BALF 31:6
propaganda purely for p. BEAV 33:9
propagandist p.'s purpose HUXL 186:5
propensities natural p. BURKE 68:1
proper held the p. opinions AUDEN 21:3
property consider himself as public p. JEFF 192:12
degrees and kinds of p. MAD 246:2
distinguished by rank or p. JUN 200:12
Every man holds his p. ROOS 311:11
from the dominion of p. GOLD 157:2
Greedy for the p. of others SALL 319:4
no right to the p. of the rich RUSK 315:8
not deprived of either p. MACH 241:6
our p. belongs to everybody RUSK 316:1
preservation of their p. LOCKE 231:7
preserve his p. LOCKE 231:5
private p. is a necessary TAWN 355:10
private p. was the original LIPP 228:2
P. is theft PRO 298:5
p.-owning democracy SKEL 340:9
p. they can call their own WASH 379:6
right of governing was not p. FOX 140:5
right of p. is the most important TAFT 354:10
system of private p. HAYEK 171:4
thereby makes it his p. LOCKE 231:4
through p. PANK 285:1
unequal distribution of p. MAD 246:4
Where p. is in question SAL 318:7
prophesy never safe to p. HEAD 172:2
prophet p. in Israel BIBLE 43:12
prophets ceased to pose as its p. POPP 295:10
proportions by p. true MARV 252:1
proposal describe a p. LYNN 235:5
propose cabinet does not p. ATTL 20:6
p. nothing DERBY 114:1
prose You govern in p. CUOMO 107:3
prospect p. of bettering MILL 259:14
prospects political p. HEAD 172:2
prosper Treason doth never p. HAR 169:1
prosperous nation great and p. BACON 23:9
p. or caring society HES 178:2
prostitutes small nations like p. KUBR 215:7
protect to p. the writer ACH 1:7
protection entitled to p. by law JACK 189:1
p. is not a principle DISR 117:16
p. is not only dead DISR 121:11
Protestant attacked me and the P. church NIEM 273:1
by my shoul 'tis a P. wind WHAR 386:3
I am the P. whore GWYN 162:7
preservation of the P. religion HAMP 167:9
printing, and the P. Religion CARL 75:12
P. ethic WEBER 381:7
P. religion BURKE 63:10
P. with a horse BEHAN 34:9
Protestantism All P. BURKE 63:10
proud man being too p. to fight WILS 392:4
prove p. anything by figures CARL 76:1
providence never could believe that P. RUMB 314:9
P. has not created mankind TOCQ 365:6
p. that protects idiots BISM 47:12
way that P. dictates HITL 179:5
province p. they have desolated GLAD 154:12
provinces defending those p. SMITH 342:3
provision decent p. for the poor JOHN 197:12
prudence p. never to practise TWAIN 372:9
Prussia military domination of P. ASQ 18:3
national industry of P. MIR 261:6
psychological p. rule KEYN 208:3
public After a lifetime in p. office GALB 146:7
aggrandizes the p. HUME 184:8
All my experience in p. life PEEL 288:3
as if I was a p. meeting VICT 374:8
at the expense of p. interests TAYL 358:11
besetting sin of p. men TAYL 358:11
burn your fingers in p. life BEAV 33:4
consult the p. good SWIFT 353:8
debate on p. issues BREN 55:11
does not describe holding p. office ACH 1:4
Every p. action CORN 103:8
excites the p. odium CLAY 97:7
failure of a listless p. SOLZ 346:4
fascination of a p. execution FOOT 138:4
for the p. good LOCKE 231:9
government and p. opinion SHAW 336:4
Great p. measures PEEL 289:10
He died by inches in p. ROS 312:6
If the British p. falls for this HAIL 163:6
loudest complainers for the p. BURKE 62:7
may be met with, in p. life TAYL 358:4
no p. institutions SMITH 343:1
one to mislead the p. ASQ 18:6
private faces in p. places AUDEN 21:1
private opulence and p. squalor GALB 145:10
promote the p. interest SMITH 342:4
p. be damned VAND 373:2
p. has to bear it PEEL 289:6
p. liberty HENRY 176:8
p. opinion BAG 24:1
p. prodigality and misconduct SMITH 342:5
p. servants, therefore TAYL 358:12
p. service carried on TAWN 355:6
p. welfare may require ROOS 311:11
p. will take care SULZ 352:8
qualities to be found in p. life DISR 121:19
require the p. expectation GALB 146:6
researchers into P. Opinion AUDEN 21:3

rainbow real r. coalition JACK 189:7
raise r. others to his own level TROL 369:6
r. the price of corn BYRON 71:5
rank However distinguished by r. JUN 200:12
r. is but the guinea's stamp BURNS 68:10
That unassailable holds on his r. SHAK 329:3
ranks closes its r. ORW 278:5
it must first close r. CARM 76:17
ransom Of the world's r. SHAK 333:4
rapine march through r. GLAD 154:16
r. and injustice SMITH 341:2
rascals r., would you live for ever FRED 143:2
rash r. and precipitate assent PEEL 288:4
rat Anyone can r. CHUR 88:5
Grey was like a r. ANON 9:4
Mr Speaker, I smell a r. ROCHE 307:4
not worth a r.'s squeak RUSK 315:11
ratio increases in a geometrical r. MALT 248:9
rational lack of r. conviction RUSS 316:6
rats r. of my own breed VOLT 376:4
ravished Or r. with the whistling POPE 295:5
razor fitter instrument than a r. PEEL 288:12
with an arse full of r. blades KEAT 202:6
reach *I r. for my pistol* JOHST 198:14
You never r. the promised land CALL 72:9
reaction Any r. which is TREV 368:6
reactionaries r. are paper tigers MAO 250:5
reactionary If r. measures are to BISM 47:7
R. is a somnambulist ROOS 309:7
recklessly r. steps BOOK 52:1
read Not that I ever r. them SHER 338:11
r. my lips: no new taxes BUSH 69:7
When I want to r. a novel DISR 121:18
Why r. the crystal BEVAN 40:8
You can r. WALP 378:10
readers by Bible r. *for* Bible r. BAIN 28:3
ready necessity of being *r.* LINC 225:9
Reagan Ronald R.... is attempting SCHR 321:8
real focus of politics on r. people HAVEL 170:5
hatreds which sound so r. TROL 370:8
realization r. of tomorrow ROOS 310:9
realm one r., one people, one leader ANON 9:11
this r., this England SHAK 333:4
reap r. the whirlwind BIBLE 44:1
reappraisal r. of basic United States DULL 126:8
reaps seed ye sow, another r. SHEL 338:4
rearming Germany was r. BALD 29:10
reason beyond the bounds of r. LINC 224:4
by their feelings than by r. ADAMS 5:6
Come now, let us r. together JOHN 196:11
dictates of r. and justice HAM 167:6
dominion of r. PRICE 298:3
influence of mere r. PEEL 289:10
r., and justice, tells me BURKE 64:5
R. and the Imagination MAC 236:6
R. herself will respect GIBB 152:2
R. to rule, but mercy to forgive DRYD 125:15
We know no r. why gunpowder ANON 13:2
With reasonable men, I will r. GARR 148:5
reasonable after r. discussion CHUR 93:11
figure of 'The R. Man' HERB 177:1
will to be rightful must be r. JEFF 192:5
With r. men, I will reason GARR 148:5
reasoning r. of tyrants GIBB 151:8
reasons R. are not like garments ESSEX 134:2
r. will certainly be wrong MANS 250:1
twenty r. why I can't BEVIN 43:1
rebel die like a true-blue r. HILL 178:9
I am *still* a r. BROWN 59:5
What is a r. CAMUS 74:6
rebelled have already r. GIBB 151:8
rebellion bring the r. to an end WILS 390:11
if r. was the certain consequence MANS 249:6
little r. now and then JEFF 191:6
r. against the United States LINC 225:11
R. lay in his way SHAK 326:5
R. to tyrants BRAD 54:8
rum, Romanism, and r. BURC 62:2
rebels One final tip to r. NIC 272:9
r. are our countrymen again GRANT 159:8
subjects are r. from principle BURKE 67:2
rebirth r. of the Union WILS 392:6
rebuild no use in attempting to r. MILL 259:6
receiver corrupts both the r. BURKE 66:13
recession It's a r. when TRUM 371:14
spend your way out of a r. CALL 72:8
reclamation It is land r. WILS 391:4
recognition We are fighting for r. MALC 248:8
reconciliation silence and r. MAC 238:8
recovery *green shoots of r.* LAM 217:1
recreational r. activities BOAZ 50:2
red better r. than dead ANON 9:1
r. men scalped each other MAC 239:4
We'll keep the r. flag flying here CONN 101:7
your raiment all r. MAC 236:3
redress r. by mob law LINC 224:3
redtape r. talking-machine CARL 76:8
refined most r. citizens SHEL 338:6
reform cured by r. or revolution BERL 39:4
fringe in all r. movements ROOS 311:13
great r. in politics if wisdom CHUR 92:14
party of progress or r. MILL 259:1
r. has dished it DISR 120:16
retrenchment, and r. BRIG 56:5
sets about r. TOCQ 367:3
To innovate is not to r. BURKE 68:4
reformation plotting some new r. DRYD 125:2
total r. is wanted in England PAINE 282:3
reforms beneficial r. THAT 362:15
odds we'll get r. are zero PEROT 290:10
refuge patriotism is the last r. JOHN 198:3
refuse thrice r.: was this ambition SHAK 330:3
war will cease when men r. ANON 14:6
wretched r. of your teeming shore LAZ 219:7

register r. of the crimes GIBB 151:6
regret Old Age a r. DISR 117:8
regrets series of congratulatory r. DISR 120:10
regulate r. matters of the mind TRUM 371:6
regulations greatest avalanche of r. BOOK 52:2
ten thousand r. CHUR 94:14
Reich *ein R., ein Volk, ein Führer* ANON 9:11
German R. is made BISM 47:5
reign George VI's r. WAUGH 380:10
His lazy, long, lascivious r. DEFOE 111:8
Long to r. over us HOGG 181:2
prince who begins early to r. BAG 26:2
reigned I have r. with your loves ELIZ 132:1
reigning capable of r. if only TAC 354:8
reigns king r., and the people THI 363:2
reinforcement r. of the State CAMUS 74:7
reins throw the r. over their necks CLAY 97:10
reject To elect, and to r. PAINE 283:7
rejoice Just r. at that news THAT 361:6
relation No cold r. is a zealous BURKE 67:9
r. of men dominating men WEBER 381:8
relations personal character and r. NAP 269:7
recognising the r. MILL 259:9
r. with Peking NIXON 274:7
relief system of outdoor r. BRIG 57:2
relieve chance to r. yourself ANON 12:9
relieved are r. SHAK 326:1
religion As to r., I hold it to be PAINE 281:9
black face and a different r. EDW 128:2
But the r. most prevalent BURKE 63:10
cult is a r. with no political WOLFE 394:1
disentangle r. from politics TREV 368:9
dominion of r. GOLD 157:2
feature of *any* r. PAINE 282:9
Freedom of r. JEFF 192:8
my r. is to do good PAINE 283:2
patriotism is a sort of r. TOCQ 365:4
politics as well as in r. JUN 200:11
politics, like r. JEFF 193:3
prefer fox-hunting—the wisest r. HAIL 163:3
r. is allowed to invade MELB 256:3
R.... is the opium of the people MARX 252:2
r., justice, counsel BACON 22:16
R. may in most of its forms RUSS 316:11
r. of humanity PAINE 283:9
r. of Socialism BEVAN 40:7
r. without a prelate BANC 31:11
reproach to r. and government PENN 289:13
religions r. considered man TOCQ 366:5
religious all r. revolution WEBER 381:10
relish deal closely and with r. MACL 242:6
reluctant Not a r. peer BENN 36:1
remedy dangerous r. FAWK 136:1
force is not a r. BRIG 57:1
prefer the grievance to the r. PEEL 289:5
r. our *enemies* have chosen SHER 339:1
Things without all r. SHAK 332:1
'Tis a sharp r., but a sure one RAL 300:5
remember Please to r. the Fifth ANON 13:2
r. what is past HAL 165:5
will little note, nor long r. LINC 226:3
remembered something to be r. ADAMS 3:6
would you like to be r. POW 297:11
remorse r. from power SHAK 328:9
remove not malignant and r. it WAUGH 380:9
render r. therefore unto Caesar BIBLE 44:7
rendezvous r. with destiny ROOS 308:10
renewed perpetually r. LIPP 228:5
Reno'd king's moll R. ANON 11:7
renounce I r. war FOSD 139:6
renovation r. of the natural order PAINE 282:11
renown land of just and old r. TENN 359:8
rent r. is that portion RIC 304:4
tear-wrung millions—why? for r. BYRON 71:6
repartee always the best r. DISR 118:8
repeal r. of bad laws GRANT 160:2
repeat condemned to r. it SANT 320:4
repel retard what we cannot r. JOHN 197:2
replace r. the pilot of the calm BAG 25:3
reply I pause for a r. SHAK 329:12
report false r., if believed MED 255:2
reporters speaking through r. CARL 76:7
reporting r., rather than debating HOGG 181:3
representation taxation and r. CAMD 73:5
taxation without r. is tyranny OTIS 279:14
representative being your r. BELL 35:2
drollery called a r. government DISR 118:7
Your r. owes you BURKE 63:8
representing r. the citizenship MACD 240:7
repression less than the price of r. DU B 126:7
reproach leave affairs of r. MACH 241:9
reproofs Even r. from authority BACON 22:12
republic England is a disguised r. BAG 27:2
essence of the R. ROB 306:9
good citizen in this R. ROOS 311:3
great R. is a Government FORD 138:12
If a r. is small, it is destroyed MONT 264:6
more corrupt the r. TAC 354:6
Only Love the Beloved R. FORS 139:5
r., if you can keep it FRAN 142:8
r. is a raft AMES 8:2
republican God is a R. and Santa O'RO 277:3
no Democratic or R. way LA G 216:5
on r. principles SHAW 335:13
R. candidate for President SIMP 340:7
R. form of Government SPEN 347:5
r. is the only form JEFF 191:10
respectable R. cloth coat NIXON 273:6
understood by r. government TOCQ 365:8
Republicans If they [the R.] STEV 350:1
We are all R. JEFF 192:4
We are R. and don't propose BURC 62:2
republics characteristic of small r. BOL 51:1
R. end in luxury MONT 264:3

R. weak BAG 25:9
repulsive Roundheads (right but r.) SELL 323:5
reputation Dear for her r. SHAK 333:4
spotless r. SHAK 333:1
requirement first r. of politics MAJOR 247:8
re-rat ingenuity to r. CHUR 88:5
researchers r. into Public Opinion AUDEN 21:3
resent I don't r. his popularity REAG 302:6
reservations no mental r. LINC 225:6
reserved I am r. for some end CLIVE 99:8
residence r. within ANON 9:13
resign says he won't r. GALB 146:2
resignation Always threatening r. BEAV 33:10
by death are few; by r. none JEFF 192:9
Has he got a r. in him BUTL 70:1
resigned Prime Minister has r. ANON 10:6
resist r. authority BAG 27:3
resistance act of intellectual r. O'BR 276:5
I am for r. by the *sword* CLAY 97:1
liberty is the history of r. WILS 391:11
refinement on the principle of r. BURKE 63:10
relation between pressure and r. NIC 271:7
r. of established ideas BERL 39:6
r. of the adversaries STAL 348:3
resolution In war: r. CHUR 93:5
r. on reflection WALP 377:10
resort God's infinite mercy, a last r. O'RO 277:2
resources r. of civilization GLAD 154:15
rock of the national r. WEBS 382:6
respect cease to r. each other TAYL 357:15
fail to get r. MACH 241:7
impartial r. for the rights BAG 27:10
insult their self-r. TAWN 355:12
respected r. persons occasionally HURD 185:8
respecter God is any r. of persons BROWN 59:2
respond To r. to evil HAVEL 170:6
responsibility Collective r. LYNN 235:9
liberty means r. SHAW 336:8
lively sense of collective r. ALD 6:9
power without r. KIPL 214:1
r. for action GALB 145:5
r. of a political party HAIL 163:4
r. without power STOP 351:7
rest all the r. were little ones ELIZ 131:9
resting history knows no r. places KISS 214:7
restricted *R.* means LYNN 235:7
restrictions finding greater r. KEIL 203:4
restructuring idea of r. [*perestroika*] GORB 158:3
results more for routine than for r. BAG 26:9
presenting the r. ROSS 313:4
retail r. mind in a wholesale LLOY 230:7
retaliation policy of r. PARN 286:6
retard r. what we cannot repel JOHN 197:2
reticence It is a r. GLAD 155:12
retirement final r. from the stage MACM 245:14
there must be no r. HAIG 163:2
retreat no r. from the principles MURR 268:4
not r. a single inch GARR 148:3
retrenchment peace, r., and reform BRIG 56:5
retrograde r. if it does not advance GIBB 151:13
retrospective r. or utopian ARON 17:7
return I shall r. MAC 235:12
revelation r. is necessarily limited PAINE 283:6
revenge Gerald Ford as his r. ABZUG 1:2
not to r. what has happened BISM 46:7
ranging for r. SHAK 329:9
take r. for slight injuries MACH 241:2
revenue abundant streams of r. WEBS 382:6
almost the whole public r. SMITH 342:5
Instead of a standing r. BURKE 64:4
Internal R. Service SULL 352:5
reverence mystic r. BAG 24:9
so poor to do him r. SHAK 330:5
take away the mystical r. JAM 190:1
revolt It is a big r. LA R 218:1
r. by all means MACM 244:10
revolution After a r., you see HAL 165:8
age of r. and reformation JEFF 192:8
cured by reform or r. BERL 39:4
day after the r. AREN 15:10
fear that the R., like Saturn VERG 373:8
I entered into this R. BROWN 59:5
make peaceful r. impossible KENN 204:11
may be fatal to a r. TOCQ 366:9
No, Sire, a big r. LA R 218:1
not the leaders of a r. CONR 102:4
poverty is the parent of r. ARIS 16:8
religion from politics in a r. TREV 368:9
restrained tyrants, averted r. BENN 36:8
r. is not the same MAO 250:2
r. of rising expectations CLEV 99:4
safeguard a r. ORW 279:7
served the cause of the r. BOL 51:2
social order destroyed by a r. TOCQ 367:3
time to stop a r. STEV 350:4
white heat of the technological r. WILS 390:5
You've had a r. GEOR 150:7
revolutionaries R. are more formalistic CALV 73:4
r. are potential ORW 278:4
revolutionary can't feel fierce and r. LINK 227:9
continent of r. change BUSH 69:9
Every r. ends as an oppressor CAMUS 74:8
fine r. phrases KHR 209:8
on the eve of r. crises BOOK 52:1
r. government is the despotism ROB 306:8
r. right to dismember LINC 225:7
r. will become a conservative AREN 15:10
revolutionists age fatal to R. DESM 114:4
revolutions collapse of the r. ROB 307:1
main cause of r. INGE 187:9
modern r. have ended CAMUS 74:7
not a nursery of future r. BURKE 66:9

revolutions (*cont.*):
R. are celebrated BOUL 53:6
R. are not made PHIL 291:8
R. have never lightened SHAW 336:6
R. in this country MACL 243:2
r. never go backward SEW 324:1
share in two r. is living PAINE 283:10
What were formerly called r. PAINE 282:11
reward act worthy of r. BROWN 59:1
should be well fed with r. TAYL 358:12
rhetoric death, without r. SIEY 340:4
rhetorician sophistical r. DISR 120:11
Rhine you think of the R. BALD 29:7
riband Just for a r. to stick BROW 60:1
rich cannot make everybody r. SEN 323:12
Chief Justice was r., quiet MAC 238:7
convenient time to tax r. people LLOY 229:13
forbids the r. FRAN 141:2
Great Britain is not r. enough REED 302:10
if the incomes of the r. SHAW 336:21
interfered in behalf of the r. BROWN 59:1
it is better to be r. than poor CECIL 79:7
poor by destroying the r. LINC 227:7
poor people in r. countries BAUER 33:1
prey of the r. on the poor JEFF 191:5
R. AND THE POOR DISR 118:2
r. enough to pay over 75% HEAL 172:7
r. have no right RUSK 315:8
r. in a more precious treasure MAC 237:7
r. man in his castle ALEX 7:1
r. man makes a bonny traitor PAINE 282:2
r. men rule the law GOLD 157:4
save the few who are r. KENN 204:3
tend to make the r. richer NEHRU 270:11
toward the r. society JOHN 196:2
When the r. wage war SART 320:5
which people can still get r. REAG 301:11
riches best r., ignorance of wealth GOLD 157:6
material and spiritual r. KHR 209:8
rid decorated, and got r. of CIC 95:13
riddle r. wrapped in a mystery CHUR 90:1
ride if you cannot r. two horses MAXT 254:5
ridiculous from the sublime to the r. NAP 269:9
no spectacle so r. as the British MAC 237:8
Ridley Be of good comfort Master R. LAT 218:5
rien *r.* LOU 233:2
right almost always in the r. SMITH 344:10
as a nation being so r. WILS 392:4
be on the r. side and lose GALB 146:1
beyond doubt that they are r. VAN 373:3
defend to the death your r. VOLT 375:11
exercise their constitutional r. LINC 225:7
folly of hereditary r. in kings PAINE 281:2
forgive those who were r. MACL 243:1
generalities of natural r. CHO 85:8
God has more r. to be obeyed JOHN 195:1
greed is r. WEIS 383:6
half of the people are r. WHITE 386:6
if r., to be kept r. SCH 322:2
know what is r. JOHN 196:6
law is demanded as a r. ROOS 311:7
majority never has r. on its side IBSEN 186:8
man of the r. MOSL 267:2
my r. is retreating FOCH 138:1
natural r. of all to the ballot ANTH 15:7
New South Wales R. WRAN 394:10
no r. in the circus MAXT 254:5
no r. to strike against the public COOL 103:1
of no government by divine r. HARR 169:7
our country, r. or wrong DEC 111:4
our r. as well as our duty PANK 284:10
put the r. man in the r. place JEFF 193:14
rather be r. than be President CLAY 97:8
r. is more precious than peace WILS 392:13
R.... is the child of law BENT 37:7
'r.' means nothing but PLATO 294:2
r. must unavoidably be politic PEEL 287:8
r. of the ignorant man CARL 76:3
r. to be consulted BAG 26:1
r. to be heard HUMP 185:4
r. to be let alone BRAN 55:2
r. to do everything the laws MONT 264:8
r. to leave any country ANON 9:13
r. to say what one pleases BLACK 48:4
r. which goes unrecognized WEIL 383:4
Roundheads (R. but Repulsive) SELL 323:5
secure of private r. DRYD 125:11
unalienable, indefeasible, divine r. ADAMS 3:4
When I am r., I get angry DE G 112:5
with firmness in the r. LINC 227:1
righteous armour of a r. cause BRYAN 60:4
rightful will to be r. JEFF 192:5
rights absolutes in our Bill of R. BLACK 48:3
adverse to the r. of other citizens MAD 246:3
Bill of R. was not ordained JORD 199:4
certain unalienable r. ANON 14:7
equal in dignity and r. ANON 8:4
equal r. JOHN 195:8
extension of women's r. FOUR 140:2
natural r. is simple nonsense BENT 37:8
refuses to defend his r. JACK 188:6
respect for the r. of all BAG 27:10
r. inherent and inalienable JEFF 191:1
r. of an Englishman JUN 201:3
r. of the smaller nationalities ASQ 18:3
theories about the r. of man BURKE 66:14
trusted to safeguard human r. SCAR 320:8
violates the inalienable r. of man ROB 306:6
war with the r. of mankind JEFF 191:10
Where all your r. become CAS 78:2
ring They now *r.* the bells WALP 378:5
When we let freedom r. KING 210:11
riot r. is at bottom KING 211:3

rule (*cont.*):
we prefer r. by amateurs ATTL 20:12
ruled others be r. ARIS 16:7
rulers conduct of their r. ADAMS 3:4
law for r. and people DAVIS 110:2
Of the best r. LAO-T 217:8
r. have no authority from God MAYH 254:7
rules by any hypercritical r. LINC 225:6
I played by the r. of politics NIXON 275:1
man of genius r. STEP 349:3
minutes r. the roost ANON 10:8
We need fixed r., not fixers HAYEK 171:8
ruling hated the r. few BENT 37:11
in the hands of the r. class STAL 348:3
refresh their r. class TREV 368:5
rum r., Romanism, and rebellion BURC 62:2
r., sodomy, prayers CHUR 93:7
rumour this, the sound and r. MORR 266:5
rumours wars and r. of wars BIBLE 44:8
rump r. Parliament—so called SELL 323:6
run country was r. by two men ROTH 313:7
I don't r. in a race MACL 243:8
In the long r. we are all dead KEYN 207:6
Now Teddy must r. KENN 206:5
They get r. down BEVAN 40:13
runner-up no second prize for the r. BRAD 54:6
running all their r. dogs MAO 250:7
can't keep on r. from labour JACK 189:8
keep r. with the pack BUTL 70:9
Rupert Prince R. DISR 117:14
R. of Debate BULW 62:1
R. of the Rhine MAC 236:4
russet-coated plain r. captain CROM 105:3
Russia action of R. CHUR 90:1
between R. and British India SAL 317:8
in R., Communism SOLZ 346:3
legislation which outlaws R. REAG 301:13
Make a good treaty with R. BISM 46:3
proletarian socialist state in R. LENIN 221:4
R. can be an empire BRZ 61:3
R. has two generals NICH 271:5
R.'s future HERZ 177:8
Whoever has really seen R. CUST 108:7
Russian not to embrace the R. CHAN 81:8
R. Ambassador CHAN 81:9
R. autocracy turned upside down HERZ 177:7
Russians keep the R. out ISMAY 188:4
R. and the Americans TOCQ 365:9

sabre keenness of his s. WALP 377:8
sack S. the lot FISH 137:3
sacked we are all s. CLARK 96:6
sacred facts are s. SCOTT 322:4
only s. thing FRAN 141:3
reserved for s. texts KAUF 202:3
sacrifice give an example of s. LLOY 230:11
great pinnacle of s. LLOY 229:6
makes undaunted the final s. SPR 348:1
people being asked to s. GING 153:3
refused a lesser s. MARY 253:7
s. to the graces BURKE 67:11
Still stands Thine ancient S. KIPL 212:11
Too long a s. YEATS 395:7
sacrificed s. to conciseness JOHN 197:5
sacrificers s., but not butchers SHAK 328:12
sacrifices s. it to your opinion BURKE 63:8
sacrilege consecrated s. DISR 119:16
sacrilegious Most s. murder SHAK 331:9
sad tell s. stories of the death SHAK 333:8
saddle put Germany in the s. BISM 46:8
saddled millions ready s. RUMB 314:9
sadly take their pleasures s. SULLY 352:7
sadness shade of s. WHIT 388:5
safe National Health Service is s. THAT 361:5
s. for democracy WILS 392:12
s. for diversity KENN 205:4
s. for hypocrisy WOLFE 393:6
s. to be unpopular STEV 350:7
safeguard one s. DEM 113:2
s. of the West WORD 394:6
safeguards destroy the juridical s. HAYEK 171:9
s. acceptable to all nations TRUM 371:4
s. of liberty have been forged FRAN 141:8
safer much s. for a prince MACH 241:3
s. than a known way HASK 170:2
safety by a politician, so has s. LYNN 234:10
every man shall eat in s. SHAK 327:9
obtain a little temporary s. FRAN 141:9
's. first' does not mean BALD 29:4
s., honour, and welfare CHAR 82:8
said if you want anything s. THAT 360:8
sailed never s. with *me* before JACK 189:3
saint seem a s. when most I play SHAK 334:11
saints Christ and His s. slept ANON 12:5
salad shit can turn to chicken s. JOHN 195:4
salmon s.'s going upstream WHITE 387:1
smoked s. and tinned s. WILS 390:4
saloon last chance s. MELL 256:7
s. keepers were Democrats GRE 161:2
salus *S. populi suprema est lex* CIC 95:6
this sentence, *s. populi* SELD 323:3
salutes see if anyone s. it ANON 11:12
salvation commence the s. of Europe PITT 293:8
mankind's s. lies exclusively SOLZ 345:11
not the s. of the Union WILS 392:6
Samaritan remember the Good S. THAT 362:1
same facing in the s. direction ROST 313:6
we must all say *the s.* MELB 256:2
sanctions financial s. WILS 390:11
sanctuary classes which need s. BALD 29:3
sandhills Everest among the s. ASQ 18:8

sang I s. a king out of three WHAR 386:4
sanguinary suffer by a s. quarrel BAG 28:1
sank They s. my boat KENN 205:11
Sansculotte *bon S. Jésus* DESM 114:4
Santa Claus going to shoot S. SMITH 343:6
in the dark besides S. HOOV 182:11
S. is a Democrat O'RO 277:3
sat everyone has s. CUMM 107:2
when they have s. down CHUR 87:5
You have s. too long here CROM 105:8
Satanic Among these dark S. mills BLAKE 49:5
satirist s. may laugh GIBB 152:2
saucepan dance like fishes in a s. KHR 209:5
savage almost a s. TOCQ 365:2
savaged s. by a dead sheep HEAL 172:10
save destroy the town to s. it ANON 11:3
God s. the king HOGG 181:2
helped s. the world KEYN 208:7
if you want to s. yourselves BALD 29:6
little less democracy to s. ATK 19:4
nobly s., or meanly lose LINC 226:1
nothing will s. WHIT 387:7
to s. the Party we love GAIT 145:1
to s. the Union LINC 226:2
To s. your world AUDEN 21:6
saved they only s. the world CHES 84:10
to be s. in this World HAL 165:3
savings If you strike at s. CHUR 88:8
say s. what you think TAC 354:7
They are to s. what they please FRED 143:4
we must all s. *the same* MELB 256:2
what they are going to s. CHUR 87:5
saying as bad as we'd been s. KENN 204:9
scabbard threw away the s. CLAR 96:1
scabbards leapt from their s. BURKE 66:15
scabs Make yourselves s. SHAK 324:4
scaffold truth forever on the s. LOW 234:2
scandal exposing a sewage s. LAW 219:1
scandalous merry monarch, s. ROCH 307:6
scarecrow not make a s. of the law SHAK 332:5
scarlet raise the s. standard high CONN 101:7
scene this our lofty s. SHAK 329:6
scent whiff of s. LLOY 230:2
sceptered this s. isle SHAK 333:4
schedule My s. is already full KISS 214:2
schemes most s. of political JOHN 197:10
Schleswig-Holstein S. question PALM 284:7
scholarship slender indications of s. CHUR 88:10
school erecting a grammar s. SHAK 327:3
every fucking grammar s. CROS 106:5
s. of Manchester DISR 121:14
went to s. without any boots BULM 61:6
schoolboy Every s. knows who MAC 238:6
schools hundred s. of thought MAO 250:6
science dismal s. CARL 76:9
founded an entire s. of Political RUSK 316:2
objective of the s. of politics ARIS 16:2
politics is not an exact s. BISM 46:4
s. of diplomacy consists ADAMS 4:10
so-called s. of poll-taking WHITE 386:7
stick to s. BEVIN 42:8
typical triumph of modern s. WAUGH 380:9
scientific Our s. power has outrun KING 211:1
s. revolution WILS 390:5
scores bridge s. in his head BUTL 70:6
scorn think foul s. that Parma ELIZ 130:9
scorning s. the base degrees SHAK 328:10
scotched We have s. the snake SHAK 332:1
Scotchmen S. are to Englishmen PEEL 288:15
Scotland grapes can be raised in S. SMITH 342:7
stands S. where it did SHAK 332:3
scoundrel last refuge of a s. JOHN 198:3
scoundrels ten obvious s. MENC 257:3
scrap s. of paper BETH 39:8
screaming Wild men s. through LLOY 229:11
scribblers teenage s. LAWS 219:4
Scripture contrary to S. TAWN 355:11
scum glittering s. CHUR 88:9
mere s. of the earth WELL 384:7
sea complaining about the s. POW 297:9
dominion of the s. COV 103:11
fed our s. for a thousand years KIPL 212:10
floats in a s. of ethics WARR 379:1
I am very much at s. CARS 77:3
in a s. of glory SHAK 327:6
revolution have ploughed the s. BOL 51:2
smiling surface of the s. PLUT 294:9
squires ride slowly towards the s. CHES 84:8
stone set in the silver s. SHAK 333:4
to the English that of the s. RICH 305:3
water in the rough rude s. SHAK 333:6
willing foe and s. room ANON 15:3
seagreen s. Incorruptible CARL 75:9
seals receives the s. of office ROS 312:9
seas troubled s. of thought GALB 145:9
seasons man for all s. WHIT 388:6
season-ticket held a s. AMERY 7:6
seat s. in the House of Commons DISR 120:18
this s. of Mars SHAK 333:4
without an office, without a s. CHUR 89:3
seated wiser when he was s. KEYN 207:4
second Finishing s. in politics NIXON 274:16
first in a village than s. at Rome CAES 71:10
have a s. profession NIC 272:9
in a race to run s. MACL 243:8
In war there is no s. prize BRAD 54:6
not a s. on the day COOK 102:5
not provide for first and s. class WILL 389:6
s. office of government JEFF 191:13
s. oldest profession REAG 301:8
secrecy greatest aid to s. TAYL 358:9
s. and a free TRUM 372:3
secret concept of the 'official s.' WEBER 381:11
s. in the Oxford sense FRAN 142:11

secret (*cont.*):
s. may be sometimes best kept TAYL 358:8
s. of happiness BRAN 54:10
s. of politics BISM 46:3
secretary s. stays and gets thinner ANON 12:12
secrets not to protect s. LYNN 235:6
sect It found them a s. MAC 238:13
persecute a s. and it holds BAG 24:8
sectaries nation of s. DISR 117:11
security common s. PAINE 282:14
freedom can make s. secure POPP 295:11
order, s. and peace JOHN 195:2
Our watchword is s. PITT 293:5
s. around the American MAIL 247:7
s. for life and property TAWN 355:9
s. in a flock of sheep CHUR 89:6
seditions surest way to prevent s. BACON 23:1
see can't s. a belt without hitting ASQ 19:2
day I was meant not to s. THAT 361:10
go and s. General Grant LEE 220:5
To s. the things thou dost not SHAK 331:5
We had better wait and s. ASQ 18:1
seed s. however broadcast PARK 285:5
s. ye sow, another reaps SHEL 338:4
seed-time s. of continental union PAINE 281:5
seek desire to s. power BACON 22:10
We still s. no wider war JOHN 196:3
seem to s. active LAW 218:6
seen I have s. war ROOS 309:1
s. to be done HEW 178:5
segregation s. now, s. tomorrow WALL 376:9
self Infusing him with s. SHAK 333:8
self-assertion s. abroad WAUGH 380:4
self-censorship s. becomes GALB 146:7
self-evident truths to be s. ANON 14:7
self-government tyranny of s. DISR 118:12
self-interest propelled by s. BAG 28:2
self love their s. SMITH 341:4
self-preservation s. in the other JEFF 193:9
self-protection number, is s. MILL 258:8
self-respect starves your s. PARR 286:11
self-satisfaction smug s. BALD 29:4
self-sufficiency s. at home WAUGH 380:4
sell To no man will we s. MAGN 247:4
selling *s. the family silver* MACM 245:11
semi-house-trained s. polecat FOOT 138:7
semi-royal s. millionairess CHAN 81:10
semper *s. aliquid novi Africam* PLINY 294:5
Sic s. tyrannis BOOTH 52:3
senator make you feel like a s. O'RO 277:5
S., you're no Jack Kennedy BENT 38:3
United States S. JOHN 195:5
senators I look at the s. HALE 164:4
s. burst with laughter AUDEN 21:5
send s. these, the homeless LAZ 219:7
senior execution of a s. colleague CLARK 96:9
sensation create a s. BROWN 58:5
sense good s. and the good faith GLAD 154:13
Let's talk s. to the American STEV 349:9
pretensions to common s. SHEL 337:6
s. kept breaking in TAYL 357:14
senseless worse than s. things SHAK 328:1
sensibilité *no word equivalent to* s. PALM 284:8
sentenced s. to death BEHAN 34:10
sententiae *Quot homines tot s.* TER 360:6
sentiment interest, not s. CHES 83:11
sentiments imaginative s. BAG 24:9
restrain the popular s. PEEL 288:8
separate as s. as the fingers WASH 379:2
forever s. GRANT 160:3
Never wholly s. in your mind BURKE 66:2
s. and equal station JEFF 190:7
separately all hang s. FRAN 142:2
separation impel them to the s. JEFF 190:7
make any real s. of powers DENN 113:7
nor are we fighting for s. MALC 248:8
prepare for a s. QUIN 299:3
seraglio s. of eunuchs FOOT 138:5
serious war is too s. a matter CLEM 98:7
Sermon S. on the Mount BRAD 54:4
servant born to be a s. TOCQ 367:2
master and s. CHUR 88:6
s. to the devil SISS 340:8
servants s. of the public GOW 158:5
talent of choosing his s. well MAC 238:14
thrice s.: s. of the sovereign BACON 22:9
serve better to s. a well-bred lion VOLT 376:4
I love to s. my country GIBR 152:3
s. our country ADD 5:8
They also s. who only stand MILT 261:5
To s. your captives' need KIPL 213:2
will not s. if elected SHER 339:4
served Had I but s. my God SHAK 327:8
have them s. to him CHUR 89:11
service aid of public s. TREV 368:1
s. and conduct of the commonwealth BURKE 63:6
s. of my love SPR 348:1
s. of our great Imperial family ELIZ 132:4
s. of the nation POMP 295:1
servitude freedom and not s. BURKE 64:1
session while the legislature is in s. ANON 12:10
setter s. up and puller down SHAK 327:4
setting against a s. sun SHAK 335:4
settlement Revolution a parent of s. BURKE 66:9
s. of America ADAMS 3:2
settling without s. it JOUB 200:7
seven Even the Almighty took s. CHUR 92:4
have the s. minutes COLL 101:5
please your Majesty, s. weeks POPH 295:9
s. feet of English ground HAR 169:4
seventy Oh, to be s. again CLEM 98:8

sewage exposing a s. scandal LAW 219:1
sewer and not the s. BIFF 44:18
sewer midst of this putrid s. TOCQ 365:2
s. and not the sewage BIFF 44:18
sewing broader than a s.-needle NIC 272:2
sex legal subordination of one s. MILL 259:8
sexes of the two s. GIBB 151:7
shackles s. and restraints GOLD 157:2
shade Within its s. CONN 101:7
shadow but it also casts a s. CHUR 91:2
shadows s. on county [cricket] MAJOR 248:2
shake rise up, and s. off LINC 224:5
Shakespeare That S. spake WORD 394:5
shaking entrusted to the s. hand VICT 374:6
shall His absolute 's.' SHAK 324:6
shambles accountable s. HUNT 185:7
shame blush of s. WHIT 388:5
monument of s. CHUR 89:5
now bound in with s. SHAK 333:4
Tory s. BEVAN 41:8
shameful s. conquest of itself SHAK 333:4
shameless most s. thing BURKE 67:4
shape our dwellings s. us CHUR 92:3
shaped s. by this one man CHUR 93:8
shapely It wiggles, it's s. ERWIN 134:1
share Thou its ruin didst not s. DOD 122:5
shares fair s. for all, is Labour's call JAY 190:5
sharks We are all s. circling CLARK 96:10
sharp s. remedy, but a sure one RAL 300:5
sheath We shall never s. the sword ASQ 18:3
shed under a s. JOHN 198:11
sheep enough pasture for all the s. WALP 378:9
savaged by a dead s. HEAL 172:10
s. are born carnivorous FAG 135:1
s. in sheep's clothing CHUR 94:17
s. on the way to the butcher CHUR 89:6
s. to pass resolutions INGE 187:5
Your s., that were wont to be MORE 265:5
sheet old England's winding s. BLAKE 49:4
turn over the s. SAND 320:2
shepherd Wilson is the nation's s. SPR 348:2
shepherds s. and butchers VOLT 375:7
shift let me s. for my self MORE 265:9
shine men who s. in a faction HAL 166:5
shines s. brightly as a king SHAK 332:11
ship bigger and more expensive s. CHUR 91:1
good old s. of the Union LINC 225:4
s. has weathered every rack WHIT 387:9
S. me somewheres east of Suez KIPL 212:8
ships far distant, storm-beaten s. MAHAN 247:6
s. empty of men NIC 271:6
shit pile of s. in a silk stocking NAP 270:4
s. can turn to chicken salad JOHN 195:4
shits he knew who the s. were CLARK 96:8
shiver s. looking for a spine KEAT 202:9
shock And we shall s. them SHAK 331:1
great s. around the age of 5 BALD 28:6
shoot s., if you must WHIT 388:5
s. me in my absence BEHAN 34:10
they shout and they s. INGE 187:8
shoots green s. of economic spring LAM 217:1
shop in the s. window WILS 391:10
shopkeepers for a nation of s. SMITH 341:6
nation of s. NAP 270:1
nation of s. are very seldom ADAMS 5:4
shopocracy abuse the s. NORTH 275:5
shore refuse of your teeming s. LAZ 219:7
shores s. of modern Conservatism HENN 175:1
short I shall be but a s. time tonight BALD 29:9
nasty, brutish, and s. HOBB 180:2
s. decisive war LYND 234:9
shortage s. of coal and fish BEVAN 40:5
shorter make you s. by the head ELIZ 130:7
shot My God! They've s. our fox BIRCH 45:6
shots best s. VOLT 375:8
shoulder looking over his s. BAR 32:9
shifted it to another s. SHAW 336:6
s. to s. on a burning deck MACL 243:6
shoulders on the s. of the saint WEBER 382:1
shout send forth a joyous s. MAC 236:3
s. and they shoot INGE 187:8
s. with the largest DICK 115:1
shouting tumult and the s. dies KIPL 212:11
show politics is just like s. business REAG 301:6
showing it is worth s. DANT 109:7
shriller I hear a tongue, s. SHAK 328:2
shrimp until a s. learns to whistle KHR 209:1
shrunk s. to this little measure SHAK 329:8
shut Men s. their doors SHAK 335:4
sick enterprise is s. SHAK 335:8
side for the good or evil s. LOW 234:1
on the s. of the angels DISR 119:10
sides works both s. of the street ROOS 310:5
siege beats back the envious s. SHAK 333:4
sight safely out of s. GALB 146:8
signed hand that s. the paper THOM 363:3
I s. my death warrant COLL 101:4
never s. off BEAV 33:10
significance No personal s. LINC 225:12
signposts s. to the socialist Utopia CROS 106:4
signs positive s. of his awareness BLUNT 49:7
silence easy step to s. AUST 21:10
ensure their s. GALB 146:13
golden Gospel of s. MORL 265:11
It is my day of s. GAND 147:6
occasional flashes of s. SMITH 344:9
period of s. on your part ATTL 19:8
s. of the law HOBB 180:5
silenced you have s. him MORL 265:10
silencing justified in s. mankind MILL 258:11
silent great s. majority NIXON 274:6
impossible to be s. BURKE 66:4
laws are s. in time of war CIC 95:12
Paris was French—and s. TUCH 372:6

treachery with a s. on its face THAT 362:13
'Twixt a prison and a s. WOTT 394:8
smiling fear the s. surface PLUT 294:9
Smith chuck it, S. CHES 84:6
Smithfield *Canterbury or S.* WALP 377:11
smoked s. salmon and tinned WILS 390:4
smoke-filled in a s. room DAUG 109:9
in a s. room SIMP 340:7
smoking found the s. pistol CON 101:6
smote He s. them hip and thigh BIBLE 43:9
snake We have scotched the s. SHAK 332:1
snatched He s. the lightning shaft TURG 372:7
snatching instead of s. his victuals CHUR 89:11
sneezes British Prime Minister s. LEVIN 222:8
snipe s. from the great Windsor NIC 271:8
snobbish not be guided by the *s.* VICT 374:7
snobs impudent s. AGNEW 6:6
snored Coolidge only s. MENC 256:13
snows Said our Lady of the S. KIPL 213:1
soapflakes going to sell Jack like s. KENN 206:1
soar creep as well as s. BURKE 68:5
sober compulsorily s. MAGEE 247:1
My mother, drunk or s. CHES 84:1
social new s. contract CALL 72:7
Piecemeal s. engineering POPP 296:2
serious source of s. unrest FRI 143:11
s. and economic experiment HOOV 182:7
s. and political problems BAL 31:8
s. contract ROUS 314:4
s. contract is left-wing DEBR 111:1
S. Contract is nothing more WELLS 385:3
s. life of great peoples CHUR 88:14
s. movements BOOK 51:7
s. position of those he meets TOCQ 365:10
s. progress, order JOHN 195:2
with a s. position ORW 277:11
socialism Can S. *possibly* STAL 348:4
democracy and s. are means NEHRU 270:10
don't really believe in S. GRIM 162:3
elephant pit of s. POW 297:2
form of paternal s. MACM 244:1
If democratic s. cannot secure FOOT 138:9
lots of ways to get s. KINN 212:3
Marxian S. must always remain KEYN 207:8
religion of S. BEVAN 40:7
restating our s. in terms of WILS 390:5
S. can only arrive by bicycle VIER 375:3
S. does not mean ORW 278:1
s. is not a stage beyond ROB 307:2
S. is nothing but the capitalism SPEN 347:7
s., its major alternative BERG 38:5
s. wandering aimlessly HEAL 172:6
s. would be worth nothing TAYL 356:5
s. would not lose its human DUBC 126:3
This is not S. SNOW 345:6
socialist build a s. society NYER 276:2
even when it is not s. TAYL 356:5
flourishing s. culture MAO 250:6
In the blood of the s. CROS 106:7
right signposts to the s. Utopia CROS 106:4
s. believes that it is better CECIL 79:7
S. philosophy is affected CHUR 88:8
s. state in Russia LENIN 221:4
typical S. is...a prim little man ORW 277:11
socialists We are all s. now HARC 168:2
society altering the *shape* of s. ORW 278:4
any particular s. TOCQ 366:5
bonds of civil s. LOCKE 231:8
build a socialist s. NYER 276:2
Corinthian capital of polished s. BURKE 67:6
democracy a s. TAWN 356:2
enter the open s. CARM 76:17
free s. is a s. where it is safe STEV 350:7
great chessboard of human s. SMITH 341:3
happiness of s. is the end ADAMS 3:10
If a free s. cannot help KENN 204:3
I get civilized s. for it HOLM 181:7
in a free s. it is master BEV 42:5
law of motion of modern s. MARX 252:8
No arts; no letters; no s. HOBB 180:2
No s. can survive GING 153:4
no such thing as s. THAT 362:2
one honest man to s. PAINE 281:4
Our s. distributes itself ARN 17:2
prosperous or caring s. HES 178:2
slow and quiet action of s. TOCQ 365:8
s. begins to act PAINE 282:14
s. exists where no happiness CUST 108:7
s. is in an organized conspiracy DOUG 124:4
s. is indeed a contract BURKE 67:5
s. needs to condemn a little MAJOR 248:1
s. would be a hell MILL 259:11
unable to live in s. ARIS 16:6
upward to the great s. JOHN 196:2
We would have a magpie s. CHUR 94:3
When s. requires to be rebuilt MILL 259:6
sodomy rum, s., prayers CHUR 93:7
soft Everybody in America is s. CHAP 82:1
s. under-belly of the Axis CHUR 91:11
soil grown from the s. BEV 42:1
powers of the s. RIC 304:4
sold I would have s. all I had CROM 105:1
what cannot be s.—liberty GRAT 160:5
Who never s. the truth TENN 360:2
soldier old s. of Tippecanoe MORR 266:4
summer s. PAINE 281:10
Your friend the British s. SHAW 336:3
soldiers if you believe the s. SAL 318:1
old s. never die MAC 235:14
solicitor few words to the s. PITT 292:8
solid s. for fluidity CHUR 89:7
solidity give an appearance of s. ORW 279:11
solution conditions for its s. MARX 252:6
either part of the s. CLE 98:2

s. more time with my family RIDL 305:5
s. more time with your family THAT 362:8
s. your way out CALL 72:8
spending s. other people's money RAND 301:3
s. the public money COOL 103:6
spider laws are like s.'s webs ANAC 8:3
spin Let the great world s. for ever TENN 359:7
spine shiver looking for a s. KEAT 202:9
spirit appeals to the Dunkirk s. WILS 390:2
bold s. in a loyal breast SHAK 333:1
'Brutus' will start a s. SHAK 328:5
done to break his s. HOLL 181:4
effects of the s. of party WASH 379:11
I believe that the s. of Dunkirk WILS 390:9
never approached my s. METT 257:9
Thy s. walks abroad SHAK 330:15
spirits Would ruffle up your s. SHAK 330:10
spiritual not being a s. people MANC 249:2
Spite In S. of Everything ZIEG 397:2
splendid It has been a s. little war HAY 171:1
s. and a happy land GOLD 157:7
splits legalize it and it s. BAG 24:8
spoils But it s. one's eye HAL 166:13
Then s. were fairly sold MAC 237:1
to the victor belong the s. MARCY 250:8
spoke He s. for an hour GARV 148:6
spoken never have s. yet CHES 84:7
spoon *Why doesn't he use a s.* LLOY 230:3
spoons faster we counted our s. EMER 133:4
sport shall Caesar bleed in s. SHAK 329:6
spot look, with a s. I damn him SHAK 330:12
spouse as the President's s. BUSH 69:3
spring green shoots of economic s. LAM 217:1
Treasury is the s. of business BAG 24:12
springs s. of the government MONT 264:13
spur I have no s. SHAK 331:8
spurs all bridle and no s. TAYL 358:4
squabbling s. nationalities ROOS 311:14
squalid s. nuisance in time of war CHUR 92:8
squalor opulence and public s. GALB 145:10
square Men must turn s. corners HOLM 181:6
to be given a s. deal ROOS 311:5
squeezed s. as a lemon is s. GEDD 148:7
squire Bless the s. and his relations DICK 115:2
squires last sad s. ride slowly CHES 84:8
world of hedges, s. and parsons BRY 60:9
stabbed My God, I've been s. INGH 188:2
stabbing s. himself in the back LEWIS 223:3
stability party of order or s. MILL 259:1
small republics is s. BOL 51:1
two roads to international s. KISS 214:10
stables s. are the real centre SHAW 336:17
staff s. of three thousand BIRCH 45:7
Stag S. at Bay with the mentality LEVIN 222:6
stage lags the vet'ran on the s. JOHN 196:14
retirement from the s. MACM 245:14
stagecoach bit like an old s. WILS 391:5
stair by a winding s. BACON 22:13
stairs kicked up s. HAL 165:1
stake deep s. they have BURKE 64:6
s. driven through O'BR 276:4
s. in the country WIND 393:1
we have at s. PITT 293:9
Stalin guilt of S. GORB 158:2
stalks starvation that s. FOSD 139:6
There he s. CHUR 95:2
stamps kill animals and stick in s. NIC 272:7
stand British soldier can s. up SHAW 336:3
By uniting we s. DICK 115:8
Here s. I LUTH 234:6
intended *to s.* DISR 116:10
Never s. when you could sit ANON 12:9
now we s. by each other SHER 339:2
They also serve who only s. MILT 261:5
standard float that s. sheet DRAKE 124:8
s. of bathing beaches POW 297:13
Then raise the scarlet s. high CONN 101:7
standing dignity by s. on it CHUR 94:13
given gladly not to be s. here JOHN 195:7
s. armies of power RADC 299:5
stands s. Scotland where it did SHAK 332:3
Stanley how S. scorns BULW 62:1
star constant as the northern s. SHAK 329:3
guiding s. of my political life CARS 77:4
s. for every State WINT 393:3
stare rule never to s. at people BALF 30:8
stars not in our s. SHAK 328:4
star-spangled 'Tis the s. banner KEY 207:1
start 'Brutus' will s. a spirit SHAK 328:5
get the s. of the majestic world SHAK 328:3
starter Few thought he was even a s. ATTL 20:9
may be a good s. CHUR 89:4
starvation s. that stalks after it FOSD 139:6
starve let our people s. so we can NYER 276:1
starving choice of working or s. JOHN 197:6
people are s. in this country REAG 302:3
s. population DISR 117:13
state all the s. powers JEFF 192:1
church and s. forever separate GRANT 160:3
councillors of s. sit plotting CARL 76:10
death of any s. HOBB 180:7
effect of s. intervention DICEY 114:7
first duty of a S. RUSK 315:9
free church in a free s. CAV 79:4
health of the s. BOUR 53:7
health of the whole s. SHAK 325:5
In seizing a s., the usurper MACH 241:8
In the youth of a s. BACON 23:7
make the s. his servant MORSE 266:7
monument was erected by the s. AUDEN 21:4
my glories and my s. depose SHAK 334:4
nation's most populous s. FEIN 136:3
neighbouring s. is in decline MONT 264:7

state (*cont.*):
no such thing as the S. AUDEN 21:2
Nothing doth more hurt in a s. BACON 22:6
partnership between the s. TAWN 355:6
pillar of the S. SOLZ 346:1
put the s. to rights for us ENN 133:9
reinforcement of the S. CAMUS 74:7
Scoffing his s. SHAK 333:8
sole employer is the S. TROT 370:14
sovereign s. power KEANE 202:5
S. business is a cruel trade HAL 166:12
S. for every Star WINT 393:3
S. is an instrument STAL 348:3
S. is a relation of men WEBER 381:8
S. is not 'abolished', *it withers* ENG 133:6
s. is or can be master BEV 42:5
S. policy, a cyclops COL 101:3
'S.' reveals itself POW 297:16
S. which dwarfs its men MILL 259:5
s. without the means BURKE 66:8
Then all were for the s. MAC 237:1
two parties which divide the s. EMER 133:2
wall between church and s. BLACK 48:2
when church and s. hold hands MITC 261:7
While the S. exists LENIN 221:7
whole machinery of the S. BRO 58:1
without the s. suffering TOCQ 365:5
states free and independent S. ADAMS 3:9
indestructible S. CHASE 83:7
In s. unborn SHAK 329:6
many sovereign S. PAGE 280:7
mental s. GAND 147:7
more s. there are to suffer BAG 28:1
number of independent s. GIBB 151:2
peoples of the several s. CARD 75:7
saved the Union of these S. WHIT 388:1
S. dissevered, discordant WEBS 382:4
sustain the rights of s. BROWN 59:5
statesman conscience of a s. TAYL 358:3
constitutional s. is in general BAG 23:14
first requirement of a s. ACH 1:6
from rising hope to elder s. FOOT 138:8
greatest gift of any s. METT 258:1
great s. MONN 262:9
he was a s. LLOY 230:6
importance to a s. to make TAYL 358:1
no gift to set a s. right YEATS 395:5
No s., be he as discreet TAYL 358:2
no s. who has committed DISR 118:13
not in Washington as a s. ASH 17:8
often a defect in a s. TOCQ 366:9
quality of the constructive s. TAYL 356:9
sole care of the s. in office TAYL 358:10
s. got into office CHUR 93:9
s. is a politician who places POMP 295:1
s. is a politician who's been TRUM 371:13
s.... must wait until he hears BISM 47:11
[s.] should steer TAYL 358:7
s. who is enamoured BIER 44:16
S., yet friend to Truth POPE 295:3
statesmanship You call that s. BEVAN 41:4
statesmen *Advice to s.* LIDD 223:5
constitutional s. BAG 23:15
faults of s. give birth WALP 377:7
government of s. or of clerks DISR 117:4
stations always know our proper s. DICK 115:2
statistic tragedy, one million is a s. STAL 348:7
statistics He uses s. as a drunken LANG 217:6
It is s. as pornography JENK 194:9
lies, damned lies and s. DISR 121:15
stature malice is of a low s. HAL 166:2
status quo little ladder called 'the s.' BENN 37:2
stay If they want to s. BEVIN 43:2
I kind of have to s. around PEROT 290:10
staying s. down with him WASH 379:4
steal I come not, friends, to s. SHAK 330:8
to s. bread FRAN 141:2
stealing not hanged for s. horses HAL 166:10
steals politician who s. is worse PLUN 294:7
s. the common from the goose ANON 14:2
steam-engine He traces the s. DISR 118:1
like a s. in trousers SMITH 344:8
steeds mounting barbèd s. SHAK 334:9
steeple North Church s. REV 303:7
steeples dreary s. of Fermanagh CHUR 88:4
Talk about the pews and s. CHES 84:6
steering Washington is a s. wheel GOOD 158:1
step One s. forward two steps back LENIN 221:2
Stephen since Matilda and S. WAUGH 380:10
steps hears the s. of God BISM 47:11
sterner made of s. stuff SHAK 330:2
stick carry a big s. ROOS 311:4
first s. that he seizes TORR 367:4
he fell like the s. PAINE 283:4
s. to science BEVIN 42:8
sticker it is a bad s. CHUR 89:4
stiffen it has had time to s. ORW 278:8
still conscience is a s. small voice ATTL 20:7
stilts nonsense upon s. BENT 37:8
stingy government ever was not s. TROL 370:4
stir Is not to s. SHAK 326:3
To s. men's blood SHAK 330:9
To s. up undisputed matters SALL 319:5
stirring s. up apathy WHIT 387:6
stock woman s. is rising CHILD 85:3
stocking hung up an empty s. SMITH 343:6
shit in a silk s. NAP 270:4
stocks great s. of Europe YEATS 396:1
stomach army marches on its s. NAP 269:11
heart and s. of a king ELIZ 130:9
patriot on an empty s. BRANN 55:5
s. of the country GLAD 154:3
stone back into the S. Age LEMAY 220:8
Can make a s. of the heart YEATS 395:7

first s. which he [the savage] TORR 367:4
precious s. set in the silver sea SHAK 333:4
stones s. of Rome to rise SHAK 330:10
stood Have s. against the world SHAK 330:5
s. four-square to all the winds TENN 359:11
stop time to s. a revolution STEV 350:4
stopped s. the engine in its tracks JENK 194:3
stories tell sad s. of the death SHAK 333:8
storm by the pilot of the s. BAG 25:3
in the west, that coming s. GLAD 154:1
storms He sought the s. DRYD 125:5
story we shall be made a s. WINT 393:2
strain Sometimes the s. is awful MACM 245:10
stranger gratitude of a s. TOCQ 365:10
strangers beaten by s. DOS 123:2
strategy industrial s. BENN 36:5
strawberry Like s. wives ELIZ 131:9
stream watching a s. of blood ANON 12:1
streams when crossing s. LINC 226:6
street works both sides of the s. ROOS 310:5
street-bred poor little s. people KIPL 212:7
streetcars as common as s. REUT 303:5
streets grow in the s. HOOV 182:10
grow in the s. of every city BRYAN 60:5
little children died in the s. AUDEN 21:5
republican way of cleaning the s. LA G 216:5
strength at length that tower of s. TENN 359:11
progress which is her present s. TROL 369:7
s. of the Empire GLAD 155:1
S. should be lord of imbecility SHAK 335:9
S. through joy LEY 223:4
To have a giant's s. SHAK 332:8
strenuous doctrine of the s. life ROOS 310:10
stretch never s. out the hand HES 177:10
stretched government are s. MONT 264:13
strife In place of s. CAST 78:3
strike no right to s. against COOL 103:1
s. the tent LEE 220:7
When you s. at a king EMER 133:5
strikes puny subject s. SHAK 333:7
string monarchy is only the s. SHEL 338:7
untune that s. SHAK 335:9
stringent s. execution GRANT 160:2
stroke at a s., reduce HEATH 173:6
stroked if not s. HAL 165:11
strong Give them a s. and a just WELL 384:1
nor the battle to the s. BIBLE 43:16
not to the s. alone HENRY 176:7
those who think they are s. BID 44:14
stronger interest of the s. party PLATO 294:2
on the side of the s. TAC 354:9
There is one thing s. ANON 13:8
struggle class s. leads MARX 252:5
long twilight s. KENN 204:6
perpetual s. for room and food MALT 248:10
struggles history of class s. MARX 253:2
struts He s. sitting down DYKS 127:3
stubbornness self-righteous s. JENK 194:6
stud-horse only a retired s. MENC 257:1
studiously apart, s. neutral WILS 392:5
study I must s. politics and war ADAMS 3:13
stuff made of sterner s. SHAK 330:2
stuffed I s. their mouths with gold BEVAN 41:10
stumbled s. over the truth CHUR 94:10
stupid governments are far more s. EIS 129:6
never be right that the s. IBSEN 186:8
s. are cocksure RUSS 316:12
stupidest s. party MILL 259:7
stupidity conscientious s. KING 210:5
simple explanation of s. LEVER 222:2
subject s. and a sovereign CHAR 82:6
s.'s duty is the king's SHAK 326:14
to be a s. ELIZ 130:6
To every s. of this land DENN 113:6
subjects from the s. of government WILS 391:11
maintains among his s. HERB 177:2
obligation of s. to the sovereign HOBB 180:6
s. are rebels from principle BURKE 67:2
subjugation conquest and s. WEBS 382:7
sublime s. to the ridiculous NAP 269:9
submission s. of men's actions HOBB 180:7
submit king do now? Must he s. SHAK 334:2
subordination legal s. of one sex MILL 259:8
subsidizes problems; it s. them REAG 301:7
subsistence s. only increases MALT 248:9
substance persons of some s. WIND 393:1
substitute no s. for victory MAC 235:13
subtlety s. of intellect MORL 266:2
subtracting without s. REED 302:11
subversion complaining about s. JUV 201:5
success generals who gain s. LINC 226:4
his s. is disgraceful MENC 256:12
judgements—s. BURKE 67:13
S. or failure lies in conforming MACH 241:11
tortured by material s. MACM 245:5
successful s. experiment JEFF 192:6
whether s. ADAMS 4:6
succession monarchy and s. PAINE 281:3
successor tie a popish s. with laws HAMP 167:9
Sudeten S. Germans HITL 179:7
Suez felt as if the S. Canal EDEN 128:1
ship me somewheres east of S. KIPL 212:8
S.—a smash and grab raid NIC 272:8
suffer Better one s. DRYD 125:9
nobody is going to s. KALD 201:10
not s. fools gladly PEAR 287:5
who clamour most, s. most PEEL 288:13
suffering cannot be s. very much GALB 146:8
loved the s. many BENT 37:11
suffice O when may it s. YEATS 395:7
sufficient not s. to keep him LLOY 231:2
suggest s. modes of taxation PEEL 289:3

suicide did not commit s. ADAMS 4:2
[Earl Haig] committed s. BEAV 34:4
it is s. MACD 240:5
longest s. note in history KAUF 202:4
s. to avoid assassination TRUM 371:6
sui generis hell, say that I am *s.* LONG 232:5
suis *J'y s., j'y reste* MACM 243:10
Sulla Rome under S. ADC 5:7
summer if it takes all s. GRANT 159:7
on a hot s. afternoon ANON 13:11
summers This many s. in a sea SHAK 327:6
summits nations touch at their s. BAG 26:5
sun against a setting s. SHAK 335:4
blushing discontented s. SHAK 334:1
has the s. in his eyes CHUR 90:2
light a candle to the s. SIDN 340:3
our own place in the s. BÜLOW 61:7
our place in the s. WILH 388:9
summer by this s. of York SHAK 334:8
s. draws its power TRUM 371:2
s. never sets NORTH 275:3
sunk s. in a bigger CHUR 91:1
sunset into the s. of my life REAG 302:8
sunshine s. patriot PAINE 281:10
superfluous s. lags the vet'ran JOHN 196:14
superior embarrass the s. SHAW 336:10
want no-one to be their *s.* TOCQ 365:1
superiors only want it with our s. BECQ 34:8
superman I teach you the s. NIET 273:3
superstition forgive his s. GIBB 151:14
s. sets the whole world VOLT 376:2
supervision national s. O'RO 277:6
suppliant s. for his own BYRON 71:3
supplies bought some new s. BREC 55:10
support depend on the s. of Paul SHAW 337:2
men who will s. me MELB 256:4
oath to s. the constitution JACK 188:9
s. of the people CLEV 99:3
s. rather than illumination LANG 217:6
without the help and s. EDW 128:5
supportable such as are s. HAL 165:14
supported not s. by the people HUMP 185:3
suppose s. what may come HAL 165:5
suppress power of s. NORT 275:7
suprema *salus populi s. est lex* CIC 95:6
supreme But if ever the S. Court TOCQ 365:5
s. power must be arbitrary HAL 165:10
surface fear the smiling s. PLUT 294:9
surplus economic s. POTT 296:3
surprised quite s. to be taken DE G 112:12
surrender immediate s. GRANT 159:6
No s. ANON 12:11
we shall never s. CHUR 90:7
survived I s. SIEY 340:5
suspicion against despots—s. DEM 113:2
Caesar's wife must be above s. CAES 71:9
democracy is the recurrent s. WHITE 386:6
suspicions s. amongst thoughts BACON 23:2
swap It is not best to s. horses LINC 226:6
swayed easily s. CLAY 97:6
sweat blood, toil, tears and s. CHUR 90:5
spending the s. of its labourers EIS 129:4
sweets bag of boiled s. CRIT 104:4
s. of place with power ROS 312:7
swift race is not to the s. BIBLE 43:16
swim that I may s. GRAH 159:2
swimming s. for his life GLAD 154:8
swooped s. down upon us ANON 9:4
sword at the point of the s. GEOR 149:3
I gave them a s. NIXON 274:14
lightning of his terrible swift s. HOWE 184:3
nation shall not lift up s. BIBLE 43:18
not to send peace, but a s. BIBLE 44:5
power of the s. CHAR 82:6
resistance by the *s.* CLAY 97:1
s. is the axis DE G 112:2
We shall never sheath the s. ASQ 18:3
when he first drew the s. CLAR 96:1
wield the s. of France DE G 112:4
swords I thought ten thousand s. BURKE 66:15
s. into plowshares BIBLE 43:18
turns our s. SHAK 330:15
sycophants s. and flatterers HARD 168:4
syllogism politicians' s. LYNN 235:11
sympathy Our s. is cold GIBB 151:11
there's no s. in politics THAT 360:9
system knocking the American s. CAP 75:6
s. of Government GLAD 154:2
they rocked the s. ROB 307:3

table people at whose t. I sit BORR 53:3
victuals from the t. CHUR 89:11
tableau t. of crimes and misfortunes VOLT 376:3
tact No more t. CAMP 74:4
tail Every time it wags its t. TOYN 367:5
which was the t. BRIG 56:9
taint any t. of legality KNOX 215:2
take big enough to t. away FORD 138:10
don't t. *everything* away SOLZ 345:10
If they t. you in the morning BALD 28:9
more blessed not to t. POW 296:6
t. away these baubles CROM 105:9
t. up the White Man's burden KIPL 213:2
taken t. at his word DE G 112:12
takes if it t. all summer GRANT 159:7
taking-off deep damnation of his t. SHAK 331:7
talent concentration of t. KENN 205:1
t. of our English nation DRYD 125:2
talents career open to the t. NAP 269:13
ministry of all the t. ANON 12:7
t. invaluable to a prince MAC 238:14
virtue and t. JEFF 193:4

talk careless t. costs lives ANON 9:7
men who t. fluently HOGB 181:1
Through t., we tamed kings BENN 36:8
talked t. for a hundred years JOHN 195:8
t. shop like a tenth muse ANON 10:7
talking if you can stop people t. ATTL 20:11
t. politics after dinner DISR 120:4
talking-machine redtape t. CARL 76:8
taller may be t. than other men HAR 169:4
tamed in one year t. MARV 251:8
Tandy I met wid Napper T. ANON 10:11
tanks Get your t. off my lawn WILS 391:1
taping t. of conversations NIXON 274:12
Tarpeian from the T. rock ARN 17:6
Tarsus which am a Jew of T. BIBLE 44:11
tart he is like the town t. BAXT 33:2
tarts by the action of two t. MACM 245:6
taste t. for freedom TOCQ 366:11
taunted I am sometimes t. PEEL 289:2
taunting grave, and not t. BACON 22:12
tax idleness and pride t. FRAN 142:1
I pay my t. bills more readily HOLM 181:7
power to t. MARS 251:3
soon be able to t. it FAR 135:4
t. collector for the welfare state GING 153:2
time to t. rich people LLOY 229:13
To t. and to please BURKE 64:15
taxation suggest modes of t. PEEL 289:3
t. and representation CAMD 73:5
t. without representation OTIS 279:14
taxes compensation for heavy t. MONT 264:15
except death and t. FRAN 142:9
just to pay our t. PEROT 290:7
little people pay t. HELM 174:4
peace, easy t. SMITH 341:1
people overlaid with t. BACON 23:4
read my lips: no new t. BUSH 69:7
taxi empty t. arrived CHUR 94:9
taxing more or less of a t. machine LOWE 233:7
taxis Labour council hiring t. KINN 211:11
taxpayer t.—that's someone REAG 301:14
tax-paying working, t. Americans GING 153:3
tea take—and sometimes t. POPE 295:2
those damned t. parties LODGE 232:2
teacher value of a true t. GARF 147:9
teaching for the t. of which SMITH 343:1
t. nations how to live MILT 260:5
team by the t. captain HOWE 184:1
tear shed one English t. MAC 238:10
t. down this wall REAG 302:5
tears blood, toil, t. and sweat CHUR 90:5
enough of blood and t. RABIN 299:4
Mine eyes are full of t. SHAK 334:7
With mine own t. I wash SHAK 334:6
technological *t. revolution* WILS 390:5
technology in relation to our t. BERR 39:7
into the sixties t. LEVIN 222:4
province of t. POPP 296:2
Ted fond of dear T. THAT 360:9
Teddy Now T. must run KENN 206:5
teenage t. scribblers LAWS 219:4
teenagers among t. FRI 143:11
teeth but he's got iron t. GROM 162:4
have three or four t. taken out HITL 179:8
Our t. are in the real meat GRIM 162:2
teetotaller usually a secret t. ORW 277:11
Teflon-coated T. Presidency SCHR 321:8
television [political] t. show MACM 245:4
tell And t. sad stories of the death SHAK 333:8
Go, t. the Spartans SIM 340:6
I t. you that which you SHAK 330:9
temper agreeable to their t. BURKE 62:6
many things including my t. NEHRU 270:9
Never lose your t. with the Press PANK 284:11
with a ruffled t. WALP 378:8
temperament But a first-class t. HOLM 181:8
temple lord's anointed t. SHAK 331:9
t. of silence and reconciliation MAC 238:8
tempora *O t., O mores* CIC 95:9
t. mutantur, et nos mutamur ANON 13:7
temporary force alone is but *t.* BURKE 64:12
temptation always a t. KIPL 213:4
temptations you may find t. KITC 214:15
tempted 'Tis one thing to be t. SHAK 332:6
ten amend the T. Commandments BIGG 45:3
I thought t. thousand swords BURKE 66:15
no T. Commandments KIPL 212:8
tenants feudal landlord abusing t. ATTL 19:7
tenement Like to a t. SHAK 333:4
tent inside the t. pissing out JOHN 196:9
strike the t. LEE 220:7
tenth He talked shop like a t. muse ANON 10:7
termination law for its own t. LINC 225:5
terminological risk of t. inexactitude CHUR 87:4
terrible t. beauty is born YEATS 395:8
territorial last t. claim HITL 179:6
territory it [the t.] is worth MAC 238:5
terror added a new t. to death WETH 386:1
For t., not to use, in time SHAK 332:4
just as great a t. LLOY 229:3
perch and not their t. SHAK 332:5
t. instituted by 'lawful authority' MACD 240:4
was the t. of the world PITT 293:4
terrorist t. and the policeman CONR 102:3
ways to starve the t. THAT 361:13
testators t. would do well HERB 176:10
Thames But the T. is liquid history BURNS 68:9
thee save t. and me OWEN 280:5
theft property is t. PRO 298:5
t. from those who hunger EIS 129:4
theme glad diviner's t. DRYD 125:7
pudding—it has no t. CHUR 95:1
theologians if you believe the t. SAL 318:1

theories seldom is it that t. stand TROL 370:5
taken up with their t. BURKE 66:14
theory *died of a t.* DAVIS 110:3
fate that for a t. is worse GILM 153:1
It is sometimes t. MAC 236:6
trickle-down t. GALB 147:1
upon a t. BURKE 65:7
there you were not t. HENR 175:3
these saved the union of t. States WHIT 388:1
thick ask the Gods for a t. skin TROL 370:1
t. skin is a gift ADEN 6:1
thicker history gets t. TAYL 357:10
thigh He smote them hip and t. BIBLE 43:9
thin those pale and t. ones PLUT 294:8
thing only t. we have to fear ROOS 308:8
There is one t. stronger ANON 13:8
this the sort of t. they like LINC 227:3
things t. fall apart YEATS 395:6
think dare to t. 'unthinkable' FULB 144:5
easier to act than to t. AREN 15:11
t. alike who t. at all PAINE 283:3
T. of your forefathers ADAMS 4:5
you may t. what you like TAC 354:7
You might very well t. DOBBS 122:4
You must t. the unthinkable ROSS 313:4
thinker Too conventional a t. MONC 261:11
thinking All t. for themselves GILB 152:9
columnists say 'Every t. man' ADAMS 2:4
modes of t. are different JOHN 198:10
never thought of t. for myself GILB 152:4
thinks He t. too much SHAK 328:7
t. he knows everything SHAW 336:13
thirst man can raise a t. KIPL 212:8
offer you hunger, t. GAR 148:1
thirty t. pieces of silver BEVAN 41:1
this t. happy breed of men SHAK 333:4
t. was a man SHAK 330:16
thorn t. in Charles's side FOX 140:4
thorns can't have the crown of t. BEVAN 41:1
this crown of t. BRYAN 60:6
thought experience is the child of t. DISR 116:4
freedom of t. HAYEK 171:7
freedom of t. and the right ADAMS 5:5
investigation and t. HALD 164:2
their modes of t. MILL 259:12
they ought to have t. ANON 12:12
troubled seas of t. GALB 145:9
thoughtcrime make t. literally ORW 279:3
thoughts I am a farmer of t. PAINE 282:1
not make t. your aim KIPL 213:3
suspicions amongst t. BACON 23:2
t. of a prisoner SOLZ 345:9
thousand difference of forty t. men WELL 384:6
end of a t. years of history GAIT 145:2
like a t. points of light BUSH 69:6
Rhodesia—not in a t. years SMITH 344:4
t. generations KINN 212:2
threatened because I t. no one BUSH 69:4
threatening t. its own demise BLAIR 49:1
three divided into t. parts CAES 71:7
little man with t. names CROM 106:2
t. corners of the world SHAK 331:1
t. kinds of lies: lies, damned DISR 121:15
throat frog in my t. MAJOR 247:10
have murder by the t. LLOY 230:1
So he has cut his t. at last BYRON 71:4
throne esteemed worthy of the t. GIBB 151:8
highest t. in the world MONT 263:9
possession of a t. GIBB 151:5
something behind the t. greater PITT 292:12
This royal t. of kings SHAK 333:4
t. of bayonets INGE 187:7
T. sent word to a Throne KIPL 213:1
t. *we* honour is the *people's* SHER 338:12
t. will sway a little CHAN 81:5
vacancy of the t. GIBB 151:1
wade through slaughter to a t. GRAY 160:8
throw t. away the dearest thing SHAK 331:6
thrown All *this* t. away for *that* MARY 253:6
Tiber River T. foaming POW 297:1
T. foaming with much blood VIRG 375:6
ticker t. tape ain't spaghetti LA G 216:4
ticket take a t. at Victoria Station BEVIN 43:4
tide [Rome] is like an incoming t. DENN 113:5
t. in the affairs of men SHAK 330:14
tiger atom bomb is a paper t. MAO 250:5
orang-outang or the t. BURKE 65:9
t. will turn vegetarian BROUN 58:4
tigers but a wilderness of t. SHAK 335:6
t. are getting hungry CHUR 89:8
tight-lipped t. mufflered men JOS 199:7
tightness t. of the magic circle MACL 242:8
tigress t. surrounded by hamsters BIFF 45:1
tiles t. on the roofs LUTH 234:7
tilling dignity in t. a field WASH 379:3
time ancient nobility is the act of t. BACON 22:14
for a moment of t. ELIZ 132:3
have not the t. to meet you KIPL 213:4
idea whose t. has come ANON 13:8
like to devote more t. FOWL 140:3
peace for our t. CHAM 81:1
plenty of t. to win DRAKE 124:7
rely upon a comfortable t.-lag WELLS 385:5
sell t., which belongs to God TAWN 355:11
spend more t. with my family RIDL 305:5
spend more t. with your family THAT 362:8
That's why it's t. for a change DEWEY 114:5
t. has come LONG 232:7
T. is on our side GLAD 154:6
t. is out of joint SHAK 325:7
T.'s noblest offspring BERK 38:4
T. spent on any item PARK 285:10
t. will come when you DISR 116:12

too much of the t. THUR 364:8
unconscionable t. dying CHAR 83:6
waste of t. and effort VEBL 373:6
week is a long t. in politics WILS 390:8
well to t. the beginnings BACON 22:7
whips and scorns of t. SHAK 325:8
you're ahead of your t. MCG 240:9
times best of t. DICK 115:4
conforming to the t. MACH 241:11
Oh, the t.! Oh, the manners CIC 95:9
our old simplicity of t. ANON 12:3
These are t. in which a genius ADAMS 2:2
t. change, and we change ANON 13:7
T. has made many ministries BAG 25:1
t. that try men's souls PAINE 281:10
t. that were are better GRE 161:1
t. will not mend PARK 285:4
timetables by railway t. TAYL 357:8
timing lucky t. of your death TAC 354:4
real bad sense of t. MCG 240:9
TINA *acronym* T. THAT 361:1
tincture Nature has left this t. DEFOE 111:12
tinhorn t. politicians WHITE 387:3
tinker don't matter a t.'s cuss SHIN 339:5
tinned t. salmon WILS 390:4
Tippecanoe old soldier of T. MORR 266:4
T. and Tyler, too ROSS 313:3
tipster racing t. TAYL 357:2
tire see if he may not t. me GEOR 149:2
tired Give me your t., your poor LAZ 219:7
tireless sound of t. voices STEV 351:3
Titanic on the deck of the T. MORT 267:1
title Who gained no t. POPE 295:3
titles T. are but nick-names PAINE 282:7
T. are shadows DEFOE 111:11
T. distinguish the mediocre SHAW 336:10
t. manifold WORD 394:5
to not freedom from, but freedom t. BERL 39:2
toadies t. of power TREV 368:7
toast My t. would be ADAMS 4:6
tobacco chew of t. LONG 232:6
today never jam t. CARR 77:2
T. is the last day YELT 396:4
toga idealism is the noble t. HUXL 186:4
toil blood, t., tears and sweat CHUR 90:5
fifty years of unrequited t. LINC 226:9
horny-handed sons of t. SAL 318:8
told Nobody t. us we could do this WEBB 381:5
tolerance continuous t. BAG 27:6
such a thing as t. WILS 392:14
tolerate at least t. one another TREV 368:3
tolerated t. the Right Honourable BEVAN 40:2
toleration t. produced GIBB 151:3
Tomnoddy My Lord T. is thirty-four BRO 57:8
tomorrow jam t. and jam yesterday CARR 77:2
jam we thought was for t. BENN 36:3
limit to our realization of t. ROOS 310:9
T. every Duchess in London MACD 240:6
tongue die, who speak the t. WORD 394:5
eye to see, nor t. to speak LENT 221:12
put a t. In every wound SHAK 330:10
t. in the balance BISM 47:13
t. to persuade CLAR 96:2
would not yield to the t. BIER 44:15
tongues with their t. doom men SHAK 335:5
tonight be but a short time t. BALD 29:9
Not t., Josephine NAP 270:3
tools give us the t. CHUR 91:6
t. to him CARL 75:13
toothpaste Once the t. is out HALD 164:3
top always room at the t. WEBS 383:1
Churchill on t. of the wave BEAV 33:5
torch t.; be yours to hold it MCCR 240:2
t. has been passed KENN 204:2
Tories both *T.*; both convinced BOSW 53:4
Mamma, are T. born wicked ANON 12:4
revolutionaries are potential T. ORW 278:4
stern and unbending T. MAC 238:1
T., every election BEVAN 40:9
T., in short, are atrophied JOHN 196:13
T. own no argument but force BROW 59:6
tormenting t. the people with trivia NAP 270:2
torrent leave it to a t. of change CHES 84:4
mere cork, dancing on a t. BALF 30:5
torture-chamber scene in a t. MACM 245:4
tortured t. by material success MACM 245:5
Tory burning hatred for the T. Party BEVAN 40:6
Disraeli was my favourite T. FOOT 138:6
I may be a T. PEEL 287:9
Let the Toryism of the T. TROL 370:6
loyalty is the T.'s secret weapon KILM 209:9
nostrils of an English T. TROL 369:2
secret weapon of the T. Party CRIT 104:9
T. and Whig in turns SMITH 344:7
T. Corps d'Armée GLAD 154:14
T. is someone who thinks POW 297:10
T. men and Whig measures DISR 117:7
T. party never panics HOSK 183:6
T. shame BEVAN 41:8
violent T. of the old school RUSK 316:4
what T. Democracy is CHUR 86:3
wise T. and a wise Whig JOHN 198:10
within the T. party MACL 243:2
Toryism T. has always been MACM 244:1
T. of the Tory TROL 370:6
total *t. solution* GOER 156:7
totalitarian lead to the t. state DENN 113:8
t. innovation O'BR 276:5
totalitarianism name of t. GAND 147:5
touch Can t. him further SHAK 332:2
little t. of Harry in the night SHAK 326:10
tough t. get going KENN 206:2
t.-minded BEN 35:7

tough (*cont.*):
T. on crime and t. on BLAIR 48:11
toughness t. doesn't have to FEIN 136:2
tower t. of strength TENN 359:11
town destroy the t. to save it ANON 11:3
t. drunkard, a t. atheist BROG 57:6
tracks stopped the engine in its t. JENK 194:3
trade autocrat: that's my t. CATH 78:4
great t. will always be attended BURKE 64:14
No nation was ever ruined by t. FRAN 142:6
none of the wheels of t. HUME 184:7
People of the same t. SMITH 341:5
pre-eminence in her Colonial t. GEOR 149:5
state business is a cruel t. HAL 166:12
There isn't any t. HERB 176:9
war is the t. of kings DRYD 126:2
world society is through free t. CHOD 85:10
trades unionists t. at heart JEV 194:11
trade Unionist British t. BEVIN 42:6
trade unions first snarl of the t. LLOY 229:1
tradition t. means giving votes CHES 84:2
traditions rooted in age-long t. BALF 30:7
tragedy first time as t. MARX 252:4
Herein lies the t. of the age DU B 126:6
One death is a t., one million STAL 348:7
trahison *t. des clercs* BENDA 35:6
train leave Powell's t. MACL 243:3
traitor find myself a t. with the rest SHAK 334:7
hate the t. DAN 109:5
rich man makes a bonny t. PAINE 282:2
traitors can see a sort of t. here SHAK 334:7
hate t. DRYD 126:1
watched the form of our t. WEST 385:9
trample If you dare t. upon these SHEL 338:6
trampled businessman has t. NIC 272:6
trampling right of t. on them CHILD 85:2
tranquillity fame and t. MONT 263:8
transgression there is no t. BIBLE 44:13
transient t. and embarrassed DISR 120:14
trapping t. of a splendid misery ROSS 313:5
traps to recognize the t. MACH 241:5
travelled care which way he t. BEAV 34:5
travelling I am weary of t. CHAR 83:4
t. round the world COOK 102:6
treachery even t. cannot trust JUN 201:2
t. of the intellectuals BENDA 35:6
t. with a smile on its face THAT 362:13
tread that I may t. safely HASK 170:2
treason bloody t. flourished over us SHAK 330:7
condoned high t. DISR 119:16
hate traitors and the t. love DRYD 126:1
If *this* be t., make the most of it HENRY 176:3
In trust I have found t. ELIZ 130:6
none dare call it t. HAR 169:1
no reason why gunpowder t. ANON 13:2
state hireling for t. to his country JOHN 197:3
That t. can but peep SHAK 326:4
though they love the t. DAN 109:5
t. has done his worst SHAK 332:2
[T.] is a question of dates TALL 355:5
treasure purest t. SHAK 333:1
Treasury If the T. were to fill old bottles KEYN 208:4
in this country is the T. WILS 391:9
on our T. Bench TROL 370:1
plaintive treble of the T. Bench DISR 118:15
T. is in power WILS 391:6
T. is the spring of business BAG 24:12
treaties t., you see, are like girls DE G 112:13
treaty hand that signed the t. THOM 363:4
Make a good t. with Russia BISM 46:3
This is not a peace t. FOCH 138:2
t. [of Rome] is like DENN 113:5
treble plaintive t. DISR 118:15
tree t. of liberty must be refreshed JEFF 191:7
Trelawny And shall T. die HAWK 170:7
tremble Indeed I t. for my country JEFF 191:3
trembles he t. as I do WELL 383:8
trembling t. most, maintain WALP 377:10
tres *est omnis divisa in partes t.* CAES 71:7
trial t. by juries JEFF 192:8
t. through which we pass LINC 225:12
tribalism It is pure t. FITT 137:6
t. is the strongest force DEL 112:15
tribunes t. with their tongues SHAK 335:5
tribute not one cent for t. HARP 169:5
Why should we pay t. SHAK 325:2
trickle-down t. theory GALB 147:1
tricks frustrate their knavish t. ANON 9:9
tried Almost everything has been t. BENN 36:5
trifle As 'twere a careless t. SHAK 331:6
trigger be one finger on the t. MACM 245:2
want on the t. ANON 15:1
trimmer This innocent word *t.* HAL 165:2
Trinity God also is a T. man BIRR 46:2
trip From fearful t. the victor ship WHIT 387:10
look forward to the t. STIN 351:5
triple t. cord, which no man BURKE 68:3
trips If he t. he must be sustained CHUR 93:6
Triton T. of the minnows SHAK 324:6
triumph for evil to t. BURKE 68:7
in t. from the north MAC 236:3
meet with t. and disaster KIPL 213:3
t. for democracy HOPE 183:2
t. of modern science WAUGH 380:9
t. of the embalmer's art VIDAL 375:2
We shall not see the t. DICK 115:5
troika like a spirited *t.* GOGOL 156:8
Trojan never know what T. 'orses BEVIN 43:5
troops march my t. GRIM 162:1
tropic Under the t. is our language WALL 377:3
trouble art of looking for t. BENN 35:8
most credit with the least t. TAYL 358:10
t. with this country ADAMS 2:5

When in t., delegate BOREN 52:6
when we are in bad t. DID 116:2
troubled see that ye be not t. BIBLE 44:8
trousers never have your best t. IBSEN 186:9
steam-engine in t. SMITH 344:8
trowel lay it on with a t. DISR 121:4
true by the people as equally t. GIBB 151:3
England to itself do rest but t. SHAK 331:1
firm state by proportions t. MARV 252:1
trumpet no use blowing the t. CHAM 80:3
Now the t. summons us KENN 204:6
trumps turn out the ace of t. CHUR 86:8
trust absolute t. SHAK 331:6
all power is a t. DISR 116:3
aroused every feeling except t. TAYL 357:12
even treachery cannot t. JUN 201:2
exercises a public t. CLEV 99:1
In t. I have found treason ELIZ 130:6
man assumes a public t. JEFF 192:12
no more than power in t. DRYD 125:8
not property but a t. FOX 140:5
t. no man living with power ADAMS 3:5
you never should t. experts SAL 318:1
trusted not to be t. with the office BROD 57:4
unfit to be t. CHES 83:12
trustworthiness Carthaginian t. SALL 319:8
truth committing ourselves to the t. NIXON 274:3
contaminated by the t. RIPP 306:3
diminution of the love of t. JOHN 197:4
economical with the t. ARMS 16:12
economy of t. BURKE 68:2
everybody can tell you the t. MACH 241:7
fiction lags after t. BURKE 64:13
fight for freedom and t. IBSEN 186:9
Give me a grain of t. WILK 389:2
His t. is marching on HOWE 184:3
I just tell the t. TRUM 371:12
innocent...To forsake this t. ROS 313:1
In the strife of T. with Falsehood LOW 234:1
is such a thing as t. BAG 24:5
Ministers are wedded to the t. SAKI 317:6
no appetite for t. in Ireland PEEL 288:1
not maintained for t. SWIFT 353:8
not t., but persuasion MAC 236:5
opinion is t. filtered PHIL 292:4
platitude is simply a t. repeated BALD 29:2
statesman, yet friend to t. POPE 295:3
stop telling the t. about them STEV 350:1
stumbled over the t. CHUR 94:10
takes two to speak the t. THOR 364:3
trusted to speak the t. BALF 30:4
T. against the world LLOY 230:14
T. forever on the scaffold LOW 234:2
T. is the first casualty JOHN 197:4
t. is the glue FORD 139:1
T. never yet fell dead PARK 285:5
t. which makes men free AGAR 6:4
unclouded face of t. SCOTT 322:4
What is t.? said jesting Pilate BACON 23:5
truths basic human t. KENN 205:8
Few new t. have ever won BERL 39:6
t. begin as blasphemies SHAW 336:20
We hold these t. to be self-evident ANON 14:7
We hold these t. to be sacred JEFF 191:1
try But above all, t. something ROOS 308:5
guiltier than him they t. SHAK 332:6
tu *Et t., Brute* CAES 71:13
Et t., Brute? Then fall, Caesar SHAK 329:4
tube toothpaste is out of the t. HALD 164:3
tumult t. and the shouting dies KIPL 212:11
tune complain about the t. BEVAN 41:2
turbulent rid me of this t. priest HENR 175:7
Turkey T. is a dying man NICH 271:4
turkeys t. have been known to vote CALL 73:1
Turkish English, not the T. court SHAK 326:8
Turks Let the T. now carry away GLAD 154:12
turned if I were t. out of the Realm ELIZ 130:4
not t. the clock back WAUGH 381:1
To be t. from one's course FAB 134:6
turning lady's not for t. THAT 361:2
Turning and t. YEATS 395:6
turnip candle in that great t. CHUR 93:3
TV politicians complain that T. MURR 268:6
twelve bringing t. good men into a box BRO 58:1
in the sworn t. have a thief SHAK 332:6
ruin himself in t. months GEOR 149:10
twentieth language of the t. century BEVAN 40:10
would the t. century SCHL 321:7
twenty given me t. reasons BEVIN 43:1
twilight burden of a long t. struggle KENN 204:6
ever fly by t. BACON 23:2
live in the grey t. ROOS 310:11
twist Let him t. slowly, slowly EHRL 128:6
two idea of the occasion in t. hours EVER 134:4
t. nations; between whom DISR 118:2
whoever could make t. ears SWIFT 353:7
two o'clock t. in the morning NAP 269:10
Tyler Tippecanoe and T., too ROSS 313:3
type highest t. of human nature SPEN 347:5
tyrannical In all t. governments BLAC 48:9
nothing more t. TROL 369:4
tyrannis *Sic semper t.* BOOTH 52:3
tyrannize t. over his bank balance KEYN 208:2
tyrannous strength, but it is t. SHAK 332:8
tyranny call it *t.* HOBB 180:8
caused by some one's t. BAG 24:11
despotism of liberty against t. ROB 306:8
ecclesiastic t.'s the worst DEFOE 111:10
grovelling t. of self-government DISR 118:12
long dark night of t. MURR 268:5
never lightened the burden of t. SHAW 336:6
not consist merely of denouncing T. BRY 60:8

tyranny (*cont.*):
submission to an unnecessary t. RUSS 316:8
T. entrenches itself SHEL 338:6
T. is always better organized PÉGUY 289:11
Under conditions of t. AREN 15:11
very definition of t. MAD 246:5
war against a monstrous t. CHUR 90:6
without representation is t. OTIS 279:14
worst sort of t. BURKE 65:4
tyrant each t., every Mob KIPL 213:5
little t. of his fields GRAY 160:8
loses the king in the t. MAYH 255:1
No t. need fear till men ARIS 16:11
When the t. has disposed PLATO 294:4
tyrants all men would be t. ADAMS 2:1
all men would be t. DEFOE 111:12
argument of t. PITT 293:7
barbarity of t. SMITH 344:6
blood of patriots and t. JEFF 191:7
curry favour with t. ZAP 397:1
kings will be t. from policy BURKE 67:2
reasoning of t. GIBB 151:8
rebellion to t. is obedience to God BRAD 54:8
sceptre from t. TURG 372:7
stuff of which t. are made BEAV 33:5
T. seldom want pretexts BURKE 67:15
we tamed kings, restrained t. BENN 36:8
Tyrone Fermanagh and T. CHUR 88:4

Ulcer I am an 8 U. Man EARLY 127:4
Ulster betrayal of U. CAIR 72:1
U. says no ANON 14:4
U. will fight CHUR 86:6
unacceptable u. face HEATH 173:8
unassailable position was u. THAT 362:6
That u. holds on his rank SHAK 329:3
unbearable in victory u. CHUR 94:5
unbeatable In defeat u.: in victory CHUR 94:5
unbribed u., there's no occasion WOLFE 393:4
unconditional u. and immediate GRANT 159:6
unconscionable u. time dying CHAR 83:6
unconstitutional u. takes KISS 214:5
uncreating before thy u. word POPE 295:8
undecided Often u. whether to BEAV 34:3
underachievers muscular u. HENN 174:8
under-belly u. of the Axis CHUR 91:11
underestimated u. for decades KOHL 215:3
underestimating lost money by u. MENC 256:11
underlings that we are u. SHAK 328:4
undermined like a rat, he u. us ANON 9:4
understand doesn't really u. the situation MURR 268:7
One has to u. the country LESS 221:13
those who u. what it is HAL 166:9
u. a little less MAJOR 248:1
u. any other BAG 25:5
understanding appeal to the u. BAG 25:9
evidence against their own u. HAL 165:9
President needs political u. TRUM 371:10
u. between France and England PEEL 289:1
understandings muddy u. BURKE 66:17
understood not as it is u. JACK 188:9
undertaking no such u. CHAM 81:3
undo mark me how I will u. myself SHAK 334:5
u. a man SHAK 327:2
unearned u. increment LLOY 229:4
u. increment of rent MILL 259:13
uneasy u. lies the head SHAK 326:7
You are u.; you never sailed JACK 189:3
uneconomic not shown it to be 'u.' SCH 322:1
uneducated government by the u. CHES 85:1
unelected u. reject politicians RIDL 305:7
unemployed from amongst the u. LLOY 229:5
retired widow and an u. youth BAG 25:4
unemployment reduce u. HEATH 173:6
u. among teenagers FRI 143:11
u. results COOL 103:7
unequal u. distribution of property MAD 246:4
u. earnings ELL 133:1
unexpected old age is the most u. TROT 370:13
unfathomable u. depths of insincerity ANON 13:10
unfinished liberty is always u. ANON 11:14
unfit other party is u. to rule MENC 257:4
u. to be trusted CHES 83:12
unforeseen contingent and the u. FISH 136:8
unfree Ireland u. shall never PEAR 287:3
unglamorous government is too u. O'RO 277:6
unhappily u. married PARK 286:2
unhappy some should be u. JOHN 198:6
u. the land that needs heroes BREC 55:6
unheard language of the u. KING 211:3
uniformity u. [of opinion] JEFF 191:2
union determined to preserve this U. HOUS 183:8
devotion to the u. CARS 77:4
fragments of a once glorious U. WEBS 382:4
good old ship of the U. LINC 225:4
knell of the U. JEFF 193:7
Liberty *and* U., now and forever WEBS 382:3
looks to an indestructible U. CHASE 83:7
music of the U. CHO 85:7
Our federal U. JACK 188:8
our u. is perfect DICK 115:9
perfect U., one and inseparable PAGE 280:7
rebirth of the U. WILS 392:6
seed-time of continental u. PAINE 281:5
strict and indissoluble U. HAM 167:5
struggle is to save the U. LINC 226:2
take the key of the U. CLAY 97:9
U., sir, is my country CLAY 97:12
U. will be dissolved COBB 100:1
unnatural a bond of u. BURKE 64:16

Was saved the U. of these States WHIT 388:1
without the U. perishing TOCQ 365:5
unions there would have been no u. BALD 29:5
when Hitler attacked the u. NIEM 273:1
unite eggheads of the world u. STEV 350:15
united neither be u. at home SHEL 337:6
That these u. colonies are LEE 220:3
We must be u. CHUR 90:11
United Colonies these U. are ADAMS 3:9
United States children, and the U. of America BISM 47:12
close to the U. DIAZ 114:6
constitution of the U. CLAY 98:1
constitution of the U. DAVIS 110:2
cowboy is President of the U. HANNA 168:1
disposition toward the U. MONR 263:6
failure of the U. BRYCE 61:2
Great Government of the U. WILS 392:9
I believe in the U. of America PAGE 280:7
in rebellion against the U. LINC 225:11
In the U. there is more space STEIN 349:2
On my arrival in the U. TOCQ 366:1
Soviet Union and the U. KENN 203:5
U.—bounded on the north FISKE 137:5
U. must be neutral in fact WILS 392:1
U. of Europe CHUR 92:11
U. themselves are essentially WHIT 387:8
uniting By u. we stand DICK 115:8
community u. peoples MONN 262:4
unity u. of our fatherland KOHL 215:5
u. of the empire BURKE 63:12
u. of the nation KOHL 215:4
universal become a u. law KANT 202:2
university u. should be a place DISR 120:2
unjust just and u. masterships RUSK 315:10
unkindest most u. cut of all SHAK 330:6
unking u. himself MAYH 255:1
unknown tread safely into the u. HASK 170:2
u. is held to be glorious TAC 354:2
u. Prime Minister [Bonar Law] ASQ 18:7
unlimited sovereignty is u. BARK 32:3
unmake people can u. it MARS 251:4
unmeritable slight u. man SHAK 330:13
unmuzzled come among you 'u.' GLAD 154:5
unnecessary u. War CHUR 92:6
unpalatable disastrous and the u. GALB 145:12
un-person abolished, an u. ORW 279:5
unpleasantness put up with u. NAP 269:5
unpolitical nearly an u. office ANON 11:9
no such thing as an u. man MAL 248:6
unpopular it is safe to be u. STEV 350:7
unselfish most u. and unsordid CHUR 92:5
unshaked u. of motion SHAK 329:3
unsoiled delicately and u. CHUR 88:3
unstable what the English call u. MACM 245:8
unthinkable dare to think 'u.' FULB 144:5
think the u., but always wear ROSS 313:4
untried against the new and u. LINC 225:3
untrue say something that is u. WALD 376:6
untying u. with the teeth BIER 44:15
unwritten that u. law D'AV 110:1
u. custom supported by popular CATT 78:6
up kicked u. stairs HAL 165:1
u. Guards and at them WELL 384:2
upmost once attains the u. round SHAK 328:10
upside turned the world u. down BIBLE 44:10
upward great one that goes u. SHAK 331:3
u. to the Great Society JOHN 196:2
urban For the u. poor the police HARR 169:6
urge u. for destruction BAK 28:4
US defeat the U. aggressors MAO 250:7
use best u. of laws is to teach PHIL 291:9
used Learn to get u. to it CHUR 90:9
useful as equally u. GIBB 151:3
usual business carried on as u. CHUR 87:6
usurper u. ought to examine MACH 241:8
usury u. is contrary to Scripture TAWN 355:11
Utopia possibly be attained in U. GLAD 155:3
principality in U. MAC 237:11
right signposts to the socialist U. CROS 106:4
U. is a blessed past KISS 214:11
utopian retrospective or u. ARON 17:7
Utopias all the static U. INGE 187:9
utterances flat, dishwatery u. ANON 13:6
U-turn catch-phrase, the U. THAT 361:2

vacancies v. to be obtained JEFF 192:9
vacancy v. of the throne GIBB 151:1
vacant no v. cover for him MALT 248:11
vae *V. victis* LIVY 228:8
valiant As he was v., I honour SHAK 329:11
value unique v. in her KEYN 207:3
values restore Victorian v. THAT 361:8
vanity Being an MP feeds your v. PARR 286:11
vapour I absorb the v. GLAD 155:11
street-bred people that v. KIPL 212:7
variety because it admits v. FORS 139:5
Vatican creeping about the V. MACM 245:12
vaulting v. ambition SHAK 331:8
veal more than cold boiled v. MAC 236:10
one of Bellamy's v. pies PITT 293:12
vegetarian often with v. leanings ORW 277:11
tiger will turn v. BROUN 58:4
vegetarianism in favour of v. INGE 187:5
vein not in the giving v. SHAK 335:3
venal v. city ripe to perish SALL 319:7
vengeance gods forbade v. CHUR 87:2
veni *v., vidi, vici* CAES 71:12
vent full of v. SHAK 324:11
venture v. to recommend them GLAD 155:6
ventures Or lose our v. SHAK 330:14
verbosity exuberance of his own v. DISR 120:11

verbs irregular v. LYNN 235:10
verdict cannot think that the v. BIRCH 45:10
verge brought to the v. of war DULL 126:9
vermin race of little odious v. SWIFT 353:6
they are lower than v. BEVAN 40:6
Vermont As Maine goes, so goes V. FARL 135:5
Versailles politics of V. MONN 262:7
verse write it out in a v. YEATS 395:8
vessel by remaining in a v. HUME 184:9
vestry of Commons as a mere v. DISR 120:16
vet'ran superfluous lags the v. JOHN 196:14
vex I believe they die to v. me MELB 255:8
vicar I will be the v. of Bray, sir ANON 10:12
vice characteristic v. a reluctance TAWN 355:7
defence of liberty is no v. GOLD 157:8
in a private man a v. MASS 254:1
render v. serviceable to the cause BOL 50:7
vice-presidency v. isn't worth GARN 148:2
Viceroy future V. must VICT 374:7
V. has been forgotten NEHRU 270:12
vices By hating v. too much BURKE 67:8
judge the v. and virtues TOCQ 366:2
victim fall v. to a big lie HITL 179:3
It marks a v.; denounces it CLAY 97:7
While he felt like a v. WALP 377:9
victims first v. of American Fascism ROS 313:2
They are its v. CONR 102:4
victis *vae v.* LIVY 228:8
victor to the v. belong the spoils MARCY 250:8
Victoria take a ticket at V. Station BEVIN 43:4
Victorian restore V. values THAT 361:8
victories few sharp v. WAUGH 380:5
liberty knows nothing but v. PHIL 292:3
peace hath her v. MILT 261:3
victorious Make him v. HOGG 181:2
victors written by the v. NEHRU 270:6
victory But 'twas a famous v. SOUT 347:2
In v.: magnanimity CHUR 93:5
in v., Revenge LYNN 235:4
in v. unbearable CHUR 94:5
knows not v. nor defeat ROOS 310:11
Let 'dig for v.' be the motto DORM 123:1
never had a v. CHUR 93:10
no substitute for v. MAC 235:13
One more such v. PYRR 299:1
peace without v. WILS 392:8
than to *v.* by a woman WEST 385:8
Together we shall achieve v. EIS 129:3
v. has a hundred fathers CIANO 95:4
victuals instead of snatching his v. CHUR 89:11
Vienna V. is nothing METT 257:10
Vietnam led to the V. War BLACK 48:5
To win in V., we will have to SPOCK 347:9
V. was lost in the living MCL 243:9
viewpoint gives their v. NEHRU 270:6
vigilance eternal v. CURR 107:4
vigour great physical v. BROW 60:3
vile v., but viler George LAND 217:5
village first in a v. CAES 71:10
Some v.-Hampden GRAY 160:8
v. fiddler after Paganini NIC 272:5
villain that v. Hitler GEOR 150:3
villany thus I clothe my naked v. SHAK 334:11
vine Under his own v. SHAK 327:9
vintage He is trampling out the v. HOWE 184:3
violate to v. would be oppression JEFF 192:5
violence I say v. is necessary BROWN 58:7
legitimate v. WEBER 381:8
organization of v. BAEZ 23:11
outburst of crime and v. TEBB 359:2
v. employed by well-meaning TOCQ 367:1
violent policy is v. HUME 184:8
v. revolution inevitable KENN 204:11
violently v. if they must QUIN 299:3
violet v. smells to him SHAK 326:12
Virginian I am not a V. HENRY 176:4
virtue characteristic v. of Englishmen TAWN 355:7
Few men have v. to withstand WASH 379:7
from v. comes money SOCR 345:8
fugitive and cloistered v. MILT 260:6
grounds of this are v. and talents JEFF 193:4
in a prince the v. MASS 254:1
practise v. afterwards HOR 183:3
serviceable to the cause of v. BOL 50:7
v. does not come from money SOCR 345:8
v. is the essence ROB 306:9
wisdom, capacity and v. SWIFT 353:8
virtues call out great v. ADAMS 2:2
his v. SHAK 331:7
in war the two cardinal v. HOBB 180:3
vices and v. of mankind TOCQ 366:2
virtuous looking upon men as v. BOL 50:6
think all men v. BURKE 63:2
visible v. governments RUSK 316:3
vision no v., the people perish BIBLE 43:15
Oh, the v. thing BUSH 69:5
To grasp and hold a v. REAG 302:7
young men's v. DRYD 125:7
visionary schemes of v. politicians BURKE 64:17
vive *V. Le Québec Libre* DE G 112:14
vocabulary diplomatist's v. TAYL 357:1
voice America, with the same v. ADAMS 4:7
prevail against the v. of a nation RUSS 317:1
saying the v. of the people ALC 6:8
v. of Rome JONS 199:3
v. of the kingdom SWIFT 353:5
v. we heard ATTL 20:1
voices sound of tireless v. STEV 351:3
want to have v. in Parliament RUSK 315:11
void against the constitution is v. OTIS 280:1
Volk *ein Reich, ein V., ein Führer* ANON 9:11

voluble In a world of v. hates TREV 368:3
volumes thirty fine v. MORL 265:11
votaries politics compels its v. VAL 372:12
vote British electors will not v. BEAV 34:6
Don't buy a single v. more KENN 203:8
if the right to v. be denied ANTH 15:7
I never v. ANON 11:1
inspire them to v. JACK 189:8
most people v. against ADAMS 2:6
not live to see women v. CHILD 85:3
not to v. is to neglect a duty PAINE 283:8
one man shall have one v. CART 77:9
v. by ballot CARL 76:15
V. early and vote often MILES 258:6
V. for the man BAR 32:7
v. for the person PET 291:1
v. just as their leaders tell GILB 152:8
voted v. at my party's call GILB 152:4
Year after year they v. BYRON 71:6
voter each is a v. SAM 320:1
Every intelligent v. ADAMS 2:4
Your every v. CLEV 99:1
votes finest brute v. in Europe BAG 26:6
giving v. to the most obscure CHES 84:2
plausibilities bring v. CARL 76:5
politicians in pursuit of v. GALB 146:10
uses his money as v. SAM 320:1
voting It's not the v. STOP 351:8
v. against Gladstone KING 210:1
vow I v. to thee, my country SPR 348:1
vox *v. populi, vox Dei* ALC 6:8
voyage all the v. of their life SHAK 330:14
its v. closed and done WHIT 387:10
vulgar all v. arts of government PEEL 288:14
vulgarity Jacksonian v. POTT 296:4

wage My home policy: I w. war CLEM 98:4
One man's w. increase WILS 391:3
You cannot lift the w. earner LINC 227:7
wages better w. and shorter hours ORW 278:1
offer you neither honours nor w. GAR 148:1
wait If you can w. and not be tired KIPL 213:3
may indeed w. for ever MAC 237:6
serve who only stand and w. MILT 261:5
want eight, and we won't w. ANON 14:10
We had better w. and see ASQ 18:1
waiting I was nearly kept w. LOU 232:10
so sorry for keeping you w. GEOR 150:2
We've been w. 700 years COLL 101:5
wake Old Country must w. up GEOR 149:5
walk no easy w.-over to freedom NEHRU 270:5
w. under his huge legs SHAK 328:4
walking w. with destiny CHUR 90:4
wall Gorbachev, tear down this w. REAG 302:5
walls in men, and not in w. NIC 271:6
wooden w. are the best COV 103:11
Walrus W. and Carpenter LEVIN 222:5
want House of W. GEOR 150:10
third is freedom from w. ROOS 309:11
w. is one only of five BEV 42:3
wants plainest physical w. BAG 24:11
wisdom to provide for human w. BURKE 66:12
war After each w. there is a little less ATK 19:4
All the business of w. WELL 384:10
All the time I wage w. CLEM 98:4
Among the calamities of w. JOHN 197:4
an end to w. or w. will put KENN 204:10
another w. in Europe BISM 47:8
anyone who wasn't against w. LOW 233:5
at peace when it's at w. KING 211:6
book that made this great w. LINC 227:4
brought to the verge of w. DULL 126:9
cold w. BAR 32:5
cold w. BAR 32:6
condemn recourse to w. BRI 56:2
condition which is called w. HOBB 179:12
country is at w. with Germany CHAM 81:3
Crimea: The W. That TAYL 356:8
cruellest and most terrible w. LLOY 229:8
dangerous as the clamour for w. PEEL 288:10
easier to make w. than CLEM 98:6
enemies in w., in peace friends JEFF 190:6
essence of w. is violence MAC 237:4
European w. might do it REDM 302:9
European w. this year BEAV 33:7
except the British W. Office SHAW 336:3
First World W. had begun TAYL 357:8
fortunes in peace and in w. CHUR 93:8
France has not lost the w. DE G 112:3
fresh to be our w. Prime Minister BALD 29:8
great protection against w. BEVIN 42:10
Grim-visaged w. SHAK 334:9
here to see the w. through HEND 174:5
If, therefore, w. should ever come BON 51:4
I hate w. ROOS 309:1
I'll furnish the w. HEAR 173:5
I must study politics and w. ADAMS 3:13
infection and the hand of w. SHAK 333:4
involve us in the wrong w. BRAD 54:7
In w. it is necessary LAW 218:6
In w.: resolution CHUR 93:5
In w. there is no second prize BRAD 54:6
In w., three-quarters turns NAP 269:7
In w., whichever side CHAM 80:8
I renounce w. FOSD 139:6
It is well that w. is so terrible LEE 220:4
I will not have another w. GEOR 149:8
killed in the w. POW 297:11
Let me have w., say I SHAK 324:11
let slip the dogs of w. SHAK 329:9
Let w. yield to peace CIC 95:7
money the sinews of w. BACON 23:3
nature of w. consisteth HOBB 180:1

war (*cont.*):
neither shall they learn w. BIBLE 43:18
never to go to w. CHAM 80:10
no declaration of w. EDEN 127:7
no interest in a w. WAUGH 380:5
older men declare w. HOOV 183:1
once lead this people into w. WILS 392:14
only w. creates order BREC 55:7
peace is harder than making w. STEV 349:6
possibility of a short decisive w. LYND 234:9
prepare for the last w. TUCH 372:4
prepare for w. like precocious giants PEAR 287:4
quickest way of ending a w. ORW 278:13
require a resort to w. JEFF 192:11
rich wage w. it's the poor SART 320:5
Second World W. the British TAYL 357:11
silent in time of w. CIC 95:12
since the second world w. LEVIN 222:9
sinews of w., unlimited money CIC 95:11
splendid little w. HAY 171:1
squalid nuisance in time of w. CHUR 92:8
stirring up some w. or other PLATO 294:4
surest way to prevent w. RAND 300:8
take a country into a w. CHAM 81:2
tell us all about the w. SOUT 347:1
There ain't gonna be no w. MACM 244:5
There never was a good w. FRAN 142:4
time of peace thinks of w. ANON 10:4
too long without a w. here BREC 55:7
unnecessary w. CHUR 92:6
very well out of the w. BALD 29:1
w. against a monstrous tyranny CHUR 90:6
W. always finds a way BREC 55:9
W. is a contagion ROOS 309:4
W. is a very rough game MONT 265:2
W. is capitalism STOP 351:9
W. is over GRANT 159:8
W. is peace ORW 279:1
w. is politics with bloodshed MAO 250:3
w. is the continuation of politics CLA 96:11
W. is the health BOUR 53:7
W. is the national industry MIR 261:6
W. is the remedy our *enemies* SHER 339:1
W. is the trade of kings DRYD 126:2
W. is too serious a matter CLEM 98:7
w. on a kindred nation BETH 39:8
w. on poverty in America JOHN 195:10
w. regarded as inevitable KENN 203:6
w. run to show the world BERR 39:7
w. situation has developed HIR 179:1
w. that will end w. WELLS 385:4
w. to 'make the world safe' ROB 307:1
w. violates the order HER 177:3
W. will cease when men refuse ANON 14:6
way to win an atomic w. BRAD 54:3
We hear w. called murder MACD 240:5
We make w. that we may live ARIS 16:3
We still seek no wider w. JOHN 196:3
We've a w., an' a debt LOW 233:8
When is a w. not a war CAMP 74:2
when there was w., he went AUDEN 21:3
When w. enters a country ANON 14:13
When w. is declared JOHN 197:4
which enable it to make w. WEIL 383:5
witnesses to the desolation of w. GEOR 149:6
Work at w. speed MORR 266:6
you must take chances in w. DULL 126:9
you want peace, prepare for w. VEG 373:7
warfare mother of arts, of w. DU B 126:4
w. must be preceded ZIN 397:4
warn right to w. BAG 26:1
w. you not to be ordinary KINN 211:10
warning w. to all Ministers WALP 378:10
warrant not a sufficient w. MILL 258:10
wars All w. are planned by old men RICE 304:5
came to an end all w. LLOY 229:8
European w. and quarrels PAINE 281:6
history is littered with the w. POW 296:9
In the w. of the European MONR 263:5
I see w., horrible wars VIRG 375:6
sent into any foreign w. ROOS 309:9
take care not to lose w. CHUR 92:12
to the beginnings of all w. ROOS 310:8
w. and rumours of w. BIBLE 44:8
W. are popular MACD 240:3
W. begin when you will MACH 242:2
W. cannot be fought MOUN 267:4
w. in history have been avoided CHUR 94:16
Warsaw order reigns in W. ANON 13:1
warship every w. launched EIS 129:4
warts *w. and all* CROM 105:14
w., and everything as you see CROM 105:14
war-war better than to w. CHUR 94:2
Warwick shameless W., peace SHAK 327:4
wash Can w. the balm SHAK 333:6
Washington come to W. to be loved GRAMM 159:4
directed from W. JEFF 193:16
government at W. lives GARF 147:8
inflation is made: that's in W. FRI 143:9
not in W. as a statesman ASH 17:8
W. has lots of those O'RO 277:5
W. is a city of southern efficiency KENN 205:12
W. is a steering wheel GOOD 158:1
what posterity will say of W. FRAN 142:3
Washingtonian W. dignity POTT 296:4
wasms All the 'isms are w. ANON 8:5
wasp exceedingly agile w. LASKI 218:2
wasps let w. and hornets SWIFT 353:4
waste Don't w. any time HILL 178:9
w. of goods VEBL 373:6
waste-paper w. basket WEBB 381:6

wasting w. the labours JEFF 192:10
watch keeping w. above his own LOW 234:2
watching BIG BROTHER IS W. YOU ORW 278:14
something out there w. over us ALLEN 7:4
watchword Our w. is security PITT 293:5
water Ah, on the w., I presume LLOY 230:12
drawers of w. BIBLE 43:8
feet are always in the w. AMES 8:2
king over the w. ANON 11:6
reached the calm of w. ADAMS 2:9
w. in the rough rude sea SHAK 333:6
Waterloo battle of W. was won WELL 384:11
Every man meets his W. at last PHIL 292:2
Probably the battle of W. *was* won ORW 278:6
That world-earthquake, W. TENN 360:1
waters bounded w. SHAK 335:9
By the w. of Babylon WALP 378:2
refreshing w. of office TROL 369:2
wave Churchill on top of the w. BEAV 33:5
way all the w. with LBJ ANON 8:6
I know really which w. I want THAT 361:14
not seem to care which w. BEAV 34:5
provided I get my own w. THAT 362:4
This is the w. the world ends ELIOT 130:2
war always finds a w. BREC 55:9
w. she disposed of an empire HARL 169:3
we w. shall not be moved ANON 14:8
w. shall overcome ANON 14:9
weak concessions of the w. BURKE 64:11
w. have one weapon BID 44:14
weakness compassion is not w. HUMP 185:6
wade into the w. of Princes JAM 190:1
w. of their imaginations BAG 25:6
weal according to the common w. JAM 190:2
wealth acquisition of w. SOCR 345:7
get w. and place POPE 295:7
greater the w., the thicker GALB 145:11
his best riches, ignorance of w. GOLD 157:6
Let w. and commerce MANN 249:5
malefactors of great w. ROOS 311:9
no increase in material w. TAWN 355:12
O citizens, first acquire w. HOR 183:3
regard the w. of their master SMITH 343:2
w. accumulates, and men decay GOLD 157:6
w. is a sacred thing FRAN 141:3
w. piled by the bond-man's LINC 226:9
w. should be found everywhere BURKE 68:8
w. ye find, another keeps SHEL 338:4
wealthy some people are very w. ARIS 16:9
weaned w. on a pickle ANON 13:12
weapon art is not a w. KENN 205:9
bayonet is a w. ANON 8:10
Loyalty is the Tory's secret w. KILM 209:9
most potent w. BIKO 45:4
weak have one w. BID 44:14
weapons books are w. ROOS 310:2
fought with nuclear w. MOUN 267:4
wearied w. me for two hours GEOR 149:2
wearing w. o' the Green ANON 10:11
weary I am w. of travelling CHAR 83:4
weasel called 'w. words' ROOS 312:1
weathercock bit like a rusty w. BENN 37:1
webs laws are like spider's w. ANAC 8:3
Webster Daniel W. struck me SMITH 344:8
wedding bride at a w. HEAD 172:1
weed ignorance is an evil w. BEV 42:4
w. that grows in every soil BURKE 64:10
week w. for preparation WILS 392:18
w. is a long time in politics WILS 390:8
weeks your Majesty, seven w. POPH 295:9
weep As make the angels w. SHAK 332:9
Babylon we sit down and w. WALP 378:2
weight punch above its w. HURD 185:9
willing to pull his w. ROOS 311:3
weights new system of w. NAP 270:2
weird As the w. women promised SHAK 331:10
welfare failures of the w. state GING 153:3
goes with the w. of the country WILS 389:7
honour, and w. of this realm CHAR 82:8
lead to the w. state DENN 113:8
led to that of the w.-state TEMP 359:5
most anxious for its w. BURKE 62:7
tax collector for the w. state GING 153:2
w. became a term of opprobrium MOYN 267:5
well golden crown like a deep w. SHAK 334:3
It is not done w.; but you JOHN 197:9
w.-placed business men YOUNG 396:6
would do very w., if they WALP 377:5
wen fate of the great w. COBB 100:3
west Cincinnatus of the W. BYRON 71:2
Go W., young man, go W. SOULE 346:8
political history of the W. HAIL 163:7
safeguard of the W. WORD 394:6
what is thought in the W. SOLZ 345:11
West End farce in the W. SMITH 343:7
western Iron Lady of the W. World THAT 360:11
w. world PAINE 281:12
Westminster brothels of W. LIV 228:7
westward w. the course of empire BERK 38:4
whale decent beached w. HENN 175:1
wharf sit on the w. for a day BEAV 34:3
wharf-rat merely a grey w. THOR 364:4
what W. did the President know ANON 14:12
W. is to be done LENIN 221:1
wheel great w. runs down a hill SHAK 331:3
wheels none of the w. of trade HUME 184:7
when w. did he know it ANON 14:12
where have they fixed the w. HAWK 170:7
w. are all the people ATTL 20:2
Whig ascendancy of the W. party MAC 238:4
first W. was the Devil JOHN 198:8
see a W. in any dress JOHN 197:14
Tory and W. in turns SMITH 344:7
Tory men and W. measures DISR 117:7

Whig (*cont.*):
wise Tory and a wise W. JOHN 198:10
Whigs caught the W. bathing DISR 117:15
For W. admit no force BROW 59:6
while w. there is a lower class DEBS 111:3
whim conform to our w. REST 303:2
whimper not with a bang but a w. ELIOT 130:2
whine thin w. of hysteria DID 116:2
Whip [W.'s duty is] to make CANN 75:5
whips Chamber selected by the W. FOOT 138:5
Like most Chief W. he knew CLARK 96:8
w. and scorns of time SHAK 325:8
whirlwind they shall reap the w. BIBLE 44:1
whisper w. of a faction RUSS 317:1
whistle until a shrimp learns to w. KHR 209:1
white acceptance of w. people BOES 50:3
between the w. and black races LINC 225:2
necessity of the American w. man BALD 28:8
nor w. so very white CANN 75:2
no 'w.' or 'coloured' signs KENN 205:5
take up the W. Man's burden KIPL 213:2
want to be the w. man's brother KING 210:2
When a w. man in Africa LESS 222:1
w. heat of the technological WILS 390:5
w. moderate KING 210:8
w. race *is* the cancer SONT 346:6
Whitehall gentleman in W. JAY 190:4
like a condottiere through W. HURD 185:8
White House From log-cabin to W. THAY 363:1
no whitewash at the W. NIXON 274:9
on the way to the W. STEV 350:9
operative W. Position ZIEG 397:3
preside over the W. BUSH 69:3
whitewash no w. at the White NIXON 274:9
who W.? Whom LENIN 221:9
wholesale in a w. business LLOY 230:7
whom Who? W. LENIN 221:9
whore I am the Protestant w. GWYN 162:7
w. and gambler BLAKE 49:4
whores parliament of w. O'RO 277:8
whose w. finger do you want ANON 15:1
why ask w. AUDEN 21:6
wicked Arthur is w. and moral CHUR 88:2
born w., and grow worse ANON 12:4
not that men are w. DU B 126:6
wickedness human w. TAYL 357:4
w. is the root of despotism ROB 306:9
widening in the w. gyre YEATS 395:6
wider We still seek no w. war JOHN 196:3
w. still and w. BENS 37:6
widow actions of a retired w. BAG 25:4
wields He who w. the knife HES 177:9
wife Aids—and that is the w. CURR 107:7
Caesar's w. must be above CAES 71:9
If I were your w. ASTOR 19:3
wig must grow to resemble a w. COCK 100:9
Wigan W. Pier BRID 56:3
wiggles It w., it's shapely ERWIN 134:1
wild one is the w. herb TOCQ 366:10
w., and incomprehensible man VICT 374:6
W. men screaming through LLOY 229:11
wilderness Rome is but a w. SHAK 335:6
savage w. into BURKE 63:11
send choice grain into this w. STO 351:12
They make a w. and call it peace TAC 354:3
wilful little group of w. men WILS 392:9
will above all, the w. ROOS 309:10
general w. rules in society ROB 306:5
his w. is not his own SHAK 325:5
not according to the common w. JAM 190:2
not to obey the w. PEEL 288:6
One single w. is necessary ROB 306:10
w. of the majority JEFF 192:5
w. to be free LIPP 228:5
Willie Prime Minister needs a W. THAT 362:12
willows not change to southern w. LEE 220:1
Wilson I suppose Mr W. HOME 182:3
W. is the nation's shepherd SPR 348:2
[Woodrow W.] thinks CLEM 98:5
win hope to w. by't SHAK 327:7
spend it, and w. KENN 206:4
To w. in Vietnam, we will have SPOCK 347:9
way to w. an atomic war BRAD 54:3
w. just one for the Gipper GIPP 153:5
wind he must lie with the w. TAYL 358:7
They have sown the w. BIBLE 44:1
to pure w. ORW 279:11
twist slowly, slowly in the w. EHRL 128:6
w. in his teeth CHUR 90:2
w. of change is blowing MACM 245:1
winding by a w. stair BACON 22:13
weave old England's w. sheet BLAKE 49:4
window broken w. pane PANK 285:2
kiss my ass in Macy's w. JOHN 196:8
they will return through the w. FRED 143:3
windows w. into men's souls ELIZ 131:7
winds W. of the World, give answer KIPL 212:7
w. that would blow then BOLT 51:3
Windsor great W. marshes NIC 271:8
wine new w. into old bottles ATTL 20:5
strong w. diluted SAL 318:1
temptations both in w. and women KITC 214:15
wings hear the beating of his w. BRIG 56:4
winners there are no w. CHAM 80:8
winning He is w. through CHAN 81:7
w. cause pleased LUCAN 234:3
Winston has to remind W. DALT 109:1
W. is back ANON 15:4
W. with his hundred-horse-power BALD 30:3
winter w. of our discontent SHAK 334:8
wisdom contrivance of human w. BURKE 66:12
conventional w. GALB 145:7

world (*cont.*):
believe all the w. to be BURKE 63:2
decide the fate of the w. DE G 112:8
Each man begins the w. afresh MONN 262:10
elect w. peace or w. destruction BAR 32:4
error to believe that the w. began CHUR 93:9
he doth bestride the narrow w. SHAK 328:4
hopes about W. Organization CHUR 92:4
hope that the w. will not narrow JOHN 195:9
instruments as the w. supplies PEEL 289:4
interest of the commercial w. BURKE 68:8
interpreted the w. MARX 252:3
in the history of the w. NIXON 274:5
into the history of the w. POPP 295:12
Let the great w. spin for ever TENN 359:7
loosed upon the w. YEATS 395:6
Marxism is now a w. faith BENN 36:7
My country is the w. PAINE 283:2
only way to a w. society CHOD 85:10
our power to begin the w. PAINE 281:8
solution for w. peace MARS 251:1
start of the majestic w. SHAK 328:3
their w. is the real one ROTH 314:1
There is a w. elsewhere SHAK 324:9
This is the way the w. ends ELIOT 130:2
This w. in arms is not spending EIS 129:4
though the w. perish FERD 136:4
three corners of the w. in arms SHAK 331:1
to be citizens of the w. ROOS 310:6
To make one half the w. fools JEFF 191:2
travelling round the w. COOK 102:6
truth against the w. LLOY 230:14
turned the w. upside down BIBLE 44:10
war run to show the w. BERR 39:7
while the w. sleeps NEHRU 270:7
w. has achieved brilliance BRAD 54:5
w. is becoming like a lunatic LLOY 230:5
w. is divided into three classes RIPP 306:2
w. must be made safe for WILS 392:12
w. of hedges, squires and parsons BRY 60:9
w. safe for diversity KENN 205:4
w. safe for hypocrisy WOLFE 393:6
w. will little note LINC 226:3
You'll never have a quiet w. SHAW 336:19
worldly breath of w. men SHAK 333:6
worms label on the can of w. CRIT 104:8
set on me in W. LUTH 234:7
worry I did not w. about it TRUM 371:7
worse from w. to better HOOK 182:6
I follow the w. OVID 280:3
It is w. than a crime BOUL 53:5
worship To w. the people BACON 22:3
various modes of w. GIBB 151:3
w. God in his own way ROOS 309:11
worshipped people is to be w. BACON 22:3
worst democracy is the w. form CHUR 93:1
it was the w. of times DICK 115:4
while the w. YEATS 395:6
w. is that which delays LLOY 229:10
You do your w. CHUR 91:5
worth wit, nor words, nor w. SHAK 330:9
would He w., wouldn't he RICE 304:8
wound first did help to w. itself SHAK 331:1
In every w. of Caesar SHAK 330:10
wrangle men w. in behalf of liberty HAL 166:3
wrath grapes of w. HOWE 184:3
wrestled I have myself w. HOWE 184:2
wring soon *w.* their hands WALP 378:5
write to read a novel, I w. one DISR 121:18
writing confine myself entirely to w. CHUR 87:7
like w. history with lightning WILS 392:2
sign the w. BIBLE 43:20
tilling a field as in w. a poem WASH 379:3
written have a w. constitution CALL 73:3
strict observance of the w. law JEFF 193:2
wromantic Wrong but W. SELL 323:5
wrong accumulated w. CAS 78:2
being disastrously w. is salutary GALB 146:5
Cavaliers (W. but Wromantic) SELL 323:5
do what both agree is w. CECIL 79:5
eloquent, impressive and w. BLYT 49:8
Englishman in the w. SHAW 335:13
Had anything been w. AUDEN 21:4
if w., to be set right SCH 322:2
involve us in the w. war BRAD 54:7
justice is ever lagging after w. GLAD 154:10
king can do no w. BLAC 48:8
people are never in the w. BURKE 62:11
when I am in the w. MELB 256:4
w. forever on the throne LOW 234:2
wrongs makes the people's w. his DRYD 125:10
wuthering that W. Height CHUR 95:2

year at the gate of the y. HASK 170:2
years end of a thousand y. of history GAIT 145:2
for five y. or fifty AUR 21:9
y. of desolation JEFF 193:11
yelps loudest y. for liberty JOHN 198:9
yes it sounds like y. PEAR 287:6
y., Minister! No, Minister CROS 106:10
yesterday eternal y. WEBER 381:9
Y., December 7, 1941 ROOS 310:1
Y.'s men (they failed before!) KING 211:5
yoke Flanders hath received our y. WALL 377:3
impertinent y. of prelaty MILT 260:4
yolks nothing to lose but your y. STEV 350:15
young But to be y. was very heaven WORD 394:7
crime of being a y. man PITT 292:7
Mine angry and defrauded y. KIPL 213:6
never dared be radical when y. FROST 144:3
too y. to understand that God BROWN 59:2
world would call y. men PEEL 288:3

y. man of promise BALF 31:6
y. men's vision DRYD 125:7
youth invite the flower of our y. TREV 368:1
traitorously corrupted the y. SHAK 327:3
unemployed y. become BAG 25:4
y., beauty, graceful action DRYD 125:10
Y. is a blunder DISR 117:8
y. is the season of credulity PITT 292:10
y. of a Nation DISR 118:6
y. to the gallows PAINE 283:1
y. who must fight and die HOOV 183:1
Yugoslavia Democratic, federal Y. TAYL 357:6

zeal holy mistaken z. in politics JUN 200:11
not the slightest z. TALL 355:3
zealous z. citizen BURKE 67:9
Zionism Z., be it right or wrong BALF 30:7
zip he did not have great z. SMITH 344:3
Zurich all the little gnomes in Z. WILS 390:1